Navigating Socialist Encounters

Africa in Global History

Edited by
Joël Glasman, Omar Gueye, Alexander Keese and
Christine Whyte

Advisory Board:
Joe Alie, Felicitas Becker, William Gervase Clarence-Smith, Lynda Day,
Scholastique Diazinga, Andreas Eckert, Babacar Fall, Toyin Falola, Matt Graham,
Emma Hunter, Erin Jessee, Isabella Kentridge, Colleen Kriger, Kristin Mann,
Patrick Manning, Conceição Neto, Vanessa S. Oliveira, Lorelle Semley,
Ibrahim Sundiata

Volume 2

Navigating Socialist Encounters

Moorings and (Dis)Entanglements between Africa and East Germany during the Cold War

Edited by
Eric Burton, Anne Dietrich, Immanuel R. Harisch, and Marcia C. Schenck

DE GRUYTER
OLDENBOURG

Gedruckt mit der freundlichen Unterstützung der Potsdam Graduate School, der Zentralen Forschungsförderung der Universität Potsdam, ‚UP - Innovative Ideen fördern' und der Philosophisch-Historischen Fakultät der Universität Innsbruck.

ISBN: 978-3-11-108789-4
eBook ISBN (PDF): 978-3-11-062354-3
eBook ISBN (EPUB): 978-3-11-062382-6
ISSN 2628-1767

This work is licensed under the Creative Commons Attribution 4.0 International License.
For details go to http://creativecommons.org/licenses/by/4.0.

Library of Congress Control Number: 2020952193

Bibliographic information published by the Deutsche Nationalbibliothek
The Deutsche Nationalbibliothek lists this publication in the Deutsche Nationalbibliografie; detailed bibliographic data are available on the Internet at http://dnb.dnb.de.

© 2022 Eric Burton et al., Walter de Gruyter GmbH, Berlin/Boston
This volume is text- and page-identical with the hardback published in 2021.
Cover image: An East German diplomat welcomes three Tanzanian journalists at Dar es Salaam airport on their return from a seminar in Berlin, ca. 1974
(courtesy of Norbert Böhme).
Printing and binding: CPI books GmbH, Leck

www.degruyter.com

Table of Contents

Marcia C. Schenck, Immanuel R. Harisch, Anne Dietrich, and Eric Burton
1   Introduction: Moorings and (Dis)Entanglements between Africa and East Germany during the Cold War —— 1

I Shaping Pioneering Institutions

Jörg Depta and Anne-Kristin Hartmetz
2   Herder vs. Goethe in Egypt: East and West German Language Courses in Cairo and the Evolution of "German as a Foreign Language" (DaF) —— 61

Christian Alvarado
3   "In the Spirit of Harambee!" Kenyan Student Unions in the German Democratic Republic and Yugoslavia, 1964–68 —— 87

Eric Angermann
4   Agency and Its Limits: African Unionists as Africa's "Vanguard" at the FDGB College in Bernau —— 115

Franziska Rantzsch
5   The Negotiations of the Contract Labor Accord between the GDR and Mozambique —— 139

II Navigating the GDR: Moorings and (Dis)Entanglements

G. Thomas Burgess
6   The Rise and Fall of a Socialist Future: Ambivalent Encounters Between Zanzibar and East Germany in the Cold War —— 169

J. A. Osei, with an annotation by Immanuel R. Harisch
7   My Impression of the German Democratic Republic [Life Itself Exposes Lies] —— 193

Fernando Agostinho Machava
8   Echoes of the Past: The Social Impact of the Returned Labor Migrants from East Germany on the City of Maputo —— 207

Marcia C. Schenck and Francisca Raposo
9   Socialist Encounters at the School of Friendship —— 235

Ibraimo Alberto and Marcia C. Schenck
10   Paths Are Made by Walking: Memories of Being a Mozambican Contract Worker in the GDR —— 247

III Sourcing Visions of Solidarity

George Bodie
11   So Close, Yet So Far: Ulrich Makosch and the GDR's Afrikabild on Screen and in Text —— 265

Paul Sprute
12   Diaries of Solidarity in the Global Cold War: The East German Friendship Brigades and their Experience in 'Modernizing' Angola —— 293

Katrin Bahr
13   Between State Mission and Everyday Life: Private Photographs of East Germans in Mozambique in the 1980s —— 319

Alexandra Piepiorka and Eduardo F. Buanaissa
14   A (Post)Socialist Memory Space? East German and Mozambican Memories of Cooperation in Education —— 351

List of Contributors —— 387

Index —— 393

Marcia C. Schenck, Immanuel R. Harisch, Anne Dietrich, and Eric Burton[1]

1 Introduction: Moorings and (Dis)Entanglements between Africa and East Germany during the Cold War

The Arusha Declaration of February 5, 1967 confirmed the intention of Tanzania's ruling party TANU (Tanganyika African National Union) to "build a socialist state."[2] The declaration affirmed that TANU planned to pursue a policy of nationalization of major industries, banks, and insurance companies.[3] Two months after the declaration, the Tanzanian trade unionist Salvatory Kaindoah wrote an enthusiastic letter to share the news of developments in his country with the Fritz Heckert Trade Union College, in the East German town of Bernau where Kaindoah had studied:

> Dear Director of the College, Dr. Kampfert,
> I am very glad when I am writing this letter to you now, being in a country which is in a way liquidating the exploitation of man by man and on the way to Socialism. Well done with your daily work. How glad were you, when you heard that our country nationalized all the banks and other big industries?[4]

Kaindoah, at that time employed at the Tanzanian National Institute for Productivity in Dar es Salaam, seemed to suggest that the Arusha Declaration meant the

---

[1] This introduction is the result of a collective thinking and writing process of all four editors. Given the ongoing benchmarkization of current academia, it is of increasing importance which author's name comes first. In order to mitigate the effects of this development, we have decided to use an alphabetical order for the edited volume and an alphabetically reversed order for the introduction. The introduction also owes much to the valuable comments, corrections, and advice of a number of people. We want to thank the two anonymous reviewers, Nele Fabian, Ingeborg Grau, and Arno Sonderegger for their careful reading and helpful suggestions. We also want to thank the members of the GDR working group at Leipzig University and Innocent Rwehabura for their comments. Last but not least we are grateful to Pieter Cordwell for skillfully editing the text and to Malte Köppen for streamlining the footnotes, cleaning up the bibliography, and creating the index.
[2] Tanganyika African National Union, "Arusha Declaration," February 5, 1967, accessed January 29, 2020, www.marxists.org/subject/africa/nyerere/1967/arusha-declaration.htm.
[3] Andrew Coulson, *Tanzania: A Political Economy* (Oxford: Oxford University Press, 2013).
[4] Salvatory Kaindoah to Karl Kampfert, Dar es Salaam, April 10, 1967, Stiftung Archiv der Parteien und Massenorganisationen der DDR im Bundesarchiv, Berlin (henceforth: SAPMO BArch), DY 79/619.

∂ OpenAccess. © 2021 Marcia C. Schenck, Immanuel R. Harisch, Anne Dietrich, and Eric Burton, published by De Gruyter. [CC BY] This work is licensed under the Creative Commons Attribution 4.0 International License. https://doi.org/10.1515/9783110623543-001

convergence of the United Republic of Tanzania with the German Democratic Republic (GDR) in a cohesive and growing world of socialism. This was to be Socialism with a capital "S," perhaps optimistically indicating that the policies of TANU and the policies of the GDR's ruling Socialist Unity Party (*Sozialistische Einheitspartei Deutschlands*, SED) led to a shared socialist future. Kaindoah's celebratory letter is one of a myriad of examples of dialogue and entanglements between African proponents of socialism, with their multiple visions of African and global futures, and East German individuals and institutions.

Many East Germans, however, were less confident about the viability of Tanzania's policies and converging paths – including those who observed these events from East Africa. Some weeks before Kaindoah's letter was written, East German experts and diplomats gathered at a meeting of the local party branch of the SED in Stone Town, the capital of Tanzania's island region of Zanzibar (it had been a separate country until it merged with Tanganyika in 1964 to create Tanzania). Their discussions revealed the urge to classify and evaluate the Arusha Declaration based on how it conformed to Marxist-Leninist dogma. According to the minutes of the party meeting, several comrades "immediately labeled the program as unscientific" and dismissed its usefulness to building socialism in Tanzania. Other members questioned the suitability of a socialist program to Tanzania. They saw Tanzania as being completely different in material and cultural terms compared to European circumstances, and at least one developmental stage away from being a "Workers' and Peasants' State," like the GDR. One member asserted that the Arusha Declaration was "based on the level of development and the mentality of Africans. Can Africans even build socialism with their ideology?" He further alluded to the fact that the East Germans had not seen the declaration coming, despite their supposedly leading role in guiding Tanzania to socialism: "Why were we surprised by the declaration?"[5] The surprise felt by the East Germans in Zanzibar stemmed from the fact that many of them took for granted the leading roles of the Soviet Union and the GDR on the road to socialist development. Thus, many found it difficult to come to terms with Tanzanian actors who were conceptualizing their own road to socialist development.

In both Tanzania and the GDR, socialism would remain official government policy for the next two decades and beyond. By 1967, both socialisms had al-

---

5 Contribution by Comrade O., no place [Zanzibar], no date [March 9, 1967], SAPMO-BArch, DY 30/98149. For a discussion of the role of East German advisers in Zanzibar, see Eric Burton, "Diverging Visions in Revolutionary Spaces: East German Advisers and Revolution from Above in Zanzibar, 1964–1970," in *Between East and South: Spaces of Interaction in the Globalizing Economy of the Cold War*, ed. Anna Calori et al. (Berlin: De Gruyter, 2019).

ready been connected by newly established modes of intercontinental exchange. These included personal migrations, new institutions, and official initiatives. Tanzanian trade unionists (such as Salvatory Kaindoah), students, and Swahili language teachers ventured to the GDR, while East German teachers, skilled workers, and technical experts were dispatched to build socialism in Tanzania. Beneath the official rhetoric of cooperation, however, ideas of internationalism and the best path to socialism often differed. Tanzania became, in the East German classification, not a "socialist country" but a country of "socialist orientation" that was still at a remove from "scientific socialism."[6] Indeed, Tanzanian president Julius Nyerere, one of the main architects of the Arusha Declaration, always kept Marxism-Leninism at arm's length and publicly chastised as "failures" the "so-called socialist countries" in which a small minority had seized power and privilege.[7]

There was thus never a universally shared or stable understanding of where the socialist world began and where it ended. At least nominally, governments in no less than 35 out of 53 countries on the African continent used the term "socialist" to characterize their politics and policies between the late 1950s and the late 1980s.[8] Many African socialisms in the 1960s and 1970s, though by no means all, shared characteristics. Examples of these traits were nationalization of key economic sectors for raw material exports, state-controlled marketing boards for agricultural produce, and universal and free education and healthcare. Ghana, Guinea, Tanzania, and Zambia are good examples of countries which followed this package of policies. Ethiopia, Tanzania, Mozambique, and Burkina Faso were the countries which attempted the most wide-ranging transformations of the all-important rural sector in the 1970s and 1980s. Many of the socialisms were also marked by "a doubling of the state into party and normal state administration, the concentration of strategic decision-making at the party

---

6 Eric Burton, "Tansanias 'Afrikanischer Sozialismus' und die Entwicklungspolitik der beiden deutschen Staaten: Akteure, Beziehungen und Handlungsspielräume, 1961–1990" (PhD diss., University of Vienna, 2017), 134–135.
7 Julius Nyerere, "Capitalism or Socialism: The Rational Choice," *New Blackfriars* 55 (1974): 447.
8 Anne M. Pitcher and Kelly M. Askew, "African Socialisms and Postsocialisms," *Africa* 76 (2006): 1. See also Eric Burton, "Socialisms in Development: Revolution, Divergence and Crisis, 1917–1991," *Journal für Entwicklungspolitik* 33 (2017): 5; Priya Lal, *African Socialism in Postcolonial Tanzania: Between the Village and the World* (Cambridge: Cambridge University Press, 2015); Mark Nash, ed., *Red Africa: Affective Communities and the Cold War* (London: Black Dog Publishing, 2016); Barry Munslow, ed., *Africa: Problems in the Transition to Socialism* (London: Zed, 1986); Edmond J. Keller and Donald S. Rothchild, ed., *Afro-Marxist Regimes: Ideology and Public Policy* (Boulder: Lynne Rienner, 1987).

leaderships, highly centralized decision-making processes and a subordination of 'mass organizations' to the party line."[9]

In view of the variety of socialisms in Africa, which often blended with "Third World" anti-imperialism and diverse forms of African nationalism, African socialist relationships with Soviet and East German Marxism-Leninism were complex. They were marked by both cooperation and tension, particularly as the anti-imperialist strand grew and diversified further.[10] The bipolar Cold War paradigm was and is unable to explain these alliances and frictions.[11] Similarly, the historiography of globalization has also ignored or marginalized these connections until very recently. As James Mark, Bogdan Iacob, Tobias Rupprecht, and Ljubica Spaskovska point out, "[t]he idea of Western capitalism as the sole engine for modernity has left us with a distorted view of socialist states as inward-looking, isolated, and cut off from global trends until the transition to capitalism in the 1990s."[12] In the globalization discourse of triumphant liberalism which emerged in the early 1990s, and decisively shaped global history as an academic discipline,[13] both Africa and Eastern Europe were neglected world regions. Too many analyses considered globalization to be a Western-led phenomenon in which neither the communist world nor African states – of varying ideo-

---

[9] Joachim Becker, "Anatomie der Sozialismen: Wirtschaft, Staat und Gesellschaft," in *Sozialismen: Entwicklungsmodelle von Lenin bis Nyerere*, ed. Joachim Becker and Rudy Weissenbacher (Wien: Promedia, 2009), 40. Our translation.
[10] William H. Friedland and Carl G. Rosberg, ed., *African Socialism* (Stanford: Stanford University Press, 1964); Allison Drew, "Communism in Africa," in *The Oxford Handbook of the History of Communism*, ed. S. A. Smith (Oxford, New York: Oxford University Press, 2014). Jodie Yuzhou Sun explores the influences of the Cold War, the political culture of individual African states (Kenya and Zambia), and their bilateral relations with communist countries, above all China, in Jodie Yuzhou Sun, "Historicizing African Socialisms: Kenyan African Socialism, Zambian Humanism, and Communist China's Entanglements," *International Journal of African Historical Studies* 52 (2019).
[11] Daniel Speich, "The Kenyan Style of 'African Socialism': Developmental Knowledge Claims and the Explanatory Limits of the Cold War," *Diplomatic History* 33 (2009); Tony Smith, "New Bottles for New Wine: A Pericentric Framework for the Study of the Cold War," *Diplomatic History* 24 (2000).
[12] James Mark et al., *1989: A Global History of Eastern Europe* (Cambridge: Cambridge University Press, 2019), 7.
[13] Sebastian Conrad, *What Is Global History?* (Princeton: Princeton University Press, 2016), 1–2. Sebastian Conrad maintains that "one of the crucial tasks of global history is to offer a critical commentary on the ongoing globalization process." Conrad, *What Is Global History?*, 212.

logical colors – were thought to be active participants until the late 1980s.¹⁴ There are, however, good reasons to say that they were.

Encounters, Moorings and (Dis)Entanglements

The title of this volume refers to how encounters between people from various African states and East Germany were navigated and negotiated by a multitude of actors, who were pursuing a wide variety of interests. As mentioned above, the meanings of socialism and the substance of socialist relations were unstable and constantly subject to negotiation. Furthermore, in many everyday encounters, socialist goals were relegated to the background, overtaken by pragmatic imperatives. On other occasions, non-socialist ideologies such as nationalism or pan-Africanism took precedence. Inevitably, such a diversity of encounters had diverse outcomes. Above all, there were encounters which led to the establishment of new institutions and the migrations which resulted from those institutions. In many instances, flows and channels between South and East were newly established after the Second World War. In the absence of direct colonial links, there was often no historical precedent from which relations could be resumed. Johanna Bockman has argued that it was this relatively blank slate that made South-East interconnections "much more global than the old hierarchic metropole-colony relations, which the neo-liberal economic policies, often mistakenly labelled as globalization, reinforced."¹⁵ The new ties represented the emergence of "alternative form[s] of global interconnectedness based on anti-imperialist geogra-

---

14 Anna Calori et al., "Alternative Globalization? Spaces and Economic Interactions between the 'Socialist Camp' and the 'Global South'," in *Between East and South: Spaces of Interaction in the Globalizing Economy of the Cold War,* ed. Anna Calori et al. (Berlin: De Gruyter, 2019), 7, our emphasis; James Mark and Tobias Rupprecht, "The Socialist World in Global History: From Absentee to Victim to Co-Producer," in *The Practice of Global History: European Perspectives,* ed. Matthias Middell (London: Bloomsbury, 2018); on the repercussions of colonialism and Africa's marginalization in history writing see Táíwò Olúfẹ́mi, "What Is 'African Studies'? African Scholars, Africanists, and the Production of Knowledge," in *Reclaiming the Human Sciences and Humanities Through African Perspectives,* ed. Helen Lauer and Kofi Anyidoho (Accra: Sub-Saharan Press, 2012); David Simo, "Writing World History in Africa: Opportunities, Constraints and Challenges," in *Global History, Globally: Research and Practice Around the World,* ed. Sven Beckert and Dominic Sachsenmaier (London: Bloomsbury, 2018).
15 Johanna Bockman, "Socialist Globalization against Capitalist Neocolonialism: The Economic Ideas behind the New International Economic Order," Humanity: An International Journal of Human Rights, Humanitarianism and Development (2015): 125–127; the quote is also used in Calori et al., "Alternative Globalization," 9.

phies."[16] Parastatal foreign trade companies engaged in barter trade as both sides often lacked the hard currency needed for exchange in a global financial system which was controlled by the United States and the international financial institutions.[17] Transnational networks of youth organizations, trade unions, and political parties had partners in Europe, Africa, the Caribbean, South America, and across Asia. This wide participation formed axes of socialist mobilities, initially envisioned to be independent of the imperial fault lines which characterized the liberal globalization which had risen from the ashes of the colonial empires.[18]

Though the contributions in this volume show a multitude of entanglements, they also demonstrate the ephemeral nature of many of the relationships, several of which were marked by tensions that allowed for rapid disentanglements. The most important rupture was, of course, the end of the GDR in 1990, when many institutionalized connections were abruptly discontinued. Even in earlier decades, however, many exchanges ended promptly and can therefore be aptly described as "temporary friendships" which passed from high hopes and enthusiasm to mutual disillusionment.[19] Pertinent examples for such a course of events include relations between Zanzibar and the GDR in the 1960s (Burgess, this volume), or the coffee trade with Ethiopia in the late 1970s, both discussed below. The temporary and fragmented character of many relations is captured in the metaphor of "moorings." The word describes the anchoring of a ship or the fixing of a moving object more generally. Some authors in mobility studies have emphasized the dialectical relationship between mobility and moorings; they argue that "mobilities cannot be described without attention to the necessary spatial, infrastructural and institutional moorings that configure and enable mobilities."[20] Mobility is only possible through the existence of multiple fixed institutions or infrastructure, and mooring is only possible if there is something

---

16 Mark et al., *1989: A Global History of Eastern Europe*, 9.
17 Vijay Prashad, *The Poorer Nations: A Possible History of the Global South* (London: Verso, 2014), 25.
18 See e.g. Ismay Milford, "More Than a Cold War Scholarship: East-Central African Anticolonial Activists, the International Union of Socialist Youth, and the Evasion of the Colonial State (1955–65)," *Stichproben: Vienna Journal of African Studies* 34 (2018); Tal Zalmanovich, "From Apartheid South Africa to Socialist Budapest and Back: Communism, Race, and Cold War Journeys," *Stichproben: Vienna Journal of African Studies* 34 (2018).
19 The term temporary friendships is borrowed from the film program "Temporary Friendships – Contract Labor and Internationalism in the GDR", bi'bak, Berlin, October 24 – November 22, 2019, bi-bak.de/en/bi-bakino/freundschaft-auf-zeit.
20 Kevin Hannam, Mimi Sheller, and John Urry, "Editorial: Mobilities, Immobilities and Moorings," *Mobilities* 1 (2006): 3, accessed December 5, 2019, doi:10.1080/17450100500489189.

immobile to moor onto.²¹ In this volume, however, we employ the mooring metaphor in a temporal rather than a physical sense. Given that few of the African and East German actors involved in the exchanges stayed abroad for the long-term, most individual experiences were moorings rather than rootings (in the sense of putting down roots). Akin to sailors who reminisce about their journeys once they get home, East German travelers to African countries and African sojourners in the GDR think back to their moorings which allowed them to learn and work abroad for a few weeks, months or even years (Burgess; Machava; Osei, annotated by Harisch; Bodie; Sprute; Bahr; Buanaissa and Piepiorka, all this volume). In the light of this, we frame the encounters between Africans and East Germans as moorings which entangled – and, with time, unmoored and disentangled – two continents through patchy personal, institutional, and linguistic webs. The contributions to this volume show how people and institutions produced new forms of transregional interconnectedness, but also how hierarchies and structures limited the possible impact of these encounters.

Historically grounded limitations impacted relations between Africa and the "East" more generally. In the economic realm, political independence did not much disrupt African dependence on vital trade links between former colonies and their erstwhile colonial powers, as governments of newly-independent states usually kept these dense economic networks with the Western capitalist states intact.²² Moreover, while the Soviet Union and the socialist states of Eastern Europe helped to diversify the sources for much sought-after foreign assistance, most investment in African economies still came from Western governments or Western multinational corporations. This was also the case in Africa's socialist states.²³ Mining contracts for Guinean bauxite or Zambian copper, or oil exploration in Congo-Brazzaville or Angola, were, for the most part, continued with Western capitalist firms. In the cultural realm, most African countries adopted the colonial language as national language and retained many aspects of the colonial education system. At the same time French, English or Portuguese were rarely taught in Eastern Europe.²⁴ These limitations, the lack of financial clout with which the Eastern Bloc could penetrate the economies of postcolonial African countries, and the inability to converse in a shared language, were only some

---

21 Ibid.
22 Iba der Thiam, James Mulira, and Christophe Wondji, "Africa and the Socialist Countries," in *Unesco General History of Africa VIII: Africa since 1935*, ed. Ali A. Mazrui and C. Wondji (California: University of California Press, 1993), 808–809.
23 Ralph A. Austen, *African Economic History: Internal Development and External Dependency* (London: James Curry, 1987), chap. 9.
24 Thiam, Mulira and Wondji, "Africa and the Socialist Countries," 809.

of the factors which hampered the establishment of more durable ties between socialist Eastern European countries and Africa. Another factor in relations was that many East German actors also carried, without much self-reflection about it, the cultural legacy of an attitude of superiority vis-à-vis Africa. This mentality dated back at least to the nineteenth century and the period of Imperial Germany's colonial possessions. It was, furthermore, compounded by the even more explicitly racist legacy of Nazi Germany. The GDR officially distanced itself both from its colonial and Nazi past, but both pasts remained largely undiscussed and unexamined with regard to individual family histories and world views.[25] East Germany was the only country in the communist Eastern Bloc with a history of colonial rule in Africa, though it was certainly not the only country whose citizens often bore an (at best) condescending attitude towards Africans. While the SED government successfully managed to distance itself from Imperial Germany in the eyes of many of its African interlocutors, the legacies of racist attitudes permeated cross-continental everyday encounters.

Although they were often of limited duration and constrained by several factors, the South-East exchanges and moorings nevertheless left their marks. During their time in the GDR, African students tried to set up associations which called for East German media to stop portraying modern Africa in the exoticizing manner which prevailed at that time (Alvarado; Angermann, this volume). Mozambican contract workers not only exchanged their labor power for education and pay in the GDR, but also brought home East German goods that changed the war economy in Maputo in ways that lasted for years (Machava, this volume). The East German and Mozambican governments established an agreement for Mozambican workers to migrate to East Germany to work and receive training, which lastingly entangled both countries economically, politically, and socially (Rantzsch, this volume). In the contribution by Schenck and Alberto we read about the personal consequences of the institutional disentanglements and the dissolution of the contract after the GDR ceased to exist. There was, therefore, a complex assemblage of multi-directional processes within these South-East relationships, which led to diverse and at times contradictory outcomes.

---

25 Peggy Piesche, "Making African Diasporic Pasts Possible: A Retrospective View of the GDR and Its Black (Step-)Children," in *Remapping Black Germany: New Perspectives on Afro-German History, Politics, and Culture*, ed. Sara. Lennox (Massachusetts: University of Massachusetts Press, 2016).

Africa and East Germany: Alternative Forms of Transcontinental Interconnectedness in Global History

The perspectives of actors from both the "South" and the "East" have been marginalized in global history.[26] This volume investigates South-East relations through a focus on global socialism and diverse transregional entanglements between actors from the African continent and the GDR.[27] It places African history into global history by highlighting connections between Africans and East Germans and their institutions during the Cold War. The volume focuses predominantly on non-elite figures and the possibilities and constraints of their agency. In this way, the scholars contributing to this collection highlight Africans' and Eastern Europeans' visions of African and global futures, which were often shaped by socialism in its numerous imaginations and manifestations. The book thus contributes to the discussions about the nature of global socialism(s), and how it shaped and was shaped by African actors and institutions. The contributions foreground "alternative form[s] of global interconnectedness"[28] by showing the many ways in which actors from different vantage points in the socialist world thought about socialism, both locally and globally, and how they navigated the new hierarchies of a global socialism in the making.

Following an interdisciplinary and initially multilingual[29] approach, this volume offers a platform for scholars from three continents (Africa, Europe, and

---

[26] Arno Sonderegger, Ingeborg Grau, and Birgit Englert, "Einleitung: Afrika im 20. Jahrhundert," in *Afrika im 20. Jahrhundert: Geschichte und Gesellschaft*, ed. Arno Sonderegger, Ingeborg Grau, and Birgit Englert (Wien: Promedia, 2011), 9–11; Calori et al., "Alternative Globalization?," 7–9.
[27] For a similar approach regarding entanglements with Vietnam, see Christina Schwenkel, "Socialist Mobilities: Crossing New Terrains in Vietnamese Migration Histories," *Central and Eastern European Migration Review* 4 (2015); see also Alena K. Alamgir, "Labor and Labor Migration in State Socialism," *Labor History* 59 (2018).
[28] Mark et al., *1989*, 9.
[29] The original contributions were based on work in English, German, and Portuguese. While scholars like Jeremy Adelman and Drayton and Motadel have rightly lamented that English is becoming "globish" and hegemonial in global history, the current publishing rules did not allow the editors of this volume to go ahead with their original plan to publish this book as a trilingual edited volume in English, German, and Portuguese. See Jeremy Adelman, "What is global history now?," Aeon, accessed October 9, 2019, https://aeon.co/essays/is-global-history-still-possible-or-has-it-had-its-moment; Richard Drayton and David Motadel, "Discussion: The Futures of Global History," *Journal of Global History* 13 (2018): 15.

North America) and various disciplines (ranging from history to German studies to education studies) to present their research. They employ a range of methodological approaches to the study of South-East relations, including oral history, the consultation of both Eastern European and African archives, the study of literature and of international academic networks. Throughout, they strive to maintain a balance between African and East German actors' perspectives. In this vein, the open access format of this volume contributes to the international accessibility of knowledge generated across national boundaries, and we invite further transregional cooperation – particularly with scholars from Africa and with researchers using African sources – in investigating the pasts and legacies of these interconnections.

With a special focus on negotiations, entanglements, and African influences on East Germany (and vice versa), the volume sheds light on personal and institutional agency, cultural cross-fertilization, migration, development, and solidarity in everyday encounters. It explores the repercussions and legacies of these South-East encounters and examines in which ways the enmeshed power structures and inequalities remain relevant up to the present day. By demonstrating the diversity of socialisms and connections to the East on the African continent, this edited volume challenges, possibly complicates, but ultimately deepens our understanding of how Africa fitted into what was, for a time, a global socialist world.

Writing South-East Relations into Global History

Global history has been on the rise for the past two decades, but, as set out above, all too often the kind of global history produced has been synonymous with a history of Western-led globalization.[30] However, recent studies have suggested that the study of alternative forms of globalization, spurred by socialism and the process of decolonization, enriches and complicates our understanding of globalization. Oscar Sanchez-Sibony, for instance, has examined the political economy of what he calls "red globalization," highlighting Soviet responses to trade initiatives from the Global South in the 1950s and 1960s.[31] Johanna Bockman has engaged with what she refers to as "socialist globalization," seeing

---

[30] Frederick Cooper, "What Is the Concept of Globalization Good for? An African Historian's Perspective," *African Affairs* 100 (2001); Lynn Hunt, *Writing History in the Global Era* (New York: Norton, 2014).
[31] Oscar Sanchez-Sibony, *Red Globalization: The Political Economy of the Soviet Cold War from Stalin to Khrushchev* (Cambridge: Cambridge University Press, 2014).

it as an alternative political project to "capitalist neocolonialism," in her work about the role of the United Nations Conference on Trade and Development (UNCTAD) in negotiating the parameters of the mooted New International Economic Order.[32] In the literature on globalization, the portrayal of state socialist Europe thus underwent a significant transformation: previously seen as an absentee from or a victim of (Western) capitalist globalization, it is now recognized as a co-producer of globalization, or as an instigator of alternative globalization(s).[33] Recent scholarship, produced mainly by historians of East Central Europe and the Soviet Union, has discussed relations between the "Second World" and the "Third World," or the Cold War East and the Global South, under terms such as "internationalism," "red globalization," and "Warsaw Pact Intervention in the Third World."[34]

The contributions to this volume demonstrate that alternative forms and ideas of globalization were about much more than just economic orders and rhetoric of political elites. We examine cultural, social, political, and economic encounters in a global socialist world. In doing so, we build on important works from other scholars who have investigated relations between Africa and the GDR. A first wave of literature arrived in the early 1990s, with many groundbreaking studies based on new archival records as well as valuable first-hand accounts of former diplomats, journalists, students, and experts. These studies generally framed relations between the GDR and Africa in mostly bilateral terms, usually highlighted East German perspectives, and frequently took a

---

[32] Bockman, "Socialist Globalization," 6.
[33] Mark and Rupprecht, "The Socialist World in Global History."
[34] Odd A. Westad, *The Global Cold War: Third World Interventions and the Making of Our Times* (Cambridge: Cambridge University Press, 2005); Maxim Matusevich, ed., *Africa in Russia, Russia in Africa: Three Centuries of Encounters* (Trenton, NJ: Africa World Press, 2007); David C. Engerman, "The Second World's Third World," *Kritika: Explorations in Russian and Eurasian History* 12 (2011); Sanchez-Sibony, *Red Globalization*; Tobias Rupprecht, *Soviet Internationalism after Stalin: Interaction and Exchange between the USSR and Latin America during the Cold War* (Cambridge: Cambridge University Press, 2015); Matthias Middell, "Weltgeschichte DDR: Die DDR in globalgeschichtlicher Perspektive," in *Die DDR als Chance: Neue Perspektiven auf ein altes Thema*, ed. Ulrich Mählert (Berlin: Metropol Verlag, 2016); Philip E. Muehlenbeck and Natalia Telepneva, ed., *Warsaw Pact Intervention in the Third World: Aid and Influence in the Cold War* (London: I.B. Tauris, 2018); Matthias Middell, "Auf dem Weg zu einer transregionalen Geschichte des Kommunismus," in *Kommunismus jenseits des Eurozentrismus: (= Jahrbuch für Historische Kommunismusforschung)*, ed. Matthias Middell, (Berlin: Metropol, 2019); James Mark, Artemy M. Kalinovsky, and Steffi Marung, ed., *Alternative Globalizations: Eastern Europe and the Postcolonial World* (Bloomington: Indiana University Press, 2020).

comparative view with West German policies and practices.³⁵ A second wave of historiographical scholarship has investigated relations between Africa (and other regions) and the GDR, focusing on power asymmetries, including reflections on the complex workings of race and the contested and ambivalent meanings of terms such as "solidarity" and "mutual benefit."³⁶ Works from either wave, however, have not explicitly discussed how relations between Africa and East Germany enrich our understanding of global history and processes of globalization.

Far from subscribing to a point of view that sees globalization as a singular homogenizing process engulfing the world, or as a Western project spreading by diffusion, we conceive of globalizations in the plural. This entails visualizing globalization "as a set of multidirectional processes stemming from different world regions."³⁷ This includes the African continent, as well as socialist Eastern Europe (in a geopolitical rather than geographical sense).³⁸ As the contributions

---

35 Ulrich van der Heyden, Ilona Schleicher, and Hans-Georg Schleicher, ed., *Die DDR und Afrika: Zwischen Klassenkampf und neuem Denken* (Münster: Lit, 1993); Ulrich van der Heyden, Ilona Schleicher, and Hans-Georg Schleicher, ed., *Engagiert für Afrika: Die DDR und Afrika II* (Münster: Lit, 1994); Jude Howell, "The End of an Era: The Rise and Fall of G.D.R. Aid," in *Journal of Modern African Studies* 32 (1994); Brigitte H. Schulz, *Development Policy in the Cold War Era: The Two Germanies and Sub-Saharan Africa, 1960–1985* (Münster: Lit, 1995); Ulf Engel and Hans-Georg Schleicher, *Die beiden deutschen Staaten in Afrika: Zwischen Konkurrenz und Koexistenz, 1949–1990* (Hamburg: Institut für Afrika-Kunde, 1998); Hans-Joachim Döring, *Es geht um unsere Existenz: Die Politik der DDR gegenüber der Dritten Welt am Beispiel von Mosambik und Äthiopien* (Berlin: Ch. Links, 1999); Ulrich van der Heyden and Franziska Benger, ed., *Kalter Krieg in Ostafrika: Die Beziehungen der DDR zu Sansibar und Tansania* (Münster: Lit, 2009). One of the few studies based on African archival materials is Haile G. Dagne, *Das entwicklungspolitische Engagement der DDR in Äthiopien: Eine Studie auf der Basis äthiopischer Quellen* (Münster: Lit, 2004).
36 Toni Weis, "The Politics Machine: On the Concept of 'Solidarity' in East German Support for SWAPO," *Journal of Southern African Studies* 37 (2011); Hubertus Büschel, *Hilfe zur Selbsthilfe: Deutsche Entwicklungsarbeit in Afrika 1960–1975* (Frankfurt am Main: Campus, 2014); Young-Sun Hong, *Cold War Germany, the Third World, and the Global Humanitarian Regime* (New York: Cambridge University Press, 2015); Quinn Slobodian, ed., *Comrades of Color: East Germany in the Cold War World* (New York: Berghahn Books, 2015).
37 Calori et al., "Alternative Globalization," 9.
38 For a thoughtful review and rethinking of the concept of the "bloc" see also Steffi Marung, Uwe Müller and Stefan Troebst, "Monolith or Experiment? The Bloc as a Spatial Format," in *Spatial Formats under the Global Condition*, ed. Matthias Middell and Steffi Marung (Berlin: De Gruyter, 2019). See also the argument by Marcia C. Schenck about the "Black East" constituting a geographic entity with blurry borders as much as a political and social entity in Marcia C. Schenck, "Constructing and Deconstructing the "Black East" – a Helpful Research Agenda: Research Note," *Stichproben Vienna Journal of African Studies* 34 (2018): 136.

to this volume and other works have shown, many instances of South-East entanglement shared certain characteristics (e. g. a focus on education, see Alvarado, this volume). At the same time, actors from countries such as Yugoslavia or China pursued globalizing strategies which differed from, or openly challenged, Soviet leadership of the anti-imperialist camp. These divisions sometimes came into play in encounters on the ground. For instance, in Zanzibar, the GDR and the People's Republic of China competed for the role of the most influential patron (Burgess, this volume). Socialist globalization can therefore be conceived of as a series of political projects in which actors chose to engage in response to global challenges and competitions. In the terminology of world-systems theory, they were often seeking both to catch up with and to challenge the capitalist core from a peripheral or semi-peripheral position.[39] Elites in many African countries were able to decide how much to invest in relations with the West, and where to engage in relations with different actors from the East to increase their bargaining power vis-à-vis the other partner (see, for instance, the example of Egypt in Depta and Hartmetz's contribution, this volume). On other occasions, such as the French retaliation after Guinea's 1958 vote for immediate independence instead of membership in the French Community, or the exodus of mostly white professional staff from Angola and Mozambique in the mid-1970s, Western hostility made stronger links to networks of socialist globalization a matter of economic survival.

While much has been written about elite actors in the Cold War, this volume demonstrates that relations were, in fact, often fostered by non-elite actors and by state projects which brought Africans together with East German partners along socialist axis to shape an alternative vision of global interconnectedness. It follows that the trend seen in the last 70-or-so years, of increasing global interconnectedness, does not automatically go hand in hand with the liberal globalization model with which it is usually associated.[40] As the contributions in this volume demonstrate, studying alternative forms of global entanglements does not have to come at the cost of national histories or "small spaces" and micro histories, and most certainly do not depoliticize these stories, as is sometimes claimed.[41] Quite to the contrary, analysis of concrete complaints about racism (Angermann, this volume), individual photos (Bahr, this volume), or entries in brigade diaries (Sprute, this volume) reveal both the reach and limits of official policies and of the socialist rhetoric of friendship and solidarity. Studying the

---

39 Mark and Rupprecht, "The Socialist World in Global History."
40 Middell, "Weltgeschichte," 153.
41 Drayton and Motadel, "Discussion," 1–3.

limits and fictions of entanglements tells us as much about their meaning as does studying their existence and achievements.

Writing Africa into Global History

The concept of globalization, when it is used to refer to a universal, Western-led process of integration, easily glosses over the complexities and diversity of actual connections and actors.[42] This does by no means imply a neglect of global dimensions. As Frederick Cooper emphasized, the "and" in DuBois' title *The World and Africa* implies two directions of causality and serves as a reminder that "African history should be studied in all its complexity, but not as if 'Africa' existed independently of the rest of the world."[43] Recent approaches – including this series, *Africa in Global History* – address the global connections which shaped African histories and which aim to fully incorporate the African continent into the "global turn". They usually embrace DuBois' and Cooper's imperative and frame Africa firmly within the study of globalizing processes. Some authors speak of "Africa in the globalizing world," others of "Africa within the global."[44] These formulations also signal that there is no consensus as to whether, and in what ways, Africa may also be seen as a producer of globalization. This is a discussion which will keep the field engaged for a while to come and to which this volume provides empirical research perspectives.[45] It offers avenues towards a global history of socialism by merging two strands of global history: Africa in global history and South-East entanglements. In the process of editing this volume we have come to appreciate the complexities of such an endeavor. It was not easy to achieve a balanced viewpoint, and in the final result more contributors and primary sources speak from the East German than from the African point of view. To a certain extent this was to be expected, given the inherent GDR-centric nature of a volume using the GDR as a unifying feature studying entanglements with socialisms across Africa. However, this volume would be

---

42 Cooper, "What Is the Concept of Globalization Good for?".
43 Cooper, *Africa in the World*, 9.
44 Ulf Engel et al., "Africa in the Globalizing World – a Research Agenda," *Comparativ* 27 (2017); Pedro Machado, "Repositioning Africa within the Global," *Africa Today* 63 (2016). See also the other insightful contributions to the section "Symposium: African Studies and the Challenge of the 'Global' in the 21st Century" in this issue of *Africa Today*.
45 James Ferguson, *Global Shadows: Africa in the Neoliberal World Order* (London: Duke University Press, 2006), especially chap. 1.

equally hard to be put together in a balanced way if it was, for example, examining Mozambique's entanglements with the Eastern Bloc.

A worthwhile future endeavor, which takes up the Afro-Asian Networks Research Collective's call to examine South-South relations, would be to examine the socialist encounters in networks created and maintained between African actors beyond the trodden paths of diplomatic relations of nation-states.[46] Yet, this volume succeeds in showing how "African actors navigated, ignored, and subverted the power dynamics of the Cold War"[47] and that many contributions actually follow a "research agenda that privileges transnational networks of affinity"[48] – and of friction – across Africa and Europe.

We should not close our eyes to the fact that there is an inequality of research output on the global socialist world that sees many more actors from the Global North engage in this research topic than scholars from the Global South. To our knowledge, current contributions in the field of South-East entanglements rarely include scholars from based in Africa who investigate these relations by drawing on archival materials and oral histories from their region of origin.[49] The multiple reasons for this global inequality of knowledge production and pitfalls of transcontinental partnerships have been discussed elsewhere,[50] but it is worth noting explicitly the effect of the different funding landscapes and intellectual freedoms, especially in the context of writing global history. For this volume we found it difficult to get contributors from African universities, reflecting that the research agendas of global history and South-East relations are currently not well established at most African institutions of higher

---

[46] Afro-Asian Networks Research Collective, "Manifesto: Networks of Decolonization in Asia and Africa," *Radical History Review* 131 (2018).
[47] Afro-Asian Networks Research Collective, "Manifesto," 178.
[48] Afro-Asian Networks Research Collective, "Manifesto," 177.
[49] An account on Ghana's relations with the Soviet Union based on Ghanaian sources by a US-based scholar is Nana Osei-Opare, "Uneasy Comrades: Postcolonial Statecraft, Race, and Citizenship, Ghana–Soviet Relations, 1957–1966," *Journal of West African History* 5 (2019). We are, however, not aware of works which are using archival documents of the MPLA or FRELIMO to examine the relations of Angola or Mozambique with socialist states as of now. Archival access seems to be an impediment to engaging with this research topic from African perspectives. For a recent discussion of Mozambican archives see Ingrid Miethe et al., *Globalization of an Educational Idea: Workers' Faculties in Eastern Germany, Vietnam, Cuba and Mozambique* (Berlin: De Gruyter, 2019), 34–35.
[50] Amina Mama, "Is it Ethical to Study Africa? Preliminary Thoughts on Scholarship and Freedom, "*African Studies Review* 50 (2007); Loren B. Landau, "Communities of Knowledge or Tyrannies of Partnership: Reflections on North–South Research Networks and the Dual Imperative," *Journal of Refugee Studies* 25 (2012).

education.⁵¹ Seen from the African research landscape today, relations with the GDR are a rather marginal topic.⁵² This suggests that the impact of the GDR was either not that profound or is a silenced topic in current political discourse, or most likely a bit of both.

Considering this, why should a volume on Africa in global history bring the GDR into the picture? There are many good reasons. Firstly, Africa – both south and north of the Sahara – serves as a crucial vantage point for investigating South-East relations and the alternative futures that these ties promised. There is a growing body of Africanist scholarship with a global history perspective, yet relations with the geopolitical Cold War "East" are often only mentioned in passing.⁵³ Similarly, connections with Africa have been absent in most of the historiography on East Germany. As Sebastian Pampuch points out, the "idea of a post-colonial world that breaks with the inequalities of capitalism through socialist modernization is one of these repressed histories." Such histories can also resituate the GDR in a transregional perspective.⁵⁴ This neglect does justice neither to African countries nor to the heterogenous socialist states. The unfolding decolonization process on the African continent in the 1950s and

---

51 Generally, one has to acknowledge the research constraints at many public African universities today that are an echo of the IMF and World Bank induced cuts on tertiary education from the late 1970s onward after the "golden age" of knowledge production at a number of African universities in the 1960s and early 1970s. See Esperanza Brizuela-Garcia, "African Historiography and the Crisis of Institutions," in *The Study of Africa Volume 1: Disciplinary and Interdisciplinary Encounters*, ed. Paul Tiyambe Zeleza (Dakar: Codesria, 2006); Mahmood Mamdani, *Scholars in the Marketplace: The Dilemmas of Neo-Liberal Reform at Makerere University, 1989–2005* (Dakar: CODESRIA Council for the Development of Social Science Research in Africa, 2007).
52 Nonetheless, two Ethiopian exceptions should be mentioned: Dagne, *Das entwicklungspolitische Engagement* and Gebru Tareke, *The Ethiopian Revolution: War in the Horn of Africa* (New Haven & London: Yale University Press, 2009). Like the majority of German historical studies on relations between Socialist Ethiopia and the GDR, however, they focus mostly on military and economic aspects and less on everyday encounters. See Hans-Joachim Döring, "*Es geht um unsere Existenz*": *Die Politik der DDR gegenüber der Dritten Welt am Beispiel von Mosambik und Äthiopien* (Berlin: Ch. Links, 1999) and Klaus Storkmann, *Geheime Solidarität. Militärbeziehungen und Militärhilfen der DDR in die "Dritte Welt"* (Berlin: Ch. Links, 2012).
53 Important exceptions include Osei-Opare, "Uneasy Comrades"; Sun, "Historicizing African Socialisms"; Jocelyn Alexander and JoAnn McGregor, "African Soldiers in the USSR: Oral Histories of ZAPU Intelligence Cadres' Soviet Training, 1964–1979," *Journal of Southern African Studies* 43 (2017); Jamie Monson, *Africa's Freedom Railway: How a Chinese Development Project Changed Lives and Livelihoods in Tanzania* (Bloomington: Indiana University Press, 2009).
54 Sebastian Pampuch, "Afrikanische Freedom Fighter im Exil der DDR: Dekoloniale Wissensbestände einer 'unerwünschten Geschichte'," in *Wissen in Bewegung: Migration und Globale Verflechtungen in der Zeitgeschichte seit 1945*, ed. Stephanie Zloch, Lars Müller, and Simone Lässig (Berlin: De Gruyter, 2018), 325. Our translation.

1960s – and the breakdown of the Portuguese Empire in the mid-1970s – breathed new life into the belief in socialist world revolution as well as postcolonial emancipation. "National democracies" in Africa were to serve as trading partners as well as crucial allies against Western capitalist neocolonialism. African actors were interested in the Eastern Bloc (whose name misleadingly suggests homogeneity and uniformity of interests[55]) as new trade partners, partners for professional and cadre training, and supporters of liberation struggles – most actively against the white minority regimes in southern Africa. These ties sometimes offered radical alternatives, but sometimes only additional elements to Western discourses on development. Colonial legacies continued to shape the opportunities and constraints of postcolonial African governments to varying degrees.[56]

These efforts to overcome peripherality are part of a longer and broader history that also includes connections across the Black Atlantic. African interests and roles in co-producing alternative forms of global interconnectedness have been bound up with the question of how to overcome the peripherality imposed by colonialism, and the asymmetries in the global order that came with it. Already in the first half of the twentieth century, African, African-American, and West Indian intellectuals, such as W. E. B. DuBois, George Padmore, C. L. R. James, Tiemoko Garan Kouyaté, and Kwame Nkrumah set up revolutionary socialist publication organs[57] and established wide anticolonial networks. These networks, at times, included the Soviet Union[58] and Western communist parties and creatively adapted Marxist and Leninist thought for use in their analyses of African affairs and their calls for decolonization.[59] In the aftermath of World War

---

[55] Marung, Müller, and Troebst, "Monolith or Experiment?".
[56] Frederick Cooper, "Possibility and Constraint: African Independence in Historical Perspective," *The Journal of African History* 49 (2008).
[57] Matthew Quest, "George Padmore's and C. L. R. James's International African Opinion," in *George Padmore: Pan African Revolutionary*, ed. Fitzroy Baptiste and Rupert Lewis (Kingston: Ian Randle, 2009).
[58] It is important to note, however, that the relationship of these mostly undogmatic Black Marxist thinkers and activists with Stalin's Soviet Union was an uneasy one; C. L. R. James, for example, favored Trotzky over Stalin and George Padmore had already broke with the Soviet Union during the 1930s. See Hakim Adi, *Pan-Africanism: A History* (London: Bloomsbury, 2018); Arno Sonderegger, "Der Panafrikanismus im 20. Jahrhundert," in *Afrika im 20. Jahrhundert: Geschichte und Gesellschaft*, ed. Arno Sonderegger, Ingeborg Grau and Birgit Englert (Wien: Promedia, 2011).
[59] Leslie James, *George Padmore and Decolonization from Below: Pan-Africanism, the Cold War, and the End of Empire* (Houndmills: Palgrave Macmillan, 2015); C. L. R. James, *A History of Negro Revolt* (Chicago: Research Associates School Times Publications, 2004 [1938]); Kwame Nkrumah, *Towards Colonial Freedom: Africa in the Struggle against World Imperialism* (London: Panaf

II, DuBois took a fresh look at the "old hierarchic metropole-colony relations" mentioned by Johanna Bockman. In *The World and Africa: An Inquiry into the Part which Africa Has Played in World History*, mentioned above, DuBois argued in 1946 that the devastating experience of the Second World War rendered it impossible for colonial business to go on as usual, providing an opening for Africans to redefine their place in the world.[60] For many aspiring African politicians after the Second World War, socialism promised an alluring break with the colonial and neocolonial order. Their experience of capitalist exploitation and institutionalized racism under European colonialism made socialism an attractive foundation on which to build their visions of modernity.

The second reason for bringing the GDR into African global history is that Afro-European encounters, under the banner of socialism, led to a dialectical process of globalizing on both sides of the equation. What Maxim Matusevich and Constantin Kastakioris have postulated for the 1960s Soviet Union[61] was true for the GDR as well. The presence of, and interactions with Africans, alongside South Asians and Latin Americans, modernized and globalized East German society. A number of chapters in this volume demonstrate these adaptive processes in detail. Depta and Hartmetz's contribution examines the institutionalization of teaching and the use of German as a foreign language. Both Alvarado and Angermann show how African student unions tested the limits of regulations laid down by the SED while individual members of these unions criticized the portrayal of Africans in GDR media. Journalists like Ulrich Makosch, as George Bodie's contribution shows, brought the struggle of the *Frente de Libertação*

Books, 1979 [1945]); George Padmore, *How Britain Rules Africa* (New York: Negro Universities Press, 1969 [1936]). See also Arno Sonderegger, "How the Empire Wrote Back: Notes on the Struggle of George Padmore and Kwame Nkrumah," in *Kwame Nkrumah 1909–1972: A Controversial African Visionary*, ed. Bea Lundt and Christoph Marx (Stuttgart: Franz Steiner Verlag, 2016).

60 W. E. B. Du Bois, *The World and Africa: An Inquiry into the Part Which Africa Has Played in World History* (New York: International Publishers, 1965 [1946]); see also Cooper, *Africa in the World*.

61 Maxim Matusevich, "Expanding the Boundaries of the Black Atlantic: Af, *Africa in the World*.

Maxim Matusevich, "Expanding the Boundaries of the Black Atlantic: African Students as Soviet Moderns," *Ab Imperio* 2 (2012), doi:10.1353/imp.2012.0060. Constantin Kastakioris, "Transferts Est-Sud. Échanges Éducatifs et Formation de Cadres Africains en Union Soviétique Pendant les Années Soixante," *Outre-mers* 94 (2007); idem, "African Intellectuals and the Soviet Union: Internationalism, Pan-Africanism, and Négritude During the Years of Decolonization: 1954–1964," *Cahiers du monde russe* 47 (2006); idem, "Students from Portuguese Africa in the Soviet Union, 1960–74: Anti-Colonialism, Education, and the Socialist Alliance," *Journal of Contemporary History* (2020), accessed August 1, 2020, doi:10.1177/0022009419893739; idem, "The Lumumba University in Moscow: Higher Education for a Soviet–Third World Alliance, 1960–91," *Journal of Global History* 14 (2019).

de Moçambique (FRELIMO) against Portuguese colonial troops into East German living rooms. Conversely, Paul Sprute shows how friendship brigades in Angola aimed to contribute to an Angolan socialist modernity by invoking the "Neuerer movement" (*Neuererwesen*), an approach which encouraged workers to propose ways to increase productivity. As Fernando Agostinho Machava shows in his chapter, East German televisions, fridges, and motorbikes, imported by former Mozambican contract workers, profoundly impacted the consumer landscape of neighborhoods in which they were received. Lastly, the possibility for East Germans to travel abroad marked another aspect of the globalizing effect of the GDR's entanglements with Africa. This is taken up in the contributions of Katrin Bahr, Alexandra Piepiorka and Eduardo F. Buanaissa, and Paul Sprute.

The third reason for the significance of the GDR to African global history is that the richness of available but frequently untapped sources lends itself to exploring the relations between Africa and the GDR in a global history perspective. In terms of archival material – often notoriously hard to come by for the post-independence period in many African countries – the GDR is a treasure trove.[62] The outstanding range and accessibility of archival documents is due to the – for the historian fortuitous – fact that the GDR as a state ceased to exist. The German Federal Republic as successor state, together with activists from the former GDR, ensured the broad availability of archival records pertaining to the state and especially the secret police (*Stasi*). With regards to Africa, the archival records of the GDR constitute a transnational "shadow archive" which holds primary documents of crucial interest for scholars of African history.[63] Several contributions in this volume draw on East German state and party archives as well as records of mass organizations (Depta/Hartmetz; Angermann; Rantzsch; Bodie; Sprute), university archives (Depta/Hartmetz), and the archives of the secret police and the ministry of foreign affairs (Rantzsch).

Of course, this is but a starting point. We believe that the GDR archives on which many of the contributions to this volume are based are useful for carving out the agency of African actors and introduce some African voices, particularly if read against the grain. It is nevertheless evident that research which makes further use of African sources is indispensable for a balanced approach. This includes archival documents on the African continent (Alvarado), oral history interviews (Machava), novels of African authors (Burgess), and African and

---

62 Steven Ellis, "Writing Histories of Contemporary Africa," *Journal of African History* 43 (2002).
63 Jean Allman, "Phantoms of the Archive: Kwame Nkrumah, a Nazi Pilot Named Hanna, and the Contingencies of Postcolonial History-Writing," *The American Historical Review* 118 (2013): 121; Kate Skinner, "West Africa's First Coup: Neo-Colonial and Pan-African Projects in Togo's 'Shadow Archives'," *African Studies Review* 6 (2019).

diaspora print cultures. The chapters in this volume thus draw on official sources, but also semi-official collective diaries of volunteer "brigades" including poems and drawings (*Brigadetagebücher*, Sprute), photographs from personal collections (Bahr), and personal memories (Schenck with Alberto, Schenck with Raposo). With this variety of sources, the contributing authors approach relations between East Germany and Africa from a variety of perspectives.

The entanglements that the alternative global formations of socialist internationalism afforded may have been marginalized by the ruthless tide of mainstream politics and history, but they are still recalled by many as powerful symbols of aspiration to alternative modernities and futures. The contributions to this volume are divided into three sections. The first section, "Shaping Pioneering Institutions," focuses on the ways in which institutions were set up for and shaped by relations between Africa and the GDR. The second section, "Navigating the GDR: Moorings and (Dis)Entanglements," brings together examples of how temporary stays and engagements led to both long-term legacies as well as rapid disentanglements. The third section, "Sourcing Visions of Solidarity," comprises contributions which discuss sources giving unique insights into the perspectives of non-elite actors, including travel writing, the collective diaries of friendship brigades, private photographs, and oral history interviews. These sources open avenues to rethink the characteristics, relevance, and scope of South-East relations in the history of the twentieth century, as well as how Africa and East Germany fit into the global perspective. The regional focus of the contributions in this volume reflect the close ties that the GDR maintained to socialist countries in Africa, especially the profound relations with Mozambique, but also with Angola, Ghana, and Tanzania – though Ethiopia, another important case study, is unfortunately absent here. The following sketch of an entangled history,[64] from the early 1950s to the late 1980s and beyond, gives an overview of socialist encounters and alternative forms of global interconnectedness.

---

64 Sebastian Conrad and Shalini Randeria, ed., *Jenseits des Eurozentrismus: Postkoloniale Perspektiven in den Geschichts- und Kulturwissenschaften* (Frankfurt: Campus Verlag, 2002); Michael Werner and Bénédicte Zimmermann, "Beyond Comparison: Histoire Croisée and the Challenge of Reflexivity," *History and Theory* 45 (2006).

A (Dis)Entangled History of Socialist Encounters between Africa and the GDR

The Dual Impulses of Decolonization and the German Division: Bandung and Hallstein in the 1950s

The establishment of the GDR in 1949 provided a zero point for the emergence of new ties between East Germany and the African continent. However, the new state was only nominally independent of the Soviet Union and remained closely tied to Stalinist policies in which the colonial world was seen as an appendage of the imperial powers. Consequently, early contacts in diplomacy, trade, and education did not, for the time being, translate into steady flows of persons, goods or ideas between Africa and the GDR. Egyptian efforts to market their cotton behind the Iron Curtain, as for example when they sent a trade delegation to East Berlin in 1950, were guided by economic concerns and accompanied by resolutely pragmatic and nationalist rhetoric.[65] Similarly, the arrival of 11 Nigerian trade unionists in 1951, the first non-European students in GDR classrooms, did not immediately lead to more intense exchanges with African countries, most of which were still colonial territories at the time.[66] The GDR's internationalism expanded beyond Europe during the early 1950s, but the expansion – involving an increasingly dense web of economic relations, the sending of experts, and the intake of students – remained largely confined to the fraternal communist parts of the world, most notably China and North Korea.[67] Two external impulses lent new diplomatic importance to the Global South. These were West Germany's Hallstein Doctrine, which from 1955 onwards sought to isolate the GDR internationally, and the Bandung moment, also in 1955.

---

65 See Depta and Hartmetz, this volume; Werner Kilian, *Die Hallstein-Doktrin: Der diplomatische Krieg zwischen der BRD und der DDR 1955–1973: aus den Akten der beiden deutschen Außenministerien* (Berlin: Duncker & Humblot, 2001), 104–108. For a broader survey, see Anne-Kristin Hartmetz, Bence Kocsev and Jan Zofka, "East-South Relations during the Global Cold War: Economic Activities and Area Studies Interests of East Central European CMEA Countries in Africa," *Working Paper Series of the Collaborative Research Center (SFB) 1199 at the University of Leipzig* 11 (2018).
66 Sara Pugach, "Eleven Nigerian Students in Cold War East Germany: Visions of Science, Modernity, and Decolonization", *Journal of Contemporary History* 54 (2019).
67 Hong, *Cold War Germany*, chapter 2; Tao Chen, "Weathering the Storms: East German Engineers in Zhengzhou,1954–1964," *The China Review* 19 (2019).

The 1955 Bandung conference in Indonesia was an important stimulus for anti-imperialist sentiments across the colonial and postcolonial world.[68] The ideas expressed at the conference were not new, but as Africans across the continent re-emphasized their right for self-government, their importance came to the fore. Despite the initial opportunities for temporary moorings, the institutionalization of South-East links between Africans and East Germans faced serious blockages. Among these obstacles were the colonial powers, who with their anti-communist agendas aimed to keep communist representatives and subversive literature from entering their territories.[69] Anti-communist sentiment was widespread among African educated elites, at least partially a result of colonial and missionaries' education programs. This too hampered contact.[70] Many freedom fighters and students, however, were willing to engage with the communist world to acquire symbolic, material and military resources for liberation struggles and opportunities for education, in some cases also actively searching alternatives to neocolonialism.[71] Contacts with the GDR were often established in the few African countries that were already independent and took an anti-imperialist stand. Cairo and Accra emerged as hubs of decolonization and served, like Conakry or (slightly later) Dar es Salaam and Algiers, as transregional meeting points for Africans from all over the continent and as points of transit to the state socialist countries in Europe.[72] Circumventing the colonial barriers described above, Africans managed to get in touch with representatives of communist countries and migrate to the East. While some traveled to universities, party schools or trade union colleges in Prague and Moscow, others came to moor at

---

[68] Vijay Prashad, *The Darker Nations: A People's History of the Third World* (New York: The New Press, 2007), 31–50.
[69] Frederick Cooper, *Decolonization and African Society: The Labor Question in French and British Africa* (Cambridge: Cambridge University Press, 1996), 436; Adi, *Pan-Africanism*, 138–140.
[70] Walter Rodney, "Education in Africa and Contemporary Tanzania," in *Education and Black Struggle: Notes from the Colonized World*, ed. Institute of the Black World (Cambridge: Harvard Educational Review, 1974).
[71] Lena Dallywater, Chris Saunders, and Helder Adegar Fonseca, ed., *Southern African Liberation Movements and the Global Cold War 'East': Transnational Activism 1960–1990* (Berlin: De Gruyter, 2019); Ilona Schleicher and Hans-Georg Schleicher, *Die DDR im südlichen Afrika: Solidarität und Kalter Krieg* (Hamburg: Institut für Afrika-Kunde, 1997).
[72] Eric Burton, "Hubs of Decolonization: African Liberation Movements and Eastern Connections in Cairo, Accra and Dar es Salaam," in *Southern African Liberation Movements and the Global Cold War 'East': Transnational Activism 1960–1990*, ed. Lena Dallywater, Helder A. Fonseca and Chris Saunders (Berlin: De Gruyter, 2019); Eric Burton, "Decolonization, the Cold War and Africans' Routes to Overseas Education, 1957–1965," *Journal of Global History* 15 (2020). See also Bodie, this volume.

Bernau or Leipzig.⁷³ One of the first relatively large groups of Africans (though they were, like Egyptians, mostly seen as "Arabs") in the GDR were Algerians involved in the war against the French (1954–62), who came, classified as "refugees" or "exiles," to undergo vocational training, attain university degrees, and receive medical treatment.⁷⁴

From the GDR's perspective, the early decolonizers of the late 1950s in Sub-Saharan Africa, such as Guinea and Ghana, were of strategic importance in breaking through the diplomatic and economic isolation which was imposed by the Hallstein Doctrine.⁷⁵ As African anti-colonialism gained momentum in the late 1950s, still with a variety of options for postcolonial visions, the GDR stepped up its efforts to become an active and respected part of the growing anti-colonial world. By establishing trade missions, consulates, and cultural institutions, the GDR undermined the Hallstein Doctrine, but still ultimately failed to win diplomatic recognition anywhere on the continent.⁷⁶ Still, governments and dominant liberation movements or trade unions were the preferred partners. Few parties in Africa embraced communism; those that did, for example in Algeria, Egypt, Senegal, Sudan, and South Africa, soon found themselves persecuted by the nationalist ruling parties, their influence limited by strong religious, ethnic, and linguistic alliances and the absence of a large working class.⁷⁷ Nevertheless, the SED government continued to establish relations with the dominant nationalist movements on the African continent.

---

73 Eric Burton, "Introduction: Journeys of Education and Struggle: African Mobility in Times of Decolonization and the Cold War," *Stichproben: Vienna Journal of African Studies* 34 (2018). Regarding military cooperation and training, see Storkmann, *Geheime Solidarität*.

74 Patrice G. Poutrus, "An den Grenzen des Proletarischen Internationalismus: Algerische Flüchtlinge in der DDR," *Zeitschrift für Geschichtswissenschaft* 55 (2007).

75 Gareth Winrow, *The Foreign Policy of the GDR in Africa* (Cambridge: Cambridge University Press, 2009[1990]), 37–46; Hans-Joachim Spanger and Lothar Brock, *Die beiden deutschen Staaten in der Dritten Welt: Die Entwicklungspolitik der DDR. Eine Herausforderung für die Bundesrepublik Deutschland?* (Opladen: Westdeutscher Verlag, 1987), 164–167.

76 Joachim Scholtyseck, *Die Außenpolitik der DDR* (München: Oldenbourg, 2003), 25. On the GDR's almost breakthrough to achieve diplomatic recognition in Guinea see Ilona Schleicher, "FDGB-Offensive in Westafrika. Der Gewerkschaftsbund im Jahr Afrikas," in *Engagiert für Afrika: Die DDR und Afrika II*, ed. Ulrich van der Heyden, Ilona Schleicher and Hans-Georg Schleicher (Münster: Lit, 1994), 83–84. Regarding the struggles over diplomatic recognition in East Africa, see George Roberts, "Press, Propaganda and the German Democratic Republic's Search for Recognition in Tanzania, 1964–72," in *Warsaw Pact Intervention in the Third World: Aid and Influence in the Cold War*, ed. Phillip E. Muehlenbeck and Natalia Telepneva (London: I. B. Tauris, 2019).

77 Thiam, Mulira, and Wondji, "Africa and the Socialist Countries," 800; Drew, "Communism in Africa".

African Decolonization and Pioneering Institutions in the 1960s

The year 1960 – dubbed the Year of Africa by the United Nations (UN) – was a turning point in East German relations with the African continent. The number of politically independent African countries rose from nine to 26, which made Africa a force to be reckoned with in international forums such as the UN. Africa's first wave of political independence evoked a sense of excitement among leading East German politicians and among functionaries in the GDR's mass organizations who imagined the socialist world system in the 1960s "as a growing, transformative object," with the Global South as a reserve of socialism or "proto-socialist" region.[78] A public declaration of the national trade union federation *Freier Deutscher Gewerkschaftsbund* (FDGB) enthusiastically welcomed the development that "[t]he 190 million Africans have now shaken off the colonial yoke," believing that the "great successes of their sacrificial struggles are an expression of the new balance of power on our planet, which is determined by the existence and growth of the enormous socialist world system."[79]

African anticolonial liberation movements and the "progressive national democracies" on the African continent were now considered crucial allies in the fight against capitalist imperialism. Updating Lenin's merger of proletarian internationalism and anti-imperialism, theoreticians and some political leaders from the GDR and across the socialist world now argued that the unfolding process of decolonization was an integral part of the world's revolutionary transition from capitalism to socialism.[80] In the euphoric mood of the early 1960s, the expectation was that the support of socialist countries for progressive "young nation-states" would enable their governments to pursue a "non-capitalist way of development," which would eventually meet the "conditions for a socialist revolution."[81]

---

[78] George Bodie, "'It Is a Shame We Are Not Neighbours': GDR Tourist Cruises to Cuba, 1961–89," *Journal of Contemporary History* (2019): 433.
[79] International Relations Department to Warnke, "Erklärung des Präsidiums des FDGB-Bundesvorstandes zum Freiheitskampf der afrikanischen Völker und Gewerkschaften", Berlin, February 10, 1961, 154, SAPMO-BArch, DY 34/16600.
[80] Ernst Hillebrand, *Das Afrika-Engagement der DDR* (Frankfurt am Main: Peter Lang, 1987); Hans-Georg Schleicher, "Entwicklungszusammenarbeit und Außenpolitik in der DDR: Das Beispiel Afrika," in *Entwicklungspolitische Zusammenarbeit in der Bundesrepublik Deutschland und der DDR*, ed. Hans-Jörg Bücking (Berlin: Duncker & Humblot, 1998).
[81] H. Amirahmadi, "The Non-Capitalist Way of Development," *Review of Radical Political Economics* 19 (1987); I. Andreyev, *The Noncapitalist Way: Soviet Experience and the Liberated Countries* (Moscow: Moscow Progress Publishers, 1977), 65–69, 101–123; Spanger and Brock, *Die bei-*

This increased interest in the African world, motivated by pragmatic considerations and visionary ideals alike, stimulated the creation of a number of pioneering institutions in the socialist countries of Eastern Europe that shaped, and were shaped by, relations with Africa. These institutions usually emerged from national motivations, rather than bloc-determined efforts, to become part of and intervene in a shared anti-imperialist world connecting South and East. These included institutes for foreigners at the Fritz Heckert Trade Union College in Bernau (founded in 1959/60) and Leipzig's Karl Marx University, the Institute for International Studies (*Institut für Ausländerstudium*, established in 1956, renamed the Herder Institute in 1961), and the Committee for Solidarity with the Peoples of Africa (founded in 1960, in 1963 renamed as the Afro-Asian Solidarity Committee). In the field of health, a newly established sub-unit at the Dorothea Erxleben nursing school in Quedlinburg took in its first students from Mali in 1961. It became the GDR's central institution for non-European nurse trainees and students in the health professions.[82]

Due to blocked diplomatic avenues, but also given ideological preferences for working class organizations, trade union relations had a particular significance. The first courses for African and (to a much smaller extent) Asian trade unionists took place first in Leipzig in 1959–60 and were in 1960/61 institutionalized at the Fritz Heckert Trade Union College in Bernau.[83] As Eric Angermann shows in his contribution to this volume, African participants at the college in Bernau challenged the course contents and institutional set-up of trade union education, although their political demands were quickly diverted. Angermann's micro-historical study looks at the attempts of the African students in Bernau to set up their own Afro-Asian committee to facilitate cultural and political exchange among their co-students. However, as Angermann emphasizes, the trade union college in Bernau was also an institution which connected Africans

---

den deutschen Staaten, 114–157; Steffi Marung, "The Provocation of Empirical Evidence: Soviet African Studies Between Enthusiasm and Discomfort," *African Identities* 16 (2018).
82 Hong, *Cold War Germany*, 201–212; Stefan Wolter, *Für die Kranken ist das Beste gerade gut genug: Klinikum Dorothea Christiane Erxleben GmbH. 100 Jahre Standort Dithfurter Weg* (Quedlinburg: Letterado-Verlag, 2007), 265–268. We thank Sebastian Pampuch for the hint to this institution.
83 Eric Angermann, "'Ihr gehört auch zur Avantgarde: Afrikanische Gewerkschafter an der FDGB-Hochschule Fritz Heckert (1961–1963)" (MA thesis, Georg-August-Universität Göttingen, 2018); George Bodie, "Global GDR? Sovereignty, Legitimacy and Decolonization in the German Democratic Republic, 1960–1989" (PhD diss., University College London, 2019), chapter 2. See also Immanuel R. Harisch, "'Mit gewerkschaftlichem Gruß!' Afrikanische GewerkschafterInnen an der FDGB-Gewerkschaftshochschule Fritz Heckert in der DDR," *Stichproben: Vienna Journal of African Studies* 43 (2018).

with each other across imperial and linguistic borders. In this way, the GDR was sometimes experienced as a pan-African rather than "Eastern" space. After all, "the opportunity to meet is better here [...] than in Africa," as one African student put it.[84] The report of a trade unionist from Ghana, J. A. Osei, who studied in Bernau, is printed in this volume as a primary source annotated by Immanuel R. Harisch. Osei's report points to the shared language of global, anti-Western socialism and visions of socialist modernity.

Another channel to establishing rapport with African audiences and countering Western anti-communist propaganda was through the media. Radio was the best-suited medium for reaching large numbers of people at a fairly low cost. In 1964, Radio Berlin International set up its Africa Service, with broadcasts in European and African languages, with employees from several African countries.[85] Broadcasters included linguistically-trained graduates of area studies courses. The establishment of area studies in the GDR in fact predated the Bandung moment, due to the initiative of academics in Leipzig who used their ties to Western leftists and who made significant advances in colonial history.[86] Africans came to the GDR as lecturers and scientific cooperators, providing the groundwork for effective language courses, co-writing dictionaries, and teaching interpreters and diplomats who would travel to Africa.[87] With the rising interest of the ruling elite, however, African Studies and related disciplines were reorganized in the 1960s in closer alignment with political aims.[88] On the other hand, East German lecturers also received invitations to teach and

---

84 Angermann, this volume.
85 "Comrade Africa," BBC World Service, Radio Documentary, 53 minutes, November 14, 2019, accessed January 29, 2020, https://www.bbc.co.uk/programmes/w3ct036t. See also Roberts, "Press, Propaganda"; James R. Brennan, "The Cold War Battle Over Global News in East Africa: Decolonization, the Free Flow of Information, and the Media Business, 1960–1980," *Journal of Global History* 10 (2015).
86 Matthias Middell, "Die Entwicklung der Area Studies in der DDR als Reaktion auf die Dekolonisierungsprozesse der 1950er/1960er Jahre," in *Kommunismus jenseits des Eurozentrismus:* (= *Jahrbuch für Historische Kommunismusforschung 2019*), ed. Matthias Middell (Berlin: Metropol, 2019).
87 Examples include Stephan Mhando and Joseph Kasella-Bantu from Tanganyika who were involved in building the good reputation of Leipzig's linguistic scholarship on Swahili and other African languages.
88 Ulrich van der Heyden, *Die Afrikawissenschaften in der DDR: Eine akademische Disziplin zwischen Exotik und Exempel. Eine wissenschaftsgeschichtliche Untersuchung* (Münster: Lit, 1999); Middell, "Die Entwicklung der Area Studies"; Waltraud Schelkle, "Die Regionalwissenschaften der DDR als Modell einer Entwicklungswissenschaft?," in *Wissenschaft und Wiedervereinigung: Asien- und Afrikawissenschaften im Umbruch*, ed. Wolf-Hagen Krauth and Ralf Wolz (Berlin: Akademie-Verlag, 1998).

establish curricula and institutions in newly independent African countries. The renowned (and headstrong) Leipzig historian Walter Markov, for instance, served as the first Director of the History Department at the University of Nsukka in Nigeria – despite the fact that he had been expelled from the SED in 1951 on charges of "Titoism."[89] These multi-directional flows in the education and media sectors were one of the most comprehensive and durable aspects of relations between the GDR and African countries.[90]

Due to its geopolitical position and diplomatic role, Nasser's Egypt had occupied a special role in the GDR's foreign policy considerations throughout the late 1950s and 1960s. In their contribution to this volume, Jörg Depta and Anne-Kristin Hartmetz demonstrate how actors from both German states strove for hegemony in German language teaching and culture transmission. They focus on the work in Cairo of the West German Goethe Institute and the East German counterinstitution that unofficially became known as the Herder Institute. The competition also enabled Egyptians to exploit these rivalries for their own ends during the maelstrom of the Six-Day War. Language instructors such as those at Cairo's "Herder Institute" exemplified Germans in Africa who combined professional and proto-diplomatic functions. Their encounters and experiences in Cairo, among other places, led to the institutionalization in the GDR of the teaching of German as a foreign language as a tool of foreign policy, before the field was even established in West Germany.

In 1963, the Politburo decided to establish another pioneering institution, the Friendship Brigades (*Brigaden der Freundschaft*) of the Free German Youth (FDJ). These groups of young East Germans, comparable to Western development volunteers, were explicitly seen as "instruments of foreign policy."[91] From 1964 until the end of the GDR in 1990, the FDJ's Central Council (*Zentralrat*) detached more than 60 friendship brigades to 26 countries in Africa, Asia, and Latin

---

89 Walter Markov, *Kognak und Königsmörder – Historisch-literarische Miniaturen* (Berlin: Aufbau-Verlag, 1979), 117–121; Matthias Middell, "Manfred Kossok: Writing World History in East Germany," *Review* (ed. Fernand Braudel Center) 38 (2015).

90 Constantin Katsakioris, "The Soviet Union, Eastern Europe, and Africa in the Cold War: The Educational Ties," *Working Paper Series of the Collaborative Research Center (SFB) 1199 at the University of Leipzig* 16 (2019); Alexandra Piepiorka, "Exploring 'Socialist Solidarity' in Higher Education: East German Advisors in Post-Independence Mozambique (1975–1992)," in *Education and Development in Colonial and Postcolonial Africa: Policies, Paradigms, and Entanglements, 1890s–1980s*, ed. Damiano Matasci, Miguel B. Jerónimo, and Hugo G. Dores (Cham: Springer Nature, 2019).

91 Eric Burton, "Solidarität und ihre Grenzen: Die 'Brigaden der Freundschaft' der DDR," in *Internationale Solidarität: Globales Engagement in der Bundesrepublik und der DDR*, ed. Frank Bösch, Caroline Moine, and Stefanie Senger (Göttingen: Wallstein, 2018), 153.

America.⁹² The first host countries in the 1960s were Mali (1964–79) and Algeria (1964–82), followed by Ghana (1965–66), Guinea (1966–85), and Tanzania/Zanzibar (1966–72).⁹³ The range of activities was broad: the mostly young and mostly male GDR citizens took up tasks in a spectrum of sectors including industry, agriculture, health services, vocational training, and transport.⁹⁴ While the early brigades' missions in the 1960s were more focused on increasing the GDR's international reputation through various types of aid projects, the late 1970s and 1980s marked a closer alignment of friendship brigades' solidarity projects with East German foreign trade interests, such as the provision of Angolan coffee or a coal mine project in Mozambique.⁹⁵

It was not only the GDR which set up new institutions and channels of exchange. As Christian Alvarado shows in his contribution to this volume, Kenyans studying in the GDR founded new institutions such as the "Kenya Students Union" to navigate the demands of East German authorities, their sending government's mission, and to help students fulfill their personal ambitions to embark on careers in the rapidly expanding Kenyan bureaucracy. Alvarado's comparative analysis of experiences of student unions in the GDR and Yugoslavia highlights how Kenyan student union members pushed against their racialized reception in Europe by campaigning for a "truer" representation of Kenya in film and other media. While GDR authorities encouraged the organization of African students in single unified national organizations, students could always turn out to be "agents of dissent" who shaped and used associations also in their own ways, sometimes across the Iron Curtain, that contrasted and often conflicted with the objectives of both sending and receiving governments.⁹⁶

---

92 Ulrich van der Heyden, "FDJ-Brigaden der Freundschaft aus der DDR – Die Peace Corps des Ostens?," in *Die eine Welt schaffen: Praktiken von "Internationaler Solidarität" und "Internationaler Entwicklung,"* ed. Berthold Unfried and Eva Himmelstoß, (Leipzig: Akademische Verlagsanstalt, 2012).
93 Ilona Schleicher, "Elemente entwicklungspolitischer Zusammenarbeit in der Tätigkeit von FDGB und FDJ," in *Entwicklungspolitische Zusammenarbeit in der Bundesrepublik Deutschland und der DDR*, ed. Hans-Jörg Bücking (Berlin: Duncker & Humblot, 1998), 136–137.
94 FDJ, Abteilung Brigaden der Freundschaft, "Historische Übersicht – 20 Jahre Brigaden der Freundschaft der FDJ", Berlin, April 1984, 8, cited in Burton, "Solidarität", 153.
95 Immanuel R. Harisch, "East German Friendship-Brigades and Specialists in Angola: A Socialist Globalization Project in the Global Cold War," in *Transregional Connections in the History of East Central Europe*, ed. Katja Naumann (Berlin: De Gruyter, forthcoming 2021).
96 Sara Pugach, "Agents of Dissent: African Student Organizations in the German Democratic Republic," *Africa* 89 (2019); Quinn Slobodian, "Bandung in Divided Germany: Managing Non-Aligned Politics in East and West, 1955–63," *The Journal of Imperial and Commonwealth History* 41 (2013).

At the same time, several African governments also established institutions to deal with global connectedness and positioning in general, and to deal with relations with socialist countries in particular. Some of these were state or party departments specializing in economic and political contacts, such as the Ghanaian State Committee for Economic Cooperation with the Soviet Union, China, and Eastern European Countries (CECEC).[97] Educational institutions also used blueprints or personnel from the GDR and other state socialist countries in Eastern Europe. This included both higher education at universities as well as party and trade union colleges, such as the Kwame Nkrumah Ideological Institute in Ghana (1961–66). Another example was Mozambique's Faculty for Former Combatants and Vanguard Workers, which was a variation of the blueprint of the workers' and peasants' faculties which had been established first in the Soviet Union, and later in the GDR, Vietnam, and Cuba.[98]

Yet already during the 1960s, some of these institutions ceased to exist as socialist African leaders such as Ghana's Kwame Nkrumah (1966) or Mali's Modibo Keïta (1968) were toppled by right-wing coups. If one were to come up with a periodization of global socialism from an African perspective, there would be no single 1989 moment to mark the end of socialist projects. Rather, there were multiple ruptures and dead ends as well as numerous fresh attempts to set up socialist polities over more than three decades. Even where there were no abrupt regime changes such as in Ghana or Mali, inflated expectations and structural constraints could easily lead to mutual disappointments in relations between Africans and the GDR. A 1967 publication from East Germany critically noted that African governments tended to economically exploit the inter-German scramble, maximizing gains without giving the GDR the recognition it was due. Ironically, with this the authors were displaying the same self-oriented attitude toward the aid competition of which they were accusing the Africans. At the same time, government leaders such as Abeid Amani Karume of Zanzibar, or Jean-Bédel Bokassa of the Central African Republic, complained about East German failures in providing effective economic aid for the modernization of their countries in the late 1960s and early 1970s.[99] As G. Thomas Burgess shows in his contribution to this volume, relations between Zanzibar and East Germany unraveled as quickly as they had emerged. However, they still left consequential

---

[97] Calori et al., "Alternative Globalization?," 1.
[98] Gerardo Serra and Frank Gerits, "The Politics of Socialist Education in Ghana: The Kwame Nkrumah Ideological Institute, 1961–1966," *Journal of African History* 60 (2019), 3, accessed November 25, 2019: Miethe et al., *Globalization of an Educational Idea*.
[99] The publication and opinions of African leaders are discussed in Winrow, *The Foreign Policy*, 76–77.

traces such as housing projects and a powerful security apparatus. Less tangible were the narratives and memories of students, technocrats, and teachers traveling back and forth between South and East. Discussing the novel *By the Sea* by Zanzibar-born writer Abdulrazak Gurnah, in which one of the main characters goes to the GDR for training, Burgess shows that sojourners could discover not only the unexpected colonial assumptions of East German citizens, but also the rich humanist heritage that lay hidden beneath socialist rhetoric. In this way, new South-East entanglements in the 1950s and 1960s, brought about by visions of socialist cooperation and anti-imperialist alliances, led to the establishment of new institutions and mobilities, unearthed legacies of colonial exploitation and discrimination, but simultaneously showed the barriers to closer or more durable alliance.

Reconfiguring Solidarity in Times of Global Crisis in the 1970s

Already in the late 1960s, East Germans' enthusiasm for revolution in Africa was waning as attention shifted towards developments in the Middle East, Latin America, and Vietnam. Yet in the mid-1970s, when the Portuguese Empire dissolved, mutual interest increased once more. The chronology of decolonization was highly uneven across the African continent. While most territories ruled by the French, British, and Belgians came to be governed by African politicians by the late 1950s and 1960s, the Portuguese dictatorship under António de Oliveira Salazar and later Marcelo Caetano resisted political decolonization and instead declared the Lusophone territories (Angola, Mozambique, Guinea-Bissau, Cape Verde, and São Tomé and Príncipe) to be overseas provinces of the mother country, namely Portugal. Another factor in the uneven chronology of decolonization was the large white population in southern Africa. South Rhodesia declared its unilateral independence under white minority rule in 1965 and South African apartheid was firmly entrenched until the late 1980s. African leaders, soldiers, and students of selected national liberation parties enjoyed sympathies and increasing financial support from the socialist camp. The GDR's Solidarity Committee campaigned for African liberation from colonial rule. Leaders from the Angolan MPLA (*Movimento Popular de Libertação de Angola*), Mozambican FRELIMO (*Frente de Libertação de Moçambique*), South African ANC (African National Congress), Rhodesia's ZAPU (Zimbabwe African People's Union), and Namibia's SWAPO (South West Africa People's Organisation) were frequent guests in East Germany throughout the 1960s, 1970s, and 1980s, often trailed by university students, trainees, and activists.[100]

Given that imagery and iconography strongly shaped the culture of solidarity in the GDR, the role of print media and television in portraying Africa deserves particular attention. Leaders from liberation movements such as FRELIMO had an urgent interest in making their views and struggles known in order to gain legitimacy and get access to resources. In this volume, George Bodie shows how journalist and SED party member Ulrich Makosch depicted Africa as simultaneously close and distant in his writing and documentaries. Relating his wanderings through the bush with the male and female guerilla fighters of FRELIMO, Makosch brought African liberation struggles and testimonies of women's emancipation home to East German living rooms. Bodie challenges the usual assumptions regarding state-led cultures of solidarity in GDR: while Makosch's influence in terms of reaching an East German audience and bolstering the spirit of solidarity was modest, his films and journalism were important weapons in FRELIMO's struggle for international recognition.

The 1970s brought an unprecedented scale of economic and political relations, entailing a mingling of solidarity and commerce. African governments and parties which pursued explicitly Marxist programs, such as in Angola, Mozambique, and Ethiopia,[101] could count on collaboration with political leaderships in the Soviet Union, Cuba, and the state socialist countries of Europe. For the GDR, connections established during the liberation struggles intensified and new opportunities opened up, as African states and independence movements sought international recognition, political and economic development aid, cultural and educational exchange, and military support. 1979, which marked the thirtieth anniversary of the GDR, represented the high point of Africa-GDR relations. A party and state delegation, led by SED General Secretary Erich Honecker, visited Libya, Angola, Zambia, Mozambique, and São Tomé

---

100 Hans-Georg Schleicher, "The German Democratic Republic (GDR) in the Liberation Struggle of Southern Africa," in *Southern African Liberation Struggles 1960–1994: Contemporaneous Documents Vol. 8*, ed. Arnold Temu and Joel das Neves Tembe (Dar es Salaam: Mkuki na Nyota, 2014); Anja Schade, "Solidarität und Alltag der DDR aus der Sicht exilierter Mitglieder des African National Congress," in *Internationale Solidarität: Globales Engagement in der Bundesrepublik und der DDR*, ed. Frank Bösch, Caroline Moine, and Stefanie Senger (Göttingen: Wallstein, 2018); Pampuch, "Afrikanische Freedom Fighter im Exil der DDR."
101 Contemporary efforts to grasp these new African varieties of socialism include Carl G. Rosberg and Thomas M. Callaghy, ed., *Socialism in Sub-Saharan Africa: A New Assessment* (Berkeley: Institute of International Studies, University of California, 1979); David Ottaway and Marina Ottaway, *Afrocommunism* (New York: Africana Publishers, 1986); Keller and Rothchild, ed., *Afro-Marxist Regimes*.

and Príncipe. They also met with delegations of SWAPO, the Patriotic Front of Zimbabwe, as well as with the ANC. Angola's MPLA and Mozambique's FRELIMO signed friendship treaties with the GDR, "the first contracts of this kind of the GDR with countries outside the socialist community."[102] In the eyes of Honecker and other high-ranking East German politicians, echoing the optimistic mood of the early 1960s, Africa was returning to the center of world revolution. As the Politburo's foreign relations operator Hermann Axen proclaimed, "this huge continent is in the process of awakening, departing from colonialist and neocolonialist exploitation to a life of freedom, independence and social progress. The world-historical transition of the peoples from exploitation to socialism has now powerfully gripped the fourth continent. The national and social liberation revolutions have taken firm root in Africa."[103]

The revived rhetoric of African revolution sugarcoated an important change in South-East relations: an increasing economization and commercialization which resulted from fundamental transformations and shocks in global financial and commodity markets, as well as the constraints of Eastern European consumer societies.[104] In the case of the GDR, the turn towards economic concerns was also facilitated by the admission of both German states to the United Nations in 1973 after which diplomatic recognition ceased to be the primary objective in foreign affairs. In economic terms, the 1970s witnessed a "new phenomenon of interdependence."[105] Price trends on global raw material and international capital markets, recessions, inflation, and banking crises had immediate repercussions in various countries in Europe, Africa, Asia, and South America.

Due to their inflexible, planned economies, many state socialist countries in Europe had difficulties in adjusting to this new situation. The GDR was no exception. On top of this, from the early 1970s socialist European states were promising a new consumer-oriented economy. Even in those regimes that were able to

---

102 Wolfgang Meyer and Freimut Keßner, *Kämpfendes Afrika: Begegnungen der Freundschaft und Solidarität* (Dresden: Zeit im Bild, 1979). Our Translation.
103 Hermann Axen at the 10th Meeting of the SED Central Committee, April 1979, cited in Meyer and Keßner, *Kämpfendes Afrika*, Preface. Our translation.
104 Sara Lorenzini, "Comecon and the South in the Years of Détente: A Study on East–South Economic Relations," *European Review of History* 21 (2014); Anne Dietrich, "Oranges and the New Black: Importing, Provisioning, and Consuming Tropical Fruits and Coffee in the GDR, 1971–89," in *The Socialist Good Life: Desire, Development, and Standards of Living in Eastern Europe*, ed. Cristofer Scarboro, Diana Mincyte, and Zsuzsa Gille (Bloomington: Indiana University Press, 2020), 104–131.
105 Niall Ferguson, "Crisis, What Crisis? The 1970s and the Shock of the Global," in *The Shock of the Global: The 1970s in Perspective*, ed. Niall Ferguson et al. (Cambridge: The Belknap Press of Harvard University Press, 2010), 15.

commit to such expenditure, this required substantial investments into housing and retail and was a costly means to guarantee popular support and maintain a stable political system.[106] Linked to both of these trends, external indebtedness burdened many such national economies and impelled leaders to act. Accordingly, trade officials in the GDR busily sought alternative sources of hard currency or ways of bypassing the world market. Above all, they had an interest in importing mineral resources, coal, and crude oil. This became particularly acute given the Soviet strategy, implemented with other countries in the Council for Mutual Economic Assistance (Comecon), of adjusting their highly subsidized oil prices to be more in line with the recent market price increases.[107] Facing skyrocketing world market prices for mineral resources and agricultural commodities like cotton, coffee, and cocoa, the GDR's economic planners intensified the principle of barter trade (*Ware-gegen-Ware*[108]). Their trading partners in Africa received trucks, weapons, turnkey facilities, and agricultural machinery. They also got East German personnel, whose tasks were often related to the GDR's material exports.[109]

Enabling the GDR to receive agricultural and mineral commodities without using precious hard currency, trade with Africa was thus "primarily a matter of the existence of the GDR," as the infamous leader of the GDR's powerful foreign trade section *Kommerzielle Koordinierung* (KoKo), Alexander Schalck-Golodkowski, put it in 1982.[110] Schalck-Golodkowski and Günter Mittag, the secretary for economy at the Central Committee of the SED, were the leading actors in the so-called *Mittag-Kommission*, a high-profile party institution established in December 1977 that came to expand, coordinate, and commercialize the GDR's relations with Africa, Asia, and Latin America. The *Mittag-Kommission* made use of good party relations and newly institutionalized political alliances with regimes

---

106 Dietrich, "Oranges and the New Black", 107–108.
107 Winrow, *The Foreign Policy of the GDR*, 160.
108 Immanuel R. Harisch, "Handel und Solidarität: Die Beziehungen der DDR mit Angola und São Tomé und Príncipe unter besonderer Berücksichtigung des Austauschs 'Ware-gegen-Ware' ca. 1975–1990" (Master Thesis, University of Vienna, 2018).
109 Anne Dietrich, "Zwischen solidarischem Handel und ungleichem Tausch: Zum Südhandel der DDR am Beispiel des Imports kubanischen Zuckers und äthiopischen Kaffees," *Journal für Entwicklungspolitik* 30 (2014), doi:10.20446/JEP-2414–3197–30–3–48; Immanuel R. Harisch, "Bartering Coffee, Cocoa and W50 Trucks: The Trade Relationships of the GDR, Angola and São Tomé in a Comparative Perspective," *Global Histories* 3 (2017), doi:10.17169/GHSJ.2017.135.
110 Döring, *Es geht um unsere Existenz*, 13. On "KoKo", see Matthias Judt, *Der Bereich Kommerzielle Koordinierung: Das DDR-Wirtschaftsimperium des Alexander Schalck-Golodkowski. Mythos und Realität* (Berlin: Ch. Links, 2013).

in Africa that embraced Marxism.[111] Following Ethiopia's 1974 revolution and embrace of Marxism-Leninism, the Derg regime desperately needed weapons to fight the Somali invasion of the Ogaden region and to suppress insurgencies within the country. The GDR seized the opportunity and KoKo's foreign traders, in coordination with the *Mittag-Kommission*, started to deliver military equipment on the basis of a barter agreement in exchange for badly-needed coffee.[112]

Economic reconfigurations were also a political matter. According to Odd Arne Westad, the 1970s and early 1980s marked an era in which the conflict between the USA and the USSR in the "Third World" reached its climax.[113] The non-aligned movement, which most African states had joined, continuously expressed its fear of a third world war brought about by nuclear armament.[114] Proxy wars were fought in the Global South, predominantly in Asia and Africa. In 1975 the United States was forced to withdraw from Vietnam. The end of US involvement there served as a fresh inspiration for revolutionaries in Africa and as a source of hope for peace, freedom, and progress.

South of the rivers Congo and Ruvuma, the late phase of decolonization also brought to power governments proclaiming socialist projects. After the Carnation Revolution of April 1974 and the cessation of the colonial war in Lusophone Africa, new independent nation-states were proclaimed, often accompanied by civil war. During the year 1975, when Angola became independent, the power struggle between the competing liberation movements led to a fierce internationalized tussle for political rule in Luanda. While Cuba and the USSR supplied the MPLA with combat troops and arms[115] to fight off the invasion of South African troops allied with UNITA (*União Nacional para a Independência Total de Angola*),

---

111 Anne Dietrich, "Kaffee in der DDR – 'Ein Politikum ersten Ranges'" in *Kaffeewelten: Historische Perspektiven auf eine globale Ware im 20. Jahrhundert*, ed. Christiane Berth et al. (Göttingen: Vandenhoeck & Ruprecht, 2015), 230–233; Döring, *Es geht um unsere Existenz*, 44; Harisch, "Bartering Coffee," 56.

112 Anne Dietrich, "Bartering Within and Outside the CMEA: The GDR's Import of Cuban Fruits and Ethiopian Coffee," in *Between East and South: Spaces of Interaction in the Globalizing Economy of the Cold War*, ed. Anna Calori et al. (Berlin: De Gruyter, 2019), 200–201; Dietrich, "Kaffee in der DDR"; Dietrich, "Zwischen solidarischem Handel und ungleichem Tausch"; Berthold Unfried, "Friendship and Education, Coffee and Weapons: Exchanges Between Socialist Ethiopia and the German Democratic Republic," *Northeast African Studies* 16 (2016).

113 Westad, *The Global Cold War*.

114 Prashad, *The Poorer Nations*.

115 Piero Gleijeses, *Visions of Freedom: Havana, Washington, Pretoria and the Struggle for Southern Africa, 1976–1991* (Chapel Hill: The University of North Carolina Press, 2016); Vladimir Shubin, *The Hot 'Cold War': The USSR in Southern Africa* (London, Scottsville: Pluto Press; University of KwaZulu-Natal Press, 2008).

the GDR continued to support the friendly MPLA government with solidarity shipments[116] and an array of experts in the fields of transport, agriculture, and education.[117] The MPLA leadership made it clear that it would expect "the utmost possible commitment of the socialist community", and that "fast acting of every country is important."[118] In the context of the 1977 *Sofortprogramm* ("immediate program", set up by high-ranked SED and MPLA party officials, including Angolan President Agostinho Neto) for the recovery of Angola's ailing coffee industry after the Portuguese exodus, a total of 217 GDR citizens, including truck drivers, coffee roasters, civil engineers, and car mechanics, were sent to Angola.[119] The friendship brigades formed the backbone of this solidarity-trade project, and during the 1980s up to eight friendship brigades (out of a total of 19 worldwide) were active in Angola.[120]

As Paul Sprute argues in his contribution to this volume, the diaries of the friendship brigades, authored collectively during the 1980s, show that the young East Germans saw themselves as modernizers for a socialist Angola in the making. In the schematic portrayals in the diaries, Angolans are firmly attributed the role of thankful beneficiaries of East German actions. Their time in Angola justified the East German order in the minds of *Brigadisten* since Angola's war-torn economy and society assured them of how much material progress had been achieved in the GDR. Emphasizing technical expertise, Sprute identifies the brigades not as a "politics machine" of the GDR's solidarity discourse (as argued by Toni Weis[121]), but rather as pursuing a "humanitarian mission of modernization" within a contest of competing East-West visions of European modernism.

In contrast to governments espousing African socialism during the 1960s and emphasizing non-alignment, the rulers of Ethiopia, Mozambique, and Angola actively encouraged closer ties to the East. This led to a reconfiguration of the global landscape. As Marcia C. Schenck argues, the socialist world seen from

---

116 Schleicher, "The (GDR) in the Liberation Struggle of Southern Africa," 503–507.
117 Bettina Husemann and Annette Neumann, "DDR – VR Angola: Fakten und Zusammenhänge zur bildungspolitischen Zusammenarbeit von 1975 bis 1989," in *Engagiert für Afrika. Die DDR und Afrika II*, ed. Ulrich van der Heyden, Ilona Schleicher and Hans-Georg Schleicher (Münster: Lit, 1994).
118 "Bericht über den Arbeitsbesuch des Premierministers der Volksrepublik Angola, Lopo do Nascimento, Mitglied des Politbüros und Sekretär des Zentralkomitees der MPLA-Partei der Arbeit, vom 6. bis 8. Februar 1978 in der DDR", February 10, 1978, 6, SAPMO-BArch, DE 1/57596, cited in Harisch, "East German Friendship-Brigades".
119 Harisch, "East German Friendship-Brigades"; Dietrich, "Kaffee in der DDR".
120 Schleicher, "Elemente entwicklungspolitischer Zusammenarbeit FDGB und FDJ," 137.
121 Weis, "The Politics Machine."

some places in Africa became closer: "For some Africans the global rise of socialism flattened the geography and led to Havana, East Berlin, Prague, and Moscow becoming likely destinations for students, workers, politicians, and experts from all over the continent; it was thus more likely that a young Mozambican school child would receive its education in geographically distant Cuba or the GDR than in neighboring South Africa or Rhodesia."[122] The plurality of encounters in school and working life – including the establishment of new educational institutions for African students in the Socialist world, the deployment of friendship (SdF) brigades, and the recruiting of contract workers – led to new entanglements between African and Eastern Bloc countries and an intensification of the flow of knowledge and ideas between the "Second" and the "Third" world.

East Germany was particularly active in the area of educational cooperation. For instance, more than 600 Angolan students came to study at institutions of higher learning in East Germany, where they had to negotiate the rigorous academic requirements and strict rules regulating their new East German lives to create spaces that conformed to their expectations of study abroad.[123] Another well-explored example of cooperation in the education sector was the Friendship School (*Schule der Freundschaft*, SdF) in Staßfurt, East Germany, which 900 Mozambican school children attended between 1982 and 1989. They were later joined by Namibian children. Officially between the ages of 12 and 14 upon their arrival, the Mozambicans underwent the equivalent of middle and high school and left the GDR with two years of professional training under their belt, leading to certificates as skilled workers, ranging from electrician to cook.[124]

---

122 Schenck, "Constructing and Deconstructing," 136.
123 Marcia C. Schenck, "Negotiating the German Democratic Republic: Angolan Student Migration During the Cold War, 1976–90," *Africa* 89 (2019).
124 Marcia C Schenck, "Small Strangers at the School of Friendship: Memories of Mozambican School Students to the German Democratic Republic," *Bulletin of the GHI* 15 (2020); Annette Scheunpflug and Jürgen Krause, *Die Schule der Freundschaft: Ein Bildungsexperiment in der DDR. Beiträge aus dem Fachbereich Pädagogik der Universität der Bundeswehr Hamburg* (Hamburg: Universität der Bundeswehr Hamburg, 2000); Mathias Tullner, "Das Experiment 'Schule der Freundschaft' im Kontext der mosambikanischen Bildungspolitik," in *Freundschaftsbande und Beziehungskisten: Die Afrikapolitik der DDR und der BRD gegenüber Mosambik*, ed. Hans-Joachim Döring and Uta Rüchel (Frankfurt am Main: Brandes & Apsel, 2005); Uta Rüchel, "'…auf Deutsch sozialistisch zu denken…' – Mosambikaner in der Schule der Freundschaft," ed. Die Landesbeauftragte für die Unterlagen des Staatssicherheitsdienstes der ehemaligen DDR in Sachsen-Anhalt, (Magdeburg, JVA Naumburg – Arbeitsverwaltung, 2001); Tanja Müller, *Legacies of Socialist Solidarity: East Germany in Mozambique* (Lanham: Lexington, 2014).

Francisca Raposo in this volume takes us with her into her own childhood as she reflects on the insecurity, the misinformation, and the weeks and months of waiting to finally leave Mozambique to become a student at the School of Friendship. In this text the reader is invited to relive the anxious anticipation of a Mozambican girl who, when imagining her future schooling in East Germany, dreamt of an unknown future paradise, unburdened by reality. The text, contextualized by Marcia C. Schenck, ends abruptly with the arrival in the GDR, leaving it up to the reader's imagination as to whether the young girl found what she was looking for once moored in the parallel universe of a boarding school in a tiny East German village.

The idea for the SdF was born in FRELIMO leadership circles at the end of the 1970s. President Samora Machel (1975–86) prioritized professional education to provide the industrializing country with skilled labor in the absence of a professional working class. This was important both ideologically and practically. Not only was the working class the revolutionary class in Marxist-socialist exegesis, but the young People's Republic of Mozambique (PRM) lacked people with professional skills. Despite the revolutionary emphasis on the working class, many Mozambicans – including parents, students, and members of the Mozambican Ministry of Education – did not value vocational training as much as general education and advanced degrees.[125] East Germany was not the only country to offer education aid to socialist-leaning African countries. Mozambicans also studied at the Isla de la Juventud in Cuba.[126] Similarly, Angolan workers went to Cuba to work and gain skills and technical training.[127] About 2,500 Angolan workers also went to East Germany between 1985 and 1990.[128] Nevertheless, the largest program of skills training was established between the GDR and Mozambique in 1979. This contract labor and training program saw about 22,000 contracts signed until its dissolution at the end of the

---

125 Tullner, "Das Experiment 'Schule der Freundschaft'," 100.
126 Hauke Dorsch, "Rites of Passage Overseas? On the Sojourn of Mozambican Students and Scholars in Cuba," *Africa Spectrum* 43 (2008); Christine Hatzky, *Kubaner in Angola: Süd-Süd Kooperation und Bildungstransfer 1976–1991* (Berlin: De Gruyter, 2012), 239–245; Michael H. Erisman, *Cuba's Foreign Relations in a Post-Soviet World* (Gainesville: University Press of Florida, 2002), 100.
127 Christine Hatzky, *Cubans in Angola: South–South Cooperation and Transfer of Knowledge, 1976–1991*, (Madison: The University of Wisconsin Press, 2015).
128 Paulino José Miguele, "Sobre o mito da solidariedade: Trabalhadores contratados moçambicanos e angolanos na RDA," in *Projekt Migration*, ed. Kölnischer Kunstverein, Dokumentationszentrum und Museum über Migration in Deutschland, Köln, Institut für Kulturanthropologie und Europäische Ethnologie der Johann Wolfgang-Goethe-Universität Frankfurt/Main, Institut für Theorie der Gestalt (Köln: DuMont, 2005), 817.

GDR.[129] As Franziska Rantzsch shows in her contribution, the negotiation process between the GDR and Mozambique did not reinvent the wheel but rather used pre-existing blueprints from prior labor migration schemes to East Germany (such as the Polish or Hungarian migrations). It also drew on labor migration experience of Mozambicans to South African mines. Initially, the negotiation process sought to arrive at an agreement that combined the interests of both countries in the name of a policy of mutual advantage. This goal became less central in the 1980s as the GDR disengaged somewhat from Mozambique due to disenchantment with the ongoing turmoil and lack of developmental progress there, and the contract labor and training program started to morph into a source of cheap labor for the GDR.

Based on oral history interviews with returned workers, Fernando Machava explores in this volume the contract labor migration and its legacies from a Mozambican perspective. His focus lies on the workers' reintegration into Maputo's various suburbs after their mass return in the 1990s. Exploring the impact of the goods the returnees brought home, he argues that they at first were able to support themselves and their families and even assumed the function of role models in their communities. Due to a lack of integration in the formal labor market the dreams and aspirations of many returnees were disappointed and some Madjermanes, as the returned workers became known in Mozambique, turned to protest as a result. These protests are still ongoing, and, as Machava highlights, are not always supported by the population at large. Solidarity as lived experience and policy came with restrictions, then and now.

Limits to Socialist Development in the 1980s

There were limits to socialist assistance. The East German ideals of anti-imperialist solidarity were challenged by the GDR's growing debt and by dissenting opinions within the heterogenous socialist world on the appropriate scope of socialist development policy. For example, the labor and training programs that were negotiated between the GDR and various countries deteriorated into work programs as numbers rose and training aspects increasingly took a back seat.[130] But it was not only the GDR's political and economic situation that

---

129 Eric Allina skillfully examines the political aspects of this labor migration in Eric Allina, "'Neue Menschen' für Mosambik: Erwartungen an und Realität von Vertragsarbeit in der DDR der 1980er-Jahre," *Arbeit, Bewegung, Geschichte: Zeitschrift für Historische Studien* 15 (2016).
130 The states from which laborers came to East Germany are listed here with the year of the signature of the bilateral agreements: Poland (1963 und 1971), Hungary (1967), Vietnam (1973

influenced economic plans. For instance, the escalation of violence in large parts of Lusophone Africa in the first half of the 1980s significantly influenced the outcomes of bilateral efforts.[131] In Angola, GDR citizens were repeatedly saved from UNITA attacks by Angolan, Cuban, and Soviet soldiers. In Mozambique, eight East German development workers were murdered in 1984 by the anti-communist *Resistência Nacional Moçambicana* (RENAMO), which enjoyed financial and logistical support from South Africa and North Atlantic Treaty Organization (NATO) members such as the US and West Germany.[132] From the early 1980s, the intensifying internationalized destabilization war against the socialist governments in Angola and Mozambique led to an East German disengagement in joint economic projects as security concerns and disillusions with the countries' war-torn economies became paramount. In 1981, Mozambique was refused entry into Comecon as most members saw another "developing country" like Vietnam or Cuba as too much of an economic burden. As Sara Lorenzini has argued, "[t]his event signaled the collapse of the rhetoric of a special East–South solidarity," showing that "[n]ot all Third World countries were equal; not all possessed the right level of development to integrate with the socialist system."[133] Only the GDR clearly advocated for the admission, which illustrates that the so-called Eastern Bloc did not represent a homogenous set of interests and opinions. The GDR had invested in the Mozambican coal mining and textile industries,

---

and 1980), Algeria (1974), Cuba (1975), Mozambique (1979), Mongolia (1982), Angola (1985), China (1986) und North Korea (1986). See Dennis Kuck, "Für den sozialen Aufbau ihrer Heimat'? Ausländische Vertragsarbeitskräfte in der DDR," in *Fremde und Fremd-Sein in der DDR: Zu historischen Ursachen der Fremdenfeindlichkeit in Ostdeutschland*, ed. Jan C. Behrends, Thomas Lindenberger und Patrice G. Poutrus (Berlin: Metropol, 2003), 272. The study of these labor programs is most advanced for the Mozambican case. The field of labor migrations to other countries in the Eastern Bloc is still wide open; see for instance Alena K. Alamgir, "From the Field to the Factory Floor: Vietnamese Government's Defense of Migrant Workers' Interests in State-Socialist Czechoslovakia," *Journal of Vietnamese Studies* 12 (2017); idem, "Socialist Internationalism at Work: Changes in the Czechoslovak-Vietnamese Labor Exchange Program, 1967–89" (PhD diss., Rutgers University, 2014).

131 Westad, *Global Cold War*, chapter 9.
132 Ulrich van der Heyden, "'Es darf nichts passieren!' Entwicklungspolitisches Engagement der DDR in Mosambik zwischen Solidarität und Risiko,'" in *Wir haben Spuren hinterlassen! Die DDR in Mosambik: Erlebnisse, Erfahrungen und Erkenntnisse aus drei Jahrzehnten*, ed. Matthias Voß (Münster: Lit, 2005); William Minter, *Apartheid's Contras: An Inquiry into the Roots of War in Angola and Mozambique*, (Johannesburg: Witwatersrand University Press, 1994).
133 Sara Lorenzini, "The Socialist Camp and the Challenge of Economic Modernization in the Third World," in *The Cambridge History of Communism, Volume 2: The Socialist Camp and World Power 1941–1960s*, ed. Norman M. Naimark, Silvio Pons, and Sophie Quinn-Judge (Cambridge: Cambridge University Press, 2017).

and planned to get involved in the development of banana plantations and the construction of a pineapple processing plant in the provinces of Sofala and Zambezia.[134] This episode is one of many that show how the GDR tried to situate itself as an independent international actor within the socialist camp by adopting a pioneering role in the Global South.

On the ground, East German friendship brigades and technical experts increasingly reached their own personal limits and faced security challenges due to the expansion of the armed conflicts in Angola and Mozambique. In her contribution, Katrin Bahr touches upon the fear and insecurity among East German experts in Mozambique that followed the aforementioned deadly attack on German agricultural experts in the province of Niassa. Focusing on private photographs taken by East Germans in Mozambique in the 1980s, Bahr shows everyday experiences of the experts and their families abroad, oscillating between working life and private sphere, and unmasking European stereotypes about "Africa" and the predominantly white male gaze of the photographers. The contribution highlights how the private photographs differ from official state photographs and provide a deeper insight into life (work and leisure) in Mozambique. Bahr claims that the private pictures also follow the narratives of the representation of Africa in the context of colonialism and colonial structures. Moreover, women were often absent in the discourse of manual aid work abroad when it came to visual representation. Rather, if portrayed in private photographs, women act within the private sphere of child rearing and leisure time.

The changing role of women that was proclaimed by all socialist regimes, and which indeed enabled female emancipation to a certain degree, remained incomplete, as the contributions to this volume demonstrate. Evenia, an 18-year-old FRELIMO fighter and instructor, assumed a role of prominent military female leadership and gained prominence as a symbol and image in the book *Das Mädchen vom Sambesi* ['The Girl from the Zambezi'] by GDR journalist Ulrich Makosch (Bodie, this volume), but her portrait was stylized. In it, she remained apart from other Mozambican women and their varied relationships with the socialist project in Mozambique. The relative absence of women in many of the histories about South-Eastern entanglements points to the gap between the rhetoric and reality of empowerment. Jörg Depta and Anne-Kristin Hartmetz show in their contribution to this volume that Egyptian housewives were considered of "little relevance" for the GDR and therefore not targeted by German language courses at the East German Cultural Institute in Cairo. In the end, it

---

134 Mission report of the Director General of the foreign trade company AHB Fruchtimex of December 21, 1978, 3–11. SAPMO-BArch, DL1/25504.

is not that female students, workers, development experts, and cooperators did not exist, but they often took a backseat to male actors in all directions and through all strata of society.

Aside from state actors and government institutions, East German grassroots associations gained more importance during the 1980s. However, they continued to be subjected to highly asymmetrical relationships with state-sponsored aid. These "Third World groups" were mostly rooted in churches and focused on solidarity, for instance with Nicaragua, but also on causes such as the anti-apartheid movement and the situation of students and contract workers in the GDR. As Maria Magdalena Verburg has highlighted, these groups criticized the failures of socialism and objected to the discrepancies between propaganda and the practices of state and party leadership.[135]

Mikhail Gorbachev's policies of *glasnost* and *perestroika* aimed to address at least some of the inherent contradictions of state socialist regimes. Gorbachev's reform attempts did not only affect the Soviet Union, but rather prepared the ground for reforms and radical changes, and ended up bringing about the implosion of the socialist camp and the end of the global order that had been established after the Second World War. The GDR government was reluctant to accept the political and economic reforms initiated by Gorbachev's new policy after 1985. Furthermore, the East German leadership was uneasy with regard to the shifting interests of the Soviet Union's foreign policy towards Africa, wishing to maintain its close relations with Mozambique, Angola, and Ethiopia. In a speech held at the 27th CPSU Congress in 1986, Gorbachev emphasized the significance of political solutions to regional conflicts in the Global South, but did not mention Mozambique, Angola, Ethiopia, and other African states. This caused some alarm among the delegates from socialist-leaning states within the region present at the congress, who feared a Soviet withdrawal from political, economic, and military support.[136]

Socialist Disentanglements and Transitions – 1989 onwards

1989 is an iconic date for the history of the Eastern Bloc but it had global implications. Ulf Engel argues that "1989 was a watershed for the African people, too" because it was "part of a 'critical juncture of globalization' in which spatializa-

---

[135] Maria Magdalena Verburg, *Ostdeutsche Dritte-Welt-Gruppen vor und nach 1989/90* (Göttingen: V&R unipress, 2012).
[136] Winrow, *The Foreign Policy of the GDR in Africa*, 207.

tions of power [were] renegotiated worldwide."[137] Indeed, the "winds of change," which British Prime Minister Harold Macmillan had famously evoked in Cape Town as many African countries turned to independence in 1960, were once again blowing through the continent in the 1990s. In South Africa, Nelson Mandela was released after 27 years in prison in 1990, President Frederik Willem de Klerk lifted the party ban on the ANC, and together they initiated the "miracle" of the end of apartheid. Among those hailing the miracle were those who had conveniently forgotten that they had supported apartheid as a bulwark against communism.[138] The same year that Mandela was released from prison, Namibia finally became independent.[139] In Zimbabwe, Robert Mugabe's one-party state evolved after the merger of ZANU and ZAPU (Zimbabwe African Peoples Union) to the ZANU-PF (Zimbabwe African National Union – Patriotic Front) on December 22, 1987.[140] Exactly one year later, in Angola, an – albeit transitory – peace process was initiated with the agreement of December 22, 1988. Cuban and Soviet troops were withdrawn from Africa shortly after.[141]

Overall, in the late 1980s, many regimes across the continent set aside their socialist convictions. Preceded by the implementation of Structural Adjustment Programs (SAPs), financed by the International Monetary Fund (IMF), and following the socialist countries' recommendation to accept Western aid and capital, various African governments began to think of – or surrendered after years of resistance to[142] – both economic and political reforms and engagement with new political institutions which mostly brought them closer to a globalizing emerging market-based world order. While 1989 was a key moment in East Germany and the Eastern Bloc, heralding rapid political changes that led to the dissolution of the GDR in 1990 and of the Soviet Union in 1991, the search for communist answers went on in Cuba, North Korea, and China. In Africa, as discussed

---

137 Ulf Engel, "Africa's '1989,'" in *1989 in a Global Perspective*, ed. Ulf Engel, Frank Hadler, and Matthias Middell (Leipzig: Leipziger Universitätsverlag, 2015).
138 Patti Ealdmeir, *Anatomy of a Miracle: The End of Apartheid and the Birth of the New South Africa* (New Brunswick: Rutgers University Press, 1997).
139 Henning Melber, *Understanding Namibia: The Trials of Independence* (London: Hurst, 2014).
140 Engel, "Africa's '1989'," 334; D.R. Kempton, "Africa in the Age of Perestroika," *Africa Today* 38 (1991).
141 Piero Gleijeses, "Moscow's Proxy? Cuba and Africa 1975–1988," *Journal of Cold War Studies* 8 (2006).
142 Aili M. Tripp, *Changing the Rules: The Politics of Liberalization and the Urban Informal Economy in Tanzania* (Berkeley: University of California Press, 1997). For the transformation process of a socialist state in Southern Africa see M. Anne Pitcher, *Transforming Mozambique: The Politics of Privatization, 1975–2000* (Cambridge: Cambridge University Press, 2002).

above, the transition was a more fragmentary and subtle process and did not proceed linearly but extended during the 1980s and early 1990s.

As made abundantly clear throughout this discussion, neither Africa nor Eastern Europe began to globalize in 1989. However, both regions now joined an exclusively Western-led vision of globalization. In doing so, they abandoned alternative projects. Towards the late 1980s in much of Eastern Europe, democratic transformation and the spread of liberal democracy coincided with the consolidation of capitalist market economies. The impact of the formal disbanding of the Comecon and the Warsaw Pact in June and July 1991 was felt in the Global South. Cuba, for instance, suffered immensely from the resulting economic disintegration, the loss of Eastern European markets, and the abrupt ending of Soviet resource flows.[143]

We should, however, resist the temptation to reify 1989 as the only significant moment of global change. What 1989 confirmed was the end of an alternative vision of global interconnectedness that was grounded in socialist, anti-imperialist geographies. This came to mean the regrouping of Europe under Western domination underlined by the decision of Eastern European countries to seek membership in a Western, "white" world replete with its racialized privileges. So it seemed, at least, from some Global South perspectives. Indeed, Gorbachev's "fateful speech in Finland [...] in which he called for a 'common European home'" sent out "shock waves [that] went through the radical Third World", as the Tanzanian leftist Abdulrahman Babu observed in 1991. In his view, Europe was "returning to its pre-World War One imperial menace – the Europe which has done so much damage to the rest of the world in conquest, slavery, colonization, settlerism, distortion and diversion of our national histories, through the massive devastation of world wars, the depletion of our resources, and the endangering of the world's environment."[144] 1989 sounded the death knell for cross-continental decolonization aspirations that had already been crumbling. Fortress Europe slowly emerged as Europe integrated and its borders were shifted outwards as new walls and fences were erected southwards in Africa. In the process borders as barriers to mobility solidified as markers of race and a prosperity gap. The Iron Curtain was lifted in 1989 but new walls emerged between Europe and Africa.[145]

---

143 Anne Dietrich, "Exploring Changes in Cuba's Ports and Hinterlands: Transition from US to Socialist Sugar Markets," *Comparativ* 27 (2017): 54.
144 A. M. Babu, "A New Europe: Consequences for Tanzania," *Review of African Political Economy* 18 (1991): 75. Parts of the quote are also cited in Mark et al., *1989*, 247.
145 See Mark et al., *1989*, 9–10. We recognize that the history of European exclusionary borders extends back to the creation of nation states.

As several of our contributions demonstrate, the end of Eastern European state-socialism and socialist projects in Africa marked a caesura – but not the end – in the multifaceted relations between people that used to live in those countries that once constituted the socialist world. The reverberations of the experiences that migrants from the Global South and the Global East had while navigating complex socialist encounters continue to impact their lives in the present. For instance, the legacies of the socialist period come to life in the biography of an individual former Mozambican contract worker, Ibraimo Alberto, who migrated to the GDR in 1981, witnessed German reunification, and stayed on in unified Germany as a German citizen (Schenck and Alberto). Ibraimo Alberto's experience was both beautiful and heartbreaking, reassuring and discouraging, as he navigated work and boxing in the two Germanies and encountered people who loved him and people who hated him because of his skin color. Xenophobia and racism have become defining features of Ibraimo Alberto's life; first as a constant negative lived experience for him and his family, and today as a topic about which he seeks to raise awareness in Germany.[146] It is necessary to explicitly state again that racism was always present and a defining feature of the lives of Africans who came to live across the Eastern Bloc.[147] Though forms of expressions varied across local context, the basic contradiction remained: racist thought and practice permeated the everyday in officially anti-racist and anti-imperialist societies, of which only East Germany had direct historical links to colonialism in Africa.[148] Racism did not disappear with the end of the socialist republics and unions but in many cases its expression worsened during the hardships of transition and remains an unsolved issue across the formerly socialist world.[149] The legacies of the socialist encounters explored in this volume

---

146 Apart from workers African students also suffered from and resided to racism in their daily lives and systemic racism in the SED regime and media in the GDR, see Sara Pugach, "African Students and the Politics of Race and Gender in the German Democratic Republic, 1957–1990," in *Comrades of Color: East Germany in the Cold War World*, ed. Quinn Slobodian (New York, Oxford: Berghan, 2015).

147 For the context in Czechoslovakia, see Alena K. Alamgir, "Race Is Elsewhere: State-Socialist Ideology and the Racialisation of Vietnamese Workers in Czechoslovakia," *Race & Class* 54 (2013). Further, African students in the USSR suffering from racism are a much-explored topic, see for instance Julie Hessler, "Death of an African Student in Moscow: Race, Politics, and the Cold War," *Cahiers Du Monde Russe* 47 (2006).

148 To understand the workings of racism and socialist chromatism in East Germany see Quinn Slobodian, ed., *Comrades of Color*.

149 For the East German context, see Patrick R. Ireland, "Socialism, Unification Policy and the Rise of Racism in Eastern Germany," *International Migration Review* 31 (1997). Eric and Jessica Allina-Pisano explore how racism permeates the lives of African Students in Russia after the

are complex and the perpetuation of racism and xenophobia in formerly East German states questions the success that international socialist migrations had in provincializing and internationalizing the GDR.

The legacies are also complex on the other side of the globe. Fernando Machava in this volume, for instance, draws out the complicated legacies of the former Mozambican contract workers who returned back to Mozambique in the early 1990s, but whose dreams and aspirations were stifled due to their traumatic reintegration into a Mozambique that remained among the world's poorest states. Back home, the Mozambican returnees from East Germany, whether workers, school students or university students, created their own communities of remembrance, as did Angolan returnees, Vietnamese returnees, and returnees elsewhere. As this volume's emphasis on Mozambique-GDR relations mirrors, the most active continuous interest was expressed by former East German citizens who were sent to Mozambique, by the Mozambican diaspora in Germany and by Mozambicans who went home. This has resulted in an attentiveness, among scholars of African history and Eastern European history alike, vis-à-vis Mozambique. In their contribution Alexandra Piepiorka and Eduardo Buanaissa examine this transcontinental Afro-European memory space from the perspective of historical actors by reading memory literature to explore how the GDR and Mozambique were remembered by Mozambicans who moored in the GDR and East Germans who went to Mozambique during the 1970s and 1980s respectively. The authors focus on the memory of the "other" to explore alternative understandings and lived experiences of socialist exchanges. On the one hand, they introduce individuals like António, a Mozambican student of economics, who bemoaned his disentanglement from East Germans whom he had gotten to know as sociable and friendly in Mozambique but who struck him as impersonal and cold once in the GDR. On the other hand, Dieter, an East German student of Portuguese, felt fully integrated in his dorm at Eduardo Mondlane University in Maputo and became entangled with the lives of his Mozambican fellow students – something for which the other East German expats, who generally did not profit as much from private intercultural exchange, envied him. Both António and Dieter were marked by their respective experiences of navigating these cross-continental socialist encounters enough to care about writing down their memories, years later.

---

transition, see Jessica Allina-Pisano and Eric Allina-Pisano, "'Friendship of Peoples' after the Fall: Violence and Pan-African Community in Post-Soviet Moscow," in *Africa in Russia, Russia in Africa: 300 Years of Encounters*, ed. Maxim Matusevich (Trenton: Africa World Press, 2007).

It was not only Mozambican and East German authors who contributed to the new genre of memory literature putting the GDR in a global context. Thomas Kunze and Thomas Vogel have collected stories in their volume "Ostalgie International,"[150] which brings together Cuban, Vietnamese, American, Nicaraguan, Namibian, Chilean, Mozambican, Syrian, Angolan, Palestinian, Iraqi, Afghan, Russian, and Mongolian voices who relate their varying memories of the GDR. In Mozambique, the majority of returned contract workers celebrate what Marcia C. Schenck terms "eastalgia" – a nostalgia for aspects of their experience in the GDR which is both similar and quite different in character and expression from the *Ostalgie* (a portmanteau of the German words for east and nostalgia) felt and expressed by former East German citizens. Many Madjermanes idolize their East German past not least as the carefree time of their youth, but also against the backdrop of their often traumatic reintegration experience in Mozambique, which leaves many struggling in relative poverty today.[151] Most importantly, public eastalgic remembering serves as criticism of the Mozambican government which has not only failed to achieve a transparent process of the repayment of withheld wages and security benefits from the workers' time in the GDR but also – from the perspective of the workers – has failed to provide stable blue-collar working life and living conditions for what was once intended to be the vanguard workforce of the People's Republic of Mozambique. Experiences collected in the GDR continue to shape how the returnees measure their lives in their home countries. The point of view of socialist cosmopolitans continues to impact the post-socialist landscape.

In sum, this edited volume challenges the view of socialism as marked by stagnation, uniformity, immobility, and isolation by investigating diverse visions and practices of socialism from a global history perspective, pointing out how they shaped – and were shaped in return – by African and European actors in numerous encounters. As illustrated by this book, however, socialist ideas and the encounters they inspired in Africa, Europe, and beyond were not dead ends which have nothing to teach; quite to the contrary, they may act as a constant reminder about the life and death of alternative visions of social, political, and economic organizations and alternative notions of globalization. It is thus a fundamental motivation of this edited volume to provide space for fresh perspectives on South-East encounters in global history and to illustrate the plethora of histori-

---

150 Thomas Kunze and Thomas Vogel, ed., *Ostalgie international: Erinnerungen an die DDR von Nicaragua bis Vietnam* (Berlin: Ch. Links, 2010).
151 Marcia C. Schenck, "A Chronology of Nostalgia: Memories of Former Angolan and Mozambican Worker Trainees to East Germany," *Labor History* 59 (2018).

cally documented ideas and practices of socialism(s) in Africa and East Germany as seen through encounters of non-elite actors, through examining institution building, and through scrutinizing visions of solidarity. In so doing we shed light on processes of (dis)entanglements, moorings, and unmoorings, and demonstrate that the study of how actors navigated the socialist world is best analyzed from several perspectives, based on multiple archives and framed within global history. This volume, therefore, contributes not only to a more complex understanding of global socialisms as well as Africa's place in the world; it also reveals a panorama of different pasts and, perhaps, futures.

Bibliography

Adelman, Jeremy. "What Is Global History Now?" *Aeon*, March 2, 2017. Accessed October 9, 2019. https://aeon.co/essays/is-global-history-still-possible-or-has-it-had-its-moment.

Adi, Hakim. *Pan-Africanism: A History*. London: Bloomsbury, 2018.

Alamgir, Alena K. "Race Is Elsewhere: State-Socialist Ideology and the Racialization of Vietnamese Workers in Czechoslovakia." *Race & Class* 54 (2013): 67–85.

Alamgir, Alena K. "Socialist Internationalism at Work: Changes in the Czechoslovak-Vietnamese Labor Exchange Program, 1967–89." PhD diss., Rutgers University, 2014.

Alamgir, Alena K. "From the Field to the Factory Floor: Vietnamese Government's Defense of Migrant Workers' Interests in State-Socialist Czechoslovakia." *Journal of Vietnamese Studies* 12 (2017): 10–43.

Alamgir, Alena K. "Labor and Labor Migration in State Socialism." *Labor History* 59 (2018): 271–276.

Alexander, Jocelyn, and JoAnn McGregor. "African Soldiers in the USSR: Oral Histories of ZAPU Intelligence Cadres' Soviet Training, 1964–1979." *Journal of Southern African Studies* 43 (2017): 49–66.

Allina, Eric. "'Neue Menschen' für Mosambik: Erwartungen an und Realität von Vertragsarbeit in der DDR der 1980er-Jahre." *Arbeit, Bewegung, Geschichte: Zeitschrift für Historische Studien* 15 (2016): 65–84.

Allina-Pisano, Jessica, and Eric Allina-Pisano. "'Friendship of Peoples' after the Fall: Violence and Pan-African Community in Post-Soviet Moscow." In *Africa in Russia, Russia in Africa: 300 Years of Encounters*, edited by Maxim Matusevich, 175–198. Trenton: Africa World Press, 2007.

Allman, Jean. "Phantoms of the Archive: Kwame Nkrumah, a Nazi Pilot Named Hanna, and the Contingencies of Postcolonial History-Writing." *The American Historical Review* 118 (2013): 104–129.

Amirahmadi, H. "The Non-Capitalist Way of Development." *Review of Radical Political Economics* 19 (1987): 22–46.

Andreyev, I. *The Noncapitalist Way: Soviet Experience and the Liberated Countries*. Moscow: Moscow Progress Publishers, 1977.

Angermann, Eric. "'Ihr gehört auch zur Avantgarde': Afrikanische Gewerkschafter an der FDGB-Hochschule Fritz Heckert (1961–1963)." Master's thesis, Georg-August-Universität Göttingen, 2018.

Austen, Ralph A. *African Economic History: Internal Development and External Dependency.* London: James Currey, 1987.

Babu, A. M. "A New Europe: Consequences for Tanzania." *Review of African Political Economy* 18 (1991): 75–78.

BBC World Service, Radio Documentary "Comrade Africa," November 14, 2019. Last modified January 11, 2020. https://www.bbc.co.uk/programmes/w3ct036 t.

Becker, Joachim. "Anatomie der Sozialismen: Wirtschaft, Staat und Gesellschaft." In *Sozialismen: Entwicklungsmodelle von Lenin bis Nyerere*, edited by Joachim Becker, and Rudy Weissenbacher, 13–56. Wien: Promedia, 2009.

Bell, Daniel. *The Coming of Post-Industrial Society: A Venture in Social Forecasting.* New York: Basic Books, 1976.

Bi'bak. "Freundschaft auf Zeit." Accessed January 11, 2020. https://bi-bak.de/en/bi-bakino/freundschaft-auf-zeit.

Bockman, Johanna. "Socialist Globalization Against Capitalist Neocolonialism: The Economic Ideas Behind the New International Economic Order." *Humanity: An International Journal of Human Rights, Humanitarianism, and Development* 6 (2015): 109–128.

Bodie, George. "Global GDR? Sovereignty, Legitimacy and Decolonization in the German Democratic Republic, 1960–1989." PhD diss., University College London, 2019.

Bodie, George. "'It Is a Shame We Are Not Neighbours': GDR Tourist Cruises to Cuba, 1961–89." *Journal of Contemporary History* 55 (2020): 411–434.

Brennan, James R. "The Cold War Battle Over Global News in East Africa: Decolonization, the Free Flow of Information, and the Media Business, 1960–1980." *Journal of Global History* 10 (2015): 333–356.

Brizuela-Garcia, Esperanza. "African Historiography and the Crisis of Institutions." In *The Study of Africa. Volume 1: Disciplinary and Interdisciplinary Encounters*, edited by Paul Tiyambe Zeleza, 135–167. Dakar: Codesria, 2006.

Burton, Eric. "Socialisms in Development: Revolution, Divergence and Crisis, 1917–1991." *Journal für Entwicklungspolitik* 33 (2017): 4–20.

Burton, Eric. "Tansanias 'Afrikanischer Sozialismus' und die Entwicklungspolitik der beiden deutschen Staaten: Akteure, Beziehungen und Handlungsspielräume, 1961–1990." PhD diss., University of Vienna, 2017.

Burton, Eric. "Introduction: Journeys of Education and Struggle: African Mobility in Times of Decolonization and the Cold War." *Stichproben. Vienna Journal of African Studies* 18 (2018): 1–17.

Burton, Eric. "Solidarität und ihre Grenzen: Die 'Brigaden der Freundschaft' der DDR." In *Internationale Solidarität: Globales Engagement in der Bundesrepublik und der DDR*, edited by Frank Bösch, Caroline Moine, and Stefanie Senger, 152–185. Göttingen: Wallstein, 2018.

Burton, Eric. "Hubs of Decolonization: African Liberation Movements and Eastern Connections in Cairo, Accra and Dar es Salaam." In *Southern African Liberation Movements and the Global Cold War 'East': Transnational Activism 1960–1990*, edited by Lena Dallywater, Helder A. Fonseca, and Chris Saunders, 25–56. Berlin: De Gruyter, 2019.

Burton, Eric. "Diverging Visions in Revolutionary Spaces: East German Advisers and Revolution from above in Zanzibar, 1964–1970." In *Between East and South: Spaces of Interaction in the Globalizing Economy of the Cold War*, edited by Anna Calori, Anne-Kristin Hartmetz, Bence Kocsev, James Mark, and Jan Zofka, 85–116. Berlin: De Gruyter, 2019.

Burton, Eric. "Decolonization, the Cold War and Africans' Routes to Overseas Education, 1957–1965." *Journal of Global History* 15 (2020): 169–191.

Büschel, Hubertus. *Hilfe zur Selbsthilfe: Deutsche Entwicklungsarbeit in Afrika 1960–1975*. Frankfurt am Main: Campus, 2014.

Calori, Anna, Anne-Kristin Hartmetz, Bence Kocsev, and Jan Zofka. "Alternative Globalization? Spaces and Economic Interactions between the 'Socialist Camp' and the 'Global South'." In *Between East and South: Spaces of Interaction in the Globalizing Economy of the Cold War*, edited by Anna Calori, Anne-Kristin Hartmetz, Bence Kocsev, James Mark, and Jan Zofka, 1–32. Berlin: De Gruyter, 2019.

Chen, Tao. "Weathering the Storms: East German Engineers in Zhengzhou, 1954–1964." *The China Review* 19 (2019): 39–64.

Cooper, Frederick. *Decolonization and African Society: The Labor Question in French and British Africa*. Cambridge: Cambridge University Press, 1996.

Cooper, Frederick. "What Is the Concept of Globalization Good for? An African Historian's Perspective." *African Affairs* 100 (2001): 189–213.

Cooper, Frederick. "Possibility and Constraint: African Independence in Historical Perspective." *The Journal of African History* 49 (2008): 167–196.

Cooper, Frederick. *Africa in the World: Capitalism, Empire, Nation-State*. Cambridge: Harvard University Press, 2014.

Conrad, Sebastian. *What Is Global History?* Princeton: Princeton University Press, 2016.

Conrad, Sebastian and Shalini Randeria, ed. *Jenseits des Eurozentrismus: Postkoloniale Perspektiven in den Geschichts- und Kulturwissenschaften*. Frankfurt: Campus Verlag, 2002.

Coulson, Andrew. *Tanzania: A Political Economy*. Second edition. Oxford: Oxford University Press, 2013.

Dagne, Haile Gabriel. *Das entwicklungspolitische Engagement der DDR in Äthiopien: Eine Studie auf der Basis äthiopischer Quellen*. Münster: Lit, 2004.

Dallywater, Lena, Chris Saunders, and Helder Adegar Fonseca, ed. *Southern African Liberation Movements and the Global Cold War 'East': Transnational Activism 1960–1990*. Berlin: De Gruyter, 2019.

Dietrich, Anne. "Zwischen solidarischem Handel und ungleichem Tausch: Zum Südhandel der DDR am Beispiel des Imports kubanischen Zuckers und äthiopischen Kaffees." *Journal für Entwicklungspolitik* 30 (2014): 48–67.

Dietrich, Anne. "Kaffee in der DDR – 'Ein Politikum ersten Ranges'." In *Kaffeewelten: Historische Perspektiven auf eine globale Ware im 20. Jahrhundert*, edited by Christiane Berth, Dorothee Wierling, and Volker Wünderich, 225–247. Göttingen: Vandenhoeck & Ruprecht, 2015.

Dietrich, Anne. "Exploring Changes in Cuba's Ports and Hinterlands: Transition from US to Socialist Sugar Markets." *Comparativ* 27 (2017): 41–57.

Dietrich, Anne. "Bartering Within and Outside the CMEA: The GDR's Import of Cuban Fruits and Ethiopian Coffee." In *Between East and South: Spaces of Interaction in the*

Globalizing Economy of the Cold War, edited by Anna Calori, Anne-Kristin Hartmetz, Bence Kocsev, James Mark, and Jan Zofka, 197–215. Berlin: De Gruyter, 2019.

Dietrich, Anne. "Oranges and the New Black: Importing, Provisioning, and Consuming Tropical Fruits and Coffee in the GDR, 1971–89." In *The Socialist Good Life: Desire, Development, and Standards of Living in Eastern Europe*, edited by Cristofer Scarboro, Diana Mincyte, and Zsuzsa Gille. Bloomington: Indiana University Press, 2020.

Dorsch, Hauke. "Rites of Passage Overseas? On the Sojourn of Mozambican Students and Scholars in Cuba." *Africa Spectrum* 43 (2008): 225–244.

Döring, Hans-Joachim. *"Es geht um unsere Existenz": Die Politik der DDR gegenüber der Dritten Welt am Beispiel von Mosambik und Äthiopien*. Berlin: Ch. Links, 1999.

Döring, Hans-Joachim and Ute Rüchel. *Freundschaftsbande und Beziehungskisten: Die Afrikapolitik der DDR und der BRD gegenüber Mosambik*. Frankfurt am Main: Brandes & Apsel, 2005.

Drayton, R., and David Motadel. "Discussion: The Futures of Global History." *Journal of Global History* 13 (2018): 1–21.

Drew, Allison. "Communism in Africa." In *The Oxford Handbook of the History of Communism*, edited by Stephen A. Smith, 285–302. Oxford: Oxford University Press, 2014.

Du Bois, W. E. Burghardt. *The World and Africa: An Inquiry into the Part Which Africa Has Played in World History*. New York: International Publishers, 1965 [1946].

Ealdmeir, Patti. *Anatomy of a Miracle: The End of Apartheid and the Birth of the New South Africa*. New Brunswick: Rutgers University Press, 1997.

Ellis, Steven. "Writing Histories of Contemporary Africa." *Journal of African History* 4 (2002): 1–26.

Engel, Ulf, and Hans-Georg Schleicher, ed. *Die beiden deutschen Staaten in Afrika: Zwischen Konkurrenz und Koexistenz, 1949–1990*. Hamburg: Institut für Afrika-Kunde, 1998.

Engel, Ulf. "Africa's '1989'." In *1989 in a Global Perspective*, edited by Ulf Engel, Frank Hadler, and Matthias Middell, 331–348. Leipzig: Leipziger Universitätsverlag, 2015.

Engel, Ulf, Matthias Middell, David Simo, and Katja Werthmann. "Africa in the Globalizing World – a Research Agenda." *Comparativ* 27 (2017): 97–110.

Engerman, David C. "The Second World's Third World." *Kritika: Explorations in Russian and Eurasian History* 12 (2011): 183–211.

Erisman, Michael H. *Cuba's Foreign Relations in a Post-Soviet World*. Gainesville: University Press of Florida, 2002.

Ferguson, James. *Global Shadows: Africa in the Neoliberal World Order*. Durham: Duke University Press, 2006.

Ferguson, Niall. "Crisis, What Crisis? The 1970s and the Shock of the Global." In *The Shock of the Global: The 1970s in Perspective*, edited by Niall Ferguson, Charles S. Maier, Erez Manela, and Daniel J. Sargent, 1–21. Cambridge: The Belknap Press of Harvard University Press, 2010.

Friedland, William H., and Carl G. Rosberg, ed. *African Socialism*. Stanford: Stanford University Press, 1964.

Gleijeses, Piero. "Moscow's Proxy? Cuba and Africa 1975–1988." *Journal of Cold War Studies* 8 (2006): 3–51.

Gleijeses, Piero. *Visions of Freedom: Havana, Washington, Pretoria and the Struggle for Southern Africa, 1976–1991*. Chapel Hill: The University of North Carolina Press, 2016.

Hannam, Kevin, Mimi Sheller, and John Urry. "Editorial: Mobilities, Immobilities and Moorings." *Mobilities* 1 (2006): 1–22. Accessed December 5, 2019. doi:10.1080/17450100500489189.

Harisch, Immanuel R. "Bartering Coffee, Cocoa and W50 Trucks: The Trade Relationships of the GDR, Angola and São Tomé in a Comparative Perspective." *Global Histories* 3 (2017): 43–60. Accessed October 28, 2019. doi:10.17169/GHSJ.2017.135.

Harisch, Immanuel R. "Handel und Solidarität: Die Beziehungen der DDR mit Angola und São Tomé und Príncipe unter besonderer Berücksichtigung des Austauschs 'Ware-gegen-Ware' ca. 1975–1990." MA thesis, University of Vienna, 2018.

Harisch, Immanuel R. "'Mit gewerkschaftlichem Gruß!' Afrikanische GewerkschafterInnen an der FDGB-Gewerkschaftshochschule Fritz Heckert in der DDR." *Stichproben. Vienna Journal of African Studies* 43 (2018): 77–109.

Harisch, Immanuel R. "East German Friendship-Brigades and Specialists in Angola: A Socialist Globalization Project in the Global Cold War," in *Transregional Connections in the History of East Central Europe*, edited by Katja Naumann. Berlin: De Gruyter, forthcoming 2021.

Hartmetz, Anne-Kristin, Bence Kocsev, and Jan Zofka. "East-South Relations during the Global Cold War: Economic Activities and Area Studies Interests of East Central European CMEA Countries in Africa." *Working Paper Series of the Collaborative Research Center (SFB) 1199 at the University of Leipzig* 11 (2018).

Hatzky, C. *Kubaner in Angola: Süd-Süd Kooperation und Bildungstransfer 1976–1991*. Berlin: De Gruyter, 2012.

Hatzky, C. *Cubans in Angola: South-South Cooperation and Transfer of Knowledge, 1976–1991*. Madison: The University of Wisconsin Press, 2015.

Hessler, Julie. "Death of an African Student in Moscow: Race, Politics, and the Cold War." *Cahiers Du Monde Russe* 47 (2006): 33–63.

Hillebrand, Ernst. *Das Afrika-Engagement der DDR*. Frankfurt am Main: Peter Lang, 1987.

Hong, Young-Sun. *Cold War Germany, the Third World, and the Global Humanitarian Regime*. New York: Cambridge University Press, 2015.

Howell, Jude. "The End of an Era: The Rise and Fall of G.D.R. Aid." *Journal of Modern African Studies* 32 (1994): 305–328.

Hunt, Lynn. *Writing History in the Global Era*. New York: Norton, 2014.

Husemann, Bettina, and Annette Neumann. "DDR – VR Angola: Fakten und Zusammenhänge zur bildungspolitischen Zusammenarbeit von 1975 bis 1989." In *Engagiert für Afrika: Die DDR und Afrika II*, edited by Ulrich van der Heyden, Ilona Schleicher, and Hans-Georg Schleicher, 158–178. Münster: Lit, 1994.

Ireland, Patrick R. "Socialism, Unification Policy and the Rise of Racism in Eastern Germany." *International Migration Review* 31 (1997): 541–68.

James, C. L. R. *A History of Negro Revolt*. Chicago: Research Associates School Times Publications, 2004 [1938].

James, Leslie. *George Padmore and Decolonization from Below: Pan-Africanism, the Cold War, and the End of Empire*. Houndmills: Palgrave Macmillan, 2015.

Judt, Matthias. *Der Bereich Kommerzielle Koordinierung: Das DDR-Wirtschaftsimperium des Alexander Schalck-Golodkowski. Mythos und Realität*. Berlin: Ch. Links, 2013.

Katsakioris, Constantin. "African Intellectuals and the Soviet Union: Internationalism, Pan-Africanism, and Negritude During the Years of Decolonization, 1954–1964." *Cahiers du Monde Russe* 47 (2006): 15–32.

Katsakioris, Constantin. "Transferts Est-Sud: Échanges Éducatifs et Formation de Cadres Africains en Union Soviétique Pendant les Années Soixante." *Outre-mers* 94 (2007): 83–106.

Katsakioris, Constantin. "The Lumumba University in Moscow: Higher Education for a Soviet–Third World Alliance, 1960–91." *Journal of Global History* 14 (2019): 281–300.

Katsakioris, Constantin. "The Soviet Union, Eastern Europe, and Africa in the Cold War: The Educational Ties." *Working Paper Series of the Collaborative Research Center (SFB) 1199 at the University of Leipzig* 16 (2019).

Katsakioris, Constantin. "Students from Portuguese Africa in the Soviet Union, 1960–74: Anti-Colonialism, Education, and the Socialist Alliance." *Journal of Contemporary History* (2020): 1–14. Accessed August 1, 2020. doi:10.1177/0022009419893739.

Keller, Edmond J., and Donald S. Rothchild, ed. *Afro-Marxist Regimes: Ideology and Public Policy.* Boulder: Lynne Rienner, 1987.

Kempton, D. R. "Africa in the Age of Perestroika." *Africa Today* 38 (1991): 7–29.

Kilian, Werner. *Die Hallstein-Doktrin: Der diplomatische Krieg zwischen der BRD und der DDR 1955–1973. Aus den Akten der beiden deutschen Außenministerien.* Berlin: Duncker & Humblot, 2001.

Kuck, Dennis. "'Für den sozialen Aufbau ihrer Heimat?' Ausländische Vertragsarbeitskräfte in der DDR." In *Fremde und Fremd-Sein in der DDR: Zu historischen Ursachen der Fremdenfeindlichkeit in Ostdeutschland*, edited by Jan C. Behrends, Thomas Lindenberger und Patrice G. Poutrus, 271–281. Berlin: Metropol, 2003.

Kunze, Thomas, and Thomas Vogel, ed. *Ostalgie international: Erinnerungen an die DDR von Nicaragua bis Vietnam.* Berlin: Ch. Links, 2010.

Lal, Priya. *African Socialism in Postcolonial Tanzania: Between the Village and the World.* Cambridge: Cambridge University Press, 2015.

Landau, Loren. B. "Communities of Knowledge or Tyrannies of Partnership: Reflections on North–South Research Networks and the Dual Imperative." *Journal of Refugee Studies* 25 (2012): 555–570.

Lorenzini, Sara. "Comecon and the South in the Years of Détente: A Study on East–South Economic Relations." *European Review of History* 21 (2014): 183–199.

Lorenzini, Sara. "The Socialist Camp and the Challenge of Economic Modernization in the Third World." In *The Cambridge History of Communism, Volume 2: The Socialist Camp and World Power 1941–1960s*, edited by Norman M. Naimark, Silvio Pons, and Sophie Quinn-Judge, 341–363. Cambridge: Cambridge University Press, 2017.

Machado, Pedro. "Repositioning Africa Within the Global." *Africa Today* 63 (2016): 88–91. Accessed December 8, 2019. doi:10.2979/africatoday.63.2.09.

Mama, A. "Is It Ethical to Study Africa? Preliminary Thoughts on Scholarship and Freedom." *African Studies Review* 50 (2007): 1–26.

Mamdani, Mahmood. *Scholars in the Marketplace: The Dilemmas of Neo-Liberal Reform at Makerere University, 1989–2005.* Dakar, Senegal: CODESRIA Council for the Development of Social Science Research in Africa, 2007.

Mark, James, and Tobias Rupprecht. "The Socialist World in Global History: From Absentee to Victim to Co-Producer." In *The Practice of Global History: European Perspectives*, edited by Matthias Middell, 81–115. London: Bloomsbury, 2018.

Mark, James, Bogdan Iacob, Tobias Rupprecht, and Ljubica Spaskovska. *1989: A Global History of Eastern Europe*. Cambridge: Cambridge University Press, 2019.

Mark, James, Artemy M. Kalinovsky, and Steffi Marung, ed. *Alternative Globalizations: Eastern Europe and the Postcolonial World*. Bloomington: Indiana University Press, 2020.

Markov, Walter. *Kognak und Königsmörder: Historisch-Literarische Miniaturen*. Berlin: Aufbau-Verlag, 1979.

Marung, Steffi. "The Provocation of Empirical Evidence: Soviet African Studies Between Enthusiasm and Discomfort." *African Identities* 16 (2018): 176–190.

Marung, Steffi, Uwe Müller, and Stefan Troebst. "Monolith or Experiment? The Bloc as a Spatial Format." In *Spatial Formats Under the Global Condition*, edited by Matthias Middell and Steffi Marung, 275–309. Berlin: De Gruyter, 2019.

Matusevich, Maxim. ed. *Africa in Russia, Russia in Africa: Three Centuries of Encounters*. Trenton: Africa World Press, 2000.

Matusevich, Maxim. "Expanding the Boundaries of the Black Atlantic: African Students as Soviet Moderns." *Ab Imperio* 2012 (2012): 325–350. doi:10.1353/imp.2012.0060.

Melber, Henning. *Understanding Namibia: The Trials of Independence*. London: Hurst, 2014.

Meyer, Wolfgang, and Freimut Keßner. *Kämpfendes Afrika: Begegnungen der Freundschaft und Solidarität*. Dresden: Zeit im Bild, 1979.

Middell, Matthias. "Manfred Kossok: Writing World History in East Germany." *Review (Fernand Braudel Center)* 38 (2015): 41–69.

Middell, Matthias. "Weltgeschichte DDR: Die DDR in globalgeschichtlicher Perspektive." In *Die DDR Als Chance: Neue Perspektiven auf ein altes Thema*, edited by Ulrich Mählert, 149–156. Berlin: Metropol Verlag, 2016.

Middell, Matthias. "Auf dem Weg zu einer transregionalen Geschichte des Kommunismus." In *Kommunismus jenseits des Eurozentrismus: (= Jahrbuch für Historische Kommunismusforschung 2019)*, edited by Matthias Middell, 1–14. Berlin: Metropol, 2019.

Middell, Matthias. "Die Entwicklung der Area Studies in der DDR als Reaktion auf die Dekolonisierungsprozesse der 1950er/1960er Jahre." In *Kommunismus jenseits des Eurozentrismus: (= Jahrbuch für Historische Kommunismusforschung 2019)*, edited by Matthias Middell, 223–254. Berlin: Metropol, 2019.

Miethe, Ingrid, Tim Kaiser, Tobias Kriele, and Alexandra Piepiorka, *Globalization of an Educational Idea: Workers' Faculties in Eastern Germany, Vietnam, Cuba and Mozambique*. Berlin: De Gruyter, 2019.

Miguele, P. J. *Sobre o mito da solidariedade: Trabalhadores contratados moçambicanos e angolanos na RDA*. Projekt Migration. Kölnischer Kunstverein, Dokumentationszentrum und Museum über Migration in Deutschland, Köln, Institut für Kulturanthropologie und Europäische Ethnologie der Johann Wolfgang Goethe Universität Frankfurt/Main, Institut für Theorie der Gestalt, 431–438. Köln: DuMont, 2005.

Milford, Ismay. "More than a Cold War Scholarship: East-Central African Anticolonial Activists, the International Union of Socialist Youth, and the Evasion of the Colonial State (1955–65)." *Stichproben. Vienna Journal of African Studies* 34 (2018): 19–43.

Minter, William. *Apartheid's Contras. An Inquiry into the Roots of War in Angola and Mozambique.* Johannesburg: Witwatersrand University Press, 1994.
Monson, Jamie. *Africa's Freedom Railway: How a Chinese Development Project Changed Lives and Livelihoods in Tanzania.* Bloomington: Indiana University Press, 2009.
Muehlenbeck, Philip E., and Natalia Telepneva, ed. *Warsaw Pact Intervention in the Third World: Aid and Influence in the Cold War.* London: I.B. Tauris, 2018.
Müller, Tanja. *Legacies of Socialist Solidarity: East Germany in Mozambique.* Lanham: Lexington Books, 2014.
Munslow, Barry, ed. *Africa: Problems in the Transition to Socialism.* London: Zed, 1986.
Nash, Mark, ed. *Red Africa: Affective Communities and the Cold War.* London: Black Dog Publishing, 2016.
Nkrumah, Kwame. *Towards Colonial Freedom: Africa in the Struggle Against World Imperialism.* London: Panaf Books, 1979 [1945].
Nyerere, Julius. "Capitalism or Socialism: The Rational Choice." *New Blackfriars* 55 (1974): 440–448.
Olúfẹ́mi, Táíwò. "What Is 'African Studies'? African Scholars, Africanists, and the Production of Knowledge." In *Reclaiming the Human Sciences and Humanities Through African Perspectives*, Volume 2, edited by Helen Lauer and Kofi Anyidoho, 966–982. Accra: Sub-Saharan Press, 2012.
Osei-Opare, Nana. "Uneasy Comrades: Postcolonial Statecraft, Race, and Citizenship, Ghana–Soviet Relations, 1957–1966." *Journal of West African History* 5 (2019): 85–111.
Ottaway David, and Marina Ottaway. *Afrocommunism.* New York: Africana Publishers, 1986.
Padmore, George. *How Britain Rules Africa.* New York: Negro Universities Press, 1969 [1936].
Pampuch, Sebastian. "Afrikanische Freedom Fighter im Exil der DDR: Dekoloniale Wissensbestände einer 'unerwünschten Geschichte'." In *Wissen in Bewegung: Migration und Globale Verflechtungen in der Zeitgeschichte seit 1945,* edited by Stephanie Zloch, Lars Müller, and Simone Lässig, 321–348. Berlin: De Gruyter, 2018.
Piepiorka, Alexandra. "Exploring 'Socialist Solidarity' in Higher Education: East German Advisors in Post-Independence Mozambique (1975–1992)." In *Education and Development in Colonial and Postcolonial Africa: Policies, Paradigms, and Entanglements, 1890s–1980s,* edited by Damiano Matasci, Miguel B. Jerónimo, and Hugo G. Dores, 289–318. Cham: Palgrave Macmillan, 2020.
Piesche, Peggy. "Making African Diasporic Pasts Possible: A Retrospective View of the GDR and Its Black (Step)Children." In *Remapping Black Germany: New Perspectives on Afro-German History, Politics, and Culture,* edited by Sara Lennox, 226–242. Massachusetts: University of Massachusetts Press, 2016.
Pitcher, M. Anne. *Transforming Mozambique: The Politics of Privatization, 1975–2000.* Cambridge: Cambridge University Press, 2002.
Pitcher, Anne M., and Kelly M. Askew. "African Socialisms and Postsocialisms." *Africa* 76 (2006): 1–14.
Poutrus, Patrice G. "An den Grenzen des Proletarischen Internationalismus: Algerische Flüchtlinge in der DDR." *Zeitschrift für Geschichtswissenschaft* 55 (2007): 162–178.
Prashad, Vijay. *The Darker Nations: A People's History of the Third World.* New York: The New Press, 2007.
Prashad, Vijay. *The Poorer Nations: A Possible History of the Global South.* London: Verso, 2014.

Pugach, Sara. "African Students and the Politics of Race and Gender in the German Democratic Republic, 1957–1990." In *Comrades of Color: East Germany in the Cold War World*, edited by Quinn Slobodian, 131–156. New York: Berghahn Books, 2015.
Pugach, Sara. "Eleven Nigerian Students in Cold War East Germany: Visions of Science, Modernity, and Decolonization." *Journal of Contemporary History* 54 (2019): 551–572.
Pugach, Sara. "Agents of Dissent: African Student Organizations in the German Democratic Republic." *Africa* 89 (2019): 90–108.
Quest, Matthew. "George Padmore's and C.L.R. James's International African Opinion." In *George Padmore: Pan African Revolutionary*, edited by Fitzroy Baptiste and Rupert Lewis, 105–132. Kingston: Ian Randle, 2009.
Roberts, George. "Press, Propaganda and the German Democratic Republic's Search for Recognition in Tanzania, 1964–72." In *Warsaw Pact Intervention in the Third World: Aid and Influence in the Cold War*, edited by Philip E. Muehlenbeck and Natalia Telepneva, 148–172. London: I. B. Tauris, 2019.
Rodney, Walter. "Education in Africa and Contemporary Tanzania." In *Education and Black Struggle: Notes from the Colonized World*, edited by Institute of the Black World, 82–99. Cambridge: Harvard Educational Review, 1974.
Rosberg, Carl G., and Thomas M. Callaghy, ed. *Socialism in Sub-Saharan Africa: A New Assessment*. Berkeley: Institute of International Studies, University of California, 1979.
Rüchel, Ute. *"…auf deutsch sozialistisch zu denken…" – Mosambikaner in der Schule der Freundschaft*. Magdeburg: JVA Naumburg – Arbeitsverwaltung, 2001.
Rupprecht, Tobias. *Soviet Internationalism After Stalin: Interaction and Exchange Between the USSR and Latin America During the Cold War*. Cambridge: Cambridge University Press, 2015.
Sanchez-Sibony, Oscar. *Red Globalization: The Political Economy of the Soviet Cold War from Stalin to Khrushchev*. Cambridge: Cambridge University Press, 2014.
Schade, Anja. "Solidarität und Alltag der DDR aus der Sicht exilierter Mitglieder des African National Congress." In *Internationale Solidarität: Globales Engagement in der Bundesrepublik und der DDR*, edited by Frank Bösch, Caroline Moine, and Stefanie Senger, 186–208. Göttingen: Wallstein, 2018.
Schelkle, Waltraud. "Die Regionalwissenschaften der DDR als Modell einer Entwicklungswissenschaft?" In *Wissenschaft und Wiedervereinigung: Asien- und Afrikawissenschaften im Umbruch*, edited by Wolf-Hagen Krauth and Ralf Wolz, 22–92. Berlin: Akademie-Verlag, 1998.
Schenck, Marcia C. "From Luanda and Maputo to Berlin: Uncovering Angolan and Mozambican Migrants' Motives to Move to the German Democratic Republic (1979–1990)." *African Economic History* 44 (2016): 203–234.
Schenck, Marcia C. "Socialist Solidarities and Their Afterlives: Histories and Memories of Angolan and Mozambican Migrants in the German Democratic Republic, 1975–2015." PhD diss., Princeton University, 2017.
Schenck, Marcia C. "Constructing and Deconstructing the 'Black East' – a Helpful Research Agenda? Research Note." *Stichproben. Vienna Journal of African Studies* 34 (2018): 135–152.
Schenck, Marcia C. "A Chronology of Nostalgia: Memories of Former Angolan and Mozambican Worker Trainees to East Germany." *Labor History* 59 (2018): 352–374.

Schenck, Marcia C. "Negotiating the German Democratic Republic: Angolan Student Migration During the Cold War, 1976–90." *Africa* 89 (2019): 144–166.

Schenck, Marcia C. "Small Strangers at the School of Friendship: Memories of Mozambican School Students to the German Democratic Republic." *Bulletin of the GHI* 15 (2020): 41–59.

Scheunpflug, Annette, and Jürgen Krause. *Die Schule der Freundschaft: Ein Bildungsexperiment in der DDR*. Hamburg, Universität der Bundeswehr Hamburg, 2000.

Schleicher, Hans-Georg. "Entwicklungszusammenarbeit und Außenpolitik in der DDR: Das Beispiel Afrika." In *Entwicklungspolitische Zusammenarbeit in der Bundesrepublik Deutschland und der DDR*, edited by Hans-Jörg Bücking, 95–110. Berlin: Duncker & Humblot, 1998.

Schleicher, Hans-Georg. "The German Democratic Republic (GDR) in the Liberation Struggle of Southern Africa." In *Southern African Liberation Struggles 1960–1994: Contemporaneous Documents, Vol. 8*, edited by Arnold Temu, and Joel das Neves Tembe, 449–561. Dar es Salaam: Mkuki na Nyota, 2014.

Schleicher, Ilona. "FDGB-Offensive in Westafrika: Der Gewerkschaftsbund im Jahr Afrikas." In *Engagiert für Afrika: Die DDR und Afrika II*, edited by Ulrich van der Heyden, Ilona Schleicher, and Hans-Georg Schleicher, 82–93. Münster: Lit, 1994.

Schleicher, Ilona. "Elemente entwicklungspolitischer Zusammenarbeit in der Tätigkeit von FDGB und FDJ." In *Entwicklungspolitische Zusammenarbeit in der Bundesrepublik Deutschland und der DDR*, edited by Hans-Jörg Bücking, 111–138. Berlin: Duncker & Humblot, 1998.

Schleicher, Ilona, and Hans-Georg Schleicher. *Die DDR im südlichen Afrika: Solidarität und Kalter Krieg*. Hamburg: Institut für Afrika-Kunde, 1997.

Scholtyseck, Joachim. *Die Außenpolitik der DDR*. Munich: Oldenbourg, 2003.

Schulz, Brigitte H. *Development Policy in the Cold War Era: The Two Germanies and Sub-Saharan Africa, 1960–1985*. Münster: Lit, 1995.

Schwenkel, Christina. "Socialist Mobilities: Crossing New Terrains in Vietnamese Migration Histories." *Central and Eastern European Migration Review* 4 (2015): 13–25.

Serra, Gerardo, and Frank Gerits. "The Politics of Socialist Education in Ghana: The Kwame Nkrumah Ideological Institute, 1961–1966." *Journal of African History* 60 (2019): 407–428.

Shubin, Vladimir. *The Hot 'Cold War': The USSR in Southern Africa*. London, Scottsville: Pluto Press, University of KwaZulu-Natal Press, 2008.

Simo, David. "Writing World History in Africa: Opportunities, Constraints and Challenges." In *Global History, Globally: Research and Practice Around the World*, edited by Sven Beckert, and Dominic Sachsenmaier, 235–250. London: Bloomsbury, 2018.

Skinner, Kate. "West Africa's First Coup: Neo-Colonial and Pan-African Projects in Togo's 'Shadow Archives'." *African Studies Review* 6 (2019): 1–24.

Slobodian, Quinn, ed. *Comrades of Color: East Germany in the Cold War World*. New York: Berghahn Books, 2015.

Slobodian, Quinn. "Bandung in Divided Germany: Managing Non-Aligned Politics in East and West, 1955–63." *The Journal of Imperial and Commonwealth History* 41 (2013): 644–662.

Smith, Tony. "New Bottles for New Wine: A Pericentric Framework for the Study of the Cold War." *Diplomatic History* 24 (2000): 567–591.

Sonderegger, Arno. "Der Panafrikanismus im 20. Jahrhundert." In *Afrika im 20. Jahrhundert: Geschichte und Gesellschaft*, edited by Arno Sonderegger, Ingeborg Grau, and Birgit Englert, 98–116. Wien: Promedia, 2011.

Sonderegger, Arno. "How the Empire Wrote Back: Notes on the Struggle of George Padmore and Kwame Nkrumah." In *Kwame Nkrumah 1909–1972: A Controversial African Visionary*, edited by Bea Lundt and Christoph Marx, 19–38. Stuttgart: Franz Steiner Verlag, 2016.

Sonderegger, Arno, Ingeborg Grau, and Birgit Englert. "Einleitung: Afrika im 20. Jahrhundert." In *Afrika im 20. Jahrhundert: Geschichte und Gesellschaft*, edited by Arno Sonderegger, Ingeborg Grau, and Birgit Englert, 9–26. Wien: Promedia, 2011.

Spanger, Hans-Joachim, and Lothar Brock. *Die beiden deutschen Staaten in der Dritten Welt: Die Entwicklungspolitik der DDR. Eine Herausforderung für die Bundesrepublik Deutschland?* Opladen: Westdeutscher Verlag, 1987.

Speich, Daniel. "The Kenyan Style of 'African Socialism': Developmental Knowledge Claims and the Explanatory Limits of the Cold War." *Diplomatic History* 33 (2009): 449–466.

Storkmann, Klaus. *Geheime Solidarität: Militärbeziehungen und Militärhilfen der DDR in die "Dritte Welt"*. Berlin: Ch. Links, 2012.

Sun, Jodie Y. "Historicizing African Socialisms: Kenyan African Socialism, Zambian Humanism, and Communist China's Entanglements." *International Journal of African Historical Studies* 52 (2019): 349–374.

Tanganyika African National Union, "Arusha Declaration," February 5, 1967. Accessed January 29, 2020. www.marxists.org/subject/africa/nyerere/1967/arusha-declaration.htm.

Thiam, Iba De, James Mulira, and Christophe Wondji. "Africa and the Socialist Countries." In *Unesco General History of Africa VIII: Africa since 1935*, edited by Ali A. Mazrui and Christophe Wondji, 798–828. Paris, Berkeley: Heinemann, University of California Press, 1993.

Tripp, Aili M. *Changing the Rules: The Politics of Liberalization and the Urban Informal Economy in Tanzania*. Berkeley: University of California Press, 1997.

Tullner, M. "Das Experiment 'Schule der Freundschaft' im Kontext der mosambikanischen Bildungspolitik." In *Freundschaftsbande und Beziehungskisten: Die Afrikapolitik der DDR und der BRD gegenüber Mosambik*, edited by Hans-Joachim Döring and Uta Rüchel, 100–109. Frankfurt am Main: Brandes & Apsel, 2005.

Unfried, Berthold. "Friendship and Education, Coffee and Weapons: Exchanges Between Socialist Ethiopia and the German Democratic Republic." *Northeast African Studies* 16 (2016): 15–38.

van der Heyden, Ulrich. *Die Afrikawissenschaften in der DDR: Eine akademische Disziplin zwischen Exotik und Exempel. Eine wissenschaftsgeschichtliche Untersuchung*. Münster: Lit, 1999.

van der Heyden, Ulrich. "Es darf nichts passieren! Entwicklungspolitisches Engagement der DDR in Mosambik zwischen Solidarität und Risiko." In *Wir haben Spuren hinterlassen! Die DDR in Mosambik: Erlebnisse, Erfahrungen und Erkenntnisse aus drei Jahrzehnten*, edited by Matthias Voß, 278–313. Münster: Lit, 2005.

van der Heyden, Ulrich. "FDJ-Brigaden der Freundschaft aus der DDR – Die Peace Corps des Ostens?" In *Die eine Welt schaffen: Praktiken von "Internationaler Solidarität" und*

"Internationaler Entwicklung", edited by Berthold Unfried and Eva Himmelstoß, 99–122. Leipzig: Akademische Verlagsanstalt, 2012.
van der Heyden, Ulrich, Ilona Schleicher, and Hans-Georg Schleicher, ed. *Die DDR und Afrika: Zwischen Klassenkampf und neuem Denken.* Münster: Lit, 1993.
van der Heyden, Ulrich, Ilona Schleicher, and Hans-Georg Schleicher, ed. *Engagiert für Afrika: Die DDR und Afrika II.* Münster: Lit, 1994.
van der Heyden, Ulrich, and Franziska Benger, ed. K*alter Krieg in Ostafrika: Die Beziehungen der DDR zu Sansibar und Tansania.* Münster: Lit, 2009.
Verburg, Maria Magdalena. *Ostdeutsche Dritte-Welt-Gruppen vor und nach 1989/90.* Göttingen: Vandenhoeck & Ruprecht, 2012.
Weis, Toni. "The Politics Machine: On the Concept of 'Solidarity' in East German Support for SWAPO." *Journal of Southern African Studies* 37 (2011): 351–367.
Werner, Michael, and Bénédicte Zimmermann. "Beyond Comparison: Histoire Croisée and the Challenge of Reflexivity." *History and Theory* 45 (2006): 30–50.
Westad, Odd Arne. *The Global Cold War: Third World Interventions and the Making of Our Times.* Cambridge: Cambridge University Press, 2005.
Winrow, Gareth M. *The Foreign Policy of the GDR in Africa.* Cambridge: Cambridge University Press, 2009 [1990].
Wolter, Stefan. *Für die Kranken ist das Beste gerade gut genug: Klinikum Dorothea Christiane Erxleben GmbH. 100 Jahre Standort Dithfurter Weg.* Quedlinburg: Letterado-Verlag, 2007.
Yuzhou Sun, Jodie. "Historicizing African Socialisms: Kenyan African Socialism, Zambian Humanism, and Communist China's Entanglements." *International Journal of African Historical Studies* 52 (2019): 349–374.
Zalmanovich, Tal. "From Apartheid South Africa to Socialist Budapest and Back: Communism, Race, and Cold War Journeys." *Stichproben. Vienna Journal of African Studies* 34 (2018): 111–134.

I Shaping Pioneering Institutions

Jörg Depta and Anne-Kristin Hartmetz
2 Herder vs. Goethe in Egypt: East and West German Language Courses in Cairo and the Evolution of "German as a Foreign Language" (DaF)

Introduction

On February 27, 1965, Egyptian Deputy Prime Minister Nureddin Tarraf along with Lotte Ulbricht, the wife of East German head of state Walter Ulbricht,[1] opened the East German Cultural Institute (*Kultur- und Informationszentrum*, KIZ) in Cairo.[2] It was situated near Cairo University in a spacious villa with a lush garden. This garden villa at the Western bank of the Nile competed directly with the West German Goethe Institute, which had been established just a few meters from the Tahir Square seven years earlier. In the memories of Egyptians, the East German cultural institute is still called the Herder Institute, although it never officially bore this name. However, it was closely related to the Herder Institute at Leipzig's Karl Marx University which offered language training to international students and other groups of foreigners arriving in the German Democratic Republic (GDR).[3] The opening of the East German cultural institute KIZ

---

[1] Walter Ulbricht was Chairman of the State Council of the German Democratic Republic.
[2] The cultural center has been given various names. It was initially known as the *Haus der Deutsch-Arabischen Gesellschaft*. Later, "Cultural Center of the GDR" was added. In East German sources, it is mostly called KIZ (*Kultur- und Informationszentrum*). We also use this name here.
[3] The beginnings of the Herder Institute in Leipzig date back to 1951, when a department for foreign students was founded for thirteen Nigerian students at the Workers' and Farmers' Faculty in Leipzig. In 1956, the department was transformed into the Institute for Foreign Students following a decision by the Council of Ministers. The institute was named after Johann Gottfried Herder in 1961 to distinguish it from the Goethe Institute. The name was based on Herder's humanistic ideas and his theories on language. The full official name was *Herder-Institut – Vorstudienanstalt für ausländische Studierende in der DDR und Stätte zur Förderung deutscher Sprachkenntnisse im Ausland* (Pre-Study Institute for Foreign Students in the GDR and Institution for the Promotion of German Language Skills Abroad). For an overview of the origins of the Herder Institute see Claus Altmayer, "50 Jahre Herder-Institut, 50 Jahre Deutsch als Fremdsprache. Traditionen und Grenzüberschreitungen," *Deutsch als Fremdsprache* 44 (2007), 67–74.

OpenAccess. © 2021 Jörg Depta and Anne-Kristin Hartmetz, published by De Gruyter. This work is licensed under the Creative Commons Attribution 4.0 International License.
https://doi.org/10.1515/9783110623543-002

was part of Ulbricht's semi-official state visit to Egypt.[4] This visit was a significant political success for East Germany in its efforts to gain international diplomatic recognition and therefore provoked outrage in West Germany. Because of this violation of the conditions of the Hallstein Doctrine, which saw the establishment of diplomatic relations with East Germany as an "unfriendly act", West German politicians had threatened to cut economic aid for Egypt or even to break off diplomatic relations to prevent the visit. But Egyptian politicians, in particular president Gamal Abdel Nasser, were unimpressed by the threats and in February 1965 Ulbricht and his wife traveled at the invitation of Nasser from Dubrovnik to Alexandria on the ship *Völkerfreundschaft* (Peoples' Friendship).[5]

In this chapter we examine the East German cultural institute KIZ in Cairo as a space for encounters and entanglements between Egyptian and German protagonists and as an experimental field for East German cultural diplomacy in the 1960s. A central part of this cultural diplomacy in the 1960s was language teaching. In the 1950s and 1960s, the teaching of German in Egypt gained importance as hundreds of young Egyptians underwent engineering education and technical training at West German universities and colleges. From 1956 onwards, young Egyptians studied in East Germany as well. It was against this background that the Goethe Institute opened a branch in Cairo in 1959. At the time, it was the largest branch of the Goethe Institute in the world and, alongside London, Paris, and New Delhi, one of the most important foreign branches.[6] When East Germany opened its cultural institute in Cairo and offered German language lessons, the KIZ entered into direct competition with the West German Goethe Institute. We argue that the German-German competition in Egypt, and Egyptian actors pursuing their interests while navigating this conflict, not only influenced and

---

4 Egypt formed a political union with Syria from 1958 to 1961. This "United Arabic Republic" (UAR) was also loosely joined by North Yemen at the end of 1958. This entity of states was meant to form the origin of a pan-Arab confederation. The UAR existed only until 1961, when Syria declared its retreat from the Union. Egypt formally called itself UAR until 1971. In this chapter we use the term Egypt, unless UAR is mentioned in (East German) sources.
5 Behind the scenes, however, the West German side struggled hard to deal with the situation. See William G. Gray, *Germany's Cold War: The Global Campaign to Isolate East Germany, 1945–1969* (Chapel Hill, London: The University of North Carolina Press, 2003), 174–182; Young-Sun Hong, *Cold War Germany, the Third World, and the Global Humanitarian Regime* (New York: Cambridge University Press, 2015), 187–89; Werner Kilian, *Die Hallstein-Doktrin. Der diplomatische Krieg zwischen der BRD und der DDR 1955–1973: Aus den Akten der beiden deutschen Außenministerien* (Berlin: Duncker & Humblot, 2001), 123–148.
6 Thomas Kramer, *Deutsch-ägyptische Beziehungen in Vergangenheit und Gegenwart* (Tübingen: Erdmann, 1974), 229.

shaped the teaching of German in Cairo. It also played an important role in the institutionalization and scientification of German as a foreign language (*Deutsch als Fremdsprache* DaF), a field that exists until today, but has its roots, partially, in Cold War competition over influence in wooing the postcolonial world.

Larger and inter-German Cold War rivalries and the West German Hallstein Doctrine are considered here as the decisive background of the events. However, we will show that developments surrounding the East German KIZ cannot be evaluated against this background alone. From an Egyptian point of view the German-German competition and the question of whether or not to fully recognize the GDR were less important. The issue was rather a tactical question for the Egyptian side.[7] Nasserism as a socialist Arab political ideology did not automatically mean that Egypt preferred socialist East Germany to West Germany. Rather, developments in the Middle East conflict played a decisive role in the GDR's relatively successful cultural and language policy in Egypt. Egyptian politicians, notably Gamal Abdel Nasser, demonstrated anti-imperialist sovereignty that did not rely exclusively on socialist countries, but included them as important partners.[8]

Drawing primarily on German archival sources,[9] we show how Egyptian agency influenced the teaching practice in the East German cultural center and back home in the GDR. The actions of Egyptians can be seen in reports from protagonists from both German states only in double refraction because East German and West German reports followed their respective ideological guidelines. Since the special constellation of German-German competition in Egypt brought about a "triangular relationship", West German agency has to be taken into account as well. In the end, however, Egyptian interests determined the scope that the two German states had for their competing cultural diplomacy in North Africa.

In the first part, we will outline the international political background as well as regional and national constellations and motives that were relevant for decisions on cooperation on the Egyptian side and in both German states. We then return, secondly, to Cairo and zoom into the practice of German-German

---

[7] Hermann Wentker, *Außenpolitik in engen Grenzen. Die DDR im internationalen System 1949–1989* (München: Oldenbourg, 2007), 172–173.
[8] The way in which the German-German sensitivities in relations with Egypt were dealt with fits into this model. The construction of the Aswan Dam with Soviet help is certainly the more prominent example.
[9] This chapter is based on archival sources from the German Federal Archives (BArch), the Archive of the Parties and Mass Organizations of the GDR (SAPMO-BArch), and the Leipzig University Archive (UAL).

language teaching after Ulbricht's state visit in 1965. Here we trace the effects of political turmoil, such as the diplomatic crisis between West Germany and the Arab states in 1965, the Six-Day War in 1967, and finally the recognition of the GDR by Egypt in 1969 on the practice of language teaching. Thirdly, we will outline how these early experiences with language teaching in Egypt influenced the institutionalization and conception of language teaching in East Germany. Our research shows that the turning of language teaching into an academic subject, and thus the invention of the subject German as a foreign language (DaF), was spearheaded by East Germany—rather than West Germany—in a process of interactions with non-native speakers. Language teaching in Egypt was an important experience in this respect and serves as an example for the impacts of relations between Africa and the GDR despite the KIZ's relatively short "mooring" in Cairo.

Goethe and Herder Go South

At this point the question arises of what interest Egyptian politicians had in the two German states and what the Germans from East and West wanted in Egypt. The long-standing German-Egyptian relations had been broken off by Egypt in 1939. Shortly after the Second World War, Egypt resumed trade relations with Germany (western occupation zones).[10] Following the 1952 revolution, Egypt reoriented its domestic and foreign policy. A decidedly socialist outlook replaced the rather liberal capitalist political orientation of the 1920s to 1940s, when British interests had shaped Egyptian policies.[11] Egypt had already turned to the Soviet Union and the socialist camp when it concluded an agreement on arms supplies with Czechoslovakia in September 1955[12] and further during the Suez Crisis and the financing and construction of the Aswan Dam from 1956 onwards.[13] Nasser admired the Soviet economic system,[14] and, although communists in

---

10 Wolfgang G. Schwanitz, "Ägypten: Zweierlei Deutsche im Kalten Krieg," *Comparativ* 16 (2006): 11–12.
11 Tarek M. Osman, *Egypt on the Brink: From the Rise of Nasser to the Fall of Mubarak* (New Haven: Yale University Press, 2011), 53–54.
12 For the arms deal see Philipp Muehlenbeck, *Czechoslovakia in Africa 1945–1968* (Basingstoke: Palgrave Macmillan, 2016), 91–93. Muehlenbeck emphasizes that connections had already been established between Prague and Cairo before 1955. Czech arms deliveries to Egypt had started in 1946.
13 For Aswan as a paradigmatic case for development projects between the frontlines of the Cold War see Dirk van Laak, *Weiße Elefanten. Anspruch und Scheitern technischer Großprojekte im 20. Jahrhundert* (Stuttgart: Deutsche Verlagsanstalt, 1999), 107–108.
14 Odd Arne Westad, *The Cold War. A World History* (New York: Basic Books, 2017), 453.

Egypt were in a difficult position because Nasser feared their political influence at that time, Nasser emphasized that he was not an anti-communist and that he wanted to further develop relations with the socialist states.[15] So while Egypt did not pursue a declared socialist policy, it was one of the countries that took up socialist ideas and was interested in closer relations with the socialist states of Eastern Europe.

However, the most important orientation that Egypt shared with the GDR was not so much a declared socialism, but rather a strong anti-imperialism. This anti-imperialism shaped Egyptian international policy. Egypt was an important player in Third World movements of the 1950s and 1960s. In the 1960s, it was one of the leading powers in the Non-Aligned Movement (NAM) and at the same time a hub of Pan-Arabism, a "sanctuary of 'revolutionists' from all over the Arab world,"[16] as well as a supporting power of political Pan-Africanism.[17] At the same time, Nasser initiated an ambitious domestic development program. Therefore, Egypt had a strong economic interest in entertaining good relations with both German states, hoping for expertise and technology as well as foreign exchange and loans.

Since Egypt was a center of political pan-Arabism and at the same time a center of the political decolonization movement in Asia and Africa, relations with Egypt were important for both German states as well. East German officials saw Egypt as an important diplomatic gateway to Africa and the Arab world[18] but were also interested in economic relations, particularly the import of cotton for its textile industry. Despite the Hallstein Doctrine, East Germany succeeded in establishing economic relations with Egypt, which laid the foundation for further

---

15 Kilian, *Hallstein-Doktrin*, 114.
16 Osman, *Egypt on the Brink*, 65–66.
17 For Egypt as a hub of decolonization and a center of the Afro-Asian movement see Eric Burton, "Hubs of Decolonization. African Liberation Movements and Eastern Connections in Cairo, Accra and Dar es Salaam", in *Southern African Liberation Movements and the Global Cold War "East": Transnational Activism 1960–1990*, ed. Lena Dallywater, Helder A. Fonseca, and Chris Saunders (Berlin: De Gruyter, 2019); Reem Abou-El-Fadl, "Building Egypt's Afro-Asian Hub: Infrastructures of Solidarity and the 1957 Cairo Conference," *Journal of World History* 30 (2019). For an overview over the Non-Aligned Movement (NAM) see Jürgen Dinkel, *The Non-Aligned Movement: Genesis, Organization and Politics, 1927–1992* (Leiden, Boston: Brill, 2018). For Egypt in the NAM see Lorenz Lüthi, "The Non-Aligned Movement and the Cold War, 1961–1973," *Journal of Cold War Studies* 18 (2016).
18 In East Germany, however, Egypt, like the entire Maghreb, was mainly categorized as belonging to the Arab world, although it is located on the African continent and had close ties to African states, especially in the 1960s. See Martin Praxenthaler, *Die Sprachverbreitungspolitik der DDR. Die deutsche Sprache als Mittel sozialistischer auswärtiger Kulturpolitik* (Frankfurt, Berlin: Peter Lang, 2002), 50–51.

cultural and later diplomatic relations. The initiative for trade relations initially came from Egypt. An Egyptian delegation visited East Berlin in July 1950 in search of new markets for cotton. The first trade agreement between the GDR and a non-aligned country was signed with Egypt in 1953 and a GDR trade agency subsequently opened in Cairo in 1954.[19] In October 1958 the German-Arabic Society (DAG) was founded in East Berlin.[20] The foundation of the society was a first step to institutionalize the cultural cooperation of the GDR with the Arab countries. The aim was to support the "Arab peoples' struggle against imperialism".[21]

West Germany wanted to maintain its economic relations with Egypt and at the same time prevent diplomatic success of East Germany by all means, fearing that a break with Egypt over the Hallstein Doctrine would compel other Arab governments to follow the Egyptian example. A crucial issue in Egypt's relations with Bonn was the question of the diplomatic recognition of Israel.[22] The relations of both German states with Egypt remained relatively stable until 1965, when the West German and British press published articles on arms deliveries from West Germany to Israel. The reports triggered a series of events that became known as the "Middle East crisis"[23] of West German foreign policy. It led to the invalidation of the Hallstein Doctrine, and eventually to diplomatic recognition of East Germany by several Arab states. After the West German-Israeli treaties had become known President Nasser saw Egypt's security interests threatened.[24] The Egyptian government now decided to restrict relations with West Germany and to develop a closer cultural and economic relationship with East Germany instead. Egypt suffered from a lack of foreign exchange during this period,

---

19 Kilian, *Hallstein-Doktrin*, 104–108.
20 SAPMO-BArch, DY 13/3340, Statut der Deutsch-Arabischen Gesellschaft in der Deutschen Demokratischen Republik, no date.
21 Liga-Akte 209: Gründungsunterlagen der Deutsch-Arabischen Gesellschaft (DAG), cited in Wolfgang Schwanitz, "Streng vertraulich? Aus den Akten der Deutsch-Arabischen Gesellschaft 1958–1969," in *Berlin-Kairo: Damals und heute. Zur Geschichte deutsch-ägyptischer Beziehungen*, ed. Wolfgang Schwanitz (Berlin: DÄG, 1991), 91.
22 For Cold War polarization in the Middle East and the conflict over Israel see Salim Yaqub. "The Cold War and the Middle East", in *The Cold War in the Third World*, ed. Robert McMahon (Oxford: Oxford University Press, 2003).
23 *Nahostkrise* (Middle East crisis) was a common term in the West German press to describe the events surrounding the recognition of Israel and the breaking off of diplomatic relations by the Arab states, e.g. "Nahostkrise: Tränen im Waldorf Astoria." *Der Spiegel* 9, February 24, 1965, 25–33.
24 "Drahtbericht Federer vom 25.01.1965", in *Akten zur auswärtigen Politik der Bundesrepublik Deutschland*, ed. Mechthild Lindemann and Rainer A. Blasius (München: Oldenbourg, 1999), 192.

and East Germany offered government loans, commercial credits, and experts.²⁵ Walter Ulbricht was invited to Cairo. In an interview with the West German news magazine *Spiegel*, Nasser replied to the question of why he had invited Ulbricht to Cairo after letting him wait for almost two years: "We felt betrayed by West Germany."²⁶

West German politicians were unsure how to react to Ulbricht's Cairo visit, discussing options of ignoring and punishing throughout February. "Stalingrad at the Nile", as a West German magazine called the disaster in a rather shrill headline, caused some turbulence.²⁷ It was feared that Egypt would ultimately recognize East Germany if West Germany exerted too much pressure. Eventually, this diplomatic confusion was the beginning of the end of the Hallstein Doctrine as West Germany could neither afford to break off relations nor act according to the doctrine.²⁸

---

25 Gray, *Germany's Cold War*, 172. The credits were granted in the East German convertible currency Valuta Mark (VM) and included VM 200 million (approximately US$50 million) in government credits and VM 130 million in commercial credits. Some of the credit commitments contained old credits from a 1958 agreement that had not been exhausted (VM 40 million). Among other things, these loans had been used to buy GDR machines for cotton processing and to set up a textile combine in Shibin el-Kom.
26 Interview by Dieter Schröder and Conrad Ahlers with Gamal Abdel Nasser, "Sie können sich doch nicht ewig erpressen lassen!" in *Der Spiegel* 9, February 25, 1965, 34. In this interview, Nasser also made it clear that Egypt would probably recognize the GDR if West Germany was to cease its economic aid because of the visit of Ulbricht to Egypt. He also stressed that Egypt would generally not react to Western threats.
27 *Christ und Welt*, February 5, 1965, quoted in Amid Das Gupta, "Ulbricht am Nil: Die deutschdeutsche Rivalität in der Dritten Welt," in *Das doppelte Deutschland: 40 Jahre Systemkonkurrenz*, ed. Udo Wengst and Hermann Wentker (Berlin: Ch. Links, 2008).
28 Gray, *Germany's Cold War*, 173–176; Kilian, *Hallstein-Doktrin*, 153. For an analysis of the West German discussions around the Ulbricht visit and its impact on the implementation of the Hallstein Doctrine see also Hong, *Cold War Germany*, 245–249.

German-German Kulturkampf[29] in Cairo

1965–1967: "Sprechen Sie Deutsch?" The First Years of Direct Competition

Competition between the two German states in Egypt was carried out through means of cultural diplomacy. Between 1957 and 1960, the Politburo of the East German ruling party, the Socialist Unity Party (SED), had passed several resolutions stipulating that cultural centers focusing on language instruction should be opened in non-socialist countries.[30] From 1965 on, language teaching became an important part of on-site cultural diplomacy in Cairo.[31] Set up in a villa near Cairo University, the newly established East German cultural institute KIZ had five large classrooms, several offices, and a library. A concert grand piano was handed over to the staff at the ceremonial opening. The grand piano later stood in the event hall, which was solemnly called the "grand hall."[32] The first director of the KIZ was the orientalist Klaus Timm, while the first chief instructor was the linguist Gerhard Helbig from Leipzig's Karl Marx University.

When Gerhard Helbig arrived in Cairo together with his wife Agnes Helbig at the end of December 1964—two months before Ulbricht's state visit to Egypt—he encountered a "completely empty, poorly maintained house." He spent the first few months supervising the preparation of classrooms and providing the complete equipment so that German lessons could take place there. At the beginning of February 1965, advertisements for a German course were placed in several Egyptian newspapers. More than 110 Egyptians personally registered with Agnes Helbig in a provisionally furnished office at the center.[33]

Paradoxically, the high number of registrations was a reason for concern rather than joy. The head of the KIZ, Klaus Timm, was originally opposed to admitting so many Egyptians to German lessons in the new institute. Due to a shortage of personnel, he only wanted to approve small courses with a maximum of six to ten participants. Gerhard Helbig, who was the only German in-

---

29 Originally the German term *Kulturkampf* (cultural struggle or culture war) refers to Chancellor Otto von Bismarck's sanctions against (political) Catholicism in 1870s Germany, but it is used for cultural conflicts in other times and places as well.
30 The first of these centers was opened in Helsinki in 1960.
31 Praxenthaler, *Sprachverbreitungspolitik*, 233–234, 260–262.
32 BArch, B 307/96, Letter Dr. Klopfer to Dr. Hutter, Goethe-Institut Zentralverwaltung Abt. I, October 21, 1965.
33 SAPMO-BArch, DR3/II/B839, Dr. Gerhard Helbig, Bericht über die Arbeit des Deutsch-Lektorats Kairo im Frühjahrssemester 1965, July 10, 1965.

structor at the KIZ during the first few months, however, managed to keep the German courses open for a larger number of interested people by referring to the competition with West German cultural diplomacy in Cairo. "For the displacement of the Goethe Institute, the effectiveness of the language institute is very important. So far, the Goethe Institute has held all these positions in its hands," Helbig explained his commitment to the East German Foreign Office (MfAA) and the Herder Institute. German lessons should be offered at more favorable conditions than at the Goethe Institute but not free of charge, as otherwise, Helbig assumed, "the value of teaching would be reduced in Arab eyes."[34]

The classes started in March 1965. Apart from regular German classes, the KIZ also offered individual lessons for Egyptian personalities considered as especially important, including not only prospective engineers or other specialists who were to study in the GDR but also members of the Egyptian elite who were interested in (East) German lessons.[35] Two state secretaries of the Egyptian Ministry of Education attended private lessons. Another visitor was Mahmoud El-Hefny, the brother-in-law of Deputy Prime Minister Nureddin Tarraf. El-Hefny was one of Egypt's most respected musicologists and chaired a club for Egyptians that had graduated in Germany (*Klub der in Deutschland graduierten Ägypter*) from 1963 to 1973. In the 1920s, El-Hefny had studied medicine and musicology in Rostock and Berlin. He had received his doctorate in musicology from the Friedrich Wilhelm University[36] of Berlin in 1931. Obviously, El-Hefny already spoke German and wanted to refresh or deepen his knowledge and invested in the maintenance of a social network.[37]

The German courses were an essential part of the KIZ, and they shaped the image of the institute to the outside world. The courses were technically good, which the West German competitors readily acknowledged. Additionally, like the Goethe Institute, the KIZ offered its visitors exhibitions and concerts, and subtitled East German films as well as scientific and political lectures and discussion evenings.

After some hesitations following Ulbricht's visit to Cairo, the West German government finally decided to impose sanctions against Egypt. West Germany announced that it would cease providing economic aid to Egypt. When Chancel-

---

34 SAPMO-BArch, DR3/II/B839, Dr. Gerhard Helbig, Bericht über die Arbeit des Deutsch-Lektorats Cairo im Frühjahrssemester 1965, July 10, 1965.
35 Ibid.
36 Now Humboldt University.
37 For biographical information about Mahmoud El-Hefny see Gerhard Höpp, *Texte aus der Fremde. Arabische politische Publizistik in Deutschland, 1896–1945. Eine Bibliographie* (Berlin: Das Arabische Buch 2000), 51–52.

lor Ludwig Erhard on March 7, 1965 announced that West Germany was willing to fully recognize Israel, Egypt and nine other Arab states broke off their relations with the Federal Republic of Germany (FRG). As a result, West Germany was forced to close its embassy in Cairo and recall the ambassador.[38] "Nowhere in the world have I seen such an impudent people as the West Germans", Nasser declared in a speech one day after Erhard's announcement to recognize Israel.[39]

Despite the breakdown of relations, the staff of the embassy's cultural department remained in Cairo.[40] The Goethe Institute and the (West) German Academic Exchange Agency DAAD (*Deutscher Akademischer Austauschdienst*) were able to continue their work for the time being. The (West German) Federal Foreign Office hoped that the Goethe Institute would be able to take on some of the diplomatic tasks of the embassy that no longer existed.[41] Although West Germany had lost its embassy in Cairo, East Germany was unable to open its own. For Nasser, political pan-Arabism was central and he refused full diplomatic recognition of East Germany not because of West German sensitivities, but to avoid conflict between the Arab states which were divided over this issue.[42]

Thus, the cultural diplomats of both German competitors were finally at eye level. Without diplomatic representation for both German states, cultural diplomacy became more central. This constellation with a "downgraded" West Germany at diplomatic eye level with East Germany is historically unique. It shows that southern agency, in this case Egyptian diplomacy, could influence and limit the scope of action of the northern partners considerably.

Although there were signals from the Egyptian side not to obstruct the work of the Goethe Institute and the DAAD, the political situation nevertheless led to restrictions. The Egyptian government banned Egyptian civil servants from visiting the Goethe Institute without ministerial permission. Appointments that the Goethe Institute had already made with ministry civil servants were cancelled at short notice, Egyptian officials rejected invitations, and the "previously approved use of venues was prohibited."[43] In the months following the diplomatic

---

[38] See Kilian, *Hallstein-Doktrin*, 132, 141–148.
[39] Nasser, cited in Kilian, *Hallstein-Doktrin*, 142.
[40] For a detailed description of the break-off of diplomatic relations see Dalia Abu Samra, "Deutschlands Außenpolitik gegenüber Ägypten: Abbruch und Wiederaufnahme der diplomatischen Beziehungen 1965–1972" (PhD diss., Freie Universität Berlin, 2002), 86–87.
[41] DAAD, Jahresbericht 1965, 158.
[42] Schwanitz, "Zweierlei Deutsche," 19–20.
[43] BArch, B 307/31, Bericht Dienstreise Direktor Werner Ross in den Nahen Osten, April 26, 1965.

withdrawal, it became increasingly difficult for the staff of the Goethe Institute and the DAAD to obtain visas and work permits for their stay in Egypt.[44]

Intra-German competition in language policy created a situation that various actors on the Egyptian side could use to their advantage. They sometimes played both German sides off against each other in order to get free German lessons or instructor positions for Egyptian universities or colleges.[45] Some examples might illustrate how the competition could be exploited for personal ends. In order to keep the Egyptians close to the West German side, the Goethe Institute decided to soften the positions of some state secretaries with small favors. Among others, State Secretary Mustafa Hassan was invited to a longer trip to Germany at the expense of the Goethe Institute, and a two-year scholarship was procured for the son of State Secretary Sayed Mohamed Roha. In addition, they promised a free additional holiday course for Egyptian German teachers in Munich. In another case the Goethe Institute responded to the GDR's offer to the Egyptian Ministry of Education for 12 teachers of German at secondary and high schools in Egypt and 20 training scholarships for German teachers in Leipzig by offering the Egyptian Ministry of Education a two-year training course for four German teachers in Munich and additional further training measures for all Egyptian German teachers with the possibility of taking part in a summer language course in West Germany.[46]

In the summer of 1965, the dean of the German department of the language school in Zeitoun, Antoum Chalaby Maher, approached the Goethe Institute and demanded two additional teachers for his institute. Otherwise he would fall back on the offer of East Germany, which had already, he claimed, promised him two teachers. The Goethe Institute responded favorably to the demand.[47] The fear of an East German breakthrough was deep-seated. The executive board of the

---

44 Several lecturers reported that the granting of visas was subject to harassing conditions. Large quantities of bribe (*baksheesh*) had to be paid and many forms signed by different authorities had to be submitted. The waiting time, begging, and errands now took several weeks of working time. BArch, B 307/31, Bericht Dienstreise Direktor Werner Ross in den Nahen Osten, April 26, 1965.
45 BArch, B 307/96, Vermerk Klopfer, Aktivitäten SBZ-Institut, April 20, 1966; BArch, B307/96, Betr.: Situation des Goethe-Institut[s] in Cairo, no date; BArch, B 307/96, Italienische Botschaft an das Auswärtige Amt, SBZ-Aktivität in Zusammenhang Deutschunterricht VAR, Lahn, June 16, 1966; SAPMO-BArch, DR3/II/B509, HA Internationale Beziehungen, Brief an Geerhardt, MfAA, October 31, 1967.
46 BArch, B 307/96, Aktennotiz Dr. Klopfer, Betr. Besuch von Dombois im Ministerium für Erziehung und Universität Cairo, February 9, 1966; BArch, B 307/96, Klopfer an Zentralverwaltung, Betr. Versuch SBZ in Deutschunterricht in Oberschulen einzudringen, March 23, 1966.
47 BArch, B 307/96, Betr.: Zur Situation des Goethe-Institut in Kairo, August 10, 1965.

Goethe Institute agreed to do everything in its power to fend off the East German advances: "If the SBZ [Soviet Occupation Zone]⁴⁸ had succeeded in making a major slump in this direction, the consequences would not be foreseeable. That's why every effort must be made to send as many good people as possible in sufficient numbers."⁴⁹

When a position as a language inspector for German lessons at the Egyptian Ministry of Education became vacant, East Germany proposed to fill it. Until then, three inspectors of the Goethe Institute had been closely involved in the professional supervision of the Egyptian German instructors. Since the Egyptian Ministry of Education postponed the decision for some time, two KIZ employees offered Egyptian German instructors jobs at the KIZ in Cairo and distributed symbolic awards such as "knowledge medals" to the course participants.⁵⁰ When the Goethe Institute protested that the previous supervision of German lessons at Egyptian schools was no longer guaranteed and that on the other hand the awarding of "FDJ [Free German Youth]⁵¹ medals" by non-authorized East German citizens at Egyptian schools was equivalent to the GDR's recognition under international law, Egyptian state secretaries replied that the West German arms deliveries to Israel had not been forgotten.⁵² Here again the Egyptians dealt with the case without showing much interest in the complicated details of German-German competition and rather bluntly asserted their focus on the Israeli case.

The existence of two German language institutes in Egypt and the ideologically charged competition led to the close observation of each other's work. In their *Kulturkampf*, Germans occasionally tried to instrumentalize Egyptians as informers and cultural saboteurs. The Goethe Institute, on the instructions of the Federal Foreign Office, encouraged its Egyptian staff to attend KIZ events in order to report on them and carry out "possible countermeasures."⁵³ On the

---

48 *Sowjetische Besatzungszone* (SBZ) was the term used for the sector of Germany which was occupied by the Soviet Union since 1945. Even after the founding of the GDR in 1949, the term was often used in West Germany instead of the abbreviation GDR, since the GDR was not recognized as a sovereign state.
49 BArch, B 307/32, Vorstandsprotokoll Goethe-Institut, March 4, 1966.
50 BArch, B 307/96, Vermerk Dvorak, Aktivitäten SBZ-Institut, April 19, 1966.
51 FDJ was the East German youth organization *Freie Deutsche Jugend*, associated with the ruling party SED.
52 BArch, B 307/96, Vermerk Klopfer, Aktivitäten SBZ-Institut, April 20, 1966. More examples of the various and sometimes absurd West German discussions about whether or not little flags, mentions of the name "GDR" in conference documentations or East German orders meant recognition of the GDR can be found in Kilian, *Hallstein Doctrine*.
53 BArch, B307/96, Schreiben Auswärtiges Amt an Goethe-Institut, Betr. Kontakte von Mitarbeitern der Kulturinstitute mit Vertretern der sowjetisch besetzten Zone, May 5, 1966.

other hand, East German language teachers visited Goethe Institute events and wrote detailed reports on them. In May 1966, the Federal Foreign Office completely prohibited the German staff of the Goethe Institute and the DAAD from contacting members of the GDR Cultural Center. Instead, their own Egyptian local staff was chosen to obtain information. They should apparently respond to the East German offer for a further training course for Egyptian German instructors, in order to learn more about the structures and working methods of the East German Institute.[54] The Egyptian instructors later stated that the East German chief instructor Peter Schumann was approaching them with special offers. He offered them to change to the East German Institute for a better salary and promised the possibility of free further training at the Herder Institute in Leipzig. The Egyptian instructor Samir Boalos, for example, reported that East Germans told him that the KIZ had excellent relations with Egyptian civil servants and secretaries of state, which would certainly benefit the professional career of German instructors.[55] Whether this East German offer really existed can only be inferred from the reports of the Egyptian instructors, but not from the documents of the GDR. It is also possible that the Egyptian instructors, in playing Germans off against each other, tried to increase their wages at the Goethe Institute and hoped for invitations to language courses in West Germany.

The East German KIZ managed to establish itself in Cairo within a few months. By fall 1966, more than 100 language students had enrolled in the courses. In instructor Gerhard Helbig's view, one reason for this was a modern, fully equipped electronic classroom, with television, film projector, and record player. It was not a widespread practice at the time to include these media in language teaching. According to Helbig, the East German classroom was looked upon with envy by West German competitors.[56] If that was the case, this might be one of the rare occasions where East German technical equipment in development cooperation was superior to West German one. From March 1967, the West German television course *Guten Tag* was broadcasted on Egyptian television.[57] The broadcasting was discontinued in the spring of 1968 and replaced by the

---

[54] BArch, B 307/96, Rundschreiben Auswärtiges Amt an Zentralverwaltung Goethe-Institut, Betr. Kontakte von Mitarbeitern der Kulturinstitute mit Vertretern der sowjetisch besetzten Zone, May 5, 1966.
[55] BArch, B 307/96, Aktennotiz Dr. Klopfer, Betr. Besuch unserer Ortskraft Samir Boalos im SBZ, February 7, 1966.
[56] SAPMO-BArch, DR3/II/B839, Bericht über die Arbeit des Deutsch-Lektorats Cairo im Frühjahrssemester 1965, Dr. Gerhard Helbig, July 10, 1965.
[57] BArch, B 370/41, Aktennotiz, betr. Internationale Erfolge des Fernsehkurses Guten Tag, October 19, 1967.

East German television course *Sprechen Sie Deutsch?* The course was meant to be a pilot project for GDR TV courses in the Arab world and other countries and was given as a gift to the Egyptian television. For a period of three years, this East German course ran weekly on the Egyptian State Channel Five.[58] Accompanying the course, the KIZ offered consultations in its own cultural center as well as in the Egyptian cultural centers in various cities.[59] The rapid successes encouraged the GDR leadership to strengthen its cultural policy work in Egypt on the basis of a decision from the GDR's Council of Ministers in summer 1966 to expand foreign information activities (*Auslandsinformation*), as the propaganda work was called, in the Arab countries. The decision provided for the opening of two new cultural centers in Aleppo and Alexandria.[60] In addition, the training and further education of Egyptian and Syrian German teachers was intensified.[61]

1967: Teaching German after the Six-Day War

The Six-Day War in June 1967[62] was a turning point for the Egyptian-German triangle relationship. Since West Germany supported Israel, the political mood and the opinion of the Egyptian authorities and in institutions quickly changed from suspicious to hostile. Politicians frequently referred to the "anti-Arab Federal Republic" in public.[63] West German instructors wrote about a "hostile attitude" of the Egyptian population in their reports. The staff of the Goethe Institute even reported that they felt a "climate of fear."[64] Egyptian authorities began to put pressure on the Goethe Institute and the DAAD as residence permits were not extended and work permits could only be obtained with great effort. The Egyptian secret service began to openly monitor employees of the Goethe Institute.[65] After Egyptian protesters in Alexandria had set the American and British consulates on fire in the name of anti-imperialism and tried to do the same at the Goethe Institute, which was protected by the police, the Goethe Institute decided to

---

58 Praxenthaler, *Sprachverbreitungspolitik*, 310–311.
59 SAPMO-BArch, DR3/II/B1022c, Tätigkeitsbericht Lektorat KIZ Kairo 1968/69, February 24, 1969.
60 Ibid.
61 SAPMO-BArch, DY30/JIV2/3/1188, Beschluß zur Verstärkung der auslandsinformatorischen Tätigkeit der DDR in den arabischen Schwerpunktländern, June 10, 1966.
62 For the Six-Day War between Israel on one side and Egypt, Jordan, and Syria on the other, which ended in a complete disaster for the Arab side see Westad, *Cold War*, 459–461.
63 BArch, B 212/21181, 000219/1 Jahresbericht DAAD Kairo 1969, Eckmann, February 11, 1970.
64 BArch, B 307/222, Tätigkeitsbericht GI Alexandria 01.01.1967–30.06.1967, July 13, 1967.
65 BArch, B 307/233, Ferkinghoff, 1. Halbjahresbericht 1967, Kulturarbeit, no date.

close the offices in Cairo and Alexandria temporarily. Language courses were discontinued and the upcoming examinations postponed until further notice. The head office in Munich was firmly expecting both branches to be permanently closed by the Egyptian government and was already planning to transfer the staff to other countries.[66]

East Germany's cultural diplomats took advantage of this situation immediately. The KIZ remained open and classes continued during the war. Just one day after the closure of the Goethe Institute, the East German KIZ advertised in Egyptian newspapers that the examinations planned by the Goethe Institute would be held by the "German Cultural Centre of the GDR – Arab-German-Society".[67] As a result, many of the Goethe Institute's language course participants, especially from the intermediate and advanced levels, moved to the KIZ.[68]

In late 1967, a brochure entitled "In the Name of Goethe – The Goethe Institute, a Weapon of West German Imperialism" appeared in Egypt. The brochure, written entirely in Arabic, was printed in East Berlin by Panorama, a publisher of the GDR's Foreign Press Agency. It was distributed free of charge in large numbers to state authorities, ministries, and the press. Excerpts from the brochure were also published in the Egyptian magazine *Al-Magalla*. The GDR obviously wanted to use the anti-imperialist, anti-Western mood and hoped to convince the supposedly communist, GDR-friendly or anti-imperialist minds in ministries, authorities, and the press of the danger represented by the Goethe Institute.[69] The campaign was seemingly successful, but this was probably due to the political circumstances rather than the persuasiveness of the East German propaganda. In a way the disaster of the Six-Day War achieved what the GDR propaganda had not in the previous years: to demonize West Germany as an imperialist power.

Since West Germany did not want to leave the field to the Eastern competitors, the Goethe Institute re-opened its doors just after a few weeks. But Ludwig Erhard's public support for Israel had taken its toll. The number of participants in language courses at the Goethe Institute dropped rapidly after the war. In September 1967, more than 30 students moved from the Goethe Institute to the KIZ. An Egyptian language student wrote to the Goethe Institute explaining his decision: "I refuse to continue taking language lessons with you. It would be embarrassing and painful for me if I continued to study in your institute which belongs

---

66 BArch, B 307/10, Protokoll Abteilungsleiterkonferenz Goethe-Institut, July 3, 1967.
67 BArch, B 307/223, H.R. Reinstrom, Vermerk, no date.
68 BArch, B 307/233, Halbjahresbericht Goethe-Institut Kairo, 1.07. – 31.12.1967, no date.
69 The brochure can be found in BArch, B 307/273, Korrespondenz Kairo, no date.

to the West German government, a government that clearly participated in the dirty, armed hostilities against the great Arab homeland."[70]

Egyptian authorities now stipulated that all West German cultural events required a permit from the Egyptian Ministry of Interior and could not take place outside the premises of the Goethe Institute.[71] Additionally, West Germany now had to pay social insurance to all local Egyptian DAAD and Goethe Institute employees which resulted in enormous bureaucratic effort and financial costs. The Goethe Institute, the DAAD and the West German Cultural Department suspected that this compulsory insurance had been introduced under pressure from East Germany.[72] This shows a characteristic pattern that shaped German-German perceptions: in the bipolar logic of system competition, both sides assumed that their (German) rivals orchestrated the restrictions and Egyptians were nothing but puppets. Egyptian initiatives and motives, such as anti-imperialism or anti-Zionism, rarely appear in the reports of both German sides. Once more, the intra-German rivalry provided several advantages for Egyptian course participants. With some skill, it was possible to get free language lessons. The director of the Egyptian Cultural Centre in Zagazig received free German lessons at the East German KIZ by mentioning that the Goethe Institute had offered him free lessons. Other German learners succeeded in enrolling late in courses of the KIZ, arguing that language courses could also be taken at the Goethe Institute.[73]

East Germany attempted to exploit the weak position of West Germany in Egypt as a result of the Six-Day War to gain a foothold in the Egyptian university landscape. In addition to three West German instructors, the Language School at Zeitoun also hired an East German instructor to run its language laboratory in September 1967. This caused problems, because the shift in Egyptian politics in favor of the GDR did not mean that all Egyptians welcomed this change. The Egyptian head of the language school, Antoum Chalaby Maher, did not conceal his sympathy for the Goethe Institute and asked the East German instructor Klaus Neubert to stick to the (West German) curriculum and teaching material. However, since Neubert had been instructed by his superiors not to use West German material for political reasons, he had to produce his own teaching material.[74]

---

[70] BArch, B 307/223, Enclosure in Halbjahresbericht Goethe-Institut Kairo, 1.07–31.12.1967, no date.
[71] BArch, B 307/222, Tätigkeitsbericht GI Alexandria 01.01.1968–30.06.1968, no date.
[72] BArch, B 307/233, Aktennotiz, May 9, 1967.
[73] SAPMO-BArch, DR3/II/B1022b, Bericht des Lektorats am KIZ Kairo WS 1967/68, March 1968.
[74] SAPMO-BArch, DR3/II/B1022b, Dietrich Engel, Bericht des Lektorats am KIZ Kairo, March 1968.

1969: Recognition

Egypt turned closer to the Soviet Union and Eastern European States after the Six-Day War. This promoted the diplomatic aims of the GDR. Cultural relations were already deepened at the end of 1968. To this end, a joint cultural commission was founded and a new joint "Working program for cultural and scientific cooperation" was concluded.[75] One of the most important goals of the program was the promotion of GDR German teaching in Egypt. The aim was to replace West Germany from its traditional positions in the field. Abdul Wahab El-Borolosy, Egyptian Minister of Research and Higher Education, and representatives of the Egyptian Ministry of Education promised at a meeting with the Cultural Department of the Consulate General and the KIZ to support the ideas of the GDR.[76]

On July 10, 1969, the Egyptian and East German governments announced the establishment of diplomatic relations. The West German Government's reaction did not contain the threat of countermeasures, which was tantamount to a change in the policy of non-recognition towards the GDR. The recognition of the GDR was still described as a hostile act by West German officials, but no retaliatory measures such as the breaking off of trade relations were used.[77] The breakthrough at the diplomatic level was also the breakthrough in the field of German as a foreign language (*Deutsch als Fremdsprache*, DaF) for the GDR in Egypt. With the opening of the embassy, the DaF working group was immediately founded, which further determined and coordinated the tasks of the cultural center and the work of East German instructors at Egyptian universities.[78] Some West German instructors were replaced by East German instructors. As one of the first measures, the East German instructors introduced GDR teaching material.[79]

The change of mood in Egypt also led to a significant increase in the number of applicants for language courses at the KIZ. In the spring of 1970, the enrolment

---

75 SAPMO-BArch, DR3/II/B837, Information über den Stand der Beziehungen auf dem Gebiet des Hochschulwesens mit der VAR, May 19, 1970.
76 SAPMO-BArch, DR3/II/B1048 Brief von Dr. Konschel an Dr. Merkel (MfAA), February 18, 1969.
77 Rainer Büren, "Die arabischen Staaten in der außenpolitischen Konzeption der Bundesrepublik Deutschland," in *Araber und Deutsche. Begegnungen in einem Jahrtausend*, ed. Friedrich Kochwasser and Hans Roemer (Tübingen/Basel: Erdmann), 22; see also Kilian, *Hallstein-Doktrin*, 162–163.
78 SAPMO-BArch, DR3/II/B1507/1a, Cheflektor Steinecke, Arbeitsplan des Lektorats Kairo für das Studienjahr 1971/72, October 13, 1971.
79 SAPMO-BArch, DR3/II/1507/1b, Erika Endesfelder, Die Einflußnahme auf den Fremdsprachenunterricht Deutsch in der VAR durch die DDR und die BRD-Institutionen, Anfang 1971, no date.

for the courses had to be stopped after only two days due to the large number of applicants. Since East German officials demanded to enroll preferably those Egyptians who "appear to be important for the foreign information objective," the tuition fees for "students and housewives" were increased by 50 percent because the DaF working group considered these to be of little relevance.[80] It becomes clear here that the main objective of the language courses was to achieve political goals. Propaganda for the GDR, the above mentioned "foreign information," was a mandatory part of the language courses.[81] The aim was to convince Egyptian society of the advantages of the socialist GDR over the "imperialist" FRG. In contrast, "housewives" and "students" were obviously not regarded as important multipliers and were therefore excluded as far as possible.

In the 1970s, however, East German propaganda became less important in language teaching and made way for a more pragmatic approach. Already in spring 1970, the KIZ began to offer the opportunity to acquire language diplomas which served to "enable the holder to take up a scientific qualification in the GDR without further linguistic preparation."[82] The course load for the language diploma comprised 480 hours and was to become mandatory in the future for an entry visa to study in East Germany. During a visit to East Germany by Abdul Wahab el Borolosy, the Egyptian minister of higher education, it was agreed that language training at the KIZ should be concentrated on those who would study in the GDR. In the future, language training should also focus on technical disciplines.

This change in the orientation of German teaching can be seen as an East German paradigm shift in the teaching of DaF. In the 1970s language teaching became more and more a tool to support educational programs. The aim was now a pragmatic preparation for university education in East Germany. Propaganda was no longer in the foreground, although the indoctrination of Egyptian instructors did not disappear completely. For economic reasons, more Egyptian instructors were hired for the teaching of beginners' and basic courses, but for political reasons they were to be "regularly instructed and controlled by East German instructors, as well as politically and methodically supervised." These

---

80 SAPMO-BArch, DR3/II/B1022d, 1. Tätigkeitsbericht des Lektorats Kairo, Studienjahr 1969/70, February 20, 1970. We found no explanation in the sources to whom the term "housewives" refers and how many of them wanted to enroll in the courses. Unfortunately, there is a general lack of information in the sources about gender of Egyptian students and teachers.
81 SAPMO-BArch, DY 13/2020, Beschlussprotokoll der Sekretariatssitzung der Deutsch-Arabischen Gesellschaft, August 3, 1966.
82 SAPMO-BArch, DR3/II/B1022c, Tätigkeitsbericht des Lektorats am Kulturzentrum in Kairo, August 12, 1969.

instructors had to attend a further training course in East Germany every two years in order to report on the GDR from their own experience.⁸³

East Germany's relative superiority vis-à-vis West Germany in the realm of cultural diplomacy was quickly ended by another change in Egypt's political scene. After Nasser's sudden death in 1970, Egyptian foreign policy under Anwar Sadat changed fundamentally. Egypt moved closer to the West without giving up cooperation with the socialist countries.⁸⁴ 1972 saw the resumption of diplomatic relations between West Germany and Egypt. With Egypt's diplomatic recognition of the GDR, cultural diplomacy in North Africa became less central for the two German states. The situation reversed, and less and less visitors were drawn to the East German cultural center.⁸⁵ German lessons continued, but while the Goethe Institute in Cairo still exists today, the GDR closed its cultural and information centers in Cairo and Alexandria in 1977. The closure of the centers was probably not only related to the diplomatic recognition of the GDR, which led to a decline of investments in cultural diplomacy, but also to the deterioration in relations between Egypt and the socialist countries under Anwar al-Sadat. From 1974, Sadat clearly moved closer to the West and, among other things, withdrew from the Treaty of Friendship with the Soviet Union in 1976.⁸⁶

German Language Courses in Egypt and the Emergence of DaF

The German-German *Kulturkampf* in Egypt played an important role in the emergence of the academic subject German as a foreign language (DaF). Egypt was the second non-socialist country after Finland in which the GDR experimented with the teaching of German as a foreign language abroad with its own instructors at its own language centers. Until then, there had been little experience with

---

83 SAPMO-BArch, DR3/II/B1022d, 1. Tätigkeitsbericht des Lektorats Kairo, Studienjahr 1969/70, February 20, 1970.
84 For an overview of the events after Nasser's death and the political change in Egypt see Westad, *Cold War*, 463–469; Christopher Andrew and Vasili Mitrokhin, *The World Was Going Our Way: The KGB and the Battle for the Third World* (New York: Basic Books, 2005), 141–142.
85 SAPMO-BArch, DR3/II/B1507/1b, Kurzbericht über das Herbstsemester 1972/73 am Lektorat des KIZ Kairo, March 13, 1973.
86 Praxenthaler, *Sprachverbreitungspolitik*, 237; Schwanitz, "Zweierlei Deutsche," 26.

teaching in a non-German-speaking environment.[87] The GDR's German classes in Egypt were also successful and attractive because they were carried out by well-trained instructors.

East German instructors were carefully selected to ensure that they had language skills in the host country. A guideline of the East German Ministry of Higher and Technical Education (MHF) for the selection of instructors stated that they should have sufficient foreign language skills "in order to be able to carry out foreign information at a high level in beginners' lessons."[88] In Egypt, this meant that almost all East German instructors were experienced language instructors or German studies experts with knowledge of English and in most cases also with Arabic language skills. Almost all the instructors had previously studied or taught at the Herder Institute in Leipzig. Egyptian authorities often pointed out to West German representatives these qualitative differences between East and West. The Federal Foreign Office therefore insisted that West German instructors should have acquired knowledge of the national language before their assignment. In reality, this could rarely be implemented. There were simply too few West German instructors with knowledge of Arabic who would have been willing to go to Egypt, either out of concern for their careers or out of fear of crisis situations flaring up again and again.[89]

In September 1966, the East German Council of Ministers decided to "establish a comprehensive system of German language teaching for foreigners." This decision formed the basis for further development of language policy as a focal point of the GDR's cultural diplomacy in order to counter West German language policy. According to the Council of Ministers of the GDR, West Germany only used language courses to "gain political influence in the developing countries and to bind the leaders in these countries to the FRG." The resolution clearly states how the influence of West Germany was to be reduced. The aim, according to the Council of Ministers, should be "to gradually reach firm contractual agreements [...] and political and cultural centers [...] through the secondment of individual instructors."[90] The decision of the Council of Ministers therefore directed that

---

[87] For GDR cultural policy in Finland see Olivia Griese, *Auswärtige Kulturpolitik und Kalter Krieg. Die Konkurrenz von Bundesrepublik und DDR in Finnland 1949–1973* (Wiesbaden: Harrassowitz, 2006).

[88] SAPMO-BArch, DR3/II/B1022b, AG Deutsch als Fremdsprache, Bericht des Lektorats am Kulturzentrum Kairo der Deutschen Demokratischen Republik in der Vereinigten Arabischen Republik, Sommersemester 1968, no date.

[89] Lothar Reinermann, "Die Außenstellen des DAAD in London und Kairo," *Spuren in die Zukunft* 1 (2000), 186.

[90] SAPMO-BArch, DC20/I/4/1412, Ministerratsbeschluss, September 8, 1966.

German as a foreign language should be underpinned theoretically and practically and had to be developed into an "independent scientific discipline."[91] In a conceptual paper on the development of German as a foreign language, the director of the Herder Institute in Leipzig, Johannes Rößler, stressed that the quantitative superiority of West Germany in the field of DaF could be countered by the qualitative superiority of the GDR. According to Rößler, this lead should be maintained at all costs.[92] It becomes once again clear at this point how much language teaching was used as a strategic weapon under the conditions of ubiquitous system competition.

Here we can see several factors that influenced German language teaching. The paradigm shift in language education from ideological to technical made it necessary to scientifically underpin language teaching. At the same time, East German party and state leaders noticed that language policy enabled them to compete with West Germany with relatively scarce resources.

In general, teaching German in Egypt was an important step for East German instructors, in their career and at the same time an opportunity to experience life abroad, as can be seen in the case of Gerhard Helbig. It was either a starting point for an international career or a once in a lifetime opportunity. Some used this opportunity for a more radical change. Although authorities took care to ensure that only well-established "cadres" were allowed to travel abroad, it was not possible to prevent the "Republikflucht" [desertion from the republic, i.e. GDR] of instructors completely.[93] For example, a married couple of instructors who had been employed in Egypt as well as the GDR instructor in Conakry in Guinea used their stay abroad to "defect" to the West.[94] This sparked a debate between the Herder Institute, the MHF, and the Foreign Office on how to prevent similar events in the future.[95]

The success of the GDR in Egypt promoted the emergence of DaF as an academic subject in the GDR. From a practice increasingly needed during the 1950s

---

91 SAPMO-BArch, DC20/I/4/1412, Beschluss Aufbau eines umfassenden Systems für den deutschen Sprachunterricht, June 8, 1966.
92 UAL, HI 028, Johannes Rößler, Problemskizze zur Entwicklung des Gegenstandes "Deutsch als Fremdsprache," August 28, 1973, 140.
93 SAPMO-BArch, DR3/II/B1022e, Günther Hänse and Horst Nalewski, Halbjahresbericht über die Arbeit an der Universität Kairo für die Zeit vom 10. Februar bis 10. Juni 1970, June 10, 1970.
94 The names of the couple are not mentioned. The lecturer from Conakry, however, became lecturer at the Goethe Institute in Munich and later Professor for DaF in Saarbrücken.
95 SAPMO-BArch, DR3/II/B1426d, Brief Leiter des Referats für Wirtschaftliche Auslandsbeziehungen MLU Halle an MHF, January 27, 1969. How many lecturers exactly used their assignment in Egypt as an opportunity to turn their backs on the GDR cannot be determined from the available sources.

and 1960s it developed into an independent scientific discipline in the GDR, several years before it was established in West Germany. On the one hand, the aim was to offer better German lessons than those of the Goethe Institute or the DAAD in countries like Egypt and thus to convince the students that the GDR was the "better Germany". On the other hand, scientific research was meant to improve and shorten the obligatory German lessons for foreign students in the GDR. At the center of these efforts was the Herder Institute in Leipzig, which from the beginning of the 1950s was the training center for the obligatory preparatory German lessons for foreign students wishing to study in the GDR. Here at the Institute, the foundations were laid for the academic subject of German as a foreign language. In 1967, a research department was founded at the institute, and in 1968, Gerhard Helbig, the former first instructor in Cairo, was appointed as the first chair for German as a foreign language.[96]

Conclusion

Cultural cooperation between Egypt and the two German states during the Cold War period was a new chapter in the long-standing Egyptian-German relations, which affected the institutions in both German states. This is particularly evident in language policy and in the genesis of the subject German as a foreign language. The debate on language teaching in Egypt had a particular influence on East German language policy, and shaped pioneering institutions like the Herder Institute and Goethe Institute in the Global North on both sides of the Iron Curtain.

The competition of the East German and West German cultural institutes in Cairo shows that Egyptian actors and institutions were in charge and shaped the discourse. For Egyptians, German-German competition was sometimes ignored but, in most cases, instrumentalized or used for tactical maneuvers in the conflict over Israel. Learning German had a long tradition in Egypt[97] and German was also needed by Egyptians who wanted to study in one of the two German countries. In this respect, teaching German in Cairo was a small piece of the puzzle in the great development project of socialist modernization under Nasser.

---

96 SAPMO-BArch, DC20/I/4/1412, Beschluss Aufbau eines umfassenden Systems für den deutschen Sprachunterricht, June 8, 1966; SAPMO-BArch, DR 3/5938, Herder-Institut der KMU Leipzig, Perspektivplan 1966/70.
97 For this tradition see Aleya Khattab, "Deutsch in Ägypten," in *Deutsch als Fremd- und Zweitsprache. Ein internationales Handbuch*, ed. Hans-Jürgen Krumm (Berlin, New York: De Gruyter, 2010), 1602–1606.

Egypt under Nasser was on its own path of socialist development and maintained close relationships with the USSR and other socialist countries. Like many non-aligned Third World countries it carefully avoided to choose one side in East West Cold War competition but rather followed its own agenda and interests. The increasingly strong relations with the socialist GDR fit into this pattern. From the Egyptian side they might have been a result of practical and strategic considerations rather than an expression of deeply felt socialist solidarity. Ideological consensus with the GDR was most likely to be found in Egypt's pronounced anti-imperialism.

Solidarity between the GDR and Egypt is perhaps better understood if it is seen not so much as political or economic altruism. Both states were interested in meeting at eye level and wanted to benefit from the exchange. This anti-imperialist win-win situation may not always have existed in practice. Nevertheless, it shaped the decisions on both sides. The East-West side of the triangular relationship described in this chapter was not central for Egypt, but system competition between East and West Germany was used by Egyptian actors to deal with both sides successfully. This is also reflected in the German-German struggle for sovereignty over the teaching of German and the changing reactions of Egyptian actors, be they learners, teachers or political functionaries, which determined the scope of action of the two German states.

In retrospect, however, the decisive question is not whether "Herder" or "Goethe" won the German-German competition in Egypt. Rather, we are challenged to examine a facet of the conflicts in the Cold War. We see the economically unequal two German states competing in one of the leading countries of the Third World movement, without diplomatic recognition by this country and at eye level to each other. We see them engaging in their tough and sometimes seemingly ridiculous cultural struggle over who should be allowed to teach German to Egyptian interested parties. German-German competition had an important side effect on the genesis and institutionalization of the subject of German as a foreign language in East Germany and subsequently also in West Germany. This shows that external missions of projecting cultural soft power in the Global South sometimes had stronger effects on the northern cultural missionaries themselves than on their southern counterparts.

Bibliography

Abou-El-Fadl, Reem. "Building Egypt's Afro-Asian Hub: Infrastructures of Solidarity and the 1957 Cairo Conference." *Journal of World History* 30 (2019): 157–192.

Abu Samra, Dalia. "Deutschlands Außenpolitik gegenüber Ägypten: Abbruch und Wiederaufnahme der diplomatischen Beziehungen 1965–1972." PhD diss., Freie Universität Berlin, 2002.

Andrew, Christopher, and Vasili Mitrokhin. *The World Was Going Our Way: The KGB and the Battle for the Third World*. New York: Basic Books, 2005.

Altmayer, Claus. "50 Jahre Herder-Institut, 50 Jahre Deutsch als Fremdsprache. Traditionen und Grenzüberschreitungen." *Deutsch als Fremdsprache* 44 (2007): 67–74.

Büren, Rainer. "Die arabischen Staaten in der außenpolitischen Konzeption der Bundesrepublik Deutschland." In *Araber und Deutsche. Begegnungen in einem Jahrtausend*, edited by Friedrich Kochwasser and Hans Roemer, 11–33. Tübingen, Basel: Erdmann, 1974.

Burton, Eric. "Hubs of Decolonization. African Liberation Movements and Eastern Connections in Cairo, Accra and Dar es Salaam." In *Southern African Liberation Movements and the Global Cold War "East": Transnational Activism 1960–1990*, edited by Lena Dallywater, Helder A. Fonseca, and Chris Saunders, 25–56. Berlin: De Gruyter, 2019.

Bracher, Karl Dietrich, Gisela Biewer, Ernst Deuerlein, eds. *Dokumente zur Deutschlandpolitik*. München: Oldenbourg, 1978.

Das Gupta, Amid. "Ulbricht am Nil: Die deutsch-deutsche Rivalität in der Dritten Welt." In *Das doppelte Deutschland: 40 Jahre Systemkonkurrenz*, edited by Udo Wengstand and Hermann Wentker, 111–134. Berlin: Ch. Links, 2008.

Dinkel, Jürgen. *The Non-Aligned Movement: Genesis, Organization and Politics, 1927–1992*. Leiden, Boston: Brill, 2018.

Gray, William G. *Germany's Cold War: The Global Campaign to Isolate East Germany, 1945–1969*. Chapel Hill, London: The University of North Carolina Press, 2003.

Griese, Olivia. *Auswärtige Kulturpolitik und Kalter Krieg. Die Konkurrenz von Bundesrepublik und DDR in Finnland 1949–1973*. Wiesbaden: Harrassowitz, 2006.

Geerhardt, Herbert. "Kultur- und Wissenschaftsbeziehungen der DDR zu Staaten Afrikas und Asiens." *Deutsche Außenpolitik* 13 (1968): 1432–1440.

Hong, Young-Sun. *Cold War Germany, the Third World, and the Global Humanitarian Regime*. New York: Cambridge University Press, 2015.

Höpp, Gerhard. *Texte aus der Fremde. Arabische politische Publizistik in Deutschland, 1896–1945. Eine Bibliographie*. Berlin: Das Arabische Buch, 2000.

Kathe, Steffen R. *Kulturpolitik um jeden Preis. Die Geschichte des Goethe-Instituts von 1951 bis 1990*. München: M. Meidenbauer, 2005.

Khattab, Aleya. "Deutsch in Ägypten". In *Deutsch als Fremd- und Zweitsprache. Ein internationales Handbuch*, edited by Hans-Jürgen Krumm, Christian Fandrych, Britta Hufeisen, and Claudia Riemer, 1602–1606. Berlin/New York: De Gruyter, 2010.

Kilian, Werner. *Die Hallstein-Doktrin. Der diplomatische Krieg zwischen der BRD und der DDR 1955–1973: Aus den Akten der beiden deutschen Außenministerien*. Berlin: Duncker & Humblot, 2001.

Kramer, Thomas. *Deutsch-ägyptische Beziehungen in Vergangenheit und Gegenwart*. Tübingen: Erdmann, 1974.

Lüthi, Lorenz. "The Non-Aligned Movement and the Cold War, 1961–1973." *Journal of Cold War Studies* 18 (2016): 98–147.

Muehlenbeck, Philipp. *Czechoslovakia in Africa 1945–1968*. Basingstoke: Palgrave Macmillan, 2016.

Osman, Tarek M. *Egypt on the Brink: From the Rise of Nasser to the Fall of Mubarak*. New Haven: Yale University Press, 2011.

Peisert, Hansgert. *Auswärtige Kulturpolitik der Bundesrepublik Deutschland, Gutachten im Auftrag des Auswärtigen Amts*. Konstanz: Auswärtiges Amt, 1971.

Porz, Helga. *Zur Entwicklung des Herder-Instituts. Von den Anfängen der Vorbereitung ausländischer Studierender auf ein Studium in der DDR bis 1966*. PhD diss, Universität Leipzig, 1972.

Praxenthaler, Martin. *Die Sprachverbreitungspolitik der DDR. Die deutsche Sprache als Mittel sozialistischer auswärtiger Kulturpolitik*. Frankfurt, Berlin: Peter Lang, 2002.

Reinermann, Lothar. "Die Außenstellen des DAAD in London und Kairo." *Spuren in die Zukunft* 1 (2000): 177–195.

Schwanitz, Wolfgang G., ed. *Berlin-Kairo damals und heute: zur Geschichte deutsch-ägyptischer Beziehungen*. Berlin: DÄG, 1991.

Schwanitz, Wolfgang G. "Ägypten: Zweierlei Deutsche im Kalten Krieg." *Comparativ* 16 (2006): 11–29.

van Laak, Dirk. *Weiße Elefanten. Anspruch und Scheitern technischer Großprojekte im 20. Jahrhundert*. Stuttgart: Deutsche Verlagsanstalt, 1999.

Wentker, Hermann. *Außenpolitik in engen Grenzen. Die DDR im internationalen System 1949–1989*. München: Oldenbourg, 2007.

Westad, Odd Arne. *The Cold War. A World History*. New York: Basic Books, 2017.

Winrow, Gareth. *The Foreign Policy of the GDR in Africa*. Cambridge et al.: Cambridge University Press, 1990.

Yaqub, Salim. "The Cold War and the Middle East". In *The Cold War in the Third World*, edited by Robert McMahon, 11–26. Oxford et al.: Oxford University Press, 2003.

Christian Alvarado

3 "In the Spirit of Harambee!" Kenyan Student Unions in the German Democratic Republic and Yugoslavia, 1964–68[1]

"We Beg to Remain in the Name of Harambee!"[2]

Situated above the signatures of the newly-minted executive committee, this phrase concludes the first official record of correspondence of the Kenya Students Union (KSU) in the German Democratic Republic (GDR). At the core of this phrase was a request: to retain, and in some ways expand, the nature of their status as Kenyan students studying abroad while also articulating a more robust and charged vision of the significance of their education to the nation-building program at home. Dated October 1, 1964, the letter was addressed to none other than Prime Minister Jomo Kenyatta himself. In naming *harambee* (a Kiswahili term typically translated as "pull[ing] together") the authors invoked the official rhetoric of the nascent Kenyatta regime, which had the year prior began using the term as "an appeal not only for self-help but for national unity as well."[3] The purpose of the KSU's letter was to notify the independent Kenyan government, only a year and some months old at this point, of the formation of a new students' union whose membership was open to all Kenyans studying in the GDR.

The KSU was not the first students' union to service Kenyans studying in East Germany. It is unclear in the historical record exactly when and how the Kenyan students whose lives this chapter explores had arrived in their respective

---

[1] I am extremely grateful to Immanuel R. Harisch and Dr. Eric Burton, whose generous insight has played a central role in shaping this chapter. Their own research, tireless and careful reviews of drafts of this piece, and recommendation of wonderful literature on the topic has benefited my work enormously. Any errors that might present are, of course, the responsibility of none other than myself. I would also like to thank The Humanities Institute at UC Santa Cruz for their generous support of this research, without which it would have been impossible.
[2] "Announcement of the Kenya Students Union in the GDR," October 1, 1964, XJ/12/24, Kenya Students Union in East Germany, Kenya National Archives, Nairobi, Kenya (henceforth "KNA").
[3] Robert Maxon, "Social & Cultural Changes," in *Decolonization and Independence in Kenya*, ed. B.A. Ogot and W.R. Ochieng (Athens, OH: Ohio University Press, 1995), 137.

ə OpenAccess. © 2021 Christian Alvarado, published by De Gruyter. This work is licensed under the Creative Commons Attribution 4.0 International License.
https://doi.org/10.1515/9783110623543-003

Eastern European host countries, but their arrival likely followed established routes taken by African students embarking for Europe during this period. To this end, Eric Burton has shown that, in general: "In the 1950s and early 1960s, South-East travels were shaped to a large extent by individual agency as a variety of trade unions, political parties, and other non-state organisations were involved in sending and receiving students and some even came on their own accord."[4] It may well be that, like their Tanzanian counterparts, these students arrived via the so-called "Nile route," "which East Africans used to get from Uganda to Sudan and Cairo, and from there to the Eastern bloc."[5] What can be said with certainty is that in East Germany a group called the Kenya Students Association (henceforth: KSA-GDR) had been founded as early as 1960 to organize and serve such students, and was chaired by a student of political economy named Owilla Olwa.[6] This organization was relatively short-lived, and by 1964 found itself marginalized within the student union landscape in the GDR. In fact, the KSU was to be a consolidation of sorts, the product of political pressure exerted by the government of the GDR who had pushed for the older union "to dissolve and join the KSU, preserving a 'united front'."[7] The dissolution of the KSA-GDR and the establishment of the KSU was also tied to domestic politics in Kenya. "By this point," writes Sara Pugach, the Kenya African National Union (KANU) "was also fracturing internally, as leading figures Jomo Kenyatta, the country's president, and Oginga Odinga, its vice president, were increasingly at odds with each other."[8]

That Kenyatta and Odinga were at odds with each other during this period puts it mildly, and the ramifications of political tensions in Nairobi extended far beyond the borders of Kenya. Contemporary observers cited the ethnic composition of both the KSU and the KSA-GDR as an extension of political strife at home, with the latter's leadership having been dominated by Luo students, the ethnic group with which Odinga was also affiliated. The creation of the KSU was thus a project responsive to the political landscapes of both the GDR and Kenya, each of which viewed student exchange programs as an aspect of diplomatic and

---

4 Eric Burton, "Navigating Global Socialism: Tanzanian Students in and beyond East Germany," *Cold War History* 19 (2019): 67.
5 Eric Burton, "Decolonization, the Cold War, and Africans' Routes to Higher Education Overseas, 1957–65," *The Journal of Global History* 15 (2020): 175.
6 Sara Pugach, "Agents of Dissent: African Student Organizations in the German Democratic Republic," *Africa* 89 (2019): 98–99.
7 Pugach, "Agents of Dissent," 101.
8 Pugach, "Agents of Dissent," 99.

foreign policy.⁹ Moreover, it is worth noting that Kenyan students now studying in Eastern Europe were profoundly shaped by their earlier lives, particularly childhoods lived during the Mau Mau era and the waning days of British colonialism. Thus, these students found themselves situated between not only the distinct racialized landscapes of the late British Empire and the GDR, but also the domestic political and social dynamics of the country they planned to return to.

The archival materials upon which this chapter is based are quite limited, consisting largely of partial records of correspondence and internal government documents, a number of which have no clear authorship.¹⁰ As one can imagine, the limitations of such an archive leave a great many questions unaddressed. Moreover, the inclusion of a chapter about Kenyan students in a volume focused on the history of exchanges between African societies and the GDR raises certain questions of its own. Despite the Kenyatta regime aligning itself explicitly with an ideal of "democratic African socialism" after independence, the Kenyan state consistently managed to cultivate the reputation of being both pro-Western and friendly to capitalist interests, be they Kenyan or foreign. "Despite the rhetoric of non-alignment and African Socialism," writes Branch, "Kenyatta's government was generally pro-West and pro-capitalism."¹¹ The period of study encompasses a time when Kenyatta and his allies successfully suppressed political opposition from the left. Indeed, by the early days of 1966 Kenyatta had effectively ousted Odinga (who harbored socialist and Maoist sympathies) from structural political influence. Thus, a chapter examining Kenyan students studying in Eastern Europe (particularly one based on rather sparse materials) appears odd on multiple fronts. I will argue, however, that it is precisely this position of these students, existing in a liminal space both in their host country and the one they called home, which makes their story particularly valuable for historians of decolonization and developmentalism.

Among other important threads, examining the experiences of these students troubles the orthodox historical ontologies about the relationship of African states and professional networks to the global Cold War, and ultimately allows for a better understanding of the contingencies of African lives during this period. This historiographical bias is nowhere clearer than in the relatively exten-

---

9 For more on the role of these programs in the realm of foreign policy, see Paul Kibiwott Kurgat, "Education as a Foreign Policy Tool: Kenyan Students' Airlifts to the Union of Soviet Socialist Republics and Eastern Europe, 1954–1991" (PhD Diss., Moi University, 2013).
10 As much as possible, I have identified documents which reflect these absences and partialities in their corresponding footnotes, including the maximum amount of information available.
11 Daniel Branch, *Kenya: Between Hope and Despair, 1963–2011* (New Haven: Yale University Press, 2011), 38.

sive amount of literature focusing on the "student airlift" coordinated by Tom Mboya and the John F. Kennedy administration, a program which shepherded hundreds of Kenyan students (including Barack Obama Sr.) to universities in the United States. Rather than reproduce such dualistic historiographical alignments, this chapter follows to an extent Marcia Schenck's articulation of "the term 'Black East' to denote the lived reality of a Black diasporic network in East Germany (German Democratic Republic, GDR) and beyond. This African diaspora owed its existence to socialist entanglements."[12] The trajectories of the students in this chapter highlight the importance of questioning the ways in which broad, national "ideological alignments" can overdetermine the manner in which we approach African intellectual history, and also show how ambiguous Kenyan futurity was felt to be during the early days of an independent Kenya. Moreover, by examining students' experiences in both the GDR and non-aligned Yugoslavia, this chapter demonstrates that a shared set of concerns and ideas existed for Kenyans completing their studies outside of more favored universities in Europe and the United States.[13] These were, broadly-speaking, the ability to play a meaningful role in Kenyan society after returning home and a sharp awareness of the significance of the cultural dimensions of national consciousness. In order to explore the significance of this dual desire, this chapter situates the KSU in the GDR in relation to both the domestic project of Kenyan nationalism and the student unions' distinct Eastern European contexts. It also examines a sister organization (a different "Kenyan Students Association," henceforth KSA-Y) which operated during roughly the same period in Yugoslavia, with the analytical aim of exploring how similar concerns were expressed in different contexts across socialist Europe.

The KSU, its Activities, and the Project of Kenyan Nationalism

The KSU in the GDR operated from 1964 to late-1967, primarily as an organization attempting to provide a bridge between Kenyan students studying in their host

---

[12] Marcia C. Schenck, "Constructing and Deconstructing the 'Black East' – A Helpful Research Agenda?", *Stichproben. Vienna Journal of African Studies* 34 (2018): 136.
[13] For more on the hierarchy imposed upon degrees according to geography see Eric Burton, "African Manpower Development during the Cold War: The Case of Tanzanian Students in the Two German States," in *Africa Research in Austria: Approaches and Perspectives*, ed. Andreas Exenberger and Ulrich Pallua (Innsbruck: Innsbruck University Press, 2016): 111–113.

country and the government at home. Its activities were most robust during the first two years of its existence, when it worked to gather information on its members in an effort to provide the Kenyan Ministry of Education with details that might allow them to facilitate employment after students completed their studies. Yet the KSU was also viewed by its members as a cultural institution, hosting Independence Day celebrations and attempting to gain access to media produced in Kenya to showcase in the GDR. It is these socio-cultural dimensions of the union that are the primary focus of this chapter, as they not only expand our understanding of the visions Kenyans studying abroad had for their country, but also highlight how these students challenged dual processes of objectification: on the one hand as commodified workers by their home government, and on the other as racialized subjects in European locales.[14]

One year after Kenya's national independence in 1963, both fluid imaginaries of what the postcolonial state could be and the nascent status of postcolonial Kenyan state ideology played pivotal roles in shaping the KSU as a political and educational formation. The tensions that existed between Kenyatta and his allies in relation to Odinga and his necessitated the careful and strategic crafting of union rhetoric about its function and operations.[15] The KSU's displacement of the earlier KSA-GDR (not to mention political strife at home) contributed to a deep and protracted emphasis on rhetoric of unity on the part of the organization, in the service of which terms in both Kiswahili and English were deployed. "Under stable Government," wrote the KSU in an early communiqué, "we feel then that we should mobilize and employ the energies of all sections of such Unity, as we took it as a noble cause everyone to consider it a privilege and duty to unite on a national basis."[16] Here, the organization positioned itself relative to the Kenyatta administration through its articulation of the "privilege" and "duties" which came with being an aspiring member of the Kenyan intelligentsia. It also suggests that, despite the fact of their studying in the GDR, it was their loyalty to Kenya that held central importance, rather than any international

---

14 The racialized experience of African students studying in the GDR has been explored in depth by (among others) Sara Pugach. For more, see Sara Pugach, "African Students and the Politics of Race and Gender in the German Democratic Republic," in *Comrades of Color: East Germany in the Cold War World*, ed. Quinn Slobodian (New York: Berghahn Books, 2015).
15 For readers interested in exploring these tensions more thoroughly, see Oginga Odinga, *Not Yet Uhuru: The Autobiography of Oginga Odinga* (London: Heineman, 1968); Tom Mboya, *Freedom and After* (London: Andre Deutsch, 1963); Poppy Cullen, "'Playing Cold War Politics': the Cold War in Anglo-Kenyan relations in the 1960s," in *Cold War History* 18 (2018).
16 "Announcement of the Kenya Students Union in the GDR," October 1, 1964, XJ/12/24, KNA. No individual author listed.

allegiance. This was, however, no simple act of pandering to the administration or a demonstration of blind and uncritical loyalty. It was tempered by laying claim to a more robust role within the project of Kenyan nation-building than had previously been offered to students in the KSU. In the same letter from October 1, 1964 mentioned above, union leadership wrote:

> the Kenya Students Union, a body consisting of both the students and the apprentices [in the GDR], so as to find out the solutions in which to implement to our constituted task in a sense of strengthening our Unity and at the same time promote our Studentship-talents in order to reflect Kenya in a lively way to the rest of the Students from different Nations as well as to the friendly country which are our hosts while abroad.[17]

While the letter goes on to outline a variety of more concrete and administrative functions of the KSU, the rhetorical emphasis on the notion of national unity is maintained throughout. So too is the idea that these students were to play a part in both the "strengthening of our Unity" and the effort to reflect Kenya "in a lively way" – this latter phrase targeting not only East Germans, but also students hailing from other European, Asian, and African nations. This sentiment was also expressed in other terms which explicitly underscored the importance of presenting Kenya as a nation among nations, rather than the mythologized entity which was the product of coverage of Mau Mau in international media. "The Kenya students in the GDR," wrote Secretary Mbianu in May of 1965, "are now about or more than 100 as the list of the Kenya Students Union shows, and we would like to participate in any Kenya National day so as to reflect Kenya as the other students from other nations do, but the arrangement of such celebrations or meetings come late and of course inadequate furthermore from too much toil."[18] This critique of the Kenyan government's unwillingness to provide support for such activities will be returned to later. For now, I wish to highlight the emphasis on national identity and unity manifested primarily through its deployment of three terms: *uhuṛu*, *harambee*, and "unity" itself. The first two of these, both Kiswahili, were often used in a largely symbolic manner. While they did appear within prose penned by the KSU and its members, they manifest far more frequently in signing phrases, letterhead, stamps, and to articulate particular ideas or claims to the official rhetoric of Kenyan nation-building.

"The *Uhuru* of Kenya," writes the KSU, "is no more than a prelude to the mobilization of our energies and resources aimed at freeing ourselves from hunger,

---

[17] "Announcement of the Kenya Students Union in the GDR," October 1, 1964, XJ/12/24, KNA. No individual author listed.
[18] Miano, Mburu, "General/5/65," May 1965, KNA.

sickness, ignorance and divisionism, etc."[19] Here, the usage of *uhuru* seems to refer specifically to formal independence as an epoch-making stage (thus its ability to serve as a "prelude"). It is used in exactly such a way elsewhere in both KSU correspondence and contemporary Kenyan political discourse more generally. Yet it is noteworthy that this understanding of the concept would make other appearances within the KSU's own time, perhaps most notably in the very title of Odinga's 1968 autobiography and critique of the Kenyan postcolonial order: *Not Yet Uhuru*.[20] Indeed, the very title of this work can be thought of in contrast to Tom Mboya's proximate work *Freedom and After*. Daniel Speich suggests that in terms of the competing political visions which dominated contemporary Kenyan thought, "the two positions are reflected in the titles of the autobiographies of the two leading politicians."[21] In other words, whether or not the country had achieved a state of *uhuru* at all remained the subject of debate throughout the 1960s (and, indeed, long afterward). While both of these usages are clearly situated within the register of national unity, they require us to think about whether a given group of Kenyans would have understood *uhuru* as having been attained with formal independence (as argued by the likes of Kenyatta and Mboya) or as something remaining to be actually realized through the destruction of what we might now identify as the neocolonial order (the perspective held by Odinga). In sum, such usages imply that the definitional status of even the most core of the organizing concepts of postcolonial Kenya were fundamentally dynamic and political, a crucial point for considering the rhetoric and experiences of Kenyan students in Eastern Europe.

Though less explicitly reliant on the stagist underpinnings of the KSU's deployment of *uhuru*, *harambee* functions in much the same politically-dynamic manner within the union's rhetoric and was also articulated to the ideal of national unity. Like *uhuru*, it is often positioned ambiguously, possibly to the end of allowing readers at the Ministry of Education to interpret it in whatever way might be most favorable to union interests (a wise maneuver in a time of tumultuous domestic politics). Typically translated as "pulling together", *harambee* held a high currency within the KSU's correspondence. This is most notable in the phrase "In the Spirit of *Harambee*," which official KSU correspondence often concluded with. On September 21, 1963, the eve of Kenyatta's departure for London to negotiate the formal process of Kenyan independence, he spoke these words: "The new era that Kenya will enter as an Independent nation—in

---

19 Miano, Mburu, "General/5/65," May 1965, KNA.
20 Odinga, *Not Yet Uhuru*.
21 Daniel Speich, "The Kenyan Style of 'African Socialism': Developmental Knowledge Claims and the Explanatory Limits of the Cold War," *Diplomatic History* 33 (2009): 454.

the spirit of 'harambee'—in December, is one which will call for dedication, hard work and unity."[22] From here, "the spirit of *harambee*" came to be a foundational concept upon which the Kenyan postcolonial order was constructed. "Pulling together" meant an attempt to manufacture a national whole from diverse and often contentious ethnic, racial, religious, and class identities. Yet even Jomo Kenyatta himself employed a notoriously slippery and vague usage of the term. In the fall of 1964, for example, he expounded on the concept at a rally by stating: "Unless the country can help itself, then it cannot develop. We must make systematic efforts to harness the spirit of self-help, and of national unity."[23] At the level of quotidian political discourse, this vagueness left open the possibility for Kenyans to articulate this concept as they saw fit. It is worth noting here that, from the earliest days of KANU, *harambee* had been connected to another phrase ("Freedom and Work" or *Uhuru na Kazi*) and conveyed a strong overtone of capitalist-oriented economic achievement.[24] Still, through the persistent invocation of the term it is reasonable to suggest that the KSU attempted to position itself as responding to the call to "harness the spirit of self-help" through serving as embodiments of Kenya abroad, rather than serving flatly as an economic resource for "the nation" as understood by the top officials of the Kenyan state.

Most frequently deployed in the actual prose of KSU communications, however, is the word "unity" itself. It often reads as almost interchangeable with *harambee*, signaling many of the same semiotic dimensions as its Kiswahili counterpart. "The future of us and of Kenya is for Kenyans to plan," wrote the KSU in October 1964, "and our judgement shall be our destiny. The Union will take a colossal measure against individualists and sectionalists, who may, in any way attempt to curtail such Unity."[25] Here, the deployment of "unity" harbors a sharp political edge. And, yet again, we see an appeal to national cohesion by Luo students during a time when tensions were flaring between Kenyatta and Odinga, and indeed between Kikuyu and Luo communities. Like *harambee*, "unity" was a core ideological concept in the service of which the KSU imagined itself as playing a crucial role. In the context of the power struggle between Kenyatta and Odinga at home, as well as the "divisionism" that had characterized the brief life of the KSA-GDR, the salience of such an emphasis on rhetoric of

---

[22] Jomo Kenyatta. *Harambee!: The Prime Minister of Kenya's Speeches 1963–1964*, ed. Anthony Cullen (London: Oxford University Press, 1964), 12.
[23] Kenyatta, *Harambee!*, 12.
[24] Branch, *Between Hope and Despair*, 248.
[25] "Announcement of the Kenya Students Union in the GDR," October 1, 1964, KNA. No individual author listed.

unity is clear. The KSU sought to position itself as an organization whose aim was to represent Kenya as a united nation as much as, if not more than, it was concerned with the individual academic achievements of its members.

Together, the KSU's deployment of *uhuru*, *harambee*, and the rhetorics of unity more generally suggests that the union considered itself to be facilitating not only the economic advancement of the home country but also the articulation of the broader, markedly cultural dimensions of a Kenyan national identity. Also noteworthy in this regard is the characterization of the intellectual composition of the KSU; both "students" at universities and "apprentices" at technical and vocational schools were eligible for membership and were considered equal members, at least in formal terms. This voicing of solidarity across the lines of class and status appealed to different rhetorical registers. Explored further below, one such example is the organization's positioning of itself under the banner of "African Democratic Socialism,"[26] though it is not further clarified in the archived correspondence what this orientation entailed for the KSU membership. Yet the union did far more than situate itself rhetorically as an integral component of the Kenyan postcolonial project; it necessarily pressed beyond this as it found its way through serving as the primary facilitator of relations between students studying abroad and their home government.

In organizational terms, the KSU positioned itself to play a significant role both in serving as an intermediary for communication between students studying in the GDR and the Ministry of Education in Kenya as well as in providing practical services to its members. This entailed a variety of distinct activities, including but not limited to: petitioning for increased levels of student funding from their home government, keeping track of the courses of study its members were pursuing, updating the Ministry in Kenya on conditions of life in the GDR, working to secure employment following the completion of students' degrees, and a host of miscellaneous administrative practicalities.[27] The KSU thus simultaneously served a reporting function and advocated, though often in vain, for remedies that would address particular problems faced by Kenyan students in the GDR. Perhaps the most emblematic examples of such a function were the efforts at tracking the experiences and courses of study for the 125–odd students present in the country during 1965. These efforts simultaneously highlight both

---

[26] On Kenya's African socialism see, more generally, Speich, "The Kenyan Style of 'African Socialism'".
[27] While allusions to forms of documentation such as those listed here are frequent in the papers of the KSU and KSA-Y, I have thus far been unable to locate many of them in archival collections.

the urgency of the KSU's requests and the immense difficulties involved in information gathering faced by the organization.

Throughout 1965, Mburu Miano, as the General Secretary of the KSU, made numerous appeals to the Ministry of Education in Kenya for both higher levels of pecuniary assistance and more robust efforts toward securing positions of employment in Kenya following the completion of students' studies. J.R. Sheffield, a prominent figure in the Ministry in Kenya, eventually responded to Miano's requests: "I am also enclosing under separate cover 150 record forms which you requested. We will be very grateful for your assistance in this important exercise since an accurate registry will help government planners and will help you and your colleagues find suitable employment upon completion of your studies."[28] While it appears that Miano did indeed undertake extensive attempts to gather the information requested (which included courses of study, institutional affiliation, and expected year of completion), his efforts ultimately bore little fruit. "I, the Secretary of the Union," Miano replied to Sheffield, "wrote to all students and supplied all copies (each to everyone) to them, but sorry to say that only 15 copies have been successfully filed and we hope to see many filled and dispatched to you soon."[29] This level of student response, no doubt at least in part a product of both the dispersion of students throughout the GDR and unsystematic paths taken by students to reach the country, is typical of such efforts conducted by the KSU during its existence.

Like student unions in the present, these types of activities (and the accompanying drudgeries of bureaucracy) were no small part of the KSU's activities, and in fact constituted the bulk of the labor performed by union leadership. Yet these administrative functions would have played a relatively limited role in shaping understandings of the KSU for the union rank-and-file. For them, interacting with the KSU primarily meant two things. First, filling out forms and paperwork (such as that lamented by Miano above) that provided insight for the government as to the courses of study of Kenyan students abroad. Another function seemed equally prominent, and indeed appears even more frequently than the information gathering efforts undertaken by the KSU: making requests for and receiving news and cultural materials from home by way of the Kenyan government. These types of resources were typically extremely limited. For example, after receiving a KSU request for 125 copies of a periodical titled *Kenya Calling*, the Ministry of Education responded: "We will only send you 50 copies of this publication which we think would be sufficient if students living together

---

[28] "Letter to Mburu Miano from J. R. Sheffield," December 9, 1965, XJ/12/24, KNA.
[29] "Letter to J. R. Sheffield from Mburu Miano," February 26, 1966, XJ/12/24, KNA.

shared the copies."³⁰ This was a solution proposed by the Ministry in Kenya without knowing even such basic information as whether it was the case that Kenyan students actually did live together, as housing arrangements varied by locale and student background.

Responses such as this suggest that, in large part, non-board members of the KSU would likely have interfaced in a very limited way with their home government, and on the occasions when they did (such as receiving copies of Kenyan periodicals or gathering personal information) faced an ambivalent ministry interested only in the nature of their studies and the occasional dissemination of extremely sparse resources. In the union's own phrasing: "Kenya Students take their different courses in different institutions of learning, but it seems to them, that, the Ministry of Education in Kenya never establish [sic] contacts with them."³¹ The overarching sentiment was, then, that the home government seemed to have little interest in interacting with Kenyan students abroad and even less in assisting with the coordination of events not deemed to be properly "educational." For example, in response to the KSU's letter announcing the foundation of the organization and requests for pecuniary support of an upcoming national independence celebration, an administrator named D.K. Ngini wrote in an internal Ministry of Education circular: "I do feel that if the students want to qualify as well and as widely as they can as a stepping stone towards contributing to the Kenya Nation building, the best course is for them to concentrate primarily on their studies."³²

Kenyan students in the GDR had other aims, even if the project of nation-building remained the ultimate guiding star. Taking seriously the intervention that the organization understood itself to be making by "reflecting Kenya in a lively way" allows for a reading of the KSU as consciously serving a pedagogical function. By describing it as an organization seeking to project a lively vision of Kenya to other students and comrades in the GDR more generally, union leadership explicitly positioned the organization as disruptive of what, by extension, must have been felt to be a static and problematic conception of life in Kenya. This is perhaps unsurprising, given the temporal proximity of the KSU to the events of the Mau Mau Emergency, during which a great deal of European media coverage had presented Kenya as a place rife with tribal antagonisms and "primitive" traditions.³³ And, while the narratives about the rebellion that

---
30 "Correspondence from J. H. Wanyoike to Mburu Miano," December 15, 1965, XJ/12/24, KNA.
31 "Correspondence from KSU to Ministry of Education," May 1965, XJ/12/24, KNA.
32 "Circular written by D. K. Ngini," October 28, 1964, XJ/12/24, KNA.
33 See, for example, Melissa Tully, "All's Well in the Colony: Newspaper Coverage of the Mau Mau Movement, 1952–56," in *Narrating War and Peace in Africa*, ed. Toyin Falola and Hetty ter

circulated in the socialist world were certainly different than those in the West, abstractions about Africa and Africanness fundamentally informed each. We might think about the KSU, then, as having understood themselves to be making a crucial correction to the narratives about Kenya that circulated in the Eastern Bloc, and perhaps Europe more generally. Moreover, the KSU's consistent appeals to national unity implies a connection between the ideological construction of Kenya as a cultural and national entity and the unique position that Kenyans studying abroad considered themselves as inhabiting: ambassadors of a certain sort.

In this light, requests for Kenyan-produced ephemera and cultural materials (and in particular films, as will be explored further later) were viewed as a means of disrupting residual mythologies attached to Kenyanness. And while I am unaware of any existing scholarship examining media representations of Mau Mau specifically in the GDR, the fact that Kenyans expressed similar sentiments in other European spaces (coupled with Pugach's work on racialization in East Germany) lends credibility to the idea that these students viewed themselves as doing a certain type of ideological work. The pedagogical core here, then, was an attempt to intervene in the channels through which information about Kenyan society in the wake of independence travelled. Moreover, this was an intervention that would present Kenya as a united and "modern" nation with the right to control its own destiny, an understandably common sentiment in the rhetoric of many African people and states in the 1960s. When the KSU positioned itself "against individualists and sectionalists, who may, in any way attempt to curtail such Unity," it did so as a means of positioning itself squarely within this national destiny.[34] Again, the idea that the Union could be a force for remedying the divisionism that had plagued both the student community in the GDR and the political landscape at home is made manifest. The KSU was thus ultimately an organization with a membership that conceived of itself as a group of politically-conscious students who sought to influence both the articulation of national identity and, in addition, the future role of Kenyans who accessed higher education in socialist Europe.

Haar (Rochester, NY: University of Rochester Press, 2010); A.S. Cleary, "The Myth of Mau Mau in its International Context," in *African Affairs* 89 (1990).
34 "Announcement of the Kenya Students Union in the GDR," October 1, 1964, KNA. No individual author listed.

Competing Visions: The Idea of Education in the KSU

In recent years, educational trajectories of Africans sojourning in the socialist world—like the GDR—have been the subject of much interest, as the compilation of this volume itself attests to.[35] With regard to the GDR's own articulation of these programs, Tanja R. Müller's recent monograph *Legacies of Socialist Solidarity* traces the contours of the complex ways in which the hegemonic ideological ethos of the GDR drew from the rhetorical registers of socialist internationalism in its construction of policies targeting relations with African states.[36] Recent work such as Müller's underscores the centrality of discourses of "development" within contemporary socialist thought. The concept has also been explored deeply within Africanist postcolonial theory, and importantly by V.Y. Mudimbe. Mudimbe has written extensively about the teleological nature of the notion of development in postcolonial Africa, calling particular attention to its ubiquity within political rhetoric across the continent. In *The Invention of Africa*, he goes so far as to agree with B. Vergaegan's characterization of this line of thinking as a "theology of development."[37] The GDR's emphasis on development should thus also be understood in relation to the concept's even greater salience for postcolonial Kenya, for whom the stakes of implementing any notion of development were felt to be far higher and operated at exactly such a quasi-theological level. The Kenyan Ministry of Education's emphasis on development, and its relation to the very idea of "education," was predicated on an understanding of education as the production of skilled "manpower."[38] Here, it is worth draw-

---

[35] See, for example, Eric Burton, "Journeys of Education and Struggle: African Mobility in Times of Decolonization and the Cold War," *Stichproben. Vienna Journal of African Studies* 34 (2018): 1–17; Marcia C. Schenck. "Negotiating the German Democratic Republic: Angolan Student Migration during the Cold War, 1976–90," Africa 89 (2019); for more on African students in Yugoslavia see Nedžad Kuč, "Southern African Students in Southeast Europe: Education and Experiences in 1960s Yugoslavia," in *Southern African Liberation Movements and the Global Cold War 'East': Transnational Activism 1960–1990*, ed. Lena Dallywater, Chris Saunders, and Helder Adegar Fonseca (Berlin: De Gruyter, 2019).
[36] Tanja Müller, *Legacies of Socialist Solidarity: East Germany in Mozambique* (Lanham: Lexington Books, 2014).
[37] V. Y. Mudimbe, *The Invention of Africa: Gnosis, Philosophy, and the Order of Knowledge* (Bloomington, IN: Indiana University Press, 1988), 179.
[38] Elsewhere, Eric Burton has explored Tanzanian discourses of "manpower" and their relationship to both the creation of an elite and positioning of education as a consumable good. For more on this, see Burton, "African Manpower Development".

ing upon the KSU's peers studying in Yugoslavia during the same period. In a 1967 exchange with the KSA-Y, for example, J.R. Sheffield wrote that: "As part of the government's programme of manpower planning and Kenyanization of both the public and private sectors, it is extremely important for us to know the supply of high-level manpower which will be returning from study overseas."[39] As we will see, the members of the KSA-Y were not particularly fond of such a one-dimensional understanding of what, exactly, their "education" was to be. Moreover, each organization rejected (sometimes explicitly, but more frequently tacitly) the purpose of an education abroad being articulated within the relatively narrow project of "Kenyanizing" the national economy.[40]

In broad strokes, during the years the KSU was active—from 1964 to 1968—the Kenyan government thus pursued an educational policy primarily concerned with increasing its intellectual manpower while students such as those involved in the union conceived their studies abroad as both this and the work of consciousness-raising. The emphasis on political consciousness was stated often and clearly by the organization. In fact, the emphasis on "consciousness" as an organizing concept more generally played an important role in the KSU's intellectual framing. In their foundational letter to Kenyatta referenced above we read that: "The Union has brought Students to the consciousness that the stage is now set for us to embark upon the next phase in our struggle for advancement."[41] Here, the relationship of students to "consciousness" functions within a somewhat stagist vision of historical development. As seen above, formal *uhuru* had served as a "prelude" which had allowed for the emergence of such a consciousness. KSU leadership insinuates that, once attained by themselves, it was the task of intellectuals such as those in the union (regardless of their field of study) to assist in proliferating political consciousness throughout the Kenyan social fabric. When considered in relation to their outline of the functions of the KSU, it is evident that the notion of "advancement" held by union members exceeded the instrumentalizing, flatly economic one being pur-

---

[39] "Letter to the President, Kenya Students Association in Yugoslavia from J.R. Sheffield," May 25, 1967, XJ/12/28, Kenya Students Association in Yugoslavia, KNA.
[40] Of course, the critique that the simple replacement of white colonial administrators with Africans did little to disrupt the political economy of colonialism was common in socialist thought of the era. Indeed, few political leaders in Kenya expressed this concern more frequently than Odinga. This perspective could also suggest the possibility that students in socialist Europe had perhaps taken some of their "ideological training" more seriously than has typically been thought to be the case, as such ideas certainly would have circulated in classrooms discussing Marxist theory and left politics.
[41] "Announcement of the Kenya Students Union in the GDR," October 1, 1964, KNA. No individual author listed.

sued by the Kenyan state. It included the role of the intelligentsia as a cultural vanguard. However, this type of function implied activities which the Ministry in Kenya was skeptical of students abroad pursuing. Moreover, the expression of this idea was also rather subtle, perhaps due to the possibility that any perceived affiliation with communist politics would have jeopardized the position of students who returned to an increasingly pro-capitalist Kenyan state.

The differences between visions of the role of the educated Kenyan was a constant site of contestation along with allegations of underfunding, poor communication, and general mismanagement.[42] What underwrote all of these tensions were two different (if deeply-entangled) conceptions of the idea of "education," what such a concept entailed and the role the foreign-educated Kenyan would play after returning home. In other words, this represented a continuous and extensive debate about the relationship between contested ideas of education within the Kenyatta regime's project of *harambee*. These contestations found themselves expressed in a variety of ways, but few were felt as acutely by KSU students as that of entering a status of commodified intellectual-laborers, toward which the state took an attitude at once ambivalent and instrumentalizing in ethos. This was not a sentiment restricted to students in the GDR, and indeed Kenyans in other European locales articulated it far more explicitly than through the "consciousness-raising" rhetoric of the KSU.

From a comparative standpoint, the KSA-Y alleged in a similar manner of their primary Ministry of Education contact that "he considers us as just 'mere trading instruments.'"[43] This was a perspective that understood the instrumentalization of students in two ways: as both pawns in international diplomacy as well as fungible workers crafted solely for the smooth operation of the postcolonial order in Kenya. The expression of such a sentiment across two different Eastern European contexts, each explicitly socialist in orientation, is intriguing. Whether couched in the affirmative terms of political unity or articulated through direct critique, it seems evident that both the KSU and the KSA-Y hoped for a far more robust vision of the role to be played by Kenyans educated in socialist Eu-

---

[42] Employment following the completion of one's course of study was a particularly robust point of concern. A general lack of communication and mismanagement in this regard produced sentiments such as the following, merely one of dozens of such inquiries: "We would like to know our positions towards our communal aim in Kenya, that is relationship between qualified manpower and Ministry of Education, at the same time Ministries which offer employment and other institutions." ("Letter to Mr. G. R. M'Mwirichia from Mburu Miano," November 5, 1965, XJ/12/24, KNA).

[43] "Letter to the Permanent Secretary, Ministry of Education from George S. Owuor and Arthur K. Owuor," February 3, 1966, XJ/12/28, KNA.

rope than was held by the Ministry of Education in Kenya. More preferable for these students was a position as harbingers of an improvement in economic circumstances, the disruptors of European mythologies about Kenya, and the articulation of an African socialist politics (however imprecisely it was defined) all at once.

Aside from direct statements—such as Ngini's insistence that "the best course is for them to concentrate primarily on their studies"[44]—the Kenyan government's aversion to student activities not considered to be part of their education-proper was expressed through the consistent rejection or inadequate fulfillment of requests for the financial support of cultural events. In a letter from November of 1965, the KSU made an appeal to the Ministry of Education in Kenya for pecuniary and material support to fund a string of events celebrating the second anniversary of Kenyan national independence. They made their case on the grounds that: "The matter of facts [sic] is that, KSU represents an image of Kenya in the front line in celebrations, advertisements, speeches and in newspapers during such national occasions."[45] This, they argued, meant that their home government had both a responsibility and a vested interest to support their activities. The response the KSU received from the Ministry was disheartening (to put it mildly) and summarized in one line: "Unfortunately, our budget does not permit our support of groups such as yours."[46] While this position loosened over time and small requests were granted on occasion, the government's assertion that they bore no real responsibility for supporting student groups focused on cultural activities and consciousness-raising remained a site of contention throughout the history of KSU-governmental relations. Thus, while the Ministry of Education in Kenya consistently displayed a preoccupation with tracking and managing the production of "manpower," they showed far less in taking seriously the political and ideological dimensions of the KSU's activities.

While visions of corrective approaches to this problem are rarely explicit, the KSU's emphasis on unity and the positioning of their organization as a cultural vanguard is telling. By articulating themselves as central to the cultural dimensions of Kenyan nationalism, it is clear that they envisioned a position relative to the Kenyan nation-building project that exceeded a status as commodified (if educated and well-paid) labor. Exacerbating this was a perception that their colleagues studying in other locales did not experience such frustrations as acutely. Daniel Branch argues that:

---

[44] "Circular by D. K. Ngini," KNA.
[45] "Correspondence from Mburu Miano to G.R. M'Mwirichia," November 5, 1965, XJ/12/24, KNA.
[46] "Letter to J.R. Sheffield from Mburu Miano," KNA.

[Students who studied in socialist Europe] expected to be the nation-builders, the economic planners and technocrats at the heart of the process of state-formation. But they found themselves excluded from the vital early stages of this process, marginalized in favour of their contemporaries who studied in Kenya itself, neighbouring Uganda, the UK and, particularly, the USA.[47]

Kenyan students in the GDR and Yugoslavia were no exception. They each had a record of communicating this precise frustration to their home government. In the KSU's phrasing: "It is to the benefit of Kenya as a Nation to see to it that, those students qualifying themselves in various fields of studies receive equal eligibility as those others in other parts of the globe."[48] The KSU's rhetoric thus suggests something of a dual-mandate for their home government: they hoped to be involved in the cultural and political dimensions of nation-building while simultaneously expressing their right to the same economic positions as Kenyan students studying in other foreign countries. Given that degrees from the "Second World" were often perceived by African governments as "second class" degrees, the KSU's request clearly demanded a position of equality in this regard.[49]

The understanding of education held by the Kenyan state thus existed in a state of deep tension with that of an organization such as the KSU, which was tacitly expressed in its foundational mission and conceptual ethos. The government's mission of creating a class of educated clerks and administrators who would serve as so many parts in the machinery of the Kenyan economic structure was a far cry from the understanding of education articulated within the cultural dimensions of KSU rhetoric, which did not shy away from fiery language. This rhetorical style was, however, tempered in order to reaffirm the organization's commitment to supporting KANU:

> We are in the mind that Party is the rallying-point of our political activities and such, we support every measure to lead to a stability of Kenya African National Union, in order to maintain African personality of every-man-Jack in both politics and economics which facilitate the building of an integrated Nation with a social structure of an African Democratic Socialism.[50]

---

47 Daniel Branch, "Political Traffic: Kenyan Students in Eastern and Central Europe, 1958–1969," *Journal of Contemporary History* 53 (2018): 831.
48 Mburu Miano. "General/5/65," May 1965, KNA.
49 Burton, "African Manpower Development," 111–113.
50 "Announcement of the Kenya Students Union in the GDR," October 1, 1964, KNA. No individual author listed.

Through simultaneously expressing their support for KANU and the nebulous project of "African Democratic Socialism," the KSU walked a fine line that both acknowledged the authority of the Kenyatta regime and challenged it to take seriously some of its own positions. It should be no surprise, then, that the sense on the part of students that they were being commodified through educational programs in the interest of a state that relegated them to an apolitical space was difficult to accept.

Through a comparative perspective, we can see that the experiences of organizations similar to the KSU in other areas of socialist Europe suggest that this perception of apathy toward (and fungibility of) students was not confined to the GDR alone. The KSA-Y also found itself perpetually frustrated by the lack of material support and the poor quality of communication between the Kenyan Ministry of Education and students abroad. In the records of the KSA-Y this manifests not only as inadequate material assistance, but also as an utter lack of knowledge on the part of the Kenyan authorities about the educational institutions they were supposedly "partnering" with. In response to a KSA-Y request for information on securing employment after completing their studies, Deputy Secretary of Education G.R. M'Mwerichia wrote: "I am writing direct to Belgrade to get a full description of the type of school you are attending and the final award you expect."[51] It should be no surprise that this statement, which constituted an open acknowledgement that the Ministry of Education lacked even such basic information as the types of schools students were attending and the degrees they could expect to be awarded, was not well received. It is worth noting that such an idea would have been completely out of line with the attention paid to those participating in the Mboya-Kennedy airlift. In a scathing retort, the KSA wrote back: "Your inquiry now into the type and system of education in Yugoslavia is a direct proof that you never cared to know why and how we were sent here."[52] In another point of consonance with the frustrations experienced by those in the KSU, the letter also argued that: "You cannot wait for a student to finish his studies and then when he comes back to Kenya you start saying you do not recognize his degree in spite of the fact that you are the one who sent him here."[53]

Contemporaries of the KSU in the GDR, the frustrations of KSA-Y members speak to the broad and deeply-rooted discontent of young Kenyan scholars studying in Eastern Europe. Namely, these shared frustrations (voiced almost

---

[51] "Correspondence from G.R. M'Mwirichia to KSA leadership," February 23, 1965, XJ/12/28, KNA.
[52] "Correspondence from KSA to G. R. M'Mwirichia," March 8, 1965, XJ/12/28, KNA.
[53] "Correspondence from KSA to G. R. M'Mwirichia," March 8, 1965, XJ/12/28, KNA.

contemporaneously a thousand kilometers apart) underscore the experiences of cohorts of scholars who felt marginalized by the national government that they hoped so dearly to play a significant role in. It should, of course, be mentioned that the level of opacity encountered by the Kenyan Ministry of Education was due in part to the absence of embassies in the GDR during this period and an ambivalent relationship to the Yugoslavian state. That the particular channels through which Kenyan students arrived in Europe were not standardized, but varied widely and occasionally even operated without the knowledge of the Kenyan state should also be understood as a source of confusion. The fact that this was apparently a widely-shared experience, however, did little to console the memberships of the KSU and KSA-Y. They perceived the Kenyan Ministry of Education as being (at best) inept, though this word understates the strong sense of exploitation and fungibility felt by the students it was allegedly responsible for supporting. These feelings toward their own government are, however, only one part of a larger picture. Equally prevalent, if even more cautiously and tacitly expressed, was the strong sense of alienation felt by African students as they navigated the landscapes of Eastern Europe.

Film and the Idea of Self-Representation

In the years following national independence, existing in European space as a Kenyan student was a lived experience fraught with tension, which laid bare the contradictions of the contemporary contours of socialist internationalism.[54] I argue that the emphasis which the KSU placed on film represented an attempt to disrupt residual forms of mythologies about Kenyans, and Africans more generally, that continued to circulate even under self-proclaimed anti-racist regimes of state socialism. To be clear, frank and explicit accusations of experiencing racial prejudice are few and far between in the limited records of these organizations to which I have access. Nonetheless, it is telling that both the KSU and KSA-Y embarked on sustained campaigns to gain access to materials that would allow for a degree of self-representation within the cultural frameworks in which they found themselves. From their home government they requested magazines, pho-

---

[54] A particularly illustrative example of this is Sara Pugach's exploration of gender dynamics in the GDR and the relation African students had to them. The antiracist posturing of the state, Pugach argues, unravels when one considers the manner in which African students were marginalized within the social body and the low-esteem in which East Germans who had sexual relations with them were held. Again, see Pugach, "African Students and the Politics of Race and Gender".

tographs, newspapers, and cultural products of all sorts with an urgency not extended even to securing employment after completing their studies. Requests for cultural materials are numerous, clear, and (this cannot be emphasized enough) expressed more emphatically even than petitions for financial support.

The final part of this chapter explores students' interest in, and perhaps even affinity for, the medium of film through extremely close analyses of the demands they made for access to these materials. This section is consciously speculative, a product of both the archival collections from which it is derived (as well as the Kenya National Archive itself) and the informational voids that existed even for those who actually participated in the experiences it examines.[55] Nevertheless, it is worthwhile to highlight what is an undeniable feature of the records that do exist, and to gesture toward the cultural and intellectual implications present within them. It is noteworthy that a preoccupation with the medium of film was by no means unique to the members of the KSU. Sarah Pugach has argued elsewhere that in 1965 the *Union der Afrikanischen Studenten und Arbeiter in der DDR* (Union of African Students and Workers in the GDR) had advocated for the relevance of film to challenge the static mythologies of Africa that circulated in East Germany.[56] In a letter from that year, the UASA argued for "compelling the *Deutsche Film-Aktiengesellschaft* (German Film Corporation or DEFA) to produce movies on contemporary Africa, since most of what they were currently making reflected only 'colonial barbarism.'"[57] As we shall see, both the KSU and the KSA-Y experienced similar debates that underscored the pedagogical utility of film.

The first mention of film in KSU correspondence dates from May of 1965, only a few months after the UASA's letter mentioned above and the second year of the Union's existence.[58] Broadly, the document in which it appears voiced frustrations felt by members of the organization which tacks between specific complaints and arguments for the importance of the work being done by the KSU. The main grievance articulated in the text, which we have already encountered, questions the equity with which students in the GDR were being treated relative

---

[55] It should be re-emphasized here that the materials examined are located at the Kenya National Archives. This institution, and the records which it houses, has been subject to colonial and neocolonial power dynamics, dynamics pertinent to contextualizing its existence and composition. I mean this not only in terms of the presence or absence of materials (the "silences" produced by what is deemed "worthy" of cataloguing in all archival bodies, and what a given Kenyan regime has believed should be made available in this institution), but also in terms of its chronic underfunding and limited (though heroic and dedicated) staff.
[56] Pugach, "Agents of Dissent," 93.
[57] Pugach, "Agents of Dissent," 103.
[58] "Correspondence from KSU to Ministry of Education," May 1965, XJ/12/24, KNA.

to Kenyan students studying in Western European and American institutions. Eric Burton has observed that African countries "sent young citizens wherever possibilities for academic training opened up, no matter if 'East', 'West', or 'South' – although Western degrees continued to enjoy the greatest prestige."[59] In their letter, the KSU claimed that in other European contexts where Kenyans studied, the impending completion of a course of study was accompanied by dialogue between would-be-graduates and the Kenyan government in order to place them in employment. This practice was rumored to be orthodox in the U.K., for example. "We remember very well," wrote KSU leadership in a circular addressed to the Ministry of Education in Kenya, "that [the] City Council of Nairobi sent its delegation to England to interview those students who were about to finish their courses (studies) so that, when they finished, they could go straight to their employment. But nothing has been done so far regarding those students in the GDR."[60] That the City Council of Nairobi would have taken a direct interest in recruiting students who had been educated in the capitalist West is striking, especially considering the Kenyatta regime's contemporary amenable positioning toward the capitalist powers of the West.

The aim of securing employment after completing one's course of study was, however, only one aspect of a much broader set of concerns for Kenyan students expressed in this letter. A special level of emphasis was reserved for underscoring the dire need for cultural materials from home. In the organization's own phrasing, the request made in their May 1965 letter was for "Financial-assistance + material assistance such as FILM in order that Kenya Students may show other people how Kenya is."[61] What exactly is meant by the phrase "how Kenya is" is not clear. Like other Kenyans studying abroad, many amongst the KSU membership would likely have hailed from privileged backgrounds. Yet it is reasonable to suggest that the trope of a "backward," violent, and "tribal" Kenya was what was being challenged here. To this end, it is worth mentioning once again that the bulk of the KSU's activities occurred scarcely a decade after the height of the Mau Mau insurgency, an event which captured the imaginations of people across the globe (both out of fear or in solidarity) and placed Kenya in a position of international notoriety.[62] What is certain in the passage above is the high degree of

---

59 Burton, "Navigating global socialism," 64.
60 Mburu Miano, "Circular, General/5/65," May 1965, KNA.
61 Mburu Miano, "Circular, General/5/65," May 1965, KNA.
62 The international legacy of Mau Mau is a phenomenon that has garnered a great deal of interest in recent years. For example, Gerald Horne has explored the legacy of the insurgency within the context of the United States. For more on this see Gerald Horne, *Mau Mau in Harlem? The U.S. and the Liberation of Kenya* (New York: Palgrave MacMillan, 2009).

emphasis placed on the word "FILM," a feature found elsewhere in the requests put forth by the KSU. In this document the word is located on the edge of the right margin, and the actual shape and place of the word itself is striking. While its specific location on the page was incidental, its impact on the reader is indicative of the importance it held for its authors. It appears as a solid block in a sea of small letters, impossible to avoid and disruptive of the measured tone and flow of the larger document. That this degree of emphasis was deemed appropriate even when requests for such basic necessities as financial sustenance were also present is particularly striking.

A second, even more explicit appeal for government-produced films to be shown at independence celebrations would find its way to the Ministry of Education in Kenya several months later. By then, the emphasis on this particular demand had grown. In November of 1965 the KSU sent the following message:

> The KSU in the GDR wish to demonstrate our standpoint and ours is for the Kenya as a whole, and therefore we would expect from you papers, photographs, maps, magazines, and even a F I L M about Kenya. Any material despatch [sic] from you, which may need preservation, the Kenya Students Union may take responsibility, such as FILM etc.[63]

Here, the high degree of emphasis experimented with in the first document comes to full fruition. Not only does the word occur twice in all capital letters, but one of these sees the insertion of a space between each letter. The effect of creating a solid visual block, absolutely impossible to ignore for the reader, cannot be overlooked as incidental or unimportant. It is, after all, not the only material requested. It is not even the only visual material on the list. Yet photographs and maps seem to hold a relatively limited importance for the KSU. Exactly why this might be the case is not, however, stated explicitly within the Union's records.

Here, it is perhaps useful to recall very briefly the history and role of the medium of film in mid-twentieth century Germany. Under the Nazis, cinema had been a staple of propaganda efforts. Racist imagery was ubiquitous, and the importance of visual contrast maintained a currency well after the fall of the regime. In his famous 1947 text *From Caligari to Hitler*, the film historian Siegfried Kracauer wrote that a primary feature of the Nazi film was: "The exploitation of physiognomical qualities by contrasting, for instance, close-ups of brute Negroes with German soldier faces."[64] The deployment of the visual dichotomies of dark

---

63 "Correspondence from Mburu Miano to G. R. M'Mwirichia," KNA.
64 Sigfried Kracauer, *From Caligari to Hitler: A Psychological History of the German Film* (Princeton: Princeton University Press, 1947), 279.

and light continued well into the period of KSU activities, and the practice and idea of contrast continued to hold a currency for film critics and audiences. As Pugach has noted, the notion that a dichotomy existed between Germans and "brute Negroes" was not erased with the establishment of an "anti-racist" regime committed to socialist internationalism. Nor was the idea that the nature of film, as a medium, held a unique ability to intervene in popular narratives of the nation. In Germany and elsewhere during the postwar era, this rested on the figural creation of outsiders, and race was a common modality deployed in their assembly. In line with this, Pugach has shown that an educative impulse extended beyond the walls of the universities that hosted African students. "The students were subject to a 'moral' education in the GDR," she writes. "This education was based on supposedly 'primal' characteristics that had been assigned to Africans much earlier, in the colonial era. It contradicted state claims that race did not matter, as well as state efforts to include blacks in the body politic."[65] More generally, these students' experiences in Germany would have been informed by what George Steinmetz has called the "devil's handwriting," or how "the inherited archives of precolonial ethnographic representations provided the ideological raw materials for almost everything that was done to colonized peoples in the modern era."[66] Such a line of analysis can easily be extended to think about how continuities in racist mythologies manifested in different areas of life in the GDR, film being only one embedded within a broader cultural landscape.

In tracking the maneuverings of the KSU and its membership, it is evident that the disruption of these mythologies was of great concern for Kenyan students in the GDR. Requests for films were made "in order that Kenya Students may show other people how Kenya is."[67] They were also made in a context wherein multiple students had been either expelled from school or jailed under questionable circumstances.[68] The attempt to resist these processes of overdetermination was at the core of requests for films depicting life in Kenya. Deploying the rhetoric of national unity, and targeted at those primarily respon-

---

65 Pugach, "The Politics of Race and Gender," 148.
66 Steinmetz, George, *The Devil's Handwriting: Precoloniality and the German Colonial State in Qungdao, Samoa, and Southwest Africa* (Chicago: The University of Chicago Press, 2007), xiv.
67 Mburu Miano, "General 5/65," KNA.
68 Over the course of the KSU's existence, it saw one student expelled from school due to a minor alcohol infraction and two others tried and imprisoned on charges of rape. Allegations of police brutality were also made by the Union against the East German authorities. For details about this see "Correspondence from E.N. Gicuchi to The Rector of Dresden Technical University," January 25, 1966, XJ/12/24, KNA; "Correspondence from J. Mwema to Ministry of Foreign Affairs," February 9, 1966, XJ/12/24, KNA; "Correspondence from J. N. Muimi to Ministry of Education," February 24, 1966, XJ/12/24, KNA.

sible for fostering such a sentiment within the nascent Kenyan republic, the desire to disrupt the existing pedagogical channels through which information about the homeland travelled found an affinity with the medium of film. It follows that the KSU may have understood it as a technology through which Europeans and Africans in the audience would receive the voice of Kenya (at least as it was portrayed by the government) without the distortions of a European lens or gaze. A Eurocentric vision of Africa would have at least some chance of being "pushed against" or "corrected." To be clear, this is not to suggest that such a representation was unproblematic, "authentic," or even an accurate analysis of the pedagogical dynamics of film. Nor was the project of Kenyan nationalism organic or untethered from colonial legacies and massive disparities in ethnic and class representation within government. Instead, the aim here is to suggest that the KSU harbored a powerful understanding of the possibilities held by the medium of film and its value for them as they navigated life in the GDR and their relations to the government at home.

While (in line with their political rhetoric more generally) the KSU signaled the importance of the medium film in a carefully coded manner, Kenyan students in Yugoslavia were less reserved. Their debates on the subject depart from the KSU's in important ways, but bear striking similarities with regard to at the level of conceptualizing the medium of film itself, and especially its ability to shape perception. As in the GDR, I suggest that it was the pedagogical power of the medium of film that served as the defining feature of these debates, although the contours of the specific circumstances are notably different. In January 1967, a bitter dispute emerged between two groups of Kenyan students within the KSA-Y over a series of films that had been screened for the previous year's independence celebrations. On January 26, Gonzaga Opundo (a rank-and-file member of the KSA) wrote to the Kenyan Ministry of Education alleging that "three foreign Embassies have engaged themselves in what seems to us a joint-work for corrupting Kenya students in Yugoslavia."[69] The three foreign powers mentioned were Britain, the United States, and West Germany, and Opundo alleged that they had targeted KSA-Y leadership. "The British and the American Embassies," wrote Opundo, "do invite 'selected' number of Kenya students to their respective Consulates or sometimes in their private homes to talk over a cup of tea. After the talks the students are shown some propaganda films and they are also provided with free newspapers."[70] Opundo went on to claim that

---

[69] "Correspondence from Gonzaga Opundo to Ministry of education: Re – Corruption by foreign embassies over Kenya students in Yugoslavia," January 26, 1967, XJ/12/28, KNA.
[70] "Correspondence from Gonzaga Opundo to Ministry of education: Re – Corruption by foreign embassies over Kenya students in Yugoslavia," January 26, 1967, XJ/12/28, KNA.

this was essentially a recruitment operation on the part of these foreign powers, which offered promises of work and financial support in exchange for information on Kenyan students studying in Yugoslavia. He also argued that these operations were based on students' political orientations, as their talks and information-gathering efforts included "Kenya politics and the parties which individuals prefer."[71] Such an attention to party affiliation must be contextualized in relation to the Kenyan political landscape, where the year prior Odinga had formally split from KANU and played a formative role in the organization of the Kenya People's Union. That Britain, the United States, and West Germany would have been interested in securing such information is to be expected. More surprising is that the particular items mentioned (films and newspapers) are the same ones petitioned for by the KSU in the GDR, is key, and underscores the widespread existence of concerns around sets of cultural materials that were understood to be "accurate" or not.

Opundo's allegations did not go unchallenged. Less than a month later, a response arrived at the Kenyan Ministry of Education from the leadership of the KSA-Y. Fadhili Lugano (the organization's Chairman) and John Omudanga (Secretary) excoriated Opundo's letter, calling his claims "baseless" and "extremely serious."[72] Opundo was, apparently, not fond of Lugano or Omudanga either, adding the phrase "whom they use as a tool" in brackets next to each of their names when listing out the students he believed had been corrupted.[73] Nevertheless, the KSA's leadership responded in-depth to his "baseless" claims. "The truth is," they wrote, "the Kenya Students Association decided to have as part of the Kenya Independence Celebration, 1966 a Kenya film, photographs and the National Anthem. We wrote to the Kenya High Commissioner in London to help us acquire some of these things."[74] They received a total of four different films for their celebration, and "nearly all Kenya students in Zagreb including Mr. Opundo saw these films."[75] Along with their rebuttal to Opundo, Lugano and Omudanga sent the titles of the films screened, writing that "It is for the Gov-

---

71 "Correspondence from Gonzaga Opundo to Ministry of education: Re – Corruption by foreign embassies over Kenya students in Yugoslavia," January 26, 1967, XJ/12/28, KNA.
72 "Letter to the Permanent Secretary, Ministry of Foreign Affairs from Fadhili B. Lugano and John Omudanga," XJ/12/28, KNA.
73 "Correspondence from Gonzaga Opundo to Ministry of education: Re – Corruption by foreign embassies over Kenya students in Yugoslavia," January 26, 1967, KNA.
74 "Letter to the Permanent Secretary from Fadhili B. Lugano and John Omudanga," February 14, 1967, XJ/12/28, KNA.
75 "Letter to the Permanent Secretary from Fadhili B. Lugano and John Omudanga," February 14, 1967, XJ/12/28, KNA.

ernment of Kenya to judge whether the above four films are propaganda films."[76] At the heart of these debates was, in essence, the question of what constituted propaganda within the medium of film. It is not the aim of this chapter to serve as arbiter to whether or not such films did indeed serve such a function. Rather, I wish only to underscore that competing understandings of Kenyanness within the medium of film clashed not only in the GDR and the Eastern Bloc, but in places such as non-aligned, socialist Yugoslavia as well. Moreover, these contestations were not simply a question of "European" representations versus "African" ones, but were suspended within a political space in which one's alignment to domestic politics in Kenya was considered to be an equally (if not more) important factor.

Conclusion

In their relatively brief periods of tenure, both the KSU and the KSA-Y established themselves as intermediaries between their members in relation to both the Kenyan government and the authorities of their host states. In a number of different ways, they sought to carve out a more expansive role for its membership in relation to each. However, with the exception of a brief influx of nursing students in late 1966 which it helped organize, the KSU witnessed a significant decline in membership after its first two years. By the beginning of 1967 the union had merged with the Kenya Students Association (a similar, smaller organization) to create the Kenya Students Organization (KSO), which at its foundation comprised only 96 members. This figure is striking when considered in relation to the fact that at its height the KSU alone had boasted a membership of over 150 students. Moreover, the activities of that organization appear to have been short-lived, and in large part consisted of collecting data about the students and (more importantly for the KSO) advocating on students' behalf for transfers to educational institutions in West Germany. The explicit rationale is only provided for two of these students, both studying agriculture, who requested to continue their education in West Germany "to develop their both theoretical and practical knowledge" at a level not offered in the GDR.[77]

The medium of film occupied a prominent space in the intellectual and political imaginaries of Kenyan students studying in both the GDR as well as other

---

[76] "Letter to the Permanent Secretary from Fadhili B. Lugano and John Omudanga," February 14, 1967, XJ/12/28, KNA.
[77] "Correspondence from Kariuki K. Njiiri to Lother [Lothar] Metw [?],"May 9, 1968, XJ/12/24, KNA.

areas of socialist Europe like Yugoslavia. The KSU's objective to "show other people how Kenya is" accounts for this in part, but their petitions for access to film produced in Kenya must also be considered alongside the manner in which they articulated their organizational politics. In treading carefully between displaying loyalty to KANU and advocating for a more robust vision within a Kenyan version of "African Democratic Socialism," the Union worked to carve out both a political and economic place for students educated in the GDR within the postcolonial order at home. So too did their comrades in Yugoslavia. The experiences of students in the KSU and the KSA-Y are thus only two episodes embedded within a much broader landscape wherein African students simultaneously pushed against both an alienated existence in Eastern Europe and the constraints and demands of their government at home. This ethos was at the heart of their project to both "represent Kenya in a lively way" and jockey for position within the Kenyan economic landscape. Following experiences abroad defined by both hope and frustration, members of these organizations would eventually return home to a Kenyan state increasingly critiqued as deeply neocolonial in practice and inattentive to its people in the wake of formal "*Uhuru.*" Through their activities and rhetoric, the leaders of the KSU (out a sense of both historical destiny and necessity) had attempted to chart a different path through the postcolonial order as they struggled in the spirit of *harambee*. More broadly, the careful analysis of groups such as the KSU and KSA-Y pursued here offers a largely unexplored avenue through which we might examine the complexities of African postcolonialisms, socialist imaginaries in the Global South, and the experiences and expressions of intellectual communities of color in white spaces during the global 1960s.

Bibliography

Branch, Daniel. *Kenya: Between Hope and Despair, 1963–2011.* New Haven: Yale University Press, 2011.
Branch, Daniel. "Political Traffic: Kenyan Students in Eastern and Central Europe, 1958–1969." *Journal of Contemporary History* 53 (2018): 811–831.
Burton, Eric. "African Manpower Development during the Cold War: The Case of Tanzanian Students in the Two German States." In *Africa Research in Austria: Approaches and Perspectives*, edited by Andreas Exenberger and Ulrich Pallua, 101–134. Innsbruck: Innsbruck University Press, 2016.
Burton, Eric. "Journeys of Education and Struggle: African Mobility in Times of Decolonization and the Cold War." *Stichproben. Vienna Journal of African Studies* 34 (2018): 1–17.
Burton, Eric. "Navigating Global Socialism: Tanzanian Students in and beyond East Germany." *Cold War History* 19 (2019): 63–83.

Burton, Eric. "Decolonization, the Cold War, and Africans' Routes to Higher Education Overseas, 1957–65." *Journal of Global History* 15 (2020): 169–191.
Cleary, A. S. "The Myth of Mau Mau in its International Context." *African Affairs* 89 (1990): 227–245.
Cullen, Poppy. "'Playing Cold War Politics': the Cold War in Anglo-Kenyan Relations in the 1960s." *Cold War History* 18 (2018): 37–54.
Horne, Gerald. *Mau Mau in Harlem? The U.S. and the Liberation of Kenya*. New York: Palgrave MacMillan, 2009.
Kenyatta, Jomo. *Harambee!: The Prime Minister of Kenya's Speeches 1963–1964*, edited by Anthony Cullen. London: Oxford University Press, 1964.
Kracauer, Siegfried. *From Caligari to Hitler: A Psychological History of the German Film*. Princeton: Princeton University Press, 1947.
Kuč, Nedžad. "Southern African Students in Southeast Europe: Education and Experiences in 1960s Yugoslavia." In *Southern African Liberation Movements and the Global Cold War 'East': Transnational Activism, 1960–1990*, edited by Lena Dallywater, Chris Saunders, and Helder Adegar Fonseca, 181–196. Berlin: de Gruyter, 2019.
Kurgat, Paul Kibiwott. "Education as a Foreign Policy Tool: Kenyan Students' Airlifts to the Union of Soviet Socialist Republics and Eastern Europe, 1954–1991." PhD Diss., Moi University, 2013.
Maxon, Robert. "Social & Cultural Changes." In *Decolonization and Independence in Kenya*, edited by B.A. Ogot and W. R. Ochieng, 110–150. Athens, OH: Ohio University Press, 1995.
Mboya, Tom. *Freedom and After*. London: Andre Deutsch, 1963.
Mudimbe, V. Y. *The Invention of Africa: Gnosis, Philosophy, and the Order of Knowledge*. Bloomington, IN: Indiana University Press, 1988.
Müller, Tanja. *Legacies of Socialist Solidarity: East Germany in Mozambique*. Lanham: Lexington Books, 2014.
Odinga, Oginga. *Not Yet Uhuru: The Autobiography of Oginga Odinga*. London: Heineman, 1968.
Pugach, Sara. "African Students and the Politics of Race and Gender in the German Democratic Republic." In *Comrades of Color: East Germany in the Cold War World*, edited by Quinn Slobodian, 131–156. New York: Berghahn Books, 2015.
Pugach, Sara. "Agents of Dissent: African Student Organizations in the German Democratic Republic." *Africa* 89 (2019): 90–108.
Schenck, Marcia C. "Constructing and Deconstructing the 'Black East' – a helpful research agenda?" *Stichproben. Vienna Journal of African Studies* 34 (2018): 135–152.
Schenck, Marcia C. "Negotiating the German Democratic Republic: Angolan Student Migration during the Cold War, 1976–90." *Africa* 89 (2019): 144–166.
Speich, Daniel. "The Kenyan Style of "African Socialism": Developmental Knowledge Claims and the Explanatory Limits of the Cold War." *Diplomatic History* 33 (2009): 449–466.
Steinmetz, George. *The Devil's Handwriting: Precoloniality and the German Colonial State in Qingdao, Samoa, and Southwest Africa*. Chicago: The University of Chicago Press, 2007.
Tully, Melissa. "All's Well in the Colony: Newspaper Coverage of the Mau Mau Movement, 1952–56." In *Narrating War and Peace in Africa*, edited by Toyin Falola and Hetty ter Haar, 56–78. Rochester, NY: University of Rochester Press, 2010.

Eric Angermann

4 Agency and Its Limits: African Unionists as Africa's "Vanguard" at the FDGB College in Bernau[1]

On January 30, 1961, Werner Raase's term of office ended abruptly. Raase had served as the first director of the *Institut für Ausländerstudium* (Institute for Foreign Students), the most recent institution added to the East German trade union college, the *Hochschule der Deutschen Gewerkschaften "Fritz Heckert"* in Bernau near Berlin. Only one day earlier, the responsible federal executive of the central trade union federation which ran the college, the *Freie Deutsche Gewerkschaftsbund* (FDGB), had decided to dismiss four persons: Raase and his deputy, a teacher and an interpreter.[2]

The FDGB executive criticized not only the theoretical and didactic shortcomings in the teaching of state-socialist Marxism-Leninism, for which Raase was held responsible. The decision to dismiss him was also based on an intervention by 17 African students, whose request for a talk led high-ranked members of the *Abteilung Internationale Verbindungen* (International Relations Department) of the federal executive to travel to Bernau.[3] The accusations subsequently collected were serious. In addition to the criticism of insufficient "political leadership" of the institute's directorate,[4] the second major point of critique were racist statements made by Raase and other teachers. For example,

---

[1] This essay is based on my MA thesis published in 2018, in which the third Afro-Asian course at the FDGB college from 1961 to 1963 is analyzed in a praxeological and microhistorical investigation. With regard to African students, the analysis focuses not only on their agency, but also on their social background and motivations for studying in the GDR as well as their actions. Passages of the work are also contained in this essay; see Eric Angermann, "'Ihr gehört auch zur Avantgarde': African trade unionists at the FDGB's academy Fritz Heckert (1961–1963)" (Master's thesis, Georg-August-Universität Göttingen, 2018). I thank Tenzin Sekhon very much for his support in the translation of my contribution into English and Immanuel R. Harisch for his helpful remarks.
[2] "Sekretariatsvorlage: Maßnahmen zur Verbesserung der Arbeit am Ausländerinstitut der Hochschule der Deutschen Gewerkschaften", January 19, 1961, 1, Stiftung Archiv der Parteien und Massenorganisationen der DDR im Bundesarchiv, Berlin (henceforth: SAPMO-BArch), DY 79/406.
[3] Ibid., 3.
[4] "Abschlußanalyse des 2. Lehrgangs für afro-asiatische Studenten an der Hochschule der Deutschen Gewerkschaften 'Fritz Heckert'", September 1960 – Mai 1961, June 2, 1961, 5, SAPMO-BArch, DY 79/406.

whilst drunk, he had supposedly claimed that in order to receive a suit in the GDR, one had to come from Africa. Similarly, the teacher who was also dismissed had allegedly said: "You come with empty suitcases and leave with full suitcases".[5] These hostile remarks pointed to the fact that the incoming students of the FDGB's trade union college were provided with clothing such as suits – a policy which aggravated social envy and xenophobia.

The "existence of nationalist arrogance", as the FDGB executive called the racist remarks, was one of the decisive reasons for their dismissal.[6] Even though the responsible FDGB offices had already criticized Raase beforehand, it was apparently the intervention of African students that was the immediate cause for his sacking. Some students had explicitly threatened to abandon their studies.[7]

It was precisely this threat by the students from Ghana and Mali, whose respective home countries were promoting socialist policies at the time, that would probably have meant a foreign policy setback for the GDR. In times of the West German Hallstein Doctrine—and several years before the GDR succeeded in establishing places of socialist encounters in the Global South[8]—was the provision of study places at the FDGB college for foreign trade unionists, mainly from African countries, who came to the GDR at the beginning of the 1960s, a significant project in East Germany's international solidarity work, in which the FDGB assumed a "leadership role".[9] The course in Bernau targeted a social group in which the FDGB invested political hopes. This was based on the ideology of Marxism-Leninism – according to George Bodie, a fundamental factor of the "pedagogical model of the GDR"[10] – which, in its historical determinism, assigned a central, progressive role in the struggle for world socialism to the trade unions prominently involved in decolonization struggles in the Global

---

5 "Sekretariatsvorlage: Maßnahmen zur Verbesserung der Arbeit am Ausländerinstitut der Hochschule der Deutschen Gewerkschaften", January 19, 1961, 4, SAPMO-BArch, DY 79/406.
6 Ibid.
7 Ibid., 3.
8 See Jörg Depta and Anne-Kristin Hartmetz, this volume.
9 Gregory Witkowski, "Between Fighters and Beggars: Socialist Philanthropy and the Imagery of Solidarity", in *Comrades of Color: East Germany in the Cold War World*, ed. Quinn Slobodian (New York: Berghahn Books, 2015), 75. For the role of the FDGB as an instrument in the foreign policy recognition efforts of the GDR see Ilona Schleicher, "Elemente entwicklungspolitischer Zusammenarbeit in der Tätigkeit von FDGB und FDJ", in *Entwicklungspolitische Zusammenarbeit in der Bundesrepublik Deutschland und der DDR*, ed. Hans-Jörg Bücking (Berlin: Duncker & Humblot, 1998), 112–113.
10 George Bodie, "Where Do Correct Ideas Come From? The FDGB Institute for Foreign Students and the Coming of the Sino-Soviet Split" (paper presented at the conference *Socialist Educational Cooperation with the Global South*, Gießen, Germany, May 11–12, 2018), 6.

South. The assessment was based on the marginal spread of communist parties, especially in sub-Saharan Africa. Furthermore, the orthodox notion of historical materialism necessitated an expectation that the working class should be united primarily in trade unions as the "class organization[s] of the proletariat".[11]

Thus, in this case it was not only a matter of the diplomatic recognition of the GDR as a sovereign state, but also of the projection of a vanguard onto the African trade unionists, who in this sense played an important role in the state-socialist ideas of a socio-political transformation.[12] In the so-called *afroasiatische Lehrgänge* (Afro-Asian courses) of the Bernau institute, then, "class-conscious, modest, sacrificial trade union functionaries" were to be instructed on how to organize and educate the "working class of Africa as the vanguard of the African peoples [...] for the improvement of working and living conditions".[13] Furthermore, these "solidarity measures" were linked to the goal of "effective support for the anti-imperialist, anti-colonial, national liberation struggles".[14]

This contribution focuses precisely on this alleged vanguard of Africa, which in the early 1960s went to study at the FDGB college as one of the most important East German places of transnational socialist encounter. In contrast to aspects of their social mobility, discussed by Immanuel R. Harisch,[15] the analysis focuses on the agency of the African trade unionists vis-à-vis the institute's directorate and the FDGB officials on the ground. I argue that, on the one hand, the (almost exclusively male) African course participants[16] knew how to use the vanguard-concept they were studying, as well as the unstable foreign policy situation of

---

11 Friedrich Engels, "Brief an Bebel", in *MEW vol. 19* (Berlin: Dietz, 1973), 6.
12 Immanuel R. Harisch, "'Mit gewerkschaftlichem Gruß!' Afrikanische GewerkschafterInnen an der FDGB-Gewerkschaftshochschule Fritz Heckert in der DDR", *Stichproben. Vienna Journal of African Studies* 34 (2018): 82–83; Schleicher, "Elemente entwicklungspolitischer Zusammenarbeit", 111–112.
13 "Sekretariatsinformation: Analyse der Arbeit im 3. afro-asiatischen Lehrgang an der Hochschule der Deutschen Gewerkschaften 'Fritz Heckert'", May 6, 1963, 2, SAPMO-BArch, DY 79/2500.
14 "Präsidiumsvorlage zur Arbeit des FDGB und seiner Gewerkschaften nach Afrika", January 11, 1960, 3–4, SAPMO-BArch, DY 79/406.
15 Harisch, 'Mit gewerkschaftlichem Gruß!', 97–100.
16 Most of the course participants (hardly surprisingly) came from the working class. Most of them were originally office workers (in public service, as teachers or in the health sector) or dock and port workers, "trade workers" or railroad workers in the transport industry. However, in retrospect it is not possible to reconstruct which trade unionists already worked as functionaries at the beginning of the course. But after their studies in Bernau, several participants took over high positions in their trade unions. For more details on their social background see Angermann, 'Ihr gehört auch zur Avantgarde', 53–61.

the GDR, to improve the teaching and living conditions at the FDGB college to their benefit. As the introductory example shows, the trade unionists of the Global South were also able to intervene against racist incidents with some success.

On the other hand, the African trade unionists, who, in their role as students in Bernau, appropriated such projections (stubbornly or *eigen-sinnig*[17]) as self-images, also had to face the limits of their agency. Although they were able to protest openly against the responsible functionaries without the risk of having to suffer repressive measures – in contrast to the East German population, which as a rule had only "silent forms of defiance"[18] at its disposal – the scope of action of the African course participants and that of the autochthonous inhabitants of the GDR were similar in terms of political options. Regardless of social origin and temporary or permanent residence, "small people" in the GDR only had "power and regulatory competence" in the surrounding lifeworlds.[19] The possibilities of influence beyond one's own, social everyday life were severely limited due to the "all unifying central power"[20] of the ruling *Sozialistische Einheitspartei Deutschlands* (SED) and its mass organizations – such as the FDGB. Given this context, the participants in the third Afro-Asian course were not in a position to water down the all-encompassing and universally valid claim to power of one party and initiate political activities that bypassed official institutions. On the contrary, despite all proclamations of international solidarity and equality, they also experienced the power techniques of SED rule. Consequentially, they were treated more as subjects of paternalist protection than as trade unionist *Kollegen* (colleagues).[21]

This will be demonstrated through a microhistorical analysis of a concrete conflict between students of the third Afro-Asian course and the institute's directorate. After half a year of study, the vast majority of the course called for an independently operating *Afro-asiatisches Komitee* (Afro-Asian Committee) to establish, amongst other things, anti-racist educational work for East German workers. In so doing, they implicitly questioned the SED's top-down claim to

---

17 For an English definition of *Eigen-Sinn* see Alf Lüdtke, *The History of Everyday Life: Reconstructing Historical Experiences and Ways of Life* (Princeton: University Press, 1995), 313–314.
18 Raul Zelik, "Nach dem Kapitalismus: Warum der Staatssozialismus ökonomisch ineffizient war und was das für Alternativen heute bedeutet", *Prokla. Zeitschrift für kritische Sozialwissenschaft* 39 (2009): 213.
19 Thomas Lindenberger, introduction to *Herrschaft und Eigen-Sinn in der Diktatur: Studien zur Gesellschaftsgeschichte der DDR* (Köln: Böhlau, 1999), 31.
20 Lindenberger, *Herrschaft und Eigen-Sinn*, 36.
21 This is the common jargon used to address course participants or trade union representatives. *Kollege* is the common form of address within or between trade unions; it symbolizes the idea of equality of all trade union members. The English equivalent is *brother* or *sister*.

sole leadership and its claims over the interpretation of social conditions in the GDR.

The presentation of this conflict outlines the different ways of interpretation of the African course participants at the college, which were heterogeneous, ambivalent, and not always consistent. Last but not least, I will show to what extent the FDGB functionaries, together with the institute's directorate, reacted to the criticism of the students they called the vanguard and made (or had to make) concessions to them, but also how they worked out disciplinary measures and partially adapted and appropriated the content of the protest.

The central arena of the conflict was the *Rat der Delegationsleiter* (Council of Heads of Delegation), which was established by the institute as a result of the intervention against the former institute's leader Werner Raase. The emergence of the council is evidence of an appropriation of agency by African trade unionists. The council was the only body through which course participants could participate in decision-making processes through their delegation representatives.[22] At first, however, they were only allowed to "help" the institute's directorate to successfully run the course by communicating "wishes".[23] The African representatives were also initially not allowed to set their own agenda items at the meetings.[24]

Even though the institutionally granted competencies were extremely limited, the Council of Heads of Delegation was nevertheless a site for voicing complaints about the institute's directorate's actions. The social conditions experienced by the African students were articulated and their objections, in some cases, even led to success. The close connection of the council to the new head of the institute, Heinz Deutschland,[25] and the institute's directorate, how-

---

[22] Each national trade union federation represented at the college by students provided a delegation. The heads of delegation were to be elected by their *Kollegen* or had already been appointed by the sending trade union in advance; see "Schulordnung der Hochschule der Deutschen Gewerkschaften 'Fritz Heckert'", no date, 7, SAPMO-BArch, DY 79/270.
[23] Ibid., 6.
[24] "Protokoll über die Sitzung des Rates der Delegationsleiter", March 20, 1962, 4, SAPMO-BArch, DY 79/2500.
[25] Shortly before the beginning of the third Afro-Asian course, Heinz Deutschland started his work as institute director. The historian, who was only 27 years old at the time, had a model East German career to this point. Born in Bernau, he came from a working class family and first learned the profession of a lathe operator. After joining the SED and the FDGB he studied economics and history in Berlin and Moscow and was a research assistant at the FDGB college, until he finally took over the directorate of the Institute for Foreign Students; see Hella Karden, "Deutschland, Heinz", in *Biographisches Handbuch der SBZ/DDR: 1945–1990. Bd. 1: Abendroth – Lyr*, ed. Gabriele Baumgartner and Dieter Hebig (München: De Gruyter Saur 1996), 119.

ever, made apparent the goals of the FDGB to control and discipline all initiatives.[26] This was also evident in the largest protest during the third course.

"Vanguardist" Complaints

On March 17, 1962, the heads of delegation of the course met informally, deliberately excluding the institute's directorate, to discuss several problems within the course.[27] The primary reason for the meeting was the discussion on the "formation of a committee" which, according to the Nigerian representative, would enable the student body to act independently "as a collective" and implement measures in the future.[28] Furthermore, his colleagues argued for a joint place for understanding trade union work,[29] "political issues", and for informing one another "about the situation of the working class in our countries"; after all, pan-

---

[26] However, Heinz Deutschland, who lives in Berlin today, emphasizes retrospectively that discussions generally took place on an equal footing under his leadership; for example, about different ideas of socialism, see Heinz Deutschland, e-mail message to Immanuel R. Harisch, September 2, 2018. Further references in the written sources also speak for a more empathetic and collegial climate under Heinz Deutschland. For example, after the end of the course, there was a regular correspondence between him, who was hardly older or even younger than many of the participants in the course, and some of the graduates for several years; see Angermann, 'Ihr gehört auch zur Avantgarde', 46–47, 75–76. Of course, these friendships could not dissolve the structural power relations at the institute.

[27] Nevertheless, there is a protocol written in German, which appears to be official. According to Heinz Deutschland, this was based on the notes of two of the institute's interpreters who were present at the meeting: "I remember that the transcript of the meeting of the heads of delegation on March 17, 1962 was made on the basis of the notes of the two interpreters Ursula Hofmann (English) and Christel Herz (French), after we [...] had heard about this meeting. Apart from their mother tongue, the African colleagues only spoke the language of the respective former or still colonial power, English or French. They had therefore asked the interpreters they knew to help them. Both colleagues had become accustomed to writing down key points or even longer sentences for their translations, because the African colleagues were not used to taking breaks and giving the interpreter the opportunity to translate. This was also necessary in this case because the explanations had to be translated first into German and then as precisely as possible into English or French. Thus, on the basis of these notes of the two colleagues, a basis existed for the reconstruction of the essential content of the explanations of the heads of delegation, partly in indirect speech and partly even literally." Heinz Deutschland, e-mail message to Immanuel R. Harisch, August 23, 2020.

[28] "Niederschrift über eine Zusammenkunft der Delegationsleiter", March 17, 1962, 1, SAPMO-BArch, DY 79/2500.

[29] "Protokoll über die Sitzung des Rates der Delegationsleiter", March 20, 1962, 13, SAPMO-BArch, DY 79/2500.

African "unity" to fight together against Western capitalist "imperialism" was the proclaimed goal.[30]

For African students adhering to a socialist-influenced pan-Africanism continental unity was paramount compared to the unity of the state-socialist camp which was propagated at the college. Thus, the dominant idea of pan-Africanism was clearly a central, thought-provoking impulse for the debate on sense and purpose of the committee. This was demonstrated at the subsequent council meetings where the heads of delegations clarified their ideas. The head of the Ghanaian delegation J. A. Osei[31] stated that "Africa in its entirety" was to be represented by the committee,[32] uniting the "builders" of the African continent.[33]

Such self-positioning revealed that the political designation as vanguard was also, in part, a self-perception. Although the political conditions in their home countries varied strongly,[34] the delegation leaders saw their role in developing "a common political strategy" for the respective "national liberation struggle" in their home countries and "against capitalism" in general. They thereby also saw their studies as an opportunity for future political struggles – after all, "the opportunity to meet is better here [...] than in Africa".[35]

The few Asian delegations, which provided just five percent of the course,[36] were also in favor of the committee. It is noticeable, however, that their African

---

30 "Niederschrift über eine Zusammenkunft der Delegationsleiter", March 17, 1962, 1, SAPMO-BArch, DY 79/2500.
31 For the Ghanaian unionist J. A. Osei see Osei, annotated by Immanuel R. Harisch, this volume.
32 "Protokoll über die Sitzung des Rates der Delegationsleiter", March 20, 1962, 12, SAPMO-BArch, DY 79/2500.
33 Ibid., 7.
34 The African students at the Bernau college came from a wide range of countries. A number of the politically independent states endured a rather peaceful transition to the postcolonial government, while others had to experience military violence and oppression of the colonial powers, Furthermore, there were the still colonial territories where African liberation movements were starting to be engaged in guerilla wars alongside the colonial settler regimes like South Africa and South-Rhodesia, where political participation and independence seemed to be far away. The independent African states which had a presence of students in Bernau varied in their political orientation – some were closer to the state-socialist countries, others to the Western-liberal bloc.
35 "Protokoll über die Sitzung des Rates der Delegationsleiter", March 20, 1962, 18, SAPMO-BArch, DY 79/2500.
36 "3. Lehrgang – September 1961–März 1963", n. d., 1–2, SAPMO-BArch, DY 79/439.

fellow students rarely made reference to Asia when they spoke of "unity".[37] Furthermore, only the Sri Lankan delegate is cited as a participant in the discussion in the protocol.[38] The East German teachers, too, generally only referred to their African students during the entire course. The social and political upheavals in Africa at the beginning of the 1960s were the most likely places of social-revolutionary imaginations for East German trade union functionaries of that period, highlighting Africans as (supposedly) revolutionary subjects.

Therefore, the broadly supported proposal of the committee is by no means to be understood as a fundamental opposition against the East German institute's directorate or state socialism in general. At the first informal meeting, several heads of delegation stressed that they did not want to openly oppose the Institute for Foreign Students and praised the commitment of their teachers. Only Tanganyika's unidentified representative, who emphasized his union's membership in the ICFTU,[39] openly criticized the situation. In his view, the students of the course had been used as a "tool" for "propaganda [...] against West Germany and America", which in the future had to be stopped by the committee.[40] His view was quickly contested by other heads of delegation who claimed that the major common enemy was imperialism.[41]

Still, a large number of other course participants were also annoyed at being objectified in the FDGB's declaration of *International Solidarity* as part of the East German state socialist agenda, which subsequently confirmed an identity-forming self-image.[42] This concerned, first and foremost, the instrumentalization of students during public events such as solidarity conferences. The institute did not even "ask" the students to participate, but "instructed" them to do so.[43] At

---

37 One of the rare examples for the reference to the Asian fellow students is the already described statement of J. A. Osei, see "Protokoll über die Sitzung des Rates der Delegationsleiter", March 20, 1962, 7, SAPMO-BArch, DY 79/2500.
38 As an example see "Protokoll über die Sitzung des Rates der Delegationsleiter", March 20, 1962, 29, SAPMO-BArch, DY 79/2500.
39 This refers to the International Confederation of Free Trade Unions (ICFTU), which brought together the Western-oriented trade unions worldwide. The ICFTU competed with the Communist World Federation of Trade Unions (WFTU) from which it split in 1949 due to strategic Cold War considerations.
40 "Niederschrift über eine Zusammenkunft der Delegationsleiter", March 17, 1962, 2, SAPMO-BArch, DY 79/2500.
41 Ibid., 3.
42 See for the problems of the East German *solidarity work* Toni Weis, "The Politics Machine: On the Concept of 'Solidarity' in East German Support für SWAPO", *Journal of Southern African Studies* 37 (2011): 352.
43 "Protokoll über die Sitzung des Rates der Delegationsleiter", March 20, 1962, 29, SAPMO-BArch, DY 79/2500.

the same time, the heads of the institutes had not communicated any information about the content of the public events in advance, while the students present on site were introduced as official representatives of their trade unions without prior notice. The South African representative Gilbert Hlabukana pointed out why this put the course participants at risk. The reporting of the conferences by the state media would endanger "50% of all the colleagues studying here" who "live in illegality" and whose "necks are put on the line".[44] Additionally, Hlabukana argued, he himself had been commissioned by his trade union confederation[45] to speak at conferences about the conditions in his country, which was "in the depths of fascism", but only on the condition that "published photos of himself were to be avoided".[46]

In the course of the discussion, it became evident that experiences of racism were the primary reason for the attempt to initiate an Afro-Asian committee as an independent institution. African course participants criticized the representation of the social conditions in their home countries in East German publications.[47] The Guinean Daouda Camara singled out a brochure entitled *Bei Freunden im freien Afrika* (With friends in free Africa), which described "an outdated state of Guinea" as a country without any car traffic.[48] The Senegalese delegation leader Amadou-Lamine Diop was angered by the racist imagery of a caricature depicting a sleeping child on the back of an elephant particularly, claiming that this was "the same propaganda" that "the imperialists spread about Africa".[49] With the planned committee, however, a possibility for intervention could be created, "in order to enlighten the people here about the real circumstances" and to enforce "that such nonsense is no longer published", the Moroccan representative announced.[50]

In this sense, not only future stereotypical representations were to be prevented, but involvement "in the upbringing and development of the masses in the GDR" with regard to the conditions in Africa was to be implemented[51] – al-

---

44 Ibid., 10.
45 This was the ANC-affiliated South African Congress of Trade Unions (SACTU).
46 "Protokoll über die Sitzung des Rates der Delegationsleiter", March 20, 1962, 10, SAPMO-BArch, DY 79/2500.
47 On this issue, see also George Bodie's contribution in this volume.
48 "Protokoll über die Sitzung des Rates der Delegationsleiter", March 20, 1962, 17, SAPMO-BArch, DY 79/2500.
49 Ibid., 32.
50 "Niederschrift über eine Zusammenkunft der Delegationsleiter", March 17, 1962, 3, SAPMO-BArch, DY 79/2500.
51 "Protokoll über die Sitzung des Rates der Delegationsleiter", April 3, 1962, 5, SAPMO-BArch, DY 79/2500.

though certain reservations also appeared in light of past experiences of racist ways of thinking, acting, and representing. A colleague from Cameroon, for example, expressed his disappointed hopes. Upon his arrival in the GDR, he would have believed "to come to a paradise" – but that was "not so", because "the European" would "always remain a European".[52] Such incidents were by no means isolated. Black students from Sub-Saharan Africa described racist behavior which they encountered on a daily basis. For example, "anonymous letters" were circulating in the vicinity of the college in which "German girls" were called upon to not "flirt with their African colleagues".[53] The Togolese representative Benoît Agbetrobu complained that the girlfriend of a fellow student from his delegation had received such a letter, an event which he called "very strange in a socialist or communist country".[54]

But even the college itself was not free of discrimination. At the beginning of the course, students had already complained to the head of the institute, Heinz Deutschland, about an employee of the school restaurant. In this specific instance, the annoyance stemmed from the fact that no consequences were noticeable.[55] Even fellow East German students stood out negatively. For example, Osée Mbaitjongue from Cameroon recalled a meeting with a guest of his *Betreuer* and room-mate,[56] who accused him of "becoming a minister and having several women" upon his return to Cameroon, and that he could provide these women if he came to visit. On top of that, another East German student at the college had grabbed his hair without offering an explanation.[57] Daouda Camara also reported on fellow East German students who had asked him whether people carried "a rifle" in Guinea "because of all the predators".[58]

---

52 "Niederschrift über eine Zusammenkunft der Delegationsleiter", March 17, 1962, 3, SAPMO-BArch, DY 79/2500.
53 "Protokoll der Sitzung des Rates der Delegationsleiter", April 10, 1962, 2, SAPMO-BArch, DY 79/2500.
54 Ibid., 6.
55 Ibid., 6, 11.
56 These mentors were students from the GDR with whom the course participants shared their double rooms; see Ilona Schleicher, "FDGB-Offensive in Westafrika: Der Gewerkschaftsverbund im Jahr Afrikas", in *Engagiert für Afrika: Die DDR und Afrika II*, ed. Ulrich van der Heyden et. al. (Münster: Lit, 1994), 89.
57 "Protokoll der Sitzung des Rates der Delegationsleiter", April 10, 1962, 22, SAPMO-BArch, DY 79/2500.
58 Ibid., 7.

These examples reveal the dominant role sexualized perceptions played in the context of racist behavior towards fellow African inhabitants in the GDR.[59] In general, and despite all official negations and an anti-fascist and anti-colonial self-idealization, they refer to the lingering effect of colonial imagery and racist ways of thinking about the exotic or original people of Africa in the GDR.[60]

Responding Hosts

Throughout the course of the conflict over the Afro-Asian Committee, the institute's directorate and the responsible representatives of the FDGB executive tried to settle the matter as quickly and quietly as possible. To this end, they engaged in lengthy discussions with the heads of delegations and made substantial concessions to them on some points. The Council of Heads of Delegation was given more time on a weekly basis in future, starting with its first official meeting after the informal meeting. In addition, the institute's directors Heinz Deutschland and Gerhard Hans expanded the opportunities for student participation by allowing delegations to submit their own agenda items.[61] Furthermore, the status of students at international solidarity events, whose central role the East German hosts repeatedly emphasized for the common "struggle" against imperialism and for the "solidarity movement" in the GDR, was to be changed to the role of "observers".[62] This could prevent them from being publicly seen as representatives, which then could have led to repression in their home countries, as the South African representative Gilbert Hlabukana had pointed out above. The institute's directorate also accepted criticism of representations in East German magazines and specialist journals voiced by the Guinean and Senegalese delegation.[63] Addressing the FDGB executive responsible for media relations, college director Karl Kampfert subsequently ordered that "all photos or other pic-

---

59 For the distribution of the image of the "lascivious African man" see Sara Pugach, "African Students and the Politics of Race and Gender in the German Democratic Republic", in *Comrades of Color: East Germany in the Cold War World*, ed. Quinn Slobodian (New York: Berghahn Books, 2015), 137–138.
60 Quinn Slobodian, "Socialist Chromatism: Race, Racism, and the Racial Rainbow in East Germany", in *Comrades of Color: East Germany in the Cold War World*, ed. Quinn Slobodian (New York: Berghahn Books, 2015), 26.
61 "Protokoll über die Sitzung des Rates der Delegationsleiter", March 20, 1962, 4, SAPMO-BArch, DY 79/2500.
62 Ibid., 5.
63 Ibid., 6.

torial material depicting Afro-Asian students from our institute for foreigners must be approved by the head of the institute before they can be published".[64]

The institute's directorate thus took up politically justifiable aspects of the students' demands, but from the outset it did not allow for the Afro-Asian committee to become an independent student initiative – even though its representatives avoided an official positioning at the first council meeting during the conflict.[65] The Council of Heads of Delegation, to which the students only wanted to assign competencies concerning the organization of studies,[66] was to be the only representative body for student interests. The "formation of such a committee", on the other hand, was supposedly unjustifiable – for it would have to subordinate itself to the "instructions of the institute's directorate", thereby limiting their right to make any independent decisions, as noted in a report on the first meeting addressed to the FDGB executive.[67] This also highlighted the concern about a loss of political control. It was strictly rejected that a possible committee run by the African students could "uniformly impose demands on the directorate of the institute" and enforce them.[68] The reason for the widespread "demand for such a committee" was not seen in the continuation of colonial relations between East Germans and the students of the Global South. Instead, those responsible in Bernau claimed that the ICFTU was trying to influence the course.[69]

The lack of self-reflection here and the reference to external manipulative forces can be explained by looking at the weaknesses of the Marxist-Leninist state doctrine.[70] This is also indicated by the fact that the report quoted here was addressed to the FDGB executive, which in the centralist structure of the

---

64 This was based on "justified complaints"; see "Brief der Hochschuldirektion an den Sekretär der Kommission für Koordinierung und Qualifizierung des FDGB-Bundesvorstands", May 4, 1962, 1–2, SAPMO-BArch, DY 79/183.
65 "Protokoll über die Sitzung des Rates der Delegationsleiter", March 20, 1962, 35, SAPMO-BArch, DY 79/2500.
66 Ibid., 12.
67 "Einige Bemerkungen und Erläuterungen zum beiliegenden Protokoll und den damit verbundenen Problemen", March 22, 1962, 4, SAPMO-BArch, DY 79/2500.
68 Ibid., 1.
69 Ibid., 3.
70 This "is based on a great optimism of progress and idealism. The idea of acting in accordance with historical laws, however, also reduces the willingness for reflection and self-criticism if the expected forecasts are not realized. If history is not understood as an open process, the absence of revolutions or even the emergence of authoritarian instead of emancipatory tendencies [or the emergence of intra-societal contradictions, note d. A.] can hardly be explained other than by manipulation of the masses and conspiracy of the ruling elites [...]"; see Moritz Zeiler, *Materialistische Staatskritik: Eine Einführung* (Stuttgart: Schmetterling Verlag, 2017), 42.

GDR Federation of Trade Unions had the final decision-making power also with regard to the Institute for Foreign Students.[71] Its directorate, with its very own motivation to create a good impression vis-à-vis the next highest authority, was itself looking for starting points for the rapid implementation of state socialist guidelines. This was accompanied by the fact that it was not so much the actual intentions of the protesting students that were at the center of the institute's own search for solutions, but rather exploring possibilities to homogenize the student collective. An external enemy had to be constructed, who would be held responsible for the "'disturbances' [...] from outside".[72] In addition to the speculations about the role of Western influence, in their criticism the institute's directorate singled out the Guinean Daouda Camara, who had been himself one of the sharpest critics of the institute's reaction, in its report from the protesters' camp. In the institute's view, Camara had allegedly tried to split the collective.[73]

The Paternalism of Comradeship

But Camara was by no means alone with his criticism. The apparent reluctance of the East German functionaries to give in to the demand for an Afro-Asian Committee was followed by incomprehension, indignation, and, in the end, intensified forms of protest on the part of the students. In the first council meeting, the heads of delegation involved in the discussion criticized the lack of approval for the committee by the institute's directorate, though some isolated voices were raised in appreciation of its efforts "to conduct the course and create favorable conditions for us".[74] In this context, Camara implicitly threatened to leak information to the West. He stressed that it was not really in the interest of the protesters to read that "you are with so-called friends who oppose your unity in the imperialist press".[75] De facto, however, he threatened to pass on the institute's

---

[71] "Einige Bemerkungen und Erläuterungen zum beiliegenden Protokoll und den damit verbundenen Problemen", March 22, 1962, 4, SAPMO-BArch, DY 79/2500.
[72] Alf Lüdtke, "'... den Menschen vergessen'? – oder: Das Maß der Sicherheit: Arbeiterverhalten der 1950er Jahre im Blick von MfS, SED, FDGB und staatlichen Leitungen", in *Akten. Eingaben. Schaufenster. Die DDR und ihre Texte. Erkundungen zu Herrschaft und Alltag*, ed. Alf Lüdtke and Peter Becker (Berlin: De Gruyter, 1997), 208–209.
[73] "Einige Bemerkungen und Erläuterungen zum beiliegenden Protokoll und den damit verbundenen Problemen", March 22, 1962, 3, SAPMO-BArch, DY 79/2500.
[74] "Protokoll über die Sitzung des Rates der Delegationsleiter", March 20, 1962, 13, SAPMO-BArch, DY 79/2500.
[75] Ibid.

disastrous assessment to the West German media if it were to oppose the formation of a committee. Camara's statement exemplifies how the students strategically used their socio-political position during the height of the Cold War to assert their own interests in the GDR.

At the following delegation council meeting two weeks later, the East German hosts nevertheless rejected the committee in the proposed form. Again, a representative of the International Relations Department of the FDGB executive was present. This "colleague Fischer" announced "on behalf of the federal executive" that, following agreements with FDGB Chairman Herbert Warnke and African trade union officials in Berlin and Prague, a "binding" decision had been made that the Council of Heads of Delegation was sufficient as the "only organ" for the institutional representation of the students.[76] Although the committee could be founded, it would only carry out a cultural function and could not deal with the FDGB directly, as this would endanger its "principle of non-interference".[77] It is obvious that Fischer here was referring to internationalist principles of Marxism-Leninism, which in terms of foreign policy included – officially – the "free self-determination" of nations and precisely "non-interference in the internal affairs of other states".[78] Therefore, the committee could only address "matters of the African colleagues among themselves"[79] and should not interfere in the home affairs of the GDR. Finally, it was argued that the Afro-Asian Committee would not have the right "to make any demands on school regulations".[80] Fischer explicitly denied discussing the position of the FDGB executive.[81]

The East German representatives were met with a wave of indignation. Hamidou Diallo from Mali called for a discussion and explained that the students

---

76 "Protokoll über die Sitzung des Rates der Delegationsleiter", April 3, 1962, 1–3, SAPMO-BArch, DY 79/2500.
77 Ibid., 18.
78 See as an exemplary contemporary source G. N. Zwektow, "Die Leninschen Prinzipien der sowjetischen Außenpolitik", *Gesellschaftswissenschaftliche Reihe* 19 (1970).
79 "Protokoll über die Sitzung des Rates der Delegationsleiter", April 3, 1962, 1–3, SAPMO-BArch, DY 79/2500, 9.
80 Ibid., 3.
81 Ibid. Looking back, Heinz Deutschland formulated an objection, which is more technical and bureaucratic than substantive: "The FDGB had contracts or agreements with the heads of the delegating organizations. These did not provide for the colleagues delegated to study in Bernau [...] to join forces with representatives of other organizations in an 'Afro-Asian committee'. We felt bound by these agreements." Heinz Deutschland, e-mail message to Immanuel R. Harisch, August 23, 2020.

felt like they were treated as "children" who did not know what they wanted.[82] This was supported by Luc Bissay from Cameroon. The students in Bernau were themselves (partially full-time) trade unionists. For them, it was therefore irrelevant what African trade union officials in Berlin or Prague thought of the idea of a committee.[83] Diallo also questioned the alleged talks with African trade union representatives and instead, together with other heads of delegation, referred to a core competence of the committee, namely educational work on life in Africa, a bottom-up approach for "the friendship between our peoples and the people of the GDR".[84] In the permitted form, however, the committee would only be a "glass bowl" with no contact to its surrounding.[85] Furthermore, it would be virtually impossible for the FDGB not to have any contact whatsoever with the committee, since without its assistance it could not be set up. Several heads of delegation also mentioned obvious distrust towards the students shown by the FDGB executive.[86] In this sense, the FDGB was apparently "afraid" of the students, as soon as they would assume an active role.[87]

Despite all objections, the institute's directorate insisted on the refusal to establish the proposed Afro-Asian committee. Heinz Deutschland responded to the broad criticism by stating that "interference in the internal affairs of the GDR", which according to the FDGB included the establishment of "relations with the workers of the GDR", was unacceptable.[88] The decision had been made "in accordance with the hundred-year-old principles of the German labour movement in relation to other foreign organisations".[89]

Other explanations for the actions of the institute's directorate and the FDGB executive appear more plausible. It is more likely that the desire to intervene in the powers of the centralist party and trade union apparatus could not be permitted. The institute's directorate was well aware that "the demand for assistance in the education of the working class in the GDR" resulted from the statement – or "accusation", as it was called by the college – "that racism exists in the GDR, and not enough was being done from the official side against it".[90] The

---

82 "Protokoll über die Sitzung des Rates der Delegationsleiter", April 3, 1962, 1–3, SAPMO-BArch, DY 79/2500, 4.
83 Ibid., 10.
84 "Protokoll über die Sitzung des Rates der Delegationsleiter", April 3, 1962, 5, 11, SAPMO-BArch DY 79/2500.
85 Ibid., 11–12.
86 Ibid., 12.
87 Ibid., 18.
88 Ibid., 6–7.
89 Ibid., 19.
90 "Einschätzung", n. d., 4, SAPMO-BArch, DY 79/2500.

creation of the committee in the form proposed by the protesters would have meant an admission of social reality in the GDR with regard to widespread racism and of the fallibility of the prevailing ideology declared as true, which consequently questioned the party's leading role in state and society. The limitation of agency of the African trade unionists to act as students in Bernau was revealed at just this point, when they had in mind a self-organized political practice without constant paternalistic subordination to the SED organs.[91]

The council meeting further escalated after this. It ended abruptly after a dispute between several heads of delegation[92] and an attempt at appeasement that was not further commented on: students were also offered to become members of the German-African Society, which was in line with the ruling party SED. They could inform them about the social conditions in Africa, without, of course, questioning positions of the SED and its associated mass organizations.[93]

As a response, the disappointed students turned to other means. The following day, the protesters declared a boycott of an excursion to the Brandenburg steel and rolling mill; apparently not a single student took part in the excursion.[94]

---

91 Two years earlier, four African students from Nigeria, Uganda, and Togo had the same limitation of their agency in the Soviet Union. The students of the state Lomonosov University in Moscow founded in September 1960 the independent "Black Africans' Student Union", for which they were expelled by the university. After returning to their home countries, the four scandalized their experienced restrictions and received great attention in Western print media; see Maxim Matusevich, "Expanding the Boundaries of the Black Atlantic: African Students as Soviet Moderns", *Ab Imperio* 2 (2012): 339–340.
92 The Congolese representative Joseph Safily, who in the previous council meeting had been the only one to express criticism of the committee's demand (see "Niederschrift über eine Zusammenkunft der Delegationsleiter", March 17, 1962, 4, SAPMO-BArch, DY 79/2500), came into the focus of his African Council colleagues. Safily accused the others of showing no real solidarity with their compatriots in times of the Congo crisis. As a result, the majority of the heads of delegations, some of whom had previously reported on trade union colleagues who had fallen in the Congo ("Protokoll über die Sitzung des Rates der Delegationsleiter", April 3, 1962, 16, SAPMO-BArch DY 79/2500), left the meeting "under loud protest"; see ibid., 20. Even after this premature end, the situation at the institute did not calm down. According to other students, Safily himself acted aggressively (see "Protokoll über die Sitzung des Rates der Delegationsleiter", April 10, 1962, 4, 20, 23, SAPMO-BArch, DY 79/2500) and was ultimately expelled from the college for this; see "3. Lehrgang – September 1961 – März 1963", n. d., 2, SAPMO-BArch, DY 79/439.
93 "Protokoll über die Sitzung des Rates der Delegationsleiter", April 3, 1962, 19, SAPMO-BArch, DY 79/2500
94 "Einschätzung", n. d., 3, SAPMO-BArch, DY 79/2500.

In order to pacify the protest at the institute and at the same time prevent the "formation of the committee as an official organ", which could potentially influence "internal affairs" and act as "appointed political representation",⁹⁵ the institute's directorate around Heinz Deutschland decided to take two steps. First, it attempted to socially "isolate" the most prominent protesters.⁹⁶ These included the delegations from Ghana and Nigeria, which had advocated for a collective refusal to take part in regular classes the day following the boycott of the excursion, but were no longer able to mobilize the majority of the course participants. Clearly, proven forms of struggle from work experience as trade unionists were used by the students in the dispute. They called their actions a "strike" and claimed that the institute directors were "capitalists", while they themselves were oppressed "workers".⁹⁷

The isolation of the main actors of the protest was supposed to happen primarily in class by the teachers; every "attempt at further political provocation" would be criticized "sharply and unequivocally".⁹⁸ This is related to the second measure adopted, namely the launch of a "comprehensive political offensive" in the course, whereby those deemed "the good forces" by the institute's directorate, essentially a large majority of the course without a clear position, would have their "back" strengthened in order to "assure their solidarity and support".⁹⁹ To this end, the institute's directorate also decided to strengthen "cultural activities" with regard to the leisure time of the course participants.¹⁰⁰ Last but not least, it planned to convene another meeting of the Council of Heads of Delegation, in order to prevent informal meetings of students which were described as "illegal".¹⁰¹ But it was also a large number of the students themselves who wanted to prevent further escalation of the committee dispute. Several representatives therefore went to one of the two deputy directors of the institute, Gerhard Hans, for a discussion in which they described the racist incidents they had experienced as one of the main reasons for their protest. This discussion, in which

---

95 Ibid., 1–2.
96 Ibid., 5.
97 "Einschätzung", n.d., 3, SAPMO-BArch, DY 79/2500.
98 Ibid., 5.
99 Ibid.
100 Ibid. This decision was also taken to prevent the West Berlin visits already criticized at this time, which were considered a bad influence; for the possibilities of visits to West Berlin see Harisch, "'Mit gewerkschaftlichem Gruß!'," 97.
101 "Einschätzung", n. d., 5, SAPMO-BArch, DY 79/2500.

the students present called for a meeting, also resulted in further unscheduled council meetings.[102]

The Triumph of Dogma

The meeting which was thus convened, and which lasted for a total of nine hours, clearly had the character of a debate. In addition to two representatives of the FDGB executive, Karl Kampfert, director of the whole FDGB college in Bernau, was present for the first time. With one exception, all heads of delegation attended the council meeting.[103]

Most of the meeting was devoted to finding a compromise on the committee question and discussing racist incidents at the college. Rolf Deubner, as one of the FDGB's executive representatives, made a clear separation between a political and a cultural sphere. He confirmed on the one hand the view that "political activity in the GDR" was not possible for the students; after all, this contradicted the "principles of proletarian internationalism", which also included "non-interference in the internal affairs of trade union organisations".[104] On the other hand, he announced that the FDGB was now quite willing to support a committee with regard to possible events – as long as it only facilitated "cultural life".[105]

Subsequently, he answered the requests of some students and, as representative of the FDGB executive, took a stand on the various accusations of racism.[106] He explained that "of course there are still numerous petty bourgeois people"—singling out people with their own small businesses and thus in possession of private property—"who are afflicted with the idea of the capitalist era".[107] According to the ruling SED's state doctrine, this population group was regarded as the manipulated mass basis which had historically given rise

---

102 "Protokoll über die Sitzung des Rates der Delegationsleiter", April 10, 1962, 13, SAPMO-BArch, DY 79/2500.
103 The Congolese student Safily was only invited as "observer" and no longer as head of delegation; see Ibid., 8.
104 Ibid., 2.
105 Ibid., 2–3.
106 One week earlier, despite an urgent request to address this issue, the institute's directorate had still ignored the complaint of the Moroccan representative about an assault in the urban area of Bernau – at least the pedantic protocols allow this evaluation; see "Protokoll über die Sitzung des Rates der Delegationsleiter", April 10, 1962, 1, SAPMO-BArch, DY 79/2500.
107 "Protokoll über die Sitzung des Rates der Delegationsleiter", April 10, 1962, 2, 24, SAPMO-BArch, DY 79/2500.

to fascism.¹⁰⁸ Deubner made them responsible for the existing racism in orthodox Marxist fashion; they still had to be educated in the socialist sense to abandon their racist worldview.¹⁰⁹

In doing so, he admitted the existence of racism in the GDR, but externalized it to a social group that was not yet socialist enough. The heads of delegation then described their own experiences at the college in an attempt to explain that racism had become a general problem of everyday life. The Cameroonian Luc Bissay tried to make his East German colleagues aware of this fundamental problem. They "should for once take our black skin, our hair" and would then "realize what problems are still open, what educational work still has to be done".¹¹⁰

In the further course of the meeting, the East German representatives insisted on their one-dimensional economist analysis of racism. Nevertheless, in response to these reports and requests, Kampfert and Deubner promised to hold talks with conspicuous employees and students.¹¹¹ "German colleagues" acting in a discriminatory way have "no place at the school", they argued.¹¹² The East German announcements in this council meeting, which ultimately concluded the conflict, were a result of the protest practices of the African trade unionists studying in Bernau. They first made it possible to address racist incidents, and also achieved partial success with other demands, even if the constitution of a Afro-Asian committee was not initiated. This is illustrated by the measures announced by Heinz Deutschland as head of the institute. He reaffirmed the active participation in council meetings, which had been promised at the start of the whole conflict, and distributed a discussion paper containing suggestions for "improving cultural work and student care".¹¹³ Amongst other things, this included students "reporting on their countries" once a month, in alphabetical order.¹¹⁴ Furthermore, the institute's directorate proposed to increase the number

---

108 See Georgi Dimitroff, "Arbeiterklasse gegen Faschismus", in *Die Offensive des Faschismus und die Aufgaben der Kommunisten im Kampf für die Volksfront gegen Krieg und Faschismus. Referate auf dem VII. Kongreß der Kommunistischen Internationale (1935)*, ed. Institut für Marxismus-Leninismus (Berlin: Dietz, 1957), 91.
109 "Protokoll über die Sitzung des Rates der Delegationsleiter", April 10, 1962, 24–25, SAPMO-BArch, DY 79/2500.
110 "Protokoll über die Sitzung des Rates der Delegationsleiter", April 10, 1962, 18, SAPMO-BArch, DY 79/2500.
111 Ibid., 12.
112 Ibid., 26.
113 Ibid., 23.
114 "Protokoll über die Sitzung des Rates der Delegationsleiter", May 11, 1962, 2, SAPMO-BArch, DY 79/2500.

of excursions, such as "sightseeing and theatre trips", and announced the establishment of a club room explicitly intended for the participants of the courses, which was also intended for political discussions amongst one another.[115] Contact with the East German population—generally supervised with East German workers of certain selected workers' brigades—was also to be strengthened from now on.[116] Just like at the beginning of the conflict, the institute's directorate carefully took up politically justifiable aspects of student demands without allowing independent student initiatives to be created; yet, subordination to the political control of the East German confederation of trade unions had to be maintained.

In the comments on the offers made by FDGB board member Deubner, one can see that despite all the disciplinary motives the imagination of a progressive – or even revolutionary – role of African trade unionists also determined the actions of their East German colleagues. According to Deubner, the "friends" from Africa "also belonged to the vanguard of the working class", which, according to the Leninist credo, stood for the "future" of their homelands.[117] It was therefore essential that trade unionists inform each other "mutually" about their "countries", "cultures", and their respective "working classes" by means of the proposals submitted.[118] It can be assumed that this political assessment of the visiting students was also a central aspect for the East German hosts' approach, which was by no means punitive and repressive, but always aimed at closer political integration.

Ultimately, the students accepted the solutions presented here.[119] Some heads of delegation even praised the institute's efforts to create a calm atmosphere for discussion and to respond to their criticism.[120] From this point on, the protocols and reports of the institute's directorate no longer contained any dissenting votes or demands for a committee; instead, several references to

---

115 "Protokoll über die Sitzung des Rates der Delegationsleiter", May 11, 1962, 2, SAPMO-BArch, DY 79/2500.
116 Ibid.
117 Ibid., 23–24.
118 Ibid., 25.
119 At the following council meeting, the heads of delegation present approved the collected proposals without dissenting votes; see "Protokoll über die Sitzung des Rates der Delegationsleiter", May 11, 1962, 2, SAPMO-BArch, DY 79/2500.
120 "Protokoll über die Sitzung des Rates der Delegationsleiter", April 10, 1962, 15–17, SAPMO-BArch, DY 79/2500.

the real implementation of the institute's proposals can be found in the corpus of sources.[121]

Conclusion

The results and the course of the conflict at the Bernau Institute for Foreign Students illustrate that African trade unionists were both seen as revolutionary subjects of Africa and treated as objects of constant paternalism. Their treatment as well as their political classification in East Germany resulted from the Leninist conception of a vanguard, in the shape of a leading party as the motor of social progress, upon which the GDR's power structure rested. Therefore, practices of all social milieus and groups were constantly subject to the "reservations of an elitist vanguard and its representatives"[122] as well as the "authoritarian-paternalistic social structure"[123] of the state-socialist one-party system.

This also applied to the African trade unionists, with their specific cadre training and their supposed vanguardist position during their temporary stay in Bernau. As one of the social groups with an ascribed special historical role on the path to world socialism, the national trade union federation FDGB, acting as the transmission belt of the SED, attempted to politically bind the course participants to this doctrine, the supposed universal validity of which lay in the "historical violence"[124] of the successful October Revolution. This motive for praxis illustrates the non-acceptance of any autonomous organizations beyond state-supporting structures, since these could have seen independent develop-

---

121 Regular contact with selected *Socialist Brigades* "in important production plants" was also implemented (see "Vorlage für die Institutsleitungssitzung am 25.5.62", May 24, 1962, 2, SAPMO-BArch DY 79/409), as was the prompt establishment of the promised clubroom, which was available in the evening with a small library and magazines in several languages; see "Schulordnung der Hochschule der Deutschen Gewerkschaften 'Fritz Heckert'", n.d., 7, SAPMO-BArch, DY 79/270. In addition, they were more actively involved in the evaluation of teaching; see "Einladung zur Sitzung der Institutsleitung mit dem Rat der Delegationsleiter am 15.11.1962 in Lektionssaal 4", n.d., SAPMO-BArch, DY 79/2500; Protokoll über die Sitzung des Rates der Delegationsleiter, December 13, 1962, 2, SAPMO-BArch DY 79/2500.
122 Lindenberger, *Herrschaft*, 31.
123 Bernd Wagner, "Zu rechtsextremen Entwicklungen in den neuen Bundesländern", in *AfrikaBilder. Studien zu Rassismus in Deutschland*, ed. Susan Arndt (Münster: Unrast, 2006), 110.
124 Hans-Jürgen Krahl, "Zu Lenin, Staat und Revolution", in *Konstitution und Klassenkampf. Zur historischen Dialektik von bürgerlicher Emanzipation und proletarischer Revolution. Schriften, Reden und Entwürfe aus den Jahren 1966–1970*, ed. Hans-Jürgen-Krahl (Frankfurt: Neue Kritik, 1971), 182.

ments, enabling political dissidence or oppositional attitudes. It is important to note that in the conflict analyzed here, those responsible in East Germany did not opt for repressive measures but for an even more intensive political integration that incorporated selected demands. However, this decision was not only based on the special position of the African trade union students, but also on their ability to make use of the unstable foreign policy situation of the GDR, thereby highlighting a particularly fragile aspect of the political control they faced. Nevertheless, the majority of the Africans studying in Bernau recognized the role of the East German trade unionists as esteemed[125] providers of "political ideas"[126] and as profound experts of socialism as an exemplary developmental model, even if a considerable part favored alternatives such as a pan-African-influenced socialism.[127]

This also points to the reproductive character of the protests. Not only did the concessions obtained help the students to interact and communicate, they also expanded the institute's directorate course repertoire. It used these new structures for propagandistic work, for example to spread the image of an imperial West Germany, which certainly did not convince all course participants.[128] They treated these new possibilities as another option for teaching Marxism-Leninism and ensuring a following in opposition to the inner-German opponent in the West. Last but not least, the protests shown here were an important step for the further establishment of studies for foreigners at the FDGB college, which 4,400 trade unionists, especially from the Global South,[129] made use of until the end of the GDR.

---

125 Letter from Bernard Obua to Heinz Deutschland, August 8, 1964, 1, SAPMO-BArch, DY 79/2511.
126 Letter from Abdelkader Djoudi to Helmut Lehmann, August 27, 1963, 1, SAPMO-BArch, DY 79/616.
127 In general, so-called "Maoist" ideas were also widespread; see Bodie, "The FDGB Institute," 22–23.
128 "Bericht über die Ergebnisse der Westberlindiskussion im 3. afro-asiatischen Lehrgang," October 9, 1962, 5, SAPMO-BArch, DY 79/2500.
129 Alfred Förster, *Die FDGB-Bundesschule "Theodor Leipart" Bernau bei Berlin* (Bernau: Verein Baudenkmal Bundesschule Bernau, 2007), 47.

Bibliography

Angermann, Eric. "'Ihr gehört auch zur Avantgarde': African trade unionists at the FDGB's academy Fritz Heckert (1961–1963)." Master thesis, Georg-August-Universität Göttingen, 2018.

Bodie, George. "Where do Correct Ideas Come From? The FDGB Institute for Foreign Students and the Coming of the Sino-Soviet Split." Paper presented at the conference *Socialist Educational Cooperation with the Global South*, Gießen, Germany, May 11–12, 2018.

Dimitroff, Georgi. "Arbeiterklasse gegen Faschismus." In *Die Offensive des Faschismus und die Aufgaben der Kommunisten im Kampf für die Volksfront gegen Krieg und Faschismus. Referate auf dem VII. Kongreß der Kommunistischen Internationale (1935)*, edited by Institut für Marxismus-Leninismus, 4–110. Berlin: Dietz, 1957.

Engels, Friedrich. "Brief an Bebel." In *MEW vol. 19*, 3–9. Berlin: Dietz, 1973.

Förster, Alfred. *Die FDGB-Bundesschule "Theodor Leipart" Bernau bei Berlin*. Bernau: Verein Baudenkmal Bundesschule Bernau, 2007.

Harisch, Immanel R. "'Mit gewerkschaftlichem Gruß!' Afrikanische GewerkschafterInnen an der FDGB-Gewerkschaftshochschule Fritz Heckert in der DDR". *Stichproben. Vienna Journal of African Studies* 34 (2018): 77–109.

Karden, Hella. "Deutschland, Heinz." In *Biographisches Handbuch der SBZ/DDR: 1945–1990. Bd. 1: Abendroth – Lyr*, edited by Gabrielle Baumgartner and Dieter Hebig, 119. München: De Gruyter Saur, 1996.

Krahl, Hans-Jürgen. "Zu Lenin, Staat und Revolution." In *Konstitution und Klassenkampf. Zur historischen Dialektik von bürgerlicher Emanzipation und proletarischer Revolution. Schriften, Reden und Entwürfe aus den Jahren 1966–1970*, edited by Hans-Jürgen-Krahl, 182–190. Frankfurt: Neue Kritik, 1971.

Lindenberger, Thomas. Introduction to *Herrschaft und Eigen-Sinn in der Diktatur: Studien zur Gesellschaftsgeschichte der DDR*, edited by Thomas Lindenberger, 13–44. Köln: Böhlau, 1999.

Lüdtke, Alf. "'… den Menschen vergessen'? – oder: Das Maß der Sicherheit: Arbeiterverhalten der 1950er Jahre im Blick von MfS, SED, FDGB und staatlichen Leitungen." In *Akten. Eingaben. Schaufenster. Die DDR und ihre Texte. Erkundungen zu Herrschaft und Alltag*, edited by Alf Lüdtke and Peter Becker, 57–75. Berlin: De Gruyter, 1997.

Lüdtke, Alf. *The History of Everyday Life: Reconstructing Historical Experiences and Ways of Life*. Princeton: University Press, 1995.

Mac Con Uladh, Damian. "Guests of the socialist nation? Foreign students and workers in the GDR, 1949–1990." PhD diss., University of London, 2005.

Matusevich, Maxim. "Expanding the Boundaries of the Black Atlantic: African Students as Soviet Moderns". *Ab Imperio* 2 (2012): 325–350.

Pugach, Sara. "African Students and the Politics of Race and Gender in the German Democratic Republic." In *Comrades of Color: East Germany in the Cold War World*, edited by Quinn Slobodian, 131–156. New York: Berghahn Books, 2015.

Schleicher, Ilona. "Elemente entwicklungspolitischer Zusammenarbeit in der Tätigkeit von FDGB und FDJ." In *Entwicklungspolitische Zusammenarbeit in der Bundesrepublik Deutschland und der DDR*, edited by Hans-Jörg Bücking, 111–138. Berlin: Duncker & Humblot, 1998.

Schleicher, Ilona. "FDGB-Offensive in Westafrika: Der Gewerkschaftsverbund im Jahr Afrikas." In *Engagiert für Afrika: Die DDR und Afrika II*, edited by Ulrich van der Heyden, Hans-Georg Schleicher, and Ilona Schleicher, 82–93. Münster: LIT-Verlag, 1994.

Slobodian, Quinn. "Socialist Chromatism: Race, Racism, and the Racial Rainbow in East Germany." In *Comrades of Color: East Germany in the Cold War World*, edited by Quinn Slobodian, 23–42. New York: Berghahn Books, 2015.

Wagner, Bernd. "Zu rechtsextremen Entwicklungen in den neuen Bundesländern." In *AfrikaBilder. Studien zu Rassismus in Deutschland*, edited by Susan Arndt, 109–120. Münster: Unrast, 2006.

Weis, Toni. "The Politics Machine: On the Concept of 'Solidarity' in East German Support für SWAPO". *Journal of Southern African Studies* 37 (2011): 351–367.

Witkowski, Gregory. "Between Fighters and Beggars: Socialist Philantrophy and the Imagery of Solidarity." In *Comrades of Color: East Germany in the Cold War World*, edited by Quinn Slobodian, 73–94. New York: Berghahn Books, 2015.

Zelik, Raul. "Nach dem Kapitalismus: Warum der Staatssozialismus ökonomisch ineffizient war und was das für Alternativen heute bedeutet". *Prokla. Zeitschrift für kritische Sozialwissenschaft* 39 (2009): 207–227.

Franziska Rantzsch
5 The Negotiations of the Contract Labor Accord between the GDR and Mozambique

In October 1980, the Berliner Zeitung, one of the biggest dailies in the German Democratic Republic (GDR), published an article written by their popular economic journalist Dr. Karl-Heinz Gerstner about a visit by Mozambique's President Samora Machel:

> The encounters with Samora Machel will be remembered for a long time. I am not only referring to the warmth of our friendly feelings. It was also nice to hear from our African friend that the GDR has really helped Mozambique so far. At the meeting with the workers of the "Schwarze Pumpe" one saw in the first rows workers from Mozambique, who received their training here. In Halle, our friend met students from his homeland studying at the Martin Luther University. In the LPG [*Landwirtschaftliche Produktionsgenossenschaft*, agricultural production cooperative, F. R.] Lützen, he watched the potato harvest with modern farm machines. At the same time, 200 harvesters from Neustadt brought in the potato harvest in the Limpopo valley in Mozambique. Specialists in the blue shirts of the FDJ [*Freie Deutsche Jugend*, Free German Youth, F. R.] helped.[1]

The article presented a general view of the various kinds of development cooperation between the GDR and Mozambique for GDR citizens. For example, the state combine "Schwarze Pumpe" Gerstner referred to was involved in the coal mining project in Moatize, in the Mozambican province Tete, which started in 1978.[2] The FDJ's Friendship Brigades helped to construct accommodation for

---

[1] Original quote: "Die Begegnungen mit Samora Machel werden uns noch lange in Erinnerung bleiben. Ich meine nicht allein die Herzlichkeit unserer freundschaftlichen Gefühle. Es war uns auch angenehm, von unserem afrikanischen Freund zu hören: Was die DDR bisher für Mocambique getan hat, ist wirklich eine Hilfe. Bei dem Meeting mit den Arbeitern der Schwarzen Pumpe sah man in den ersten Reihen Arbeiter aus Mocambique, die hier ihre Ausbildung erhalten. In Halle traf unser Freund Studenten aus seiner Heimat, die an der Martin-Luther-Universität studieren. In der LPG Lützen beobachtete er die Kartoffelernte mit modernen Rodeladern. Zur gleichen Zeit fuhren im Tal des Reises bei Limpopo in Mocambique 200 Mähdrescher aus Neustadt die Ernte ein. Spezialisten im Blauhemd der FDJ halfen dabei". See Dr. Karl-Heinz Gerstner, "Hilfeleistung bei Lichte besehen," *Berliner Zeitung*, October 11, 1980, 9. Own translation.
[2] Heide Künanz, "Das Steinkohleprojekt Moatize zwischen solidarischer Hilfeleistung und kommerziellen Anspruch," in *Die DDR und Afrika: Zwischen Klassenkampf und neuem Denken*, ed. Ulrich van der Heyden et al. (Münster: Lit, 1993), 174–191.

miners at Moatize.³ Especially interesting is the fact that the article mentions the recruitment of contract workers from Mozambique among the numerous joint activities by the GDR and Mozambique that actually benefit Mozambique. In this respect, the article differs from the historical research on this subject. Most studies that focus on the economic history of the GDR read the recruitment of foreign workers as a strategy pursued solely to benefit the domestic economy of the GDR, not as part of a broadly conceived cooperation between the GDR and its allies in Africa and Asia.⁴ This approach has recently been questioned more frequently in historical research and instead analyses concentrate on the recruitment of contract workers from Mozambique in the context of the broader relations between the GDR and its partners.⁵ Admittedly, economic motives were crucial for the GDR's recruitment of contract workers, but nevertheless, in the Cold War era political-ideological motives were also important.

On February 24, 1979, the People's Republic of Mozambique and the GDR signed an accord on the temporary employment of Mozambican workers in socialist enterprises of the GDR in Maputo.⁶ This bilateral contract included nine-

---

3 Eric Burton, "Solidarität und ihre Grenzen: Die 'Brigaden der Freundschaft' der DDR," in *Internationale Solidarität: Globales Engagement in der Bundesrepublik und der DDR*, ed. Frank Bösch et al. (Göttingen: Wallstein Verlag, 2018), 152–185; Landolf Scherzer, "Meine Ankunft in Mosambik," in *Mosambikanische Vertragsarbeiter in der DDR-Wirtschaft: Hintergrund – Verlauf – Folgen*, ed. Ulrich van der Heyden et al. (Münster: Lit, 2014), 143–149.
4 Cf. Sandra Gruner-Domić, "Zur Geschichte der Arbeitskräftemigration in die DDR: Die bilateralen Verträge zur Beschäftigung ausländischer Arbeiter, 1961–1989", *Internationale wissenschaftliche Korrespondenz zur Geschichte der deutschen Arbeiterbewegung* 32 (1996): 204–230; Mirjam Schulz, "Migrationspolitik in der DDR: Bilaterale Anwerbungsverträge von Vertragsarbeitnehmern," in *Transit. Transfer: Politik und Praxis der Einwanderung in die DDR 1945– 1990*, ed. Kim Christian Priemel (Berlin: be.bra wissenschaft verlag, 2011), 143–168; Andreas Müggenburg, *Die ausländischen Vertragsarbeitnehmer in der ehemaligen DDR: Darstellung und Dokumentation* (Berlin: Die Beauftragte der Bundesregierung für die Belange der Ausländer, 1996).
5 Cf. Ulrich van der Heyden, *Das gescheiterte Experiment: Vertragsarbeiter aus Mosambik in der DDR-Wirtschaft (1979–1990)* (Leipzig: Leipziger Universitätsverlag, 2019), 394; Marcia Schenck, "Between Hammer, Machete, and Kalashnikov: Contract Labor Migration from Angola and Mozambique to East Germany, 1979–1990," *Europe Now* 15 (2018), accessed March 2018, https://www.europenowjournal.org/2018/02/28/between-hammer-machete-and-kalashnikov-contract-labor-migration-from-angola-and-mozambique-to-east-germany-1979-1990/.
6 Agreement between the Government of the GDR and the Government of the People's Republic of Mozambique on the temporary employment of Mozambican workers in socialist enterprises in the GDR (February 24, 1979) [Abkommen zwischen der Regierung der DDR und der Regierung der VR Mosambik über die zeitweilige Beschäftigung mosambikanischer Werktätiger in sozialistischen Betrieben der DDR (24. Februar 1979)], Political Archive of the Federal Foreign Office, Archives of the Ministry of Foreign Affairs of the GDR [Politisches Archiv des Auswärtigen Amtes,

teen articles and was amended or supplemented by annual protocols and subsequent agreements. The content of the accord was broad and supposed to regulate almost every detail of the procedure. Next to the scope and duration of the assignment, it also determined the precise definition of the areas of application, the organization of health checks for the workers, and the allocation of repatriation costs in case of death. This detailed subdivision can also be found in other contract labor accords, which the GDR concluded with Poland (1963) and Hungary (1967), but also with Cuba (1975) and Vietnam (1980).[7] The historical research often uses the finalized versions of the international accords as an analytical starting point. That the GDR profited from the contract labor accords cannot be denied, but it is also important to take a closer look at the interests of the sending country or in this case the Mozambican workers themselves.[8] As Ulrich van der Heyden noted in his extensive analysis of Mozambican contract workers, neither state has been outright forced to sign a contract labor accord. Nor were the Mozambican workers physically forced to report for deployment in the GDR. Instead, he pointed out that this was a project of development policy that was intended to benefit both sides.[9] I argue that an examination of the drafting and the process of negotiation of these accords as evidenced in the East German archives can contribute to a broader perspective on contract labor practices in the GDR. In this way, one can trace the range of possibilities in these negotiations, which allows us to draw conclusions about diplomatic relations between the GDR and Mozambique. Therefore, this analysis not only examines the intentions and demands that were made on both sides of the agree-

---

Archiv des Ministeriums für Auswärtige Angelegenheiten der DDR], Berlin (henceforth: PA AA, MfAA), ZR 970/87.

7 Cf. Rita Röhr, "Die Beschäftigung polnischer Arbeitskräfte in der DDR 1966–1990: Die vertraglichen Grundlagen und ihre Umsetzung," *Archiv für Sozialgeschichte* 42 (2002): 211–236; Katalin Jarosi, "Umschwärmte Kavaliere und gewinnbringende Ehemänner: Ungarische Vertragsarbeiter in der DDR," in *Arbeitsmigration: WanderarbeiterInnen auf dem Weltmarkt für Arbeitskraft*, ed. Thomas Geisen (Frankfurt a. M.: IKO, 2005), 197–216; Sandra Gruner-Domić, *Kubanische Arbeitsmigration in die DDR 1978–1989: Das Arbeitskräfteabkommen Kuba – DDR und dessen Realisierung* (Berlin: Ed. Parabolis, 1997); Christina Schwenkel, "Socialist Mobilities: Crossing New Terrains in Vietnamese Migration Histories," *Central and Eastern European Migration Review* 4 (2015): 13–25; Damian Mac Con Uladh, "Die Alltagserfahrungen ausländischer Vertragsarbeiter in der DDR: Vietnamesen, Kubaner, Mosambikaner, Ungarn und andere," in *Erfolg in der Nische? Die Vietnamesen in der DDR und in Ostdeutschland*, ed. Karin Weiss and Dennis Mike (Münster: Lit, 2005), 51–67.

8 See Machava, and Ibraimo and Schenck, this volume.

9 van der Heyden, *Das gescheiterte Experiment*, 394.

ment, but also, as far as possible, under what conditions the diplomatic negotiations were conducted.

In the first section, I discuss the historical precedents in creating labor migration agreements for both the GDR and Mozambique. Especially for the Mozambican side it is necessary to recognize, that the negotiation process of the contract labor accord constitutes a socialist encounter that stood at the end of the entangled labor history with South Africa and at the beginning of a new history of entanglement between the GDR and Mozambique and entailed new moorings, linked to the resulting labor migration to East Germany. After that, I focus on the role of the contract labor accord as part of a process of intensifying political relations between those states. In addition, it is important to take into account the development politics of the GDR in the "Third World,"[10] and especially in states that officially proclaimed a socialist political course, as this deeply influenced the ideological conceptions of contract labor accords. Thus, the meaning of "international solidarity" as an expression of mutual advantage as part of the creation of the bilateral accord will also be questioned. The analysis is based on negotiating guidelines and reports from the Secretariat for Labor and Wages and the related decisions of the Council of Ministers of the GDR, as well as agreements signed by the Secretariat for Labor and Wages and the Ministry of Labor of the People's Republic of Mozambique. These documents primarily help to reconstruct the intensions of the GDR, but they also give limited insight into the demands and reactions of the Mozambican side. Unfortunately, these documents cannot reflect the planning processes of the Mozambican government. The analysis takes place from the perspective of the GDR and its dealings with the Mozambican side in the negotiation process. What demands did the GDR make on Mozambique and how did the GDR deal with the demands of the Mozambican side? In this context, it will be demonstrated that Mozambique had a voice in shaping the agreement and that controversies arose on both sides due to a lack of knowledge about each other, which had a lasting impact on the negotiations. Finally, a brief outlook on the further course of the labor agreement will be given.

---

10 In the GDR, and elsewhere in the post-war era, the term "Third World" was used to denote new states that emerged in Asia, Africa, and Latin America as part of the decolonization process that did not clearly fit into a bipolar Cold War division of the world. Based on theories of modernization these countries were also considered as being economically backward and thus "underdeveloped"; see Jürgen Dinkel, "'Dritte Welt' – Geschichte und Semantiken, Version: 1.0," *Docupedia-Zeitgeschichte* (2014), accessed October 6, 2014, doi:10.14765/zzf.dok.2.596.v1.

Previous Labor Migration Agreements

By 1978, the GDR was able to look back on extensive experience in the negotiation of labor migration agreements. The first accord on the employment of foreign workers was concluded by the Socialist Unity Party (*Sozialistische Einheitspartei Deutschlands*, SED) with Poland in 1963. After that, a whole series of other bilateral agreements with socialist or at least socialist-leaning states followed: Hungary (1967), Algeria (1974), and Cuba (1975).[11] Although the authorities had gained some experience in dealing with foreign workers since the 1960s, the specific characteristics of every country forced the responsible bureaucrats to adapt individually to the new foreign workers after each agreement – a task that involved the Ministry of State Security (MfS or Stasi), especially in monitoring the foreign workers. Thus, it was not unusual for the Stasi to prepare an evaluation of the planned agreement with Mozambique.[12] Since the surveillance of foreigners fell within the remit of state security, the so-called "Foreigners Working Group" (*AG Ausländer*) was created as part of the Department of Counterintelligence in 1980 to centralize this task. According to the Stasi, foreigners (*Ausländer*) were defined as "all people, who are not GDR citizens who reside in the territory of the GDR."[13] This included Soviet occupying forces, political emigrants, foreign students, and also contract workers from Africa, Asia, and Latin America. The special observation status was justified by the SED government, on the one hand, based on the almost paranoid fear of hostile attacks against the GDR and, on the other hand, the concerns for GDR prestige abroad.

For Mozambique, state-induced temporary labor migration was also not a novelty. Since the nineteenth century, labor migration between southern Mozambique and South African mines was one of the most significant aspects of the

---

[11] Cf. Röhr, "Die Beschäftigung polnischer Arbeitskräfte in der DDR 1966–1990," 211–236; Jarosi, "Umschwärmte Kavaliere und gewinnbringende Ehemänner: Ungarische Vertragsarbeiter in der DDR," 197–216; Gruner-Domić, *Kubanische Arbeitsmigration in die DDR 1978–1989*; Mac Con Uladh, "Die Alltagserfahrungen ausländischer Vertragsarbeiter in der DDR," 51–67.
[12] Opinion on the draft decision about the deployment of Mozambican workers in the GDR (March 26, 1979) [Meinungsäußerung zum Beschlussentwurf über den Einsatz mosambikanischer Werktätiger in der DDR (26. März 1979)], Federal Commissioner for the Records of the State Security Service of the former German Democratic Republic Stasi Records Agency [Bundesbeauftragte für die Unterlagen des Staatssicherheitsdienstes der ehemaligen Deutschen Demokratischen Republik], Berlin (henceforth: BStU), MfS, Abt. X, Nr. 812, sheet 129–130.
[13] Lecture as part of a political-technical training by the Ministry of State Security (undated) [Vortrag im Rahmen einer politisch-technischen Ausbildung durch das Ministerium für Staatssicherheit (undatiert)], BStU, MfS, HA II, Nr. 28659, sheet 7–49. Own translation.

two countries' economic and social relationship. During Portuguese colonial rule, nearly one third of the male population in the south of Mozambique was contracted to the mines for between 12 and 18 months at a time; the vast majority of the migration took place within a state-managed framework, a few migrants found their way to South Africa along different routes.[14] The migration of Mozambican miners was an important economic factor for the Portuguese and also for the British colonial rulers in South Africa. For example, in 1928, it was agreed that at least 65,000 Mozambican workers should work in the mines in South Africa. This number increased to nearly 100,000 by the mid 1930s. The Great Depression of 1929, however, had a negative impact on almost all sectors of the South African economy and gold mining was no exception. As a result, many South Africans sought work in the mines, which eventually led to a decline in demand of Mozambican labor.[15] However, the number of Mozambicans working in the mines was still very high. That did not change until the mid 1970s. After Mozambique gained its independence under the leadership of the Mozambique Liberation Front (Frente de Libertação de Moçambique, FRELIMO) in 1975, the bilateral contracts for labor migration with South Africa remained basically in place, although the number of recruits dropped significantly. The main reasons for this were the consequences of investing in the mechanization of work, the will of mine operators to be less dependent on migrant workers, and the increased price of gold, which made it possible to pay higher wages and make work more attractive to the local population. While not all Mozambican migrant workers were dismissed because their experience could not be easily replaced, hardly any new workers were recruited.[16]

After independence, Mozambique faced major economic problems. The colonial economy the Portuguese rulers had built primarily based on the production of agricultural goods was labor export-oriented. Also the rapid exodus of the formerly Portuguese settlers—including many skilled workers—during and after the independence process left the Mozambican economy in disarray and was anoth-

---

14 Barry Munslow, "State Intervention in Agriculture: The Mozambican Experience," *The Journal of Modern African Studies* 22 (1984): 200; see also Sara Mercandalli, Christopher Changwe Nshimbi, and Inocent Moyo, "Mozambican Labour Migrations, Remittances and Development: Evidence, Practices and Implications for Policy," in *Migration, Cross-Border Trade and Development in Africa: Exploring the Role of Non-State Actors in the SADC Region*, ed. Sara Mercandalli et al. (Cham: Palgrave Macmillan, 2017), 18.
15 Napoleão Gaspar, "The Reduction of Mozambican Workers in South African Mines, 1975–1992: A Case Study of the Consequences for Gaza Province – District of Chibuto" (PhD diss., Universidade Eduardo Mondlane, 2006), accessed May 16, 2008, hdl.handle.net/10539/4839, 31–32.
16 Gaspar, "The Reduction of Mozambican Workers in South African Mines," 41–42.

er obstacle to the industrialization of the country.[17] The decline in the use of migrant labor in the 1930s had already shown how much Mozambique was dependent on the South African economy, especially its labor market. Therefore, the leaders of FRELIMO initially stuck to this concept, because they were unable to create employment alternatives for migrant workers in the south of the country after taking power.[18] In the long term, however, FRELIMO decided that sending miners to South Africa should be discontinued. The Mozambican government, especially after the party congress in 1977, pursued a Marxist-Leninist policy that explicitly aimed to break away from dependence on the South African economy. Its new leaders believed that industrialization, strengthening of the public sector, and the development of collective peasant structures would finally raise Mozambique to the status of a developed socialist state.[19] To this end, FRELIMO aimed to change the dynamics that created labor migration, mainly focused on the migrant workers to South Africa, and to productively reintegrate them into the Mozambican economy. Nevertheless, new methods had to be found to sustainably relieve the pressure on the domestic labor market and the intensification of relations with the GDR offered the Mozambican government an opportunity in this area. The sending of workers to the GDR was intended to remove unemployed unskilled workers from the domestic labor market for a certain period of time and then to reintegrate them after that as skilled workers into the domestic economy. Unlike the previous migrations to South Africa this time skills training was an important factor for the Mozambican government preparing to build a more industrialized country. After independence and the resulting departure of Portuguese skilled labor, it was urgently necessary for the Mozambican economy to make up for the ensuing shortage.[20]

---

17 Allen Isaacman and Barbara Isaacman, *Mozambique: From Colonialism to Revolution, 1900 – 1982* (Boulder et al.: Westview Press 1983), 145.
18 Ramos Cardoso Muanamoha, "The Dynamics of Undocumented Mozambican Labour Migration to South Africa" (PhD diss., University of KwaZulu-Natal, 2008), accessed March 2008, http://www.repositorio.uem.mz/handle/123456789/278, 39 – 40.
19 Hector Guerra Hernandez, "Cooperación para el desarrollo en tiempos de internacionalismo: Los hombres nuevos de Machel," *Vibrant – Virtual Brazilian Anthropology* 9 (2012): 567; Grete Brochmann, "Migrant Labour and Foreign Policy: The Case of Mozambique," *Journal of Peace Research* 22 (1985): 337.
20 Cf. Hector Guerra Hernandez, "Ma(d)jermanes: passado colonial e presente diasporizado: reconstrução etnográfica de um dos últimos vestígios do socialismo colonial europeu" (PhD diss., Universidade Estadual de Campinas, 2011), accessed August 19, 2018, http://www.repositorio.unicamp.br/handle/REPOSIP/280790; Hector Guerra Hernandez, "RAND à RDA? Modernização compulsória e práticas sociais e estratégias de mobilidade social," *(con) textos: Revista d'antropologia i investigació social* 3 (2009): 61 – 83.

Intensification of Foreign Relations

After the official founding of the People's Republic of Mozambique in 1975, the country faced numerous problems. Although FRELIMO had prevailed, a civil war lasting over 15 years against the anti-communist Mozambican National Resistance (Resistência Nacional Moçambicana, RENAMO), backed primarily by South Africa, the USA and West Germany, followed formal independence.[21] Apartheid South Africa, an important trading partner of the former colony Mozambique, also tried to undermine the new state and its economy. Furthermore, after the exodus of Portuguese settlers, Mozambique required skilled workers to develop its industries.[22] Thus, the new government under the leadership of FRELIMO sought supporters. It focused mainly on the states of the Eastern bloc and, to an extent, to Scandinavian countries and their solidarity committees, because the NATO members had—if not officially, at least in their de facto politics—sided with their partner Portugal in the struggle over who was to rule Mozambique. Since the middle of the 1960s, the GDR had financially supported FRELIMO as a liberation movement against Portuguese colonialism. Based on this early financial aid FRELIMO hoped for a deepening of economic and political ties with East Berlin after it seized power. Around that time West Germany had abandoned its claim to be the only representative of Germany (in accordance with the so-called "Hallstein Doctrine"). In 1973, both states were admitted to join the United Nations and consequently East Berlin started opening embassies all over the world. At first, however, the GDR hesitated to upgrade its relations with Mozambique, because FRELIMO had not so far announced its economic and social orientation now that it had taken control of the former colony. Only in February 1977, after President Samora Machel clearly declared his support for socialism to the SED envoy Werner Lamberz[23] at the Third FRELIMO Congress

---

21 Odd Arne Westad, *The Global Cold War: Third World Interventions and the Making of Our Times* (Cambridge: Cambridge University Press, 2007), 207–218; Margaret Hall and Tom Young, *Confronting Leviathan: Mozambique since Independence* (London: Hurst & Company 1997), 131–133.
22 Peter Meyns, *Konflikt und Entwicklung im südlichen Afrika* (Opladen: Leske + Budrich, 2000), 181.
23 Werner Lamberz (1929–1978): since 1967 Lamberz was secretary of the Central Committee and since 1971 member of the SED-Politburo. He was founding vice president of the German-African Society and had considerable influence on the re-profiling of the Africa policy of the GDR. He died in a helicopter crash in Libya on March 6, 1978; see Ulf Engel and Hans-Georg Schleicher, *Die beiden deutschen Staaten in Afrika: Zwischen Konkurrenz und Koexistenz 1949–1990* (Hamburg: Institut für Afrika-Kunde, 1998), 110–113.

did the GDR agree to forge closer ties.[24] With its official commitment to socialism, Mozambique became one of the most important countries for the GDR's foreign policy of international solidarity in the ideological conflict between capitalism and socialism.

As a result, an "immediate program" (*Sofortprogramm*) was agreed upon by the two nations that same year at the Leipzig Autumn Trade Fair, which set in motion the deepening of economic ties between the two states. In November 1977, an "Agreement on Economic and Scientific-Technical Cooperation", signed by Horst Sölle (Minister of Foreign Trade) and Marcelino dos Santos (Minister of Planning and Development), followed. It included a variety of joint projects for the extraction of raw materials in Mozambique, especially pit coal. Among other things, the GDR was supposed to send experts and advisors to provide and set up industrial equipment. The culmination of this partnership were Erich Honecker's trips to Africa in February and November 1979, visiting Libya, Angola, Zambia, Mozambique, and Ethiopia. He was accompanied by a high-ranked delegation consisting of Willi Stoph (Chairman of the Council of Ministers), Hermann Axen (Secretary of the Central Committee, foreign policy commission), Günter Mittag (Secretary of the Central Committee, economic issues), Oskar Fischer (Minister for Foreign Affairs), Julian Hollender (Ambassador of the GDR to the People's Republic of Mozambique, 1978–1981) and also by a group of "experts" from the Department of International Connections of the Central Committee of the SED, the Ministry of Foreign Affairs and the Ministry of Foreign Trade.[25] At the end of their visit to Mozambique, a "Treaty of Friendship and Cooperation" was signed in Maputo. The conclusion of further agreements of a political or economic nature, including an agreement on the temporary employment of Mozambican workers in the GDR, followed during Honecker's stay in Mozambique.[26]

---

24 Hans-Joachim Döring, *"Es geht um unsere Existenz." Die Politik der DDR gegenüber der Dritten Welt am Beispiel von Mosambik und Äthiopien* (Berlin: Ch. Links, 2001), 143–150.
25 Schedule for the visit of the GDR party and state delegation headed by Erich Honecker in the People's Republic of Mozambique (February 1979) [Zeitplan für den Besuch der DDR-Partei und der Staatsdelegation unter der Leitung von Erich Honecker in der Volksrepublik Mosambik (Februar 1979)], PA AA, MfAA ZR, 2288/89.
26 Döring, *"Es geht um unsere Existenz,"* 159–161.

Planning and Shaping of "International Solidarity"

In view of diplomatic relations and the contracts concluded up to that point, at this time—from a GDR perspective—it was possible to speak of an "equal partnership" between the GDR and Mozambique. Though Mozambique was not indeed on the same level of experience in the negotiation of labor migration as the GDR, according to the official discourse, their economic relations would be following the principle of mutual benefit. According to the GDR Foreign Policy Dictionary of 1980, the term "international solidarity" encompasses an extension of the class-based behavioral principles of "togetherness, consensus, mutual support and commitment, support and sacrifice." "International solidarity" in this context stood for the "fraternal cohesion of the revolutionary department of a country with the international revolutionary labor movement, with all allies in the anti-imperialist struggle." In the correlation with development policy, priority has been given to the principle of so-called "socialist economic aid," which according to the dictionary definition was founded "on the basis of equality, non-discrimination and mutual benefit" and should serve "free of exploitation, acquisition of property and sovereignty-infringing conditions [...] political independence, development of the national economy in general and social progress of young states."[27] Socialist economic aid was closely linked to the concept of "international solidarity." However, with the Commercial Coordination Division (*Bereich Kommerzielle Koordinierung*, commonly known as KoKo), under direction of Alexander Schalck-Golodkowski and responsible for the procurement of convertible foreign currency, there was another level that had a lasting impact on the GDR's economic cooperation with countries in the Global South. As Berthold Unfried shows, it is difficult to draw a clear dividing line between regular economic relations and development policy measures, since the two levels often influenced each other.[28] That is what happened in regard to the contract labor accord between the GDR and Mozambique – educational aid merged with economic interests.

---

27 Institut für Internationale Beziehungen an der Akademie für Staats- und Rechtswissenschaft der DDR, ed., *Wörterbuch der Außenpolitik und des Völkerrechts* (Berlin: Dietz Verlag, 1980), 150–152, 528. Own translation.
28 Berthold Unfried, "Instrumente und Praktiken von 'Solidarität' Ost und 'Entwicklungshilfe' West: Blickpunkt auf das entsandte Personal," in *Die eine Welt schaffen: Praktiken von 'Internationaler Solidarität' und 'Internationaler Entwicklung'*, ed. Berthold Unfried and Eva Himmelstoss (Leipzig: AVA, 2012), 77.

Already at the beginning of the 1980s, the GDR was facing rapidly increasing economic problems and Mozambique was no longer able to adhere to the terms of the treaties due to its intensifying civil war. This was the beginning, when the balance ran aground. Mainly because the railway connecting the pit coal mining complex Moatize with the port of Beira suffered from continuous sabotage from RENAMO rebels, Mozambique was not able to fulfill its coal delivery agreements; so as a result, debt began to accumulate towards the GDR.[29] Also, the GDR faced increasing economic problems and actively pursued the acquisition of foreign exchange. Thus, both states were confronted with problems that came to have a lasting effect on the further course of the contract labor migration.

The international development policy commitments of the GDR consisted of several branches: First, in the realm of foreign trade, there were preferential price contracts, awarding of favorable loans, bartering, and free services. This was intended to strengthen the economic relations between the GDR and Mozambique and, in accordance with the socialist principle of trade, both sides should benefit. As a result, the GDR countered its counterparties' lending terms and paid amounts well above normal market prices due to closed preference price agreements for commodity imports. Because of constant shortages of foreign exchange, which resulted mainly from the existing import surpluses, trade with Mozambique was mostly based on a direct exchange of commodities for commodities.[30] It is important to emphasize that bartering with countries of the Global South was in many cases beneficial for the GDR, as it enabled to cheaply buy raw materials, thus saved important foreign exchange.[31] In addition to GDR development policy involvement, such as the supply of agricultural machinery and the assistance of Free German Youth (FDJ) brigades, the support also included "educational aid."[32] For example, the GDR Solidarity Committee promoted the training of foreign students with scholarships.[33] However, the training

---

29 Künanz, "Das Steinkohleprojekt Moatize zwischen solidarischer Hilfeleistung und kommerziellen Anspruch," 179–184.
30 Verburg, Maria Magdalena, *Ostdeutsche Dritte-Welt-Gruppen vor und nach 1989/90* (Göttingen: V & R Unipress, 2012), 24.
31 Cf. Anne Dietrich, "Kaffee in der DDR – 'Ein Politikum ersten Ranges'," in *Kaffeewelten: Historische Perspektiven auf eine globale Ware im 20. Jahrhundert*, ed. Christiane Berth et al. (Göttingen: Vandenhoeck & Ruprecht, 2015), 225–247; Immanuel R. Harisch, "Bartering Coffee, Cocoa and W50 Trucks: The Trade Relationships of the GDR, Angola and São Tomé in a Comparative Perspective," *Global Histories* 3 (2017): 43–60.
32 See Piepiorka and Buanaissa, this volume.
33 There was no overarching ministry in the GDR that coordinated development measures. Instead, the management of the projects and the negotiation of agreements with the countries concerned fell within the area of responsibility of the respective state authorities, such as the Min-

of Mozambican workers was a mixture of development aid and economic benefits. Already in the run-up to the "Agreement on Economic and Scientific-Technical Cooperation," concluded on November 15, 1977, the Mozambican government asked the GDR, if it is possible to send 50 to 100 Mozambican workers to the GDR for vocational training. Thus, from September 1978, the first group of 65 workers came to the GDR and was trained to work in the cement industry, the transporting sector, and in the sugar industry. This sector selection was based on the key industries of the Mozambican economy. The trainees had to complete a five-month language course in German before starting the two-year vocational training. The Ministry of Foreign Trade and the relevant Ministries of Economic Affairs were primarily responsible for the organization, financing, and implementation of the vocational qualification.[34]

At this point, it is important to emphasize that the vocational training of workers based on the "Agreement on Economic and Scientific-Technical Cooperation" – was not the same type of vocational training that was later part of the contract labor accord from 1979. Instead of vocational training, the contract labor accord stipulated that the assignment was linked to the simultaneous provision of practical work experience as a part of providing productive activity and vocational education and training in the context of in-company adult qualification.[35] In contrast to direct financial support, this form of "development aid" was feasible for the GDR since it was resource-efficient enough to be financed on the

---

istry of Foreign Affairs or the Secretariat for Labor and Wages. Despite this division of competence areas, all positions were subject to the instructions of the Central Committee of the SED. The only institution that commanded a concentrated coordination center for "development aid" was the Solidarity Committee of the GDR. This social organization was primarily responsible for the implementation of "international solidarity". The area of responsibility of the committee included the procurement of financial and material funds for development policy projects as well as the support of anti-imperialist liberation movements in Asia, Africa, and Latin America; see Hans-Joachim Spanger, and Lothar Brock, *Die beiden deutschen Staaten in der Dritten Welt: Die Entwicklungspolitik der DDR – Eine Herausforderung für die Bundesrepublik Deutschland?* (Opladen: Westdeutscher Verlag, 1987), 214–217.

34 Presidium of the Council of Ministers of the GDR, resolution on the proposal on the professional qualification of citizens of Mozambique in the GDR (October 27, 1977) [Präsidium des Ministerrats der DDR, Beschluss zum Vorschlag über die berufliche Qualifizierung von Bürgern der VR Mosambik in der DDR (27. Oktober 1977)], BStU, MfS, HA II, Nr. 32490, sheet 4–8.

35 Agreement between the Government of the GDR and the Government of the People's Republic of Mozambique on the temporary employment of Mozambican workers in socialist enterprises in the GDR (February 24, 1979) [Abkommen zwischen der Regierung der DDR und der Regierung der VR Mosambik über die zeitweilige Beschäftigung mosambikanischer Werktätiger in sozialistischen Betrieben der DDR (24. Februar 1979)], PA AA, MfAA, ZR 970/87.

limited East German budget of convertible currencies. Moreover, such an approach was seen to be not only economically, but also ideologically useful.[36]

In the first draft of the contract labor accord it was already stated that the vocational qualification was oriented both to the existing technical installations in Mozambique and to the key industries of the national economy. Furthermore, workers should only be employed in areas in which they had already gained practical experience.[37] This was intended to ensure that the workers could actually use the acquired knowledge after their return to Mozambique. It was also stipulated that workers should be given the opportunity to continue their professional education at GDR enterprises after their regular working time. In general, however, the Secretariat for Labor and Wages did not undertake any obligation to achieve specific qualification goals in its concept paper.[38] These were instead ultimately determined between the workers and the companies through respective qualification contracts.[39] This practice gave the contract workers a certain degree of individual responsibility, which was, however, fundamentally dependent on the actual implementation of the requirements of the enterprises.

Since the civil servants in the Secretariat for Labor and Wages, like Horst Rademacher (1967–1977), and later Wolfgang Beyreuther (1977–1989) already had some experience in the preparation of such negotiations, it took only a few months to finalize the negotiation plans with Mozambique. In September 1978, initial calculations were made internally to determine and optimize the economic value of the contract labor. In a letter to Wolfgang Beyreuther, an employee of the Ministry of Foreign Affairs indicated that the "additional financial burden of training a foreign citizen to become a skilled worker" would cost between 8,000 and 9,000 East German Marks (DDM) per year, with the extra output generated in production amounting to 12,000 to 15,000 DDM. As a result, Beyreuther was ad-

---

36 Eric Allina, " 'Neue Menschen für Mosambik.' Erwartungen an und Realität von Vertragsarbeit in der DDR der 1980er-Jahre," *Arbeit, Bewegung, Geschichte: Zeitschrift für historische Studien* 3 (2016): 66.
37 Concept paper for the temporary employment of working people from developing countries in the production process of national enterprises of the GDR (September 6, 1978) [Konzeption zur zeitweiligen Beschäftigung von Werktätigen aus Entwicklungsländern im Produktionsprozess volkseigener Betriebe der DDR (6. September 1978)], BStU, MfS, HA II, Nr. 32493, sheet 63–67.
38 Ibid.
39 See article 9, paragraph 2 in Agreement between the Government of the GDR and the Government of the People's Republic of Mozambique on the temporary employment of Mozambican workers in socialist enterprises in the GDR (February 24, 1979) [Abkommen zwischen der Regierung der DDR und der Regierung der VR Mosambik über die zeitweilige Beschäftigung mosambikanischer Werktätiger in sozialistischen Betrieben der DDR (24. Februar 1979)], PA AA, MfAA, ZR 970/87.

vised to suggest to the Council of Ministers "that it would be more expedient for the GDR from 1982 onwards—and with a lower foreign exchange burden—to aim for two years of vocational training followed by 2–3 years of work in the GDR."[40] A more detailed breakdown of these calculations can be found in an appraisal of the economic costs and benefits of using Mozambicans in GDR enterprises in the formal decision to implement the agreement of May 1979. It calculated that, for 2,000 Mozambican contract workers, the cost for the GDR would be around 15 million DDM, whereas the annual production value of the additional labor force was estimated to be 20 million DDM. Thus, the letter concluded: "Expenditure and economic benefits of the employment of Mozambican workers for the GDR are likely to balance each other."[41] The GDR would not make a large profit, but would be able to maintain its own production.

The training of workers was also an important aspect of the FRELIMO policy program.

> Increasing training of workers and peasants in the field of the science and technique of the productive process is a decisive front in the battle for complete independence. On a par with the development of education, all structures—state or private—should, in a co-ordinated way, launch permanent and successive professional training activities for the nation's workers.[42]

Overcoming colonial structures and building up an independent economy was the top priority for Mozambique. In this context, especially the integration of young people into the labor market was particularly important.

> We must give special attention to involving young people who have completed their studies in productive activity. To put an end to anarchy in the labour market, a body must be set up

---

40 Note on the draft accord (September 19, 1978) [Anmerkung zum Abkommensentwurf (19. September 1978)], Federal Archives, Foundation Archives of Political Parties and Mass Organizations in the GDR [Stiftung Archiv der Parteien und Massenorganisationen der DDR im Bundesarchiv], Berlin (henceforth: SAPMO-BArch), DQ3/1026. Own translation.
41 Decision of the Presidium of the Council of Ministers of the GDR on the implementation of the Agreement (February 24, 1979) with the Government of the People's Republic of Mozambique on the temporary employment of Mozambican working people in socialist enterprises in the GDR (May 31, 1979) [Beschluss des Präsidium des Ministerrates der DDR vom 31. Mai 1979 über die Durchführung des Abkommens vom 24. Februar 1979 mit der Regierung der VR Mosambik über die zeitweilige Beschäftigung mosambikanischer Werktätiger in sozialistischen Betrieben der DDR], BStU, MfS, HA II, Nr. 32490, sheet 32–44.
42 Samora Moisés Machel, "Central Committee Report [to the Third Congress], Maputo" (published June 6, 1978. Translation into English by the Mozambique-Angola-Guiné Information Centre (MAGIC), London), 56–57.

to make sure these young people are employed in a planned way, taking into consideration their technical and political qualities, and the priorities for the country's development.[43]

The labor accord with the GDR promised to carry out the economic plans, which were formulated on the Third Congress of FRELIMO, held in February 1977.

The agreement was supposed to benefit both sides. Mozambique profited from the training of its workers, the relief of the domestic labor market and the creation of professional prospects for young people. For the GDR, it solved the labor shortage that seriously threatened economic production. To maintain and increase production was a central aspect of the SED government's claim to power. After all, with his program of "unity of economic and social policy" (*Einheit von Wirtschafts- und Sozialpolitik*) Honecker had promised an increase in the standard of living in the GDR.[44] In addition, the training of skilled workers in the designated workers' and peasants' state GDR represented a form of truly "international solidarity" for the SED leadership and its propaganda machine.

The Negotiations of the Contract Labor Accord

On October 12, 1978, one month after the initial calculations, the Presidium of the Council of Ministers of the GDR decided to enter into negotiations with the Mozambican government for a contract labor accord that worked independently of the "Agreement on Economic and Scientific-Technical Cooperation."[45] These documents formed the basis for the first talks on the draft accord with a delega-

---

43 Ibid., 64.
44 Joint decision of the Central Committee of the SED, the Federal Executive of the FDGB and the Council of Ministers of the GDR on social policy measures in the implementation of the main task of the five-year plan decided on at the 8th SED Party Congress, (April 28, 1972) [Gemeinsamer Beschluss des Zentralkomitees der SED, der Bundesleitung des FDGB und des Ministerrates der DDR über sozialpolitische Maßnahmen zur Umsetzung der Hauptaufgabe des auf dem 8. SED-Parteitag beschlossenen Fünfjahresplans (28. April 1972)], printed in Günter Benser, ed., *Dokumente zur Geschichte der SED, Vol. 3: 1971–1986* (Berlin: Dietz Verlag, 1986), 73–74.
45 Decision on the guideline for negotiations with the Government of the Republic of Mozambique about the preparation of an intergovernmental agreement on the temporary employment of Mozambican workers in socialist enterprises in the GDR (October 12, 1978) [Beschluss zur Direktive für die Verhandlungen mit der Regierung der VR Mosambik zur Vorbereitung eines Regierungsabkommens über die zeitweilige Beschäftigung mosambikanischer Werktätiger in sozialistischen Betrieben der DDR (12. Oktober 1978)], BStU, MfS, HA II, Nr. 32490, sheet 9–22.

tion from Mozambique, under the direction of Amandio Chongo[46] (Ministry of Labor, Department for Vocational Training), held in East Berlin.[47] As part of these negotiations, some questions, for example the determination of health suitability, early termination of the employment contract and vacation trips of the workers to Mozambique, remained open and had to be clarified internally by the SED. In addition, the Mozambican representatives had made some new proposals, like a vacation day for Mozambican workers on the Mozambican national day and the supply of workers with press products from Mozambique, which also needed to be discussed.[48] At the beginning of February 1979, a delegation of the Secretariat for Labor and Wages, consisting of Ingolf Noack (deputy), Ernst-Otto Jacobs (head of inspection) and Lutz Hoepner (interpreter), traveled to Mozambique to continue the negotiation of the agreement with the Mozambican Ministry of Labor, under direction of Alberto Cassimo (Minister of Labor).[49] Based on the revised version of the negotiating guideline, it is easy to understand which critical points had to be discussed in detail during this

---

46 Amandio Rafael Moises Chongo (*1945) joined FRELIMO in Tanzania in the mid-1960s. There he received his first military training, which he perfected especially in the field of artillery with a training period in the Soviet Union in 1966. After that he was then an active military fighter but also took care of the military and political training of guerrillas. In the summer of 1970, he lost a leg during a fight and worked until 1976 as a diplomatic relations manager for FRELIMO in Italy. Then he joined the Ministry of Labor, Department for Vocational Training; source: "Amandio Rafael Moises Chongo", Archive portal of the IBC network of Emilia-Romagna, accessed July 26, 2020, http://archivi.ibc.regione.emilia-romagna.it/ibc-cms/cms.find?&id=produttori&.titolo=chongo&numDoc=8&munu_str=0_1_2&.date=&archType=auther&perpage=30&realTemplate=templateRicercaProduttori&flagfind=customXdamsFindProduttori&.q=&fromId=y&qrId=3se4482248f8810101&physDoc=961&pos=0&archType=auther#nogo.

47 Joint minutes of the delegation visit by representatives of the Mozambican Ministry of Labor in Berlin (November 6, 1978) [Gemeinsames Protokoll zum Delegationsbesuch von Vertretern des mosambikanischen Arbeitsministeriums in Berlin (6. November 1978)], SAPMO-BArch, DQ3/1026.

48 Guideline for the negotiations with a delegation of the Ministry of Labor of the Republic of Mozambique in Maputo (February 1979) about the preparation of the intergovernmental Agreement on the temporary employment of Mozambican workers in the GDR (undated) [Direktive für die Verhandlungen mit einer Delegation des Arbeitsministeriums der Volksrepublik Mosambik in Maputo (Februar 1979) über die Vorbereitung eines zwischenstaatlichen Abkommens zur befristeten Beschäftigung mosambikanischer Werktätiger in der DDR (undatiert)], BStU, MfS, HA II, Nr. 32490, sheet 23–30.

49 Telegram from the GDR ambassador Julian Hollender about the preparation of the delegation talks between the Secretariat for Labor and Wages of the GDR and the Ministry of Labor in Mozambique (January 17, 1979) [Telegramm des DDR-Botschafters Julian Hollender über die Vorbereitung der Delegationsgespräche zwischen dem Staatssekretariat für Arbeit und Löhne der DDR und dem Arbeitsministerium in Mosambik (17. Januar 1979)], SAPMO-BArch, DQ3/1026.

time. In it, individual paragraphs of the first draft accord were listed and clearly formulated along with how many concessions could be granted by the GDR representatives to the Mozambican delegation. These formulations were partially supplemented with detailed justifications.

As a first example, the GDR demanded a joint medical commission to determine the fitness of prospective contract workers. The primary aim was that Mozambique should cover all costs for East German doctors to travel to Mozambique as well as their room and board once they arrived. If this proposal was not approved by Alberto Cassimo, the delegation members could propose to share the costs, so that the GDR took over the travel expenses while Mozambique would finance the accommodation. If this should be rejected by the Mozambicans as well, it could also be agreed that the investigation be carried out by doctors from Mozambique alone. The guideline stipulated, however, that this provision should then be carefully enforced and that an involvement of foreign doctors presently deployed in Mozambique, mainly Chinese or Portuguese, should be excluded.[50] The results of the negotiations can be found in the report of the Secretariat for Labor and Wages from February 23, 1979, one day before the accord was signed: In the end, the Mozambican side agreed to take over the subsistence costs of the GDR doctors, which meant that the Mozambican government had rejected assuming the full cost of the inspections.[51] This point shows that the GDR was willing to compromise, and that the SED negotiators did not aim to impose its demands by any means necessary, especially because the GDR economy would also benefit from the envisaged contract.

As we can see on the basis of the archived protocols of the negotiation process, the Mozambican representatives of FRELIMO were not merely reactive players during the phase of negotiations, and they brought their own interests and

---

50 Guideline for the negotiations with a delegation of the Ministry of Labor of the Republic of Mozambique in Maputo (February 1979) about the preparation of the intergovernmental Agreement on the temporary employment of Mozambican workers in the GDR (undated) [Direktive für die Verhandlungen mit einer Delegation des Arbeitsministeriums der Volksrepublik Mosambik in Maputo (Februar 1979) über die Vorbereitung eines zwischenstaatlichen Abkommens zur befristeten Beschäftigung mosambikanischer Werktätiger in der DDR (undatiert)], BStU, MfS, HA II, Nr. 32490, sheet 23–30.
51 Report of the Secretariat for Labor and Wages on the negotiations on the Agreement between the Government of the GDR and the People's Republic of Mozambique (February 13–20, 1979) about the temporary employment of Mozambican working people in the GDR in Maputo (February 23, 1979) [Bericht des SAL über die Verhandlungen zum Abkommen zwischen der Regierung der DDR und der VR Mosambik (13.–20. Februar 1979) über die zeitweilige Beschäftigung mosambikanischer Werktätiger in der DDR in Maputo (23. Februar 1979)], BStU, MfS, HA II, Nr. 32490, sheet 91–96.

ideas to the discussion. In the draft prepared by the GDR, the section on premature termination of employment contracts stipulate that this could be done if the worker made himself liable to punishment, violated so-called "socialist labor discipline,"[52] or if he was out of work for more than three months due to illness.[53] In return, Alberto Cassimo demanded, that it should be possible to initiate a premature termination of the employment contract in the event of a breach of duty by GDR enterprises or due to extenuating Mozambican state interests. Cassimo justified this demand with the fact that the party leadership of FRELIMO decided that workers who do not stick to their revolutionary mandate should be sent back immediately.[54] The GDR agreed to this proposal without protest. The report also stated, however, that further arrangements still had to be made in this regard. They decided that if an East German company does not fulfill its obligations, the employment relationship could but did not necessarily have to be dissolved. In cooperation with the Mozambican partner, it should be explored if the transfer of a worker to another enterprise could possibly solve the problem instead.[55]

In retrospect, the contract's paragraph on extenuating state interests introduced by Mozambican officials seems to have been a kind of back door that allowed the Mozambican state to bring home workers from the GDR without a specific substantiation. The reason why the GDR did not oppose the installation of

---

52 In the GDR labor code (Gesetzbuch der Arbeit, § 106), the term "socialist labor discipline" was defined as: "Socialist labor discipline manifests itself in the conscious action of the working people in asserting the common interests of all working people in the socialist society. It is based on the fundamental correspondence between the interests of society and the individual, and includes comradely cooperation, mutual help and respect, and the conscientious fulfillment of all work tasks for the realization of the operational plans. It is a crucial basis of the socialist organization of labor." Own translation.
53 See article 5, paragraph 4 in Agreement between the Government of the GDR and the Government of the People's Republic of Mozambique on the temporary employment of Mozambican workers in socialist enterprises in the GDR (February 24, 1979) [Abkommen zwischen der Regierung der DDR und der Regierung der VR Mosambik über die zeitweilige Beschäftigung mosambikanischer Werktätiger in sozialistischen Betrieben der DDR (24. Februar 1979)], PA AA, MfAA, ZR 970/87.
54 Report of the Secretariat for Labor and Wages on the negotiations on the Agreement between the Government of the GDR and the People's Republic of Mozambique (February 13–20, 1979) about the temporary employment of Mozambican working people in the GDR in Maputo (February 23, 1979) [Bericht des SAL über die Verhandlungen zum Abkommen zwischen der Regierung der DDR und der VR Mosambik (13.–20. Februar 1979) über die zeitweilige Beschäftigung mosambikanischer Werktätiger in der DDR in Maputo (23. Februar 1979)], BStU, MfS, HA II, Nr. 32490, sheet 91–96.
55 Ibid.

such a back door could probably be found in the previous paragraph. With the undefined passage "violation of socialist labor discipline," the GDR also had the option of dissolving an employment relationship without stating specific reasons. Whether and to what extent these two loopholes were actually used in practice cannot be reconstructed, but it ultimately leads to the question of whether they were deliberately used for concealment. After all, both sides were interested in making the agreement a success.

A question that—in the view of Mozambique—was actually not a real question arose in relation to the leave entitlement. According to the GDR's understanding of the labor law, Mozambican workers were to be given one paid vacation back home during the four-year operational period of their contract. Based on the experience of designing earlier bilateral contract labor agreements, it was also required from GDR representatives that the holiday entitlements should be clearly regulated on the intergovernmental level, especially since this was ultimately about the payment of travel expenses. At this point, differences in the conception of labor law between the GDR and Mozambique came to the fore. For the GDR, it was logical to guarantee the foreign workers a paid holiday to return home during their vocational training period. For the Mozambican representatives, however, this practice was not particularly relevant in their understanding of the draft of the contract labor agreement. Thus, the report of the Secretariat for Labor and Wages stated, that the Mozambican side was not in a position to express a binding position on these issues.[56] It cannot clearly be identified, whether paid leave was simply seen as a luxury or whether considerations such as associated costs of getting the workers to their home provinces were seen as obstacles. Maybe there were concerns about security of internal travel and drafting of workers during the civil war in Mozambique. In order to avoid an unnecessary delay during the negotiations in Maputo, the request of the Mozambican representatives was accepted and no clear formulation regarding the regulations about paid vacations was included.

The last section of the negotiation report reveals how important the conclusion of the contract labor accord was for the Mozambican government. During their visit, the members of the GDR delegation were taken to a cement factory

---

56 Report of the Secretariat for Labor and Wages on the negotiations on the Agreement between the Government of the GDR and the People's Republic of Mozambique (February 13–20, 1979) about the temporary employment of Mozambican working people in the GDR in Maputo (February 23, 1979) [Bericht des SAL über die Verhandlungen zum Abkommen zwischen der Regierung der DDR und der VR Mosambik (13.–20. Februar 1979) über die zeitweilige Beschäftigung mosambikanischer Werktätiger in der DDR in Maputo (23. Februar 1979)], BStU, MfS, HA II, Nr. 32490, sheet 91–96.

and some railway repair centers in Maputo. This excursion shows that on site the Mozambican representatives repeatedly pointed out how urgently trained workers were needed. They emphasized that there was a large backlog, especially in the repair and maintenance of plant installations, since usually only one sufficiently qualified worker was available at any given point in time.[57] For the Mozambicans, it was important to demonstrate the social and economic needs that the deal would fulfill as part of the socialist revolution taking place in the country during the negotiation process.

The Further Course of the Contract Labor Accord

This contract labor accord was never fixed; instead it was subsequently amended or supplemented only by annual protocols and subsequent agreements that were negotiated in cooperation with the Mozambican Ministry of Labor. The first annual protocol from 1979 determined that only 440 Mozambican workers should be employed in the GDR. 300 of them were sent to the coal industry, where they were able to get a skilled worker training as a maintenance mechanic, electrician, motor vehicle repairman or vulcanizer – which was especially important for the pit coal project in Moatize. Another 100 workers should be employed in the smelting industry to get qualifications as metal craftsmen.[58] Before the training started, the Mozambican had to attend a compulsory language course in German. Of these, 40 people had to attend an intensive language course so that they could later be used as "language mediators" in the companies. The fulfillment of this condition was very important for the further course of the labor migration accord. The recruiting of more workers in this year was dependent on how quickly the training of Mozambican translators progressed.[59] The deployment of the contract workers should be carried out in groups of 50 people, a size that often varied in reality. In each group one worker was assigned by the Mozambican representative in East Germany as a so-called "group leader". Ac-

---

[57] Ibid.
[58] Annual protocol 1979 of the Secretariat for Labor and Wages on the agreement between the Government of the GDR and the Government of the People's Republic of Mozambique on the temporary employment of Mozambican workers in socialist enterprises in the GDR (undated) [Jahresprotokoll 1979 des Staatssekretariats für Arbeit und Löhne über das Abkommen zwischen der Regierung der DDR und der Regierung der Volksrepublik Mosambik über die befristete Beschäftigung mosambikanischer Werktätiger in sozialistischen Betrieben der DDR (undatiert)], BStU, MfS, HA II, Nr. 32490, sheet 49–52.
[59] Ibid.

cording to the agreement, the group leaders must contribute to the close cooperation between Mozambican workers and the East German company manager. They also should take care of the fulfillment of the tasks, the observance of the work discipline and the political and cultural education in the group.[60] According to the 1980 annual protocol, another 2,000 Mozambican workers should enter the GDR, and this time 100 of them should be trained as a language mediator.[61]

However, the numbers on the size of the recruited workers agreed on within these protocols, did not correspond to reality, because in 1980 over 2,800 and, in 1981 over 2,600 Mozambican workers arrived in the GDR. But during the three following years, the total number of new arrivals was just 382.[62] In 1985 there were about 5,000 Mozambican contract workers in the GDR. Because of the planned rotation principle and the maximal duration of four years enshrined in the agreement, many contracts were about to expire in the mid 1980s. Thus, the GDR created an agreement, which should regulate the procedure in the case of contractual extensions, in October 1984.[63] Both, the East German government and the employed contract workers in the GDR had an interest in contractual extensions. As a result, the Mozambican government agreed to an extension of deploy-

---

60 Agreement between the Government of the GDR and the Government of the People's Republic of Mozambique on the temporary employment of Mozambican workers in socialist enterprises in the GDR (February 24, 1979) [Abkommen zwischen der Regierung der DDR und der Regierung der VR Mosambik über die zeitweilige Beschäftigung mosambikanischer Werktätiger in sozialistischen Betrieben der DDR (24. Februar 1979)], PA AA, MfAA, ZR 970/87.
61 Annual protocol 1980 of the Secretariat for Labor and Wages on the agreement between the Government of the GDR and the Government of the People's Republic of Mozambique on the temporary employment of Mozambican workers in socialist enterprises in the GDR (undated) [Jahresprotokoll 1980 des Staatssekretariats für Arbeit und Löhne über das Abkommen zwischen der Regierung der DDR und der Regierung der Volksrepublik Mosambik über die befristete Beschäftigung mosambikanischer Arbeitnehmer in sozialistischen Unternehmen in der DDR (undatiert)], BStU, MfS, HA II, Nr. 32490, sheet 54–59.
62 Secretariat for Labor and Wages: Overview on the development of the contract labor accord between Mozambique and the GDR (April 1989) [Staatssekretariat für Arbeit und Löhne: Überblick über die Entwicklung des Vertragsarbeitsabkommens zwischen Mosambik und der DDR (April 1989)], SAPMO-BArch, DQ 3/1813.
63 Arrangement on Article 1 (3) on the agreement between the Government of the GDR and the Government of the People's Republic of Mozambique on the temporary employment of Mozambican workers in socialist enterprises in the GDR (October 26, 1984) [Vereinbarung zu Artikel 1 Absatz 3 des Abkommens zwischen der Regierung der DDR und der Regierung der Volksrepublik Mosambik über die befristete Beschäftigung mosambikanischer Werktätiger in sozialistischen Betrieben der DDR (26. Oktober 1984)], PA AA, MfAA, ZR 2331/89.

ment with a maximum of operational time of up to ten years.[64] Although at this time the decline in foreign trade relations between Mozambique and the GDR began, the number of contract workers continued to increase from the mid 1980s. Since 1987, the temporary employment of Mozambican workers in East German enterprises had been used as the primary clearinghouse for Mozambique's debt reduction to the GDR. As a result, from 1987 to 1989, a total of over 11,500 additional workers arrived, a number of which consisted of workers returning on a second contract.[65]

In their internal correspondence, the responsible actors[66] in the GDR did not stop to emphasize that the mission should continue to be linked to professional qualification, as this was of "high political and practical importance" for the People's Republic of Mozambique.[67] Until the collapse of the GDR, the promise of vocational training formed an integral part of the contract workers' agreements. Testimonies by former contract workers, too, reported that they had always received training. Though, the quality of training and the tasks of the workers greatly varied from monotonous factory work to excellent vocational training opportunities.[68] And even if a worker could not complete his training successfully, he was offered opportunities in the GDR to achieve further "partial qualifications."[69] But previous research has argued that, with the increase in contract

---

[64] Information on the situation among Mozambican workers in the GDR economy (September 24, 1987) [Information zur Situation der mosambikanischen Werktätigen in der DDR-Wirtschaft (24. September 1987)], BStU, MfS, HA XVIII, Nr. 19422, sheet 9–14.
[65] Döring, "Es geht um unsere Existenz," 237.
[66] Paul Gerhard Schürer (Chairman of the State Planning Commission at the Council of Ministers of the GDR and member of the Politburo), Kurt Singhuber (Minister of Heavy Industry), Gerhard Beil (Minister of Foreign Trade), Alexander Schalck-Golodkowski (Head of the Commercial Coordination Division at the Ministry of Foreign Trade), Oskar Fischer (Minister for Foreign Affairs), Wolfgang Beyreuther (Secretary of State for Labor and Wages), and Ernst Höfner (Minister of Finance).
[67] Measures for the organization of the economic relations between the GDR and the VR Mozambique until 1995 in the sense of a mutually satisfactory solution to the reduction of the credit of the GDR (June 23, 1988), quoted according to Müggenburg, *Die ausländischen Vertragsarbeitnehmer in der ehemaligen DDR*, 63–73.
[68] Marcia C. Schenck, "From Luanda and Maputo to Berlin: Uncovering Angolan and Mozambican Migrants' Motives to Move to the German Democratic Republic (1979–1990)," *African Economic History* 44 (2016): 214–216.
[69] Julio Mussane, "Es war immer jemand da, der half, Probleme zu lösen: Interview mit Julio Mussane am 29. April 2013 durch Ralf Straßburg," in *Mosambikanische Vertragsarbeiter in der DDR-Wirtschaft: Hintergrund – Verlauf – Folgen*, ed. Ulrich van der Heyden et al. (Münster: Lit, 2014), 229; Jose Reis, "Keine leichten Lebensumstände in der DDR: Interview mit Jose Reis am 31. Mai 2013 durch Ralf Straßburg," in *Mosambikanische Vertragsarbeiter in der DDR-*

workers from the mid 1980s on, the vocational qualifications defined in the agreements were no longer fully met.[70]

Furthermore, the integration of workers trained in East Germany into GDR-financed enterprises in Mozambique continued to be a decisive factor. To illustrate this point, I would like to quote an internal letter from the Commercial Coordination Division from November 9, 1984. In this letter, its leader Alexander Schalck-Golodkowski was informed by Klaus-Dieter Uhlig[71] that a textile combine plant built by the GDR in Mocuba, a town in central Mozambique, was still under construction and would not be operational until two years later.[72] In case their stay in Germany was extended, the trained Mozambican skilled workers could immediately start their work in this company after their return. He also warned that if the request to extend the period of residence was rejected, the returnees would not find work in Mozambique. Instead, they would be integrated into the armed forces, leading to a loss of skilled workforce.[73] This letter also stressed that Mozambique was also very interested in extending the period of residence because of its own economic problems. The arguments made demonstrate that the GDR was interested in furthering and securing its projects in the spirit of "international solidarity" and of course, it was also to boost exports as the machinery was usually bought by the recipient countries, either through barter with local goods or through credit lines with interest. However, it also clearly demonstrates that the recruitment policy of the GDR cannot be explained solely in the context of the GDR's domestic economic history. Instead, all joint activities with Mozambique need to be taken into consideration to properly analyze the GDR's contract labor policy.

Wirtschaft: Hintergrund – Verlauf – Folgen, ed. Ulrich van der Heyden et al. (Münster: Lit, 2014), 235.

70 Müggenburg, *Die ausländischen Vertragsarbeitnehmer in der ehemaligen DDR*, 10; Andrzej Stach and Saleh Hussain, *Ausländer in der DDR: Ein Rückblick* (Berlin: Ausländerbeauftragte des Senats, 1994), 11; Gruner-Domić, *Geschichte der Arbeitskräftemigration*, 228.

71 Klaus-Dieter Uhlig was head of the trade policy department at the Commercial Coordination Division, responsible for the foreign offices in Tehran, Maputo, and Cairo.

72 See Bahr, this volume.

73 Internal letter from the Department of Commercial Coordination Division regarding the extension of the period of residence for Mozambican workers in the GDR (November 9, 1984) [Internes Schreiben der Abteilung für Kommerzielle Koordinierung über die Verlängerung der Aufenthaltsdauer für mosambikanische Werktätige in der DDR (9. November 1984)], SAPMO-BArch, DL 226/1682.

Conclusion

Relations between the GDR and Mozambique date back to the time before the declaration of independence of 1975 when the GDR aimed to gain international recognition as a sovereign state in the 1960s and the SED regime sought diplomatic contacts with FRELIMO. The early support of the Marxist-oriented Mozambican liberation movement meant that once FRELIMO was in power, the two states moved closer to one another in the 1970s. On the part of the GDR, this was mainly due to the prestige-oriented idea of class struggle within the context of the East-West conflict. The Mozambican government was faced with the exodus of skilled personnel and simultaneously had to overcome the colonial legacies in the economic realm. The "Treaty of Friendship and Cooperation" concluded in February 1979 laid the foundation for further cooperation between Mozambique and the GDR. At the same time, the treaty formed the basis for a number of arrangements, including the agreement on the employment of Mozambican contract workers at GDR state-owned enterprises. According to the identity of the GDR's ideological conception of "international solidarity," the labor agreement had to be linked to a vocational qualification, but economic interests have always been part of the considerations. The education and training of workers should benefit Mozambique in the long term, whereas the GDR was able to counteract its shortage of labor in industrial production in the short term. For the Mozambican government, the sending of workers to the GDR provided an opportunity to further its economic development. The long tradition of sending miners to South Africa was to be discontinued and replaced by the transfer of these workers to the GDR instead. This practice not only made it possible to relieve the pressures on the Mozambican domestic labor market in the short term, but also contained the potential to develop much-needed skilled workers for their own economy.

The central requirement of the agreement was that both sides should benefit. On the part of the GDR, the drafting took into account a balanced cost-benefit principle. From a financial point of view, the GDR was not to incur any additional burden that could not be offset by the economic benefits. Although the framework agreements provided for the possibility of acquiring qualifications, successful completion of vocational training was not compulsory. The workers had to gain such qualifications through academic achievements; they were not awarded automatically at the end of their employment in the GDR. In this way, the workers were given personal responsibilities, which ultimately absolved the GDR from further obligations to the Mozambican government. Alberto Cassimo[74] also emphasized that Mozambican workers who do not stick to their revolutionary duty should be sent back immediately. This ideological claim was a decisive aspect of the labor agreement, which the Mozambican side took very seriously. In the selection of the areas in which this would be applied, however, the decision lay on the Mozambican side. The negotiators of the ruling party FRELIMO were able to decide which economic sectors skilled workers were needed for, and thus could also participate in shaping the transfer of its labor force.

As shown by the examples, the path to the accord was characterized on the one hand by mutual willingness to compromise and on the other hand by different understandings of the nature of certain aspects of contract labor migration. Both negotiating partners were able to bring their own ideas and even build in arbitrary loopholes that made early termination of contracts possible. The workers themselves, however, had no voice at this point in the process. In retrospect, the recruitment of foreign workers combined with vocational training was certainly a concept with potential and the agreement was supposed to benefit both sides. Mozambique was to profit from the training of its workers, the relief of the domestic labor market and the creation of professional prospects for young people. For the GDR, it contributed to addressing the labor shortage that seriously threatened economic production. In theory, the advantages outweighed the disadvantages for both sides according to the concept of "mutual benefit." In practice, however, the implementation of the agreement was influenced by political and economic constraints that came with the end of the Cold War on both sides.

Bibliography

Allina, Eric. "'Neue Menschen für Mosambik': Erwartungen an und Realität von Vertragsarbeit in der DDR der 1980er-Jahre." *Arbeit, Bewegung, Geschichte. Zeitschrift für historische Studien* 3 (2016): 65–84.

Archive portal of the IBC network of Emilia-Romagna. "Amandio Rafael Moises Chongo." Accessed July 26, 2020. http://archivi.ibc.regione.emilia-romagna.it/ibc-cms/cms.find?&id=produttori&.titolo=chongo&numDoc=8&munu_str=0_1_2&.date=&archType=auther&perpage=30&realTemplate=templateRicercaProduttori&flagfind=custom

---

74 Alberto Cassimo's commitment is still recognized in Mozambique. On November 1, 2016 the *Instituto de Formação Profissional e Estudos Laborais Alberto Cassimo / Institute of Vocational Training and the Labor Studies Alberto Cassimo* was founded. IFPELAC is a public vocational training institution headquartered in Maputo and overseen by the Ministry of Labor, Employment and Social Security.

XdamsFindProduttori&.q=&fromId=y&qrId=3se4482248f8810101&physDoc=961&pos=0&archType=auther#nogo.

Brochmann, Grete. "Migrant Labour and Foreign Policy: The Case of Mozambique." *Journal of Peace Research* 22 (1985): 335–344.

Burton, Eric. "Solidarität und ihre Grenzen: Die 'Brigaden der Freundschaft' der DDR." In *Internationale Solidarität: Globales Engagement in der Bundesrepublik und der DDR*, edited by Frank Bösch, Caroline Moine, and Stefanie Senger, 152–185. Göttingen: Wallstein Verlag, 2018.

Dietrich, Anne. "Kaffee in der DDR – 'Ein Politikum ersten Ranges'." In *Kaffeewelten: Historische Perspektiven auf eine globale Ware im 20. Jahrhundert*, edited by, Christiane Berth, Dorothee Wierling, and Volker Wünderich, 225–247. Göttingen: Vandenhoeck & Ruprecht, 2015.

Dinkel, Jürgen. "'Dritte Welt' – Geschichte und Semantiken, Version: 1.0." *Docupedia-Zeitgeschichte* (2014). Accessed October 6, 2014. doi:/10.14765/zzf.dok.2.596.v1.

Döring, Hans-Joachim. *"Es geht um unsere Existenz." Die Politik der DDR gegenüber der Dritten Welt am Beispiel von Mosambik und Äthiopien*, 2nd ed. Berlin: Ch. Links, 2001.

Engel, Ulf, and Hans-Georg Schleicher. *Die beiden deutschen Staaten in Afrika: Zwischen Konkurrenz und Koexistenz 1949–1990*. Hamburg: Institut für Afrika-Kunde, 1998.

Gaspar, Napoleão. "The Reduction of Mozambican Workers in South African Mines, 1975–1992: A Case Study of the Consequences for Gaza Province – District of Chibuto." PhD diss., Universidade Eduardo Mondlane, 2006. Accessed May 16, 2008. http://hdl.handle.net/10539/4839.

Gerstner, Karl-Heinz. "Hilfeleistung bei Lichte besehen", *Berliner Zeitung*, October 11, 1980.

Gruner-Domić, Sandra. *Kubanische Arbeitsmigration in die DDR 1978–1989: Das Arbeitskräfteabkommen Kuba – DDR und dessen Realisierung*. Berlin: Ed. Parabolis, 1997.

Gruner-Domić, Sandra. "Zur Geschichte der Arbeitskräftemigration in die DDR: Die bilateralen Verträge zur Beschäftigung ausländischer Arbeiter, 1961–1989." *Internationale wissenschaftliche Korrespondenz zur Geschichte der deutschen Arbeiterbewegung* 32 (1996): 204–230.

Guerra Hernandez, Hector. "Cooperación para el desarrollo en tiempos de internacionalismo: Los hombres nuevos de Machel." *Vibrant – Virtual Brazilian Anthropology* 9 (2012): 541–573.

Guerra Hernandez, Hector. "Ma(d)jermanes: passado colonial e presente diasporizado: reconstrução etnográfica de um dos últimos vestígios do socialismo colonial europeu." PhD diss., Universidade Estadual de Campinas, 2011. Accessed August 19, 2018. http://www.repositorio.unicamp.br/handle/REPOSIP/280790.

Guerra Hernandez, Hector. "RAND à RDA? Modernização compulsória e práticas sociais e estratégias de mobilidade social." *(con) textos: Revista d'antropologia i investigació social* 3 (2009): 61–83.

Hall, Margaret, and Tom Young. *Confronting Leviathan: Mozambique since Independence*. London: Hurst & Company, 1997.

Harisch, Immanuel R. "Bartering Coffee, Cocoa and W50 Trucks: The Trade Relationships of the GDR, Angola and São Tomé in a Comparative Perspective." *Global Histories* 3 (2017): 43–60.

Institut für Internationale Beziehungen an der Akademie für Staats- und Rechtswissenschaft der DDR, ed. *Wörterbuch der Außenpolitik und des Völkerrechts*. Berlin: Dietz Verlag, 1980.

Isaacman, Allen, and Barbara Isaacman. *Mozambique: From Colonialism to Revolution, 1900–1982*. Boulder: Westview Press, 1983.

Jarosi, Katalin. "Umschwärmte Kavaliere und gewinnbringende Ehemänner. Ungarische Vertragsarbeiter in der DDR." In *Arbeitsmigration: WanderarbeiterInnen auf dem Weltmarkt für Arbeitskraft*, edited by Thomas Geisen, 197–216. Frankfurt a.M.: IKO, 2005.

Joint decision of the Central Committee of the SED, the Federal Executive of the FDGB and the Council of Ministers of the GDR on social policy measures in the implementation of the main task of the five-year plan decided on at the 8th SED Party Congress, (April 28, 1972) [Gemeinsamer Beschluss des Zentralkomitees der SED, der Bundesleitung des FDGB und des Ministerrates der DDR über sozialpolitische Maßnahmen zur Umsetzung der Hauptaufgabe des auf dem 8. SED-Parteitag beschlossenen Fünfjahresplans (28. April 1972)]. In *Dokumente zur Geschichte der SED, Vol. 3: 1971–1986*, edited by Günter Benser, 73–74. Berlin: Dietz Verlag, 1986.

Künanz, Heide. "Das Steinkohleprojekt Moatize zwischen solidarischer Hilfeleistung und kommerziellen Anspruch." In *Die DDR und Afrika: Zwischen Klassenkampf und neuem Denken*, edited by Ulrich van der Heyden, Ilona Schleicher, and Hans-Georg Schleicher, 174–191. Münster: Lit, 1993.

Mac Con Uladh, Damian "Die Alltagserfahrungen ausländischer Vertragsarbeiter in der DDR. Vietnamesen, Kubaner, Mosambikaner, Ungarn und andere." In *Erfolg in der Nische? Die Vietnamesen in der DDR und in Ostdeutschland*, edited by Karin Weiss, and Dennis Mike, 51–67. Münster: Lit, 2005.

Machel, Samora Moisés. "Central Committee Report [to the Third Congress], Maputo". Published June 6, 1978. Translation into English by the Mozambique-Angola-Guiné Information Centre (MAGIC), London.

Meyns, Peter. *Konflikt und Entwicklung im südlichen Afrika*. Opladen: Leske + Budrich, 2000.

Mercandalli, Sara, Christopher Changwe Nshimbi, and Inocent Moyo. "Mozambican Labour Migrations, Remittances and Development: Evidence, Practices and Implications for Policy." In *Migration, Cross-Border Trade and Development in Africa: Exploring the Role of Non-State Actors in the SADC Region*, edited by Sara Mercandalli, Christopher Changwe Nshimbi, and Inocent Moyo, 15–42. Cham: Palgrave Macmillan, 2017.

Muanamoha, Ramos Cardoso. "The Dynamics of Undocumented Mozambican Labour Migration to South Africa". PhD diss., University of KwaZulu-Natal, 2008. Accessed March 2008. http://www.repositorio.uem.mz/handle/123456789/278.

Müggenburg, Andreas. *Die ausländischen Vertragsarbeitnehmer in der ehemaligen DDR: Darstellung und Dokumentation*. Berlin: Die Beauftragte der Bundesregierung für die Belange der Ausländer, 1996.

Munslow, Barry. "State Intervention in Agriculture: The Mozambican Experience." *The Journal of Modern African Studies* 22 (1984): 199–221.

Mussane, Julio. "Es war immer jemand da, der half, Probleme zu lösen: Interview mit Julio Mussane am 29. April 2013 durch Ralf Straßburg." In *Mosambikanische Vertragsarbeiter in der DDR-Wirtschaft: Hintergrund – Verlauf – Folgen*, edited by Ulrich van der Heyden, Wolfgang Semmler, and Ralf Straßburg, 226–230. Berlin: Lit-Verlag, 2014.

Reis, Jose. "Keine leichten Lebensumstände in der DDR: Interview mit Jose Reis am 31. Mai 2013 durch Ralf Straßburg." In *Mosambikanische Vertragsarbeiter in der DDR-Wirtschaft. Hintergrund – Verlauf – Folgen*, edited by Ulrich van der Heyden, Wolfgang Semmler, and Ralf Straßburg, 231–236. Münter: Lit, 2014.

Röhr, Rita. "Die Beschäftigung polnischer Arbeitskräfte in der DDR 1966–1990: Die vertraglichen Grundlagen und ihre Umsetzung." *Archiv für Sozialgeschichte* 42 (2002): 211–236.

Schenck, Marcia. "Between Hammer, Machete, and Kalashnikov: Contract Labor Migration from Angola and Mozambique to East Germany, 1979–1990." *Europe Now* 15 (2018). Accessed March 2018. https://www.europenowjournal.org/2018/02/28/between-hammer-machete-and-kalashnikov-contract-labor-migration-from-angola-and-mozambique-to-east-germany-1979-1990/.

Schenck, Marcia C. "From Luanda and Maputo to Berlin: Uncovering Angolan and Mozambican Migrants' Motives to Move to the German Democratic Republic (1979–1990)." *African Economic History* 44 (2016): 202–234.

Scherzer, Landolf. "Meine Ankunft in Mosambik." In *Mosambikanische Vertragsarbeiter in der DDR-Wirtschaft: Hintergrund – Verlauf – Folgen*, edited by Ulrich van der Heyden, Wolfgang Semmler und Ralf Straßburg, 143–149. Münster: Lit, 2014.

Schulz, Mirjam. "Migrationspolitik in der DDR: Bilaterale Anwerbungsverträge von Vertragsarbeitnehmern." In *Transit. Transfer: Politik und Praxis der Einwanderung in die DDR 1945–1990*, edited by Kim Christian Priemel, 143–168. Berlin: be.bra wissenschaft verlag, 2011.

Schwenkel, Christina. "Socialist Mobilities: Crossing New Terrains in Vietnamese Migration Histories." *Central and Eastern European Migration Review* 4 (2015): 13–25.

Spanger, Hans-Joachim, and Lothar Brock. *Die beiden deutschen Staaten in der Dritten Welt: Die Entwicklungspolitik der DDR – Eine Herausforderung für die Bundesrepublik Deutschland?* Opladen: Westdeutscher Verlag, 1987.

Stach, Andrzej, and Saleh Hussain, *Ausländer in der DDR: Ein Rückblick*. Berlin: Ausländerbeauftragte des Senats, 1994.

Unfried, Berthold. "Instrumente und Praktiken von 'Solidarität' Ost und 'Entwicklungshilfe' West: Blickpunkt auf das entsandte Personal." In *Die eine Welt schaffen: Praktiken von 'Internationaler Solidarität' und 'Internationaler Entwicklung'*, edited by Berthold Unfried and Eva Himmelstoss, 73–98. Leipzig: AVA, 2012.

van der Heyden, Ulrich. *Das gescheiterte Experiment: Vertragsarbeiter aus Mosambik in der DDR-Wirtschaft (1979–1990)*. Leipzig: Leipziger Universitätsverlag, 2019.

Verburg, Maria Magdalena. *Ostdeutsche Dritte-Welt-Gruppen vor und nach 1989/90*. Göttingen: Vandenhoeck & Ruprecht, 2012.

Westad, Odd Arne. *The Global Cold War: Third World Interventions and the Making of Our Times*. Cambridge: Cambridge University Press, 2007.

II Navigating the GDR: Moorings and (Dis)Entanglements

G. Thomas Burgess
6 The Rise and Fall of a Socialist Future: Ambivalent Encounters Between Zanzibar and East Germany in the Cold War

Less than a month into its existence, the People's Republic of Zanzibar in January 1964 opened a relationship with the German Democratic Republic that would have far-reaching consequences, particularly for Zanzibaris.[1] In competition with the Chinese, who also saw their relationship to the incipient island state as a means by which to break out of their diplomatic isolation, East Germany offered a generous package of aid and expertise. Although in late April 1964 Zanzibar federated with Tanganyika—its much larger neighbor on the East African mainland—and although this meant the downgrading of the newly-established East German embassy in the islands, the new union did not short-circuit GDR-Zanzibar relations. Throughout the 1960s Zanzibar retained most of the accoutrements of an independent state: its own president, ruling party, bureaucracy, and security forces. Zanzibar also continued to enjoy some autonomy in foreign affairs. And so with a relatively free hand, islanders leaned heavily on East German aid and advice, which played an influential role in shaping Zanzibar's revolutionary experiment.

East Germany sent a regular flow of experts to Zanzibar, and in turn received a steady stream of Zanzibari students in search of training and education. Such encounters were sustained by a common vision of the solidarity of like-minded socialist nations, all supposedly sharing the same uplifting image of a future world characterized by equality, selflessness, and abundance. Officials in both Eastern Europe and Africa believed Zanzibar, with its relatively small size and population, could serve as a showcase for this future-in-the-making. At relatively

---

[1] For East German relations with Zanzibar during the Cold War, see Abdulrahman Mohamed Babu, "I Was the First Third World Minister to Recognize the GDR," in *I Saw the Future and It Works: Essays Celebrating the Life of Comrade Abdulrahman Mohamed Babu, 1924–1996*, ed. Haroub Othman (Dar es Salaam, Tanzania: E & D Limited, 2001), 48–58; Eric Burton, "Diverging Visions in Revolutionary Spaces: East German Advisors and Revolution from Above in Zanzibar, 1964–1970," in *Between East and South: Spaces of Ineraction in the Globalizing Economy of the Cold War*, ed. Anna Calori et al. (Berlin, Boston: De Gruyter Oldenbourg, 2019); Antony Clayton, *The Zanzibar Revolution and its Aftermath* (Hamden, CT: Archon Books, 1978); Heinz Schneppen, *Zanzibar and the Germans: A Special Relationship, 1844–1966* (Dar es Salaam, Tanzania: National Museums of Tanzania, 1998).

OpenAccess. © 2021 G. Thomas Burgess, published by De Gruyter. This work is licensed under the Creative Commons Attribution 4.0 International License.
https://doi.org/10.1515/9783110623543-006

little cost, a small nation like East Germany could make a highly visible impact by rendering decisive assistance to an even smaller territory struggling to achieve a better life for its citizens. Together East Germany and Zanzibar could realize the socialist vision of a society free of capitalist exploitation and neo-colonial domination. Zanzibar could serve as a revolutionary model to neighbors still dependent on the West for aid, trade, and expertise.

As historians turn to the study of East-South relations during the Cold War, and recover an often forgotten and yet highly consequential world of linkages, moorings, entanglements, and disentanglements, we should consider the ideas that animated such encounters.[2] This essay demonstrates that at least on one level the East Germans and Zanzibaris were in agreement: the future would be one in which Africans would not only enjoy the blessings of freedom and sovereignty in islands where many of their ancestors once toiled as slaves. They would also experience "development," and enjoy such modern amenities as electricity, running water, and indoor plumbing. Throughout the 1960s, this future sustained a relationship between two nations separated by thousands of miles of land and sea, as well as highly dissimilar cultural traditions.

Such cooperation between Zanzibar and East Germany may be placed within the context of an historic moment when socialist internationalism appeared to possess real promise in orienting recently decolonized territories in Africa and Asia towards the socialist East. The East beckoned with aid, friendship, and discursive support, and was an emerging and enticing counterpoint to Western nations implicated by colonialism. Later in the Cold War, East Germany would form close ties with other movements and nations of the developing world, and Zanzibar would look to China for aid and expertise. Nevertheless, for both Zanzibaris and East Germans, their once close relationship contained all the romance, frustrations, and misunderstandings of a first love.[3] Believing socialism and African nationalism were natural allies in the struggle against imperialism, racism, and inequality, they rushed into a relationship that seemed to offer a bright future and benefits to both sides, and yet which led instead to mutual disillusionment.

This chapter will discuss why Zanzibar's ties with East Germany quickly waxed, and eventually waned. It will examine East Germany's influence on Zanzibar's fledgling revolution, the initial violence of which had only recently been

---

2 For a broad picture, see Philip Muehlenbeck and Natalia Telepneva, eds., *Warsaw Pact Intervention in the Third World: Aid and Influence in the Cold War* (London: I.B. Tauris, 2018).
3 Soviet-Cuban ties also contained a strong element of romance in the 1960s. For a study that emphasizes how Soviets imagined the relationship, see Anne Gorsuch, "'Cuba, My Love:' The Romance of Revolutionary Cuba in the Soviet Sixties," *American Historical Review* 120 (2015).

brought under state control by the time GDR representatives made their first appearance in the islands in early-1964. In addition to oral and archival sources that give some indication of the impact of this relationship on the popular level, I will examine the novel *By the Sea*, in which Zanzibari author Abdulrazak Gurnah provides a compelling narrative of Latif Mahmud, who at the age of 18 sets out to study in the GDR.[4] Latif is something of a composite character, inspired by the memories and narratives of Gurnah's former classmates who set out with high hopes to study in East Germany in the 1960s.[5] Their experience is emblematic of an era of inflated expectations, when Africans newly-liberated from colonial rule hoped to achieve all their nation building ambitions, and turned to wise men from the East bearing gifts of credit, scholarships, and technology. After the end of colonialism and before the onset of the African debt crisis of the 1980s there were relatively few limits on futurist discourses. In the 1960s, the "socialist transnational imaginary"[6] was in full swing, producing a series of images of the future that animated a steady stream of students, technocrats, and teachers traveling back and forth between East and South. Such encounters, linkages, and connections helped shape Zanzibar's revolutionary experiment, and were but one component of a project of socialist globalization that forged new and consequential ties between Africa and the East.

The Rise of a Socialist Vanguard

When in the early twentieth century the British began to establish schools in Zanzibar along western lines it had to overcome considerable resistance among parents and village leaders convinced such institutions would corrupt the minds of the next generation, and undermine their faith in Islam. Only after the colonial state moved in the 1940s to incorporate Islam into the curriculum did the schools begin to gain widespread favor and acceptance.[7] The experiment proved so successful that after World War II more and more Zanzibaris began to look further afield for opportunities to pursue higher education. Those who came to physical maturity in the Cold War era were uniquely advantaged in

---

4 Abdulrazak Gurnah, *By the Sea* (New York: New Press, 2001).
5 Personal email communication from Abdulrazak Gurnah to the author, August 14, 2019.
6 James Mark and Péter Apor, "Socialism Goes Global: Decolonization and the Making of a New Culture of Internationalism in Socialist Hungary, 1956–1989," *The Journal of Modern History* 87 (2015): 890.
7 Norman Bennett, *A History of the Arab State of Zanzibar* (Cambridge, MA: Methuen and Co., 1978), 222–33, 244.

this respect; not only were the British offering more scholarships—primarily to study at Uganda's Makerere University, or in the United Kingdom—families were also more willing than ever to sponsor promising children anxious to acquire higher education overseas.[8] And by the late 1950s a rising generation of young Zanzibaris could also look to the East for patronage and support. Recognizing an opportunity to influence an emerging Third World elite, the socialist fraternity of nations began to arrange for a growing number of Africans to visit carefully stage-managed tours, or to stay for longer periods of study and training. The GDR was one of a constellation of states that also included the Soviet Union and China willing to invest scarce state resources in an attempt to inculcate Third World nationalists in socialist theory and belief.[9]

By the late 1950s the British also signaled their intention to eventually withdraw from Zanzibar, which triggered a bitter partisan dispute over the colonial inheritance. Two rival nationalist party coalitions emerged, and access to foreign scholarships was just one of the ways in which they competed. Of the two, the Zanzibar Nationalist Party (ZNP) was more aggressive in obtaining and disseminating scholarships; indeed, the party could not find enough applicants to fill the number of offered scholarships.[10] Party leader Ali Muhsin persuaded Gamal Abdel Nasser to sponsor dozens of Zanzibari students to come and study in Egypt.[11] Sent to Cairo in 1960 to represent the ZNP and supervise the students, Ali Sultan Issa contacted Eastern Bloc embassy officials, and requested scholarships. He estimates that through his and others' efforts over 300 Zanzibaris went to the GDR in the 1960s for short courses in trade unionism and cooperatives, or for full degree programs in such fields as medicine and engineering.[12]

The presence in the islands of a small but increasingly significant cohort of youth who had been exposed to life in the East had far-reaching consequences,

---

8 See G. Thomas Burgess, "Youth and the Revolution: Mobility and Discipline in Zanzibar, 1950–80" (PhD. diss., Indiana University, 2001), 84.
9 The Bandung Conference of 1955 was a major stimulus to Chinese efforts; see G. Thomas Burgess, "Mao in Zanzibar: Nationalism, Discipline, and the (De)Construction of Afro-Asian Solidarities," in *Making a World After Empire: The Bandung Moment and Its Political Afterlives*, ed. Christopher Lee (Athens, OH: Ohio University Press, 2010).
10 Burgess, "Youth and the Revolution," 84.
11 Ali Muhsin Al Barwani, *Conflicts and Harmony in Zanzibar (Memoirs)* (no publisher: 1997), 98–105.
12 G. Thomas Burgess, *Race, Revolution, and the Struggle for Human Rights in Zanzibar: The Memoirs of Ali Sultan Issa and Seif Sharif Hamad* (Athens, OH: Ohio University Press, 2009), 66. Most went after independence, when the GDR became Zanzibar's leading educational patron.

which will only be outlined here.¹³ It encouraged a growing divide within the ZNP between the more conservative party mainstream and a leftist faction led by Abdulrahman Mohamed Babu, the party's secretary general and principal founder of the ZNP youth wing, known as the Youth's Own Union (YOU). In mid-1963 Babu resigned from the ZNP to help found the Umma Party, which gained the support of most of those who had returned from the East. The new party was based overwhelmingly in Zanzibar Town, and accommodated members who espoused everything from Maoism to anarchism, nationalism, and social democracy.¹⁴ Umma began to criticize the ZNP as a party of reactionary feudalists and capitalists; it also formed a tactical alliance with the ZNP's main rival, the Afro-Shirazi Party (ASP), even though in previous years Babu had repeatedly attacked that party for its divisive racial polemics.¹⁵

As Zanzibar approached independence these three parties presented widely contrasting electoral appeals. In a society in which a large majority of voters were poor Muslims of at least partial African ancestry, they disagreed as to how that majority ought to be identified, and from what it ought to be protected. The ZNP claimed Zanzibaris were first and foremost Muslims who needed to be protected from the political domination of newly independent states like Kenya and Tanganyika lacking clear Muslim majorities. They also needed to preserve Zanzibar's unique Muslim culture from "hordes" of unwanted migrants from the African mainland. The ASP, meanwhile, claimed most Zanzibaris were Africans who needed to defend themselves from Arab cruelty and domination.¹⁶ And for its part Umma claimed most islanders were members of downtrodden classes that required protection from exploitative capitalists and feudalists. The three parties also differed dramatically when it came to which global leaders they found most inspiring, and to which they looked for material support. The ZNP claimed to eschew racial politics, and yet aligned itself with Gamal Abdel Nasser's version of anti-colonial Arab nationalism. The ASP for its part openly embraced racial politics, yet drew inspiration from Julius Nyerere, the non-racialist

---

13 See G. Thomas Burgess, "An Imagined Generation: Umma Youth in Nationalist Zanzibar," in *In Search of a Nation: Histories of Authority and Dissidence from Tanzania: Essays in Honor of I.M. Kimambo*, ed. Gregory Maddox et al. (London: James Currey Publishers, 2005), 216–249.
14 For a particularly laudatory account, see Amrit Wilson, *The Threat of Liberation: Imperialism and Revolution in Zanzibar* (London: Pluto Press, 2013). Wilson draws heavily from Babu's writings and recollections.
15 The ASP, in turn, criticized the ZNP for its "communist" element. Jonathon Glassman, *War of Words, War of Stones, Racial Thought and Violence in Colonial Zanzibar* (Bloomington: Indiana University Press, 2011), 271–272.
16 See Glassman, *War of Words*.

leader of Tanganyika's independence movement. Umma, meanwhile, looked further afield for allies and ideological cousins, revering socialist nations as sources of inspiration and support.[17]

Umma's very existence was only possible through Eastern patronage; despite the triangular symmetry of the partisan contest, socialism was not an organic plant that sprouted naturally from an island population that traditionally saw the world in terms of class struggle. The only thing "traditional" about socialism in Zanzibar was its cosmopolitanism; socialism drew much of its strength and vitality from the travel experiences of a rising generation precocious in its cultural and intellectual appropriations. While Zanzibaris coming to maturity during the height of the Cold War were uniquely eager and able to go abroad, and while they ventured much further than their predecessors, for at least a thousand years Zanzibar had been a key link in a cosmopolitan network of trade and migration encompassing the islands and coasts of the western Indian Ocean.[18] In the waning years of colonialism the GDR and other socialist nations of the East managed to attract a growing number of aspiring young islanders, many of whom upon their return to Zanzibar gravitated towards Umma, and embraced "scientific" solutions to the islands' chronic racial and class divisions. Never a party that enjoyed mass appeal, Umma may be described as a small but effective party in the Leninist vanguard tradition. In the mid-1960s Umma would play an instrumental role in pushing Zanzibar towards the GDR and other nations of the East.

A New East-South Partnership

After a final round of elections, in December 1963 the British transferred power to the ZNP and its sister party, the Zanzibar and Pemba People's Party (ZPPP). Barely a month later the independent ZNP-ZPPP coalition government was overthrown in an ASP uprising that triggered weeks of violence. The seizure of power quickly captured international headlines, in part because it was not clear who was behind it, or whether the new regime would align with the East, the West, or remain neutral in the Cold War. While the violence was definitely racialized, and directed primarily against Arabs as the allegedly arrogant descendants of slave owners, Umma comrades were also active in the revolution, including

---

17 See Burgess, "Mao in Zanzibar."
18 See, for example, Randal Pouwels, *The Horn and the Crescent: Cultural change and traditional Islam on the East African Coast, 800–1900* (Cambridge: Cambridge University Press, 1987).

those of Arab ancestry. And since over a dozen had received military training in Cuba, and could be heard shouting Spanish revolutionary slogans over the radio in Zanzibar, there was even brief media speculation that the revolution was the work of Fidel Castro's regime.[19]

Umma cooperation with the ASP in early 1964 was a function of their common opposition to the ZNP-ZPPP alliance; but it also stemmed from the fact that race and class identities were slippery, and easily, conflated. It was not difficult for ASP revolutionaries to recast Arabs as feudalists and South Asians as capitalists—especially when, in the context of the Cold War, such an appropriation of socialist vocabulary earned the new regime a modicum of international respect, as well as inclusion in the global narrative of the dawning of a new and more equitable socialist epoch. A further reason for the willingness of ASP leaders to accept Umma comrades into their ranks was a desperate manpower shortage caused by the death or flight of so many supporters of the former regime, some of whom were among the islands' more educated citizens.

Umma officially merged with the ASP in March 1964, by which time Babu and his cohort of leftists had assumed positions of influence in the new regime. In fact, as Minister of External Affairs and Trade, Babu was instrumental in Zanzibar's decision to recognize the GDR in late January 1964.[20] According to West Germany's Hallstein Doctrine, no nation except the Soviet Union could have relations with both West and East Germany. By siding with the GDR, the new regime clearly signaled its intentions to depart from the general trend of African non-alignment in the Cold War. Markus Wolf, who at the time was the GDR's director of foreign intelligence in the ministry of state security, reasoned that diplomatic recognition came about through the influence of Zanzibaris who studied in the GDR, and returned with positive feelings towards the East.[21] Those who visited other socialist lands instead were also in support of recognition.

Relatively uneducated, and a moderate when it came to the global contest between East and West, President Abeid Karume was encircled by ministers like Babu who had traveled to the East and embraced a socialist vision of the future. Though they sometimes disagreed as to what that would actually entail,

---

19 Keith Kyle, "The Zanzibar Coup," *The Spectator*, January 25, 1964; Keith Kyle, "How it Happened," *The Spectator*, February 14, 1964; cf. Piero Gleijeses, *Conflicting Missions: Havana, Washington, and Africa, 1959–1976* (Chapel Hill: University of North Carolina Press, 2002), 59–60; cf. Burgess, *Race, Revolution, and the Struggle for Human Rights*, 84.
20 Schneppen, *Zanzibar and the Germans*, 12. See also Babu, "I Was the First Third World Minister," 53.
21 Markus Wolf, with Anne McElvoy, *Man Without a Face: The Autobiography of Communism's Greatest Spymaster* (New York: Random House, 1997), 252.

at least some were convinced of the need to oust or at least sideline Karume in order for their cherished People's Republic to take its rightful place in the progressive march of humanity. After considerable maneuvering on all sides, as well as continual American and British strategizing as to how to best neutralize the perceived communist threat in the islands, in late April 1964 Karume consented to a federation with Tanganyika, Zanzibar's closest neighbor on the continent. This allowed him to transfer to the mainland men like Babu and Vice President Kassim Hanga considered to be hostile and/or actively plotting against him.[22]

If the federation purchased Karume some short-term political security, it set up an immediate confrontation with Tanganyika over the issue of Zanzibar's recognition of the GDR. The GDR had already offered a generous aid package, which Karume saw as vital to his ambitions for nation building and racial uplift. He was not prepared to abandon such aid in order to placate Julius Nyerere, his partner in the union and now president of the United Republic of Tanzania. Tanganyika, meanwhile, was the largest recipient of West German aid in sub-Saharan Africa, and among other projects the Bonn government provided key technical and material assistance to the air wing of the Tanganyikan army. All of this was now in jeopardy due to the Hallstein Doctrine. The issue was so serious it threatened to break the union; Karume refused to abandon his East German "friends," and Nyerere was convinced the GDR was trying to sabotage the union.[23] He eventually persuaded the East Germans to accept the demotion of their embassy in Zanzibar in exchange for the right to open a consulate general in Dar es Salaam. When the West Germans interpreted this as a violation of the Hallstein Doctrine, and announced in early-1965 they would be withholding their military aid, Nyerere renounced all aid ties with the Federal Republic.[24] Karume was the only real winner in all these negotiations, since the East Germans were forced to increase their aid pledges so as to keep him on their side.

The New Zanzibar

From 1964 to 1968 the GDR competed with China as Zanzibar's leading patron. In his vivid memoir, Markus Wolf describes the beginnings of a relationship that would fall into a familiar pattern of East-South relationships during the Cold

---

22 See Burgess, "Youth and the Revolution," 258–275.
23 Issa Shivji, *Pan-Africanism or Pragmatism? Lessons of Tanganyika-Zanzibar Union* (Dar es Salaam, Tanzania: Mkuki na Nyota Publishers, 2008), 103.
24 Schneppen, *Zanzibar and the Germans*, 14–20; Clayton, *Zanzibar Revolution*, 147–148.

War. It included farcical moments, as when upon his arrival in February 1964 Wolf was asked to inspect a guard of honor to the "lilting strains" of a police orchestra playing Viennese waltzes. In celebration of May Day, he watched as singers "praised the beauty and richness" of the GDR as a kind of "fairytale land of plenty."[25] Clearly, Zanzibari officials saw the GDR as a potentially endless source of patronage. And the GDR did nothing to disabuse such notions, but instead offered an aid program that would have gone a long way towards "developing" Zanzibar, and realizing a modernist vision of the future shared by President Karume and his new East German friends.

Though the GDR did not deliver on all its initial promises, it did send medical personnel and secondary school teachers to help make up for the exodus of British expatriates and skilled Zanzibaris victimized by the revolution.[26] Officials of the *Freie Deutsche Jugend*, the East German youth organization, also advised the ASP on how to mobilize the younger generation in support of socialist nation building imperatives. Abdulla Said Natepe and Aboud Talib traveled to the GDR to receive training in how to establish their own version of the Young Pioneers, an institution first established in the Soviet Union in the early-1920s, which over the decades had become ubiquitous in the socialist East. Rajab Kheri told a Zanzibari student audience in 1965 that "our problem is that we are backward, and we have to be in harmony with our friends who are the long time founders of these children development programs. ... their children have achieved high development levels. We have to construct a bridge of friendship with them and unite with them. In this way we can achieve that same level of development."[27] The youth labor camp was another fixture of life in the socialist East, and the GDR assisted Zanzibar in establishing its own set of camps by sending tractors

---

25 Wolf and McElvoy, *Man Without a Face*, 253–254. Wolf reasoned Zanzibaris had chosen the GDR as a major patron so as to not offend neighboring states like Kenya still economically tied to Great Britain, and who might be anxious about too close of ties with the Soviet Union: "We were economically advanced enough to be a useful supplier of advice ... but small enough not to annoy any other sources of income." Ibid., 255.
26 Clayton, *Zanzibar Revolution*, 144, 146. To compare East German aid with that of the USSR and China, see also Burton, "Diverging Visions;" Burgess, "Mao in Zanzibar"; and G. Thomas Burgess, "A Socialist Diaspora: Ali Sultan Issa, the Soviet Union, and the Zanzibari Revolution," in *Africa in Russia, Russia in Africa: Three Centuries of Encounters*, ed. Maxim Matusevich (Trenton, NJ: Africa World Press, 2007).
27 Thomas Burgess, "The Young Pioneers and the Rituals of Citizenship in Revolutionary Zanzibar," *Africa Today* 51 (2005): 10.

and instructors to impart practical skills in plumbing, for example.²⁸ Finally, the GDR ramped up the number of scholarships on offer; in 1966, for example, 123 Zanzibari students were in the GDR—more than in any other foreign country, and nearly double the combined number of those studying in China and the USSR.²⁹

While the GDR sponsored the construction of a dairy plant it had a more significant economic impact in the realm of finance. The Moscow-trained Abdul Aziz Twala, Zanzibar's Minister of Finance, leaned heavily on the advice of Martin Gentsch, who although East German was asked to chair the Public Finance Control Commission. In early 1966 the commission was instrumental in establishing the People's Bank of Zanzibar (*Benki ya Wananchi wa Zanzibar*). As Eric Burton describes, Twala and Gentsch were close personal friends, and agreed that Zanzibar needed to reduce its dependency on the capitalist West, while also maintaining financial autonomy from the Tanzanian mainland. They were also convinced of the need for East German instruction in the principles of socialist economics, management, and bookkeeping. In addition to arranging for islanders to receive such training in the GDR, Gentsch and Twala collaborated on the opening of a "School of Economics," which when it opened in Zanzibar in April 1967 boasted over a hundred students.³⁰

While the GDR had an impact in the realms of finance, education, and youth mobilization, East Germany is especially remembered for its assistance in housing and security. From early-1964 Karume was an enthusiastic supporter of East German plans to house the entire population of the islands in massive new apartment blocks that would boast modern amenities such as running water, indoor plumbing, and electricity.³¹ As an African nationalist who cut his political teeth in the streets of Zanzibar Town, it is not hard to imagine Karume's rapturous response to such proposals. By the mid-twentieth century the capital was divided between the largely Arab and South Asian neighborhoods of Stone Town, and the mostly African area known as Ng'ambo, or literally "the other side." Stone Town enjoyed cooling sea breezes and close proximity to the palaces of the sultans, high colonial officials, and wealthy grandees of island society.

---

28 G. Thomas Burgess, "To Differentiate Rice from Grass: Youth Labor Camps in Revolutionary Zanzibar" in *Generations Past: Youth in East African History*, ed. Andrew Burton and Hélène Charton-Bigot (Athens, OH: Ohio University Press, 2010), 227.
29 Burgess, "A Socialist Diaspora," 281.
30 Burton, "Diverging Visions," 91–92, 95, 109. See also Shivji, *Pan-Africanism or Pragmatism*, 133–141; Clayton, *Zanzibar Revolution*, 144.
31 Garth Andrew Myers, *Verandahs of Power: Colonialism and Space in Urban Africa* (Syracuse: Syracuse University Press, 2003), 109.

It also boasted an array of cafes, movie theaters, and public gardens. Meanwhile the African residents of Ng'ambo rented housing of widely varying quality and amenity.[32] Thus if East Germany followed through on its promise to provide Africans with "modern" housing it would rectify one of Zanzibar's most visible, galling, and visceral reminders of racial inequality.

Such grandiose plans were, however, soon scaled down to the demolition and reconstruction of two Ng'ambo neighborhoods, Kikwajuni and Kilimani. In 1968, however, architect Hubert Scholz and a team of East German experts proposed to extend these pilot projects over the rest of Ng'ambo. The plan called for the construction of 6,992 flats in an area that already included 5,163 homes deemed to be in good or fair condition.[33] Ultimately, through GDR support and the forced and unpaid labor of urban Zanzibaris citizens, the regime managed to construct only 1,102 flats. These new units in the urban area Michenzani suffered from chronic problems with water pressure, and along with those in Kikwajuni and Kilimani represented an addition of less than a thousand flats to Ng'ambo's pre-existing housing stock.[34] Yet in terms of square footage the Michenzani apartment blocks were the largest buildings ever constructed in Zanzibar, and their sheer scale did manage to impress some islanders, and grant the regime's development schemes a measure of legitimacy. For many islanders, however, the massive apartment blocks are stark reminders of the thousands of hours of forced labor required for their construction. And according to this author's own subjective aesthetic, they have aged about as well as most of their modernist Eastern European predecessors.[35]

A plan to demolish homes, relocate citizens, and force them to contribute unpaid labor to the construction of flats intended for only a relative few was controversial enough; even more so was the GDR's central role in setting up Zanzibar's notorious security apparatus. Markus Wolf recalls that almost as soon as diplomatic relations were established the Zanzibaris requested training in intelligence gathering—no doubt due to the GDR's excellent reputation in such matters. Karume's regime hoped to employ such expertise against potentially disloyal islanders. Wolf recalls:

---

32 See Laura Fair, *Pastimes and Politics: Culture, Community, and Identity in Post-Abolition Urban Zanzibar, 1890–1945* (Athens, OH: Ohio University Press, 2001).
33 Myers, *Verandahs of Power*, 111–112.
34 Ibid., 115, 123.
35 The regime's dependence on forced labor to build the new flats in Ng'ambo, as well as for other public works projects, is one of the most vividly remembered and well known facets of the revolutionary project. See, for example, Burgess, *Race, Revolution, and the Struggle for Human Rights*.

> In many ways we were naïve about the effects of our intervention in Third World countries. Our intelligence-gathering skills, honed by the experience of the Second World War and the Cold War, were transferred through our well-trained liaison officers and specialists. Prompted by their diligence, the security service in Zanzibar reached ridiculous dimensions. Relative to the size of the population, it was soon far bigger than our own, and it rapidly acquired a dynamic of its own over which we had no more influence.[36]

In hindsight, Wolf is defensive and apologetic about the consequences of such training. He must certainly have been aware of the willingness of people like Seif Bakari, Zanzibar's director of intelligence, to resort to torture and extra-judicial murder. Until research is undertaken in the *Stasi* archives, much will remain unknown about this murky relationship.[37] It is known that Seif Bakari and other islanders received security training in the GDR,[38] and that under Bakari's direction thousands of Zanzibaris were arrested in the decade following the 1964 Revolution. Many were tortured, and some were killed. Citizens were kept in a permanent state of fear; informants were believed to be everywhere, continually feeding information to security agents. Ali Sultan Issa, who served Karume's regime as Minister of Education, recalls:

> In those days, we could not trust even our own wives because they sometimes informed on their husbands to the state security, trained by the East Germans. And we all know how the East Germans controlled their people, so almost the same system applied here. ... We used to have a saying that "among three people one is not yours." We thought the walls had ears, they could be bugged.[39]

Kjersti Larsen notes that in her anthropological fieldwork, "elderly people recall the system of denunciation ... where neighbors, even family members, informed on each other."[40] Charles Swift, an American mental health officer assigned to Zanzibar in the late-1960s, recalls the atmosphere as "heavy with suspicion and apprehension. ... About the only people who spoke their minds were the patients at the psychiatric hospital."[41] While in popular memories the GDR is usu-

---

36 Wolf and McElvoy, *Man Without a Face*, 256.
37 See Anna Warda's project on The Ministry of Security in the "Third World", which includes a case study on Zanzibar: https://zzf potsdam.de/de/forschung/projekte/die-tatigkeiten-des-mfs.
38 Interview by author, Seif Bakari, Dodoma, Tanzania, May 1, 1995.
39 Burgess, *Race, Revolution and the Struggle for Human Rights*, 126–127.
40 Kjersti Larsen, "Silenced Voices, Recaptured Memories: Historical Imprints Within a Zanzibari Life-World," in *Social Memory, Silenced Voices, and Political Struggle: Remembering the Revolution in Zanzibar*, ed. William Cunningham Bissell and Marie-Aude Fouéré (Dar es Salaam: Mkuki na Nyota Publishers, Ltd., 2018), 259.
41 Charles Swift, *Dar Days: The Early Years in Tanzania* (New York: University Press of America, 2002), 98.

ally remembered as the patron and mentor of this hated security apparatus, locals tend to blame its cruelty on officials like Bakari, animated as they were by a lethal combination of paranoia and racial animus.

East-South Encounters in Memory

In oral histories of the revolution, Zanzibaris remember East Germany mostly for its investments in housing and security. Those who studied in the GDR, however, often have more vivid, personal memories. Such recollections inspired Abdulrazak Gurnah—Zanzibar's most respected novelist and twice a nominee for the Booker Prize—to provide us with the evocative story of Latif Muhammed, who in *By the Sea* obtains a scholarship to study dentistry in the GDR in the 1960s, and thus escape a series of tragedies that have engulfed his family.[42] His father is considered the town drunkard, and his mother is indiscrete in her infidelities. His older brother, meanwhile, is seduced by a visiting Persian merchant, who convinces him to board a dhow and follow him over the horizon. To compound the family's shame, the Persian merchant also tricks the father into relinquishing ownership of his house; the family suffers eviction, and the loss of their possessions.

Latif is laconic about his family's descent into poverty and disgrace. He merely notes that he wants to escape from his parents, to never "see them again, to leave them to their indignant decline and their poisoned lives."[43] Literature becomes a refuge—the books and magazines available at his school library, and at the United States Information Service (USIS). He praises America for offering air-conditioning, jazz recordings, and "beautiful" books he could actually borrow, and return. Through such American largesse Latif becomes exposed to Emerson, Hawthorne, Melville and other authors who excite "a noble curiosity," and which—unlike British authors—are unconnected to "a discourse of [colonial] tutelage and hierarchy." As "the Emperor of Hollywood and rock'n'roll," President Kennedy also impresses him. America's glamorous image is tainted, however, by the murder of Patrice Lumumba, footage of American police roughly handling black civil rights activists, and the CIA's reputation for "manipulating and controlling every small and big thing that caught their attention."[44]

---

[42] Gurnah interviewed his former classmates who studied in the GDR in the 1960s. Personal email communication from Abdulrazak Gurnah to the author, August 14, 2019. It bears notice that in *By the Sea* Latif's story represents only a fractional component of a much larger narrative.
[43] Gurnah, *By the Sea*, 115.
[44] Ibid., 106–107.

In his hunger for the cultural and intellectual capital of distant lands, Latif also visits the East German "Information Institute," where he discovers Schiller, Chekov, and Mikhail Sholokhov. And then as the mistress of the Minister of Education, Latif's mother manages to secure for her son a coveted scholarship to the GDR. Having sworn off alcohol, and become deeply religious, Latif's father worries Latif will lose his religious beliefs among the communist atheists of the East. He takes him to the mosque, where he leads the men in prayer, and then dispenses some fatherly advice: "When you get to that godless place, don't forget to pray. ... Whatever else you do, don't lose God, don't lose your way. There's darkness there." Blaming his father for his family's dissolution, Latif finds his newly found piety laughable.[45]

Latif's first impressions of the GDR are not favorable; the place strikes him as wet and gloomy, and his student hostel is cramped and poorly heated. It is a "catacomb" set aside for "dark" male students from Africa like himself. Uprooted and thrust into this artificial environment, the students jostle one another for respect and primacy. They create "an order of precedence and exclusions and dislikes" that is "detailed and precise, despite the appearance of raucous, romping disorder." Having never "lived amid such noise and play and violence before," Latif relishes "most of it cautiously, without questioning or wonder."[46] His roommate, Ali, hails from Guinea and immediately demonstrates his "sneering dislike," and need for deference. Full of "scorn and mockery and knowingness," Ali has a low opinion of the GDR's rank among the nations. "This is Eastern Europe," he says. "They don't have anything here. It's just as bad as Africa." He speculates that the meat in the cafeteria stew is not really meat, but goat feces, or asbestos.[47]

In such cynical company, Latif quickly loses any belief he may have had of being on a personal mission to help realize his country's future as a "developed" socialist society. Early on he declares to Ali: "I came to GDR to study, to learn a skill. As soon as I've done that, I'll go back home and do what I can to help my people." Ali just laughs, and dismisses Latif's attempt at idealism:

> Is that why you came, you Young Pioneer? I did not want to come here. I wanted to go to France, but the only scholarships available were to fraternal socialist countries, either to come here or go to the Soviet Union to learn to drive a snow plough. I think all the students here would prefer to be somewhere else.

---

45 Ibid., 111.
46 Ibid., 114.
47 Ibid.

Latif then concedes: "We all wanted to be in the land of Coca-Cola and blue jeans, even if it wasn't just for those refined pleasures that we wanted to be there."[48]

Though Latif is an avid student, and earns the respect of his German instructors, he observes a relationship between them and the rest of the students rife with "misunderstanding and insolence and mischief."[49] As a whole, the teachers are neither very fond of nor impressed by their African charges. And in turn, the students

> acted superior to the teachers, as if we knew about things which the teachers had no inkling of – useful and complicated things, not just a couple of wedding songs or a sonorous prayer or how to play a harmonica. I wondered then, and still wonder now, who did we think we were? Perhaps we knew that we were beggar pawns in somebody else's plans, captured and delivered there. Held there. Perhaps the scorn was like the prisoner's sly refusal of the gaoler's authority, stopping short of insurrection. Or perhaps most of us were reluctant students, and reluctant students are always like that with their teachers. Or perhaps still, something stern and unyielding and despising in our teacher's demeanor made us resistant to them. Or perhaps even further still, as one of the teachers told us, the heat in our countries and in our food had sapped our motivation and drive, and made us prisoners to instinct and self-indulgence.[50]

Thus despite the rhetoric of socialist solidarity Latif's German instructors possess attitudes and draw conclusions about their "dark" students that mirror colonial and Orientalist tropes of equatorial idleness and hedonism. They see their students' less than stellar academic performance as indicative of broad cultural and racial norms. The students, meanwhile, do not view their instructors as comrades in the great progressive march of humanity, but rather as curmudgeonly and mean-spirited prison guards, whose austere and often disdainful attitudes deserve only mischief and mockery in return. And yet Gurnah goes further than merely setting out a well-worn dialectic between European paternalism and post-colonial pride. Through Latif he asks: "who did we think we were?" Did the students really know more than their teachers?

Though Latif includes himself in this question, he is clearly open to new understandings. For him, East Germany is "like a gleaming new order, intimidating in its earnest and brutal self-assurance."[51] He does not, however, expound much further on his personal impressions of this socialist new order, other than to note

---

48 Ibid., 119.
49 Ibid., 115.
50 Ibid.
51 Ibid., 104.

the local town's unwelcoming architecture and wind-swept emptiness, which may be read as a metaphor for sterile bureaucratic central planning. He also refers to the "authoritarian degradations of the GDR," but without elaboration.[52] Otherwise, his interpretations of life in the East are free of socialist references, and could be the impressions of any African traveler coming to Germany long before or after the Cold War. Accompanying Ali on a walk around town on a Sunday afternoon, they encounter racist or at least socially obtuse behavior. A clutch of male German youths approach on the sidewalk; Ali tenses for an altercation, but the boys merely laugh and exclaim, "*Afrikernische.*"[53] Latif remarks: "their swagger and their laughter made the word ugly. It was shocking, that casual mockery, but there would be time to get used to that and worse, to learn to recover from such smug disregard."[54]

Later, while riding a nearly empty bus a German man "wearing a dark, heavy workman's coat" leans over the back of his seat and stares at Latif "for about five minutes without interruption." When Latif eventually "glanced back into the bus, it was to find the man's liquid eyes resting watchfully on me, unraveling a deep mystery. ... After his five minutes were up, the man made a snorting noise and turned to face the front again."[55] Aside from whatever may be deduced from a snort and a stare, Latif's encounters with ordinary East Germans are devoid of violence and overt abuse. And on a trip to Dresden Latif is amazed to learn of the city's "medieval triumphs, its great industries, its beautiful buildings," as well as devastation suffered in the recent war. He regrets that his colonial education was limited to the historic doings of the British, and made no mention of Dresden, "or a multitude of other Dresdens. They had been there for all these centuries despite me, ignorant of me, oblivious of my existence. It was a staggering thought, how little it had been possible to know and remain contented."[56]

Latif's visit to Dresden figures as part of a growing awareness of a very humanist side of the socialist East, first glimpsed in the works of Schiller and Chekov. Further nurturing this awareness is a pen pal relationship with a young German woman named Elleke, who sends Latif a photo of herself wearing a leopard-

---

52 Ibid., 135–136.
53 This might refer to the German adjective "afrikanische."
54 Ibid., 119.
55 Ibid., 135.
56 Ibid., 122.

skin coat and a "friendly satirical smile."⁵⁷ The two agree to meet; and Ali begs to come along as a sort of bodyguard, in case he is harassed by "German thugs." Ali says "You are so young. ... So inexperienced. Such a sad creature from the bush. You'll need some worldly advice when you meet up with the leopard-skin coat."⁵⁸

Latif goes alone, however, and is approached by a young man named Jan, who announces he is Elleke—that he impersonated a young woman in their correspondence as a prank that went further than intended. It all began when a speaker came to his college "to talk about the work that the GDR was doing in Africa," which Jan dismissed as "the usual campaigning rubbish about fraternal relations." He decided to invent Elleke as a sort of secret slap against the authorities, but which to his surprise yielded a letter from Latif, and the beginning of a very satisfying correspondence.⁵⁹ A student of automobile design at a local college, Jan introduces Latif to his mother who is tall, graceful, and a former beauty. Both he and his mother are well read, fluent in English, and pepper their conversation with literary allusions rather than socialist rhetoric. Indeed, though having lived through two world wars, and seen the rise of both fascism and socialism, the mother is remarkably independent in her thinking. Above all, she may be described as an irrepressible humanist, who through life's many vicissitudes retains a passionate attachment to literature and philosophy.⁶⁰

Latif is surprised to discover the mother also has her own deep well of African stories to tell, as well as scathing ruminations on the morality of settler colonialism. Before World War One her parents were wealthy landowners in Austria; when Austria lost the war the family booked passage to Kenya, and purchased a coffee farm. They felt they had a right to "places that were only occupied by people with dark skins and frizzy hair." Her parents didn't inquire much into the "duplicity and force" of colonial rule; all that mattered was "the natives were pacified and labour was cheap." And life continued that way until 1938, when they were informed that if war erupted in Europe they would be interned. So they sold their farm, moved to Dresden, and with their

---

57 Ibid., 117. For Gurnah, this pen pal relationship was autobiographical. However, unlike in *By the Sea*, he and Elleke never met in real life. Personal email communication from Abdulrazak Gurnah to the author, August 14, 2019.
58 Gurnah, *By the Sea*, 122–123.
59 Ibid., 124. For a thoughtful examination of Hungary's contemporaneous attempts to nurture a youth culture of international socialist solidarity, see Mark and Apor, "Socialism Goes Global."
60 Gurnah, *By the Sea*, 125–128.

life's savings bought a large and imposing home. After the war the new socialist regime confiscated their home and divided it into smaller apartments.[61]

When Jan mentions his mother wrote a memoir of her time in Africa, she dismisses it as "lying nostalgia." She says,

> If I were writing it now, I would also tell the horrible stories and depress everyone, like a boring old woman. ... My father was fond of saying that our superiority over the natives was only possible with their consent. ... Poor Papa, he didn't think that it was torture and murder that were committed in our name which gave us that authority in the first place. He thought it was something mysterious to do with justice and temperate conduct, something we acquired from reading Hegel and Schiller, and going to Mass. Never mind the exclusions and expulsions, and the summary judgements delivered with contemptuous assurance. ... It was our moral superiority which made the natives afraid of us.[62]

If anything in East Germany strikes Latif as especially admirable, it is this sort of ruthless honesty. Years later, Latif recalls the way Jan and his mother "treated every question as if it tested their integrity, as if they had to guard against the duplicitous revision which alters the balance of a story and turns it into something heroic." He praises their "sustained passion for ideas that could not be destroyed completely, not even by living through the obscenities of colonialism, nor the inhumanities of the Nazi war and the Holocaust, nor by the authoritarian degradations of the GDR."[63] Latif admires their obstinate belief in humanist values, and unwillingness to conform to hegemonic narratives and ways of seeing the world.

While initially willing to at least try and sound like an idealistic Young Pioneer, Latif comes to see the great distance between the transcendent rhetoric of fraternal East-South relations and the depressing realities of life in the GDR, including an ever-present fear of arrest and imprisonment. He becomes an accomplice in Jan's elaborate plan of escape. The two pose as tourists visiting Yugoslavia; from there they board a train to Austria, where the authorities send them on to Munich. The two then separate, with Jan staying in Germany, and Latif continuing on to further studies in England. Thus we see how, in an effort to escape his tragic family circumstances, a shy and precocious young Zanzibari male accepts an opportunity to study in the GDR, and there loses any faith he may have had in the socialist project. Within a few months he takes an opportunity to travel to London, the capital of British imperialism, and yet also a center of humanist learning and scholarship.

---

61 Ibid., 131–132.
62 Ibid., 132–133.
63 Ibid., 135–136.

Although a work of fiction, Latif's story is inspired by Gurnah's own life experiences, in that he left Zanzibar in the 1960s to study literature in Great Britain, where he has resided for most of his adult life. Like Latif in *By the Sea*, Gurnah eventually became a university lecturer, as well as a noted author of both novels and literary criticism. While he did not spend time in the GDR as a student, Gurnah developed his account of Latif from the recollections of fellow Zanzibaris who had. And although highly mediated, *By the Sea* nevertheless proposes a way for us to view the Zanzibari encounter with East Germany in the 1960s as one in which African students were on the surface willing to respect the basic tenets of the socialist project. Yet because they were not consulted in the role they were to play in this project, they sometimes felt they were "beggar pawns in somebody else's plans."[64] And though their presence in the GDR was meant as living proof of the socialist fraternity of nations, for some this fraternity remained abstract, and less real or impactful than the personal connections they made with German citizens while abroad.[65] Anxious over where such unscripted encounters might lead, the GDR's notion of "solidarity" did not actually encourage such personal associations. As Toni Weis observes, the GDR was far more interested in the solidarity of abstract peoples than of real, flesh-and-blood people.[66] And yet some Africans were able to leave their student hostels and form associations with East Germans, through which they were introduced to a surprising world of private passions and subjective experience.[67]

Conclusion

Back in Zanzibar, the effort to turn the theory of socialist internationalism into the reality of modernist development was facing unforeseen obstacles. When Wolf first arrived in the islands in 1964, he soon realized Zanzibaris had exaggerated ideas of what sort of aid the GDR could provide: "They would mournfully

---

64 Ibid., 115.
65 For another perspective, based upon oral histories of Tanzanian students in the GDR, see also Eric Burton, "Navigating Global Socialism: Tanzanian Students in and Beyond East Germany," *Cold War History* 19 (2019); Eric Burton, "Introduction: Journeys of Education and Struggle: African Mobility in Times of Decolonization and Cold War." *Stichproben. Vienna Journal of African Studies* 18 (2018).
66 Toni Weis, "The Politics Machine: On the Concept of 'Solidarity' in East German Support for SWAPO," *Journal of Southern African Studies* 37 (2011).
67 For other perhaps less mediated perspectives on how African students remembered their time in the GDR, see Alberto and Schenck; Osei, annotated by Harisch; Piepiorka and Buanaissa; Schenck and Raposo, all in this volume.

show us crumbling boats, old radios, and fraying telephone cables left behind by the British, hoping that we could restore the infrastructure of their entire country."[68] If islanders saw the GDR as a source of endless munificence, and if East Germans saw their relationship with Zanzibar as a means by which to break out of their diplomatic isolation, and build idealistic ties with a state that met their standards of socialist authenticity, the disillusionment was on both sides. By 1968 President Karume was increasingly upset with the poor results and/or high cost of GDR-sponsored fishing and dairy projects, the poor English skills of East German instructors, and the amount Zanzibar was expected to pay back on interest-bearing loans. He became impatient with any foreign expertise that could not be obtained at minimal cost—and by "minimal cost" he meant the Chinese, who offered grants and interest-free loans, and sent experts and advisors willing to subsist on very little. Some of Karume's frustration with the East Germans percolated down to the popular level. An East German biology teacher, when asked by his students in 1967 about the size of his salary, was duly informed that for the same amount Zanzibar could support five or ten Chinese instructors, all of whom could live in the house he alone occupied.[69]

Karume's attitude became one of suspicion of all forms of technocratic expertise; hence his closure of the short-lived GDR-sponsored "School of Economics," and decision in the late-1960s to dramatically curtail the numbers of Zanzibaris sent overseas for training and education.[70] He began to say at rallies, "*Tumesoma hatukujua, lakini tumejifunza tulijua,*" which roughly translates as "We studied and didn't understand, but then we learned through practical experience."[71] Karume's disdain for experts was an extension of his general dislike for educated persons, since from the 1950s they were the ones in the ASP most likely to challenge his authority. Yet Karume also parted ways with the GDR over his unwillingness to follow any "scientific" blueprint for socialism that entailed collectivization of agriculture, for example, or curbing the privileges of the political elite. And as Eric Burton observes, the East Germans were sometimes put off by the racial animosity that animated many of Karume's

---

68 Wolf and McElvoy, *Man Without a Face*, 254. For an engaging American perspective on the Cold War rivalries playing out in Zanzibar, see Don Petterson, *Revolution in Zanzibar: An American Cold War Tale* (Boulder, CO: Westview Press, 2002).
69 Interview by author, Eckhart Schultz, Zanzibar Town, July 22, 2004.
70 Burton, "Diverging Visions," 108–109.
71 Interview by author, Rubesa Hafidh Rubesa, Mtambwe Nyale, Zanzibar, June 21, 2010. These words were featured on a large banner strung up on the government-built Michenzani flats, suggesting Zanzibaris did not need East German expertise to complete the project (photograph in author's possession).

most cherished initiatives. Though they once viewed him as an "anti-imperialist progressive," by 1970 he was a "nationalist conservative" who "artificially fuelled racial tensions for personal interests."[72] By then China had supplanted the GDR as Zanzibar's leading foreign patron, and about 200 East German teachers and "experts" in Zanzibar had already left, or were on their way home.[73]

The disillusionment was mutual—East Germans were convinced Karume was not a true socialist, and Karume felt that other than in the realm of security the GDR had failed to live up to expectations. It wasn't only the obstacles of language, culture, and distance that eventually brought an end to the flow of students, technicians, and teachers between East Germany and Zanzibar. By 1970 it was clear to both sides their shared vision of a socialist future was hollow, superficial, and unable to paper over serious differences of interest and ideology. The political elite of both countries felt it was time to be more selective in their international partners, and to be more aware of the potentially shallow quality of an imagined future that, while possessing immense appeal, was unable to reconcile diverging concepts of revolution, development, and solidarity.[74]

Thus just as Zanzibar achieved sovereignty during the height of the Cold War, the GDR was poised and ready to break out of its diplomatic isolation and conduct its first major development projects in Africa. Believing they were part of a global drama in which one people after another would embrace socialism and achieve modernist development, East Germans felt they were playing a significant and honorable role in advancing the irreversible progressive momentum of history. By 1990, however, the GDR had merged with West Germany, and Zanzibar had lost key aspects of its sovereignty: its presidents were now selected by Tanzania's ruling party based overwhelmingly on the mainland. Severe economic decline had also compelled Zanzibar to roll back one revolutionary initiative after another, and to abandon anything more than lip service to socialism. Instead of gazing eastward, state officials now looked to the West and Middle East for aid, expertise, and tourists to fill the many hotels now clustered along Zanzibar's fine white sand beaches. And Abdulrazak Gurnah was now asking his friends and former classmates who studied in the GDR—caught up as they were in an era of high idealism and socialist solidarity—how they managed to negotiate the disparate avenues of opportunity suddenly presented to them.

---

72 Burton, "Diverging Visions," 111.
73 Burgess, "A Socialist Diaspora," 282; Clayton, *Zanzibar Revolution*, 148.
74 For the difference between "development" and "solidarity," see Weis, "The Politics Machine," 352, 357.

Bibliography

Al Barwani, Ali Muhsin. *Conflicts and Harmony in Zanzibar (Memoirs)*. No publisher, 1997.
Babu, Abdulrahman Mohamed. "I Was the First Third World Minister to Recognize the GDR." In *I Saw the Future and It Works: Essays Celebrating the Life of Comrade Abdulrahman Mohamed Babu, 1924–1996*, edited by Haroub Othman, 48–58. Dar es Salaam, Tanzania: E & D Limited, 2001.
Bennett, Norman. *A History of the Arab State of Zanzibar*. Cambridge, MA: Methuen and Co., 1978.
Burgess, G. Thomas. "Mao in Zanzibar: Nationalism, Discipline, and the (De)Construction of Afro-Asian Solidarities." In *Making a World After Empire: The Bandung Moment and Its Political Afterlives*, edited by Christopher Lee, 196–234. Athens, OH: Ohio University Press, 2010.
Burgess, G. Thomas. "To Differentiate Rice from Grass: Youth Labor Camps in Revolutionary Zanzibar." In *Generations Past: Youth in East African History*, edited by Andrew Burton and Hélène Charton-Bigot, 221–236. Athens, OH: Ohio University Press, 2010.
Burgess, G. Thomas. *Race, Revolution, and the Struggle for Human Rights in Zanzibar: The Memoirs of Ali Sultan Issa and Seif Sharif Hamad*. Athens, OH: Ohio University Press, 2009.
Burgess, G. Thomas. "A Socialist Diaspora: Ali Sultan Issa, the Soviet Union, and the Zanzibari Revolution." In *Africa in Russia, Russia in Africa: Three Centuries of Encounters*, edited by Maxim Matusevich, 263–291. Trenton, NJ: Africa World Press, 2007.
Burgess, G. Thomas. "An Imagined Generation: Umma Youth in Nationalist Zanzibar." In *In Search of a Nation: Histories of Authority and Dissidence from Tanzania: Essays in Honor of I.M. Kimambo*, edited by Gregory Maddox, James Giblin, and Y.Q. Lawi, 216–249. London: James Currey Publishers, 2005.
Burgess, G. Thomas. "The Young Pioneers and the Rituals of Citizenship in Revolutionary Zanzibar." *Africa Today* 51 (2005): 3–29.
Burgess, G. Thomas. "Youth and the Revolution: Mobility and Discipline in Zanzibar, 1950–80." PhD. diss., Indiana University, 2001.
Burton, Eric. "Diverging Visions in Revolutionary Spaces: East German Advisors and Revolution from Above in Zanzibar, 1964–1970." In *Between East and South: Spaces of Ineraction in the Globalizing Economy of the Cold War*, edited by Anna Calori, Anne-Kristen Hartmetz, Bence Kocsev, James Mark, and Jan Zofka, 85–115. Berlin, Boston: De Gruyter Oldenbourg, 2019.
Burton, Eric. "Navigating Global Socialism: Tanzanian Students in and Beyond East Germany." *Cold War History* 19 (2019): 63–83.
Burton, Eric. "Introduction: Journeys of Education and Struggle: African Mobility in Times of Decolonization and Cold War." *Stichproben. Vienna Journal of African Studies* 18 (2018): 1–17.
Clayton, Anthony. *The Zanzibar Revolution and its Aftermath*. Hamden, CT: Archon Books, 1978.
Glassman, Jonathon. *War of Words, War of Stones, Racial Thought and Violence in Colonial Zanzibar*. Bloomington: Indiana University Press, 2011.

Gleijeses, Piero. *Conflicting Missions: Havana, Washington, and Africa, 1959–1976*. Chapel Hill: University of North Carolina Press, 2002.

Gorsuch, Anne. "'Cuba, My Love:' The Romance of Revolutionary Cuba in the Soviet Sixties." *American Historical Review* 120 (2015): 497–526.

Gurnah, Abdulrazak. *By the Sea*. New York: New Press, 2001.

Kyle, Keith. "The Zanzibar Coup." *The Spectator*, January 25, 1964.

Kyle, Keith. "How it Happened." *The Spectator*, February 14, 1964.

Larsen, Kjersti. "Silenced Voices, Recaptured Memories: Historical Imprints Within a Zanzibari Life-World." In *Social Memory, Silenced Voices, and Political Struggle: Remembering the Revolution in Zanzibar*, edited by William Cunningham Bissell and Marie-Aude Fouéré, 251–278. Dar es Salaam: Mkuki na Nyota Publishers, 2018.

Mark, James, and Péter Apor, "Socialism Goes Global: Decolonization and the Making of a New Culture of Internationalism in Socialist Hungary, 1956–1989." *The Journal of Modern History* 87 (2015): 852–891.

Muehlenbeck, Philip E., and Natalia Telepneva, eds. *Warsaw Pact Intervention in the Third World: Aid and Influence in the Cold War*. London: I.B. Tauris, 2018.

Myers, Garth Andrew. *Verandahs of Power: Colonialism and Space in Urban Africa*. Syracuse: Syracuse University Press, 2003.

Petterson, Don. *Revolution in Zanzibar: An American Cold War Tale*. Boulder, CO: Westview Press, 2002.

Pouwels, Randal. *The Horn and the Crescent: Cultural change and traditional Islam on the East African coast, 800–1900*. Cambridge: Cambridge University Press, 1987.

Shivji, Issa. *Pan-Africanism or Pragmatism? Lessons of Tanganyika-Zanzibar Union*. Dar es Salaam, Tanzania: Mkuki na Nyota Publishers, 2008.

Schneppen, Heinz. *Zanzibar and the Germans: A Special Relationship, 1844–1966*. Dar es Salaam, Tanzania: National Museums of Tanzania, 1998.

Swift, Charles. *Dar Days: The Early Years in Tanzania*. New York: University Press of America, 2002.

Weis, Toni. "The Politics Machine: On the Concept of 'Solidarity' in East German Support for SWAPO." *Journal of Southern African Studies* 37 (2011): 351–367.

Wilson, Amrit. *The Threat of Liberation: Imperialism and Revolution in Zanzibar*. London: Pluto Press, 2013.

Wolf, Markus, with Anne McElvoy. *Man Without a Face: The Autobiography of Communism's Greatest Spymaster*. New York: Random House, 1997.

J. A. Osei, with an annotation by Immanuel R. Harisch[1]
7 My Impression of the German Democratic Republic [Life Itself Exposes Lies][2]

Editor's note

J. A. Osei's report of his sojourn in the GDR, which is fully reproduced below, is to be found in J. A. Osei to Heinz Deutschland, Accra, July 22, 1964, SAPMO-BArch, DY 79/615. The original title Osei had chosen for his report – "My impression of the German Democratic Republic" – was crossed out by one (anonymous) member of the editorial board of the journal *Correspondence* and changed to "Life itself exposes lies". Ultimately, Osei's contribution was printed in *Correspondence* under the title "Reality exposes lies" without, to my knowledge, any further queries by the editorial board.[3] *Correspondence* was the quarterly bulletin of the Faculty for Foreign Students[4] at the Bernau college. From 1964 to 1966 it was edited and published in both English and French by the staff of the faculty, with the editorial team usually consisting of six to eight members. It was sent to all alumni of the trade union college and was "meant to report on your and our

---

1 I would like to thank the anonymous reviewer as well as my colleagues and co-editors Eric Burton and Marcia C. Schenck for their encouragement and valuable comments on this annotation. My gratitude also goes to Esther Asenso-Agyemang from the University of Legon for discussing Osei's letters and for help in obtaining literature on the Ghana TUC, and to Nana Osei-Opare for sharing his manuscript on workers' discontent in Ghana with me.
2 The undertaking to have African and Asian alumni write about their experiences in East Germany was linked to the fifteenth anniversary of the GDR. In June 1964, the Institute for Foreign Students (*Ausländerinstitut*) of the FDGB's trade union college Fritz Heckert in Bernau, close to Berlin (see Angermann, this volume), had actively contacted 42 alumni of the first three courses and asked them to send back a paper on the topic "I lived and studied 18 months in the GDR". Twenty-four former students, among them Osei, responded to the call. In 1964, a selected number of them were published in the third issue of *Correspondence* in both English and French. See Heinz Deutschland to Karl Kampfert, n. d. [1964], Stiftung Archiv der Parteien und Massenorganisationen der DDR im Bundesarchiv, Berlin (henceforth: SAPMO-BArch), DY 79/403.
3 See J. A. Osei, "Reality exposes lies," *Correspondence. Informationsbulletin Nr. 3 der Fakultät für Ausländerstudium an der Hochschule der Deutschen Gewerkschaften "Fritz Heckert" Bernau* (1964).
4 Also commonly referred to as Institute for Foreign Students.

∂ OpenAccess. © 2021 J. A. Osei, with an annotation by Immanuel R. Harisch, published by De Gruyter. This work is licensed under the Creative Commons Attribution 4.0 International License.
https://doi.org/10.1515/9783110623543-007

activities. It is meant to convey aid and instructions to assist you in your further studies and to tighten the bonds of friendship connecting us forever."[5]

In order to give our readers an impression of the original source, Osei's report is reproduced here without corrections. Mistakes are not indicated with [sic!] so as to facilitate a smoother reading. I believe that the handwritten comments by the East German members of the editorial board of *Correspondence*, which are marked in the letter by square brackets and strikethrough, offer interesting insights into what the editorial board in the GDR deemed unacceptable and where they polished phrases for the final version.

* * *

In September, 1961 the Trade Union Congress of Ghana[6] sent a number of students to be trained in the College of the Confederation of Free German Trade Un-

---

[5] See "Editorial," *Correspondence Informationsbulletin Nr. 1 der Fakultät für Ausländerstudium an der Hochschule der Deutschen Gewerkschaften "Fritz Heckert" Bernau* (1964), 3. Digital copy in the possession of Immanuel R. Harisch. I thank the former director of the Institute for Foreign Students, Heinz Deutschland, for allowing me to digitize several issues of *Correspondence*.

[6] The predecessor of the Ghana TUC was founded in 1943 under the name of the Gold Coast Trade Union Congress (GCTUC) and was modeled after British industrial relations. In 1950, during the early struggle for self-government, the GCTUC organized a general strike which decisively shaped the outcome of the campaign for the benefit of the Convention People's Party (CPP) led by Kwame Nkrumah. During the 1950s, however, the CPP joined the British colonial office in the crusade against left-wing, Marxist trade unionists who sought to establish contact to the World Federation of Trade Unions (WFTU). Internationally, the GCTUC remained in the Western, anti-communist camp of the rivalrous International Confederation of Free Trade Unions (ICFTU). Accra was host to one of the two ICFTU informational centers on the African continent as well as to the ICFTU's first African Regional Conference. With the passing of the Industrial Relations Act (IRA) in parliament in 1958, however, the Ghana TUC prepared the ground for its disaffiliation from the ICFTU in 1959 and was reorganized, now to consist of 16 industrial unions – the Timber & Woodworkers' Union, of which J. A. Osei was deputy general secretary after his return from the GDR, being one of them. The changes due to the IRA, criticized by the ICFTU and International Labour Organization (ILO), were far-reaching: to be a member of the Ghana TUC became obligatory for workers; Ghana's industrial unions had to affiliate with the TUC central in Accra, where the TUC had built a new headquarters with money lent from the CPP government; the "check-off" system was introduced, which allowed the companies to deduct membership fees from the workers' salary; and the right to strike was severely curtailed. The Ghana TUC general secretary was a minister of the CPP government at the same time. As a result, the Ghana TUC became severely restricted in its agency, although it profited from a strong financial and organizational base after the integration into the CPP's political machine. See Douglas G. Anglin, "Ghana, the West, and the Soviet Union," *The Canadian Journal of Economics and Political Science / Revue Canadienne d'Economique et de Science Politique* 24 (1958): 161, 164; Imanuel Geiss, *Gewerkschaften in Afrika* (Hannover: Verlag für Literatur und Zeitgeschehen, 1965), 197–

ions in Bernau/Berlin. I happened to be one of the luckiest chaps selected for this course.[7] The time of our journey coincided with the closing down of the border between the East and West Berlin which happened on 13th August, 1961. [i. e. the erection of the antifascist protection wall].

It is an admitted fact that any attempt by any state to obstruct capitalist intrigues and wicked machinations, designed to undermine the progress and development of that state, is always repulsed by the capitalist press with vile and slanderous propaganda. Immediately after the closing down of this border, an attempt to safeguard the G.D.R.'s economy, the newspapers of the Western Al-

---

198; Ioan Davies, *African Trade Unions* (Harmondsworth: Penguin Books, 1966), 174–180; John Kraus, "The Political Economy of Industrial Relations in Ghana," in Industrial Relations in Africa, ed. Ukandi G. Damachi, Dieter H. Seibel, and Lester Trachtman (London: Macmillan, 1979), 132; Paul Tiyambe Zeleza, "Pan-African Trade Unionism: Unity and Discord," *Transafrican Journal of History* 15 (1986): 182; Peter Blay Arthiabah and Harry Tham Mbiah, *Half a Century of Toil, Trouble and Progress: The History of the Trades Union Congress of Ghana 1939–1995* (Accra: Gold-Type Publications, 1995), 55–98; Frederick Cooper, *Decolonization and African Society. The Labor Question in French and British Africa* (Cambridge: Cambridge University Press, 1996), 432–438; Naaborko Sackeyfio-Lenoch, "The Ghana Trades Union Congress and the Politics of International Labor Alliances, 1957–1971," *International Review of Social History* 62 (2017): 194, 203, 213.

7 During his stay in the GDR, Osei acted as leader of the 13-person Ghanaian delegation, which was delegated by the Ghana TUC. Following a cooperation agreement with the East German national trade union federation *Freier Deutscher Gewerkschaftsbund* (FDGB), the Ghana TUC dispatched between 10 and 15 students to study on each course at the trade union college in Bernau. Prior to his stay abroad, Osei had completed 10 years of primary and secondary schooling. At college in the GDR, the Ghanaian unionist graduated from an 18-months long-term course, taking political-ideological subjects such as "The socialist world system," "The revolutionary international workers' movement," "The national liberation movement" and "Inquiries into problems of socialist economics." The program was complemented by more practical lessons on "Problems of trade union organization" as well as by a polytechnic education and internships in GDR companies, an accordance with the students' interests. See "Jahresarbeitsbericht für die Zeit vom 1.9. Bis 31.12.1961," n. d. [January 1962], SAPMO-BArch, DY 79/83; "Lehrplan des 3. afro-asiatischen Lehrgangs 1962/63, " n. d. [1962], SAPMO-BArch, DY 79/271. For the traineeships see e. g. "Zur Auswertung des praktischen Einsatzes vom 12.–26. Januar 1963," February 7, 1963, SAPMO-BArch, DY 79/2500, among others; for an analysis of the third course (1961–63) at the college, consult Eric Angermann, "'Ihr Gehört Auch Zur Avantgarde': Afrikanische Gewerkschafter an der FDGB-Hochschule Fritz Heckert (1961–1963)" (Master's thesis, Georg-August-Universität Göttingen, 2018) and Chapter Two "Where do Correct Ideas Come From? The FDGB Institute for Foreign Students and the Coming of the Sino-Soviet Split" in George Bodie, "Global GDR? Sovereignty, Legitimacy and Decolonization in the German Democratic Republic, 1960–1989" (PhD diss., University College London, 2019). For a micro-historical analysis of African students' agency at the college and their attempts to set up an independent committee, see Angermann's chapter in this volume.

lies carried false news perpetrated against the Sovereign State of the German Democratic Republic. One of such news was captioned: "Running from Hell to Heaven." This news gave horrible account of the G.D.R. as how the inhabitants were not free and how they could not get food sufficiently to feed themselves and their families, and therefore were escaping from East Berlin to the West and so on and so forth. Really, it was only the person who was determined in purpose who could defy those wicked propaganda to go to East Germany at that moment.

Determined as we were to train and harden ourselves to oust the final remains of capitalism from our new state of Ghana[8] we were not disturbed at all by these news. Finally, therefore, on 6th September, 1961 we flew from the Accra International Airport to for Democratic Berlin and to hear, see and learn for ourselves what the European Capitalists had been saying of that country.

---

[8] Osei's witty writing style and his socialist rhetoric were certainly shaped both by his stay in the GDR and by the socialist modernization project that Ghana's CPP, led by Kwame Nkrumah, was undertaking at the time of writing. That Osei strongly identified with the CPP's aims and policies becomes evident in his personal correspondence with the faculty's staff. See the correspondence between Osei and the director of the Institute for Foreign Students, Heinz Deutschland, in the signatures SAPMO-BArch, DY 79/615, DY 79/614, DY 79/615, DY 79/616 and DY 79/617, which contain thousands of letters between the mainly African alumni of the college and the institute's employees. Historian Sara Pugach has noted that these letters present crucial insights into the lifeworlds of the returning students in their home contexts. See Sara Pugach, "African Students in Cold War Leipzig: Using University Archives to Recover a Forgotten History," in *Sources and Methods for African History and Culture: Essays in Honour of Adam Jones*, ed. Geert Castryck et al. (Leipzig: Leipziger Universitätsverlag, 2016), 551–552. Works which have made use of these letters are Angermann, "Ihr Gehört auch zur Avantgarde" and Immanuel R. Harisch, "'Mit Gewerkschaftlichem Gruß!' Afrikanische GewerkschafterInnen an der FDGB-Gewerkschaftshochschule Fritz Heckert in der DDR," *Stichproben. Vienna Journal of African Studies* 18 (2018). For a look on the CPP's mobilization strategies for the "labouring masses towards work and happiness", see Kate Skinner, "Who Knew the Minds of the People? Specialist Knowledge and Developmentalist Authoritarianism in Postcolonial Ghana," *The Journal of Imperial and Commonwealth History* 39 (2011). A recent panorama on the Nkrumah years can be found in *Kwame Nkrumah 1909–1972: A Controversial African Visionary*, ed. Bea Lundt and Christoph Marx (Stuttgart: Franz Steiner Verlag, 2016). For Ghana's relations with the USSR during the Nkrumah years, see Nana Osei-Opare, "Uneasy Comrades: Postcolonial Statecraft, Race, and Citizenship, Ghana–Soviet Relations, 1957–1966," *Journal of West African History* 5 (2019): 85–111; on workers' discontent with the CPP and the Ghana TUC, see Nana Osei-Opare, "'If You Trouble a Hungry Snake, You Will Force It to Bite You': Rethinking Archival Pessimism, Worker Discontent, and Petition Writing in Ghana, 1957–66," *Journal of African History* (forthcoming).

First Lie Nailed Down:

The Polish two engined plane which took us from Amsterdam touched the beautiful Berlin Schönefeld Airport at exactly 4.30 p. m. We were in a different country with different people with different language. Contrary to our expectations a member of the Airport Unit of the People's Police of the G.D.R., who could not speak English approached us and by his action seemed to ask as to whether he could help us. He was smart and neat, wearing a cheerful countenance which depicted his kindness. This gentle Officer led us through all the custom formalities without any of my Comrades encountering any inconveniences.

Just as we could [had] finish[ed] with the Airport and Custom Officials, a 6 foot tall and well built man arrived at the Airport and hastily came to us. He introduced himself as Comrade Horst Thomas, a lecturer of the Fritz Heckert College, where we were to go and that he was to be our guide. The simple but impressive receptions accorded [to] us by Comrade Thomas and the Airport Authorities were quite sufficient to disbelieve the lies told in the Western Press about the G.D.R.

At the College

After some minutes drive we arrived at the "Fritz Heckert Institute" [College]. Contrary to the assertion that the College is a "Concentration Camp"[9] I found to my amazement magnificent buildings with beautiful surroundings; this environment alone is quite sufficient to satisfy the whims of any ambitious student.[10]

---

9 Unfortunately, I was unable to retrieve this particular report, allegedly from a media outlet in a Western capitalist country.
10 Since the Weimar Republic, the German Trade Union College (*Hochschule der Deutschen Gewerkschaften*) Fritz Heckert offered various courses for German trade unionists in Bernau, a suburb of Berlin. The college, which was inaugurated in 1930, was designed by the Swiss architect Hannes Meyer, director of the *Bauhaus* in Dessau. In 1933, the national socialists converted the school into a training center for fascist leaders (*Reichsführerschule*). From 1947 onward, the newly founded FDGB held seminars in the Soviet occupation zone. After the foundation of the GDR in 1949 and under the directorship of anti-fascist trade unionist Hermann Duncker, the college expanded to train union functionaries of the FDGB. In 1960, the Institute for Foreign Students was moved from Leipzig-Leutzsch to the site of the Bernau college where new facilities had been constructed and additional staff was hired. See Alfred Förster, "Zur Geschichte der Gewerkschafts-Schule in Bernau (1928–90)," in *Der Freie Deutsche Gewerkschaftsbund. Seine Rechte und Leistungen. Tatsachen, Erfahrungen, Standpunkte*, ed. Horst Bednarek, Harald Bühl, and Werner Koch (Berlin: Verlag am Park, 2006).

In the Institute's Dining Room both the Whites and the Blacks dined together.[11] The mixture of both Whites and Blacks in such a room reminds one of the keyboard of a piano. This completely relieved us of any fear that haunted our minds because of those obnoxious publications about the G.D.R.[12]

After seeing all these and many more I said to myself that "HELL" is an imaginary place of permanent torment of fire, (with apology to the Bible) and if one is to believe that the G.D.R. is a "HELL", as indicated by the Western Press, then to me Hell is a comfortable and happier place to live.

---

11 As Yevette Richards has shown for the ICFTU's own trade union college, the African Labour College in Uganda's capital Kampala, the fact that a trade union college's dining room like the one in Bernau was shared by black and white students and staff was by no means universal in the late 1950s and early 1960s. In the early period of the ICFTU college, the white personnel dined in the main dining hall of Kampala's exclusive Imperial Hotel while the black students, the Kenyan deputy principal Odero-Jowi, and the black U.S.-American teacher McCray sat at tables in another hall, close to the kitchen. In January 1959, when two African students were refused entry to the main dining hall and the white racist hotel management threatened them with expulsion, the students collectively refused to eat and asked for airline tickets home. They fiercely criticized the hypocritical ICFTU, which campaigned for "free trade unionism" and "democracy." See Yevette Richards, *Maida Springer: Pan-Africanist and International Labor Leader* (Pittsburgh: University of Pittsburgh Press, 2000), 154.

12 In his report, Osei omits the fact that racist incidents did repeatedly happen in the socialist states of Europe and the USSR in the early 1960s. For scholarly accounts, see, for example, Ilona Schleicher, "FDGB-Offensive in Westafrika. Der Gewerkschaftsbund im Jahr Afrikas," in *Engagiert für Afrika. Die DDR und Afrika II*, ed. Ulrich van der Heyden, Ilona Schleicher, and Hans-Georg Schleicher (Münster: Lit, 1994), 89–90; Sara Pugach, "African Students and the Politics of Race and Gender in the German Democratic Republic," in *Comrades of Color: East Germany in the Cold War World*, ed. Quinn Slobodian (New York: Berghahn, 2015); Young-sun Hong, *Cold War Germany, the Third World, and the Global Humanitarian Regime* (Cambridge: Cambridge University Press, 2015); Daniel Branch, "Political Traffic: Kenyan Students in Eastern and Central Europe, 1958–69," *Journal of Contemporary History* 53 (2018); Maxim Matusevich, "Expanding the Boundaries of the Black Atlantic: African Students as Soviet Moderns," *Ab Imperio* 2012 (2012); Julie Hessler, "Death of an African Student in Moscow," *Cahiers Du Monde Russe* 47 (2006). Moreover, as leader of the Ghanaian delegation during his stay, Osei regularly attended the council of the delegations' leaders (*Rat der Delegationsleiter*), where the African delegates discussed xenophobic behavior of some shopkeepers in Bernau or anonymous letters sent to East German women telling them not to engage with the African students. See "Protokoll der Sitzung des Rates der Delegationsleiter am 10. April 1962", n. d. [April 1962], SAPMO-BArch, DY 79/2500. For the council of delegation leaders' meetings, see also the chapter by Angermann in this volume.

Care for the Foreign Students

All Foreign Students have the same right as the German students in the College. Every Foreign Student receives for every month, a stipend of 400 ~~Deutsch~~ [German] Marks and it is made as follows: 150 D. M. for food and 250 D. M. for books and other minor expenses.

~~Major meals are served 3 times a day and in addition intermediate meals are served at every 10 a. m. between breakfast and lunch at 3 p. m. between lunch and supper.~~

Freedom of Movement

All foreigners, respectable of their color or creed, are free to move everywhere and see anything as any other German citizen. As students, who were willing to learn and know everything, we joined German families at week-ends in their homes. We found to our amazement that every average family has sufficient food to feed upon. They live in spacious flats at very low rentage.

The German Democratic Republic has no unemployment questions to solve. All ~~and sundry~~ work to earn a decent living.[13] I was mostly impressed to see graduated young women engineers in the "Sachsenwerk" Electric Motor Factory in Dresden. Their agile fingers doing and undoing parts on electric motors are delightful to the eye to watch.[14]

---

13 The idyllic picture Osei painted of the East German workers can be brought into dialogue with the concept of relative deprivation – "the idea that how one judges one's own situation and circumstances depends on the person or group to whom or to which one is comparing oneself." See Andrew I. Port, "'Awkward Encounters': East German Relations with the Third-World 'Other'," *German History* 35 (2017): 630. A 1962 report, written by two FDGB labor advisors who were dispatched to the Ghana TUC for eight months in order to act as Ghana TUC general secretary John K. Tettegah's right-hand men, stated that 65% of the workers and 36% of white-collar workers earned a salary below the minimum subsistence level as defined by the Ghanaian government. See "Bericht über einige Fragen der Entwicklung Ghanas und des Ghana TUC", Berlin, 11.1.1962, 54, SAPMO-BArch, DY 34/3475. Richard Jeffries has examined the declining real wages for Ghanaian railwaymen in detail; see Richard Jeffries, *Class, Power and Ideology in Ghana: The Railwaymen of Sekondi* (Cambridge: Cambridge University Press, 1978). To summarize, in Imanuel Geiss' words, the austerity measures introduced by the CPP in 1961 made the toiling masses suffer. See Geiss, *Gewerkschaften in Afrika*, 195.

14 Osei's admiration for the female engineers – expressed in the above paragraph with an erotic and somewhat belittling undertone – paralleled the CPP's progressive policies with regard to women in the Nkrumah years. Female traders had been a crucial pillar of support for Nkrumah's

Socialist Construction

In that modern model city of Eisenhuttenstadt[15], which I call the city of "Socialism", we were highly impressed to see how every worker works willingly, freely and diligently without any emotion. Prior to the Second World War this city which is situated in a heart of a thick forest, did not exist. After the war the G.D.R. workers under the banner of the Socialist Unity PARTY built this industrial city with its most modern Steel Factory. The city is therefore the workers city. What I gathered from this city of Eisenhuttenstadt is the oneness of purpose with which the workers work and live. Workers families, previously unknown to one another, are joined together in a common alliance which is the mood of production. They meet in club houses to discuss how best they can produce and to produce abundantly to enable them to create more to improve their own living condition. "Each worker is not for himself and gold [god] for them all" as it is said in the Capitalist countries but rather every worker in this Steel Factory is his brother's keeper. This means that the concern of one worker is the concern of all workers. They are knitted together by the steel they produce and "behold how good and how pleasant it is for workers to live together in Socialism".[16]

CPP during the anti-colonial struggle and since then had contributed considerably to its success through their financial and organizational efforts. During the CPP's rule, women entered institutions of higher learning in increasing numbers and soon gained access to male-dominated domains such as aviation and engineering. See Edzodzinam Tsikata, "Women's Political Organisations 1951–1987," in *The State, Development and Politics in Ghana*, ed. Emmanuel Hansen and Kwame A. Ninsin, (London: Codesria, 1989), 77; June Milne, *Kwame Nkrumah – a Biography* (London: Panaf Books, 2006), 109.

15 The East German model city of modernity, Eisenhüttenstadt (literally "ironworks city" in German, from 1953 to 1961 named Stalinstadt), which Osei called the "city of 'Socialism,'", was designed on the drawing board. It was founded in 1950 in order to provide the workers of the nearby steelworks with housing. Located in the state of Brandenburg close to the Polish border, the city had roughly 25,000 inhabitants by 1960.

16 Osei's idea of workers' unity is guided by a productionist language echoing the CPP's understanding of labor. Work was meant to "unite Ghanaians of all walks of life in the party-led and party-defined nation-building project." See Jeffrey S. Ahlman, *Living with Nkrumahism: Nation, State, and Pan-Africanism in Ghana* (Athens, Ohio: Ohio University Press, 2017), 116.

Seeing is Believing

We had the pleasure to visit the port of Rostock. This is the shipping port of the G.D.R. with its modern Harbour. It has also a fishing harbour attached and employs about 30,000 workers. The Workers of the German Democratic Republic have every cause to be happy. The Government and the people chose the socialist order of living and they are enjoying the fruits of their toils and sacrifices.

~~Many Holiday and Convalescent Homes are built for the workers and their families. After every 12 continuous months' work a worker chooses one of these Holiday Homes where to relax for just 30 D. Marks for the days of his leave. All kinds of entertainments and modern clinics as well as Post Offices are attached to each home. We had the opportunity of visiting and staying in some of these Homes; Klink-on the-Müritz near Waren in the region of Neubrandenburg and also in Friedrichsroda in the Thuringen Forest in the region of Erfurt.~~

We had [also] trips ~~also~~ to Heringdorf at the Baltic Sea near the Polish border. There we met thousands of workers and their families from many Socialist countries enjoying their holidays together with the G.D.R. workers.[17]

Our trip also took us to the Spreewald in the District of Cottbus. This is one of the most interesting places for tourist's attraction. The cruise on the long, narrow, winding stream offers a frolic spree [for] fine recreation. And least I forget: The voyage on the Muritz Lake through series of canals to the village of Plau cannot be short of enjoyment. These and many others are reserved for the workers

---

17 Here Osei affirms the official script of socialist internationalism, the idea of one socialist community made up of socialist brother countries. With regard to the recreational sphere, the FDGB's holiday service (see note below) aimed at providing its members with affordable enjoyment as a constitutive part of its mission to raise overall productivity. In Ghana, the CPP perceived the trade unions as the vehicle of the government's productionist dreams within the discourses of development and progress. The TUC also engaged in a number of socio-economic activities for its members, like workers' recreational centers with sports facilities, cinemas and bars, vegetable farms, housing projects, and two professional dance bands "for the entertainment of workers in compliance with the Convention People [sic!] Party's slogan of 'WORK AND HAPPINESS'." See Arthiabah and Mbiah, *Half a Century of Toil, Trouble and Progress*, 127–37. While Ghanaian workers, grosso modo, could secure some social and security benefits, real wages, however, stagnated and the CPP government cracked down on the right to strike and to protest in the early 1960s, most prominently after the 1961 strike. See Osei-Opare, "'If you trouble a hungry snake,'" 36, and Jeffries, *Class, Power and Ideology in Ghana*, 71–101. See also footnote 13.

and [the] people of the G.D.R. for their enjoyment.¹⁸ Who then can say that the citizens of the G.D.R. are not free? Can there be any other freedom and liberty more than these? Away then! Mr. Capitalist, with your intrigues and wicked machinations. We have seen and we bear testimony of the good things in the German Democratic Republic.

"Some people went to the G.D.R. to sit and stink; But we went there to sit and think."

Respect of Colour

The people of the German Democratic Republic are kind and loving. Wherever we went during our 18 months' stay, either in groups or in singles, ~~either officially or privately,~~ we were accorded with warm reception and hospitality.

In the drinking bars, restaurants and in the dancing rooms too, the Black is as well welcome as the White. Unlike the capitalist countries in Europe, people of all races are regarded as equal.

Peace Loving

The German Democratic Republic is a peace-loving country. The Government and people of this country have endured series of provocations from the people of West Germany without reiteration. This patience of the people of the G.D.R. has saved the whole world and mankind from what would had flared up to another dangerous World War. One could recollect the cold murder of the G.D.R. soldiers on the Jerusalem Strasse on the Border ~~in East~~ Berlin [to West] and other places.¹⁹ The killing of the Prince of Sarajavo [Sarajevo] in 1914 kindled

---

18 The FDGB, as the umbrella organization of all trade unions in the GDR, also played a crucial social and cultural role. The FDGB's *Feriendienst* (holiday service) provided roughly half of the GDR's population with recreational facilities for their holidays, like the holiday villages in Waren-Klink at Lake Müritz. A series of canals connects Lake Müritz with Lake Plauen with the village Plau on its Western shore. See Fritz Rösel, "Der Feriendienst des FDGB," in *Der Freie Deutsche Gewerkschaftsbund. Seine Rechte und Leistungen. Tatsachen, Erfahrungen, Standpunkte*, ed. Horst Bednarek, Harald Bühl, and Werner Koch (Berlin: Verlag am Park, 2006); Bodie, "Global GDR?," 45–48.
19 Here Osei is probably referring to the killing of GDR soldier Reinhold Huhn at the Berlin Wall in June 1962. Huhn was patrolling the German-German border in the center of Berlin. From the West Berlin side, the frequent border trespasser (*Grenzgänger*) Rudolf Müller and his aides dug a tunnel to a cellar in East Berlin with the aim to bring Müller's wife, their two children, and his

the first World War and would not the killing of more people by another people justify a Great War? But the G.D.R. Government bore these provocations ~~cooly and collectedly~~ for the interest of mankind. This alone is a living testimony that the Communist detests war.

Friendliness

The large number of German Students of the College of the Confederation of Free German Trade Unions and friends and families from many parts of the country who saw us off on Sunday March 24th, 1963 at the Berlin Schönefeld Airport, wailing and weeping because of the friends they would perhaps see no more is a good sign of the friendliness of the people of the German Democratic Republic.

I have never stop[ped] recollecting the happy days I had in this wonderful country and I have every ambition to visit this country in the near future to pay homage to my Alma Mater and to meet also friends and families of auld langsyne.

I have every hope that the German Democratic Republic will grow in strength and might to accomplish its ultimate task of building complete socialism where continuous abundance will flow for the people and their dependents and where greed, avarice, fraud and exploitation will never exist.

J. A. Osei

Deputy General Secretary Timber & Woodworkers Union of T. U. C. (Ghana)

---

sister-in-law to West Berlin. After Müller had picked up his family at a meeting point, the group was examined by Huhn on their way to the entrance of the tunnel. Müller pulled a pistol and shot Huhn in the chest. Huhn died and Müller's family managed to escape. In the Federal Republic, Müller denied that he had shot Huhn; the West German court closed the investigation in November 1962. The case was reopened after German reunification in 1996 and Müller confessed to shooting Huhn. Müller was sentenced for involuntary manslaughter in self-defense, which, was changed to homicide upon appeal at the Federal Court in 2000. See Hans-Hermann Hertle and Maria Nooke, *Die Todesopfer an der Berliner Mauer 1961–1989. Ein Biographisches Handbuch* (Berlin: Zentrum für Zeithistorische Forschung Potsdam und der Stiftung Berliner Mauer, 2009) and Dietmar Arnold and Rudolf Müller, *Kein Licht am Ende des Tunnels. Berlin 1962. Die tragische Flucht einer Familie* (Berlin: Ch. Links, 2018).

Bibliography

Ahlman, Jeffrey S. *Living with Nkrumahism: Nation, State, and Pan-Africanism in Ghana.* Athens, Ohio: Ohio University Press, 2017.
Angermann, Eric. "'Ihr Gehört Auch Zur Avantgarde'. Afrikanische Gewerkschafter an der FDGB-Hochschule Fritz Heckert (1961–1963)." Master's thesis, Georg-August-Universität Göttingen, 2018.
Anglin, Douglas G. "Ghana, the West, and the Soviet Union." *The Canadian Journal of Economics and Political Science / Revue Canadienne d'Economique et de Science Politique* 24 (1958): 152–65.
Arnold, Dietmar, and Rudolf Müller. *Kein Licht Am Ende des Tunnels. Berlin 1962. Die tragische Flucht einer Familie.* Berlin: Ch. Links, 2018.
Arthiabah, Peter Blay, and Harry Tham Mbiah. *Half a Century of Toil, Trouble and Progress: The History of the Trades Union Congress of Ghana 1939–1995.* Accra: Gold-Type Publications, 1995.
Bodie, George. "Global GDR? Sovereignty, Legitimacy and Decolonization in the German Democratic Republic, 1960–1989." PhD diss., University College London, 2019.
Branch, Daniel. "Political Traffic: Kenyan Students in Eastern and Central Europe, 1958–69." *Journal of Contemporary History* 53 (2018): 811–31. Accessed July 27, 2020. doi:10.1177/0022009418761194.
Cooper, Frederick. *Decolonization and African Society. The Labor Question in French and British Africa.* Cambridge: Cambridge University Press, 1996.
Davies, Ioan. *African Trade Unions.* Harmondsworth: Penguin Books, 1966.
Editorial Board. "Editorial." *Correspondence Informationsbulletin Nr. 1 der Fakultät für Ausländerstudium an der Hochschule der Deutschen Gewerkschaften "Fritz Heckert" Bernau* (1964): 3.
Förster, Alfred. "Zur Geschichte der Gewerkschafts-Schule in Bernau (1928–90)." In *Der Freie Deutsche Gewerkschaftsbund. Seine Rechte und Leistungen. Tatsachen, Erfahrungen, Standpunkte,* edited by Horst Bednarek, Harald Bühl, and Werner Koch, 366–88. Berlin: Verlag am Park, 2006.
Geiss, Imanuel. *Gewerkschaften in Afrika.* Hannover: Verlag für Literatur und Zeitgeschehen, 1965.
Harisch, Immanuel R. "'Mit Gewerkschaftlichem Gruß!' Afrikanische GewerkschafterInnen an der FDGB-Gewerkschaftshochschule Fritz Heckert in der DDR'." *Stichproben: Vienna Journal of African Studies* 18 (2018): 77–109.
Hertle, Hans-Hermann, and Maria Nooke. *Die Todesopfer an der Berliner Mauer 1961–1989. Ein biographisches Handbuch.* Berlin: Zentrum für Zeithistorische Forschung Potsdam und der Stiftung Berliner Mauer, 2009.
Hessler, Julie. "Death of an African Student in Moscow." *Cahiers du monde russe* 47 (2006): 33–63.
Jeffries, Richard. *Class, Power and Ideology in Ghana: The Railwaymen of Sekondi.* Cambridge: Cambridge University Press, 1978.
Kraus, John. "The Political Economy of Industrial Relations in Ghana." In *Industrial Relations in Africa,* edited by Ukandi G. Damachi, Dieter H. Seibel, and Lester Trachtman, 106–68. London: Macmillan, 1979.

Lundt, Bea, and Christoph Marx, eds. *Kwame Nkrumah 1909–1972: A Controversial African Visionary.* Stuttgart: Franz Steiner, 2016.
Matusevich, Maxim. "Expanding the Boundaries of the Black Atlantic: African Students as Soviet Moderns." *Ab Imperio* (2012): 325–50. Accessed July 27, 2020. doi:10.1353/imp.2012.0060.
Milne, June. *Kwame Nkrumah – A Biography.* London: Panaf Books, 2006.
Osei, J. A. "Reality Exposes Lies." *Correspondence Informationsbulletin Nr. 3 der Fakultät für Ausländerstudium an der Hochschule der Deutschen Gewerkschaften "Fritz Heckert" Bernau* (1964): 3–8.
Osei-Opare, Nana. "Uneasy Comrades: Postcolonial Statecraft, Race, and Citizenship, Ghana-Soviet Relations, 1957–1966." *Journal of West African History* 5 (2019): 85–111.
Osei-Opare, Nana. "'If You Trouble a Hungry Snake, You Will Force It to Bite You': Rethinking Archival Pessimism, Worker Discontent, and Petition Writing in Ghana, 1957–66." *Journal of African History*, forthcoming.
Port, Andrew I. "'Awkward Encounters': East German Relations with the Third-World 'Other'." *German History* 35 (2017): 630–37. Accessed July 27, 2020. doi:10.1093/gerhis/ghx086.
Pugach, Sara. "African Students and the Politics of Race and Gender in the German Democratic Republic." In *Comrades of Color*, edited by Quinn Slobodian, 131–56. New York: Berghahn, 2015.
Pugach, Sara. "African Students in Cold War Leipzig: Using University Archives to Recover a Forgotten History." In *Sources and Methods for African History and Culture: Essays in Honour of Adam Jones*, edited by Geert Castryck, Silke Strickrodt, Katja Werthmann, and Adam Jones, 541–64. Leipzig: Leipziger Universitätsverlag, 2016.
Richards, Yevette. *Maida Springer: Pan-Africanist and International Labor Leader.* Pittsburgh: University of Pittsburgh Press, 2000.
Rösel, Fritz. "Der Feriendienst des FDGB." In *Der Freie Deutsche Gewerkschaftsbund. Seine Rechte und Leistungen. Tatsachen, Erfahrungen, Standpunkte*, edited by Horst Bednarek, Harald Bühl, and Werner Koch, 225–34. Berlin: Verlag am Park, 2006.
Sackeyfio-Lenoch, Naaborko. "The Ghana Trades Union Congress and the Politics of International Labor Alliances, 1957–1971." *International Review of Social History* 62 (2017): 191–213. Accessed July 27, 2020. doi:10.1017/S0020859017000189.
Schleicher, Ilona. "FDGB-Offensive in Westafrika. Der Gewerkschaftsbund im Jahr Afrikas." In *Engagiert für Afrika. Die DDR und Afrika II*, edited by Ulrich van der Heyden, Ilona Schleicher, and Hans-Georg Schleicher, 82–93. Münster: Lit, 1994.
Skinner, Kate. "Who Knew the Minds of the People? Specialist Knowledge and Developmentalist Authoritarianism in Postcolonial Ghana." *The Journal of Imperial and Commonwealth History* 39 (2011): 297–323. Accessed July 27, 2020. doi:10.1080/03086534.2011.568756.
Tsikata, Edzodzinam. "Women's Political Organisations 1951–1987." In *The State, Development and Politics in Ghana*, edited by Emmanuel Hansen and Kwame A. Ninsin, 73–93. London: Codesria, 1989.
Zeleza, Paul Tiyambe. "Pan-African Trade Unionism: Unity and Discord." *Transafrican Journal of History* 15 (1986): 164–90.

Fernando Agostinho Machava
8 Echoes of the Past: The Social Impact of the Returned Labor Migrants from East Germany on the City of Maputo

Introduction[1]

On an intensely hot afternoon in the city of Maputo in 2011, I was traveling by public transport towards the city center. When we arrived at the crossroads formed by *Avenida 24 de Julho* and *Avenida Guerra Popular,* our journey was interrupted by a crowd of people singing and dancing in the middle of the road. They carried with them banners, flags, and homemade posters. Singing and dancing at the junction of the two avenues, they obstructed traffic in both directions. In our bus, the passengers were exhausted by the delay and started to complain. One of the passengers said it was the fault of the *"Madjermanes"* and explained that they were a group of Mozambicans who had been in East Germany from 1979 to 1990. I came to learn that from 1980 to 1992, they formed a kind of neighborhood elite especially in the suburban districts of Maputo, such as the one in which I grew up. These returnees used to wear stylish clothes, so everyone in their districts wanted to hang out with them. I listened intently to the passenger and my curiosity was aroused. I later found out that during my childhood, my parents had owned a television set bought from a returnee from East Germany. As a result, on many evenings our house would fill up with neighbors who came to be entertained by our television set. I resolved to discover more about this group of people who once sold my parents the television set. Their legacies are still visible as they walk through the streets brandishing placards and demonstrating against the government and as they continue to occupy the public park *Jardim 28 de Maio,* better known as the "Garden of the Madjermanes." What follows is the story of the return of these former labor migrants.

The name *Madjerman* became widespread in Mozambique when returnees from East Germany created a black market of what was perceived to be luxury

---

[1] This text was translated from Portuguese to English by Mark Beresford. I would also like to thank Marcia C. Schenck for allowing me to use her interviews with Mozambican workers to the GDR and for her guidance during the writing process. Many thanks to her and Immanuel R. Harisch for their editorial support.

products, called Red Star. It was named after a school in its proximity in the Alto Maé district of Maputo, a location about which I will speak later on. Here all sorts of used goods could be obtained at competitive prices ranging from television sets to fridges and kitchenware. This market helped to supply residents of the capital city with goods which until then had been scarce or even completely unavailable in Maputo.[2]

The young migrants that were to become known as Madjermanes had gone to the German Democratic Republic (GDR) as a consequence of bilateral cooperation agreements aimed at giving them qualifications across various industries, after which they would return to their home country to deploy their knowledge in Mozambique. Franziska Rantzsch in this volume elaborates on the contract that governed the labor migration from Mozambique to East Germany. This migration served as a refuge for many young Mozambicans who did not want to be recruited by the Armed Forces at a time when the country was suffering from civil war. Many young migrants further wanted to escape the hunger that had been caused by the nationwide drought in the 1980s and the ensuing food supply shortages. Europe further exercised a strong pull over the imaginations of the young Mozambicans.[3]

It is important to highlight that these young people left their country to gain work experience in what was known as a "brother nation" in the socialist world, and in the process were to disconnect from colonial labor values and to be transformed into socialist workers, the *"Homem Novo."*[4] It is my argument that they returned indeed as new men and women but not so much in the socialist sense; they returned as women and men of some modest wealth, who, much like the gayisa—Mozambican men who work in the South African mining industry—had accumulated material possessions abroad.[5] Their moment of glory was, however, short-lived as many had to part with their goods in order to finance

---

[2] Alice Samuel Sengo, "Processos de enriquecimento do léxico do português de Moçambique" (MA diss., Universidade do Porto, 2010).
[3] For an analysis of the various reasons for the young Mozambicans employed migrating to East Germany, see Marcia C. Schenck, "From Luanda and Maputo to Berlin: Uncovering Angolan and Mozambican Migrants' Motives to Move to the German Democratic Republic (1979–1990)," *African Economic History* 44 (2016), accessed October 20, 2019, doi:10.1353/aeh.2016.0008.
[4] The main characteristics of the *Homem Novo* that emerged in FRELIMO discourse were to be "free forever from ignorance, obscurantism, superstition and [...] conscious of the obligations of solidarity". The new man was to serve a crucial role in the construction of a communal socialist Mozambique. The role of the FRELIMO party was paramount. See Tanja R. Müller, *Legacies of Socialist Solidarity: East Germany in Mozambique* (Lanham, Md: Lexington Books, 2014), 2–3.
[5] Franziska Rantzsch (in this volume) goes into detail on the parallels between labor migration from Mozambique to South Africa and to East Germany.

their survival after their return. Many labor migrants thus fell back into lives at the margins of Mozambican society. Their story is one of socialist entanglements and socialist encounters as well as post-socialist disentanglements and isolation.

In the GDR, the young Mozambicans were allocated job positions in which they had frequent contact with people of other nationalities, meaning they were continuously navigating diverse socialist encounters. In the process of labor assimilation and socialization with East German culture, they not only acquired socialist values but also experiences and ideas closely linked to notions of autonomy and adulthood and "the good life," notions that came to define their behavior post-return.[6] Mozambican migrants were also faced with adverse circumstances: racist expressions and open conflicts involving Mozambicans were common, mainly in places of leisure and entertainment such as bars and discos.

The migration program ended after the fall of the Berlin wall in 1989, a caesura in the lives of many of the Mozambican workers who returned home in the changing circumstances within East Germany and as the bilateral agreement was dissolved in 1990.[7] Many foreigners who were in the country at the time, such as the Mozambicans, went back to their own countries after their work contracts were cancelled, uncertain which procedures they had to follow to remain in East Germany and also concerned by the wave of xenophobic violence that affected many German cities after the fall of the wall.[8]

While most existing studies on the Madjermanes focus on their experiences in the GDR, my contribution interrogates their impact upon return. It transpires that not only does the story of their return mirror that of the male Mozambican workers in the South African mining industry, but they also returned as new men and women, albeit not in a socialist sense.[9] Many Madjermanes had left their homes as ordinary youth and returned to become figures of admiration who had a modest transformative impact on their communities. These young workers

---

6 See Marcia C. Schenck and Ibraimo Alberto in this volume for a depiction of the life of a Mozambican worker in the GDR.
7 Almuth Berger, "Vertragsarbeiter: Arbeiter Der Freundschaft? Die Verhandlungen in Maputo 1990," in *Wir haben Spuren hinterlassen!: Die DDR in Mosambik: Erlebnisse, Erfahrungen und Erkenntnisse aus drei Jahrzehnten*, ed. Matthias Voss (Münster: Lit, 2005).
8 Aníbal Fernando Lucas, "Mão de obra Moçambicana na ex-República Democrática Alemã, 1979–1990" (Graduate thesis, UEM, 2002).
9 For a classic scholarship on Mozambican workers in South Africa, see Patrick Harries, *Work, Culture, and Identity: Migrant Laborers in Mozambique and South Africa, c.1860–1910* (Portsmouth, NH: Heinemann, 1994); Dunbar T. Moodie and Vivienne Ndatshe, *Going for Gold: Men, Mines, and Migration* (Berkeley: University of California Press, 1994); Ruth First, *Black Gold: The Mozambican Miner, Proletarian and Peasant* (New York: St. Martin's Press, 1983).

were not the only group to return to Mozambique from the GDR. As discussed by Marcia C. Schenck and Francisca Raposo (Chapter 9 in this volume) and Tanja Müller, school students for instance were only allocated pocket money and were thus not able to assemble goods in the same way as the workers. Most school students had to serve military service upon their return and while some later managed to become part of Mozambique's middle class, others fell back into the poverty from which they emerged.[10] Mozambican university students who studied in the GDR were in the long run among the economically most successful returnees as many became part of the middle and upper classes in Mozambique, from which quite a few originated.[11] Upon the return of these groups, the country as a whole was undergoing profound economic transformations in connection with the end of the socialist period and the Economic Rehabilitation Program.[12]

Based on 10 cited interviews with Madjermanes and with people close to them who witnessed their return, and on song lyrics, this text explores the social impact of the return of the Mozambican migrants from East Germany.[13] It examines the social dynamics that developed after the return of the Madjermanes at a time when Mozambique was undergoing the upheavals caused by civil war and by the transition from a centralized economy to a political and economic system based on a free market. I explain how the products that the Madjermanes brought with them led their families into relatively privileged positions, at a time of great changes in Mozambique, and highlight how the feelings of pride

---

10 Tanja Müller, *"Legacies of Socialist Solidarity: East Germany in Mozambique"* (Lanham, Md: Lexington Books, 2014).
11 A systematic study of Mozambican university students to East Germany remains a desideratum.
12 The Economic Rehabilitation Program (PRE) emerged in 1987, after talks between Mozambique and the Bretton Woods institutions and led to profound political, economic, and social transformations in the country. See João Mosca, *A Experiência "socialista" em Moçambique (1975 – 1986)* (Lisbon: Instituto Piaget, 1999), 163 – 174; João Mosca, *Economia de Moçambique século XX* (Lisbon: Instituto Piaget, 2005), 309 – 400.
13 Interviewing people who had been in East Germany and returned after reunification posed a significant challenge. Most of them were not interested in sharing their experiences and some even replied aggressively, triggered by the money that Mozambican authorities allegedly still owe them. Nevertheless, the information I could obtain from the Madjermanes and from people who witnessed their return has been invaluable. I cite here only 10 interviews but I have read about 200 interviews (of which I have transcribed many) conducted by Marcia C. Schenck for her PhD dissertation "Socialist solidarities and their afterlives: Histories and memories of Angolan and Mozambican migrants in the German Democratic Republic, 1975 – 2015" (PhD diss., Princeton University, 2017) and therefore can confidently state that what I cite here is representative for a wider pool of interviews.

derived from their stay in Germany and from having returned with fancy clothes, vehicles, and even European girlfriends or wives distinguished the Madjermanes and their families in their communities. I argue that these young people, returning from a developed European country, were first treated with high levels of respect and admiration. For their communities they indeed returned as New Men, however, not as initially idealized by the party and the state but rather as icons of fashion and bringers of essential and "luxury" goods. They initially were seen as an example for other family members and neighbors to follow until they failed to obtain stable work and had to sell their possessions. Importantly, I maintain that we should not forget, despite the narrative of social decline that is present in the current literature on this topic, that the return of the Madjermanes served to inject new life into peripheral districts, especially in the capital city.[14] In some cases, the Madjermanes even helped support training and job creation by setting up small businesses after they returned to their country.

This contribution is divided into two main sections. The first examines the circumstances of the Mozambican labor migration to the GDR and the memories that former migrants express about this migration today. In the second part, I then move on to elaborate in four subsections the social and economic impacts of the mass return of many former worker-trainees to Maputo by tracing the rise and fall of the Madjerman as social groups within their Maputo communities.

Labor Migration Agreements: From Mozambique to East Germany

During the socialist period from 1975 to 1990, Mozambique signed agreements with various countries of similar political orientation. One such cooperation agreement was signed with the German Democratic Republic (GDR), one of Mozambique's most important partners. Of all the accords signed with East Germany, the one with the highest public profile was the agreement to send young people to work on contracts with companies in Germany.[15] In February 1979, Erich Honecker, then General Secretary of the Socialist Unity Party of Germany, visited

---

[14] For an analysis of the decline in living standards on the returnees' psyches see for instance Marcia C. Schenck, "A Chronology of Nostalgia: Memories of Former Angolan and Mozambican Worker Trainees to East Germany," *Labor History* 59 (2018), accessed April 4, 2019, doi:10.1080/0023656X.2018.1429187.

[15] Franziska Rantzsch (in this volume) studies the agreements between the governments of the GDR and Mozambique. She affirms that economic motives were crucial for the GDR's recruitment of contract workers, as were the Cold War era political-ideological motives.

Maputo to sign a friendship agreement and a series of commercial deals. The relevant agreement was signed on February 24, 1979 by representatives from the parties of both countries.[16] The Bilateral Commissions, which met alternately in Maputo and Berlin, then developed the details of the cooperation between the two states.[17]

Mozambique was experiencing an almost total paralysis of its administrative and economic system, as a result of the shortage of personnel qualified to hold the positions vacated by the Portuguese. Furthermore, most of the young people found in migration a way of escaping recruitment for the armed forces and for the front line in the civil war. Allen Isaacman and Barbara Isaacman state that between 1974 and 1977, the Portuguese community fell from 250,000 to approximately 20,000. This exodus resulted in a severe shortage of technicians and professionals, as the Portuguese were the only group to enjoy access to higher education in the colonial period, as a result of their privileged racial and class position. Consequently, there were no engineers, mechanics, accountants or agronomists left in the country who had administered Mozambique during the colonial period but also limited qualified textile workers, harbor managers, and coal miners.[18] The country's manufacturing industry faced a series of critical problems which forced the state to intervene immediately.[19] At the same time,

---

[16] The agreement was signed by Marcelino dos Santos, the then Minister of Planning for Mozambique, and by Günter Mittag, Secretary for Economics of the Committee of the Unified Socialist Party of Germany. See Agreement on temporary employment of Mozambican workers in the GDR, 1979, in Aníbal. F. Lucas, "Mão de obra Moçambicana na ex-República Democrática Alemã, 1979–1990" (Graduate thesis, UEM, 2002).

[17] Marcia C. Schenck, "Socialist Solidarities and Their Afterlives: Histories and Memories of Angolan and Mozambican Migrants in the German Democratic Republic, 1975–2015" (PhD diss., Princeton University, 2017).

[18] Allen Isaacman and Barbara Isaacman, *Mozambique: From Colonialism to Revolution* (Boulder, CO.: Westview Press, 1983), 145.

[19] After the Lusaka Accord of 1974 and the implementation of a post-independence transition government, the Mozambican industry, which had been highly dependent on serving the Portuguese economy and the few Portuguese citizens in the country, entered into crisis for a number of reasons: firstly, because former Portuguese owners abandoned and sabotaged their companies; secondly, there was a shortage of qualified technicians to replace the foreigners who had left the country; thirdly, the agricultural distribution network, which had also been under colonial management, collapsed; and fourthly, the physical condition of equipment deteriorated and maintenance proved very difficult, leading to the almost complete collapse of industrial infrastructure. As a result, there was a 35% drop in industrial production from 1974 to 1976, forcing the state to intervene to rescue an industry in decline. See Carlos Nuno Castel-Branco, "Problemas estruturais de Industrialização," in *Moçambique: Perspetivas Económicas*, ed. Carlos Nuno Castel-Branco (*Maputo: UEM*, 1994), 96.

East Germany was suffering from the loss of some of its young people to the Federal Republic of Germany, the more populous capitalist part of Germany which was outperforming the GDR economically and technologically.[20]

For Mozambique, as well as encouraging migration for work, the agreement enabled the technical and professional training of young Mozambicans who in the future would return and deploy their skills in businesses and factories across the country. There are similarities to note between the recruitment of Mozambicans for East German companies and the recruitment for South African mines (see Rantzsch in this volume). However, one of the major differences between the two migrations was the existence of a system for training the young migrants on the job so that many returned with a certificate that marked them as skilled laborers, which did not occur with those Mozambicans who migrated to the mines of South Africa.[21] This fact is featured centrally in former migrants' memories to which I turn now.

Migrants' Memories of their Reasons to Migrate[22]

Many young Mozambicans who wanted to receive professional training went to East Germany. They came mostly from families with humble backgrounds and low income, with no chance of continuing their studies. Migration to East Germany was a dream for many young citizens of Mozambique, because of the political and military situation of their own country and because of the chance to discover a western country. Abílio Forquilha talks of his feeling of privilege on being chosen to go to (East) Germany, both because of the professional experience and the chance to continue his studies:

---

20 Lucas, "Mão-de-obra Moçambicana."
21 Schenck, "Socialist Solidarities." Héctor H. Guerra makes a comparison between recruitment and migration for South Africa and recruitment for East Germany, noting the similarities and differences between both processes. Apart from the deferred payment systems established by both agreements, the author points to social and political factors as the driving forces for migration. While a desire to escape the forced labor system resulted in the massive migration to the Rand mines in the colonial period, in contrast it was the post-independence civil conflict and a desire to escape the draft that were the main reasons for migration to East Germany. Héctor Hernández Guerra, "Do Rand à RDA? Modernização Compulsória e Práticas Sociais e Estratégias de Mobilidade Social," *Revista d'antropologia i investigació social* 3 (2009): 61–83.
22 Alexandra Piepiorka and Eduardo Buanaissa (Chapter 14 in this volume) write about memory-scapes that exist between Mozambique and (East) Germany and consist of various memories from travelers of both countries about their lives in the other country. They also engage with Mozambican workers' memories about the GDR.

> Being selected to go to Germany was not easy and was a challenge for students with scholarships and for workers. Everybody wanted to go to Germany, plus there was a war in Mozambique at that time and Germany was a relatively calm country with an impressive level of development and a decent lifestyle. Every young person wanted to go. So, when we left we felt that it was a time of good fortune for us. We were the lucky ones. In many cases the work and the training were successful, and we also had all the basics that a person needs to live. It was very good.[23]

Inocêncio Honwana, a resident of Manhiça in Maputo province, remembers the following general feeling:

> Armed conflict in Mozambique had erupted and death was getting closer all the time. At night, death took youngsters, pregnant women, children, the sick. It was tough to live in Manhiça and to wake up to see people mourning for a victim who the day before had been a companion. It was also sad to think about fleeing from Maluana, which had become a real slaughterhouse. I was obsessed by the desire to leave for a distant land [...]. It was more exciting than dreaming of making love to a nymphomaniac.[24]

In the 1980s Mozambique was afflicted by natural disasters, in particular by a famine which had left many families in hunger and deprived the shops and cooperatives of food. In a collection of memories, Moisés Alberto writes:

> At that time there were shortages of everything except tea leaves. Youngsters were growing up with an uncertain future, with very few vacancies for education or employment. The only solution was the army, but all young people were afraid and wanted to escape from certain death.[25]

Faced by these difficulties, many young people chose to migrate to neighboring countries or even distant lands and specially to take up work contracts in East Germany. The idea of escaping hunger and war, obtaining a job, and discovering a developed European country was fascinating to young people, who signed up at registration posts all over the country eager to temporarily moor in a new region of the socialist world.

---

23 Abílio Forquilha, March 5, 2014, Maputo, interview with Marcia C. Schenck.
24 Inocêncio Domingos Honwana, "Berlim: Um paraíso Suspenso na Memóri," in *Moçambique – Alemanha, Ida E Volta: Vivências Dos Moçambicanos Antes, Durante E Depois De Estadia Na Alemanha*, ed. Ulf Dieter Klemm (Maputo: ICMA, 2005), 89.
25 Moisés João M. Alberto, "Untitled," in *Moçambique – Alemanha, Ida E Volta: Vivências Dos Moçambicanos Antes, Durante E Depois De Estadia Na Alemanha*, ed. Ulf Dieter Klemm (Maputo: ICMA, 2005), 191.

Memories of Former Labor Migrants in East Germany

The memories migrants share of their stay in East Germany are often quite positive, to the surprise of many German analysts, to whom the living and working conditions of most foreign workers in the GDR seem unattractive. Mozambican listeners on the contrary expect tales of adventure and riches to confirm their positive associations of Europe as the land of milk and honey. The exception to the nostalgic memories, which Marcia C. Schenck has termed "eastalgic" memories, are memories of racist incidents which ranged from verbal expressions to physical violence and even murder.[26]

Regarding the working environment that labor migrants encountered in East Germany, experiences were mixed but most interviews record being satisfied overall with their work. Abdenego Levi Matsinhe, who went to Germany in the late 1980s, recalls:

> I worked for a paper company called *"Zellstoff- und Papierfabrik"* in a small location near the city of Dresden. We worked in shifts [and groups] made up of Mozambicans, Germans, Angolans and Vietnamese [...]. We got on well with each other and there was not a lot of racism in the workplace because the laws were harsh.[27]

And Rogério Cumbane concurs that, during official business, there was no space for racist expressions:

> At the company where I worked there were no problems with racism, only some people from outside, mainly in bars, did not like us, especially because German girls preferred to go out with us rather than with them.[28]

As the two testimonies above and other conversations with returnees show, racism was curtailed in the official domain of the anti-racist state but broke out in unpoliced spaces.[29] This is not to suggest that all private spaces were marred by racism. As Marcia C. Schenck observes, intercultural relationships were spaces for intercultural learning. In East Germany there were loving relationships between Angolan and Mozambican men and German women, or the other way

---

26 Schenck, "A Chronology of Nostalgia."
27 Abednego Levi Matsinhe, February 24, 2014, Maputo, interview with Marcia C. Schenck and Fernando Machava.
28 Rogério Cumbane, February 17, 2014, Maputo, interview with Marcia C. Schenck and Fernando Machava.
29 Quinn Slobodian, ed., *Comrades of Color: East Germany in the Cold War World* (New York, Oxford: Berghahn, 2015).

around. This served to support the integration of the migrants in a foreign world.³⁰

During their time in the GDR, young migrants could also buy goods for personal use in their homes during their free time. Because many young Mozambicans did not like German cuisine and preferred to make their own meals, many of them bought freezers to conserve food in their homes. In the interview, Marcos, who moved in with his East German partner, states:

> It was difficult for me to get used to German cooking (...) so I prepared my own meals when I was at home, as this was not forbidden. In my room I had a small fridge where I left food, I had bought to make meals. When I moved into my girlfriend's house, I took the fridge with me, along with the television set, the HiFi [High Fidelity] and other things that I had bought over there.³¹

Statements such as these show the complex nature of relations between Mozambicans and East Germans. These relations varied from affectionate and private relationships to professional relationships and ranged from love affairs and marriage to hatred and xenophobia.

The same cannot be said when the immigrants were in entertainment venues such as bars and discotheques. Many interviewees say they suffered threats or even aggression, mainly because the Mozambicans would interact with the German women in these places. Ilda Melembe remembers shocking experiences with violent racism from the last months of her time in Germany:

> In Berlin we had a lot of problems with young men. We had to move out of our accommodation and go to Potsdam because there was so much racism. Before leaving the company dormitory we were assaulted by some young [German] men. I was one of the victims. I was hit by a stone when our building was invaded. After that we moved to another boarding house where we spent almost two months before returning to Mozambique but it was not easy. We suffered a lot. I did not know that in Germany we would suffer so much in the last days. We lived on apples, milk, boiled eggs and bread for the time that we were in the new boarding institution.³²

Rogério Cumbane concurs and speaks about his experience of xenophobia in East Germany:

---

30 Schenck, "Socialist Solidarities."
31 Marcos Rungo, July 21, 2016, interview with Fernando Machava.
32 Ilda Melembe, Rosita Lucas, Beatriz Simão et al., August 31, 2011, interview with Marcia C. Schenck.

After the fall of the Wall I remember that there were xenophobic leaflets around and that the Germans did not want to see any foreigners anymore. They only wanted to live among other Germans. From that time on, no black person could leave their accommodation without permission, because they could be beaten up or killed in the street. [33]

This sort of intolerance from a part of German society led many young Mozambicans to fear for their safety and to start avoiding public spaces. After the fall of the Berlin Wall and the reunification of Germany the vast majority of migrants came home.

The Labor Migrants' Return to Mozambique

The political scenario in Germany in 1989 was dominated by a series of demonstrations, culminating in November with the fall of the Berlin Wall.[34] As a result of the breakdown of the GDR, the commissioner for foreigners Almuth Berger and her team negotiated the early termination of the agreements in Mozambique and thousands of Mozambicans who had come to Germany to work under the agreements returned.[35] The last agreement signed between the governments of the GDR and Mozambique in May 1990 established that, in the event of dismissals, workers had the right to three months of 70% of the gross salary previously earned, to stay at the company's home, and to a return ticket to Mozambique. In addition, dismissed workers and those who were willing to leave the GDR had right to an indemnity payment of DM 3000.[36] Many workers received these payments at a time when products from West Germany where already introduced, quickly replacing East German products in their popularity and lowering the prices of local products. It was then that many migrants bought the products to support their whole families and their own construction of a new family.

The mass return of workers led to a lack of coordination between the German government and Mozambican authorities when it came to scheduling the return flights back to Mozambique. An example of this can be found in a news report in Tempo magazine on October 14, 1990, which discusses an "unex-

---

33 Rogério Cumbane, February 17, 2014, Maputo, interview with Marcia Schenck and Fernando Machava.
34 Lucas, "Mão-de-obra Moçambicana."
35 Berger, "Vertragsarbeiter: Arbeiter Der Freundschaft? Die Verhandlungen in Maputo 1990."
36 See Jochen Oppenheimer, "Mozambican Worker Migration to the Former German Democratic Republic: Serving Socialism and Struggling under Democracy," *Portuguese Studies Review* 12 (2004): 163–187; Lucas, "Mão-de-obra Moçambicana."

pected return," referring to the return of about 16,000 Mozambicans from the newly unified country of Germany. The repatriation of the young Mozambicans was disorderly and often "unplanned," as the events of September 17, 1990 demonstrates:

> A group of youngsters coming back from former East Germany was arriving at Maputo on an unscheduled flight, without the authorities at the International Airport of Maputo or the relevant Mozambican authorities being aware. The airport did not authorize the landing of the airplane, which had to go on to South Africa. From there, however, the Mozambicans were sent back to Europe, even though their luggage had been taken off the airplane in South Africa [...].[37]

In Maputo, returning workers, especially those who did not have a fixed abode or any family in the city, were received at a provisional housing facility for outgoing and returning workers in the neighborhood of Machava close to the airport and the lodges of the Mozambican railway company. However, because of the high number of people these sites became too small to cope with so many returnees at once, which meant that they had to find alternative accommodation. Some of the returnees soon bought land on the outskirts of the city of Maputo and began to build their makeshift or even stone houses there.[38]

Another cause that led many returnees to stay in the capital city was the reception of their goods, which were usually chartered by sea and, therefore, arrived later – if at all. Many tell stories about the late arrival of their products that were only released after paying customs. Due to having to raise the money to be able to receive the goods, many prolonged their stays. Moreover, the costs of air tickets to the provinces, especially those of the center and north of the country, were high but it was very difficult and dangerous to travel by land because of the civil war. Thus paying for the costs of customs clearance and the transport of their goods in many cases exhausted funds to pay for onward travel to their home regions.[39]

Francisco Macaringue remembers the following:

> I was actually very anxious to return to the land where I was born (the province of Sofala), but we had to wait for a long time for the goods which were all supposed to arrive here in Maputo. When they arrived, I had to pay a large sum of money for customs clearance and then I also had to pay to transport them to my province, which was very expensive and

---

37 António Elias, "Moçambicanos na RDA: O Regresso Inesperado," *Tempo Magazine*, October 14, 1990, 22–25.
38 Ibid.
39 Lucas, "Mão-de-obra Moçambicana."

which I could not afford. I went to visit my family, taking with me only the products I had bought for my family, while the other items stayed behind in Maputo at a family house because I could not take them all home.⁴⁰

Although the government erected a temporary camp for returnees in Machava, the returning Mozambicans encountered problems in receiving their payments, and, when they finally received them, found that the calculation had not taken inflation into account. These and other factors resulted in most of the returning Mozambicans who were from the provinces setting up homes in Maputo, with a major impact on the city. Although living conditions did not approach the level of German cities, it was the location in Mozambique where they felt most comfortable and safe from the impacts of the civil war. Furthermore, the Mozambican Labor Ministry, which was in charge of the affairs of former workers in East Germany, was located in Maputo and hence easy for them to reach if required.

In response to demands uttered across the country, in September 2001 the government carried out the first nationwide census of former workers in East Germany, using criteria such as the presentation of documents which confirmed their residence and employment in Germany, including passports and employment cards with the company name. This first census registered 11,252 former workers with the right to receive social security repayments. Of this number, it is important to note that around 6,000 people had set up their residences in Maputo City.⁴¹

Social Impact of the Madjermanes across Maputo

Originally, the workers were sent to East Germany in a revolutionary context with the objective of educating the "Homem Novo." However, in East Germany the migrants were exposed to new forms of socialization, not all of which were in line with the SED and FRELIMO politics. Labor migrants returned as New Men, although not in the socialist context as previously envisioned by their representatives. Instead, they returned as an embryonic class in ascension, accumulating a material and even monetary wealth that to a certain degree impacted the lives of the people around them, before it disappeared again. Thus, the cycle closed, and many returned to the lives they unmoored from to migrate to East Germany. What migrants had in their baggage, apart from material goods, were practices such as

---

40 Francisco Macaringue, July 21, 2016, interview with Fernando Machava.
41 Lucas Xavier Canjale, "O Fórum dos ex-trabalhadores da ex-RDA na Cidade de Maputo (1996–2006)" (Graduate thesis, UEM, 2007).

protests and invoking notions of self-esteem and social inclusion.[42] Notions of autonomy and adulthood had a long tradition in transnational Mozambican labor migrations but were not part of the socialist goals of solidarity and the collective. Where governments expected political and technical education along a real socialist exegesis as practiced in East Germany at the time, quite a few labor migrants began to practice indiscipline, alcoholism, and violations of dormitory rules in an attempt to ensure personal freedoms so abhorred by both governments.

The Madjermanes who returned and established themselves in Maputo stimulated the curiosity of numerous residents of the city. Many people were keen to get to know these men (and some women) who were returning from a western country with a vast range of experiences. Returnee Adevaldo Banze recalls that "People were amazed. They all wanted to see the Madjermanes, as we were affectionately known. We were men who commanded economic respect from anyone who showed up."[43] Carlos Cossa, a resident of the Ferroviário neighborhood in Maputo, remembers:

> When the young people from East Germany returned, the neighborhood became very exciting. Their houses were nearly always full of people, family members as well as neighbors. Every young person wanted to hang out with them because they had money and there was nearly always a party in their homes. Their houses were full of quality things, whether food and drink or things to watch. People wanted to be close to them. They were always dressed very differently. I remember that one of them who brought back a motorbike would make a lot of noise when he left home and all the kids would run to watch him go by.[44]

Another kind of transformation resulting from the return of the Madjermanes took place in their residences. Some of the youngsters returned and invested their money in improving the living conditions of their families, especially in building houses of brick and stone. These houses were equipped with electrical appliances from East Germany which were very hard to find in the suburbs and even in the most expensive parts of the city. Adevaldo Banze states that on his return one of his priorities was to build a decent home for his family and to fur-

---

[42] See Eric Allina, "From 'New Man' to Superman: The Politics of Work and Socialism, from Maputo to Karl-Marx-Stadt, c. 1982," (WISER: Wits Institute for Social and Economic Research, 2016).
[43] Adevaldo Banze, "Berlim: um Paraíso Suspenso na Memória," in *Moçambique – Alemanha, Ida e Volta: Vivências dos Moçambicanos antes, durante e depois de estadia na Alemanha*, ed. Ulf Dieter Klemm (Maputo: ICMA, 2005), 37–39.
[44] Alfredo Mandlate and Carlos Cossa, July 18, 2016, interview with Fernando Machava.

nish it with "television sets, fridges, radios, videos and many more, plus the famous MZ motorbike,⁴⁵ which was the flag of Germany in Mozambique."⁴⁶

At this time, it was seen as a major privilege to have traveled to East Germany. When migrants returned, they were seen as individuals with valuable life experience. João Raimundo, a resident of the Ferroviário neighborhood in Maputo, states:

> When the youngsters who were in East Germany returned home, many young people wanted to be close to them. They thought that they had more experience of life because of their time in Europe, where things were more dynamic [...]. For example, they wanted to know what sort of clothes went well together or how to get with a girl. They also wanted to be close to them to increase their popularity and even to be seen with them by a woman in whom they were interested. Some people would borrow their clothes or even their motorbikes to make an impression.⁴⁷

Some of the returnees also impressed by bringing with them their European girlfriends,⁴⁸ partners or wives, something which—as a relic of colonial times—was seen as an honor for the neighborhoods where they lived. This was not simply an affinity for the foreign read as exotic and exciting, but it mattered that these women where white, the color of power.

In his song "*Miboba*" (2000), José Guimarães describes the joy of the Mozambicans who went to (East) Germany and their delight in seeing the beauty of German cities. The same music talks of the return in triumph of some of the Madjermanes, who came home with German girlfriends or motorbikes, to the amazement and admiration of the locals, singing "*A Loko aho ku tivha Nwana mamany, a uta Tsaka, a Skambalene*⁴⁹ [...] *Vhanwany Vhafana, vha*

---

45 The MZ refers to an East German brand of motorbikes produced by IFA (Industrieverband Fahrzeugbau), which many of the young Mozambicans acquired in the GDR second hand. This was one of the most visible assets upon the return of the Madjermanes, leading to the expression "German flag in Mozambique." It was characteristic in the whole city to see young people on these motorbikes for years until they disappeared one by one as they broke down and could not be repaired for lack of spare parts.
46 Banze, "Berlim: Um paraíso Suspenso na Memória," 37–39.
47 João Raimundo, July 29, 2019, interview with Fernando Machava.
48 According to several interviewees, some young East German women accompanied their partners to Mozambique. However, given the differences in climate, living standard, and culture, most did not last long before they eventually returned, in some cases with their partners, in others alone. At present no East German woman still in Mozambique was identified either by the author or Marcia C. Schenck during her dissertation research in 2014.
49 Unfortunately, the composer of this song has died and it was not possible to ask him about the meaning of this word. Based on the story told by the song, the word refers to a city in East

vhuhy ni swithuthuthu, niswy lunguana, a Skambalene [...]."⁵⁰ In this music, the artist sings of the beauty of German cities, for which many returnees felt strong nostalgia when they had to return to Mozambique after the end of the socialist regime in East Germany.⁵¹ The song also mentions the labor migrants who returned from East Germany not only with goods (motorbikes) but also with "white girls" (East German women), to the widespread admiration of their families and local community.⁵² At that time it was not common for a young Mozambican man, especially one from a suburban neighborhood, to go out with a white woman or to have a white wife. A colonial legacy, white women were still considered to be members of the elite, so these young people enjoyed a privileged position in their neighborhood by virtue of an assumption about the economic and social position of their East German partners. Regardless of the East German background the white women actually came from, their skin color privileged them in the Maputo of the early 1990s.

We should also note that the returning men were highly attractive to some local women, again based on an assumption about material wealth but also fascinating as somebody who had seen Europe personally and could tell interesting stories. Many new relationships between Maputo's women and returning migrants were formed immediately after their return, sometimes culminating in marriage and family creation. The country was still feeling the devastating effects of the civil war and its economy was extremely weak. This had an impact above all on families in poor suburbs across the country. Some Mozambican women were keen to have relationships with young men returning from their work experience in East Germany, who apparently had goods and money. Samuel Manjate, a resident near the temporary camp in Machava, which was established on an old farm to process male returnees, says:

Germany. Many returnees whom I was able to interview could not say exactly what it refers to, but everything suggests that the word denotes a real or fictitious city. The song discusses the beauty of European cities and the joy that young people who had been in Europe felt when remembering the place.

50 This translates to "If you met my brother you would be happy in Skambalene [...] Other kids came back with motorbikes, with white girls from Germany [...]", José Guimarães. *Miboba*. Rádio Moçambique, 2000.
51 See for instance Schenck, "Socialist Solidarities."
52 Marcia Schenck describes the reverse process in East Germany, where black husbands and boyfriends were often not approved of in East German families and communities; see Schenck, "Socialist Solidarities."

> The area near that place used to be full of women who had relationships with the Madjermanes, thinking that they could get on in life that way. These people had come from Europe and the women thought they had a lot of money which wouldn't run out soon.[53]

Before the money ran out, many Madjermanes were role models to the young people in their neighborhoods but life changed for everybody, young and old, for better or for worse. Alfredo Mandlate and Carlos Cossa, both residents of Ferroviário, saw how some of the young returnees from Germany moved close to their homes and remember:

> A lot of things changed here when they arrived. Everyone would go to one of their houses to watch TV, which only they had. They were basically the first people with stereos and they played very loud music which was totally different to what we were used to. (...) There were always people with them and sometimes we could not sleep because of the noise they made when they had a party.[54]

The return of the Madjermanes led to changes in the habits and customs of the neighborhoods, as thousands of youngsters arrived bringing their experiences of Germany with them and influencing other residents. The returnees were similar in many ways, but also different from the migrants who had been to the South African mines. They had emigrated to Europe in a state-organized program targeted at job training while the miners had emigrated within the region and often for personal reasons such as marriage, improved living conditions, or traditions in the family or community. Both, however, made an impact in their communities, not least through the goods they brought.[55]

Improvement in Living Conditions Thanks to New Products

One of the most significant legacies of the cooperation between Mozambique and East Germany was constituted by the material goods brought back by thousands of Mozambicans. Thousands of containers full of products arrived, includ-

---

[53] Samuel Manjate, July 15, 2016, interview with Fernando Machava.
[54] Alfredo Mandlate and Carlos Cossa, July 18, 2016, interview with Fernando Machava.
[55] Consumption is also a theme familiar from southern African labor history; see Emmanuel Kreike, *Recreating Eden: Land Use, Environment, and Society in Southern Angola and Northern Namibia*, Social History of Africa (Portsmouth, NH: Heinemann, 2004), Chapter 5; Patrick Harries, *Work, Culture, and Identity: Migrant Laborers in Mozambique and South Africa, c.1860 – 1910* (Portsmouth, NH: Heinemann, 1994).

ing electrical appliances, clothes, vehicles, and other items, which were unloaded in the port of Maputo after being shipped from East Germany.

Most of the youngsters had enjoyed good living conditions in East Germany, with subsidized food, accommodation, and leisure activities resulting in an economically stable, if not prosperous, life. The migrants bought two kinds of goods: goods for immediate consumption and use and goods for their return to Mozambique. In Germany, many bought food and a fridge to be able to cook their own Mozambican food, but also a television set, radio and HiFi for their entertainment. For their return, migrants bought everything they considered useful for their families or that could be sold to substantiate their meager income. But many also prioritized their own creation of a future household.

The material items that the returnees brought with them, for instance appliances such as television sets, sound systems, motorbikes and even vehicles, which until then had been scarce or non-existent in the suburban communities of Maputo, converted the Madjermanes into a local elite. Their style and clothes inspired a new way of dressing and a new look and they made a major impression with their haircuts and ripped jeans. These items also led to major changes in their families and the surrounding communities, for example by increasing the capacity to preserve food in freezers and fridges and also by increasing access to information and entertainment from radio and television, with informal cinemas in the community known as "videos." Many of the new appliances were still reliant on local electricity and thus their use was not possible at all times or in all places.

Most of the migrants to East Germany and their families had experienced scarcity of almost all types of products prior to migrating. When they received their wages abroad, they prioritized buying the goods they deemed useful and prestigious. Workers like Manuel Loureço, who was among the workers who received compensation pay after the early termination of his contract due to the German re-unification, used that money to go on a shopping spree and buy Western and formerly Eastern goods for home:

> With the money that I received in Germany when the company I was working for was shut down, I bought some things to use here in Mozambique and for all the family. I knew there was not a lot here so I invested in things that would be useful to me. I already had some items I used over there, such as a fridge, record player, dishes and an MZ motorbike for myself I just bought some more clothes and then a lot of stuff for my family.[56]

---

56 Manuel Loureço, June 29, 2019, interview with Fernando Machava.

Aware of the difficulties that their families were experiencing, Mozambicans in East Germany tried to cover the full range of a family's needs when buying goods. When they returned home, these items would serve to distinguish the families of Madjermanes, who stood out because of the way they dressed.

Florêncio Obadias mirrors the intention to build his own household with the goods acquired during the migration process:

> I bought clothes, a fridge, television set, dishes and other utensils which I could use at home. I was coming back with my girlfriend and she chose most of the things as she said we had to arrive and build our home. I remember there were a lot of dishes and sheets and that we even brought curtains with us.[57]

When they returned, electrical appliances gave these families of the returnees an advantage in life that they had not enjoyed before, such as the ability to conserve food in the freezers and refrigerators brought by the Madjermanes from East Germany. As one interviewee explains:

> [...] I brought a fridge which helped a lot at home, especially in the summer when food goes bad quickly. It was not easy in our humble families of farmers to find someone with fridge or a freezer. Many of our neighbors would come to store their things here, mainly fish and meat products, which before they had stuffed with salt [...] so that they did not rot.[58]

These domestic appliances increased a family's capacity to conserve food and hence enhanced their ability to buy perishable food products in large volumes, as they could be preserved without difficulty.

Another benefit from these goods of high prestige was the possibility they provided of increased access to televised information and entertainment. Televised football games and soap operas gave the families and neighbors of the Madjermanes access to more entertainment. Normally, a Madjerman's house would be full of people of all ages looking for some form of content to watch on their televisions. For the communities, these appliances gave more access to entertainment and, even more importantly, more choices when accessing information. Another important opportunity for entertainment came from films on video cassettes, which until then had been very scarce in families in the suburbs of Maputo. The return of the Madjermanes saw video players arrive in these homes, providing families and neighbors with a new form of entertainment. Interviewee Alfredo Mandlate remembers:

---

57 Florêncio Obadias, June 27, 2019, interview with Fernando Machava.
58 Alfredo Mandlate, July 18, 2016, interview with Fernando Machava.

> [...] We used to go to the home of our neighbor who had come back from Germany to watch his TV, mainly when there were football matches from Portugal. We sat down and watched the games with people of all ages because television sets were rare around here. On days when there were no matches, we would watch the news, soap operas and some films they had brought from Germany. It was something new that had never been seen before and the house used to fill up. Some people saw that their houses were getting full and started to charge entry. On normal days there was one price, on days when there was a football game there was another price.[59]

As this interview shows, people would flock to the house of a Madjerman to enjoy audiovisual entertainment. With their sound systems and records, the Madjermanes introduced new music which began to captivate and delight the listeners. The Madjermanes thereby introduced to the community western music that was not very well known in Mozambique at the time. As we have seen in this section, the goods of the Madjerman changed the lifestyle of the local Maputo communities into which the returnees integrated in many small ways.

From Prestige Goods to Opportunities for Financial Gains

Some of the returnees also made the most of the training they had received in East Germany and created small businesses to support themselves and their families. They brought with them and acquired materials to help them in their work, such as equipment for metalworking and mechanical work and they set up businesses supplying the local population. Apart from being the economic foundation of their livelihoods, these businesses created employment for young people to acquire trading skills and earn an income, albeit mostly in the informal economy:

> When my contract with the [East German] company where I was assigned ended and I knew that I had to come home [to Mozambique], I began to buy materials to come and open a small metalworking shop to produce pieces for people. At the start my idea was not to make the things myself: it was to train people so that they could make the items while I was at work in the company that would be allocated for me when I arrived home. When I saw that things were not working out as had been planned, I assumed personal responsibility for the project. Even today I am still working in the area in which I received training in East Germany.

---

[59] Alfredo Mandlate, July 18, 2016, interview with Fernando Machava.

> With the small company that I opened I managed to support my parents and brothers and then form my own family, all supported by my small business.⁶⁰

With the small enterprises that they established, some of the returnees not only made full use of the knowledge they acquired in East Germany but also trained people, created job positions, and produced or repaired items for neighboring communities.

Another way of raising funds came from the informal cinemas. Conventional cinemas were normally the preserve of well-off people in the city itself. The Madjermanes, however, began to introduce to the suburbs cinemas which were known as "videos." When finances began to become tighter, these young people would not only sell goods from East Germany but also entertain youngsters with video films they had brought with them from East Germany. These informal cinemas had another impact on society, which was the change in the name of robbers from "*Mabandidos*", the name they had during the civil war, to "*Ninjas*", which had become famous thanks to the films shown in the cinemas set up by the Madjermanes. One interviewee states:

> There were no Ninjas here. The Madjermanes brought them with their martial arts films. A few years later a martial arts training area was even set up in the Xikhelene zone. Before that there were only "*Bandidos*" or "*Mabandidos*", but after the Madjermanes came back there started to be people who assaulted and beat up their victims, wearing those hoods that cover the face. The only thing you could see was the eyes and the nose [...].⁶¹

The films from the Madjermanes created the space for a new form of behavior by people who caused trouble and carried out looting in the communities. Thus, some of the aspects of the mixing of cultures had tangible disadvantages.

The goods that the Madjermanes brought with them from East Germany initially gave them a considerable privilege. With that came many friends and many expenses. Most of the money they had brought from East Germany was soon spent on parties, drinks, and fun with friends. As their money ran out, and with no income coming from the payment transfers they had made when they were in Germany, they began to sell their goods to survive and support their habits. Adevaldo Banze says in his memoirs:

> The days began to darken and day after day became even darker, with no payments or anything. The time had come to find a job, but no jobs appeared. I can still remember the sad

---

60 Marcos Rungo, July 21, 2016, interview with Fernando Machava.
61 Samuel Manjate, July 15, 2016, interview with Fernando Machava.

time when I gave up my goods, day after day, piece after piece. I got rid of my television, my radio, even my famous and beloved MZ, because I had to live [...].[62]

The first sales of products brought from Germany began in the 1990s, when some returnees put their belongings up for sale in the area that today is known as the Red Star Market. When their products ran out, these people then began to sell the products of other Madjermanes who were also in financial difficulties. One of the interviewees says:

> The Red Star market became famous for selling products from people who had returned from East Germany. From 1990 to 1997–1998 people would show up to sell the appliances they had bought in Germany. When we came back from Germany and we had not been employed or received the value of the transfers, we had to find other ways to survive. The only way out we found was to sell the items that we had brought from Germany. This became our employment. The business began with one person and after a while there were around 20 Madjermanes selling products from Germany, either their own goods or those of other people who had sold them to us for resale or just to sell for a certain commission.[63]

As the interviewee confirms, those responsible for selling the products of the Madjermanes were other returnees, who would sell the products of their colleagues for a commission. When the goods of the Madjermanes began to run out, they started to sell other products. To this day, they continue in the same business. This section has shown that while many returnees did not gain a place of employment in Mozambique's formal economy in the industry for which they have been trained, some still used their skills on the informal market to create small businesses, rooted in their local communities.

From the Elite to the Margins: The Social Legacy of the Madjermanes

For a certain period, the Madjermanes constituted an elite in Mozambican society and they seemed firmly moored back home. Many of these youngsters were still enthused by their time in Europe and expected to quickly be assigned a job where they could put into practice the skills they had learned. As a result, with the cash they momentarily possessed and the money they expected to receive, a certain complacency set in.

---

62 Banze, "Berlim: Um paraíso Suspenso na Memória," 37–39.
63 Grupo Mercado Estrela Vermelha, interview with Marcia C. Schenck, April 21, 2014.

Their dreams were destroyed, however, not least by the change in the political and economic systems as socialism unraveled and the armed fighting continued and the abandonment of Mozambique's socialist projects for which thousands of youngsters were sent to third countries to receive professional training. With few formal employment opportunities and no goods left from East Germany to support them, some of the returnees migrated again, this time to the mines of South Africa. Others looked for jobs locally, and yet others started small businesses. Most Madjermanes continued to wait for the money the Mozambican government owed them from the payments made when they were in East Germany, regardless of how they created their income. Before long, the situation of the unemployed returning migrants became desperate, culminating in a demonstration in front of the Ministry of Employment in late December 1990, when the Madjermanes demanded the money that was owed to them. Many of them expressed regret for having returned to the country, maintaining that those who remained in reunified Germany had better opportunities than those who planned to fulfill President Samora Machel's dream of developing Mozambique through a trained vanguard working class.[64]

As well as financial problems and unemployment, the Madjermanes faced the problem of social reintegration, as they were to a degree discriminated against and prevented from accessing employment opportunities because they had a reputation for participating in protest marches. They began to be referred to as "Madjermanes," "ninjas," or even "*molwenes* of the district," and thus their name was tainted with associations of troublemakers and indeed a few Madjermans slid into a life of crime, though that is by no means representative of the population as a whole.[65]

Time went by and the Madjermanes became older. During the period of their protests and demands, which began shortly after their return and intensified in the decade following the mid 1990s, there were countless confrontations between the returnees and not only governmental authorities but also ordinary citizens, who would sometimes suffer the consequences of the frustrations of the Madjermanes. As a result, their reputation considerably deteriorated over the course of the years.

---

64 Ibraimo Alberto is an example of Mozambican labor migrant who decided to stay in Germany after its reunification. He obtained German nationality, founded a family, retrained and worked in integration and anti-racism work; see Marcia C. Schenck and Ibraimo Alberto, Chapter 10 in this volume.
65 Lucas, "Mão-de-obra Moçambicana."

Conclusion

Many Mozambicans, especially the generation born after the 1990s, have little inkling of the history behind the social changes that the Madjermanes experienced and the protests they provoked upon returning to their home country in the early 1990s. Faced overall with a decline of prestige and living standards, expressions of Madjermanes' frustrations continue to be tangible up to the present day in the form of marching through the city with placards and occasionally inciting violence. Nowadays, the Madjermanes as a whole have a reputation of being violent troublemakers and stone throwers, mainly because of the violence that has occasionally broken out at their protests and in the park that they occupy. However, as I have highlighted in this contribution, they have suffered from intense social and economic changes in a short period of time. Moreover, many of the returnees were in their early twenties as they returned to Mozambique and have since grown old with their frustrations and disappointments.

The chance of migrating to a "developed" and above all "peaceful" European country, the dream of being in an industrialized nation, of acquiring goods with which to improve the standard of living, of having contact with other peoples and of opening new horizons—all this inspired many young people to sign up for a working experience in the socialist country GDR.

On the one hand the young men and women had the chance to emigrate to East Germany, to receive training, live in decent accommodations, and enjoy acceptable working conditions. They had the opportunity to acquire goods such as fridges, television sets, and HiFi systems, which were at once useful in their daily lives in East Germany and increased their status in their post-return lives in Mozambique. On the other hand, their work contracts were suddenly canceled, and they had to return en masse to Mozambique where they neither encountered the money that had been subtracted from their wages nor regular jobs in the positions for which they had been trained. When they arrived in their home country, they were initially seen as popular and wise key figures across Maputo, but their reputation began to tumble as their poverty increased.

The Madjermanes exercised an impact on the communities where they settled. For example, their arrival with television sets increased access to information. Their fridges and freezers helped expand people's ability to preserve food. Culturally, they brought new genres of music, a new style, and a new look. Their arrival also inspired acquisitiveness and a new capacity for protest for demands. Yet, as I have illustrated, the socioeconomic status and prestige of the Madjermanes was subject to rapid change. Their disappointment at not being allocated to jobs after their return, their loss of importance in the communities where they lived, and their increasing criminalization led some of the Madjermanes to become more violent in order to try to convince authorities to settle the demands they had relating to their social security and deferred wage payments. Today, when some of the Madjermanes participate in marches to demand their rights, street traffic builds up rapidly. Car windows are shattered by stones, sticks, and other instruments. Occasionally people are insulted or assaulted by the Madjermanes. Resorting to violence in lieu of wielding political and economic power to claim their payments, the Madjermanes are not as important now as they were once perceived to be. The desperate demonstrations are mere echoes of a past remembered as affluent.

Bibliography

Primary sources

Written sources

Agreement between the Government of the People's Republic of Mozambique and the Government of the German Democratic Republic concerning the Temporary Employment of Mozambican Workers in Socialist Companies of the German Democratic Republic, 1979.

Oral sources

Cumbane, Rogério. February 17, 2014. Maputo, interview with Marcia Schenck and Fernando Machava.
Loureço, Manuel. June 29, 2019. Maputo, interview with Fernando Machava.
Matsinhe, Abednego Levi. February 24, 2014. Maputo, interview with Marcia Schenck and Fernando Machava.
Macaringue, Francisco. July 21, 2016. Maputo, interview with Fernando Machava.
Mandlate, Alfredo, and Carlos Cossa. July 18, 2016. Maputo, interview with Fernando Machava.
Manjate, Samuel. July 15, 2016. Maputo, interview with Fernando Machava.
Melembe, Ilda. October 28, 2011. Maputo, interview with Marcia Schenck.
Obadias, Florêncio. June 27, 2019. Maputo, interview with Fernando Machava.
Raimundo, João. June 29, 2019. Maputo, interview with Fernando Machava.
Rungo, Marcos. July 21, 2016. Maputo, interview with Fernando Machava.

Secondary sources

Allina, Eric. *From "New Man" to Superman: The Politics of Work and Socialism, from Maputo to Karl-Marx-Stadt, C. 1982*. Wiser: Wits Institute for Social and Economic Research, 2016.
Isaacman, Allen, and Barbara Isaacman. *Mozambique: From Colonialism to Revolution*. Boulder, CO: Westview Press, 1983.
First, Ruth. *"O Mineiro Moçambicano: Um estudo sobre a exportação de mão de obra em Inhambane"*. Maputo: UEM, 1998.
Castel-Branco, Carlos N. "Problemas Estruturais de Industrialização." In *Moçambique: Perspetivas Económicas*, edited by Carlos Nuno Castel-Branco, 87–157. Maputo: UEM, 1994.
Elias, António. "Moçambicanos na RDA: O regresso Inesperado." *Revista Tempo* 14 (1990).
First, Ruth. *Black Gold: The Mozambican Miner, Proletarian and Peasant*. New York: St. Martin's Press, 1983.
Guerra, Héctor Hernández. "Do Rand À RDA? Modernização Compulsória e Práticas Sociais E Estratégias De Mobilidade Social." *Revista d'antropologia i investigació social* 3 (2009).
Harries, Patrick. *Work, Culture, and Identity: Migrant Laborers in Mozambique and South Africa, c.1860–1910*. Portsmouth, NH: Heinemann, 1994.
Klemm, Ulf Dieter. *"Moçambique – Alemanha, Ida E Volta: Vivências Dos Moçambicanos Antes, Durante E Depois De Estadia Na Alemanha"*. Maputo: Instituto Cultural Mocambique – Alemanha (ICMA), 2005.
Kreike, Emmanuel. *Recreating Eden: Land Use, Environment, and Society in Southern Angola and Northern Namibia*. Portsmouth, NH: Heinemann, 2004.
Lucas, Aníbal Fernando. "Mão-De-Obra Moçambicana Emigrante Na Ex. Republica Democratica Alema, 1979–1990." Graduate thesis, UEM, 2002.
Moodie, Dunbar T., and Vivienne Ndatshe. *Going for Gold: Men, Mines, and Migration*. Berkeley: University of California Press, 1994.
Müller, Tanja. *"Legacies of Socialist Solidarity: East Germany in Mozambique."* Lanham, Md: Lexington Books, 2014.
Oppenheimer, Jochen. "Mozambican Worker Migration to the Former German Democratic Republic: Serving Socialism and Struggling under Democracy." *Portuguese Studies Review* 12 (2004): 163–87.
Port, Andrew I. "'Awkward Encounters': East German Relations with the Third-World 'Other.'" *German History* 35 (2017): 630–637. Accessed February 1, 2020. doi:10.1093/gerhis/ghx086.
Schenck, Marcia C. "From Luanda and Maputo to Berlin: Uncovering Angolan and Mozambican Migrants' Motives to Move to the German Democratic Republic (1979–90)." *African Economic History* 44 (2016): 202–234. Accessed October 20, 2019. doi:10.1353/aeh.2016.0008.
Schenck, Marcia C. "Socialist Solidarities and Their Afterlives: Histories and Memories of Angolan and Mozambican Migrants in the German Democratic Republic, 1975–2015." PhD diss., Princeton University, 2017.
Schenck, Marcia C. "A Chronology of Nostalgia: Memories of Former Angolan and Mozambican Worker Trainees to East Germany." *Labor History* 59 (2018): 352–374. Accessed April 4, 2019. doi:10.1080/0023656X.2018.1429187.

Schenck, Marcia C. "Small Strangers at the School of Friendship: Memories of Mozambican School Students to the German Democratic Republic." *German Historical Institute Washington DC, Bulletin, Vol. 15*, 2020 forthcoming.

Sengo, Alice Samuel. *Processos de enriquecimento do léxico do português de moçambique.* Maputo, Porto: Universidade do Porto, 2010.

Serra, Carlos, ed. História de Moçambique Vol. 1. Maputo: UEM, 2000.

Slobodian, Quinn, ed. *Comrades of Color: East Germany in the Cold War World.* New York, Oxford: Berghahn, 2015.

Marcia C. Schenck and Francisca Raposo
9 Socialist Encounters at the School of Friendship

> Education is our principal instrument in forming the New Man; a man, liberated from old ideas, from a mentality that was contaminated by the colonial-capitalist mindset; a man educated by the ideas and practices of socialism.[1]
>
> Mozambican President Samora Machel

When Mozambique achieved independence in 1975, there arose new opportunities for knowledge exchange and socialist encounters in the education sector. The socialist alignment of the Mozambican Liberation Front (FRELIMO) allowed the country to tap into international knowledge networks connecting socialist countries across the world. Young Mozambicans attended schools in Cuba and the German Democratic Republic (GDR), while adults received vocational and military training or attended universities all over the Eastern Bloc, as part of state-initiated knowledge transmission migrations.[2] The idea for the School of Friendship (Schule der Freundschaft, SdF) was born in FRELIMO leadership circles at the end of the 1970s. President Samora Machel (1975–86) prioritized professional education to provide the industrializing country with skilled labor in the absence of a professional working class. This was important both ideologically and practically. Not only was the working class the revolutionary class in the Marxist-socialist exegesis favored by Machel, but in the aftermath of colonial neglect of education and the exodus of Portuguese settlers, the young People's Republic of Mozambique (PRM) lacked people with professional skills.[3] The SdF was to provide its 900 students with both general knowledge and vocational training to return skilled socialist workers as New Men (and Women) for the Mo-

---

[1] Samora Machel, "Organizar a sociedade para vencer o subdesenvolvimento," [Organize society to fight underdevelopment] *Colecção Estudos e Orientações* 14 (1982): 4.
[2] Hauke Dorsch, "Rites of Passage Overseas?: On the Sojourn of Mozambican Students and Scholars in Cuba," *Africa Spectrum* 43 (2008): 225–44. Prior to independence, Mozambicans had already migrated to other African countries for instance to attend school in Dar es Salaam; see Michael G. Panzer, "The Pedagogy of Revolution: Youth, Generational Conflict, and Education in the Development of Mozambican Nationalism and the State, 1962–1970," *Journal of Southern African Studies* 35 (2009).
[3] Mathias Tullner, "Das Experiment 'Schule der Freundschaft' im Kontext der Mosambikanischen Bildungspolitik," in *Freundschaftsbande und Beziehungskisten: Die Afrikapolitik der DDR und der BRD gegenüber Mosambik*, ed. Hans-Joachim Döring and Uta Rüchel, (Frankfurt am Main: Brandes & Apsel, 2005), 100.

zambican socialist and industrial revolution. The East German Socialist Unity Party (SED) leadership also took up the idea in the late 1970s and developed the SdF, not least because this goal was congruent with the SED's political values, its aspiration to aid the socialist development of so-called brother nations, and its economic interests in Mozambique. The SdF can be read in a broader tradition of East German institutions of learning targeted at the African and international vanguard. Other examples of these institutions explored in this volume include the FDGB college in Bernau, discussed by Eric Angermann in Chapter 4, the Herder Institute, discussed by Jörg Depta and Anne-Kristin Hartmetz in Chapter 2, and the higher education student exchanges discussed by Christian Alvarado in Chapter 3.

Existing studies dedicated specifically to the SdF are overwhelmingly based on the German archival record and aim to understand what the experiment can tell us about the successes and failures of schooling children from socialist brother states.[4] Some researchers have given particular attention to the socialist dimension of this education migration project.[5] Education scholars focus on the education aspect.[6] This contribution combines an analytical section with a firsthand account and is divided into two parts. The first provides background and historical context to understand the second part. This second section, which, similarly to Chapter 10, delves into one life-history, is a first-person account by a former student of the SdF, Francisca Raposo. Ms. Raposo pays particular attention to the process of her unmooring from Mozambican life to prepare for her new life in the GDR. She describes how she navigated personal disentanglements from familiar social structures and contexts, while forming new connections as she made new friends from all over Mozambique even before she arrived in the GDR. We can interpret her account using the metaphor of mooring and unmooring, discussed in the introduction to this volume. The metaphor comes into play here both in a spatial and a temporal sense.

---

4 See Annette Scheunpflug and Jürgen Krause, *Die Schule der Freundschaft: Ein Bildungsexperiment in der DDR*, Beiträge aus dem Fachbereich Pädagogik der Universität der Bundeswehr Hamburg (Hamburg: Universität der Bundeswehr Hamburg, 2000); Lutz R. Reuter and Annette Scheunpflug, *Eine Fallstudie zur Bildungszusammenarbeit zwischen der DDR und Mosambik* (Münster: Waxmann Verlag, 2006).
5 Uta Rüchel, "...*Auf Deutsch sozialistisch zu denken...*" – *Mosambikaner in der Schule der Freundschaft*, ed. Die Landesbeauftragte für die Unterlagen des Staatssicherheitsdienstes der ehemaligen DDR in Sachsen-Anhalt (Magdeburg: JVA Naumburg – Arbeitsverwaltung, 2001); Tanja Müller, *Legacies of Socialist Solidarity: East Germany in Mozambique* (Lanham, Md: Lexington Books, 2014).
6 Scheunpflug and Krause, *Die Schule der Freundschaft: Ein Bildungsexperiment*; Reuter and Scheunpflug, *Eine Fallstudie*.

Why did 900 young Mozambicans have to travel thousands of kilometers northward to attend an East German school to become skilled workers? For the FRELIMO leadership circle, establishing the school in Mozambique was out of the question, due to the ongoing war, a scarcity of internship opportunities, and funding challenges. Under these circumstances, it did not seem possible to maintain an isolated school with elite conditions in the country itself – it was more prudent to transfer the children. The SdF was to be a vision of Mozambique's scientific-Marxist future, one in which "tribalism," "occultism," and "poor work routine" were to be overcome and Mozambican traditions were to become nothing but folklore.[7] The few hundred square meters of an idealized Mozambique, embodied in the school's campus in Staßfurt, were dedicated to the socialist venture of educating the New Man.[8] In the language of the time, it was a symbol of international solidarity, but it also played into the political and economic interests of the GDR.[9] The content and concept of the SdF were intentionally left in German hands; Mozambique was interested in East German, not Mozambican, standards.[10] This produced an in-betweenness, where an idealized Mozambique was constructed in Staßfurt. The school remained isolated, foreign visitors were not allowed in, and initially the Mozambican students were only allowed to go out in supervised groups. Thus the young migrants traversed a whole continent, only to find themselves practically immobile, at least in the beginning.[11] As the students became older and spoke better German, they were able to leave the premises by themselves, especially to visit their East German host families, or friends at the weekends. Many students remember their overall experience in a rather positive light, but they were also subjected to racism and found their freedom curtailed in other ways. For instance, the possibilities for students to enact their faiths or live in accordance with religious commandments were limited at best.[12] This is, therefore, a case study for political

---

[7] Allen F. Isaacman and Barbara Isaacman, *Mozambique: From Colonialism to Revolution, 1900–1982* (Boulder: Westview Press, 1983), 93–99.
[8] Tullner, "Das Experiment 'Schule der Freundschaft'," 103.
[9] Katrin Lohrmann and Daniel Paasch, "Die 'Schule der Freundschaft' in Staßfurt," in *Freundschaftsbande und Beziehungskisten*, ed. Hans-Joachim Döring and Uta Rüchel (Frankfurt am Main: Brandes & Apsel, 2005), 95–98.
[10] Tullner, "Das Experiment 'Schule der Freundschaft'," 105.
[11] Scheunpflug and Krause, *Die Schule der Freundschaft: Ein Bildungsexperiment*, 82, 128.
[12] Müller, *Legacies of Socialist Solidarity*, 86–90; Marcia C. Schenck, "Small Strangers at the School of Friendship: Memories of Mozambican School Students to the German Democratic Republic," *Bulletin of the GHI* 15 (2020): 49–50; Emilia Francisco, "A Presença de Skinheads em Stassfurt?," in *Moçambique – Alemanha, Ida e Volta: vivências dos moçambicanos antes, durante e depois de estadia na Alemanha*, ed. Ulf Dieter Klemm (Maputo: ICMA, 2005), 81–84.

entanglements between two countries but on the social level of the school project entanglements remained temporary encounters, transitory moorings rather than roots. This story ended with political disengagement of the two governments, a process that reverberated on the individual level long after the participants had returned to Mozambique.

Who were the students, like Francisca Raposo, and how were they recruited and selected? The Mozambican Minister of Education, Graça Machel, had the prospective students recruited from across provinces to foster the unity of the Mozambican nation state which the government was trying to create.[13] Students were often approached in their local schools, as Francisca describes in her account. Once they were convinced, they often had to persuade their parents, many of whom were afraid of selling their children into slavery: a fear based on their and their ancestors' experience with Portuguese colonialism, forced labor, and slavery.[14] Other parents placed their trust in the FRELIMO government and immediately supported their children's decision to pursue their education abroad.[15] Francisca's experience lay somewhere in the middle of these extremes. What drew many children, including Francisca, was a thirst for adventure, the will to leave behind a life of relative poverty, and a desire to further pursue their education.[16] Most, like Francisca, were making a leap into the complete unknown.

As regards the operation of the SdF, in the summer of 1982 a total of 900 Mozambican children arrived in Staßfurt. They were between 12 and 14 years of age, and had completed at least a fourth-grade education in Mozambique. Contrary to official documentation, the new students did not constitute a homogeneous group. Rather, the 200 girls and 700 boys, from all over Mozambique, arrived with various levels of education and an actual age range of nine to 16.[17] The result was a potpourri of religions, languages, customs, and class origins. This diversity was, however, all but ignored. The students were to grow into socialist Mozambican citizens, overcoming ethnic and religious identities. It was irrelevant whether they were Makonde or Makua, Shangaan or Shona, animist, Muslim, or Christian. For the students, this meant that by the time they were brought together in holding centers all over Mozambique—even prior to reaching Maputo—their ties with their home regions, languages, and customs were slowly loosened and they learned, as

---

13 Tullner, "Das Experiment 'Schule der Freundschaft'," 103.
14 Albino Forquilha, interview conducted by the author, Maputo, September 2, 2011; Pedro Munhamasse, interview conducted by the author, Quelimane, June 7, 2014.
15 Forquilha, interview.
16 Pedro Munhamasse, Pascoa Rodrigues, and Narguice Ibrahim Jamal, interview conducted by the author, Quelimane, June 8, 2014.
17 Reuter and Scheunpflug, *Eine Fallstudie*, 78.

Francisca vividly describes, to engage on new terms with children from all over the country. As Francisca left her home region further behind, the group diversity increased and she gradually had to communicate in Portuguese and concentrate on what she shared with the other children: being young, curious Mozambican citizens.[18] The more Francisca and the children met children with other mother tongues, customs, and lived realities, the more they were encouraged to shed these distinguishing features and to form a new identity: that of a shared Mozambican-ness. This process was intensified once they were living and studying in the closed cosmos of the SdF, in a small East German village. The aim was to become Mozambique's vanguard workforce of the future.

In Francisca Raposo's contribution, we are invited to step into her shoes as a Mozambican girl, not yet a teenager. For her this story was decidedly not a political story about education cooperation between brother nations, but a personal story of liberation and emancipation from a life of work and service to family members. Her tools of liberation were her mind – she was always an excellent student – and the opportunity to travel to the GDR. The story Francisca chooses to share leaves no doubt that she sees her child-self as the main protagonist. In other words, it was her who made the decision to leave at all costs and managed to talk her parents into letting her go. The larger political context, socialism, and government agreements play no role in her story. Her account highlights the level of misinformation, rumors, and speculation that were rife in the general population in Mozambique as regards to the government's international education initiatives. Despite all the distorted reports that young Francisca heard about the GDR, she chose to trust in the information her teachers provided and placed all her hopes and anticipations for a better life in her journey to an unknown land. There is, however, more context and background to these rumors (p. 242) than Francisca knew when she came across them as a girl. There is a long history of rumors in different parts of Africa asserting that slavers were cannibals.[19] Witches and vampires served as metaphors to talk about exploitation and reveal anxieties and concerns of those speaking about them.[20] Where violence was concerned, fact and fiction often merged.[21] These rumors likely then indicate, in the minds of those spreading them, a continuity between the

---

18 Munhamasse, interview.
19 John Thornton, "Cannibals, Witches, and Slave Traders in the Atlantic World," *The William and Mary Quarterly* 60 (2003).
20 Luise White, *Speaking with Vampires: Rumor and History in Colonial Africa*, Studies on the History of Society and Culture (Berkeley, Cal.; London: University of California Press, 2000).
21 Ann Laura Stoler, "'In Cold Blood': Hierarchies of Credibility and the Politics of Colonial Narratives," *Representations* 37 (1992).

slave trade, colonialism, and the GDR. Despite official rhetoric that the new partners in the socialist east (who claimed to be anti-racist and anti-imperialist) were to be radically different from the former colonizers, people appear to have been less than convinced, as they continued to associate overseas countries with white inhabitants with a centuries-long history of forced migration, labor exploitation, and unfreedom. This might open up a new perspective on stories told by migrants to the GDR about racism and exploitative working conditions. On the other hand, this particular form of labor migration had only been active for two years at the time when Ms. Raposo heard these rumors.

This story focuses on the long path that young Francisca had to travel before she ever set foot on East German soil. With that, this contribution deals with a little-explored topic, namely the migration process from selection to arrival at the SdF. Francisca Raposo reflects on her childhood as a girl growing up in central Mozambique between the Zambezi River and the city of Quelimane. She also presents her perspective as one of the only 200 female students at the SdF. Another important feature of her story is its theme of unity between the students from all walks of life and all corners of Mozambique. This unity of the student body, which was later to become a socialist collective, is something that alumni all over Mozambique continue to emphasize to the present day, and which even led to the establishment of many alumni groups across the country.[22] The special connection that many former students maintain with one another, but also with the SdF as an institution and with Germany, as heir to the GDR, is also a motivation for women like Ms. Raposo who chose to travel across continents again to speak about her time as a student at the School of Friendship, 30 years after her return to Mozambique. In contributing her recollections to this volume, she also chose to defy personal circumstances and the personal consequences of devastating cyclones, demonstrating the importance of her SdF experience to her personal story.

* * *

What follows now is Francisca Raposo's narrative:[23]

---

22 Müller, *Legacies of Socialist Solidarity*, Chapter 3; Schenck, "Small Strangers," 57. During 2015, Marcia C. Schenck spent six months travelling through Mozambique and interviewed just about 200 returned workers, school children, and students who had spent part of their formative years in the GDR. In the process she met with many active alumni groups.
23 Thank you to Immanuel Harisch and Marcia C. Schenck for providing feedback and editing the narrative and to Marcia Schenck for translating it from German into English. Marcia C. Schenck and Francisca Raposo met at the conference "Respekt und Anerkennung" (Respect and Acknowledgement) in Magdeburg, Germany, February 22–24, 2019. Ms. Raposo agreed to

A Long Way to School: My Memories of Making My Way to the GDR

In December 1981, my school director announced that the government would select the best students between 11 and 13 years of age to fly to the German Democratic Republic to continue their studies. I lived in a small village called Conho, which is located 18 kilometers from the town of Mopeia. I was almost 13 years old at the time. At the time, in fifth grade, I was one of the best students in my class. I did not know what GDR meant and could not even imagine what the country looked like. But I was curious and wanted to go.

I really wanted to fly far away with other students because my life at home was not easy. I lived with my aunt and had to do a lot of housework and take care of my cousins. Sometimes I also lived with my grandmother, the mother of my father. I had to go to the forest for firewood with my friends. We didn't have an electric cooker or a gas stove. To buy school supplies, I had to work in the fields to earn money. Once I was given a lot of school materials as a gift because I was one of the best students. That was a relief for me, but I had to share some school materials with my brothers and sisters. My older sister studied in another school, in another place called Luabo. We saw little of each other. She was in a dormitory and sometimes, when she had no money to pay for the dormitory, she lived with my aunt, my mother's sister.

The Dream of the Unknown

Given this life at home, the option of flying to the GDR was a relief for me – and a very big chance. I was a girl with no concept of the GDR, but that didn't interest me. Whether it looked nice there or not, whether there were nice people or not, none of that mattered to me. I only wanted to go to the GDR – that became my primary goal.

Finally, the six best students between 11 and 13 years among us were chosen. Our parents were informed by the school director about our trip. At first, my parents did not agree to my leaving, because they had no idea what it meant to learn in the GDR either. Illiteracy was a problem for my parents' generation

---

write a contribution for this book. During the writing process, she was hit hard by Cyclone Idai, family tragedies, and the Corona pandemic, which made writing much more challenging than anticipated.

and the population in Mozambique in general at the time. Thus, speculation was rife and wrong attitudes about white people prevailed. For example, people were convinced that the GDR made sardines out of us. Some children, people said, will return to Mozambique in crates, or we will never return home at all. I was not scared easily. For me it didn't matter whether they made sardines out of me or killed me, I just wanted to get away from what to me was an unbearable life. To dispel the rumors and allow us children to go, the headmaster tried to explain to the people that it was not true that people were making sardines or something else out of us. He also said that white people do not eat human flesh, but many didn't believe it. It was clear to my parents that it was unlikely we would end up as sardines because they trusted the government. Yet, my mother still didn't want me to fly to the GDR but eventually, after many explanations, she agreed.

An Inner Mozambican Odyssey to the GDR... Quelimane first

After our parents agreed, we thought we were ready to go; but before we could start, we had to have many health checks. Fortunately, I was healthy and so were my fellow students. Next we all had to go to Quelimane, the state capital, where we met other students from other county towns. When we finally arrived in Quelimane one evening, everyone was tired and exhausted but also curious about what was waiting for us. I already knew Quelimane because I had been there several times with my aunt. It is a very beautiful city with many coconut trees.

In Quelimane I started a different life, without my aunt, my cousins, without my brothers and sisters, and without housework. The girls were separated from the boys. We were placed in a boarding school. After three days we could visit the boys. Our boarding school was small and better than the boys'. In the meantime, students from different districts of the Zambézia Province also came. They looked just like me: exhausted and curious. We immediately made friends and learned our names. All the girls were very nice and everyone wanted to know about everything. Each of us spoke about life at home and at school, about what we wanted to play and other such matters on the mind of young girls. I quickly made new girlfriends: Arminda, Laura, Narguisse, Bernadette, Gloria, Angelina, Laurinda, and others. We were treated very well and had enough to eat. Although the boys were in a different home, we almost always met.

... Then onto Nampula

After staying in Quelimane for about three weeks we went to Nampula. There, in the north of Mozambique, we stayed for three months. The trip to Nampula was not as easy as I had imagined because the roads were in very bad condition. Once in Nampula, we were to meet other students from other provinces, namely from Cabo Delgado, Niassa, and also Zambézia. Once again a new life began for me – different faces, many different languages, different habits, and expectations. In Mozambique, each province and even subregions have their own language, but everybody uses Portuguese to communicate and so it was the same for us.

... And Finally Maputo

When three months had passed, we had to travel again, this time by plane to Maputo, the capital of Mozambique. It was not the first time I flew, because I had flown once before from Quelimane to Beira together with my aunt.[24] But for most of the others, it was the first time and they were afraid.

In Maputo I met even more children from yet other provinces: Maputo, Tete, Sofala, Inhambane, Gaza, Cabo Delgado, Niassa, Nampula, Manica, and Zambézia. Now the whole country was gathered. And we all established friendships despite the many new languages, new faces, new cultures, and new habits. We were housed in a home called Pousada dos Caminhos de Ferro de Moçambique. The home belonged to the Mozambican railway. We were about 1,500 students. Five hundred of them flew to Cuba and only 900 were allowed into the GDR. This meant that 100 students were too many – once we learned that nobody slept peacefully anymore. We were so afraid that our name might not be on the right list, or worse yet, on no list at all. It didn't help matters that we stayed in Maputo for about four or five months. We had to do different examinations again but otherwise spent a lot of time waiting and fretting about who would go. After about two months, people from the ministry came with lists and passports. All of us were called to gather. They told us that this time a group of 70 students could fly. I was glad of that. I thought this time I was going to fly for sure. The names were read out, from one to seventy, but my name was not among

---

24 Flying was something very special to be remembered by every child in this story. At the same time, given the civil war, it was the only safe way to travel between the provinces for much our post-independence history and whoever could afford it would prefer that way of travel.

them. Every time new groups were read out, I intently listened for my name, but every single time I was disappointed and left even more anxious than before. Eventually, my name was read out in the ninth group. I was thrilled and beside myself with relief, joy, and expectation. But I did not have much time for feelings as I had to prepare for the journey.

The day of all days then came quickly. We took a truck to the airport. I was trembling all the time because I was afraid that someone would tell me I wasn't allowed to fly because I was sick, or the names got mixed up, or something similar. But our flight left Maputo at 10:00 a.m.

And Then – My First Night in the GDR

Between 11:00 p.m. and 12:00 a.m. we finally landed in Berlin. It was the middle of the night, and pitch dark, but I could see many things because of the lights. I saw a very large city with so many colorful lights I had never seen before. We slept in a hotel in Berlin, well most of us didn't sleep that much. But the next day, we drove on to the village of Staßfurt, to the School of Friendship, where our colleagues, educators, and teachers were already waiting for us. And there we finally arrived.

Bibliography

Dorsch, Hauke. "Rites of Passage Overseas? On the Sojourn of Mozambican Students and Scholars in Cuba." *Africa Spectrum* 43 (2008): 225–244.
Francisco, Emilia. *A Presença de Skinheads em Stassfurt? Moçambique – Alemanha, Ida e Volta: vivências dos Moçambicanos antes, durante e depois de estadia na Alemanha*, edited by Ulf Dieter Klemm, 81–84. Maputo: Instituto Cultural Mocambique – Alemanha (ICMA), 2005.
Isaacman, Allen F., and Barbara Isaacman. *Mozambique: From Colonialism to Revolution, 1900–1982*. Boulder, Colo: Westview Press, 1983.
Lohrmann, Katrin, and Daniel Paasch. "Die 'Schule der Freundschaft' in Straßfurt." In *Freundschaftsbande und Beziehungskisten: die Afrikapolitik der DDR und der BRD gegenüber Mosambik*, edited by Hans-Joachim Döring and Uta Rüchel, 91–99. Frankfurt am Main: Brandes & Apsel, 2005.
Machel, Samora M. "Organizar a Sociedade para Vencer o Subdesenvolvimento." *Colecção estudos e orientações* 14 (1982).
Müller, Tanja. *Legacies of Socialist Solidarity: East Germany in Mozambique*. Lanham, Md: Lexington Books, 2014.

Panzer, Michael G. "The Pedagogy of Revolution: Youth, Generational Conflict, and Education in the Development of Mozambican Nationalism and the State, 1962–1970." *Journal of Southern African Studies* 35 (2009): 803–820.

Reuter, Lutz-Rainer, and Annette Scheunpflug. *Eine Fallstudie zur Bildungszusammenarbeit zwischen der DDR und Mosambik*. Münster, New York, Munich, Berlin: Waxmann Verlag GmbH, 2006.

Rüchel, Ute. *"...auf deutsch sozialistisch zu denken..." – Mosambikaner in der Schule der Freundschaft*. Magdeburg: JVA Naumburg – Arbeitsverwaltung, 2001.

Schenck, Marcia C. "Small Strangers at the School of Friendship: Memories of Mozambican School Students to the German Democratic Republic." *Bulletin of the GHI* 15 (2020): 41–59.

Scheunpflug, Annette, and Jürgen Krause. *Die Schule der Freundschaft: ein Bildungsexperiment in der DDR*. Hamburg: Universität der Bundeswehr Hamburg, 2000.

Stoler, Ann Laura. "'In Cold Blood': Hierarchies of Credibility and the Politics of Colonial Narratives." *Representations* 37 (1992): 151–189.

Thornton, John. "Cannibals, Witches, and Slave Traders in the Atlantic World." *The William and Mary Quarterly* 60 (2003): 273–294.

Tullner, Mathias. "Das Experiment 'Schule der Freundschaft' im Kontext der mosambikanischen Bildungspolitik." In *Freundschaftsbande und Beziehungskisten: die Afrikapolitik der DDR und der BRD gegenüber Mosambik*, edited by Hans-Joachim Döring and Uta Rüchel, 100–109. Frankfurt am Main: Brandes & Apsel, 2005.

White, Luise. *Speaking with Vampires: Rumor and History in Colonial Africa*. Studies on the History of Society and Culture. Berkeley, Cal.; London: University of California Press, 2000.

Ibraimo Alberto and Marcia C. Schenck[1]
10 Paths Are Made by Walking: Memories of Being a Mozambican Contract Worker in the GDR

When I meet Ibraimo Alberto, I recognize him immediately. He is the man with the hat. Today, it is a narrow-brimmed black hat, very similar to the one he is wearing on the cover of his autobiography. During our interview, I see pictures of Ibraimo wearing a cowboy hat, a broad-brimmed hat, the color of which is hard to determine in the black and white photograph, and various other headdresses. Today, Ibraimo asks whether the hat can stay on during the interview. It is part of his style, an expression of his personality, and timelessly fashionable, he remarks with a grin. The hat has stayed with Ibraimo throughout his often-tumultuous life.

Ibraimo's story begins to take shape for me like an extensive collage that spreads out over the big conference table that stands between us as we talk. Pictures emerge: a certificate of excellence for Ibraimo's work in the GDR, a pennant of his sports club after reunification. These artefacts appear like flags to mark the unclaimed territory on the tabletop. There are constantly reemerging themes: Ibraimo the protector, Ibraimo the boxer, Ibraimo the hat connoisseur. Ibraimo artfully spins the web of his life in front of me, using the artefacts and themes to signpost his winding path. He speaks intently, often relating stories in the

---

[1] First of all, I would like to thank Ibraimo Alberto, without whose patience and generous willingness to share his memories this contribution would not have been possible. When I approached Ibraimo with this idea, he was immediately keen, on the condition that he did the talking and I did the writing. So, here we are. As the co-author of this piece I have taken off my academic hat and slipped into a new role, that of Ibraimo's hand and pen. I have thus not fact-checked or otherwise verified this story but have written down the memories that Ibraimo wanted to share with me about his life in the GDR and beyond. I have decided against using a first-person perspective because I want to make explicit the layers of interpretation inherent in the co-creation of this text. During May and June 2019, Ibraimo and I met in Berlin and he told me stories which were intended for a wider audience. I listened and transformed them into a piece of writing, which we then edited together. In the process, our subjective lenses combined into the present text. A note on language: our conversations took place in German and Portuguese and I wrote this text in English, which I then translated back for Ibraimo during the editing process. Further, I would also like to extend my thanks to the International Research Center Work and Human Lifecycle in Global History at the Humboldt Universität zu Berlin for allowing us to use their wonderful facilities for our meetings. And lastly, I would like to say thank you to Daniela Lehmann, Eric Burton, and Immanuel Harisch for their helpful comments and suggestions.

OpenAccess. © 2021 Ibraimo Alberto and Marcia C. Schenck, published by De Gruyter. This work is licensed under the Creative Commons Attribution 4.0 International License.
https://doi.org/10.1515/9783110623543-010

form of direct dialogue. His hands underscore his stories with emphatic gestures. Ibraimo takes this chance to talk about his life seriously. It is important to him to speak about the wonders but also the injustices that he has experienced as a black man in the GDR, and later in unified Germany. It is his larger goal to foster intercultural understanding through the sharing of memories. That is why he has agreed to share his recollections of life in the GDR, and of its legacies with which he continues to live.

Ibraimo has written his autobiography together with Daniel Bachmann, published in German in 2014.[2] This article is not just an English short version but zooms in on Ibraimo's life as a boxer in the GDR and is grounded in his memories as he shared them with me in 2019. Alexandra Piepiorka and Eduardo Buanaissa, in this volume, analyze the memoryscape that emerges as a result of the lived experiences that saw people travel along the axes of the socialist world. They reflect in detail on the role of memory in the production of intercultural spaces of remembrance. I will now turn towards Ibraimo's memories.

The Travels of the Man with the Hat

When I first met Ibraimo at a conference in Magdeburg in February 2019, I had already read his book and thus approached him to ask whether he would be interested in contributing a chapter to our edited volume.[3] He said he was willing to do so—provided he could do the talking and I did the writing—offered me the informal *Du*, gave me a big hug, and handed me his business card. The motto on his business card reads: "Wege entstehen dadurch, dass man sie geht" ("paths are made by walking"). Nothing could be more appropriate for a life such as Ibraimo's, including as it has migrations big and small, forced and voluntary.

Ibraimo's first transcontinental journey took him to Europe, straight into the heart of East-West divisions, into a city where cold war rivalries had become

---

[2] Ibraimo Alberto and Daniel Bachmann, *Ich wollte leben wie die Götter: Was in Deutschland aus meinen afrikanischen Träumen wurde* (Köln: Kiepenhauer & Witsch, 2014).

[3] The symposium "Respekt und Anerkennung" [Respect and Recognition] brought together former Mozambican contract workers and former Mozambican school children in East Germany with East German experts who worked in Mozambique and actors from politics, the development sector, the Lutheran church and the academy and took place in Magdeburg, February 22–24, 2019. The conference proceedings have been published; see Birgit Neumann-Becker and Hans-Joachim Döring, ed., *Für Respekt und Anerkennung: Die mosambikanischen Vertragsarbeiter und das schwierige Erbe aus der DDR*, Studienreihe der Landesbeauftragten (Halle/Saale: Mitteldeutscher Verlag, 2020).

Image 1: Ibraimo in cowboy hat and jeans posing at a photographer's studio in Berlin at the beginning of the 1980s (image in the possession of Ibraimo Alberto).

manifest in the very cityscape: to East Berlin. Ibraimo came to the German Democratic Republic (GDR, or East Germany) on June 16, 1981, as an 18-year-old teenager thirsting for life, eager to embrace the new world he was about to encounter, to absorb all the education he could before returning home. He and his two third-grade friends, Fernando António Macajo and Manuel João Diego, had decided together to migrate to the GDR because they wanted to take the opportunity to receive an education.[4] Neither of them had the faintest idea about the

---

4 See Franziska Rantzsch in this volume for a study on the negotiations between the representatives of the GDR and Mozambique with regard to the labor mobility scheme that brought Ibraimo Alberto and his friends to the GDR. See Marcia C. Schenck and Francisca Raposo in this volume for a discussion of an education migration scheme between Mozambique and the GDR.

GDR or what life there might look like. They only knew that it was a country in Europe, inhabited by white people. Ibraimo, the cowboy, was ready to explore the Wild East and the urban jungle of East Berlin. His hat made him invincible and his glasses (Ibraimo needed no glasses except for fashion reasons) let him see the world in a new way.

Ibraimo felt like he now was somebody: a traveler, a learner, an important young man, making an investment in his and his country's future. Intertwined, both futures would follow a path to success: while the young, recently-independent People's Republic of Mozambique was to develop through industrialization, Ibraimo was to learn a profession and return as skilled laborer and eligible bachelor who had explored Europe and in the process amassed not only stories but also material goods with which to support both his extended family and future nuclear family in Mozambique. "Nos somos continuadores!" is the slogan that comes to Ibraimo's mind, nearly 40 years later: "We are the continuation of the Mozambican revolution!" That was a sentiment close to young Ibraimo's heart. Aiding the revolution and working towards personal success were not exclusionary, but on the contrary, were interlocking goals, as Ibraimo understood the objective of his future return migration. Asked about this, more than a quarter of a century after the collapse of socialism in both Mozambique and East Germany, Ibraimo is not sure whether he ever believed in socialism. He was proud of Mozambique and he wanted development for his home country. He found himself living in two socialist people's republics and as such was active in the respective party organizations, but he cannot remember having been a particularly fervent supporter of socialism as a political doctrine.

At first, the young migrants were still very much connected to their previous lives in their respective home regions across Mozambique. This was a time before cellphones. Most migrants were only able to write letters home, but much more important than the written word (with which sometimes neither migrants nor their parents were overly familiar) were photos. Ibraimo and his friends sat for professional portraits in photo studios across East Berlin to document their journey. These were carefully orchestrated displays of a life Ibraimo and the other young workers lived as much—if not more—in their dreams as in reality. They wanted to send home images of successful young men and women who could afford to buy the latest fashionable clothes and pose with consumer goods. Their pictures also illustrated friendships (sometimes with white friends or extras, more often with one another) and playfulness. I am young, I am strong, I have travelled a long way, and I am invincible, these photos seem to say. They do not show the drudgery and long hours of work, the darkness and cold, the unfamiliar food, and the struggle to learn a foreign language (German) through another language (Portuguese) that was rarely the migrants' mother tongue.⁵ This was also the case for Ibraimo. Looking at the young Mozambican cowboy, who is exploring the city of East Berlin not on horseback but on foot, not guarding cattle but hunting for consumer goods and enjoying touristic sites, I recall the motto on Ibraimo's business card: paths are made by walking. With these professional photos, Ibraimo and his friends wanted to convey to their friends and families at home that the path they were walking now was a prosperous one. The temporarily lost sons and daughters were basking in material attainments and enjoying their explorations of a far-away land in Europe, inhabited by foreign white people.

What these photos did not show was the shock that Ibraimo and others experienced upon arriving in East Germany. Ibraimo, who says of himself that he is an anxious person, suffered from disappointment and alienation, and struggled to adapt to the different climate and cuisine during his first few weeks. He felt isolated, betrayed, and at the mercy of those around him. Living in a country about which he knew nothing, where he could neither speak the language, nor any other language that would help him communicate with the inhabitants, was a deeply unsettling experience for Ibraimo. He felt that he had been lured to Germany under the false promise of education and was instead confronted with menial work in an industrial slaughter house. He wanted to return. But he believed that were he to return before his time was up, he would spend 14 years in a labor camp in Mozambique working off his travel costs. Not knowing what to do, he stopped eating. In the period immediately after his arrival, Ibraimo's chosen path looked gloomy and dangerous.

Becoming a Boxer

It might have all ended disastrously, had Ibraimo not had a dream. On the bus back from Schönefeld airport on the fateful day of June 16, 1981, a fight broke out. Teenage Ibraimo did what he always did. He went straight up to the aggressor and demanded: "Beat me, not him. But I will hit back!" Fifty-two heads turned, eyes expectantly on Ibraimo the protector. And in this moment Ibraimo's dream crystalized in his mind. He was going to learn how to box in East Germany.

He lost no time in asking the Mozambican intermediary and translator where he could learn boxing in this new land. The translator was used to many ques-

---

5 Katrin Bahr's text in this volume examines the other side of the coin, namely photographs taken by East Germans in Mozambique.

Image 2: Ibraimo and his friend Manuel João Diego training (image in the possession of Ibraimo Alberto).

tions from the recently arrived, but never before had he encountered such a request with such urgency. He did not know, but the German teacher assigned to the new worker-trainees of the meat processing plant, *VEB Fleischkombinat Berlin*, promised to inquire. Two months after his arrival in the GDR, Ibraimo started boxing at *Tiefbau Berlin*, a sports club of the *VEB Tiefbau*, a publicly-owned civil engineering enterprise. At 18, Ibraimo had no formal knowledge of boxing, so he started with the very young boys of 12 to 16, but that did not deter him. He was still wary of moving about the city by himself and so he persuaded his friend Manuel João Diego to accompany him. That was the beginning of two amateur sports careers that made headlines in East Germany.

To Ibraimo, boxing was not just a sport: it became central to his self-image. When he tells the story of his life, it begins with a small boy in the North of Mozambique who had an innate drive to protect the weak and needy. There was not a single fight in the boy's village or the boy's school that took place without that boy going up to the aggressor and stating: "Before you hit him, hit me!" The reply would come: "But you are a good person, we want to attack the boy behind you." And the little boy Ibraimo would reply: "But he is as good a person as I am. We are all good people." Sometimes the fight would dispel as quickly as it had brewed. In other instances, young Ibraimo would have to physically fight and sometimes got badly beaten. Ibraimo the boy not only got into fights for noble reasons, but also for necessity. He had to protect his food from older youths who attacked him on his way to school, and to defend himself in class from older boys during unsupervised school hours. With all this fighting, young Ibraimo dreamed of learning how to box—not simply to be more effective in terms of self-defense, the older Ibraimo underscores—but to be a better protector. Yet, Ibraimo could not find boxing training anywhere near him in Manica and so he buried the dream and kept on fighting the only way he knew. Until one day on the bus from Schönefeld airport, an opportunity emerged to finally become a boxer.

Boxing in the GDR

Ibraimo's travels half way around the globe, to an unfamiliar country called the GDR, would have meant nothing to him had he not been able to start an amateur boxing career which saw him become Berlin Champion in September 1983. Even today, boxing is more to Ibraimo than a sport. It has been a valve, a mental challenge, an avenue for integration, and a tool for self-defense. Boxing was what made his life in the GDR enjoyable and protected him from overt and covert racism. Without boxing, his life in the GDR would have been miserable, Ibraimo states bluntly. But boxing gave him a purpose and a social network of teammates and trainers on which he was able to rely. His successes in the ring gave him a reason to feel proud and provided his life with the purpose and mental challenge that he could not find in his work. He worked in a meat-processing factory, *VEB Fleischkombinat Berlin*, from 1981 to 1986, and later as group leader in a glass factory, *VEB Glaswerk Stralau*, from 1986 to November 1990.

At work, Ibraimo was always successful. He was elected as head of his brigade as early as 1982. His gregarious and open character and his reputation as protector of the weak made him an obvious choice for his colleagues. In 1988, Ibraimo received a medal from the mayor of East Berlin for "excellent productivity in the socialist competition."⁶ Yet, his work was never a source of satisfaction for Ibraimo. Ibraimo spent much of his time doing sports. He organized soccer competitions between Mozambicans from different companies across East Germany, and he played in an otherwise all-German team, *Turbine Treptow*. His real passion though was boxing.

Ibraimo describes boxing as a conversation using one's hands. It requires awareness and concentration. It is not brute violence, but physical interactions that are governed by strict rules. Ibraimo thinks of boxing as an exchange. In many ways, boxing to 18-year old Ibraimo became the conversations he could not have otherwise, because he still only spoke a few words of German. It became the cultural exchange that rarely took place outside the training room and boxing ring for him. Ibraimo lived in a hostel near Tierpark that only housed foreign workers, a living arrangement he remembers as fun because of the parties that were thrown every weekend, but also as isolating from East German society. His brigade at the meat-processing plant combined workers from different nationalities, including Mozambican, Mongolian, Polish, and German, and relations were generally amicable, but during break time, everybody went to sit with their own national groups in the company canteen. Not so with boxing. In Ibraimo's memory, he and his friend João became inseparable, trained together, travelled together to and from training and supported each other. But the support did not stop there. Their East German trainers and the other boxers from their club, young and old, stood behind them. They taught the two young Mozambicans the ins and outs of boxing and physically protected them from racist attacks.

Ibraimo recalls his first fight as if it were yesterday. He had been training for a year, when his coach Rainer Kühn told him that he was ready to compete. They chose an opponent who was a good match for his weight class and experience level, but on the day of the competition, the opponent bailed. Ibraimo was furious because he wanted nothing more than to fight. In the end they found a man who already had experience of seven fights. Despite the experience mismatch, Ibraimo decided to brave it out. He won. It was the moment in which Ibraimo found his style. The minute he entered the ring, Ibraimo says he became a wild animal that needed to defend its territory. He mercilessly attacked and attacked, and attacked, and attacked again.

---

6 The full German text reads: "In Anerkennung hoher Leistungen und beispielgebender Initiativen im sozialistischen Wettbewerb wird Ibraime (sic) Alberto als Mitglied eines sozialistischen Kollektivs die Medaille für ausgezeichnete Leistungen im Wettbewerb verliehen. Berlin 7. Oktober 1988."

That style served him well, and only one year later Ibraimo had boxed himself to the top of Berlin's amateur sports scene and became city champion. During this time Ibraimo represented Berlin in different cities and was loaned to different clubs such as *Berlin TLC* and *Dynamo Berlin*. He remembers that when the others in his team had fun on the bus to competitions, he sat by himself and went through all the different scenarios of a fight. He would discuss the different strategies with his trainers and teammates. Ibraimo did not allow himself to lose focus. He had a goal. He had a passion. He had a mission.

Ibraimo's focus paid off. From 1985 onwards, he and João competed internationally for Mozambique. They bought training suits and designed the Mozambican national outfit for boxing. When Ibraimo recounts these stories his eyes still light up. He was proud to be able to bring fame to his home country. Ibraimo recounts how his East German coach became the Mozambican national trainer. Sadly though, the trainer had no emotional connection to the country and there was no money in it. That was the end of the Mozambican boxing team. Ibraimo's disappointment is still palpable many years later.

Being a black boxer in a white man's country was an ambivalent thing for Ibraimo from the start. In his East German opponents' minds, it was often not Ibraimo Alberto who entered the ring, but Muhammad Ali or George Foreman. Some were already afraid before the fight began, and Ibraimo quickly learned how to incorporate that into his strategy. But there were just as many fights when Ibraimo was not met by awe but by blank hatred. Especially when his team went to fight in Dresden and Magdeburg, Ibraimo felt racism emanating from both the audience and his opponents. That, he says, made him fight like a predatory animal. His trainers, he recounts, would never understand what came over him at these occasions. Only he knew. He was defending himself from much more than just the fists of his opponents. They were fighting about something more important than winning or losing this or that competition. Ibraimo felt the weight of defending his personal honor and the honor of every black man on planet earth. He needed to make the audience see that this "ape" knew a thing or two about boxing. He needed to make his opponents crumble under his fists because he knew how hopeless it all was. In the face of racism, Ibraimo felt himself standing on the losing side. Even when he walked away victoriously, his team would have to wait just outside the ring and embrace him with their masses of sweaty, muscular bodies to guard him safely back to the bus, back to Berlin. Ibraimo remembers these moments as sweet moments of boxing success, but also tainted forever with racism.

Boxing, however, did more than just expose the bigotry of some parts of the GDR. Boxing also allowed Ibraimo and João privileges that other Mozambican worker-trainees and workers did not have, such as mobility but also—paradoxi-

Image 3: Ibraimo fighting a boxer from VEB "Schwarze Pumpe" (image in the possession of Ibraimo Alberto).

cally—the opportunity to settle. For instance, Ibraimo proudly remembers international boxing competitions in Copenhagen, Moscow, and Budapest. Travel to the other side of the iron curtain was prohibited for the average Mozambican worker-trainee, but sport let Ibraimo cross what, even to most GDR citizens, was the insurmountable anti-fascist bulwark. And while boxing allowed Ibraimo to be mobile and travel along new paths to different countries, it also afforded him the ability to continue on the path on which he had set out in East Germany: it allowed him to put down roots. Ibraimo tells me he became a GDR citizen in 1988, a process that in the end needed him to make the tough decision to give up his Mozambican citizenship. Ibraimo, unlike his boxing partner João, did not lose much sleep over that issue, because he saw the center of his life to be in

East Germany.[7] Overall, Ibraimo declares, life in the GDR was good because of the sports. The GDR fully supported Ibraimo's boxing career and once he had a contract, he was released from work to attend training camps. Between work, sports, and parties in his free time, time passed, the GDR fell, and the machines around Ibraimo came to a grinding halt.

Boxing in a Brave New World

While the GDR crumbled, Ibraimo boxed. When his Mozambican co-workers at the *Glaswerk* on the Stralau peninsula phased out of his life and returned to Mozambique, he took it out on the punchbag. João, his partner in crime for many years, also left and Ibraimo found himself alone. Ibraimo trained some more. As the world fell to pieces around Ibraimo, the sport gave him focus and strength.

The winds of change blew through East Germany like a cyclone, swept Ibraimo up, and dumped him in the small and isolated town of Schwedt. The town lies in Brandenburg state, on the left bank of the river Oder which marks the border with Poland. Schwedt has a special history, marked by substantial growth during the early days of the GDR—from 6,000 to 52,000 inhabitants—due to the petrochemical industry (PCK-Raffinerie). It then saw rapid decline in employment possibilities after German reunification, resulting in the outmigration of almost half of its population.[8] Here, against the dramatic changes of the reunification period, emerged a personal treasure: Ibraimo was in love and soon his family began to grow. Still, the city of Schwedt and its surroundings proved less welcoming to Ibraimo and his family as time passed. Once again, boxing remained as Ibraimo's constant, the pillar of his self-worth, and the defining characteristic of his place in the community at large. While all the East German box-

---

[7] Unlike Ibraimo, the majority of workers decided to return. Fernando Machava, in this volume, examines how fellow worker-trainees fared after their return back to Mozambique, describing a return in the expectation of riches and the good life but soon falling from grace and struggling to survive.

[8] Schwedt was situated at the very fringes of the GDR but connected to the Druzhba pipeline which was constructed in the early 1960s as Comecon project to connect Russian oil to several countries in the Eastern bloc. While this was hugely important, the city was, apart from oil, also known as the country's biggest potato supplier, for paper factories and for the notorious NVA (the army of the GDR) prison. See Marc Langebeck and Alexander Goligowski's *Brandenburg aktuell*, May 6, 2014 special on the future of Brandenburg, "Die Kunst des Schrumpfens," published on May 7, 2014, https://www.rbb24.de/politik/thema/2014/gehen-oder-bleiben/bei traege/gehen-oder-bleiben-die-kunst-des-schrumpfens.html, accessed July 2, 2020.

ing clubs changed their names, and no longer were affiliated with the socialist factories from which many had originated, the boxers stayed. Ibraimo now boxed for what had been the club of the *PCK Chemie* in Schwedt but was now known as *Uckermärkischer Boxverein 1948 Schwedt e.V* (Uckermark Boxing Club 1948 Schwedt). Ibraimo began boxing in the national second division and moved up after one year to the first division (the Bundesliga). Ibraimo remembers that his success was untarnished. He had a secret weapon. He was able to lose weight, or what he calls to "make weight", like nobody else. His nickname from that time—"Ali, the world champion of making weight"—attests to that. His normal weight would have been about 75 kg, but he managed to slim down to 63 kg for fights. Ibraimo's amateur boxing career was the center of his life until he had to retire at the age of 37. But even then, he did not hang up his gloves but continued to train the next generation and got certified as a coach and referee. By the time of his retirement from competitive amateur boxing, the world around Ibraimo had fallen to pieces and was in the process of putting itself back together. The GDR was no more and its former citizens were now struggling to make a living in unified Germany.

At first, Ibraimo thought he had escaped the worst upheavals of the reunification ramifications. He married Birgit, an East German nurse who he had met after a boxing accident in Schwedt hospital in the fall of 1989. Their first child, a daughter, arrived in November 1990. With that, it was clear to Ibraimo that his future would be in Germany. A second child, a son, followed. The family still lived in Schwedt. During that time, Ibraimo remembers working for intercultural understanding, against all odds. He often had to take on the role that he was so familiar with from his childhood, that of a protector. He protected not only his family and himself, but also other migrants and Germans who needed his protection, in his role as representative for foreigners' issues. While his wife continued working as a nurse, Ibraimo worked for the city of Schwedt as translator and advisor to the many refugees and asylum-seekers who arrived from Yugoslavia and elsewhere in the early 1990s. Ibraimo became very successful, not only knowing how to knock out his opponents in the boxing ring, but also interacting with and mediating for the many international sojourners who found a new home in Schwedt. As a result of his work fostering integration and intercultural understanding, Ibraimo studied social work at a college in Potsdam from 1997–2002. He still works as social worker with refugees in Berlin and remains active in anti-racism work.

Despite his evident people skills, one day it all became too much even for Ibraimo the protector. After a group of Neo-Nazis came to one of his son's soccer games and threatened to kill him and another boy of Vietnamese heritage, Ibraimo felt that he could no longer guarantee the safety of his family. They packed their belongings and left Schwedt under cover of darkness that very night. Their idea was to look for "inner German refuge" as Ibraimo calls it, in the "West", meaning the former West Germany. Ibraimo says that I should have no trouble locating this tragic event in the newspapers because at that time he became famous for another reason, as "the last black man" fleeing Schwedt. At first, the family stayed in a rented holiday home close to Stuttgart until they received an offer that they could move into a flat in Karlsruhe. Ibraimo remembers thinking that life in Karlsruhe was far from perfect, but that he noticed that people were different, in that they sat next to him on public transport. According to Ibraimo, this was impossible in Schwedt. In Karlsruhe, life returned to a new normal and every family member worked through their own trauma of having survived racism in various forms. Eventually, however, the marriage broke apart and Ibraimo now found himself back where it had all started, in Berlin.

Image 4: Ibraimo never loses focus.

New Paths on Old Routes

When Ibraimo walks through Berlin today (yes, more often with a hat than without), he, like any East German Berliner, sees two cities. He walks the streets of the capital of the united Federal Republic of Germany and his eyes meet those of the hipsters, businessmen and women, politicians, migrants, and tourists who dominate the streets today. But in his mind, he sees the East German Friedrichshain and Stralau peninsula, where he used to work in the 1980s. His memories of the rather greyer and more dilapidated city are juxtaposed with the new information his retina sends to his brain. What emerges is a city of memories, in a city where new memories are made daily.

Ibraimo's current life as a German citizen in Berlin is a legacy of the socialist dreams that expanded the world for Mozambicans like Ibraimo. Young Mozambican boys, girls, men and women were sent to Cuba, East Germany, the Soviet Union, and other countries of the Eastern Bloc, to go to school, to work, to attend universities, to take part in military training and professional job development workshops. Without the labor migration program that brought up to 21,000 Mozambican workers in their late teens and early twenties to East Germany, he would have never set foot on East German soil. Without setting foot on East German soil, he would not have had a boxing career, he would not have met his East German wife, and they would not have had children. If he had stayed at home, or if he had returned in 1990, there are countless scenarios of what might have happened. The two extremes are that Ibraimo might be dead as a result of the 16-year war in Mozambique, or alternatively he might have become successful at home with a combination of luck, relationships, and his boxing knowledge. Either way, he would most certainly not be sitting in Berlin with me today to talk about his past.

When asked how he remembers the GDR, Ibraimo brings up the metaphor of an oven. He explains that just like in an iron oven, it is nice and warm inside, and good things are in the process of being cooked. Yet, looking from the outside, you do not have a clue what is happening inside. It might get too hot, and, when you finally open the oven, you see that everything has already burned. When he first arrived, he knew nothing about the GDR. Later, there was a lot that Ibraimo came to enjoy. The friendships he formed, the parties they had, the clothes and consumer products he was able to buy, the travels he was able to undertake, the soccer matches he played with Mozambicans and Germans, and of course his boxing. But—and it is a big but—his memories of the GDR, just like his memories of his traumatic post-GDR experience in reunified Germany, circle back to the experience of racism. He remembers two types of racism. Firstly, the everyday, chronic, verbal kind; a poison that slowly sets about decomposing the self-worth even of a boxing champion and protector of the weak. Secondly, he remembers the immediate, acute, life-threatening kind of racism. Both seep into your very being, rewire your memories, stay with you forever. It was the latter, though, that made Ibraimo leave everything behind after his son was threatened. All Ibraimo had to protect him until the police arrived was his own muscle strength, against the odds of a group of more than 10 ferocious Neo-Nazi boys. Nobody bothered to look into the oven. It is too late now. Everything is burned. The fear has never left Ibraimo.

Ibraimo accuses the average GDR citizen of a lack of interest in the people that came from abroad to work and train in the GDR. While he established friendships, he also encountered indifference and hostility. He credits a certain measure of protection from racist expressions in the GDR to the *Volkspolizei* (People's Police) and to their omnipresence. Ibraimo was not surprised at the outbreak of racist violence after reunification. To him, these actions were on a continuum with the GDR he had experienced before, where the illegality of racism merely led to it being capped and contained, not eradicated. In the end, in places like Schwedt, racism and xenophobia were able to grow to such proportions that Ibraimo reports even his friends became afraid of inviting him over for fear of themselves becoming targets of the wrath of the xenophobic. Ibraimo felt he could no longer trust the police to protect him and his family. But Ibraimo also gives a glimpse into the complicated notions of belonging in Schwedt, in that local people who he describes as Neo-Nazis protected him against outside Neo-Nazis, claiming the boxer is "one of us." In this complicated interplay between notions of masculinity, race, and belonging, we can see why Ibraimo might have seen hope in fighting for a peaceful and multicultural Schwedt during his 20 years in that town. For everything he has lived through, he has maintained a forgiving attitude. He speaks of the possibilities of understanding between people of different colors and life experiences and he takes us as an example. Our sitting at a table, a black man in his fifties and a white woman in her thirties, my listening to him telling his stories. Our project of giving voice to his memories so readers might gain an insight into a Mozambican former contract worker's recollection about his life in East Germany and the legacies thereof.

As Ibraimo and I are walking towards Friedrichstraße station on our respective ways home, he looks at me and relates a story that is at once funny and sad. In 1981, shortly after his arrival, he was exploring Berlin with a friend. They were taking in the new sights and taking pictures as any tourist would. When they came to Friedrichstraße, they did the same. Very soon, they found themselves handcuffed and held by the East German police for the afternoon. They did not have the faintest idea what was happening to them or why they were spending hours in police custody. When their translator finally arrived, after what seemed like an eternity to the two frightened teenagers, they learned that they had stumbled upon an inner-German border where it was strictly prohibited to take pictures. Today, Ibraimo, along with everybody else, can take pictures and traverse Friedrichstraße in whichever direction he likes. This is his freedom as a German citizen. That citizenship, and the rights that come with it, are an important legacy of the pan-socialist links which connected Mozambique to East Germany, and which continue to reverberate into the present, embodied in the lives of people like Ibraimo.

Bibliography

Alberto, Ibraimo, and Daniel Bachmann. *Ich wollte leben wie die Götter: Was in Deutschland aus meinen afrikanischen Träumen wurde.* Köln: Kiepenhauer & Witsch, 2014.

Neumann-Becker, Birgit, and Hans-Joachim Döring, eds. *Für Respekt und Anerkennung: Die mosambikanischen Vertragsarbeiter und das schwierige Erbe aus der DDR.* Edited by Beauftragte des Landes Sachsen-Anhalt zur Aufarbeitung der SED-Diktatur, Studienreihe der Landesbeauftragten. Halle/Saale: Mitteldeutscher Verlag, 2020.

III Sourcing Visions of Solidarity

George Bodie
11 So Close, Yet So Far: Ulrich Makosch and the GDR's Afrikabild on Screen and in Text

> Although our two states are located on different continents, Socialist Ethiopia is close and dear to every citizen of our country.
> Erich Honecker to Mengistu Haile Mariam, 1978.[1]

The GDR is often described as a "closed" society.[2] This metaphor has a number of implications, mostly related to the very real restrictions placed on travel, goods, and exchange by the state. Indeed, travel restrictions have in many ways come to define it in both popular memory and the historiographical literature. In the order of the GDR's symbolic associations, the Berlin Wall remains primary, its figurative importance matched only by the vital practical role it played in perpetuating the state's existence. But were physical restrictions matched by similar limitations on ideas or images? Did state-produced media mirror the GDR's border regime, shielding citizens from the outside world? Or was such imagery and reportage used to make up for a lack of opportunity to travel? In a state where travel beyond the Eastern Bloc was difficult for most citizens, what role did reportage on the outside world play?

Thanks to a growing literature on the subject, we now know that international solidarity—particularly the variety practiced with non-European nations and

---

[1] Stiftung Archiv der Parteien und Massenorganisationen der DDR im Bundesarchiv (hereafter SAPMO-BArch), DY 30/2419, "Toast während des Essens zu Ehren Mengistu Haile Mariams," 1.
[2] The GDR has frequently been depicted as deliberately resisting global forces; see, for example Charles S. Maier, *Dissolution: The Crisis of Communism and the End of East Germany* (Princeton: Princeton University Press, 1999), 104; Gareth Dale, *Between State Capitalism and Globalisation : The Collapse of the East German Economy* (Oxford: Peter Lang, 2004), 340; Olaf Klenke, *Ist die DDR an der Globalisierung gescheitert? : Autarke Wirtschaftspolitik versus internationale Weltwirtschaft ; das Beispiel Mikroelektronik* (Frankfurt am Main: Peter Lang, 2001), 111; Christoph Buchheim, "Die Achillesferse der DDR – der Aussenhandel," in *Überholen ohne einzuholen : die DDR-Wirtschaft als Fußnote der deutschen Geschichte?*, ed. André Steiner, Forschungen zur DDR-Gesellschaft (Berlin: Ch. Links, 2006), 91; Peter Grieder, *The German Democratic Republic* (Basingstoke: Palgrave Macmillan, 2012). No state in the world has ever been completely autarchic, of course. Some scholars have acknowledged that state-socialist countries traded with the rest of the world, although still argue for autarchy—or at least "near-autarchy"—on the basis that these states didn't take part in "outward-orientated developmental strategy" or "international specialization". See for example Jan Winiecki, *Shortcut or Piecemeal: Economic Development Strategies and Structural Change* (Budapest: Central European University Press, 2016), 24.

OpenAccess. © 2021 George Bodie, published by De Gruyter. This work is licensed under the Creative Commons Attribution 4.0 International License. https://doi.org/10.1515/9783110623543-011

movements—played an important role in GDR culture, political discourse, and everyday life. For the most part, this culture of solidarity was rooted in imagery and iconography. As Quinn Slobodian has shown, "for the great majority of the East German population, icons and contributions rather than personal experience remained the means of engaging with the global South and activists of colour."[3] A number of scholars have explored the shape and form of this iconography.[4] Very little work has been done on the content of foreign news reporting however, which was one of the most quotidian and widespread mediums through which this iconography was disseminated: an absence that is perhaps unsurprising given the Cold War consensus that news, to quote Simon Huxtable, "was alien to the communist world view."[5]

The GDR's cultures of solidarity were not monodirectional, however: they also grew from the strategic concerns of national liberation movements in Africa. Socialist journalists from the Eastern Bloc sought to convey the image of a growing socialist world to their fellow citizens, but they were also used by national liberation movements and newly independent states to spread their own messages, creating transnational entanglement. In the throes of anti-colonial struggle or the early days of independence, such movements and states were often reliant upon foreign bureaus.[6] As Matthew Connolly has shown in the case of the National Liberation Front (FLN) in Algeria, "human rights reports, press conferences, and youth congresses" were among the most important weapons of anti-colonial struggle, with world opinion and international law more than important than conventional military objectives.[7] Hakan Thörn illustrates in his transnational history of the anti-apartheid movement that national liberation movements were centrally concerned with a "struggle for representation" that took

---

[3] Quinn Slobodian, "Socialist Chromatism: Race, Racism and the Racial Rainbow in East Germany," in *Comrades of Color: East Germany in the Cold War World*, ed. Quinn Slobodian (New York: Berghahn Books, 2015), 32.
[4] See, for example, Gregory Witkowski, "Between Fighters and Beggars: Socialist Philanthropy and the Imagery of Solidarity in East Germany," in *Comrades of Color: East Germany in the Cold War World*, ed. Quinn Slobodian (New York: Berghahn Books, 2015).
[5] Simon Huxtable, "Making News Soviet: Rethinking Journalistic Professionalism after Stalin, 1953–1970," *Contemporary European History* 27 (2018): 59.
[6] George Roberts, "Press, Propaganda and the German Democratic Republic's Search for Recognition in Tanzania, 1964–72," in *Warsaw Pact Intervention in the Third World: Aid and Influence in the Cold War*, ed. Natalia Telepneva and Philip Muehlenbeck (London: I.B.Tauris, 2018), 151.
[7] Matthew Connelly, *A Diplomatic Revolution: Algeria's Fight for Independence and the Origins of the Post-Cold War Era* (New York: Oxford University Press, 2003), 4.

place in a "transnational media space."⁸ In this space, partisan socialist journalists were important actors to be utilized by anti-colonial forces.

It was events across the continents of Africa and Asia which sparked the growth of an extra-European-centered solidarity culture in the GDR, specifically the acceleration of decolonization in the early 1960s. This acceleration led GDR elites to believe that they were entering what Politburo member Hermann Axen would later call a "new revolutionary moment."⁹ The states produced by this new revolutionary moment were not simply potential allies for the socialist world, but rather viewed as being "objectively anti-imperialist" according to Soviet premier Nikita Khrushchev.¹⁰ As a Soviet academic wrote at the time, "the national liberation movement is an inseparable part of the world revolutionary process."¹¹

In the GDR, the state made a concerted effort to depict Africa as a site of friendly, revolutionary, anti-imperialist movements and peoples, educating its citizens both about the existence of this revolutionary world and their need to practice solidarity with it. Erich Honecker, the General Secretary of the ruling Socialist Unity Party of Germany (SED), frequently boasted to African leaders that they were popular figures in the GDR: despite geographical distance, as he told Ethiopian leader Mengistu Haile Mariam in 1978, "socialist Ethiopia is close and dear to every citizen of our country."¹² A year earlier, Joachim Yhombi-Opango—the head of state of the Marxist-Leninist People's Republic of the Congo—had traveled to East Berlin, where Honecker assured him that he was a household name. "In our country," he told the Congolese leader, "it is very well known how much the People's Republic of the Congo is doing for the final liberation of the African Continent from colonialism and racism."¹³ As Honecker would go on to tell Yhombi-Opango, he was not the only African leader to play a prominent role in everyday life in the GDR, noting that streets and buildings in the

---

8 Håkan Thörn, *Anti-Apartheid and the Emergence of a Global Civil Society* (Basingstoke: Palgrave Macmillan, 2006), 17.
9 Hermann Axen and Harald Neubert, *Ich war ein Diener der Partei: autobiographische Gespräche mit Harald Neubert* (Berlin: Edition Ost, 1996), 400.
10 Donald S. Carlisle, "The Changing Soviet Perception of the Development Process in the Afro-Asian World," *Midwest Journal of Political Science* 8 (1964): 386.
11 Cited in Roger E. Kanet, "Soviet Propaganda and the Process of National Liberation," in *The Soviet Union, Eastern Europe and the Third World*, ed. Roger E. Kanet (Cambridge: Cambridge University Press, 1987), 91.
12 SAPMO-BArch, DY 30/2419, "Toast während des Essens zu Ehren Mengistu Haile Mariam," 1.
13 SAPMO-BArch, DY 30/2459, "Toast des Generalsekretärs des ZK der SED und Vorsitzenden des Staatsrates der DDR, Erich Honecker", 31.

country had recently been named after Patrice Lumumba, Amílcar Cabral, and another Congolese Marxist, Marien N'Gouabi.[14]

This chapter will analyze this depiction both on screen and in text, focusing on the output of a figure whose work spanned both media forms: Ulrich Makosch. It will show how GDR media sought to elide distance between Africa and the GDR, while at the time reproducing gendered and othering depictions which distanced the continent from the East German state. In particular, it will focus on the output from a trip Makosch made as a guest of the Mozambique Liberation Front (FRELIMO) to Tete province in the early 1970s, which resulted in several articles, a book, and three documentaries. This output represented both sides of the dual role taken on by socialist foreign reporters in this era: created both as propaganda for GDR citizens at home and as an object of international diplomacy. As we will see, Makosch's work ultimately proved to be more successful as the latter than the former.

Depicting a Revolutionary World: GDR Foreign Reportage

How were different media to present this image of Africa to the GDR population? Each one, as former Socialist Unity Party (SED) propaganda chief Werner Lamberz noted in 1976, had "its own place, its own specific potential impact. Together they form our reliable ideological orchestra. And in opposition to certain composers, we prefer neither the strings nor the brass, nor also the flutes. The Party's score has enough notes for all."[15] The orchestral metaphor, of course, depends on absolute state control of media sources. In societies where media is subject to competition (or, as is often the reality, oligarchic monopoly), newspapers and television often exist in competition with one another. But in the GDR, the different sections of media were merely different outlets of the same body sharing the same message, meaning that their different attributes came into sharper focus.

For GDR propagandists keen to efface the geographical space between the GDR and national liberation movements abroad, television and film were exciting media. They were also vital weapons in the struggle for national liberation, with movements such as FRELIMO using radical filmmaking in order to garner solidarity across continents. As Radina Vučetić has shown in the case of Yugo-

---

14 Ibid., 33.
15 SAPMO-BArch, DY 30/477, "Schlusswort des Genossen Werner Lamberz," 1–2.

slavia, FRELIMO had been cooperating with foreign socialist powers in order to produce propaganda films since the late 1960s if not earlier.¹⁶ Beyond the socialist world, R. Joseph Parrot has highlighted the influence of Robert Van Lierup's *A Luta Continua* (The Struggle Continues), a collaborative film produced with FRELIMO, which played an instrumental role in the growth of African American solidarity with liberation movements in Southern Africa.¹⁷

In an often isolated GDR, television could elide distance, thus domesticating the political vision of socialist internationalism and translating grand ideology into everyday entertainment. In this regard, news programming was naturally seen to have a hugely important role. In terms of timescales of appearance, the development of news programming in the GDR largely mirrored West Germany (the Federal Republic, or FRG): the GDR state broadcaster *Deutscher Fernsehfunk's* (DFF) flagship newscast *Aktuelle Kamera* (Current Camera) first aired in December 1952 with a report on Stalin's birthday, with daily broadcasts beginning in 1957. The West German *Tagesschau* premiered five days after *Aktuelle Kamera* and began appearing daily in 1956. The content of the two programs was different, however, both in form as well as focus. Communist news bore its own very specific temporality. Domestic news was often thematically planned weeks or months in advance: the front pages of the SED's official newspaper, the *Neues Deutschland*, usually covered statements from party officials and reported breakthroughs or economic achievements, official celebrations or anniversaries, or party functions.¹⁸ In theory, one might expect foreign news reportage to be different: more reactive, or guided by events, and of course, more unpredictable. But foreign news could also be selective: reports on the capitalist world focused on poverty, drug addiction, weapons-trading and the far right, drawn together with anti-imperialist developments worldwide. As author and television critic Uwe Johnson once summarized, communist news was "news regarding the advantages of the East and the disadvantages of the West."¹⁹

DFF polling of citizens' views on television, so-called *Sofortresonanzen* ("immediate response") often picked up criticisms regarding GDR television's selectivity in this regard. One, from January 1969, noted that three different respondents had demanded that *Aktuelle Kamera*—which focused on the socialist and

---

16 Radina Vučetić, "We Shall Win: Yugoslav Film Cooperation with FRELIMO," *Revista Crítica de Ciências Sociais* 118 (2019).
17 R. Joseph Parrott, "A Luta Continua: Radical Filmmaking, Pan-African Liberation and Communal Empowerment," *Race & Class* 57 (2015).
18 On the Soviet case, see Huxtable, "Making News Soviet," 66.
19 Cited in Knut Hickethier, *Geschichte der Fernsehkritik in Deutschland* (Baden-Baden: Sigma, 1994), 88.

anti-imperialist world—showed more reports from "all of the world," the clear implication and emphasis on the word "all" suggesting that what was really meant was the West.[20] We should, of course, be wary of presenting this as a cut-and-dried case of socialist propaganda in contrast to journalistic integrity in the West. Instead, the question of comparison is better thought of in terms of form. Socialist media systems might not have been more political than capitalist media, if such calculation were meaningful or indeed possible. But socialist media was intentionally political and those who controlled it imbued it with explicitly political purposes. Discussing the East German state film studio DEFA, for example, Seán Allan and Sebastian Heiduschke argue that to describe film as a propaganda tool is reductive, but that is very literally how film, alongside other media, was understood, at least by those in charge.[21] Socialist media systems were defined by the Leninist notion of "agitprop": propaganda explains the "capitalistic nature of crises," agitation rouses the masses to action.[22] As Kristin Roth-Ey explains in her history of Soviet television, the mass media boom in the Soviet Union was similar to that in the West, but the socialist ideal of culture was a key differentiating factor; communist culture was elitist and pedagogical because it saw itself as carrying out a spiritual mission of cultural uplift.[23] At the same time, it is misleading to speak, as Kochanowski, Trültzsch and Viehoff do, of "political indoctrination."[24] The goal of socialist media was, rather, to create independent and ideologically literate socialist subjects.

Ulrich Makosch and Mozambique

As the GDR's best known foreign correspondent, Ulrich Makosch was one of the foremost examples of this media landscape. As the DFF's chief foreign correspondent from 1965 until 1971 and then the face of *Objektiv*, the GDR's weekly political television program based on foreign affairs and international news, Ma-

---

20 BArch, DR 8/131, "Ergebnisse der 2. (26.) Sofortresonanz vom 25 Januar 1969," Anhang, 1.
21 Seán Allan and Sebastien Heiduschke, "Introduction," in *Re-Imagining Defa: East German Cinema in Its National and Transnational Contexts*, ed. Seán Allan and Sebastian Heiduschke (New York: Berghahn Books, 2016), 5.
22 See especially Chapter 3 of V. I. Lenin, *What Is to Be Done?* (Harmondsworth: Penguin, 1988).
23 Kristin Roth-Ey, *Moscow Prime Time: How the Soviet Union Built the Media Empire That Lost the Cultural Cold War* (Ithaca: Cornell University Press, 2011).
24 Katja Kochanowski, Sascha Trueltzsch, and Reinhold Viehoff, "An Evening with Friends and Enemies: Political Indoctrination in Popular East German Family Series," in *Popular Television in Eastern Europe During and Since Socialism*, ed. Timothy Havens and Kati Lustyik (London: Routledge, 2013).

kosch was a prominent exponent of the GDR's state-led *Afrikabild*. He also served on the board of the GDR-Mozambique Friendship Committee, a state-led organization consisting of various journalists, politicians, and other public figures which existed to promote GDR-Mozambique relations, and was a prolific author of African and Asian travelogues. Born in Brandenburg in 1933, Makosch studied journalism at the Karl Marx University in Leipzig, joining the Journalists Union (Verband der Journalisten der DDR, or VDJ) in 1952 and graduating in 1955. He began work in local radio as an editor at the *Landessender Schwerin* where he worked from 1955 to 1956, when he became editor and travel correspondent for the national broadcasting committee. He joined the SED in 1963, and in 1965 became radio and television correspondent for the DFF in Asia, based in Jakarta, before being forced to leave for Singapore in 1968 following Suharto's takeover.[25] His early books and reportage were travel reports from Asia: featuring Japan (*Heute in Japan: Aufgezeichnet zwischen Tokio und Hiroschima*, 1959), multiple Asian countries (*Zwischen Fudschijama und Himalaja*, 1963, and *Jahre in Asien, Eindrücke und Begegnungen*, 1970), and Ceylon (now Sri Lanka) (*Paradies im Ozean: Begegnungen in Ceylon*, 1966).

Makosch moved away from foreign based reportage in the 1970s, taking key editorial roles in Berlin. He became editor in chief of reportage and documentaries at the DFF in 1972, editor-in-chief of *Aktuelle Kamera* in 1975, and a member of the SED district leadership in Berlin in 1976. At the same time, his focus switched to events in Southern Africa and became more explicitly political. Both of these shifts were the result of the marriage of personal circumstances and broader political changes in the GDR. The mid- to late 1970s were the heyday of internationalist solidarity in the country. Honecker's ascendance as leader preceded the collapse of the Hallstein doctrine and the entrance of the GDR and the FRG into the United Nations, leading to widespread diplomatic recognition.[26] Many scholars have claimed that the GDR's emphasis on discourses of international solidarity existed as a means to circumvent diplomatic isolation:[27] paradoxically, however, the discourse of solidarity actually grew following wide-

---

[25] See a letter regarding Makosch's redeployment, SAPMO-BArch, DR 8/362, Letter from Adamek to Kiesewetter, July 2, 1968.
[26] The Hallstein doctrine was a West German foreign policy principle which stated that the FRG would not maintain or establish relations with any nation that recognized the GDR. It was largely successful in preventing widespread diplomatic recognition of the GDR until it was abandoned in favor of *Ostpolitik* in the early 1970s. See Rüdiger Marco Booz, *Hallsteinzeit: Deutsche Aussenpolitik 1955–1972* (Bonn: Bouvier, 1995).
[27] For an illustrative example, see Toni Weis, "The Politics Machine: On the Concept of 'Solidarity' in East German Support for SWAPO," *Journal of Southern African Studies* 37 (2011): 362.

spread recognition. As Gregory Witkowski has shown, usage of the term "solidarity" in the GDR press peaked in 1973, the same year as entrance to the UN.[28]

Makosch's rise to prominence also coincided with an increased focus on Lusophone Africa in the GDR. Portuguese efforts to hold on to their colonial possessions in Angola, Guinea-Bissau, and Mozambique had faced armed insurgency since the early 1960s, but events came to a head in terms of international attention in the 1970s. Tanzania—which bordered Mozambique and had seen an influx of Mozambican refugees since the beginning of the anti-colonial insurgency—was an important site of entanglement for the GDR and FRELIMO. GDR officials had maintained relations with Lusophone resistance movements since the mid-1960s, especially through its consulate in Dar es Salaam, which, as Eric Burton has shown, became a hub for revolutionaries and the leaders of national liberation movements in this period.[29] The existence of a GDR consulate—which had survived Julius Nyerere's abortive diplomatic recognition of the country—meant that GDR diplomat Helmut Matthes was able to meet and establish links to these movements, including FRELIMO, the Angolan MPLA, and the Guinean PAIGC in the 1960s.[30] Peter Spacek, a reporter with the East German state news agency, the *Allgemeiner Deutscher Nachrichtendienst* (ADN), was also based in Dar es Salaam from 1965 and reported for the *Neues Deutschland* on developments in Tanzania and East Africa. Spacek's reports often relied upon contacts and bulletins from national liberation movements based in the city during that period, which included FRELIMO, the South African ANC, Namibian SWAPO, as well as the Zimbabwean organizations ZAPU and ZANU and the head of the Angolan MPLA, Agostinho Neto.[31]

---

28 Witkowski, "Between Fighters and Beggars: Socialist Philanthropy and the Imagery of Solidarity in East Germany," 73.
29 Eric Burton, "Hubs of Decolonization. African Liberation Movements and 'Eastern' Connections in Cairo, Accra, and Dar es Salaam," in *Southern African Liberation Movements and the Global Cold War "East": Transnational Activism 1960–990*, ed. Lena Dallywater, Chris Saunders, and Helder Adegar Fonseca (Boston, MA: De Gruyter Oldenbourg, 2019), 47–55; See also Andrew Ivaska, "Movement Youth in a Global Sixties Hub: The Everyday Lives of Transnational Activists in Postcolonial Dar es Salaam," in *Transnational Histories of Youth in the Twentieth Century*, ed. Richard Ivan Jobs and David M. Pomfret (London: Palgrave Macmillan UK, 2015), 188–210.
30 Matthias Voß and Helmut Matthes, "Die Beziehungen DDR – VR Mosambik zwischen Erwartungen und Wirklichkeit," in *Wir haben Spuren hinterlassen!: die DDR in Mosambik: Erlebnisse, Erfahrungen und Erkenntnisse aus drei Jahrzehnten*, ed. Matthias Voß (Münster: LIT Verlag, 2005), 15.
31 Peter Spacek, "Mit der FRELIMO im Busch," in *Wir haben Spuren hinterlassen!: die DDR in Mosambik: Erlebnisse, Erfahrungen und Erkenntnisse aus drei Jahrzehnten*, ed. Matthias Voß (Münster: LIT Verlag, 2005), 47.

In the early 1970s, these links would be exploited to great effect as a newly confident, internationally recognized GDR expanded its international influence, and organizations such as FRELIMO increasingly sought to bring their struggles to international attention. A key feature of FRELIMO propaganda at this time was an emphasis on "liberated zones": areas of northern Mozambique that the organization claimed to have liberated from colonial rule. Photography and film were important means through which these liberated zones could be depicted. As Drew A. Thompson has shown, FRELIMO's Dar es Salaam-based Department of Information and Propaganda placed particular importance on photography: as a FRELMO photographer would later explain, sending photographs "all over the world ... was necessary to make [audiences] understand the objectives of our struggle."[32] In this regard, the work of foreign photographers in liberated areas was particularly valuable due to FRELIMO's self-perceived deficits in both equipment and credibility, turning "propaganda," as Thompson puts it, into "information."[33]

Foreign press visits to liberated zones were a constant feature in *Mozambique Revolution*, FRELIMO's English-language periodical which was published in Dar es Salaam using a printing press donated by Finnish students from 1963–1975. The periodical was intended for an international audience, and visitors came from across the globe, including West Germany, the United Kingdom, Canada, and Italy. Official state visits were limited to the socialist countries, however. The December 1969 edition of *Mozambique Revolution* reported messages of solidarity sent to FRELIMO by the GDR's Afro-Asian Solidarity Committee and reports of a FRELIMO delegation visit to the GDR in June.[34] The next edition, from March 1970, featured a report from Peter Spacek, who had traveled to a liberated zone and proudly proclaimed himself to be the "first German to visit the free part of Mozambique." While there, Spacek reported witnessing a West German-produced military plane, a Dornier DO 27, drop bombs on civilians.[35]

The intra-German conflict was, of course, a key theme of GDR propaganda efforts, especially in the era of the Hallstein doctrine. What may have otherwise been an obscure provincial European conflict to FRELIMO was made important, however, by West German relations with Portugal, which had grown throughout the 1960s to encompass a significant amount of Portuguese arms imports and

---

32 Drew A. Thompson, "Visualising FRELIMO's Liberated Zones in Mozambique, 1962–1974," *Social Dynamics* 39 (2013): 28.
33 Ibid., 29.
34 *Mozambique Revolution*, no. 41, October – December 1969, 38.
35 *Mozambique Revolution*, no. 42, January – March 1970, 17.

foreign investment.³⁶ During the early 1970s, a key FRELIMO demand was West German divestment from the Cahora Bassa dam project: international pressure had already forced Swedish and British companies to withdraw from the scheme.³⁷ According to *Mozambique Revolution*, not only were German companies providing key services in the construction of the dam, but there were also widespread campaigns to settle white Europeans—including West Germans—on the arable lands that would be created by the project.³⁸

In the immediate period following the election of Willy Brandt as Chancellor in 1969, FRELIMO reached out to the West German leader, hoping to persuade him to draw back FRG support for Portugal.³⁹ Although these efforts were unsuccessful, grassroots support for the national liberation movements in Lusophone Africa among the membership of Brandt's party, the SPD, did lead to a FRELIMO delegation visiting Bonn in July 1973. SPD support did not mean government support, however, and the FRELIMO delegation, led by vice-president Marcelino dos Santos, left Germany disappointed by their inability to extract concrete assurances on Cahora Bassa or official recognition of FRELIMO as government in exile.⁴⁰

The summer of 1973 saw FRELIMO come more firmly down on the side of the socialist camp. A June 1973 article in *Mozambique Revolution* delineated a hierarchy of international solidarity, with African nations at the top, and the socialist camp coming in a close second: "Africa is leading the solidarity movement," the article claimed, but the "Socialist countries have also increased their support. Although far from meeting our needs, this support has played a very important role in our successes."⁴¹ It was in this atmosphere of increased cooperation that Ulrich Makosch began to focus on Mozambique in the summer of 1973. His first mention of events in Africa in the *Neues Deutschland* came on July 20. An ADN report entitled "GDR Journalists visited the site of Portuguese massacre" detailed a press conference held by a delegation of the GDR Journalist's Union in Lusaka, Zambia, in which Makosch, as the leader of the delegation, stated that

---

36 As Luís Nuno Rodrigues has shown, West Germany became a key supplier of arms for Salazar's Portugal in the 1960s, filling a gap created by John F. Kennedy's (short-lived) withdrawal of US support for the regime. Luís Nuno Rodrigues, "The International Dimensions of Portuguese Colonial Crisis," in *The Ends of European Colonial Empires: Cases and Comparisons*, ed. Miguel Bandeira Jerónimo and António Costa Pinto (London: Palgrave Macmillan, 2016), 257–261.
37 *Mozambique Revolution*, no. 42, January – March 1970, 30–32.
38 *Mozambique Revolution*, no. 45, October – December 1970, 14.
39 Rui Lopes, *West Germany and the Portuguese Dictatorship, 1968–1974: Between Cold War and Colonialism* (London: Palgrave Macmillan, 2014), 20.
40 Ibid., 225–227.
41 *Mozambique Revolution*, no. 55, April – June 1973, 1.

he had visited the charred remains of a village in Mozambique whose inhabitants had been murdered by colonial troops. Having traveled to the country on a two-week "information trip," Makosch also asserted that he had met 68 children in an orphanage, and uncovered evidence that Portuguese troops were being supported by Rhodesian and South African units.[42] The date of Makosch's claims was interesting, coming seven months after the Wiriyamu massacre, which occurred in December 1972, and just ten days after the massacre was first reported in the Western press, in the *Times*, on July 10, 1973.[43] The *Times* report came from a former British missionary, Adrian Hastings, who had received the information via survivors who had reported the massacre to local Spanish missionaries.[44] When Makosch's account of the trip was later published in book format, however, the book only mentioned the burnt remains of a village "where the inhabitations appeared to have got out just in time."[45] It seems the intention of the *Neues Deutschland* article was to suggest that Makosch had visited Wiriyamu: in his later published book, Makosch mentions the outcry regarding Wiriyamu following Hastings' report, but does not claim to have visited the site himself.

This book, entitled *The Girl from the Zambezi*, [*Das Mädchen vom Sambesi*] was based on Makosch's experiences in Mozambique in the summer of 1973, when he traveled as part of a three man team to the liberated zone of Tete to collect material for work that would span the GDR media landscape, including film, articles in the East German press, and an article for *Mozambique Revolution*.[46] Makosch's account of his trip, adapted from articles in *Neues Deutschland* and other journals, appeared as the first monograph in a new series of "current-political" texts from Leipzig publisher F. A. Brockhaus in early 1975, just months before Mozambique achieved formal independence in June. A review in the *Neues Deutschland* praised its accounts of personal encounters with both ordinary people and FRELIMO leaders and the "self-sacrificing struggle" against the colonial regime, claiming that it "explains the issues of the national liberation movements in concrete detail."[47]

---

42 "DDR-Journalisten waren am Ort portugiesischer Massaker", *Neues Deutschland*, July 20, 1973, 5.
43 On the massacre, see Mustafah Dhada, *The Portuguese Massacre of Wiriyamu in Colonial Mozambique, 1964–2013* (London: Bloomsbury Publishing, 2017).
44 "Portuguese massacre reported by priests", *The Times*, July 10, 1973, 1.
45 Ulrich Makosch, *Das Mädchen vom Sambesi* (Leipzig: F. A. Brockhaus, 1975), 9.
46 *Mozambique Revolution*, no. 56, July – September 1973, 14.
47 "Start zur aktuell-politischen Reihe bei F. A. Brockhaus", *Neues Deutschland*, May 21, 1975, 14.

In the book, Mozambique was presented as being both at the center of a global socialist community, but also fundamentally different: both distant and close. In an article written following the end of the Cold War, Makosch admitted to knowing very little "about Mozambique, about the structure of FRELIMO, or the different influences in this African area of tension" at the time.[48] What followed from this was a work of representation: of Makosch's experiences in Mozambique, but also of the wider significance of events in Mozambique for the socialist world. For Samora Machel, the leader of FRELIMO, these issues of representation were central to revolutionary praxis. In conversation with Erich Honecker later in the decade, Machel complained that

> [w]hen people speak of Africa, they often have a particular notion. It is one that says: we will help the Africans. The African is one who lives in misery, walks barefoot, is plagued by illness, who walks through the desert. That is to say that the image of the African is a timeless one, one rooted in the past. When European tourists come here, they want to take photos. But when they see me, they aren't interested, because I wear a suit and tie: I am not African enough. They want to see Africans whose ribs can be counted, who are hungry, dirty, and barefoot. This mentality has still not been dispelled.[49]

As Gregory Witkowski has argued, GDR solidarity campaigns towed a thin line between emphasizing the "superiority of the donor as much as the bond of solidarity between donor and recipient," depicting non-white recipients as somewhere between "fighters and beggars."[50] In his literature and prodigious literary output on Mozambique, Makosch towed this same line, claiming that he "experienced Africa, in pain, sorrow and confidence and with the smile of victory."[51]

In the text's opening pages, the socialist optimism of the mid-1970s is palpable, with the GDR's new-found international confidence coinciding with the collapse of the Portuguese empire. Both the Carnation Revolution itself and the Marxist-inspired nature of the liberation movements that fought the Portuguese in Africa were a huge source of hope for GDR ideologues. Indeed, the impression made by the success of these movements was not limited to GDR apparatchiks:

---

48 Ulrich Makosch, "Was bleibt... Afrika in den Medien der DDR," in *Engagiert für Afrika: die DDR und Afrika II*, ed. Ulrich van der Heyden, Ilona Schleicher and Hans-Georg Schleicher (Münster: LIT Verlag, 1994), 267.
49 SAPMO-BArch, DY 30/2470, "Stenografische Niederschrift der offiziellen Gespräche des Generalsekretärs des ZK der SED, Genossen Erich Honecker, mit dem Präsidenten der Frelimo und der Volksrepublik Moçambique, Genossen Samora Machel, in Maputo, 22. Februar 1979", 47.
50 Witkowski, "Between Fighters and Beggars: Socialist Philanthropy and the Imagery of Solidarity in East Germany."
51 Makosch, *Das Mädchen vom Sambesi*, 13.

as US international relations expert and future emeritus senior Hoover fellow Thomas H. Henriksen noted in 1978, the victories of PAIGC and FRELIMO could be interpreted as the "first successful indigenous Marxist revolutions accompanied by prolonged fighting not growing directly from the conditions of international war."[52] These successes also fit into a pattern discerned by GDR foreign policy experts in the 1970s. Hermann Axen later remembered that the Portuguese revolution had played "an important role" in elite thinking: not only had it shown that revolution could take place in a small, agrarian country, but it had also been led by a small group of army generals. These developments were part of a broader global trend, Axen noted, that "appeared to show was that we were arriving at a new moment, where not only the intellectuals, but also the military were joining the revolutionary movement—Nasser in Egypt, Assad in Syria, the Portuguese military."[53] Makosch himself played an important role in articulating the importance of Portugal to GDR audiences, appearing on a program in 1974 to outline "how this victory of the democratic forces in Portugal became possible, and what difficulties still exist in consolidating the progressive forces."[54]

The opening passages of Makosch's book show this revolutionary optimism through the prism of transnational linkage. In the opening scene, Makosch discusses attending the founding of the PAIGC's youth organization in newly freed Guinea-Bissau with Soviet, Portuguese, Guinean, and Mozambican comrades:

> And while we all still carried the red dust of the runway in Guinea on our face and in our hair, one of us... gave a spontaneous comparison of the stone thrown into the water, generating waves, which in turn produce further waves on the far shore. This refers to the emergence of the states of the socialist community with the Soviet Union at the head, the emergence of revolutionary-democratic governments such as in Tanzania and Guinea, which in turn made the stream of solidarity for the national liberation movements more powerful, a struggle which has now led to success.[55]

Such a metaphor was typical of the confidence of the socialist 1970s: highlighting the power of transnational effects; the vital, if not always clearly perceptible role played by socialist movements in the success of national liberation movement, while always making sure to note the key role played by the Soviet Union. It was also typical of a certain socialist "mooring" in the decade: the

---

52 Thomas H. Henriksen, "Marxism and Mozambique," *African Affairs* 77 (1978): 441.
53 Nasser had actually died in 1970, but his successor, Anwar Sadat, was also a member of the military. Axen and Neubert, *Ich war ein Diener der Partei*, 401.
54 "Information und Eindruck", *Neues Deutschland*, June 25, 1974.
55 Makosch, *Das Mädchen vom Sambesi*, 10–11.

fleeting collision of state-socialist confidence and national liberation in Lusophone Africa. Later, Makosch notes, the group "hear the historic speech of Brezhnev, and over the long distance his voice penetrates into the camp of Madina do Boe, a greeting to the peoples of Africa."[56]

The world-historical importance of developments in Lusophone Africa was a key element of Makosch's account here, noting that the "last two decades have seen my journalistic work take me to various showplaces of international events in Asia and Africa: to the culminating points in the result of the interaction of the revolutionary mainstreams, as in Vietnam, as in Mozambique, as a witness of anti-colonialist revolutions, which themselves became powerful accelerators of modern history."[57] Makosch was keen to highlight the GDR's role in these events. In keeping with GDR solidarity discourses, notions of development were prominent: "Earlier, every serious illness led to death. There is a hospital with a grass roof now. For almost 400 years here, there was no development to speak of."[58] The pedagogical work of FRELIMO was also a key focus. Here again, the GDR's influence was felt strongly: "Here, that [freedom] means the overcoming of illiteracy and a real right to education. A maths course book, developed and printed with the help of the GDR, shows the power of the socialist community, here in a mountainous province."[59] This form of cooperation would expand following Mozambican independence to encompass a wide variety of education exchange programs, as Marcia Schenck's chapter in this volume illustrates. One chapter of Makosch's text, entitled "Bridges of Solidarity," centered on this theme: the influence of the GDR framed through a developmentalist and "stageist" conception of history. Revealingly, Makosch quotes Marcus Mobote, then a commander with FRELIMO, who told him that "the medicine in our hospitals, some of the books in the schools, the material for our uniforms and much more—it comes from you."[60] This claim is followed by a comparison of the two countries, which imagined similarities between anticolonial and antifascist struggle: "you have also liberated yourselves, many years ago. Now you govern yourselves, and can help us because you have built up your country... although you live far away, divided by the sea, you feel like us, think like us, and we have the same enemy."[61]

---

56 Ibid., 11.
57 Ibid., 11.
58 Ibid., 23.
59 Ibid., 23.
60 Ibid., 109.
61 Ibid.

For Makosch, Mozambique was at the forefront of a global community of socialist struggle and development. Its struggles were closely tied to that of the GDR, but at the same time the text relies on gendered, othering tropes which present Mozambique as fundamentally foreign. On one level, this difference was articulated through age-old climatic stereotypes: Makosch frequently mentions the biting cold at night, something he admits he "never would have thought" was possible in Africa.[62] Camera operator Hans Anderssohn was more explicit in his usage of the traditional tropes of Western charity, talking of children with "big eyes" who looked "sad and intimidated."[63] Children featured heavily in the text, mostly as orphans who had lost parents to the Portuguese and were now under the care of FRELIMO: as we will see later, of all of Makosch's output, it was that which focused on children that was most successful among GDR viewers. As Makosch himself later noted, knowing very little about Mozambique, what struck him most upon arrival was the children: "That was the saddest thing I have had to view in my life... The children, many very small, some of them adolescents, had no shoes. They froze miserably in the night and in the mornings."[64]

The title of Makosch's travelogue, *The Girl from Zambesi*, is a reference to a FRELIMO instructor named Evenia that Makosch met on the trail and to whom a chapter is devoted, as well as half of the front cover. At 18 years of age, Evenia had been with FRELIMO for three years when Makosch met her. Much of his introduction is based on her appearance: "I estimated then—she looked almost like a boy—that she was about 16."[65] By contemporary standards, Evenia was a child soldier. She would have been one of many recruited by FRELIMO: almost half of the FRELIMO fighters questioned for a study in Mozambique's Manica province were younger than 18 when they joined the organization.[66] At the time Makosch was writing, however, it was common for socialist writers to celebrate imagery of armed women and children engaged in political struggle: there is no sense in the text of any issue with Evenia's age. Conversely, as Harry G. West has shown, it was common at the time for female teenage and child soldiers to be celebrated in 1960s propaganda, making them "legends of them not only in southern Africa but, more broadly, among leftist and feminist

---

62 Ibid., 18.
63 "Kinder der FRELIMO", *Neues Deutschland*, May 13, 1974, 7.
64 Makosch, "Was bleibt... Afrika in den Medien der DDR," 267.
65 Ibid., 30.
66 Jessica Schafer, "The Use of Patriarchal Imagery in the Civil War in Mozambique and Its Implications for the Reintegration of Child Soldiers," in *Children and Youth on the Front Line*, ed. Jo Boyden and Joanna de Berry (New York: Berghahn Books, 2004), 87.

militants worldwide."⁶⁷ Indeed, it was only in the 1980s and 1990s that the phenomenon of child soldiers began to take center stage in international human rights campaigns. One of the key architects of this new discourse was Graça Machel, former FRELIMO member and Mozambique's first Minister of Education and Culture, who authored an influential UN report on the issue in 1996.⁶⁸

Makosch's description of Evenia is also typical of the focus on female fighters which dominated GDR coverage of national liberation struggles. Thanks in part to FRELIMO propaganda, women in Mozambique became international icons of revolutionary feminism in the 1960s.⁶⁹ While throughout the book most of Makosch's conversations are with men, it is Evenia who gains prominence as a symbol and image. We are introduced to her as a "source of the excitement and attraction" in a FRELIMO camp.⁷⁰ Her appearance is detailed much more than any of the men profiled, beginning with her face, which looked "like a particularly realistic Makonde woodcutting, a colorful cloth often covering frizzy hair... in her backpack, among a thousand other things, a mirror and a comb... and a machine gun over the shoulder."⁷¹

As Katrin Bahr shows in this volume, a refusal to engage with European colonial legacies—despite their anticolonial intentions—manifested in GDR citizens frequently reproducing the colonial gaze in Mozambique.⁷² Although the references to Evenia's appearance represent a typically European example of the male gaze, they stop short of the overt sexualization and exoticization seen in other GDR solidarity campaigns.⁷³ Instead, Makosch is keen to present Evenia as a symbol of female emancipation: "calm and composed, passionate in discussions, self-sacrificing, friendly to us, tough when it comes to her opponents."⁷⁴ Coded within this notion are a number of assumptions. Makosch initially presents Evenia as running the field kitchen, and moves on the later describe her running, to his surprise, a military maneuver. "Evenia works as an instructor

---

67 Harry G. West, "Girls with Guns: Narrating the Experience of War of FRELIMO's 'Female Detachment,'" in *Children and Youth on the Front Line*, ed. Jo Boyden and Joanna de Berry (New York: Berghahn Books, 2004), 112.
68 See Graça Machel, *Impact of Armed Conflict on Children* (New York: United Nations, 1996).
69 Kathleen E. Sheldon, *Pounders of Grain: A History of Women, Work and Politics in Mozambique* (Portsmouth, NH: Heinemann Educational Books, 2002), 142.
70 Makosch, *Das Mädchen vom Sambesi*, 29.
71 Ibid.
72 Bahr, this volume.
73 See, for example, depictions of Cuban women in the literature surrounding the practice of tourism to the island in George Bodie, "'It Is a Shame We Are Not Neighbours': GDR Tourist Cruises to Cuba, 1961–89," *Journal of Contemporary History*, August 28, 2019.
74 Makosch, *Das Mädchen vom Sambesi*, 30.

here, accepted by all her male compatriots who find nothing wrong with it", Makosch notes.[75] Evenia's role is clearly portrayed as an outcome of FRELIMO's success: Makosch quotes a pamphlet he claims to have found in a village, which argues that in the colonial system women "were doubly exploited: first through the traditional society and second through the hungry capitalist regime, which gobbled up the material and cultural wealth of our people."[76] This notion of a doubled exploitation was ironically a key theme of feminist literature in the GDR, which focused on the dual oppressions of workforce involvement and unpaid domestic labor, but this appears to pass Makosch by.[77]

The feminism presented in Makosch's text is clearly rooted in developmentalist conceptions of history: patriarchy was colonial, but also a remnant of feudalism. As Makosch writes, despite the overcoming of colonial forces, "there exists psychological factors which hold some women back from the realisation of their dreams: the inferiority complex, which resides in the conjunction of traditional worldviews and the colonial system."[78] Evenia notes to Makosch that "contradictions" between men and women have existed for a long time, but she asks rhetorically if these are not "representative of the contradiction between the obsolete societal order and our lives?"[79] When Makosch asks Evenia about the difficulties of commanding men, her answer is revealing: answering in the affirmative, she notes that her role "was probably only unusual for some at the beginning. Tradition and superstition are often just old habits, but our chairman, who spent some time in the GDR, said that it also wasn't easy there... and some people still do not quite understand it today."[80]

Although Makosch's text was not guilty of a sexualized depiction of Evenia, her foregrounding raises questions. To a large extent, state-led feminism in the GDR, as Donna Harsch notes, retained the gender norms of previous social systems: and being state-led almost always meant being led by men.[81] Scholars such as Celia Donert have alerted us to the previously underexamined importance that official (and, to a lesser extent, unofficial) women's organizations

---

75 Ibid., 31.
76 Ibid.
77 On this, see Lorna Martens, *The Promised Land?: Feminist Writing in the German Democratic Republic* (New York: SUNY Press, 2001), 171–80.
78 Makosch, *Das Mädchen vom Sambesi*, 36.
79 Ibid., 31.
80 Ibid.
81 Donna Harsch, "Communism and Women," in *The Oxford Handbook of the History of Communism*, ed. Stephen A. Smith (Oxford: Oxford University Press, 2014), 488.

played in the global Cold War.⁸² But the patriarchal nature of socialist power structures meant that official feminist discourses emanated from male voices as much as, if not more than, female ones. Because foreign reporters and journalists in the GDR tended to be men, the focus on female emancipation in Africa thus came almost exclusively from male voices.

Makosch's text is a striking example of this ventriloquism: references to interpreters in the text make it unlikely that Makosch understood or could speak Portuguese, but large sections of the book consist of direct quotations from his subjects, and these quotations often sound remarkably similar to the Party (in this case, either FRELIMO or the SED) line.⁸³ Evenia's notion of a double oppression under patriarchy and colonialism was also a theme for Samora Machel, who claimed in 1973 that "Generally speaking, women are the most oppressed, humiliated, and exploited beings in society. A woman is even exploited by a man who is himself exploited, beaten by the man who is lacerated by the *palmatoria*, humiliated by the man who is crushed under the boot of the boss and the settler."⁸⁴ In a particularly jarring example of this ventriloquism, a 1972 text was published featuring writing from Makosch and three other male writers entitled "Salaam Fatima! Women of an Awakening World" [*Salaam Fatima! Frauen der erwachenden Welt*], focusing on "women's issues in Africa, Asia and Latin America" and heavily illustrated with pictures.⁸⁵ This, of course, was a world in which the punishment for a television presenter deemed to have crossed the line in making sexist remarks on air was to be summoned to the office of a male boss and given a copy of August Bebel's *Women and Socialism*, as happened to Heinz Quermann: that is to say, not one where issues of representation or female voices were often considered in any great detail.⁸⁶

---

82 Celia Donert, "Feminism, Communism and Global Socialism: Encounters and Entanglements," in *The Cambridge History of Communism, Volume 2: Everyday Socialism and Lived Experiences*, ed. Juliane Fürst, Silvio Pons, and Mark Selden (Cambridge: Cambridge University Press, 2017); Celia Donert, "From Communist Internationalism to Human Rights: Gender, Violence and International Law in the Women's International Democratic Federation Mission to North Korea, 1951," *Contemporary European History* 25 (2016).
83 Makosch, *Das Mädchen vom Sambesi*, 9.
84 Samora Machel, "The Liberation of Women is a Fundamental Necessity for the Revolution", https://www.marxists.org/subject/africa/machel/1973/liberation-women.htm, accessed December 15, 2019. I am grateful to Dr. Eric Burton for this reference.
85 Otto Marquardt et al., *salaam fatima! Frauen der erwachenden Welt* (Leipzig: F.A. Brockhaus, 1975).
86 Heather L. Gumbert, *Envisioning Socialism: Television and the Cold War in the German Democratic Republic* (Ann Arbor: University of Michigan Press, 2014), 115–16.

Africa on Screen: Socialist Internationalism as Entertainment

Probably the most prominent outputs from Makosch's trip were three documentary films: "Mozambique – The Struggle Continues," [*Der Kampf geht weiter*] first screened on GDR television screens in September 1973 and later at the sixteenth International Leipzig Documentary and Short Film Week in late November; "FRELIMO's Children" [*Kinder der FRELIMO*], first screened on GDR television on May 14, 1974; and "Victors on the Zambezi" [*Sieger am Sambesi*], which focused on the challenges of the new Mozambican state and first aired, also on GDR television, on July 16, 1975. While the reception of his book is difficult to gauge, television audience research produced by the DFF provides some useful insight into the relative success—or otherwise—of Makosch's televisual output.[87] As already noted, Makosch was an important figure within GDR foreign news journalism, which had grown from the late 1950s onward into a particularly important feature of television programming. As Heather Gumbert has shown, the state broadcaster in the GDR, the *Deutscher Fernsehfunk*, or DFF, had been chastised by the Politbüro for being outflanked and outpaced by Western news agencies in their coverage of the Hungarian uprising in 1956.[88] From the late 1950s onwards, then, there was an increased focus on "current-political" (*aktuell-politisch*) programming, with a particular emphasis on anti-imperialist struggle in Africa and the Middle East.[89] This domestic development combined with events worldwide, where decolonization and the increasing momentum of various forms of national liberation were attracting the attention of the socialist state. The DFF were already demanding in 1958 that television raise awareness among the GDR population regarding "fraternal socialist countries."[90]

This focus lasted only a decade, however. It is a central claim of the historiography that from the late 1960s onward, GDR television moved toward a focus on entertainment as information and news-based programming failed to have

---

[87] The qualitative data produced by such research comes with obvious reservations, but viewership figures would seem to relatively unproblematic. For a detailed discussion of Zuschauerforschung, see Michael Meyen, *Einschalten, Umschalten, Ausschalten? das Fernsehen im DDR-Alltag* (Leipzig: Leipziger Universitätsverlag, 2003), 18–29.
[88] Gumbert, *Envisioning Socialism*, 71.
[89] Ibid., 78.
[90] Ibid., 142.

the desired propagandistic effect.[91] Michael Meyen's study of GDR television made similar findings via both interviews and contemporary viewer research.[92] Claudia Dittmar traces this shift to the late 1960s and early 1970s, as does Heather Gumbert, citing a commonly quoted Honecker speech in 1971 which exhorted programmers to overcome a "certain boredom" among GDR viewers.[93] As Sasha Trültzsch and Uwe Breitenborn have shown, the GDR television program corresponded similarly to other countries—including the FRG—in terms of genre-share by the 1970s, eschewing an earlier focus on factual programming.[94]

Despite the decline of factual programming, the DFF's own research convinced it that foreign news reportage remained both popular and important for GDR viewers. This was true of events close to home, such as the Prague Spring in 1968, which prompted a demand for more informational and educational programming in a similar fashion to the Hungarian uprising.[95] But the GDR's growing international confidence and widespread optimism in the socialist world during the 1970s led to opportunities for more foreign news reporting in Africa too, of which Makosch's Mozambique films were a notable example. DFF researchers found that foreign reporting was the fourth most desired form of programming in the early 1970s, and that GDR-produced foreign reportage was lacking in the program, with existing foreign reportage-based programs proving popular.[96]

Makosch became *Objektiv*'s frontman in the late 1960s, presiding over a slump in the show's viewership, from an average of 20.9 percent in 1968 to 8.2 percent in 1972.[97] Given international events, one might have expected a growth in audience, but instead viewership declined throughout the decade,

---

91 Sascha Trültzsch and Reinhold Viehoff, "Undercover: How the East German Political System Presented Itself in Television Series," in *Popular Television in Authoritarian Europe*, ed. Peter Goddard (Manchester: Manchester University Press, 2013), 142. Carol Anne Costabile-Heming makes the same claim. See Carol Anne Costabile-Heming, "'Rezensur': A Case Study of Censorship and Programmatic Reception in the GDR," *Monatshefte* 92 (2000): 54.
92 Meyen, *Einschalten, Umschalten, Ausschalten?*, 80.
93 Gumbert, *Envisioning Socialism*, 161.
94 Sasha Trültzsch and Uwe Breitenborn, "Program Structure Analysis of the GDR Television 1956 to 1991," *Siegener Periodicum zur internationalen empirischen Literaturwissenschaft* 25 (2006): 266.
95 Deutsches Rundfunk Archiv (hereafter DRA), H008–02–04–0023, "Analyse der Bisherigen Forschungsergebnisse zur Wirkung der Journalistischen Sendungen im Programm des Deutschen Fernsehfunks", 18–19.
96 Ibid., 51.
97 DRA, H074–00–02–0082, "Einige Ergebnisse zu Objektiv", July 4, 1972, 1.

continuing on a steady decline into the 1980s.[98] DFF reports noted that viewership was significantly higher among SED members.[99] While Makosch's reportage was increasingly viewed as unpopular and messages regarding socialist internationalism were increasingly finding more traction via entertainment, GDR viewers were also increasingly getting their information and news from television.[100] DFF leaders obviously hoped that films like Makosch's could fill this gap.

"The Struggle Continues" was the most heavily touted of the three films and appeared on GDR television screens first, on the important 8 p.m. slot on the DDR 1 channel on September 25, 1973.[101] GDR press reported on its success with rapturous acclaim. "The documentary-maker's search for truth often goes hand in hand with unfamiliar physical efforts," a review of the film's first screening claimed: "Ulrich Makosch and Hans Anderssohn walked 200 km through hard-to-reach areas in an unfamiliar climate for their half-hour GDR feature film 'Mozambique – The Struggle Continues,' in constant danger of discovery by Portuguese colonial troops."[102] Despite the fanfare, however, the initial screening defied the high expectations that earlier DFF reports had placed on foreign reportage. Research showed that only 5.5 percent of viewers watched the show, which was "well under the average for journalism in the Tuesday 8pm slot and well under the average for foreign reportage."[103] These numbers were put down to the fact that the film had been screened at short notice and not widely advertised, and the report noted that those viewers who had seen the show evaluated it favorably.[104] The film was screened again during the Christmas period and highlighted in a Christmas television guide in *Neues Deutschland*.[105] This time round, however, viewership was even worse: audience researchers were unable to find a single viewer among their research subjects.[106] The follow up film, "Victors on the Zambezi," which used Makosch's footage to

---

98 Klaus Behling, *Fernsehen aus Adlershof: Das Fernsehen der DDR vom Start bis zum Sendeschluss* (Berlin: Edition Berolina, 2016), 57.
99 DRA, H074–00–02–0082, "Einige Ergebnisse zu Objektiv", 2.
100 DRA, H074–00–02–0082, "Zusammenfassende Darstellung aller bisherigen Erfahrungen der Zuschauerforschung auf dem Gebiet: Allgemeine Einstellungen zum Fernsehen und Probleme der Programmstruktur", May 1971, 4.
101 "Fernsehen Aktuell", *Neues Deutschland*, September 25, 1973, 6.
102 "In der vordersten Frontlinie des Klassenkampfes", *Neues Deutschland*, 29.10.1973, 4.
103 DRA, H081–03–02–0053, "Ergebnisse der 39./193. Sofortresonanz vom 28.09.1973", 16–17.
104 Ibid., 16–17.
105 "Was es an den Festtagen zu sehen gibt", *Neues Deutschland*, 12.12.1973, 4.
106 The film was screened on the GDR's less popular second channel this time round, but these numbers are nevertheless surprisingly low. DRA, H081–03–02–0053, "Ergebnisse der 52./206. Sofortresonanz vom 27.12.1953", 16.

put together a film anticipating the forthcoming Mozambican independence celebrations, also struggled to attract audiences despite media previews.[107] Notably, a third film, "The Children of FRELIMO," which aired in May 1974 and focused on the orphans Makosch had encountered in Mozambique, received almost double the viewership of the previous two, at ten percent.[108]

The evidence suggests that Makosch's films were more important as objects of high diplomacy than a means of generating solidarity among the GDR population. In this regard there was a curious mirroring with the work of FRELIMO's Department of Information and Propaganda, which drew distinct lines between its domestic and international audiences, belying claims to transnational unity in the process.[109] As the initial review of "The Struggle Continues" in *Neues Deutschland* noted, quoting Makosch's press briefing in Leipzig, the film was to serve the elision of distance between the GDR and FRELIMO, serving to "bring us closer to the fight of FRELIMO, allowing us to look into the faces of people who, because they love life, have learned not to fear death in battle."[110] But it was also made to be used as propaganda for FRELIMO themselves, and thus as an instrument of the "solidaric unity" between the two sides.[111]

Makosch's visit to Mozambique's liberated zones came at a time of increased cooperation between FRELIMO and the GDR: the very existence of the trip and resulting film may have been more important than its reception in the GDR. In contrast with low viewership figures, the film was greeted with much international fanfare. At the 1973 Leipzig film week, which featured delegations from almost 40 nations, the film was well received, receiving a Silver Dove award.[112] The Palestinian delegation to the festival awarded it the first "Palestine Prize," which was given to films "which depicted the struggle of a people against imperialism and whose struggle resembled that of the Palestinians."[113] Later reports suggested the film was sold to "many Asian and African nations" at the festival.[114] In December Samora Machel (misspelt "Marchel" in the *Neues Deutschland* article

---

107 DRA, H081–03–02–0068, "Sehbeteiligung und -bewertung der Sendungen der 29. Woche", 3.
108 DRA, H081–03–02/0067, "Ergebnisse der 21. (227.) repräsentativen Umfrage vom 22. Mai 1974", 12.
109 Thompson, "Visualising FRELIMO's Liberated Zones in Mozambique, 1962–1974," 38.
110 "In der vordersten Frontlinie des Klassenkampfes", *Neues Deutschland*, 29. October 1973, 4.
111 Ibid., 4.
112 "Was es an den Festtagen zu sehen gibt", *Neues Deutschland*, December 12, 1973, 4.
113 Nadia Yaqub, *Palestinian Cinema in the Days of Revolution* (Austin: University of Texas Press, 2018), 134.
114 "DDR-Künstler solidarisch mit den kämpfenden Völkern", *Neues Deutschland*, December 29, 1973, 2.

reporting the event) wrote a letter to Erich Honecker thanking him for the production of the film, which had been screened to a delegation consisting of the vice president of FRELIMO, the Tanzanian information minister, and the deputy General Secretary of the Organisation for African Unity National Liberation Committee at the tenth World Festival of Youth and Students in Berlin.[115] Machel would note his gratitude to Honecker in person at a meeting in 1979, praising the "fruitful cooperation" that FRELIMO had with the journalists and press organs of the GDR, "who disseminated the news of our struggle" and noting that many of them, like Makosch, had "visited liberated areas and areas of conflict."[116] The impact of the film itself remained fleeting, a temporary act of solidarity, or mooring. It does not appear in a recent study of similar foreign-made films in Mozambique during this period by Ros Gray, for example, and references to it beyond the 1970s are difficult to find.[117]

Conclusion

Ulrich Makosch was a party journalist in the purest sense. His reporting on Africa, then, was political and pedagogical: it was agitprop, seeking to depict Africa as "close" to the GDR in the abstract. Makosch was deeply involved and implicated in some of the more unsavory implications of agitprop: in 1985, for example, he presented a Stasi-produced program entitled "Returned: Interviews with the Disillusioned" [*Zurückgekehrt – Interview mit Enttäuschten*], which featured interviews with people who had fled the GDR and returned, agreeing in arrangements with the Stasi to appear on the program in the hopes of a comfortable resettlement.[118] Makosch himself was, for a number of years, an "IM" or unofficial collaborator with the Stasi, which was almost certainly a requirement of his role. Following the fall of the Wall, he renounced agitprop and spoke of being "ready, with pleasure to work along journalistic lines."[119] He subsequently worked for US

---

115 "FRELIMO dankt DDR für Film über Befreiungskampf", *Neues Deutschland*, December 20, 1973, 2.
116 SAPMO-BArch, DY 30/2470, "Stenografische Niederschrift der offiziellen Gespräche des Generalsekretärs des ZK der SED, Genossen Erich Honecker, mit dem Präesidenten der Frelimo und der Volksrepublik Moçambique, Genossen Samora Machel, in Maputo, 22. Februar 1979", 42.
117 Ros Gray, *Cinemas of the Mozambican Revolution* (Woodbridge: James Currey, 2020), 15–64.
118 See https://www.stasi-mediathek.de/medien/propagandavideo-zurueckgekehrt-interview-mit-enttaeuschten-ueber-rueckkehrer-in-die-ddr/, accessed November 11, 2019.
119 "East Germany: Putting the Pieces Together Again", *Broadcasting*, June 2, 1990, 55.

broadcaster CNN for a couple of years. Freed from the dictates of GDR agitprop, Makosch's work saw a shift in register, highlighted by a contribution to an edited volume on GDR-Mozambican relations in 2005: in contrast to the air of impending victory found in his 1970s texts, Makosch spoke of encountering a "sad and tired existence" among Mozambicans in that period.[120]

If the newspaper was the dominant medium for foreign news reportage at the beginning of the GDR's existence, then television would have assumed this mantle by the end of its existence. Television, particularly on location filming, boasted an ability to sever the physical divisions between viewer and viewed. The German word for television, *Fernsehen*, is a calque derived from English, thus sharing its literal connotation of "distance viewing." The technical ability to remove distance, as the great theorist of television Raymond Williams noted, created specific forms of cultural power; during the Falklands War, Williams criticized a particular mode of distancing in contemporary coverage, which "distorts the imagination and permits the fantasies of models and of convictions without experience."[121] Williams' concern was television's ability to create distance from reality and thus soften the effect of war, so that "the sovereign power to order war operates within the cultural power to distance."[122] Television abstracted what was real. Depictions of Africa in the GDR, conversely, began with an abstract ideal and sought to reify it. The GDR was a confined state, but one that imagined itself, through the medium of Marxist-Leninist theory, to be part of an objectively defined global political movement. Unlike the news reportage that Williams chastised, GDR television's depictions of this world thus sought to elide, rather than create, distance.

Ulrich Makosch's output on Mozambique was an important example of this attempt to create elision. In this sense, it was a paradoxical success. In a post-*Wende* evaluation of the GDR's *Afrikabild*, Makosch struck a largely defiant tone. If this image was to be criticized, Makosch noted, such criticism ought to center on its inability to draw out "differentiation," arguing that "great proximity and differentiation are usually mutually exclusive, an experience that is to be discerned in the African reporting of the GDR media."[123] For Makosch, the problem was over-identification: "one suffered with the guest state," and fears regarding the utilization of criticism by mutual enemies led to the creation of

---

120 Ulrich Makosch, "Salz auf der Hand...," in *Wir haben Spuren hinterlassen!: die DDR in Mosambik: Erlebnisse, Erfahrungen und Erkenntnisse aus drei Jahrzehnten*, ed. Matthias Voss (Münster: LIT Verlag, 2005), 577.
121 Raymond Williams, "Distance," *London Review of Books*, June 17, 1982, 20.
122 Ibid., 20.
123 Makosch, "Was bleibt...Afrika in den Medien der DDR," 275.

an "idealised image."[124] The notion of such proximity reveals the mutual advantage found in foreign reportage between Makosch and his Mozambican partners: the importance of such reportage lay in the international sphere, in the transnational world of anti-imperialist politics. But this proximity was not reproduced on the domestic level: evident both in his othering and ventriloquizing of Mozambican subjects, and in the lack of success and viewership that Makosch's films found at home. In the end, elision worked only on an international level: preaching to the converted, but failing in its promise to bring the struggles of FRELIMO home for GDR citizens.

Such findings may not come as surprise to those familiar with the GDR's cultural output. "Nothing did more harm to the GDR," Stefan Wolle has claimed, "than its own propaganda."[125] But the failure of Makosch's work to have an impact at home challenges the usual assumptions regarding state-led cultures of solidarity in GDR, which have long been viewed as primarily existing to promote the state's legitimacy among the GDR population at large. The case here seems to indicate that rather than existing as a symbolic projection for a credulous East German public, the real importance of Makosch's work lay abroad. For the leadership of FRELIMO, figures such as Makosch were important weapons in the fight for international recognition and support. And for the exponents of international socialism in the 1970s, it seemed to confirm the growing strength of the socialist world. In the longer term, the importance of Makosch's work would prove fleeting, an imperfect mooring: the optimism of the early to mid-1970s dwindled toward the end of the decade as Mozambique and the GDR descended into civil war and a fiscal crisis respectively.

Bibliography

Allan, Seán, and Sebastien Heiduschke. "Introduction." In *Re-Imagining Defa: East German Cinema in Its National and Transnational Contexts*, edited by Seán Allan and Sebastian Heiduschke, 1–19. New York: Berghahn Books, 2016.

Axen, Hermann, and Harald Neubert. *Ich war ein Diener der Partei: autobiographische Gespräche mit Harald Neubert*. Rote Reihe. Berlin: Edition Ost, 1996.

Behling, Klaus. *Fernsehen aus Adlershof: Das Fernsehen der DDR vom Start bis zum Sendeschluss*. Berlin: Edition Berolina, 2016.

Bodie, George. "'It Is a Shame We Are Not Neighbours': GDR Tourist Cruises to Cuba, 1961–89:" *Journal of Contemporary History*, August 28, 2019.

---

124 Ibid., 275.
125 Stefan Wolle, *Die heile Welt der Diktatur: Alltag und Herrschaft in der DDR 1971–1989* (Berlin: Links Christoph Verlag, 2013), 70.

Booz, Rüdiger Marco. *Hallsteinzeit: Deutsche Aussenpolitik 1955–1972.* Bonn: Bouvier, 1995.
Buchheim, Christoph. "Die Achillesferse der DDR – der Aussenhandel." In *Überholen ohne einzuholen: die DDR-Wirtschaft als Fußnote der deutschen Geschichte?*, edited by André Steiner, 91–103. Berlin: Ch. Links, 2006.
Burton, Eric. "Hubs of Decolonization. African Liberation Movements and 'Eastern' Connections in Cairo, Accra, and Dar es Salaam." In *Southern African Liberation Movements and the Global Cold War "East": Transnational Activism 1960–1990*, edited by Lena Dallywater, Chris Saunders, and Helder Adegar Fonseca, 25–56. Boston, MA: De Gruyter Oldenbourg, 2019.
Carlisle, Donald S. "The Changing Soviet Perception of the Development Process in the Afro-Asian World." *Midwest Journal of Political Science* 8 (1964): 385–407.
Connelly, Matthew. *A Diplomatic Revolution: Algeria's Fight for Independence and the Origins of the Post-Cold War Era.* New York: Oxford University Press, 2003.
Costabile-Heming, Carol Anne. "'Rezensur': A Case Study of Censorship and Programmatic Reception in the GDR." *Monatshefte* 92 (2000): 53–67.
Dale, Gareth. *Between State Capitalism and Globalisation: The Collapse of the East German Economy.* Oxford: Peter Lang, 2004.
Dhada, Mustafah. *The Portuguese Massacre of Wiriyamu in Colonial Mozambique, 1964–2013.* London: Bloomsbury Publishing, 2017.
Donert, Celia. "Feminism, Communism and Global Socialism: Encounters and Entanglements." In *The Cambridge History of Communism, Volume 2: Everyday Socialism and Lived Experiences*, edited by Juliane Fürst, Silvio Pons, and Mark Selden, 399–421. Cambridge: Cambridge University Press, 2017.
Donert, Celia. "From Communist Internationalism to Human Rights: Gender, Violence and International Law in the Women's International Democratic Federation Mission to North Korea, 1951." *Contemporary European History* 25 (2016): 313–333.
Gray, Ros. *Cinemas of the Mozambican Revolution.* Woodbridge: James Currey, 2020.
Grieder, Peter. *The German Democratic Republic.* Basingstoke: Palgrave Macmillan, 2012.
Gumbert, Heather L. *Envisioning Socialism: Television and the Cold War in the German Democratic Republic.* Ann Arbor: University of Michigan Press, 2014.
Harsch, Donna. "Communism and Women." In *The Oxford Handbook of the History of Communism*, edited by Stephen A. Smith, 488–504. Oxford: Oxford University Press, 2014.
Henriksen, Thomas H. "Marxism and Mozambique." *African Affairs* 77 (1978): 441–62.
Hickethier, Knut. *Geschichte der Fernsehkritik in Deutschland.* Baden-Baden: Sigma, 1994.
Huxtable, Simon. "Making News Soviet: Rethinking Journalistic Professionalism after Stalin, 1953–1970." *Contemporary European History* 27 (2018): 59–84.
Ivaska, Andrew. "Movement Youth in a Global Sixties Hub: The Everyday Lives of Transnational Activists in Postcolonial Dar es Salaam." In *Transnational Histories of Youth in the Twentieth Century*, edited by Richard Ivan Jobs and David M. Pomfret, 188–210. London: Palgrave Macmillan UK, 2015.
Kanet, Roger E. "Soviet Propaganda and the Process of National Liberation." In *The Soviet Union, Eastern Europe and the Third World*, edited by Roger E. Kanet, 84–121. Cambridge: Cambridge University Press, 1987.

Klenke, Olaf. *Ist die DDR an der Globalisierung gescheitert?: Autarke Wirtschaftspolitik versus internationale Weltwirtschaft; das Beispiel Mikroelektronik*. Frankfurt am Main: Peter Lang, 2001.
Kochanowski, Katja, Sascha Trueltzsch, and Reinhold Viehoff. "An Evening with Friends and Enemies: Political Indoctrination in Popular East German Family Series." In *Popular Television in Eastern Europe During and Since Socialism*, edited by Timothy Havens and Kati Lustyik, 81–101. London: Routledge, 2013.
Lenin, V. I. *What Is to Be Done?* Harmondsworth: Penguin, 1988.
Lopes, Rui. *West Germany and the Portuguese Dictatorship, 1968–1974: Between Cold War and Colonialism*. London: Palgrave Macmillan, 2014.
Machel, Graça. *Impact of Armed Conflict on Children*. New York: United Nations, 1996.
Maier, Charles S. *Dissolution: The Crisis of Communism and the End of East Germany*. Princeton: Princeton University Press, 1999.
Makosch, Ulrich. *Das Mädchen vom Sambesi*. Leipzig: F. A. Brockhaus, 1975.
Makosch, Ulrich. "Salz auf der Hand..." In *Wir haben Spuren hinterlassen!: die DDR in Mosambik: Erlebnisse, Erfahrungen und Erkenntnisse aus drei Jahrzehnten*, edited by Matthias Voss, 577–580. Münster: LIT Verlag, 2005.
Makosch, Ulrich. "Was bleibt ... Afrika in den Medien der DDR." In *Engagiert für Afrika: Die DDR und Afrika II*, edited by Ulrich van der Heyden, Ilona Schleicher, and Hans-Georg Schleicher, 266–277. Münster: LIT Verlag, 1994.
Marquardt, Otto, Ulrich Makosch, Günter Nerlich, and Konrad Schmidt. *salaam fatima! Frauen der erwachenden Welt*. Leipzig: F.A. Brockhaus, 1975.
Martens, Lorna. *The Promised Land?: Feminist Writing in the German Democratic Republic*. New York: SUNY Press, 2001.
Meyen, Michael. *Einschalten, Umschalten, Ausschalten? das Fernsehen im DDR-Alltag*. Leipzig: Leipziger Universitätsverlag, 2003.
Parrott, R. Joseph. "A Luta Continua: Radical Filmmaking, Pan-African Liberation and Communal Empowerment." *Race & Class* 57 (2015): 20–38.
Pugach, Sarah. "African Students and the Politics of Race and Gender in the German Democratic Republic." In *Comrades of Color: East Germany in the Cold War World*, edited by Quinn Slobodian, 131–157. New York: Berghahn Books, 2015.
Roberts, George. "Press, Propaganda and the German Democratic Republic's Search for Recognition in Tanzania, 1964–72." In *Warsaw Pact Intervention in the Third World: Aid and Influence in the Cold War*, edited by Natalia Telepneva and Philip Muehlenbeck, 148–173. London: I.B. Tauris, 2018.
Rodrigues, Luís Nuno. "The International Dimensions of Portuguese Colonial Crisis." In *The Ends of European Colonial Empires: Cases and Comparisons*, edited by Miguel Bandeira Jerónimo and António Costa Pinto, 243–268. London: Palgrave Macmillan, 2016.
Roth-Ey, Kristin. *Moscow Prime Time: How the Soviet Union Built the Media Empire That Lost the Cultural Cold War*. Ithaca: Cornell University Press, 2011.
Schafer, Jessica. "The Use of Patriarchal Imagery in the Civil War in Mozambique and Its Implications for the Reintegration of Child Soldiers." In *Children and Youth on the Front Line*, edited by Jo Boyden and Joanna de Berry, 87–104. New York: Berghahn Books, 2004.
Sheldon, Kathleen E. *Pounders of Grain: A History of Women, Work and Politics in Mozambique*. Portsmouth, NH: Heinemann Educational Books, 2002.

Slobodian, Quinn. "Socialist Chromatism: Race, Racism and the Racial Rainbow in East Germany." In *Comrades of Color: East Germany in the Cold War World*, edited by Quinn Slobodian, 23–43. New York: Berghahn Books, 2015.

Thompson, Drew A. "Visualising FRELIMO's Liberated Zones in Mozambique, 1962–1974." *Social Dynamics* 39 (2013): 24–50.

Thörn, Håkan. *Anti-Apartheid and the Emergence of a Global Civil Society.* St Antony's Series. Basingstoke: Palgrave Macmillan, 2006.

Trültzsch, Sascha, and Reinhold Viehoff. "Undercover: How the East German Political System Presented Itself in Television Series." In *Popular Television in Authoritarian Europe*, edited by Peter Goddard, 141–158. Manchester: Manchester University Press, 2013.

Trültzsch, Sasha, and Uwe Breitenborn. "Program Structure Analysis of the GDR Television 1956 to 1991." *Siegener Periodicum zur internationalen empirischen Literaturwissenschaft* 25 (2006): 16.

Voß, Matthias, and Helmut Matthes. "Die Beziehungen DDR – VR Mosambik zwischen Erwartungen und Wirklichkeit." In *Wir haben Spuren hinterlassen!: die DDR in Mosambik: Erlebnisse, Erfahrungen und Erkenntnisse aus drei Jahrzehnten*, edited by Matthias Voß, 12–33. Münster: LIT Verlag, 2005.

Vučetić, Radina. "We Shall Win: Yugoslav Film Cooperation with FRELIMO." *Revista Crítica de Ciências Sociais* (2019): 131–50.

Weis, Toni. "The Politics Machine: On the Concept of 'Solidarity' in East German Support for SWAPO." *Journal of Southern African Studies* 37 (2011): 351–67.

West, Harry G. "Girls with Guns: Narrating the Experience of War of FRELIMO's 'Female Detachment.'" In *Children and Youth on the Front Line*, edited by Jo Boyden and Joanna de Berry, 105–29. New York: Berghahn Books, 2004.

Williams, Raymond. "Distance." *London Review of Books*, June 17, 1982.

Winiecki, Jan. *Shortcut or Piecemeal: Economic Development Strategies and Structural Change.* Budapest: Central European University Press, 2016.

Witkowski, Gregory. "Between Fighters and Beggars: Socialist Philanthropy and the Imagery of Solidarity in East Germany." In *Comrades of Color: East Germany in the Cold War World*, edited by Quinn Slobodian, 73–95. New York: Berghahn Books, 2015.

Wolle, Stefan. *Die heile Welt der Diktatur: Alltag und Herrschaft in der DDR 1971–1989.* Berlin: Ch. Links, 2013.

Yaqub, Nadia. *Palestinian Cinema in the Days of Revolution.* Austin: University of Texas Press, 2018.

Paul Sprute
12 Diaries of Solidarity in the Global Cold War: The East German Friendship Brigades and their Experience in 'Modernizing' Angola[1]

> *Solidarisch eng verbunden*
> *mit Angola das geschunden*
> *Stolz erhoben dieses Land*
> *Kämpfen mit Ihm Hand in Hand*[2]
>
> *Wir zogen an, das ist schon wahr*
> *Ersatzteile aber blieben stets rar!*
> *Drum war Erfindergeist gefragt*
> *Und jeder brachte uns 'ne Tat*[3]
>
> In solidarity closely connected
> with Angola sorely tormented
> this proudly risen land
> with whom we fight hand in hand
>
> We held fast, that is true for sure
> but in spare parts we remained ever poor
> inventive spirits were in demand
> and everyone gave us a hand.

Introduction

In his monthly poems, Rudi reflected on the routines of his deployment in a *Brigade der Freundschaft* (also called *Freundschaftsbrigade*, "Friendship Brigade") in Angola. These collectives of young citizens of the German Democratic Republic (GDR) were sent to the "newly independent nation states" of the post-colonial world in order to enact the "international solidarity" that the GDR leadership

---

[1] I am very grateful to the editors of this piece, Eric Burton and Immanuel R. Harisch, who made all the necessary and extremely helpful editorial suggestions. What is more, both were so kind to share their great expertise gained from working on the otherwise little-studied *Freundschaftsbrigaden* themselves.
[2] "Gedanken," Rudi S., April 1984, Stiftung Archiv der Parteien und Massenorganisationen der DDR im Bundesarchiv (hereafter SAPMO-BArch, DY 24/19129.
[3] "Freude," Rudi S., February 1984, SAPMO-BArch, DY 24/19129.

OpenAccess. © 2021 Paul Sprute, published by De Gruyter. This work is licensed under the Creative Commons Attribution 4.0 International License. https://doi.org/10.1515/9783110623543-012

proclaimed as one of its basic political principles. The *Brigaden* of the GDR's official youth organization *Freie Deutsche Jugend* (FDJ, "Free German Youth") provided social services or training and supported local economies by directly engaging in agriculture, transport, or construction.[4]

Rudi's poem echoed official solidarity discourses—namely as a unified struggle of African and German actors—but also reflected the practical dilemmas of exercising solidarity in Angola. Taking up this lead, my contribution seeks to reconsider the roles of young East Germans in the *Freundschaftsbrigaden* within the Cold War—which became a "hot war" in the vast and resource-rich country of Angola.[5] My central aim is to examine the perspectives that the brigade collectives assumed and presented of their deployment to socialist Angola in the last decade of the GDR's existence. Particular attention is put on their views of the mission of "friendship" and "international solidarity" within their work environment and (official) encounters with the Angolan youth and project partners.

The discussion on the impact of official state solidarity and its ramifications in reality for this specific group of East German actors is inspired by Odd Arne Westad's emphasis on the importance of the interventionist and modernist polit-

---

[4] This contribution relies on the solid basis of Immanuel R. Harisch's research on the deployment of the GDR's *Freundschaftsbrigaden* in Angola in the larger context of economic relations between the two countries. Apart from a general overview of the numbers, Harisch touches upon the issues of motivation, choice, and selection of the *Brigadisten*, the bilateral negotiations preparing their deployment, their remuneration as well as supply, provisioning, and accommodation, but also the fields, places, and results of their work, as well as instances of disciplining, racism, and corruption; Immanuel R. Harisch, "Handel und Solidarität: Die Beziehungen der DDR mit Angola und São Tomé und Príncipe unter besonderer Berücksichtigung des Austauschs 'Ware-gegen-Ware' ca. 1975–1990" (M.A. thesis, Universität Wien, 2018), 111–169. Ulrike Gödeke's study of the political organization of *Freundschaftsbrigaden* in Africa is equally very helpful to come to an overview of their role in the political context of the GDR; Ulrike Gödeke, "Zwischen brüderlicher Hilfe und allseitiger Stärkung der DDR: Die Freundschaftsbrigaden der FDJ in Afrika 1964 bis 1990" (Diploma thesis, Freie Unversität Berlin, 2002). While the scholarly literature on the *Brigaden* is generally scarce, Eric Burton has recently highlighted the entanglements of the brigades' activities with state interests as well as work relations and personal motives in his contribution "Solidarität und ihre Grenzen: Die Brigaden der Freundschaft der DDR," in *Internationale Solidarität: Globales Engagement in der Bundesrepublik und der DDR*, ed. Frank Bösch, Caroline Moine, and Stefanie Senger (Göttingen: Wallstein Verlag, 2018). For an apologetic account that still gives a good overview, see Ulrich van der Heyden, "FDJ-Brigaden der Freundschaft aus der DDR – die Peace Corps des Ostens?," in *Die eine Welt schaffen: Praktiken von 'Internationaler Solidarität, und 'Internationaler Entwicklung,'* ed. Berthold Unfried and Eva Himmelstoss (Leipzig: Akademische Verlagsanstalt, 2012).
[5] Vladimir Shubin, *The Hot 'Cold War': The USSR in Southern Africa* (London: Pluto Press, 2008).

ical ideologies on both sides of the bloc divide for perpetuating the global Cold War.[6] Westad states that "injustice and oppression became more visible in the 20th century ... [and] people—*especially young people—felt the need to remedy these ills. Cold War ideologies offered immediate solutions to complex problems.*"[7] The commitment of the young East Germans within the context of the "anti-imperialist struggle" of Angola turns this group of actors into a relevant test case for Westad's assumptions. The *Freundschaftsbrigaden* were directly and personally affected by the global Cold War. Still, they have been mostly neglected in the existing literature on the GDR's international solidarity as well as in the literature on Angola's Cold War more generally.

The GDR's official and state party documentation indicates the interlinkages and entanglements of the *Freundschaftsbrigaden*'s deployment in Angola with profane economic interests.[8] In retrospect, this view is also shared by former brigade members dismissing the GDR's solidarity as "plundering among friends."[9] Other memory accounts of brigade members rather stress apolitical understandings of an "adventurist journey."[10]

My approach, focusing on the contemporary motivations and their discussion in the *Freundschaftsbrigaden*, complements these views of former brigade members as well as recent scholarship.[11] The analysis focusses on the *Brigadetagebücher*, annual "brigade diaries" that were written and compiled by the col-

---

6 Odd Arne Westad, *The Global Cold War: Third World Interventions and the Making of Our Times* (Cambridge: Cambridge University Press, 2005), 4–5; 39–73.
7 Odd Arne Westad, "The Cold War and America's Delusion of Victory," *New York Times*, August 28, 2017, accessed January 20, 2020, https://www.nytimes.com/2017/08/28/opinion/cold-war-american-soviet-victory.html. Apart from Westad, other historians, such as David Engerman or Sara Lorenzini, have also offered reflections on the links between "developmentalist" and Cold War ideologies. David Engerman, "Development Politics and the Cold War," *Diplomatic History* 41 (2017); Sara Lorenzini, *Global Development: A Cold War History* (Princeton: Princeton University Press, 2019).
8 Albrecht to Günter Mittag, "Abkommen über den weiteren Einsatz von FDJ-Brigaden," February 12, 1981, 103, SAPMO-BArch, DY 3023/1464.
9 "Franke," "Mein Angola 1984," Angola Forum, accessed January 20, 2020, http://www.angola-forum.de/thread.php?board=3&thread=1.
10 "Mit einer FDJ-Freundschaftsbrigade in Angola," MDR.de, January 13, 2011, accessed January 20, 2020, https://www.mdr.de/damals/archiv/artikel105354.html. For an exemplary analysis of not only East German but also Lusophone African (in this case Mozambican) memories of cooperation, see Piepiorka and Buanaissa, this volume.
11 Here I follow the suggestions of Berthold Unfried, "Instrumente und Praktiken von 'Solidarität' Ost und 'Entwicklungshilfe' West: Blickpunkt auf das entsandte Personal," in *Die eine Welt schaffen. Praktiken von 'Internationaler Solidarität, und 'Internationaler Entwicklung,'* ed. Berthold Unfried and Eva Himmelstoss (Leipzig: Akademische Verlagsanstalt, 2012), 77.

lectives themselves. These diaries were in line with similar documentation of economic and political collectives in the GDR.[12] In the diaries, brigade members dutifully chronicled their deployment but also engaged in broader reflections.[13] The entries in these diaries give insight into a dense network of official socialist encounters with Angolan counterparts of the socialist ruling party *Movimento Popular de Libertação de Angola* (MPLA) or the brigades' counterparts of the MPLA's official youth organization, the *Juventude* (JMPLA). Consequently, the *Brigadetagebücher* are unique and compact sources offering insights into concrete practices shaped by non-elite East German conceptions of international solidarity. They showcase the subjectivities of *Brigadisten* as well as the possibilities of their communication within the forum of the collective. Their perspectives were constrained by the expected audience, balancing different communicative demands. The "semi-official" diaries were part of the competition for collective awards and thereby favored entries by individual brigade members situating their mission within publicly condoned narratives.[14]

As I show in this contribution, the image of Angolans within the *Tagebücher* largely remained confined to the GDR's official framework of solidarity. The brigade members' mediated and fragmentary perspective on the Angolan counterparts presents the latter as willing and thankful beneficiaries of East German actions rather than complex individuals or even political allies. The *Tagebücher* only rarely give proof of direct repercussions that encounters with Angolans had for *Brigadisten* or point to potential criticisms against GDR policies emerging from the ruptures in their experiences. These limitations are due to the character of the sources as well as the rigidly controlled structured realities of the *Brigaden*'s deployment.

Still, a close reading of the *Brigadetagebücher* can reveal how the dichotomy between the "modern" GDR and the "backwardness" of post-colonial Angola turned into a central interpretative frame for individual brigade members. The

---

[12] Emerging out of the East German brigade movement of work collectives, brigade diaries were promoted as chronicles of collective work life to take account of participation in work competitions. See Jörg Roesler, "Berichtsbuch, Beschwerdeschrift oder Bilderfolge? Unterschiedliche Vorstellungen zum Inhalt von Brigadetagebüchern in den Anfangstagen der 'sozialistischen Kollektive,'" in *Vorwärts und nichts vergessen. Sprache in der DDR – was war, was ist, was bleibt*, ed. Ruth Reiher and Antje Baumann (Berlin: Aufbau, 2004).
[13] For a broader introduction to the *Brigadetagebücher* as sources, see Immanuel R. Harisch and Eric Burton, "Sozialistische Globalisierung. Tagebücher der DDR-Freundschaftsbrigaden in Afrika, Asien und Lateinamerika," unpublished manuscript, forthcoming in *Zeithistorische Forschungen*.
[14] The *Brigadetagebücher* were read and assessed by superiors. See Harisch and Burton, "Sozialistische Globalisierung."

task of "modernization" was understood as the fundamental transformation of the Angolan society by mirroring attributes that the East German actors assumed to be central for the basic set-up of their own society, such as rationalism and industrialization.[15]

I argue that the *Brigadisten* presented their deployment as a crucial factor in contributing to Angola's "modernization" along socialist lines through the transfer of knowledge and values. In practice, the *Brigadisten* strongly focused on their immediate surroundings as well as their concrete possibilities to this contribution and providing "humanitarian" relief as their main objectives. These practical concerns frequently contradicted the official GDR's cliché phrases of internationalism and anti-imperialism.

My findings therefore relativize arguments which stress the immediate centrality of socialist ideology for this group of exposed East Germans in the Cold War. Still, they also underline the emphasis in Odd Arne Westad's writing on the "modernizing" mission as a central dimension of Cold War ideologies with respect to nation building in countries such as socialist Angola. Remarkably, the members of the friendship brigades in Angola rarely engaged explicitly with the need for socialism. Instead of projecting a "politicized" understanding of their activities, I show how their "interventionism" focused on tangible practices of aid and the mechanics of modernization instead.

The tensions between the collectivist and individualist perspectives within these sources show how far the collectivist ideal within the brigades actually extended and how visions of solidarity were sourced between individual emphases and common proclamations. Not least, this collective source undermines common tropes contrasting African collectivism with European individualism, as a European collectivism comes into view. The taken micro-historical approach of a close focus on the brigades helps to trace the intensity and ambiguities of the brigades' socialist encounters, but also the extent of their (dis)entanglement with the political conditions in Angola as the *Brigaden* moored in this crucial locale of the Global Cold War.

---

15 This take on 'modernization' draws from Frederick Cooper, *Colonialism in Question: Theory, Knowledge, History* (Berkeley: University of California Press, 2005), 113, 120–122.

International Solidarity in the GDR's Global Cold War

The *Brigaden der Freundschaft* and its members were active within the wider context of the GDR's foreign policy's focus on the "newly independent nation states" of the post-colonial world. Throughout the GDR's existence, the involvement with these countries was presented as international solidarity which even carried constitutional weight from 1974.[16] The GDR would stand "united" with these states in a joint struggle against "imperialism" and "capitalism."[17] Conceptually, international solidarity was presented as a quasi-natural life praxis of "true" and "mutual" friendship on an equal footing in no need of profound theoretical deliberations.[18]

In the GDR public sphere, officially condoned solidarity was legitimized and popularized by the state-socialist organizations from state-coordinated media to education. International solidarity was present(ed) as an ideological argument for the continued benefits of the East German political order despite the GDR's lethargic state.[19] At the same time, non-state actors promoted values of international solidarity as well, but were marginalized by the official GDR.[20] The "omnipresence" of this "mission" instilled it as an integral part of the political consciousness of GDR citizens.

With regards to the discursive functions of international solidarity within the GDR, Gregory Witkowski argues that the campaign for solidarity was supposed to mobilize East Germans into action by stressing the dependency of its recipients but also calling for a change of consciousness among GDR citizens. The predominant narrative of the already socialist East German state seeking to spread this remedy for continuing political ills was to position the GDR society "on the

---

16 "Artikel 6,"*Verfassung der Deutschen Demokratischen Republik*, October 7, 1974, accessed January 6, 2020, http://www.documentarchiv.de/ddr/verfddr.html.
17 Hans-Joachim Spanger and Lothar Brock, *Die beiden deutschen Staaten in der Dritten Welt: Die Entwicklungspolitik der DDR – eine Herausforderung für die Bundesrepublik Deutschland?* (Opladen: Westdeutscher Verlag, 1987), 39–49.
18 Hubertus Büschel, *Hilfe zur Selbsthilfe: Deutsche Entwicklungsarbeit in Afrika 1960–1975* (Frankfurt: Campus, 2014), 77–78.
19 Ulrich Mählert and Gerd-Rüdiger Stephan, *Blaue Hemden – Rote Fahnen: Die Geschichte der Freien Deutschen Jugend* (Opladen: Leske und Budrich, 1996), 187–188.
20 Maria Magdalena Verburg, *Ostdeutsche Dritte-Welt-Gruppen vor und nach 1989/90* (Göttingen: V&R unipress, 2012).

side of moral righteousness,"[21] and perpetuated a hierarchical and even racialized worldview.[22]

Toni Weis equally stresses the importance of the anti-colonial imaginary of solidarity and describes it as a vague ethic at the same time.[23] Weis rejects discussions about its imposition or genuineness, underlining how solidarity was endorsed "to different degrees and for a variety of reasons."[24] Indeed, GDR citizens fundamentally agreed with the benevolence of East German support for anti-imperialist, anti-colonialist, and anti-capitalist causes, that could, at the same time, be acknowledged as genuine and state-imposed.

Exploring the reasons for the perpetual stability of the discourse, Weis introduces the picture of a "working misunderstanding" in the political relations of East German and African actors: the "rhetoric of solidarity remained abstract enough to be filled with different contents by the two partners and used for their own respective agendas."[25] With regards to the discourse within the GDR, Weis assesses how "[t]he image of the 'other' was confined to the framework of solidarity, which in turn reflected back—ideally in a positive way—on the GDR itself."[26]

FDJ-Friendship Brigades in Socialist Angola

By exploring the *Freundschaftsbrigaden*, set up in 1963 as a main actor of the GDR's practice of international solidarity, it is possible to reconsider the concrete implications of the solidarity framework. As tools of their foreign policy, detached to over 20 countries on three continents in total, the *Brigaden* were used by the SED leadership to woo "newly independent nation states" and their socialist alignment.[27] From the mid-1970s onwards, the *Freundschaftsbrigaden* had a strong focus on Ethiopia, Mozambique, and particularly Angola as "socialist-ori-

---

21 Gregory Witkowski, "Between Fighters and Beggars: Socialist Philanthropy and the Imagery of Solidarity in East Germany," in *Comrades of Color: East Germany in the Cold War World*, ed. Quinn Slobodian (New York: Berghahn, 2014), 76.
22 Witkowski, "Between Fighters and Beggars," 88–89.
23 Toni Weis, "The Politics Machine: On the Concept of 'Solidarity' in East German Support for SWAPO," *Journal of Southern African Studies* 37 (2011): 352.
24 Weis, "Politics Machine," 359.
25 Weis, "Politics Machine," 352.
26 Weis, "Politics Machine," 363–364.
27 Ulrike Gödeke, "Zwischen brüderlicher Hilfe und allseitiger Stärkung der DDR."

ented countries."²⁸ Their deployment was entangled with trade and export interests as well as it was linked to "solidarity efforts," such as the support of vocational training and donations organized by societal organizations of the GDR.²⁹ In these countries, the alignment with the socialist bloc remained fragile and at times contested so that the East German employment of brigades served to continuously underline the benefits of cooperating with the GDR as a comparatively weak socialist economic and political partner.

The *Freundschaftsbrigaden* were joined by young men and (fewer) women of different professions who lived and worked as "collectives" in their countries of deployment. Before they traveled abroad, the brigade members were thoroughly checked for their political reliability and underwent training. Whereas the services of the *Brigaden* were usually provided free of charge, the host government was responsible for food and accommodation.³⁰

In 1989, the FDJ celebrated the *Freundschaftsbrigaden*'s mission to overcome colonial legacies and their role as the "bridges of friendship" to the youth of the postcolonial world.³¹ The FDJ named the provision of (vocational) training and possibilities for academic study as well as contributions to construction projects, or their work in industry, transport, and agriculture, as central objectives of the *Freundschaftsbrigaden*. Transport and agriculture were of particular importance to the activities of the *Freundschaftsbrigaden* in Angola.³² The GDR had emerged as a trusted partner among other socialist states for the ruling Marxist MPLA since at least the early 1960s.³³ Its international relations to socialist countries were of vital importance to the MPLA to seize government control after Angolan

---

28 For a detailed list of the dispatched brigades from 1964 to 1989 see Ilona Schleicher, "Elemente entwicklungspolitischer Zusammenarbeit in der Tätigkeit von FDGB und FDJ," in *Entwicklungspolitische Zusammenarbeit in der Bundesrepublik Deutschland und der DDR*, ed. Hans-Jörg Bücking (Berlin: Duncker & Humblot, 1998), 136–137.
29 Burton, "Die Grenzen der Solidarität," 157–161.
30 Immanuel R. Harisch, "Bartering Coffee, Cocoa and W50 Trucks: The Trade Relationships of the GDR, Angola and São Tomé in a Comparative Perspective," *Global Histories* 3 (2017): 44.
31 Zentralkomitee der FDJ, "25 Jahre Brigaden der Freundschaft – Berlin 28. Juli 1989," SAPMO-BArch, DY 24/19631.
32 For a thorough account of the *Freundschaftschaftsbrigaden*'s actitivities in Angola see Immanuel R. Harisch, "East German Friendship-Brigades and Specialists in Angola: A Socialist Globalization Project in the Global Cold War," in *Transregional Connections in the History of East Central Europe*, ed. Katja Naumann (Berlin: De Gruyter, forthcoming 2021).
33 Zentralkomitee der Sozialistischen Einheitspartei Deutschlands – Abteilung Internationale Verbindungen, "Angola," 95–191, SAPMO-BArch, DY 30/98121. See also Hans-Georg Schleicher, "The German Democratic Republic (GDR) in the Liberation Struggle of Southern Africa," in *Southern African Liberation Struggles 1960–1994: Contemporaneous Documents*, ed. Arnold Temu and Joel das Neves Tembe (Dar es Salaam: Mkuki na Nyota, 2014).

independence from Portugal in 1975 with the help of Cuban soldiers and Soviet arms.[34]

Both should remain vital for the MPLA's hold to power with the continuation of Angola's anti-colonial liberation war as an internationalized civil war. The MPLA leadership's rule over the country was challenged by internal opposition within the party resulting in an attempted *coup d'état* in May 1977 and the continuing onslaught by competing former liberation movements. The interests of these armed groups were interwoven with those of neighboring states, such as Zaire, as well as South Africa which had control of Namibia. The dynamics of the Cold War, but also commercial interests in Angola's diamond and most importantly oil resources, guaranteed the longevity of conflict.[35]

Over the years following independence, the GDR leadership took strong interest in its political as well as economic relations with Angola. Seeing Angola as a model for other African states, an official of the East German Ministry of Foreign Affairs noted accordingly: "For the first time, a developing country with the foundations of a modern economy is on our side."[36] Angola became not only a major and politically relevant supplier of coffee, but also an important export destination for GDR machinery and technologies, most notably the IFA W50 trucks.[37]

The deployment of GDR personnel to Angola as technical and administrative experts as well as political advisers was an integral part of trade and cooperation.[38] In late 1977, these GDR experts were joined by over 130 members of the

---

34 For an overview of Angola's history before and after independence see David Birmingham, "Angola," in *A History of Postcolonial Lusophone Africa*, ed. Patrick Chabal (London: Hurst, 2002).
35 For an overview of the longer-term entanglements of these interests, see Birmingham, "Angola," 155–179. For Cuba's paramount importance in the support of the MPLA government stressing a course of action independent from the Soviet Union, see Piero Gleijeses, *Visions of Freedom: Havana, Washington, Pretoria and the Struggle for Southern Africa* (Chapel Hill: The University of North Carolina Press, 2013). Gleijeses' further argument of Cuban "revolutionary idealism" stands in contrast to Christine Hatzky's who has pitted the importance of economic motivations for the lasting service of Cuban experts in Angola. Christine Hatzky, *Cubans in Angola: South-South Cooperation and Transfer of Knowledge, 1976–1991* (Madison: University of Wisconsin Press, 2015), 181–188. For an account of the Soviet Union's role in this context, see Shubin, *The Hot Cold War*, 67–115.
36 Generalsekretär des Ministeriums für Auswärtige Angelegenheiten, A. B. Neumann, "Information über die Reise einer Delegation des MfAA in die Volksrepublik Angola," September 1, 1977, SAPMO-BArch, DY 3023/1463.
37 Harisch, "Coffee, Cocoa, and W50 Trucks."
38 Alexander Schalck to Günter Mittag, "Informationen über Aufenthalt Klaus Häntzschel, 5.–14.10.1983 in Angola," SAPMO-BArch, DY 3023/1464.

Freundschaftsbrigaden on the explicit request of the Angolan President Agostinho Neto who had himself once lived next to a brigade in his Tanzanian exile.³⁹ The *Brigaden* were to mainly facilitate and guarantee the servicing of W50 trucks and coffee exports, mostly by familiarizing Angolans with (the repair of) the trucks as well as maintaining other agricultural machinery.⁴⁰ Internal sources explicitly refer to such tasks as *"Kundendienst,"* customer service, a term reflecting the brigades' integration into economic supply lines and inclusion into trade relations overall.⁴¹

The MPLA's youth organization, the *Juventude do Movimento Popular de Libertação de Angola* (JMPLA), was the direct counterpart of the FDJ in the deployment of the *Freundschaftsbrigaden*, an awkward fit as the JMPLA was a tiny cadre organization by comparison.⁴² Apart from their frequent exchanges with the JMPLA, the brigades also cooperated with other official organizations of the Angolan socialist society, such as the women's organization and the trade unions, but also the armed forces, most notably the regular army *Forças Armadas Populares de Libertação de Angola* (FAPLA).⁴³ The East Germans were one group in a lively sphere of "internationalists" from the Soviet Union, Bulgaria, Vietnam, and Cuba among others—fertile ground for "socialist encounters".

The *Brigaden* of around 10 to 20 Germans were first based in the urban centers Luanda, Gabela, N'Dalatando, and Uíge. In later years, further *Brigaden* set up "repair stations" for GDR machinery and vehicles. From the beginning, the conditions of their service were plagued with problems, leading to dissatisfaction among the *Brigadisten*, but also fueling political dispute between the Ger-

---

39 A.B. Neumann, "Information über die Reise," 34, SAPMO-BArch, DY 3023/1463.
40 Harisch, "East German Friendship-Brigades and Specialists in Angola."
41 Erich Honecker to Günter Mittag, "Informationen über beendete Beratungen des Gemeinsamen Wirtschaftsausschusses DDR/VRA Angola," March 8, 1981, SAPMO-BArch DY 3023/1464. Interlinkages between economic and solidarity relations were characteristic of the East German interactions with "newly independent nation states" beyond Angola as well. One prominent example is the coal plant in the Mozambican town Moatize.
42 While the JMPLA only had a few thousand members at times, the FDJ included the vast share of young GDR citizens, e. g. 2.3 million members in 1981, more than 77% of GDR citizens between 14 and 25 years of age. Unfortunately, there is hardly any secondary literature on the JMPLA; for some basic information refer to Michael Wolfers and Jane Bergerol, *Angola in the Frontline* (London: Zed Press, 1983). For an official historical account by the MPLA see Movimento Popular de Libertação de Angola, "História Da JMPLA," no date, accessed November 25, 2019, http://www.mpla.ao/jmpla.39/historia.40.html.
43 Wolfers and Bergerol, *Angola in the Frontline*, 166; Keith Somerville, *Angola: Politics, Economics, and Society* (London: Pinter Publishers, 1986).

man and Angolan sides.⁴⁴ The prolonged internationalized civil war resulted in severe risks for the safety of the dispatched brigades due to which the ones in Gabela and Malanje were, for example, evacuated in 1983.⁴⁵ Security concerns also co-determined the extent to which the brigades isolated themselves or engaged with the partners and society surrounding them, underlining the impression of limited and finite moorings with the possibility of sudden departure. Nonetheless, the deployment of *Brigaden* was continued until 1989.

The Structured Practice of Solidarity in the GDR Collective

The five *Brigadetagebücher* analyzed here⁴⁶ were authored by four different brigades and jointly cover a time period from 1982 to 1986. These "diaries" were produced by the brigades themselves over the course of their deployment. Supposed to "represent the interesting life of the collective,"⁴⁷ the diaries included written texts as well as various forms of illustrations⁴⁸ from multiple authors and were part of wider documentation obligations.⁴⁹ They gave "calendar sheet" reports reflecting the cycles of deployment and others on political meet-

---

44 Alexander Schalck to Günter Mittag, "Bericht über die Reise der Genossen Stritzke und Büttner nach Luanda/VR Angola," November 29, 1977, Eberhard Feister to Paul Markowski, October 30, 1977, SAPMO-BArch, DY 3023/1463.
45 "Basiswechsel," SAPMO-BArch, DY 24/20215. In Mozambique, which had also officially embarked on a socialist path in 1977, rebels of the Western-financed *Resistência Nacional Moçambicana* (RENAMO) killed eight agricultural specialists from the GDR in 1984. See Bahr in this volume.
46 The archive *Stiftung Archiv der Parteien und Massenorganisationen der DDR im Bundesarchiv* (SAPMO) holds a number of these "brigade diaries" (SAPMO-BArch/DY 24). It remains unclear where other diaries may be found. The respective titles are: "Brigadetagebücher der Ernte und Reperaturbrigaden 'Comandante Bula' in Samba Caju und N' Dalatando, Angola, 1983–1984," SAPMO-BArch, DY 24/19129; "Brigadetagebuch der Brigade 'Daniel Dangereux' in Uige, Angola, 1982–1983," SAPMO-BArch, DY 24/20213; "Brigadetagebuch der Brigade der Freundschaft in Gabela, Angola, 1983," SAPMO-BArch, DY 24/20215; "Brigadetagebuch der Brigade "Comandante Kassange" in Lobito, Angola, 1985–1986," SAPMO-BArch, DY 24/20214.
47 "Daniel Dangereux," SAPMO-BArch, DY 24/20213.
48 While my analysis focuses on the writings of the *Brigadisten*, these illustrations—including clippings from publications, drawings, and photos—often assembled into collages, would be compelling sources in their own right. For an analysis of private photographs taken by East Germans during their stays abroad in the 1980s in Mozambique, consult Bahr's contribution in this volume.
49 See Harisch and Burton, "Sozialistische Globalisierung."

ings or the fulfillment of work requirements, but also covered the extraordinary events of brigade life. These events included festivities and get-togethers with the members of the JMPLA or other "internationalists," but also recreational activities. Moreover, there was space for reflections of individual brigade members on their personal situation within the brigade collective. Taken together, the "diaries" feature relatively unguided and sometimes quite personal contents and perspectives—diverse takes on brigade life with strong individual emphases—next to more official takes on conventional markers of socialist life in the collective abroad.

The diaries represent the collectives' activities as tightly structured around the political space of the GDR and official encounters with the Angolan side confirming their mission of solidarity and mutual friendship. Reflective of their continuing close integration into the GDR's socio-political structures were the brigades' participation in work competitions for honorary titles,[50] but also their duties to present solidarity donations to beneficiaries in Angola.[51] Here, the brigades acted as representatives of East German organizations and companies that usually exercised their solidarity through collections from afar.[52] Reports on the occasion of national political events in the GDR or certain initiatives of the Free German Youth (FDJ)—for example by transplanting "peace marches" to Angola—further underlined how East German political rituals were perpetuated in the social life of the *Freundschaftsbrigaden:*

> It wasn't that easy to explain without an interpreter why we should take to the streets together and that peace marches took place everywhere in the world and that the youth of the GDR also demonstrated at the same hour for the same goals. [...] Everyone of us was a little proud that we had succeeded in getting the people out of their huts and houses according to the peace contingent of the FDJ.[53]

---

[50] "Öffentliche Veranstaltung zur Antragstellung zur Auszeichnung mit dem Ehrentitel 'Kollektiv der Sozialistischen Arbeit'," SAPMO-BArch, DY 24/20215.
[51] "Unsere Patenklasse und die Solidarität," SAPMO-BArch, DY 24/19129; "Solidaritätsgüter aus der DDR für die Waisenkinder von 'Kipuco'," SAPMO-BArch, DY 24/20215.
[52] "VEB Kraftwerkskombinat Dresden – Liebe Jugendfreunde!," March 21, 1983, SAPMO-BArch, DY 24/20213.
[53] "Es war nicht ganz einfach, ohne Dolmetscherin zu erklären, weshalb wir gemeinsam auf die Straße gehen wollten und daß Friedensmärsche überall in der Welt stattfinden und auch die Jugend der DDR zur gleichen Stunde, für die gleichen Ziele wie hier, demonstriert. ... Jeder von uns war ein bißchen stolz darauf, daß es uns gelungen war, entsprechend dem 'Friedensaufgebot der FDJ' die Menschen aus den Hütten und Häusern zu holen." "'Keine Atomwaffen für Südafrika!' Sofortige Beendigung des unerklärten Krieges gegen die VR Angola!...," SAPMO-BArch, DY 24/20215.

Importantly, the actual work of the brigades was not necessarily linked to these reports. The political axioms in the diaries therefore often only served as general confirmations of the GDR's official political causes, extended and copied into a new environment.[54] These rituals gave limited opportunity for exchange: the "peace march" was, for example, aimed against US and South African aggression as an immediate concern through which the *Brigaden* attested to the urgency of the GDR's anti-imperialist mission in Angola and beyond. However, while the brigades sought to mobilize the Angolan population and partners, the extension of such rituals "according to the FDJ" did not envisage their creative transformation through exchange. These rituals seem as attempts to create socialist encounters and confirm the different partners of their entangled political realities. However, the challenges to their translation and adaption rather underline how they ultimately remained rooted in the East German political space and detached from their surroundings.

The diaries further give account of a dense network of socialist encounters with other internationalists from socialist countries, representatives of the MPLA, and local leaders of the Angolan military, economy or state to strengthen the internationalist friendship.[55] Delegations of the brigades were constantly invited to central political events, such as the oath-taking of Angolan soldiers,[56] to which the Germans contributed short messages reaffirming their internationalist mission.[57] The reports on such encounters, just as well as the ones on interlinkages with the GDR, were rife with the parlance and set phrases of solidarity as a "class duty."[58]

These encounters were completed by the cooperation between the brigades of the FDJ and representatives of the party youth organization JMPLA as their official counterparts.[59] Purged, and kept under strict control by the MPLA after the JMPLA's implication in the attempted coup by a disillusioned faction of the MPLA against its leadership in 1977, the JMPLA only had around 4,000 members

---

54 "Abzeichenprüfung für gutes Wissen," SAPMO-BArch, DY 24/20215.
55 "Marx-Gedenken bei unseren Freunden der FAPLA"; "Zu Gast bei unseren kubanischen Freunden," SAPMO-BArch, DY 24/20215.
56 "Vereidigung bei der FAPLA," SAPMO-BArch, DY 24/19129; "Vereidigung der Kämpfer der ODP," SAPMO-BArch, DY 24/20215.
57 "FDJ – Freundschaftsbrigade – Basis Gabela An das Sekretariat des Kreiskomitees von Amboim der JMPLA-JdP Gabela," SAPMO-BArch, DY 24/20215; "Grussadresse," SAPMO-BArch, DY 24/19129.
58 "FDJ-Freundschaftsbrigade – Basis Gabela An das Sekretariat des Kreiskomitees," SAPMO-BArch, DY 24/20215.
59 Unfortunately, there is hardly any literature on the JMPLA and it proved impossible to retrieve perspectives of (former) JMPLA functionaries in contact with the brigades.

after "rectification." It was a small cadre organization with limited pervasion in the Angolan society.[60] The MPLA also identified serious deficiencies in the JMPLA with regards to its level of activity, politicization, and social responsibilities towards the country's youth.[61] Documents by the FDJ's central committee show that it understood its relations to the JMPLA as privileged, but was also staunchly critical of "parasitic tendencies" within the JMPLA.[62] The FDJ and JMPLA agreed that the brigades were supposed to contribute to the political profile of the JMPLA and support its development into a mass organization.[63] The FDJ offered material support to the JMPLA, inter alia by printing brochures. The brigades themselves joined through work services, for example by setting up a JMPLA youth club in premises that had been "in colonial times a night club, called *To the Black Diamond*."[64]

The *Brigaden* were further integrated into political cooperation by the leadership of both youth organizations as they were expected to offer political training to JMPLA functionaries. Together with the local JMPLA, the *Brigaden* therefore drafted working programs and held joint political forums or information events on various East German political customs or events.[65] The JMPLA chapters respectively celebrated important Angolan political occasions with the brigades. Representatives of the JMPLA served the *Brigaden* as gate keepers and intermediaries to the political reality of Angola and accompanied them on excursions to Angolan companies or the remote rural area.[66]

The official encounters between members of the FDJ and the Angolan youth of the JMPLA were not limited to Angola. Five places at the Wilhelm Pieck academy of the FDJ in Bogensee were reserved for JMPLA members throughout the

---

[60] Somerville, *Angola*, 92–94.
[61] Somerville, *Angola*, 90–91.
[62] "Information über den Aufenthalt einer Delegation des Zentralrates der FDJ in der VR Angola vom 25.10.–2.11.1989," SAPMO-BArch, DY 24/14424.
[63] "Vereinbarung über Freundschaft und Zusammenarbeit zwischen der Freien Deutschen Jugend (FDJ) und der JMPLA – Jugend der Partei für die Jahre 1980–1982," SAPMO-BArch, DY 24/22466.
[64] "Eine schöne Aufgabe. Jugendclub der JMPLA 'Ché-Guevarra,'" SAPMO-BArch, DY 24/20213.
[65] "Forum mit JMPLA-FDJ Freundschaftsbrigade 'Kommandante Kassange' und der Besatzung der MS 'Inselsee'," "Vorbereitung des 40. Jahrestages der FDJ," SAPMO-BArch, DY 24/20214.
[66] Besichtigung des Radio- und Fernsehwerkes von Lobito," SAPMO-BArch, DY 24/20214; "Ein Lepradorf- Quitunga," SAPMO-BArch, DY 24/19129. Considering the limited exposure of brigade members to their Angolan environment, the brigades were in dire need of guides. To give an example, a brigade got into trouble on an unaccompanied excursion as they had unknowingly (and uncaringly) cut down a banana tree ignorant of a local farmer's ownership. "'Frühschoppen oder Organisieren' Von Bananen im Botanischen!" SAPMO-BArch, DY 24/19129.

1980s and a permanent representative of the JMPLA supervised young Angolans studying and working in the GDR in the second half of the 1980s.[67] Furthermore, information, formalized greetings, and delegations were exchanged steadily. In March 1980, a JMPLA delegation visited Ludwigsfelde where the IFA W50 trucks exported to Angola were manufactured. Extending a practice known from Angola and interlinking their respective activities, a local youth brigade in the factory was awarded the honorary title "Dr. Agostinho Neto" to celebrate their contribution.[68]

In fact, the most significant recurring moment of the mutual confirmation of solidarity within Angola was the annual bestowal of the brigade's honorary title, the name of an Angolan "martyr" to the "revolution," awarded by the Angolan side.[69] Names like "Daniel Dangereux," a member of the FAPLA general staff who had been killed during the attempted coup in May 1977,[70] signified that the Angolan army and the German brigades were leading one unified struggle. This subtly confirmed the assumed intrinsic links between everyday acts, such as the maintenance of W50 trucks, and the global cause of anti-imperialism. In its struggle for the honorary title, the friendship brigade "Comandante Bula," also named after a victim of the coup, accordingly argued: "His name is honor and obligation to us. [...] But the disputes continue. [...] The support which we can offer to the country [of Angola], is to guarantee the operability of the agrarian technology in our province."[71]

The internationalist role of the brigades was further reflected by the diaries in the frequent exchanges with Soviet, Bulgarian, or Vietnamese personnel next to the dominating Cuban presence.[72] The collectives of internationalists shared

---

67 "Information über den Aufenthalt einer Delegation des Zentralrates der FDJ in der VR Angola vom 25.10.–2.11.1989," SAPMO-BArch, DY 24/14424". For a contribution on Angolan students in the GDR see Marcia C. Schenck, "Negotiating the German Democratic Republic: Angolan Student Migration During the Cold War, 1976–90," *Africa* 89 (2019).
68 "Jugenddelegation bei Automobilwerken," *Neues Deutschland*, March 8, 1980, 2.
69 "HOJI YA HENDA – Der 14. April"; "Hoji Ya Henda würdige Verteidigung des Ehrennamens," SAPMO-BArch, DY 24/20215.
70 Paul Fauvet, "Angola: the Rise and Fall of Nito Alves," *Review of African Political Economy* 9 (1977): 101. An Angolan student association was named after "Commandante Dangereux" as well.
71 "Dieser Name ist für uns Ehre und Verpflichtung zugleich. [...] Aber die Auseinandersetzungen gehen weiter. [...] Die Unterstützung die wir dem Land geeben können, ist die Gewährleistung der landwirtschaftlichen Technik in unserer Provinz." "Kampf um Ehrentitel," SAPMO-BArch, DY 24/19129.
72 Concerning the Cuban presence see Gleijeses, *Visions of Freedom*.

extensive social contacts of friendly visits or good-spirited sports competitions,[73] for example marking the International Worker's Day as a globalized event now also linked to anti-colonialist causes.[74] Beyond these official expressions of friendship with Angolans and internationalists emphasizing a common sense of mission,[75] the brigade diaries also occasionally mentioned more "spontaneous" and "surprising" get-togethers, implicitly giving accounts of their usually structured, mediated, and planned character:[76] "On the eve of January 22, where actually nothing special was going on, ten youth friends of the JMPLA suddenly came to us [...]. They brought tapes with Angolan music with them and asked us to the play those for them as they didn't have a cassette deck. [...] For us it was interesting as well to get to know the Angolan folk, *Schlager* pop songs and rock music for once."

These types of diary entries always referred to the brigade as a whole, while individual members only featured as representatives of a larger collective and its common struggle. This was because of fundamental collectivist orientations in GDR society,[77] but also due to their nature as collectively produced sources for the perusal of a limited public. This collectivist rather than individualized framing, with its most direct expression in the almost exclusive use of "we" throughout the respective articles, was reinforced by the fact that the brigade members spent their free time mostly together due to constantly bemoaned language barrier as well as concerns of political control among the GDR authorities and security risks.[78]

At the same time, the sources omit mentioning more informal encounters between the brigade members and the Angolan counterparts or other internation-

---

[73] "Eine schöne Aufgabe – Jugendklub der JMPLA 'Ché-Guevarra,'" SAPMO-BArch DY 24/20213; "Unser Klubleben," SAPMO-BArch DY 24/20213; "Cabambe – Hier treffen sich Freunde," SAPMO-BArch, DY 24/19129; "Protest," SAPMO-BArch, DY 24/20215.
[74] "1. Mai 1983 in Sumbe," SAPMO-BArch, DY 24/20215; "66. Jahrestag der Oktoberrevolution 1917," SAPMO-BArch, DY 24/19129.
[75] "KAMPFPROGRAMM zur Führung des sozialistischen Wettbewerbs der FDJ-Freundschaftsbrigade Lobito im 9. Einsatzjahr 1985/86 in der VR Angola," SAPMO-BArch, DY 24/20214.
[76] "Am Abend des 22. Januar, wo eigentlich nichts besonderes los war, kamen plötzlich 10 Jugendfreunde der JMPLA zu uns [...]. Sie brachten einige Kassetten mit angolanischer Musik mit und baten uns, diese für sie abzuspielen, da sie kein Kassettengerät hätten. [...] Es war auch für uns interessant mal die angolanische Volksmusik, Schlager und Rockmusik kennen zu lernen." *Schlager* is a sub-genre of German popular music, dealing with romantic themes and often delving into exoticism. "Ein unerwartet schöner Abend," SAPMO-BArch, DY 24/20123.
[77] See Thomas Reichel, *'Sozialistisch arbeiten, lernen und leben': die Brigadebewegung in der DDR (1959–1989)* (Köln: Böhlau, 2011), 287–294; Mählert and Stephan, *Blaue Hemden*, 213–216.
[78] Harisch, "East German Friendship Brigades."

alists beyond the recourse to official socialist group encounters. The Angolan addressees of East German solidarity mostly appeared in the diaries as willing apprentices of East German skills in the workplace and political activists in socialist organizations. Apart from the bestowal of individual honorary titles, namely for the "best Angolan colleagues" of the month, the Angolan contacts were subsumed under amorphous abbreviations and collective descriptions such as "the JMPLA," "Angolan friends," or just as "Angolans."

Given that unofficial contacts, not to speak of intimate relationships, were discouraged by the SED functionaries who ran the operational command in Luanda, and probably the brigade leaders in each brigade as well, they would not have been included in the *Tagebücher*. This lack of reports on individual encounters underlines the impression of the tight rigidity of the *Brigaden*'s officially acceptable (inter)actions. Entries on festivities to official occasions do, however, often hint to more informal possibilities "to cement the friendship" usually during or after banquets.[79]

The Exercise of Solidarity: Seeing like a Brigadist

The reports in the diaries presented in the chapter above reflected the brigade collectives' mission of "enacting solidarity":[80] the diaries immediately connected work duties with the struggle of the MPLA for a socialist society in the official affirmative reports of solidarity. However, the reports written from a stronger personal perspective in the focus of this chapter went beyond the officialized solidarity discourse—and possibly cliché. While the section above was seeing with us like an East German state,[81] this one seeks to source the visions of solidarity of individual *Brigadisten*.

The *Brigadisten* themselves still dedicated the most space and reflection on their daily work and its impact, which stressed a practical interpretation of the brigades' presence. The *Brigadisten* frequently identified material shortages or technical difficulties as the ultimate challenges to "modernization" in Angola.[82]

---

79 "Zweiter Sanza Pombo Report," SAPMO-BArch, DY 24/20213.
80 "Es lebe der proletarische Internationalismus! Es lebe unsere Freundschaft!" SAPMO-BArch, DY 24/19129.
81 James C. Scott, *Seeing like a State: How Certain Schemes to Improve the Human Condition Have Failed* (New Haven: Yale University Press, 1998).
82 "Meine Arbeit in der Küche!," SAPMO-BArch, DY 24/20213.

This reflects a rather technocratic understanding of their contribution as well as the fact that such language could serve as a safeguard against the shallows of political phrasing. In this context, the brigade members sought to stimulate technical innovations by giving *Neuerervorschläge*, "innovation proposals" common in the GDR, to overcome specific technical problems.[83] The so-called "innovators' movement" (*Neuererbewegung*), as an official GDR policy and means to get extra payments for successful innovations,[84] aimed at promoting individual initiatives to increase economic productivity. Transplanting this "movement" to Angola was an attempt to export characteristic means of East German work organization.[85] The innovation proposals documented in the diaries reflected understandings of standardized and regularized work organization and the assumed possibility to directly transfer them to war-torn Angola as well.[86]

As such work processes were described in great detail throughout the diaries,[87] the Germans perceived "creativity" and "ingenuity" as their most important qualities: their individual initiative and readiness to take inconvenient steps were presented as indispensable assets within the Angolan context. The *Brigadisten* understood this set of skills and qualities as honed in the GDR in response to material shortages and technological deficiencies. They assumed that they could make use of these skills in the Angolan economy, in their view characterized by similar problems. Both the assumption of ingenuity as a typical East German skill as well as the link drawn between the economic conditions illustrate how the experiences in Angola illuminated the own background of the *Brigadisten* to them and how they deduced their role in Angola from it.

Through their day-to-day work in the car workshops, repair missions for coffee harvesting machines, and in vocational training, the *Brigadisten* were sure to not only achieve tangible economic progress but also directly impact their Angolan partners: "Our work did not only have statistical value but had an absolutely

---

[83] "Bericht über die Verwirklichung des Neuerervorschlages 'Wie kann unser Waschautomat ständig und zu jeder Zeit genutzt werden," SAPMO-BArch, DY 24/20123; "Ein Vorschlag zum Neuererwesen," SAPMO-BArch, DY 24/20215.
[84] *FDGB-Lexikon, s.v.* "Neuererbewegung," Berlin 2009, accessed August 8, 2020, http://library.fes.de/FDGB-Lexikon/texte/sachteil/n/Neuererbewegung.html.
[85] Inge Tvedten, *Angola: Struggle for Peace and Reconstruction* (Boulder: Westview, 1997), 70–77; see also M. R. Bhagavan, "Establishing the Conditions for Socialism: The Case of Angola," in *Africa: Problems in the Transition to Socialism*, ed. Barry Munslow (London: Zed, 1986).
[86] "Packen wir es an es gibt viel zu tun," "Einige Gedanken zu den Ergebnissen unserer Zusammenarbeit mit Enama; Unsere Werkstatt," SAPMO-BArch, DY 24/20123.
[87] "Die Kaffeeschälanlage in Puri," "Aktion Sanza Bombo vom 19.–22.9.1982," SAPMO-BArch, DY 24/20123.

real effect for our Angolan friends."[88] In this context, the brigade members understood themselves as irreplaceable mentors: "Who but us could attend to that work?"[89] Thereby, the East Germans positioned themselves as "benefactor" of the Angolans, since the former presented themselves as the bearers of further progressed knowledge to be passed on to the Angolan colleagues. The aim was for the Angolans to pick up the East German dedication to work to "raise the individual responsibility and interest in participation," as one *Brigadist* described the mission.[90] The Angolan co-workers were generally assumed to be willing learners, but still lacking these necessary qualities so that "responsibilities [could] only slowly be transferred."[91] In this way the *Brigadisten* also legitimized their continued presence. The *Brigadisten*'s focus on the dissemination of knowledge and their positioning as educators of the Angolans highlights the projection of inequality and hierarchization in supposedly horizontal solidarity relations.[92]

The focus on practical work, still communicated within the collective as common and shared experiences, was supplemented by broader reflections of the individual *Brigadisten* on their own "African adventure,"[93] as it was an extraordinary privilege for GDR citizens to travel overseas.[94] The exoticist expectations of *Brigadisten*[95] reporting on their first day in Angola were, however, reliably curbed by impressions of dirt, the staggeringly frequent mention of which speaks to the anticipation of an unspoiled "Africa" (but possibly also of their lacking prep-

---

[88] "Zweiter Sanza Pombo Report," SAPMO-BArch, DY 24/20213.
[89] "Zweiter Sanza Pombo Report," SAPMO-BArch, DY 24/20213.
[90] "Einige Gedanken zu den Ergebnissen unserer Zusammenarbeit mit Enama," SAPMO-BArch, DY 24/20123.
[91] "Unsere Werkstatt," SAPMO-BArch, DY 24/20123.
[92] To a large extent, the idea of international solidarity in the GDR was based on the assumption of a shared opposition between East Germans and their partners in solidarity against global forces, such as imperialism. From this perspective, the hierarchized understanding of solidarity seems ill-fitting. On the other hand, solidarity has been described as a contradictory concept, which could also include the connection to a group perceived as different, or in need, finding an expression in humanitarian action. While not represented to a large extent in the GDR's solidarity discourse, the perspectives of the *Brigadisten* rather have their roots in the latter form. See Kurt Bayertz, *Solidarität: Begriff und Problem* (Frankfurt: Suhrkamp, 1998), 49.
[93] "Meine Einreise in die VR Angola und die Fahrt nach Uíge," SAPMO-BArch, DY 24/20213.
[94] "Aus dem täglichen Leben der FDJ-Freundschaftsbrigade Gabela," SAPMO-BArch, DY 24/20215; "Exkursion nach Massangano," "Erste Eindrücke," SAPMO-BArch DY 24/19129.
[95] The expectations communicated in such reports, which come close to travelogues, had been co-shaped by East German media coverage. For an analysis of the projections by a prominent East German journalist, see Bodie's contribution in this volume.

aration or German babbittry).[96] As one brigade member observed: "The capital of Angola made a very depressing impression on me, since everything was still different as I had imagined. [...] I spent three days in Luanda and slowly got used to half-finished houses, ever changing scents, and auto wrecks along the roads."[97]

Similarly, the misery observed among Angolans was addressed throughout the diaries, raising the awareness of "how much help this country needed to eliminate all the poverty still present."[98] This writer's explicit disgust with the presence of "shoe shine boys" is telling because their service represented to him the continuation of exploitative economic structures in a post-colonial setting. As it was not possible to criticize the MPLA's nascent socialism, such continuing deficiencies were understood and presented as remnants of capitalism or neo-colonialism.

Indeed, the writers of the *Brigadetagebücher* often pointed to Angolan "backwardness," "ignorance," and even "darkness" in opposition to East German progress showcasing how myriad forms of hierarchical thinking were beneath the language of solidarity.[99] Adopting the anti-colonial discourse common in the GDR, they located the causes of these miseries in the legacies of Portuguese colonial rule. These were discovered and discussed by the *Brigadisten* in reports on excursions to the splendor of churches, graveyards, or resorts of the colonial era juxtaposed with concrete impressions of hardships, for example in leprosy villages. Reassuringly, these contradictions were about to be overcome by the MPLA state with the active support of the *Brigaden* themselves.[100]

Against the backdrop of their perceptions of Angolan "backwardness," many writers in the *Tagebücher* expressed their own humanitarian concern and desires

---

[96] "Anleitung in Bezug auf Sauberkeit und Hygiene," "Neu in N'Dalatando," SAPMO-BArch, DY 24/19129; The term babbittry refers to a kind of narrow-minded self-satisfaction with an unthinking attachment to middle-class values and materialism after the main character in Sinclair Lewis' novel *Babbitt*.
[97] "Die Hauptstadt Angolas macht einen sehr deprimierenden Eindruck auf mich, weil alles noch anders war, wie ich es mir vorgestellt hatte. [...] Mit diesen Eindrücken verbrachte ich drei Tage in Luanda und gewöhnte mich langsam an halbfertige Häuser, ständig wechselnde Gerüche und Autowracks am Straßenrand." "Erste Eindrücke," SAPMO-BArch, DY 24/19129. Next to the here mentioned smell the unpunctuality of life in Angola was another frequently invoked negative impression.
[98] "Meine Einreise in die VR Angola und die Fahrt nach Uíge," SAPMO-BArch, DY 24/20213.
[99] "Meine Einreise in die VR Angola und die Fahrt nach Uíge," SAPMO-BArch, DY 24/20213; "Hospitation in der Patenklasse," SAPMO-BArch, DY 24/20214; "O.M.A. Die Teilnahme der angolanischen Frau an den Aufgaben der Revolution," SAPMO-BArch, DY 24/20215.
[100] "Hospitation in der Patenklasse," SAPMO-BArch, DY 24/20214; "Stadtrundfahrt in Luanda," SAPMO-BArch, DY 24/19129.

to relieve Angolans from the starkest effects of poverty. The occasions of such reflections were found in the handover of donations, for example of clothes collected in the GDR, collective work services, or visits to partner classes in Angolan schools. The *Brigadisten* showered neighboring children, clothed them or fed them with German-style sandwiches (*Stullen*).[101] Individual brigade members thereby set up their own "aid projects" reflective of their self-image as benefactors. This certainly attests to the potential for independent positioning among brigade members.

Despite the fact that individual *Brigadisten* put their own emphases in their activities, the personal reflections in the *Brigadetagebücher* expectedly did not criticize the politics of GDR solidarity. The Angolan partners were not directly criticized either. Their praise, for example of the "open atmosphere" in Angolan political conventions, is telling, however. It points to the opinion of individual *Brigadisten* that such a spirit was lacking in their own organization.[102]

The futility of relief as well as work efforts,[103] not least due to the lack of supplies, found frequent expression in the diaries. Open dissatisfaction and doubts seemed acceptable in a context that explicitly subscribed to the pursuit of solidarity duties and their insufficient fulfillment. Brigade members, the initially quoted poet Rudi among them, often criticized the lack of spare parts. The expressions of discontent even extended to direct, collectively voiced criticism of the organizational priorities among superiors. This was the case when assigned tasks did not seem to align with the brigades' central objective and their Angolan partners' assumed main interest to maintain trucks: "One was not pleased, however, that just in the last week of our deployment [...] a part of our *Brigadisten* was kept from repairing the ENAMA trucks. [...] Whether this was actually necessary? On whose costs is surely beyond question—isn't it???"[104]

---

101 "1. Juni 1983," SAPMO-BArch DY 24/20215; "Kinderfest auf unserer Basis," SAPMO-BArch, DY 24/19129; see also "Aus dem täglichen Leben der FDJ-Freundschaftsbrigade Gabela," SAPMO-BArch, DY 24/20215.

102 "Gewerkschaftsversammlung mit der UNTA," SAPMO-BArch, DY 24/20215.,

103 "Gedanken zum Weltgesundheitstag am 7. April 1983," SAPMO-BArch, DY 24/20215, "Werkstattkollegen August und Manuel," SAPMO-BArch, DY 24/20215.

104 Please note the use of the German neuter pronoun in this case of collectively voiced criticism. "Nicht erfreut war man jedoch das ausgerechnet in der letzten Woche unseres Einsatzes [eine Maßnahme] einen Teil unserer Brigadisten von Reparaturen [...] fernhielt. [...] Ob das wohl nötig war? Auf wessen Kosten wohl steht außer Frage – oder???" "Kraftakt – auf wessen Kosten???" SAPMO-BArch, DY 24/20215. The *Empresa Nacional e Mecanização Agrícola* (ENAMA), National Enterprise for the Mechanization of Agriculture, was the brigades' economic partner.

Conclusion

The diaries reflect a variety of "socialist encounters" between the *Freundschaftsbrigaden* and their Angolan colleagues or political partners as well as their consequences. Within this context, this contribution has focused on the expressed subjectivities of the *Brigadisten*, presenting a range of perspectives originating in solidarity conceptions common in the GDR, but also emerging from their experiences on the spot in their temporary Angolan workplaces. Overall, the individual reflections of *Brigadisten* on their service were shaped by their emphasis on the impact of their work and on their position mediating the technologies to overcome the assumed "ignorance" of the Angolan society as well as relieving Angolans of crass expressions of misery.

The *Brigadisten* believed it their mission to help "modernize" a MPLA-ruled Angola along socialist lines. Regarding their work assignments, they emphasized skills and concrete techniques of management known from the GDR as solutions to be adopted and adapted in the nascent socialist economy of Angola. In their living environments, the *Brigadisten* were acutely unsettled by the encountered social realities of Angolan life in response to which they spontaneously took on the responsibility to provide aid, for example through concrete humanitarian action. Such relief efforts as well as the fact that the *Brigadisten* saw themselves as "agents of modernization" at the workplace reaffirmed hierarchical relations between the East German benefactors and their supposedly dependent beneficiaries. This stood in an uneasy relationship with the equality proclaimed as a basic principle of solidarity by the GDR's leadership, but can still be rooted within the contradictory implications of the solidarity concept.[105]

Schematic portrayals of their Angolan counterparts remained prevalent in the "diaries." These sources therefore are in many instances of limited use to understand the reciprocal effects of the relations; in their unilateral nature they mostly hint at certain entanglements. Moving on from this study, it would be crucial to find ways to account for the question of how African actors (re)produced, reflected, and rejected specific perspectives on solidarity relations in co-dependence and interaction with their Eastern "friends," whom they often located in the global North given their relative wealth.[106]

---

105 Bayertz, *Solidarität*, 49.
106 The impressions of Angolans and Mozambicans studying in the GDR are emphasized in Marcia C. Schenck, "A Chronology of Nostalgia: Memories of Former Angolan and Mozambican Worker Trainees to East Germany," *Labor History* 59 (2018): 1.

Still, despite their imbalances and limitations in portraying African actors and dynamics of entanglements, the sources give a clear indication of the positioning of the East German *Brigadisten*. The image of the Angolan realities presented in the diaries positively reflected on the GDR through the lens of solidarity. The service in Angola had the potential to stabilize the East German order in the minds of *Brigadisten* since Angolan misery proved to them how much material progress had already been achieved in the GDR, for example in the social sector: "Our life and our work in a developing country is instructive to us all and fills us with gratitude and recognition of our socialist health care and its achievements."[107]

Yet, the brigade members did not present themselves as actors in a pressing ideological confrontation—although correspondent reflections on anti-colonialism and anti-imperialism would have seemed self-evident concerns in the context of the internationalized civil war in Angola. Whereas Toni Weis identifies a "politics machine" at work in the GDR's solidarity discourse and practices, the diary entries of the *Brigadisten* do not transmit an explicitly "politicized" understanding or ideologized expressions of their activities, focusing on actual mechanics of aid instead. The GDR leadership's official politicized statements of solidarity co-existed with the brigade members' emphasis on managing the concrete challenges to (socialist) modernization. Thereby, they established their own "working misunderstanding" within the structure of the *Freundschaftsbrigaden*, accommodating quite different emphases in interpretations of the GDR's role in Angola, even if both were within the scope of international solidarity at large.

The brigade members' assumed role as agents of modernization partly confirms Westad's emphasis on interventions in the name of modernization as a useful frame for the interpretation of the global Cold War. The diaries do, however, challenge Westad's focus on pronouncedly ideological, that is explicitly political, interpretations of such modernization and, by consequence, diminish the importance of competition with its capitalist or imperialist variation for the case of the *Brigadisten*. Although it was a self-evident opportunity to fill the space of the "diaries" with cliché phrases of anti-imperialism, the *Brigadisten* did not engage in political rhetoric.[108] Rather, their writing highlights the impact of a "de-

---

107 "Unser Leben und unsere Arbeit in einem Entwicklungsland ist für uns alle sehr lehrreich u. erfüllt uns mit Dank u. Anerkennung für unser sozialistisches Gesundheitswesen und seine Errungenschaften." "Gedanken zum Weltgesundheitstag am 7. April 1983," SAPMO-BArch, DY 24/20215; "Tag des Gesundheitswesens," SAPMO-BArch, DY 24/19129.
108 While it is certainly hardly possible to interpret 'modernization' with its baked-in teleology and aspirations in non-ideological terms and thereby extract ideology from it, my argument is

velopmentalist paradigm" understood as a "humanitarian mission of modernization" as the guiding interpretation of their experiences in the postcolonial world.[109] In this spirit, the brigade poet Rudi concluded the typical brigade member's accomplishments relating to their perceived modernizing as well as humanitarian mission to the occasion of their "disentanglement," their heaving out:

> Du lerntest wahre Not erkennen,
> warst stets bereit Dich zu bekennen.
> Tratst ein für Fortschritt und Verstand,
> und gabst dein Wissen unverwandt.
>
> You came to see real distress,
> you were ever ready to profess.
> You stood up for progress and reason.
> and steadfastly, you gave your ken.[110]

Bibliography

Bayertz, Kurt. *Solidarität: Begriff und Problem*. Frankfurt: Suhrkamp, 1998.
Bergerol, Jane, and Michael Wolfers. *Angola in the Frontline*. London: Zed Press, 1983.
Bhagavan, M. R. "Establishing the Conditions for Socialism: The Case of Angola." In *Africa: Problems in the Transition to Socialism*, edited by Barry Munslow. London: Zed, 1986.
Birmingham, David. "Angola." In *A History of Postcolonial Lusophone Africa*, edited by Patrick Chabal, 137–185. London: Hurst, 2002.
Brock, Lothar, and Hans-Joachim Spanger. *Die beiden deutschen Staaten in der Dritten Welt: Die Entwicklungspolitik der DDR – eine Herausforderung für die Bundesrepublik Deutschland?* Opladen: Westdeutscher Verlag, 1987.
Burton, Eric. "Solidarität und ihre Grenzen: Die Brigaden der Freundschaft der DDR." In *Internationale Solidarität: Globales Engagement in der Bundesrepublik und der DDR*, edited by Frank Bösch, Caroline Moine, and Stefanie Senger, 152–185. Göttingen: Wallstein Verlag, 2018.
Büschel, Hubertus. *Hilfe zur Selbsthilfe: Deutsche Entwicklungsarbeit in Afrika 1960–1975*. Frankfurt: Campus, 2014.
Cooper, Frederick. *Colonialism in Question: Theory, Knowledge, History*. Berkeley: University of California Press, 2005.
Engerman, David. "Development Politics and the Cold War." *Diplomatic History* 41 (2017): 1–19.

---

that the expressly ideological conflict of the Cold War played a diminished role in this case. For the relevant take on modernization, please see Cooper, *Colonialism in Question*, 113–149.
109 For the establishment of this paradigm see Katrina M. Hagen, "Internationalism in Cold War Germany," (Ph.D. diss., University of Washington, 2008), 42.
110 "Abschied von N'dalantando!" SAPMO-BArch, DY 24/19129.

Fauvet, Paul. "Angola: The Rise and Fall of Nito Alves." *Review of African Political Economy* 4 (1977): 88–104.
FDGB-Lexikon. s.v. "Neuererbewegung." Berlin 2009. Accessed August 8, 2020. http://library.fes.de/FDGB-Lexikon/texte/sachteil/n/Neuererbewegung.html.
"Franke." "Mein Angola 1984." Angola Forum. Accessed January 21, 2020. http://www.angola-forum.de/thread.php?board=3&thread=1.
Gleijeses, Piero. *Visions of Freedom: Havana, Washington, Pretoria and the Struggle for Southern Africa, 1976–1991*. Chapel Hill: University of North Carolina Press, 2016.
Gödeke, Ulrike. "Zwischen brüderlicher Hilfe und allseitiger Stärkung der DDR: Die Freundschaftsbrigaden der FDJ in Afrika 1964 bis 1990." Diploma thesis, Freie Unversität Berlin, 2002.
Hagen, Katrina M. "Internationalism in Cold War Germany." Ph.D. dissertation, University of Washington, 2008.
Harisch, Immanuel R. "Bartering Coffee, Cocoa and W50 Trucks: The Trade Relationships of the GDR, Angola and São Tomé in a Comparative Perspective." *Global Histories* 3 (2017): 43–59.
Harisch, Immanuel R. "Handel und Solidarität: Die Beziehungen der DDR mit Angola und São Tomé und Príncipe unter besonderer Berücksichtigung des Austauschs 'Ware-gegen-Ware' ca. 1975–1990." Master's thesis, Universität Wien, 2018.
Harisch, Immanuel R. "East German Friendship-Brigades and Specialists in Angola: A Socialist Globalization Project in the Global Cold War." In *Transregional Connections in the History of East Central Europe*, edited by Katja Naumann. Berlin: de Gruyter, forthcoming 2021.
Harisch, Immanuel R., and Eric Burton. "Alltagszeugnisse sozialistischer Globalisierung: Die Tagebücher der DDR-Freundschaftsbrigaden." Unpublished manuscript. Forthcoming in *Zeithistorische Forschungen*.
Hatzky, Christine. *Cubans in Angola: South-South Cooperation and Transfer of Knowledge, 1976–1991*. Madison: University of Wisconsin Press, 2015.
Lorenzini, Sara. *Global Development: A Cold War History*. Princeton: Princeton University Press, 2019.
Mählert, Ulrich, and Gerd-Rüdiger Stephan. *Blaue Hemden – Rote Fahnen: Die Geschichte der Freien Deutschen Jugend*. Opladen: Leske und Budrich, 1996.
MDR.de. "Mit einer FDJ-Freundschaftsbrigade in Angola." January 31, 2011. Accessed November 25, 2019. https://www.mdr.de/damals/archiv/artikel105354.html.
Movimento Popular de Libertação de Angola. "História Da JMPLA." Accessed November 25, 2019. http://www.mpla.ao/jmpla.39/historia.40.html.
Reichel, Thomas. *'Sozialistisch arbeiten, lernen und leben': Die Brigadebewegung in der DDR (1959–1989)*. Köln: Böhlau, 2011.
Roesler, Jörg. "Berichtsbuch, Beschwerdeschrift oder Bilderfolge? Unterschiedliche Vorstellungen zum Inhalt von Brigadetagebüchern in den Anfangstagen der 'sozialistischen Kollektive.'" In *Vorwärts und nichts vergessen. Sprache in der DDR – was war, was ist, was bleibt*, edited by Ruth Reiher and Antje Baumann, 206–214. Berlin: Aufbau, 2004.
Schenck, Marcia C. "A Chronology of Nostalgia: Memories of Former Angolan and Mozambican Worker Trainees to East Germany." *Labor History* 59 (2018): 352–374.

Schenck, Marcia C. "Negotiating the German Democratic Republic: Angolan Student Migration During the Cold War, 1976–90." *Africa* 89 (2019): 144–166.

Schleicher, Hans-Georg. "The German Democratic Republic (GDR) in the Liberation Struggle of Southern Africa." In *Southern African Liberation Struggles 1960–1994: Contemporaneous Documents*, edited by Arnold Temu and Joel das Neves Tembe. Dar es Salaam: Mkuki na Nyota, 2014.

Schleicher, Ilona. "Elemente entwicklungspolitischer Zusammenarbeit in der Tätigkeit von FDGB und FDJ." In *Entwicklungspolitische Zusammenarbeit in der Bundesrepublik Deutschland und der DDR*, edited by Hans-Jörg Bücking. Berlin: Duncker & Humblot, 1998.

Scott, James C. *Seeing like a State: How Certain Schemes to Improve the Human Condition Have Failed.* New Haven: Yale University Press, 1998.

Shubin, Vladimir. *The Hot 'Cold War': The USSR in Southern Africa.* London: Pluto Press, 2008.

Somerville, Keith. *Angola: Politics, Economics, and Society.* London: Pinter Publishers, 1986.

Tvedten, Inge. *Angola: Struggle for Peace and Reconstruction.* Boulder: Westview, 1997.

Unfried, Berthold. "Instrumente und Praktiken von 'Solidarität' Ost und 'Entwicklungshilfe' West: Blickpunkt auf das entsandte Personal." In *Die eine Welt schaffen: Praktiken von 'Internationaler Solidarität' und 'Internationaler Entwicklung.'*, edited by Berthold Unfried and Eva Himmelstoss, 73–98. Leipzig: Akademische Verlagsanstalt, 2012.

van der Heyden, Ulrich. "FDJ-Brigaden der Freundschaft aus der DDR – die Peace Corps des Ostens?" In *Die eine Welt schaffen: Praktiken von 'Internationaler Solidarität' und 'Internationaler Entwicklung.'*, edited by Berthold Unfried and Eva Himmelstoss, 99–122. Leipzig: Akademische Verlagsanstalt, 2012.

Weis, Toni. "The Politics Machine: On the Concept of 'Solidarity' in East German Support for SWAPO." *Journal of Southern African Studies* 37 (2011): 351–367.

Westad, Odd Arne. *The Global Cold War: Third World Interventions and the Making of Our Times.* Cambridge: Cambridge University Press, 2005.

Westad Odd Arne. "The Cold War and America's Delusion of Victory." *New York Times*, August 28, 2017. Accessed November 25, 2019. https://www.nytimes.com/2017/08/28/opinion/cold-war-american-soviet-victory.html.

Witkowski, Gregory. "Between Fighters and Beggars: Socialist Philanthropy and the Imagery of Solidarity in East Germany." In *Comrades of Color: East Germany in the Cold War World*, edited by Quinn Slobodian, 73–95. New York: Berghahn, 2014.

Katrin Bahr
13 Between State Mission and Everyday Life: Private Photographs of East Germans in Mozambique in the 1980s

As the Second World War came to an end, African colonies underwent tremendous political, social, and economic changes. The colonial powers Great Britain and France saw their economic base severely weakened after the Second World War, as newly founded liberation movements in those colonies began to revolt against their colonial rulers. As a result, most of the formerly colonized African countries achieved independence during the 1960s. Each state, however, faced similar problems in its attempt to overcome colonial legacies and to implement well-suited political systems. While few African countries consciously chose a capitalist path, many African governments at least theoretically pursued one form or another of socialism—derived from the assumption that capitalism was an extension of colonialism and imperialism.[1] Socialism, therefore, was seen as a way to achieve liberation and future development.

Beginning with the armed struggle in 1964, it took the liberation movement *Frente de Libertação de Moçambique* (FRELIMO) until 1975 to achieve political independence in Mozambique. While British and French colonies followed a classic "neocolonial solution," Portugal remained uncompromising and refused to surrender its colonies.[2] Following the Carnation Revolution in Portugal in April 1974, and the uprising in the other Portuguese colonies Angola and Guinea-Bissau, the colonial power was now unwilling and felt increasingly unable to retain its grip on power; ultimately, this condition, paired with FRELIMO's struggle for independence, resulted in the sovereignty of Mozambique on June 25, 1975. Though Portugal's presence in Mozambique was limited to the coastlines and specific trade routes in the hinterland for many centuries, the colonized had suffered greatly under the Portuguese, including from the exploitation of its people and resources to other foreign interests; forced labor and slavery, underdevelopment in the agricultural and economic sectors, illiteracy, malnutri-

---

[1] Allen F. Isaacman and Barbara Isaacman, *Mozambique: From Colonialism to Revolution* (Boulder: Westview Press, 1985), 3; Bruce R. Bartlett, "Capitalism in Africa: A Survey," *The Journal of Developing Areas* 24 (1990).
[2] John S. Saul, *A Difficult Road: The Transition to Socialism in Mozambique* (New York: Monthly Review Press, 1985), 9.

OpenAccess. © 2021 Katrin Bahr, published by De Gruyter. This work is licensed under the Creative Commons Attribution 4.0 International License. https://doi.org/10.1515/9783110623543-013

tion, tribalism, and racism had turned Mozambique into one of the poorest African countries.[3]

The experience of Portuguese colonialism, marked by economic exploitation, and the foreseen threat of neighboring anti-communist countries, led FRELIMO to direct its political mission towards socialist countries and to establish a "Socialism with a Mozambican face."[4] One of FRELIMO's allies was the German Democratic Republic (GDR)—which, due to the West German Hallstein Doctrine, itself struggled for state recognition since 1955. First contacts between the GDR's ruling Socialist Unity Party (SED) and FRELIMO were established in the 1960s when the East German government agreed to train Mozambican FRELIMO fighters in the GDR, financed by the Solidarity Committee of the GDR.[5] Additionally, a handful of East German specialists[6] were sent to Mozambique to teach in the camps of FRELIMO.[7] The exodus of Portuguese settlers on the eve of Mozambique's political independence left the country devastated with neither trained personnel nor the infrastructure and technical equipment to reconstruct its economy. Based on the cordial relations established during FRELIMO's liberation struggle, the SED government intensified its collaboration with Mozambique. Those first socialist encounters led to the signing of the Treaty of Friendship (*Freundschaftsvertrag*) on February 24, 1979.[8] Furthermore, they strengthened the relations between the two countries and paved the way for thousands of East German specialists and their families who would visit the country over the next ten years.[9] In the GDR's official discourse, these specialists arrived under the prospect of international solidarity. As a concept, international solid-

---

[3] Saul, *A Difficult Road*, 36–48; Isaacman and Isaacman, *Mozambique*, 3, 27–60.
[4] Isaacman and Isaacman, *Mozambique*, 3; Saul, *A Difficult Road*, 9–31.
[5] See Ilona Schleicher, "Berufsbildung und Wirtschaftsbeziehungen der DDR-Mosambik," in *Engagiert für Afrika: Die DDR und Afrika II*, ed. Ulrich van der Heyden, Ilona Schleicher, and Hans-Georg Schleicher (Münster: Lit, 1994), 179–180; Hans-Georg Schleicher, "The German Democratic Republic (GDR) in the Liberation Struggle of Southern Africa," in *Southern African Liberation Struggles: Contemporaneous Documents, 1960–1994*, ed. A. J. Temu and Joel das Neves Tembe (Dar es Salaam, Tanzania: Mkuki na Nyota Publishers, 2014), 507–598.
[6] In the bureaucratic jargon of the GDR, the term specialist (*Spezialist*) referred to citizens working abroad.
[7] Matthias Voß, "Um de nós – einer von uns! Gespräch mit Achim Kindler, der als Lehrer im Auftrag des Solidaritätskomitees der DDR als erster DDR-Bürger bei der FRELIMO arbeitete," in *Wir haben Spuren hinterlassen! Die DDR in Mosambik: Erlebnisse, Erfahrungen und Erkenntnisse aus drei Jahrzehnten*, ed. Matthias Voß (Münster: Lit, 2005), 34–46.
[8] Schleicher, "Berufsbildung und Wirtschaftsbeziehungen DDR-Mosambik," 179–195.
[9] For more information on the negotiations of the contract labor accord between the GDR and Mozambique and the sending of Mozambican contract workers (*Vertragsarbeiter*) to the GDR see Franziska Rantzsch in this volume.

arity was seen as the counter-project to the Western understanding of development aid, and was interpreted as a relationship among equals; "instead of continuity with the past, it emphasized rupture; instead of otherness, likeness; instead of differentiation, integration; and instead of continuing subjugation, political emancipation."[10] Depending on the work assignments, East German specialists remained in Mozambique for a period of six months to three years, and were deployed across the country, with the majority living in the capital Maputo.[11] Beyond their solidarity, GDR citizens brought their technical knowledge—occupations ranged from railway engineers, mechanics, and bricklayers to teachers, doctors, and geologists. Equipped with their cameras, East Germans took snapshots both at their workplaces and in their domestic environments. Largely, though, the people who took these private photographs were amateurs in our current understanding of the word.

While scholars became increasingly interested in the foreign policy of the GDR in the early 1990s, most of the resulting research remained limited to the political and economic sphere.[12] More recent studies have begun to look at the everyday life experiences of East Germans, focusing on the working and living conditions abroad and the collaborations with their respective counterparts.[13]

---

10 Toni Weis, "The Politics Machine: On the Concept of 'Solidarity' in East German Support for SWAPO," *Journal of Southern African Studies* 37 (2011).

11 They were divided into three groups: *Reisekader* (short-term deployment up to six months and business trips), *Auslandskader* (long-term deployment up to three years), and *FDJ-Brigadisten* (young people from the Free German Youth Brigades, the official youth organization of the GDR). Only the *Auslandskader* and sometimes also the FDJ brigade leaders were allowed to bring along their families (with restriction). See also Jens Niederhut, *Die Reisekader: Auswahl und Disziplinierung einer privilegierten Minderheit in der DDR* (Leipzig: Evangelische Verlagsanstalt, 2005) and Informationen über das Kollektiv der DDR-Bürger in der VRM, Botschaft der DDR in der VRM, Maputo 5.7.1989, Stiftung Archiv der Parteien und Massenorganisationen der DDR im Bundesarchiv, Berlin (henceforth: SAPMO-BArch, DY 30/14095.

12 Some pioneering works worth mentioning are Siegfried Baske and Gottfried Zieger, *Die Dritte Welt und die beiden Staaten in Deutschland* (Asperg: Edition Meyn, 1983); Gareth M. Winrow, *The Foreign Policy of the GDR in Africa* (Cambridge: Cambridge University Press, 1990); Ilona Schleicher and Hans-Georg Schleicher, *Die DDR im südlichen Afrika: Solidarität und Kalter Krieg* (Hamburg: Institut für Afrikakunde, 1997).

13 Iris Christina Obernhummer, "Experten der 'wissenschaftlich-technischen Zusammenarbeit' der DDR in Afrika: Alltag und Lebensweisen zwischen DDR-Richtlinien und angespannter Sicherheitslage in den 1970er und 1980er Jahren" (diploma thesis, University of Vienna, 2010); Hubertus Büschel, *Hilfe zur Selbsthilfe: Deutsche Entwicklungsarbeit in Afrika 1960–1975* (Frankfurt am Main: Campus Verlag, 2014); Alexandra Piepiorka, "Exploring 'Socialist Solidarity' in Higher Education: East German Advisors in Post-Independence Mozambique (1975–1992)," in *Education and Development in Colonial and Postcolonial Africa, Global Histories of Education: Policies, Para-*

Edited volumes that include interviews with former specialists about their experiences in Mozambique established another narrative of the GDR's participation in Africa.[14] Researchers became increasingly interested in the visual representation of everyday life within the GDR, but have not yet looked across the borders of the nation state. While researchers have begun to discuss the representation of international solidarity in official state photographs,[15] scholars have yet to make use of private photographs taken by East Germans documenting socialist encounters, solidarity, and the everyday life in African and other non-European countries.

In this chapter, I show that private photographs are documents of vital importance for the discussion of the GDR's participation in development activities abroad, and, more specifically for this work, in Mozambique. Firstly, private photographs give insights into the different lives of East Germans and their individual interactions and entanglements with Mozambicans. They combine a personal-political message of the state and the photographer's own endeavor to apply international solidarity in that moment and space. The everyday life (*Alltagsleben*)[16] that East Germans experienced abroad contrasted with their lives in the GDR. Importantly, the private pictures that East Germans took serve as a counter narrative to the existing photographs of the *Allgemeiner Deutscher Nachrichtendienst* (ADN)—the main state news agency that published its photographs in various newspapers and magazines.[17] While most of the official photographs only portray the (overwhelmingly male) specialists at work, the private photographs, in contrast, portray a number of aspects of the everyday life abroad that were usually absent in the state-official portrayals. In this context, a more gendered

---

digms, and Entanglements, 1890s–1980s, ed. Damiano Matasci et al. (Cham: Palgrave Macmillan, 2020), 289–318; Alexandra Piepiorka and Eduardo F. Buanaissa, this volume.
14 Two edited volumes should be mentioned here: Matthias Voß, *Wir haben Spuren hinterlassen! Die DDR in Mosambik: Erlebnisse, Erfahrungen und Erkenntnisse aus drei Jahrzehnten* (Münster: Lit, 2005); Hans-Joachim Döring and Uta Rüchel, *Freundschaftsbande und Beziehungskisten: Die Afrikapolitik der DDR und der BRD gegenüber Mosambik* (Frankfurt am Main: Brandes und Apsel, 2005).
15 Büschel, *Hilfe zur Selbsthilfe*, 271–274; Gregory Witkowski, "Between Fighter and Beggars," in *Comrades of Color: East Germany in the Cold War World*, ed. Quinn Slobodian (New York: Berghahn Books, 2015), 73–94.
16 Alf Lüdtke, *Alltagsgeschichte: Zur Rekonstruktion historischer Erfahrungen und Lebensweisen* (Frankfurt: Campus, 2018 [1989]), 21.
17 Photographs addressing the development of African countries can be found in the daily newspapers *Neues Deutschland* (ND) and *Junge Welt* (JW), and the weekly magazine for international politics *Horizont*, *Neue Berliner Illustrierte* (NBI) and the illustrated magazine for women *Für Dich*.

perspective becomes visible. Crucially, the pictures illuminate the various roles of women within the concept of international solidarity and their participation in the preservation of a Eurocentric idea at home. Women are portrayed organizing solidarity bazaars with other socialist countries and undertaking leisurely activities such as knitting *Macramé* (a knitting technique to create wall hangings, tablecloths, and other home furnishings). And finally, while those photographs are private snapshots, they also show how colonial structures were perpetuated by the concept of solidarity. The photographs highlight that the state ideology of anti-racism and anti-colonialism did not hold off the white male gaze but rather assumed a certain superiority towards their subjects of interest.

To substantiate my claims, I will first explore the meaning of photography as a medium that reflects on *Alltagsleben*. In this context, it is important to examine the various genres of photography that were used in the GDR in order to be able to embed private photographs in the broader discourse of GDR amateur photography and its representation of GDR culture. Secondly, I will discuss the representation of East German specialists and their Mozambican counterparts in official state photographs and how those photographs were connected to the understanding of international solidarity and the GDR's state mission. Having set the foundation for the use of photographs to discuss the GDR's involvement in Africa, I will then analyze the meaning of private photographs. During a research trip to Germany in 2016, I received over 2,000 photographs from my German interview partners who were on long-term deployment in Mozambique in the 1980s. Most of these photos came without caption and can therefore only be discussed on an image-based analysis. The photographs discussed in this chapter all appear with context provided by my interview partners—as such, a text-based analysis accompanies these photos. The historical contribution of the aforementioned interviews, however, has to be evaluated critically as they constitute constructions of memories that partly aim to justify one's own action.[18]

Moreover, I discuss photographs of two travel reports published by GDR specialists working in Mozambique during the 1980s. In my analysis, I differentiate between work and leisure time, and show the personal lens East Germans applied when taking photographs. Importantly, I will also include the types of representation of East German women in those pictures. In closing, I trace colonial continuities in both the official and private photographs I have analyzed.

---

18 Cf. Piepiorka and Buanaissa, this volume.

Photographs as a Medium to Document *Alltagsleben*

The use of photography as a medium for documenting everyday life creates a relationship between those people who take and those who view photographs. Pictures taken with a camera are socially distinct objects that exist and interact in a certain time and space, moving between the past and the present, and therefore reflect on the social and cultural experiences of the photographers. They tell stories that are carried on visually and orally. Photographs are social objects that have a certain effect in conveying the stories and experiences of the photographers and incorporate real-life experiences, biographical narratives, and agency.[19]

In evaluating East German photographs, researchers have mainly focused on the artistic or professional photography produced of the SED government.[20] Studies on amateur photographs as part of the state's project mostly refer to the pictures of *Betriebsfotogruppen*, photographic circles which operated in many state-owned companies abbreviated *VEBs* (*Volkseigene Betriebe*).[21] In the 1950s it was the German Cultural Association (*Deutscher Kulturbund*) and the Free German Trade Union Confederation (*Freier Deutscher Gewerkschaftsbund*, aka FDGB), which tried to establish amateur photography (*Hobbyfotografie*) as part of "photo work in the service of socialism,"—a classification that was consequently meant to also control its people.[22] In her book *Greif zur Kamera, Kumpel!*, cultural historian Regine Schiermeyer points out that in the eyes of the GDR

---

[19] Elizabeth Edwards, "Photography and the Material Performance of the Past," *History and Theory* 48 (2009); Elizabeth Edwards and Janice Hart, "Introduction: Photographs as Objects," in *Photographs Objects Histories: On the Materiality of Images*, ed. Elizabeth Edwards and Janice Hart (London: Routledge, 2010); Susan Sontag, *Regarding the Pain of Others* (New York: Picador, 2003), 85; Tina M. Campt, *Image Matter: Archive, Photography, and the African Diaspora in Europe* (Durham/London: Duke University Press, 2012), 6–7.

[20] One of the most recent publications is Candice Hamelin's dissertation "Behind Immaterial and Material Divides: East German Photography 1949–1989" (PhD diss., University of Michigan, 2016).

[21] Regine Schiermeyer, *Greif Zur Kamera, Kumpel! Die Geschichte der Betriebsfotogruppen in der DDR* (Berlin: Ch. Links, 2015), 165–166.

[22] Karin Hartewig, "Einleitung," in *Die DDR im Bild: Zum Gebrauch der Fotografie im anderen deutschen Staat*, ed. Karin Hartewig and Alf Lüdtke (Göttingen: Wallstein, 2004), 10. For a short overview about the *Kulturbund* see also Kurt Ludwig, "Zwischen Anspruch und Anpassung: Der Kulturbund im kulturellen Alltag der DDR," in *Die DDR zwischen Mauerbau und Mauerfall*, ed. Heiner Timmermann (Münster: Lit, 2003), 126–138.

state, amateur photography was an "organized hobby photography with an artistic claim."[23] According to cultural historian Karin Hartewig, the state differentiated between "serious amateur photographers" (*ernsthafte Amateure*) and "unreflective amateur photographers" (*gedankenlose Knipser*), who took pictures for their own private use.[24] The state, however, was more interested in the "serious amateur photographers" who took pictures for their *Brigadetagebücher*, the brigade journals that documented the work of the brigade collective.[25] In contrast to official GDR photographers, the so-called "unreflective amateur photographers" were those who took photographs without a primarily socialist intention, and whose pictures were therefore considered meaningless products.

Researchers have maintained the division between professional and amateur photographs in so far that the former are embedded in the narrative of presumed socialist success and achievement.[26] But it was the "unreflective amateur photographers" who provided their own projections, with niches and forms of expression becoming increasingly important. Art historian Catherine Zuromski defines these private photographs as snapshots that do not belong to a clearly defined genre. A "subjective purity" differentiates them from other photographic genres and challenges the notion of a defined style or convention of any kind based on the plentiful number of photographs and the paradoxes they present.[27] In the case of the GDR, those pictures are individual, non-normative, and unexpected, therefore, in complete contrast to the regime of control and standardization that the East German regime implemented. What makes them so interesting, moreover, is that they are not professionally shot rather sometimes blurred or improperly exposed. Most important is the setting in which they are "viewed, touched, framed, exchanged, discussed, remembered, collected, and, on certain occasions, defaced."[28] By embedding them into social conventions and cultural patterns, the photographs document special events within the sphere of the individual, the family, or immediate relatives and friends. They follow a chronology

---

23 Schiermeyer, *Greif zur Kamera, Kumpel!*, 12.
24 Hartewig, "Einleitung," 10.
25 See Gerhard Henniger, *Zur gesellschaftlichen Wirksamkeit der Amateurfotografie in der DDR: Hinweise und Erfahrungen* (Berlin: Dt. Kulturbund, 1965), 5–6. *Brigadetagebücher* were also kept abroad by the friendship brigades of the FDJ working in African countries like Mali, Guinea, Zanzibar, and Angola. On the *Brigadetagebücher* of various friendship brigades working in Angola see Paul Sprute in this volume.
26 Hartewig, "Einleitung," 11.
27 Catherine Zuromski, *Snapshot Photography: The Lives of Images* (Cambridge: The MIT Press, 2013), 8–9.
28 Zuromski, *Snapshot Photography*, 48.

that reveals the everyday life of the photographers and the people being photographed.

The Power of Images: Official State Photographs

In a 1988 interview conducted with the *Horizont*— a weekly magazine reporting on international politics and economy—Kurt Seibt, chairman of the Central Revision Commission of the SED and Chairman of the Solidarity Committee of the GDR, spoke about the importance of promoting solidarity with other peoples and nations. While the GDR already had a history of almost three decades of solidarity aid in African, Latin American, and Asian countries, Seibt stressed the continuing effort to anchor the idea of solidarity with those countries in the consciousness of the East German population. Although a continuous increase in public donations was fundamental to the solidarity campaigns, it was also considered important "that the unifying idea of solidarity is supported in all collectives and in all families. This is even more effective [...] when we bring our citizens closer to the struggle, the suffering and hopes of the people of Asia, Africa, and Latin America."[29] In this sense, photographs became an important part in showing the struggle in those countries firsthand.[30]

Besides depicting poverty and destruction in the aforementioned regions,— which Susan Sontag describes as a "gazing on other people's reality with curiosity but also detachment"—these photographs also highlighted East German accomplishments.[31] Showing one's own accomplishment was not a new concept and had already accompanied the intrusion of Europeans before the advent of colonialism.[32] In this context, photography was used as a tool "through which

---

[29] "[...] dass die völkerverbindende Idee der Solidarität in alle Kollektive, in alle Familien getragen wird. Das wird um so wirkungsvoller gelingen, [...] wenn wir unseren Bürgern den Kampf, das Leid und die Hoffnungen der Menschen Asiens, Afrikas und Lateinamerikas nahebringen." Ein festes Band von Managua bis Hanoi: interview with Kurt Seibt, chairman of the Central Revision Commission of the Socialist Unity Party of Germany (SED) and chairman of the Solidarity Committee of the GDR, *Horizont*, 8/1988, 3–4. Author's own translation.
[30] For a discussion on the representation of development work in East German newsreels, see also George Bodie in this volume.
[31] Susan Sontag, *On Photography* (New York: Picador, 1973), 55.
[32] See, for instance, Willeke Sandler's article "Deutsche Heimat in Afrika: Colonial Revisionism and the Construction of Germanness through Photography," *Journal of Women's History* 25 (2013), doi:10.1353/jowh.2013.0000; Henrik Stahr, *Fotojournalismus zwischen Exotismus und Rassismus: Darstellungen von Schwarzen und Indianern in Foto-Text-Artikeln deutscher Wochenillustrierter 1919–1939*, (Hamburg: Kovač, 2004).

Europeans sought to establish, stabilize and disseminate concepts about African pasts and imaginaries about African futures."³³ Photographs served as documentation of the work of missionaries in Africa, including their construction of missionary schools and hospitals. Photographs also served to legitimate and illustrate one's own missionary work abroad and were used to raise donations in the home country.³⁴ As scholars Richard Vokes and Darren Newbury state, "the photograph's orientation towards the future emerges not only from the semiotics of their representations but also from the ways in which they are circulated and deployed."³⁵ It is therefore not a surprise that those concepts continued to exist with decolonization and postcolonial independence in the making following the Second World War. While the Cold War saw an arms race between the East and West, it also highlighted competing ideologies. Within this rivalry, both the United States and the Soviet Union used photography as part of their mission in Africa. The resulting images were meant to represent solidarity in building a future that each country had in mind for its African "recipient country".³⁶

The GDR engaged itself in shaping narratives. Solidarity in the GDR was supposed to be everyone's concern, and therefore had to be staged accordingly. The "staging of help" on television and in newspapers and magazines promoted, on the one hand, the willingness of the population to donate. On the other hand, it promoted political and ideological education.³⁷ Portrayals of encounters involving socialist assistance and support were personalized by the faces of East German specialists and the friendship brigades (*Freundschaftsbrigaden*) of the Free German Youth, or FDJ (*Freie Deutsche Jugend*). As historian Hubertus Büschel ar-

---

33 Richard Vokes and Darren Newbury, "Editorial: Photography and African futures," *Visual Studies*, 33 (2018): 2. doi:10.1080/1472586X.2018.1424988. On the definition of images as objects see also Elizabeth Edwards, "Objects of Affect: Photography beyond the Image," *Annual Review of Anthropology* 41 (2012): 221–234, doi:10.1146/annurev-anthro-092611-145708.
34 Joachim Zeller, and Peter Weiss, *Weisse Blicke, schwarze Körper: Afrikaner im Spiegel westlicher Alltagskultur* (Erfurt: Sutton Verlag, 2010); T. Jack Thompson, *Light on Darkness? Missionary Photography of Africa in the Nineteenth and Early Twentieth Centuries* (Grand Rapids, Mich: Eerdmans Publ., 2012); Nina Berman and Klaus Mühlhahn and Patrice Nganang, eds., *German Colonialism Revisited: African, Asian, and Oceanic Experiences* (Ann Arbor: Michigan Press, 2018).
35 Vokes and Newbury, "Editorial: Photography and African futures," 2.
36 Vokes and Newbury, "Editorial: Photography and African futures," 4.
37 Witkowski, "Between Fighter and Beggars," 74–80; Quinn Slobodian, "Socialist Chromatism: Race, Racism, and the Racial Rainbow in East Germany," in *Comrades of Color: East Germany in the Cold War World*, ed. Quinn Slobodian (New York: Berghahn Books, 2015), 23–39. See also Bodie, this volume.

gues, the photographs of the specialists' work abroad created a narrative of the "developed" GDR with a "still-in-development" Africa.[38] According to historian Jürgen Osterhammel, the "civilizing mission" (*Zivilisierungsmission*) from colonial times carries on into the present day.[39] During the Cold War, the civilizing mission transformed into a new developmental strategy of strategic support, the *Hilfe zur Selbsthilfe* or solidarity for self-help, in order to create a lasting order of ideologies from the supporting countries.[40] Education and training was the focus of the GDR's development policies and the success of such solidarity projects was documented in the state's newspapers and magazines. Photographs depicting East Germans with their counterparts often showed East Germans explaining the handling of machinery and equipment to Africans, all while the latter appeared to be watching closely. Africans are thereby depicted as the ones who must pave the path to modernity, to catch up, and to make progress.[41] This is the very same narrative Büschel describes for the West German specialists who appeared in scientific journals and newspapers. The photographs also connect to patterns used in the GDR's representation of work and its worker in the 1950s, in which we often see an experienced worker explaining something to his colleagues gathered around him. The speaker usually points with a distinctive hand gesture at the discussed object, such as a part of a machine. As art historian Agneta Maria Jilek further notes, these types of images were meant to establish an authentic atmosphere of a newly created world.[42]

The theme of labor as a representation of establishing socialism and economic wealth was already incorporated in the state's art photography in the GDR in the 1950s. In doing so, the human being was seen as a major player in the construction of the socialist society and state.[43] This image motif and the creation of the "New Man"—the development of a new socialist personality—were also being used for the development work in African countries. Within these representations, the East German worker was seen as a symbol for the successful

---

38 Hubertus Büschel, "In Afrika helfen: Akteure westdeutscher 'Entwicklungshilfe' und ostdeutscher 'Solidarität' 1955–1975," in *Dekolonisation: Prozesse und Verflechtungen 1945–1990*, ed. Anja Kruke (Bonn: Dietz, 2009), 350.
39 Jürgen Osterhammel, "'The Great Work of Uplifting Mankind'": Zivilisierungsmission und Moderne," in *Zivilisierungsmissionen: Imperiale Weltverbesserung seit dem 18. Jahrhundert*, ed. Boris Barth and Jürgen Osterhammel (Konstanz: UVK, 2005), 422.
40 On the concept of "Hilfe zur Selbsthilfe" see Büschel, *Hilfe zur Selbsthilfe*, 85–115, 116–178.
41 Büschel, "In Afrika helfen," 350; Büschel, *Hilfe zur Selbsthilfe*, 271–274.
42 Agneta Maria Jilek, "'Laßt uns pflügen, laßt uns bauen': Brigadebilder und Typenporträts in der DDR-Fotografie der frühen fünfziger Jahre," in *Die DDR im Blick II: Ein zeithistorisches Lesebuch*, ed. Anja Hertel, Franziska Kuschel, and Markus Böick (Berlin: Metropol, 2012), 151.
43 Jilek, "'Laßt uns pflügen, laßt uns bauen'," 146.

implementation of socialism, whose role now was to pass on the achievements to Africans. Mozambique's first president Samora Machel was eager to adapt this model since he himself believed that the country needed a fresh start by shaking off the shackles of colonialism and focusing on the future and the community to rebuild the country. The internationally deployed friendship brigades—who exported the GDR's socialist worker—were therefore a favored image motif in the representation of the personified development work; their work was not expressed as a contribution of the individual, but as a representation of the collective.[44]

Images of men at work served not only as a statement of productivity, but also as a representation of international solidarity. The East German specialists depicted in official photographs embodied this international solidarity and assistance themselves and served as a personification of development cooperation in a way that GDR citizens "back home," who donated money for the cause, could identify with. Personal stories and experiences were rarely reported in the East German press, and if so, only in smaller local newspapers.[45] The photographs in newspapers and journals usually served as the visual background to report on the merits of the GDR in the development of cooperation.[46] It was important to show the East German donors that GDR specialists utilized their money in a useful and monitored way.[47]

Authenticity also became an indicator for the definition and representation of the "other". As already mentioned, in addition to the motif of the work, which shows the achievements of the GDR, images of the local population also appeared in these newspapers and magazines. The camera captured everything that might be of interest to those at home who supported the solidarity efforts. Those photographs depict the local population in their everyday activities, sometimes staged with people standing in front of their huts, children presenting self-made toys, or children sitting around a table playing with donated toys they received from the Solidarity Committee. For the most part, the photographs also meant to show the cultural differences, for instance children dancing in their traditional costumes. It was the GDR that defined how Mozambique and its citizens would be represented and, moreover, what needed to be seen. The cultural dif-

---

44 See Immanuel R. Harisch and Eric Burton, "Sozialistische Globalisierung: Tagebücher der DDR-Freundschaftsbrigaden in Afrika, Asien und Lateinamerika," forthcoming in *Zeithistorische Forschungen / Studies in Contemporary History*.
45 Interview with a former ADN journalist in Mozambique 1987–1990, conducted on June 15, 2016 in Berlin.
46 See *Junge Generation*, a theoretical magazine of the FDJ, 3–88, 50 and *NBI* 7/82, 29.
47 See *Für Dich*, 10/84, 12, 19.

ferences as presented in those photographs continued to create a picture of colonizer and colonized.[48]

The Power of Images: Everyday Life Abroad

Most of the official state photographs were taken by professionals who were sent to Mozambique by the ADN to document the GDR's projects abroad. Their job assignments were precisely defined, with usually one place and one project to be visited during that time. In contrast, private photographs took on a completely new meaning, as they not only allowed amateur photographers to be their own narrators, but also illustrated how those amateur photographers positioned themselves and others in the context of the political, social, and cultural environment in Mozambique. This "other view" moved away from the state propaganda image towards the portrayal of the everyday life of the individual. In this context, the presented themes, the origin of the photograph, the time when the photograph was taken, and the historical background played decisive roles in narrating these photographs.

Based on the owners of the photographs I received and the subjects depicted in these photographs, one can assume that it was usually the East German men who had their cameras with them at work or when traveling through the country. The main reason for this was the number of East German men deployed abroad, which exceeded the number of women working.[49] However, an interesting question that deserves further research is the question of the male and female gaze and if there was a difference in the pictures taken by women compared with those taken by men. Most of these private photographs were taken as souvenirs to document the workplace and surroundings in Mozambique, and later shared with friends, family or relatives in the GDR. Some of the photographers also showed their pictures in presentations at school or at work after they had re-

---

[48] Homi Bhabha. "Framing Fanon, Foreword," in *The Wretched of the Earth*, ed. Frantz Fanon et al. (New York: Grove Press, 2004 [1961]), ix.

[49] In 1989, 342 East Germans were deployed in Mozambique, 194 of them were men, 135 women, and 13 children. Looking at the positions occupied by East Germans, it becomes clear that the number of working women was below 100. For a specific example see Maputo with the largest group of specialists in the country: APO I (embassy and advisors/65), APO II (Council of Ministers Working Group/47), APO III (department of trade policy/30), APO IV (advisors and specialists/35), APO V (national education/28), APO VI (university/12), Informationen über das Kollektiv der DDR-Bürger in der VRM, Botschaft der DDR in der VRM, Maputo 5.7.1989, SAPMO-BArch, DY 30/14095.

turned. For this purpose, the photos were usually developed as slides to facilitate projection.[50] Although color films were expensive, most of the photos displayed appeared in color. Usually, the film rolls were brought home undeveloped during vacation in the GDR or were given to other East Germans who went home for vacation or whose time abroad had come to an end. This procedure bypassed the formal requirement of the state to have all correspondence (for security reasons) sent through the dispatch of the embassy, as well as random checks for material that the GDR state might find inappropriate and counterproductive for its display of solidarity.[51]

The photographs I analyze span over a period of ten years and show recurring similarities in themes that reflect everyday life of East Germans in Mozambique. Based on those similarities, photographs can be roughly divided into the following categories: family life, work and labor, leisure activities, work collective, nature, and representation of the local population. For this contribution, I focus on the themes of family life, work and labor, leisure activities, and representation of the local population. I argue that these photographs must be viewed in the context of the place and time of the deployment, the profession of the East Germans, and above all, the interest behind the motifs. Due to their work assignments, some East Germans traveled more frequently than others throughout the country, and thus had more opportunities to capture their varying impressions with the camera. As the internationally supported civil war in Mozambique spread in the mid-1980s, excursions into the countryside consequently diminished. These trips came to a complete halt with the vicious attack on nine GDR agriculture specialists on December 6, 1984, in which eight of them died.[52] They had worked at one of the state farms in Lichinga and were ambushed while leaving their homes to drive to the nearby farm they worked at. After this event, the fear for the safety of the East Germans increased. As a result, the photographs that depicted travels of East Germans in the country decreased and photographs of the private sphere came more to the fore. What the photographs also show in that respect is how the safety mea-

---

50 All of the photographs I received from my interview partners came as slides.
51 Interview with former specialist B. about the mailing of film material back to the GDR, conducted on June 2, 2016 in Berlin.
52 Monika Smardz, "Bis zu jenem Tag im Dezember – Eine Farm mitten in der Savanne," in *Wir haben Spuren hinterlassen! Die DDR in Mosambik: Erlebnisse, Erfahrungen und Erkenntnisse aus drei Jahrzehnten*, ed. Matthias Voß (Münster: Lit, 2005), 270–277; Ulrich van der Heyden, "Es darf nichts passieren! Entwicklungspolitisches Engagement der DDR in Mosambik zwischen Solidarität und Risiko," in *Wir haben Spuren hinterlassen! Die DDR in Mosambik: Erlebnisse, Erfahrungen und Erkenntnisse aus drei Jahrzehnten*, ed. Matthias Voß (Münster: Lit, 2005), 278–313.

sures[53] of the GDR impacted the everyday life of East Germans, especially when traveling or exploring the city. The photographs prove that East Germans always had to travel in groups, never alone. The existing tense political situation prohibited individual explorations. Therefore, East Germans not only photographed their workplaces, their homes or luxury goods—which they could purchase at the Intershop, a state-run retail store offering high-quality products made in GDR and western goods—but also the attacks or assaults on their workplaces. For example, there are numerous photographs of the Beira-Machipanda railway line, where the tracks and a bridge were constantly being destroyed. They also photographed gatherings and private parties with Mozambicans, contacts that they were not officially allowed to have.[54]

The Photographer: The Moving Self

While official state photographs provide a very clear and defined portrayal of development work by depicting projects on site and their impact on the Mozambican society, private photographs offer personal insights into the lives of East German specialists and their relationships with their Mozambican colleagues. In some of these photographs, the viewers are presented with group shots in which they can learn about the working environment and which encourage them to reflect on stories of collaboration and friendship.

Figure 1 shows a group shot of 14 Mozambican students with their East German teacher Rainer Grajek posing in front of the *Centro de Formação dos Instrutores*, the Trainee Center for Teachers in Maputo. Grajek was sent to train the students to become teachers in history and Marxism-Leninism.[55] After a successful completion of the course, the students were then sent out to the countryside to teach their own classes. It is noticeable to the observer that most of the students are men. The photograph also shows two younger children, a baby resting on the

---

[53] Mitteilung der Abteilung Auslandsdienstreisen Nr. 02/1988, Schulungsmaterial zu den "Grundsätzen und Hinweisen für die Vorbereitung dienstlicher Reisen und für das Verhalten von dienstlich im Ausland weilenden Bürgern der DDR," SAPMO-BArch, DC 20/11976.
[54] Mitteilung der Abteilung Auslandsdienstreisen Nr 02/1988, SAPMO-BArch, DC 20/11976.
[55] When Grajek first met the national director for the cadre training program in the Ministry of Education, the director explained to him that the country was in need of teachers. One of the requirements to train good teachers is the availability of qualified instructors. It was for this very reason that Grajek was sent to help train those cadres; Rainer Grajek, *Berichte aus dem Morgengrauen: Als Entwicklungshelfer der DDR in Mosambik* (Großbothen: Bücherwerkstadt & Verlag Ute Vallentin, 2005), 64. For further details on Grajek's deployment in Mozambique see also Piepiorka and Buanaissa in this volume.

Figure 1: Rainer Grajek with his students in front of the Centro de Formação dos Instrutores (Training Center for Teachers) in Maputo. Source: Private Archive R.G.

arm of the East German instructor and a young girl standing in front of her mother. The woman is also the mother of the baby as can be inferred from the fact that she looks to the side to check on her child. She smiles comfortably as she looks at the East German holding her baby. In his memoir *Berichte aus dem Morgengrauen*, we learn about the special relationship between Grajek and that woman, Madalena Lhomulo. Growing up in the countryside, Lhomulo decided to attend missionary school in Lourenço Marques (today Maputo) where she finished the fourth grade in 1972. Due to racial discrimination, she only finished the introductory course in the secondary school she attended. She soon got married and gave birth to her first child. In 1976, she decided to go back to school while pregnant with her second child. After the birth of her third daughter in the 1980s, her husband decided to separate since she had not born him a son. While they were still living together, she gave birth to another child in 1982, this time a boy. However, the husband abandoned the family shortly after which left her alone to take care of their children. To make ends meet, she picked up evening courses and taught in several schools in Maputo. It was also in 1982 when she decided to join a training program to become an official teacher. During this time, she also gave birth to the baby featured in the photograph. Grajek and Lhomulo became very close during the time of the training. Both had children of the same age—a commonality that served as a starting point beyond the regular conversation of homework and work material. She started to take her newborn with her to classes, sometimes accompanied by her younger daughter who looked after her son while she was in class. Grajek and his wife visited Lhomulo several times at the boarding school where she stayed since she was not able to go back to her house in the Maputo suburbs due to war conflict. Grajek was impressed by her energy to juggle the many responsibilities she had to endure, which might have been the reason that he reached out to her. He was aware of her struggle and described it as such in his memoir: "It seemed like she was carrying an invisible weight on her slender, always bent, shoulders. […] When she spoke one recognized optimism and confidence. When you looked into her eyes, you could also see fear."[56] Because women were expected to fulfill the traditional role of caretakers, it is not surprising to see so few women participating in such courses. Grajek wanted her to be successful because he saw her potential. The group pictures, however, allow us to reflect on another aspect of representation; they are never meant to be for the Mozambicans, but rather for the East Germans to draw attention to their students and apprentices. Those photographs not only validated their work abroad but also depicted the "other" again in the binaries of teacher and student, and therefore played an important role in the portrayal of the relationships between the subjects.

Occasionally, the East Germans also had portraits taken of themselves. For the majority of the East Germans, the impressions and experiences they captured in photographs contrasted with their lives in the GDR. Being aware that their work and travel abroad was a one-time opportunity from which most East Germans were excluded, the urge to document life abroad in all its details is understandable. With photographs, every important moment was captured as evidence and memory for later when they would have already returned home. Other photographs document the East Germans individually or with their families in their homes. While most of the East German specialists—who were deployed up to three years—were accompanied by their spouses with or without children, it also happened that the husband left for Mozambique first, followed by his family soon after. It was sometimes also the case that his wife and children had to stay behind during the time of his employment. In this situation, photographs added a visual element to the letters that were sent home. However, in the next photo-

---

56 "Sie schien eine unsichtbare Last auf ihren schmalen, stets etwas gebeugten Schultern zu tragen. […]. Wenn sie sprach, erkannte man ihre Zuversicht. Wer in ihre Augen blickte, sah, dass in ihnen auch Angst wohnte." Grajek, *Berichte aus dem Morgengrauen*, 76.

graph, the East German who worked for the CFM (*Caminhos de Ferro*) in Beira, the Mozambican Ports and Railways authority, had to travel occasionally to various places in the hinterland to help with the installation of railroad tracks.

Figure 2: East German sitting at a table eating. Messica, 1983. Source: Private Archive T.B.

In Figure 2 we see the man sitting at the table and eating. The table is set for only one person. He is cautiously smiling into the camera, ready to dig into his food that was prepared for him by a Mozambican cook. The picture was taken in one of the houses in Ifloma, a woodwork factory in the small town of Messica in central Mozambique, which was turned into a guesthouse after the Swedish specialists—who had built those houses— unexpectedly left. It is a private moment, a portrait photograph, meant to serve as evidence that everything was going well abroad and that wife and family at home did not have to worry about their husband and father. Although those pictures mainly served a private purpose, they also show that the local supply in the northern and central region of Mozambique was more than sufficient with enough meat, fruits, and vegetables at hand. It was the coastal region neighboring Beira that did not receive supplies due to the destruction of the Moatize-Beira railroad and therefore failed to deliver the basic necessities.[57] While the East Germans wanted to support as many projects

---

[57] Jahresbericht 1980, Botschaft der DDR in der VRM, Maputo 5. Februar 1981, Politisches Archiv des Auswärtigen Amtes, Archiv des Ministeriums für Auswärtige Angelegenheiten der DDR, Berlin (henceforth PA AA), M 31 MfAA ZR 1658/83; Helmut Matthes, "Die Beziehungen der DDR-VR Mosambik zwischen Erwartungen und Wirklichkeit: Ein Gespräch," in *Wir haben Spuren hinterlassen! Die DDR in Mosambik: Erlebnisse, Erfahrungen und Erkenntnisse aus drei Jahrzehnten*, ed. Matthias Voß (Münster: Lit, 2005), 12–33.

as possible, the attacks of the resistant movement *Resistência Nacional Moçambicana* (RENAMO), and the small number of specialists working at institutions like the CFM, rendered them unable to sufficiently fulfill the needs for help and assistance. In fact, the coal production in Moatize started to decrease in 1982, and the installation of the textile factory in Mocuba, as well as the railroad corridor Beira-Moatize, were never fully completed.[58]

Where Are the Women? Between Absence and Presence

So far, studies of East Germans abroad have mainly been devoted to the labor of male specialists.[59] Even though women worked as doctors, nurses, and teachers in Africa, their voices remain silent in the portrayal of mostly male specialists in official state photographs.[60] This one-sided view of the male specialists in the workplace is challenged by private photographs. Although the photographers were primarily men, they made East German women in Mozambique visible— in their workplace, domestic environment, and with friends or at outings. One of the main privileges enjoyed by long-term East German specialists was the opportunity to bring their families with them. The prerequisite was that they met certain conditions, such as that they only brought children under or above a certain age, were loyal to the party and in good health. Women who accompanied their husbands on their work assignments were labeled as "accompanying spouses" (*mitreisende Ehepartner*). Although this term was theoretically for both men and women, it became apparent over the years that those co-travelling

---

[58] Heide Künanz, "Das Steinkohleprojekt Moatize zwischen solidarischer Hilfeleistung und kommerziellem Anspruch," in *Die DDR und Afrika: zwischen Klassenkampf und neuem Denken*, ed. Ulrich van der Heyden, Ilona Schleicher, and Hans-Georg Schleicher (Münster: Lit, 1993), 174–191; Matthes, "Die Beziehungen der DDR zur Volksrepublik Mosambik in der Afrikapolitik der DDR," 39–52.
[59] Although material on women's work as specialists abroad is rare, the women's magazine *Für Dich* published on women working within the FDJ friendship brigades, for example a portrait of FDJ brigadier Margitta Bernstein who worked as a nurse in Angola, *Für Dich* 30/84, "Vom Glück helfen zu können," 27–29.
[60] In her 2014 book *Mocambique – Marcou-Nos Para A Vida. Grupo de Mulheres Internacionalistas 1980–1984*, Elisa Fuchs interviewed 15 women who worked in Mozambique as doctors, teachers, urban planners, lawyers, researchers, economists, and as professionals in ministries and public services. Not one of these women was from the former GDR. Fuchs is, however, so far, the only one writing about the deployment of women and their accomplishments in Mozambique.

family members remained mostly women. The photographs show that the accompanying wives shaped how East German men understood their experience in Mozambique. Photographs outside the home were usually connected to the work environments of the husbands. In contrast, photographs inside the home were limited to women and their roles as housewives and mothers. These photographs typically focused on raising children, cooking, or meeting with other women. Photographs of women taking care of their children at home or during outdoor activities are a symbol of all-round childcare, a distraction for women during the day while their husbands were at work. It was a rare occasion that women also worked as specialists if there were children in the household. This housewife existence (*Hausfrauendasein*) contrasted sharply with the situation in the GDR, where the state expected women to work, and where children attended public kindergartens.[61] The photographs also created an image of an GDR idyll abroad including typical East German activities, customs, and traditions, with children playing with an imported toy shop (*Kaufmannsladen*), the documentation of the first day at school with a sugar cone (*Zuckertüte*) in hand, or an Easter egg hunt (*Ostereiersuche*) in springtime. They show the clear assignment of gender roles within the marriage and seemingly fail to show the way in which women also contributed to the success or preservation of the projects in place. Instead, the viewer gets the impression of a protective and patronizing environment, which is reinforced by the man as photographer and decision-maker of the image motifs. The photographs show how men wanted to document women in this way, not how women experienced their lives in Mozambique.

Despite the male gaze of the private photographs that presented women in a domestic role, a few photographs showed East German women's activism in the premise of solidarity. Figure 3 is a collection from a photo album with various photographs stacked together on one page. A detailed look reveals that this collection did not depict one event but rather shots taken at various solidarity bazaars and events organized by these women. The solidarity events were celebrations in which so-called "solidarity packages" sent by the DFD, the Democratic Women's League of the GDR, were officially handed over to the OMM, the Organization of Mozambican Women in the presence of members of the national sec-

---

61 While it is difficult to get an exact number of how many men and women worked in Mozambique, archival material from the Federal Archive in Berlin such as *Kaderakten* and minutes of party meetings show a predominantly male presence. Most of the specialists in consulting positions were men while women filled the jobs of secretaries, teachers, doctors, and nurses.

retariat of the OMM in Maputo and the FRELIMO party.⁶² Other events, such as those seen in Figure 3, were organized by East German women who had accompanied their husbands to Mozambique.

Figure 3: East German women organize a solidarity bazaar with other socialist countries in Maputo. Source: Private Archive K.L.

The above photograph depicts a group of East German women standing in front of the East German flag. They are participating in the annual solidarity bazaar at Maputo's main exhibition site. Every embassy had set up a booth to collect money. East German women sold clothing that they had brought back from the GDR while on vacation.⁶³ The women stand in what seems to be their booth, proudly peering into the camera. Another photograph, which was used as a postcard, gives further information about what these women did: "This was your mom in action at the solidarity bazaar of socialist and sympathizing countries while decorating and setting up the booth. The other person here is the director of Intercoop, who coordinated the whole thing as the advertising expert. We were sweating which, fortunately, you can't see. But what you can see is your mother

---

62 Zusammenarbeit des DFD mit der Organisation der Mocambiquanischen Frau (OMM), Delegationsaustausch – Solidaritätssendungen, 1986–1988, SAPMO-BArch, DY 31/1461.
63 Interview with former accompanying wife L., conducted on April 27, 2016 in Petershagen.

aging (unfortunately)."⁶⁴ This postcard was sent to one of the women's children who had stayed at home. Instead of sending a letter that would describe the day of the solidarity bazaar, she decided to illustrate the event in form of a photograph as a documentation of her being "in action." Informing the children about their mothers' work abroad showed that the East German women in Mozambique understood themselves as part of the political project of promoting socialism and did not see themselves as mere domestic caregivers.

Private Photographs and the "Other": Mozambique and Mozambicans

As mentioned previously, official photographs taken by photo agencies played into the GDR's concept of solidarity and willingness to donate to legitimize its expatriates' work abroad. Representations of Africa and Africans in photographs and texts gave the GDR an opportunity to have their citizens reflect upon their own privileged living conditions, especially in times of crises, when East Germans would disapprove the state's policies or travel restrictions. The interplay of inferiority and superiority became particularly important through the representation of the "Other."⁶⁵ Like the Soviet Union, the GDR struggled with its presence in Africa and the complex entanglements of race, exoticization, otherness, and stereotyping when the ideology—internationalism, solidarity, and humanist communism—clashed with realities on the ground.⁶⁶

So, how do the private photographs fit into the concept of "othering"? And how were Mozambique and Mozambicans portrayed in the photographs? In his 2011 book *Unter Moçambicanern: Arbeit – Leben – Abenteuer, 1979–1985*, Udo Heiland, an East German specialist who worked for the planning commission in Maputo, describes one of his encounters with Mozambican women as follows: "As I started to take pictures of them, they got cranky and I stopped. There would

---

64 "Das war Eure Mutter in Aktion beim Solibasar der sozialistischen und sympathisierenden Länder beim Ausgestalten und Aufbau des Standes. Der andere Akteur ist der Leiter Intercoop, der als Werbefachmann natürlich den Hut aufhatte. Wie wir dabei geschwitzt haben, sieht man leider nicht, aber wie Eure Mutter eben auch älter wird (leider)." Postcard from L. to her children, date unknown, private archive. Author's own translation.
65 Stuart Hall, "Die zwei Paradigmen der Cultural Studies," in *Widerspenstige Kulturen: Cultural Studies als Herausforderung*, ed. Karl H. Hönring and Rainer Winter (Frankfurt/M.: Suhrkamp, 1999), 13–42.
66 Quinn Slobodian, "Introduction," in *Comrades of Color: East Germany in the Cold War World*, ed. Quinn Slobodian (New York: Berghahn Books, 2015), 3.

be another opportunity later. Some black people at the beach seemed to be more open-minded. They sat in the water up to their belly and chuckled like children. (…) One of those beauties even spoke a few words of German."[67]

As Heiland's observation shows, there was no need for a visual representation to imagine the described scene. Above all, this statement clearly illustrates how many East German men chose their photo subjects and how they captured them. In that context, the photographs support Susan Sontag's argument that the camera is a weapon that can "intrude, trespass, distort, and exploit."[68] The East Germans' photographs illustrate that taking pictures is more than just an innocent encounter. Instead, the encounter between the photographer —the GDR specialist on the one side and the Mozambican being photographed on the other—resembles a photographic assault, an invasion, in which the Mozambican women and men are at the photographer's mercy. The general interest of getting to know the "Other" has not remained merely in silent observation, on walks, shopping in the city, or writing about what those specialists experienced. Instead, everything is documented in photographs. They show what the feminist and film scholar Ann Kaplan meant in distinguishing between two concepts of observing someone or something: the "look" and the "gaze". While the former can be attributed to a process of seeing and observing in a way to understand one's own surroundings and relations to people, the latter receives special attention in a postcolonial discourse. The gaze here describes a "one-way subjective vision."[69] As an active process, the gaze consumes the subject's own anxiety, whereby the object becomes a threat.[70] In particular, traveling promotes an awareness of one's own national identity: "People's identities when they are traveling are often more self-consciously national than when they stay home. In addition, travel provokes conscious attention to gender and racial difference."[71] In their travels and excursions to the countryside, East Germans participated in this kind of gaze.

---

67 "Als ich sie fotografieren wollte, hatten sie sich zickig, und ich ließ es sein. Es würde sich später noch Gelegenheit finden. Aufgeschlossener waren einige Schwarze am Strand. Sie saßen bis zum Bauch im Wasser und freuten sich wie Kinder, als wir ein Gespräch mit ihnen begannen. Eine der Schönen sprach sogar einige Brocken Deutsch." Udo Heiland, *Unter Moçambicanern: Arbeit – Leben – Abenteuer, 1979–1985* (Leipzig: Engelsdorfer Verlag, 2013), 40. Author's own translation.
68 Sontag, *On Photography*, 13.
69 Anne E. Kaplan, *Looking for the Other: Feminism, Film, and the Imperial Gaze* (New York: Routledge, 1997), xvi.
70 Kaplan, *Looking for the Other*, xviii.
71 Kaplan, *Looking for the Other*, 6.

Most of the photographs reveal the surprise or discomfort of Mozambicans. They are photographed from close up or far away, and it seems that most of the shots were taken without asking for permission. In his 2013 travel memoir *Als Auslandskader in Mosambik*, the East German specialist Günter Mosler, who worked in the coalmine in Moatize during the 1980s, includes a series of photographs portraying his Mozambican colleagues.[72] Those workers are seemingly placed in front of huts, be it in front of their own homes or local shops. All of them are depicted in the narrative of a "simple lifestyle". While Mosler refers to the house of one of his colleagues as *Hütte* (hut), another photograph showing Mosler's wife, their poodle Buffy, and his friends in front of their house which he captions as *casa* (house). We then observe how their privileged lifestyle is interrupted by begging children. To visually underpin the situation, Mosler introduces us to a 14-year-old boy named Boa Tard[e], Portuguese for "Good Afternoon". However, it is not only Boa Tard[e] begging for food, but he and his team, as Mosler captioned the picture he took of the group. The team refers to a situation that Mosler's wife experienced when she gave two begging children some bread, only to return later to a group of 20 children screaming and asking for food. This seemingly terrifying moment is then reinforced through the detailed description of Boa Tard[e] dressed in rags, smelling miserably with his feet and hands covered in wounds.[73]

Another method of taking authentic snapshots with the locals was to make use of one's own children. The natural urge of children to play with other children, who, in contrast to their parents, did not have to worry about a communication ban with the Mozambican population, served as a perfect basis for snapshots of everyday life. While some East Germans had no problems with their children playing with Mozambican children, there were some incidents in which women complained about the lack of hygiene of Mozambican children and their fear of diseases.[74] However, the photographs that show East German children together with Mozambican children suggest that the separate housing arrangements of the East Germans in Mozambique did not impact the everyday relationships and contacts, at least when it came to children.

---

[72] Günter Mosler, *Als DDR-Auslandskader in Mosambik, 1979–1982: Zwischen Dschungel, Taiga, Savanne, Wüste und Heimat* (Leipzig: Engelsdorfer Verlag, 2013), 48, 51, 53.
[73] Mosler, *Als DDR-Auslandskader in Mosambik (1979–1982)*, 61.
[74] Interview with accompanying wife G. about her life in Mozambique, conducted on November 29, 2015 in Riesa.

Figure 4: Two East German children with a Mozambican boy. Beira 1984. Source: Private archive T.B.

Often, the locals that were photographed were unknown to the photographer.[75] Instead, they served as a general representation of the country and its people. In Figure 4, two East German children seem to be looking confidently into the camera; in contrast, the Mozambican adolescent looks into the camera reluctantly and his body language seems to be more defensive and insecure. This appearance of reluctance and discomfort can be seen in many other pictures as well. Although colonialism had in practice vanished, the memories and the various practices of how colonialism was implemented were still very present—especially in Mozambique. This trauma is described by Frantz Fanon as a constant state of anxiety in which the colonized looks for signs that place him in the racially divided world.[76] In this vein, Mozambicans' encounters and interactions with white Europeans were still affected by the colonial past. While the GDR proudly looked upon its rhetoric of anti-colonialism and anti-racism, the East Germans' awareness of their place in the history of colonialism was largely ignored. For this very reason, the colonial gaze continued.[77] Compared to the photographs depicting labor, in which East Germans pose with their colleagues and apprentices, the above photograph appears staged because there is no apparent relationship

---

75 My interview partners confirmed that photographs with Mozambican children taken at the beach or in the countryside were usually without any personal connection.
76 Bhabha, "Framing Fanon," ix.
77 Zeller and Weiss, *Weisse Blicke, schwarze Körper*, 7.

between the people being photographed. With staging attempts that imitated an anchoring in local life, the East Germans tried to show that they had found entries and moorings in Mozambican society.

Figure 5: East German adolescent boy in front of a group of Mozambican children in Maputo. Source: Private Archive G.K.

The boy in Figure 5 had just arrived in Mozambique to visit his parents. This is one of the cases in which children were not allowed to accompany their parents because they were too old. The composition of this shot is a reminder of the established binaries of colonial representation. The boy is placed in the center of the frame with a group of young children and young adults in the background. It seems that children played at this spot—an opportunity that the East German photographer seized upon by placing his child in front. The photograph suggests that there is no relation between the photographer and the children in the background. Most of the children pay little attention to the photographic setup and seem to be more interested in something going on in the distance. The photograph looks like a collage of two photographs, which is due to the fact that the East German boy is so far away from the group of Mozambican children. Sontag describes such a situation as a duel moment, which "offers [...] both participation and alienation in our own lives and those of others—allowing us to participate, while confirming alienation.[78]

Compared to the young woman's confidence and the other children's indifference in the background of the picture, the East German boy seems to feel uncomfortable, posing with one hand in his pocket. His eyes are focused on the camera, behind which we can imagine the photographer asking him to smile. Although some of the children look intrigued with one young woman posing for the camera, the overall impression is that such encounters with white Europeans were not a rare incident but rather part of their everyday life.[79] Under colonial rule, Mozambicans were consistently objectified due to their racial signifiers. The white gaze, an indicator for power, hegemony, and privilege, is what philosopher George Yancy calls a "historical achievement—a specific historical practice, socially collective and intersubjective, a process that is dutifully maintained."[80] Within this white power, objectification of the black body was normalized. Especially in bigger cities such as Maputo or Beira, or in joint projects such as the coalmine in Moatize the number of international specialists was higher than in the more remote areas in the hinterlands. Assuming that other international specialists took similar photographs, the children were not only used to being photographed but also exposed to the camera's intrusion.

Conclusion: The Use of Private Photographs in the Context of GDR Memory and Beyond

Private photographs reveal what the official GDR rhetoric did not dare to say and what did not fit into the socialist image of the GDR. In fact, private photographs taken by East Germans in Mozambique represent more than just a technology for documenting life; like most technologies, they are themselves powerful agents. The socialist encounters of East Germans with Mozambicans show a different part of the everyday life in the East German society, namely that beyond the state apparatus and enactment. Today, these private photographs are important documents for researchers and even more important for the biographical stories

---

78 Sontag, *On Photography*, 167.
79 There are some studies that focus on body language and how the "look" can be identified as part of resistance. See Viktoria Schmidt-Linsenhoff, *Ethnizität und Geschlecht: (Post-) Koloniale Verhandlungen in Geschichte, Kunst und Medien* (Köln: Böhlau, 2005).
80 George Yancy, *Black Bodies, White Gaze: The Continuing Significance of Race in America* (Lanham: Rowman & Littlefield, 2016), 243.

of people whose lives have changed significantly since reunification. The visual portrayals of the work of East Germans abroad have yet to find access into the collective memory of the GDR.[81] They show how East Germans saw themselves situated in the country among their Mozambican and international colleagues and apprentices, sometimes contrary to what the GDR had tried to implement.[82] Furthermore, the framework of postcolonial theory I have used for analyzing some of the pictures reveals the enormous importance of photographs for investigating the East German relationships with Mozambique and Mozambicans then and now under the premise of Germany's colonial history.

Incorporating private photography into scholarly research challenges four underlying assumptions and opens further fields of research. Firstly, photographs facilitate the understanding of the work and life of East German citizens in the 1980s beyond the narrative of propaganda. This also includes different perspectives, such as that of East German women and their active engagement. Secondly, photographs place the perspectives of family, work, and travel in dialogue with different deployment locations and times that the East Germans spent in Mozambique. Furthermore, they help identify differences and similarities in studies of comparative systems such as those of the Federal Republic of Germany, the former Soviet Union, or other socialist and non-socialist countries that deployed their citizens on the African continent. Finally, an examination of photographs raises the question of how private pictures of East Germans fit into the representation of an "underdeveloped" Mozambique and how they contributed to—or challenged—that narrative. Private photographs can be interpreted as case studies into postcolonialism in their own right. Lastly, the private photographs serve as documentation of Mozambique's construction period as well as its wartime experiences during the 1980s. The photographs firmly place Mozambique within its own context of postcolonial history on the African continent.

---

[81] The same can be said about the memory of Mozambican contract workers (*Vertragsarbeiter*) who returned to Mozambique after the unification of the two Germanys. For more information see Fernando Agostinho Machava's chapter in this volume, and Ibraimo Alberto and Marcia C. Schenck's chapter in this volume.

[82] Including, for instance, travel restrictions, prohibited contacts to international, especially non-socialists colleagues, and individual explorations of a city or countryside.

Bibliography

Baske, Siegfried, and Gottfried Zieger. *Die Dritte Welt und die beiden Staaten in Deutschland*. Asperg: Edition Meyn, 1983.
Bhabha, Homi. "Framing Fanon, Foreword." In *The Wretched of the Earth*, edited by Frantz Fanon, Richard Philcox, and Jean-Paul Sartre, vii–xli. New York: Grove Press, 2004 [1961].
Berman, Nina, Klaus Mühlhahn, and Patrice Nganang, eds. *German Colonialism Revisited: African, Asian, and Oceanic Experiences*. Ann Arbor: Michigan Press, 2018.
Büschel, Hubertus. *Hilfe zur Selbsthilfe: Deutsche Entwicklungsarbeit in Afrika 1960–1975*. Frankfurt am Main: Campus Verlag, 2014.
Büschel, Hubertus. "In Afrika helfen: Akteure westdeutscher "Entwicklungshilfe" und ostdeutscher "Solidarität" 1955–1975." In *Dekolonisation: Prozesse und Verflechtungen 1945–1990*, edited by Anja Kruke, 333–365. Bonn: Dietz, 2009.
Bartlett, Bruce R. "Capitalism in Africa: A Survey." *The Journal of Developing Areas* 24 (1990): 327–350. www.jstor.org/stable/4191873.
Campt, Tina M. *Image Matter: Archive, Photography, and the African Diaspora in Europe*. Durham/London: Duke University Press, 2012.
Döring, Hans-Joachim, and Uta Rüchel. *Freundschaftsbande und Beziehungskisten: Die Afrikapolitik der DDR und der BRD gegenüber Mosambik*. Frankfurt am Main: Brandes und Apsel, 2005.
Edwards, Elizabeth. "Photography and the Material Performance of the Past." *History and Theory* 48 (2009): 130–150.
Edwards, Elizabeth, and Janice Hart, "Introduction: Photographs as Objects." In *Photographs Objects Histories: On the Materiality of Images*, edited by Elizabeth Edwards and Janice Hart, 1–15. London: Routledge, 2010.
Edwards, Elizabeth. "Objects of Affect: Photography beyond the Image." *Annual Review of Anthropology* 41 (2012): 221–234. doi:10.1146/annurev-anthro-092611-145708.
Fuchs, Elisa. *Moçambique: Marcou-nos Para a Vida: Grupo De Mulheres Internacionalistas 1980–1984 Retratos E Depoimentos*. Maputo: Ciedima, 2014.
Grajek, Rainer. *Berichte aus dem Morgengrauen: Als Entwicklungshelfer der DDR in Mosambik*. Großbothen: Bücherwerkstadt & Verlag Ute Vallentin, 2005.
Hall, Stuart. "Die zwei Paradigmen der Cultural Studies." In *Widerspenstige Kulturen. Cultural Studies als Herausforderung*, edited by Karl H. Hönring and Rainer Winter, 13–42. Frankfurt/M.: Suhrkamp, 1999.
Hamelin, Candice. "Behind Immaterial and Material Divides: East German Photography 1949–1989." PhD diss., University of Michigan, 2016.
Harisch, Immanuel R., and Eric Burton. "Sozialistische Globalisierung: Tagebücher der DDR-Freundschaftsbrigaden in Afrika, Asien und Lateinamerika." Forthcoming in *Zeithistorische Forschungen / Studies in Contemporary History*.
Hartewig, Karin. "Einleitung." In *Die DDR im Bild: Zum Gebrauch der Fotografie im anderen deutschen Staat*, edited by Karin Hartewig and Alf Lüdtke, 7–12. Göttingen: Wallstein, 2004.
Heiland, Udo. *Unter Moçambicanern: Arbeit – Leben – Abenteuer, 1979–1985*. Leipzig: Engelsdorfer Verlag, 2013.

Henniger, Gerhard. *Zur gesellschaftlichen Wirksamkeit der Amateurfotografie in der DDR: Hinweise und Erfahrungen.* Berlin: Dt. Kulturbund, 1965.
Isaacman, Allen F., and Barbara Isaacman. *Mozambique: From Colonialism to Revolution.* Boulder: Westview Press, 1985.
Jilek, Agneta Maria. "'Laßt uns pflügen, laßt uns bauen': Brigadebilder und Typenporträts in der DDR-Fotografie der frühen fünfziger Jahre." In *Die DDR im Blick II: Ein zeithistorisches Lesebuch,* edited by Anja Hertel, Franziska Kuschel, and Markus Böick, 145–154. Berlin: Metropol, 2012.
Kaplan, Anne E. *Looking for the Other: Feminism, Film, and the Imperial Gaze.* New York: Routledge, 1997.
Künanz, Heide. "Das Steinkohleprojekt Moatize zwischen solidarischer Hilfeleistung und kommerziellem Anspruch." In *Die DDR und Afrika: Zwischen Klassenkampf und neuem Denken,* edited by Ulrich van der Heyden, Ilona Schleicher, and Hans-Georg Schleicher, 174–191. Münster: Lit, 1993.
Ludwig, Kurt. "Zwischen Anspruch und Anpassung: Der Kulturbund im kulturellen Alltag der DDR." In *Die DDR zwischen Mauerbau und Mauerfall,* edited by Heiner Timmermann, 126–138. Münster: Lit, 2003.
Lüdtke, Alf. *Alltagsgeschichte: Zur Rekonstruktion historischer Erfahrungen und Lebensweisen.* Frankfurt: Campus, 2018 [1989].
Matthes, Helmut. "Die Beziehungen der DDR-VR Mosambik zwischen Erwartungen und Wirklichkeit: Ein Gespräch." In *Wir haben Spuren hinterlassen! Die DDR in Mosambik: Erlebnisse, Erfahrungen und Erkenntnisse aus drei Jahrzehnten,* edited by Matthias Voß, 12–33. Münster: Lit, 2005.
Mosler, Günter. *Als DDR-Auslandskader in Mosambik, 1979–1982: Zwischen Dschungel, Taiga, Savanne, Wüste und Heimat.* Leipzig: Engelsdorfer Verlag, 2013.
Niederhut, Jens. *Die Reisekader: Auswahl und Disziplinierung einer privilegierten Minderheit in der DDR.* Leipzig: Evangelische Verlagsanstalt, 2005.
Obernhummer, Iris Christina. "Experten der 'wissenschaftlich-technischen Zusammenarbeit' der DDR in Afrika: Alltag und Lebensweisen zwischen DDR- Richtlinien und angespannter Sicherheitslage in den 1970er und 1980er Jahren." Diploma thesis, University of Vienna, 2010.
Osterhammel, Jürgen. "'The Great Work of Uplifting Mankind': Zivilisierungsmission und Moderne." In *Zivilisierungsmissionen: Imperiale Weltverbesserung seit dem 18. Jahrhundert,* edited by Boris Barth and Jürgen Osterhammel, 363–425. Konstanz: UVK, 2005.
Piepiorka, Alexandra. "Exploring "Socialist Solidarity" in Higher Education: East German Advisors in Post-Independence Mozambique (1975–1992)." In *Education and Development in Colonial and Postcolonial Africa, Global Histories of Education: Policies, Paradigms, and Entanglements, 1890s–1980s,* edited by Damiano Matasci et al., 289–318. Cham: Palgrave Macmillan, 2020.
Sandler, Willeke. "Deutsche Heimat in Afrika: Colonial Revisionism and the Construction of Germanness through Photography." *Journal of Women's History* 25 (2013): 37–61. doi:10.1353/jowh.2013.0000.
Saul, John S. *A Difficult Road: The Transition to Socialism in Mozambique.* New York: Monthly Review Press, 1985.

Schiermeyer, Regine. *Greif Zur Kamera, Kumpel! Die Geschichte der Betriebsfotogruppen in der DDR.* Berlin: Ch. Links, 2015.
Schleicher, Ilona, and Hans-Georg Schleicher. *Die DDR im südlichen Afrika: Solidarität und Kalter Krieg.* Hamburg: Institut für Afrikakunde, 1997.
Schleicher, Ilona. "Berufsbildung und Wirtschaftsbeziehungen der DDR-Mosambik." In *Engagiert für Afrika: Die DDR und Afrika II*, edited by Ulrich van der Heyden, Ilona Schleicher, and Hans-Georg Schleicher, 179–195. Münster: Lit, 1994.
Schleicher, Hans-Georg. "The German Democratic Republic (GDR) in the Liberation Struggle of Southern Africa." In *Southern African liberation struggles: contemporaneous documents, 1960–1994*, edited by A. J. Temu, and Joel das Neves Tembe, 507–598. Dar es Salaam: Mkuki na Nyota Publishers, 2014.
Schmidt-Linsenhoff, Viktoria. *Ethnizität und Geschlecht: (Post-) Koloniale Verhandlungen in Geschichte, Kunst und Medien.* Köln: Böhlau, 2005.
Slobodian, Quinn. "Introduction," In *Comrades of Color: East Germany in the Cold War World*, edited by Quinn Slobodian, 1–19. New York: Berghahn Books, 2015.
Slobodian, Quinn. "Socialist Chromatism: Race, Racism, and the Racial Rainbow in East Germany." In *Comrades of Color: East Germany in the Cold War World*, edited by Quinn Slobodian, 23–39. New York: Berghahn Books, 2015.
Smardz, Monika. "Bis zu jenem Tag im Dezember – Eine Farm mitten in der Savanne." In *Wir haben Spuren hinterlassen! Die DDR in Mosambik: Erlebnisse, Erfahrungen und Erkenntnisse aus drei Jahrzehnten*, edited by Matthias Voß, 270–277. Münster: Lit, 2005.
Sontag, Susan. *On Photography.* New York: Picador, 1973.
Sontag, Susan. *Regarding the Pain of Others.* New York: Picador, 2003.
Stahr, Henrik. *Fotojournalismus zwischen Exotismus und Rassismus: Darstellungen von Schwarzen und Indianern in Foto-Text-Artikeln deutscher Wochenillustrierter 1919–1939.* Hamburg: Kovač, 2004.
Thompson, T. Jack. *Light on Darkness? Missionary Photography of Africa in the Nineteenth and Early Twentieth Centuries.* Grand Rapids: Eerdmans Publ., 2012.
van der Heyden, Ulrich. "Es darf nichts passieren! Entwicklungspolitisches Engagement der DDR in Mosambik zwischen Solidarität und Risiko." In *Wir haben Spuren hinterlassen! Die DDR in Mosambik: Erlebnisse, Erfahrungen und Erkenntnisse aus drei Jahrzehnten*, edited by Matthias Voß, 278–313. Münster: Lit, 2005.
Vokes, Richard, and Darren Newbury. "Editorial: Photography and African futures." *Visual Studies*, 33, no. 1 (2018): 1–10. doi: 10.1080/1472586X.2018.1424988.
Voß, Matthias. "Um de nós – einer von uns! Gespräch mit Achim Kindler, der als Lehrer im Auftrag des Solidaritätskomitees der DDR als erster DDR-Bürger bei der FRELIMO arbeitete." In *Wir haben Spuren hinterlassen! Die DDR in Mosambik: Erlebnisse, Erfahrungen und Erkenntnisse aus drei Jahrzehnten*, edited by Matthias Voß, 34–46. Münster: Lit, 2005.
Voß, Matthias. *Wir haben Spuren hinterlassen! Die DDR in Mosambik: Erlebnisse, Erfahrungen und Erkenntnisse aus drei Jahrzehnten.* Münster: Lit, 2005.
Weis, Toni. "The Politics Machine: On the Concept of 'Solidarity' in East German Support for SWAPO." *Journal of Southern African Studies* 37 (2011): 351–367. doi:10.1080/03057070.2011.579443.
Winrow, Gareth M. *The Foreign Policy of the GDR in Africa.* Cambridge: Cambridge University Press, 1990.

Witkowski, Gregory. "Between Fighter and Beggars." In *Comrades of Color: East Germany in the Cold War World*, edited by Quinn Slobodian, 73–94. New York: Berghahn Books, 2015.

Yancy, George. *Black Bodies, White Gaze: The Continuing Significance of Race in America*. Lanham: Rowman & Littlefield, 2016.

Zeller, Joachim, and Peter Weiss, *Weisse Blicke, schwarze Körper: Afrikaner im Spiegel westlicher Alltagskultur*. Erfurt: Sutton Verlag, 2010.

Zuromski, Catherine. *Snapshot Photography: The Lives of Images*. Cambridge: The MIT Press, 2013.

Magazines

Horizont
Für Dich
Junge Generation
NBI

Interviews

Interview with former ADN journalist in Mozambique 1987–1990, conducted on June 15, 2016 in Berlin.

Interview with former specialist B. about the mailing of film material back to the GDR, conducted on June 2, 2016 in Berlin.

Interview with former accompanying wife L., conducted on April 27, 2016 in Petershagen.

Interview with accompanying wife G. about her life in Mozambique, conducted on November 29, 2015 in Riesa.

Alexandra Piepiorka and Eduardo F. Buanaissa
14 A (Post)Socialist Memory Space? East German and Mozambican Memories of Cooperation in Education

Introduction

In the socialist world, international contacts between national education systems usually developed in the context of bilateral agreements on cooperation and friendship. This was also the case for the People's Republic of Mozambique (PRM) and the German Democratic Republic (GDR). Nevertheless, in publications by contemporary actors, the starting point of East German and Mozambican cooperation in education is dated back to the years before Mozambican independence, when several GDR citizens began to work as teachers in underground schools run by the Mozambican liberation movement Frente de Libertação de Moçambique (FRELIMO) in the late 1960s.[1] In historiographic representation on behalf of the GDR, this early cooperation in education during the liberation struggle against Portugal is depicted as the cornerstone for further cooperation between the two countries after Mozambican independence in 1975.[2] In the 1970s and 1980s a rapidly growing number of East German educational advisors and educators departed to Maputo, with the mission to contribute to the reconstruction of a postcolonial and socialist education system in Mozambique.[3] Likewise, Mozambican students entered the GDR to continue their secondary education at the "School of Friendship"[4] or to undergo vocational training,[5] while

---

[1] Herbert Graf, "Vor der Unabhängigkeitserklärung Mosambiks – Erinnerungen und Reflexionen," in *Wir haben Spuren hinterlassen!*, ed. Matthias Voß (Münster: Lit, 2005), 62. Hans-Jochen Roos, "Unterricht unter Palmen: Als Biologielehrer an der FRELIMO-Schule in Bagamoyo," in *Wir haben Spuren hinterlassen!*, ed. Matthias Voß (Münster: Lit, 2005).
[2] For official self-representation see for instance Erich Honecker, *Aus meinem Leben* (Berlin: Dietz, 1981), 406. A similar argumentation can be traced in GDR documents with reference to Angola, see Immanuel Rafael Harisch, "Bartering Coffee, Cocoa and W50 Trucks: The Trade Relations of the GDR, Angola and São Tomé in a Comparative Perspective," *Global Histories* 3/2 (2017), 49, accessed November 7, 2019, doi:10.17169/GHSJ.2017.135.
[3] Mathias Tullner, "Die Zusammenarbeit der DDR und Mosambiks auf dem Gebiet der Bildung und die Tätigkeit der Bildungsexperten der DDR in Mosambik," in *Wir haben Spuren hinterlassen!*, ed. Matthias Voß (Münster: Lit, 2005).
[4] Lutz R. Reuter and Annette Scheunpflug, *Die Schule der Freundschaft: Eine Fallstudie zur Bildungszusammenarbeit zwischen der DDR und Mosambik* (Münster: Waxmann, 2006).

ə OpenAccess. © 2021 Alexandra Piepiorka and Eduardo F. Buanaissa, published by De Gruyter.
This work is licensed under the Creative Commons Attribution 4.0 International License.
https://doi.org/10.1515/9783110623543-014

other young Mozambicans merely hoped to receive vocational education in the framework of contract labor in East German enterprises.[6]

Although Mozambican and East German educational trajectories differed quite remarkably, the common experience to work through a foreign and socialist education system offers space for some *geteilte Erinnerungen* ("shared experiences")[7] from protagonists on both sides. In this context we assume the possibility of a small-scale Afro-European "memory space,"[8] which would presumably lie in between the GDR and Mozambique, nestled in the common educational history of both. This memory space may seem relatively small, but nevertheless bears the potential of having conserved rich memories of the PRM and the GDR – two formerly socialist (education) systems, whose place in the overall memory culture in the respective countries is still being negotiated. Complementary to the overarching national debates, this article focuses on the written and personal memories of protagonists, who were engaged in cross-border educational endeavors and encounters between the PRM and the GDR. In search of such memories, we consulted publications that can be combined under the label of "memory literature."[9] Our analysis aims at catching a glimpse of (post)socialist worlds

---

[5] Ilona Schleicher, "Berufsbildung und Wirtschaftsbeziehungen DDR – Mosambik," in *Engagiert für Afrika: Die DDR und Afrika II*, ed. Ulrich van der Heyden (Münster: Lit, 1994).

[6] Ulrich van der Heyden, Wolfgang Semmler and Ralf Straßburg, *Mosambikanische Vertragsarbeiter in der DDR-Wirtschaft: Hintergrund – Verlauf – Folgen* (Münster: Lit, 2014); Marcia C. Schenck, "From Luanda and Maputo to Berlin: Uncovering Angolan and Mozambican migrants' motives to move to the German Democratic Republic (1979–1990)," *African Economic History* 44 (2016).

[7] The German term *geteilte Erinnerung* has a double meaning, containing a notion of shared and divided memory at the same time.

[8] For the concept of memory spaces see Aleida Assmann, *Erinnerungsräume: Formen und Wandlungen des kulturellen Gedächtnisses* (Munich: C. H. Beck, 1999).

[9] Memory literature does encompass a variety of written sources, reaching from historically inspired and sometimes bestselling novels to self-published memoirs and autobiographical stories. In literature studies especially, but also in interdisciplinary research dealing with collective memory, researchers seem to favor historical novels as objects of analysis. However, for our analysis we selected autobiographically inspired books written by amateur authors and contemporary witnesses from the former GDR and Mozambique, that offer personal views on the socialist past in the respectively other country. For a discussion of German memory literature see Aleida Assmann, "Wem gehört Geschichte? Fakten und Fiktion in der neueren deutschen Erinnerungsliteratur," *Internationales Archiv für Sozialgeschichte der deutschen Literatur* 36 (2011). See also Friederike Eigler, *Gedächtnis und Geschichte in Generationenromanen seit der Wende* (Berlin: Erich Schmidt Verlag, 2005). For Mozambican memory literature see Ana Margarida Fonseca, "(Re)Configurations of Identity: Memory and Creation in the Narrative of Mia Couto," in *Mozambique on the Move: Challenges and Reflections*, ed. Sheila Pereira Khan, Maria Paula Meneses, and Bjørn Enge Bertelsen (Leiden and Boston: Brill, 2018). Also consult

of memory, which might have emerged in the context of GDR-Mozambican cooperation in education. Our argument is that a collective memory concerned with state socialism does exist separately in both formerly socialist states. At the same time, personal memory of certain East Germans and Mozambicans transverse these national memory horizons by offering common as well as differing memories of the socialist past of both countries – resulting in a multiplicity of (post)socialist memory spaces. Accordingly, Millei et al. refer to "(post)socialist spaces" in the plural to "highlight this complexity of the time-spaces of historical socialism and what followed."[10]

In the following, we first discuss the role of memory literature in the context of post-socialist and cross-national remembering processes. Secondly, we summarize memory debates on the socialist phase in reunited Germany and in post-socialist Mozambique. Thirdly, we present our interpretation of post-socialist memory literature, and finally we discuss the post-socialist memory space in between East Germany and Mozambique.

Theoretical Considerations on Post-socialist Memory Making

As a starting point, we want to raise the question whether or not memories of Mozambican and East German expatriates do play a part in (a) post-socialist "memory space" of both countries.[11] Picking up this point, we started wondering about the role of memory literature in the overall memory making in post-socialist spaces like East Germany and Mozambique. In Assmann's considerations, memory literature constitutes a genre that combines personal experience, historic events, and elements of fiction into a literary text and eventually works out historical perspectives that hitherto did not make it into the collective memory of a given society.[12] Consequently, memory literature appears to offer a space for subliminal memories, situated somewhere in between the canonized cultural

---

Maria do Carmo Ferraz Tedesco, "Reconfiguração da Moçambicanidade nos romances de Mia Couto e Paulina Chiziane," *Revista Mosaico* 3 (2010). For the role of testimony books in Mozambican memory discourse see João Paulo Borges Coelho, "Politics and Contemporary History in Mozambique: A Set of Epistemological Notes," *Kronos* 39 (2013), 29.
10 Zsuzsa Millei, Iveta Silova, and Susanne Gannon, "Thinking Through Memories of Childhood in (Post)Socialist Spaces: Ordinary Lives in Extraordinary Times," in *Children's Geographies*, published online, August 1, 2019, doi:10.1080/14733285.2019.1648759.
11 Assmann, *Erinnerungsräume*.
12 Assmann, "Wem gehört Geschichte," 216–217.

memory of a given society and the inter-generational communicative memory of certain groups within this society.[13] As memory literature may deliberately integrate autobiographical and fictional features into the storyline, such texts are less reliable in terms of historical accuracy.[14] However, she states that memory literature offers a platform for a wide range of little stories that reflect the bigger history, but which remained previously untold and unheard and are not part of the official narrative.[15] In line with Assmann's ideas, we consider memory literature as a valuable non-academic and personal contribution to collective memory making on socialist times in both Germany and Mozambique.[16]

As the memories under examination emerged in at least two national contexts and were (re)told by de facto migrants,[17] we would like to address spatiality here. To our understanding, Assmann's notion of "memory spaces" refers to (subjective or collective) memories of specific places, and to (inanimate) spaces of remembrance like historical monuments, that transcend personal memory.[18] This understanding of space in memory processes builds upon the concept of *lieux de mémoire* (translated to "realms of memory") as introduced by Pierre Nora. Nora and colleagues started to explore French history and collective identity through a constructivist analysis of concrete memory sites, like the Eiffel

---

[13] For the different forms of individual and collective memory see Aleida Assmann, "Memory, Individual and Collective," in *The Oxford Handbook of Contextual Political Analysis*, ed. Robert E. Goodin and Charles Tilly (Oxford: Oxford University Press, 2006), 210–224. Also see Harald Welzer, *Das kommunikative Gedächtnis: Eine Theorie der Erinnerung* (Munich: C. H. Beck, 2002).
[14] Assmann, "Memory, Individual and Collective," 223. According to Assmann, in memory literature a generous portion of "fiction" is added into the overall storyline – e.g. events are described rather from an aesthetic point of view, but with no reference to time or place; or fictional characters are added into the plot to make the text more consistent and to synthesize past events for the reader. Even though fiction or selective remembering often triumph over "accuracy" in historical novels and autobiographical memoires, such literary products still serve as valuable sources for understanding past events or past emotions.
[15] Assmann, "Memory, Individual and Collective," 222.
[16] Assmann discusses the function of collective memory as a unifying framework for groups or nations with reference to Maurice Halbwachs and Pierre Nora. But she also reflects on the potential of latent and "dysfunctional memories" that may eventually delegitimize, correct or complement the official memory framework; see Assmann, *Erinnerungsräume*, 131–142. In a way, memory literature and autobiographical testimonies may serve as corresponding supplements to official memory making. Also consult Maurice Halbwachs, *Das kollektive Gedächtnis* (Stuttgart: Enke, 1967).
[17] For migrant memory see an overview by Julia Creet, "Introduction: The Migration of Memory and Memories of Migration," in *Memory and Migration: Multidisciplinary Approaches to Memory Studies*, ed. Julia Creet and Andreas Kitzmann (Toronto: University of Toronto Press, 2011).
[18] Assmann, *Erinnerungsräume*.

tower, but also through immaterial sites, like symbols or social divisions within the country.[19] Although these *lieux* were highly relevant for France's national identity, Nora's initial selection was critiqued for overlooking transnational aspects of French identity, such as *lieux* connected to France's inglorious colonial past.[20] Nevertheless, Nora's concept proved useful for similar projects in other European countries.[21] In addition to such national adaptations, Nora's concept of *lieux* fostered an international discussion on the possibility of collective memory making beyond the "national container" as a spatial unit.[22] Over the years, scholars have reworked Assmann's "memory spaces" and Nora's *lieux de mémoire* by applying their concepts to the transnational level.[23]

But how can one capture rather immaterial memory landscapes on socialist pasts that seem entangled in-between two countries (and continents)? For our purpose, we found the concept of "travelling memory"[24] and the corresponding discussion about transnationality in the field of memory studies helpful.[25] Within this framework memories rather emerge from cross-border movement of people and media[26] then from circumscribed places or national boundaries.[27] As we

---

19 Pierre Nora and Lawrence D. Kritzmann, *Realms of Memory: Rethinking the French Past*, Vol. 1–3 (New York: Columbia University Press, 1996–1998).
20 Etienne Achille, Charles Forsdick, Lydie Moudileno, *Postcolonial Realms of Memory: Sites and Symbols in Modern France* (Liverpool: Liverpool University Press, 2020). This critique is especially true to Nora's publications on the French republic and nation, whereas the later volumes on "Les Frances" did also explore the historical role of migrants or religious minorities within French society. See relevant chapters in Nora and Kritzmann, *Realms of Memory*.
21 For Germany see Etienne François and Hagen Schulze, *Deutsche Erinnerungsorte – Eine Auswahl* (Munich: C. H. Beck, 2005). Martin Sabrow, *Erinnerungsorte der DDR* (Munich: C. H. Beck, 2009).
22 See Indra Sengupta, "Introduction. Locating *lieux de mémoire*: A (Post)colonial Perspective," in *Memory, History, and Colonialism: Engaging with Pierre Nora in Colonial and Postcolonial Contexts*, ed. Indra Sengupta (London: German Historical Institute, 2009). Hans Henning Hahn, Robert Traba, and Peter Oliver Lowe, *Deutsch-Polnische Erinnerungsorte*, Vol. 1–5 (Paderborn: Schöningh, 2012–2015).
23 Pim den Boer, *Europäische Erinnerungsorte, Volume 3: Europa und die Welt* (Munich: Oldenbourg, 2012); Ulrike Schmieder, "Orte des Erinnerns und Vergessens: Denkmäler, Museen und historische Schauplätze von Sklaverei und Sklavenhandel," in *Comparativ* 22 (2012).
24 Astrid Erll, "Travelling Memory," *Parallax* 17 (2011).
25 Chiara De Cesari and Ann Rigney, *Transnational Memory: Circulation, Articulation, Scales* (Berlin: De Gruyter, 2014); Astrid Erll, *Kollektives Gedächtnis und Erinnerungskulturen: Eine Einführung*, third edition (Stuttgart: J.B. Metzler, 2017), 123–126.
26 An impressive example of travelling memory items may be found in East German media products, like popular music or video cassettes that were brought to Maputo suburbs by Mozambican worker-trainees returning from the GDR. The long-lasting impact of this group of returnees and their souvenirs on urban culture in Maputo is documented in this volume (see Fernando

navigate within the context of global socialism and analyze written testimonies on binational exchanges in education, we find the perspective of travelling memories intriguing. Although plots connected to transnational identity building are highlighted in this strand of research, researchers rarely focus on the transnational, socialist experience in memory literature.[28] A remarkable contribution is the study of Gronenthal, who dived into a world of nostalgia in East German and Polish literature and worked out post-socialist nostalgia as a transnational phenomenon.[29] Furthermore, there is an interdisciplinary interest in what was labeled "Eastalgia"[30] or "post-communist nostalgia"[31] within memory literature, but many contributions stay focused on the European memory space.[32] So, how to examine the Afro-European experience of remembering socialism?

Agostinho Machava). See also Malte Wandel, *Einheit, Arbeit, Wachsamkeit: Die DDR in Mosambik* (Heidelberg, Berlin: Kehrer Verlag: 2012).
27 Erll, *Kollektives Gedächtnis*, 126.
28 Transnationality in memory literature is usually discussed with reference to diaspora and the experience of loss, as well as (forced) migration or collective trauma. For transnational melancholy see for instance Stephanie Siewert, "Die Topographie der Melancholie in transnationaler Perspektive," in *Raum und Gefühl: Der Spatial Turn und die neue Emotionsforschung*, ed. Gertrud Lehnert (Bielefeld: Transcript, 2011). For a discussion of transnational memory in the context of diaspora and migration, see the edited volume by De Cesari and Rigney, *Transnational* Memory. For collective trauma in memory literature consult Anja Tippner and Anna Artwińska, *Narrative of Annihilation, Confinement, and Survival: Camp Literature in a Transnational Perspective* (Berlin: De Gruyter, 2019).
29 Mariell C. Gronenthal, *Nostalgie und Sozialismus: Emotionale Erinnerung in der deutschen und polnischen Gegenwartsliteratur* (Bielefeld: Transcript, 2018).
30 Thomas Kunze and Thomas Vogel, *Ostalgie international: Erinnerungen an die DDR von Nicaragua bis Vietnam* (Berlin: Ch. Links, 2010); Marcia C. Schenck, "A *Chronology* of *Nostalgia: Memories* of *Former Angolan* and *Mozambican Worker Trainees* to *East Germany*," in *Labor History* 59 (2018), doi:10.1080/0023656X.2018.1429187.
31 Maria Todorova and Zsuzsa Gille, *Post-Communist Nostalgia* (Oxford: Berghahn 2010). See also Enzo Traverso, *Left-Wing Melancholia: Marxism, History, and Memory* (New York: Columbia University Press, 2016).
32 Nevertheless, there is a strand of research on memories of foreign students in the former GDR; for instance, for Cuban students consult relevant chapters in Wolf-Dieter Vogel and Verona Wunderlich, *Abenteuer DDR: Kubanerinnen und Kubaner im deutschen Sozialismus* (Berlin: Karl Dietz, 2011); Susanne Ritschel, *Kubanische Studierende in der DDR: Ambivalentes Erinnern zwischen Zeitzeuge und Archiv* (Hildesheim: Georg Olms, 2015). For Latin American students in the Soviet Union see Tobias Rupprecht, *Soviet Internationalism After Stalin: Interaction and Exchange Between the USSR and Latin America During the Cold War* (Cambridge: Cambridge University Press, 2015), 191–229.

In this regard we find the discussion connected to "post-socialism" in educational science inspiring,[33] because the authors do not stay within the European framework, but decisively transverse the global scale when researching socialist experiences of schooling, education, and childhood from all over the world.[34] The authors approach the socialist past through personal memories and contrast these memories with official narratives on childhood in socialist states, as well as evaluations on this past in scientific and public discourses. During their analysis, the researchers seek to "think with" memories while "thinking through" childhood and the everyday life in socialist education systems. In that framework, they give attention to collective negotiation processes of that socialist past in the post-socialist space and also examine their own role in such processes – both as memory holders and as scientists engaged in the generation of knowledge about the socialist past.[35] Before moving to our analysis of individual memories by formerly educational travelers, we wish to briefly explore the course of collective remembering in both post-socialist societies. For that purpose, we will dive into public debates on the socialist past in post-socialist Germany and Mozambique and compare remembrance in both local contexts.

---

33 Iveta Silova, *Post-Socialism Is Not Dead: (Re)Reading the Global in Comparative Education* (Bingley: Emerald Group Publishing, 2010); Iveta Silova et al.,, *Reimagining Utopias: Theory and Method for Educational Research in Post-Socialist Contexts* (Rotterdam: Sense Publishers, 2017).
34 Iveta Silova, Nelli Piattoeva, and Zsuzsa Millei, *Childhood and Schooling in (Post)Socialist Societies: Memories of Everyday Life* (Cham: Springer International Publishing, 2018).
35 Millei, Silova, and Gannon, "Thinking Through," 3. We fit into the category of researches born in socialist systems (Poland and Mozambique), and to a certain extent we share the experience of childhood in socialism with the authors cited above. At the same time, we share this experience with the authors of the memory books we use for our analysis of cross-national remembering of socialism. Therefore, we agree with Millei et al. that writing about a socialist past that – in bits and pieces – seems related to one's own biography can be a methodologically challenging venture, especially were "collective biography collapses the binary that separates the knowledge generating expert from the layperson remembering." Ibid.

Remembering Socialism in Post-socialist Germany and Mozambique

In German and Central European memory debates, state socialism is considered a significant period for contemporary historiography.[36] Historians conducted research on state socialism from the 1990s onwards and results on socialist education in the former GDR were gradually woven into the overall German memory discourse. Studies on socialist education in the GDR examined political indoctrination in schools and mechanisms of sanction within the education system, among other rather unpleasant topics.[37] These negative aspects of GRD education were discussed publicly and received a prominent place in the collective memory making in unified Germany.[38]

Nevertheless, the collective memory on the former GDR lived through considerable inner-German controversies in the post-1990s era and, interestingly enough, it remains a contested memory space up-to-date.[39] What lies at the core of such controversies? The German historian Martin Sabrow sums up that at least three narratives are concurring for hegemony in GDR historiography. The first focuses on totalitarianism and the malice of dictatorship (official mem-

---

[36] Martin Sabrow, "Zeitgeschichte als Aufarbeitung: Der Fall DDR," in *Aufarbeitung der Aufarbeitung: Die DDR im geschichtskulturellen Diskurs*, ed. Saskia Handro (Schwalbach: Wochenschau-Verlag, 2011), 23.
[37] Gert Geissler and Ulrich Wiegmann, *Schule und Erziehung in der DDR: Studien und Dokumente* (Neuwied: Hermann Luchterhand, 1995); Tilman Grammes, Henning Schluß, and Hans-Joachim Vogler, *Staatsbürgerkunde in der DDR: Ein Dokumentenband* (Wiesbaden: VS Verlag, 2006); Andreas Gratzemann, *Die Erziehung zum "neuen" Menschen im Jugendwerkhof Torgau: Ein Beitrag zum kulturellen Gedächtnis* (Berlin: Lit, 2008).
[38] Gronenthal, *Nostalgie und Sozialismus*, 38–41. Official GDR memorial sites, for instance, were placed in former special status prisons of the Ministry for State Security (MfS or Stasi), a "Berlin Wall" museum opened up in 1998, and former Stasi headquarters were turned into museums in Leipzig and Berlin. See Carola S. Rudnick, *Die andere Hälfte der Erinnerung: Die DDR in der deutschen Geschichtspolitik nach 1989* (Bielefeld: Transcript, 2011). A wider variety of memory perspectives was adapted in cinematographic productions on the GDR, which would address topics like persecution or monotony in state socialism, but also encompass comedic elements and Eastalgia; see Gerhard J. Lüdeker, *Kollektive Erinnerung und nationale Identität: Nationalsozialismus, DDR und Wiedervereinigung im deutschen Spielfilm nach 1989* (Munich: Ed. Text + Kritik, 2012), 206–272. On representations of everyday life in GDR museums see Regina Göschl, *DDR-Alltag im Museum: Geschichtskulturelle Diskurse, Funktionen und Fallbeispiele im vereinigten Deutschland* (Münster: Lit, 2019).
[39] Sebastian Klinge, *1989 und wir: Geschichtspolitik und Erinnerungskultur nach dem Mauerfall* (Bielefeld: Transcript, 2015).

ory politics), the second praises the fruits of socialist progress (former GDR functionaries and supporters of the system), and the third paints a picture of adjustment and "coming to terms" with the GDR system ("*Arrangementgedächtnis*" of average GDR citizens).[40] Although in 1998 the Federal Foundation for the Reappraisal of the SED Dictatorship was initiated to deal with the various aspects of life in the GDR and a common German memory discourse,[41] critics observe that in public debate the SED state's surveillance apparatus and the one-party dictatorship of the SED prevailed as a major topic. With this emphasis, public attention was rightly paid to the victims of the SED state, but the memory horizon of a probably large majority of GDR citizens was disregarded. Many of the less spectacular tales on everyday life in the GDR ended up being less visible in the collective memory of unified Germany, but stayed conserved in the communicative memory of East Germans. This may be exemplified by the diverging perceptions of GDR history as expressed by school pupils from East and West.[42] West German pupils tend to associate the GDR with repression, as told in school, and horrifying stories about "passing the inner-German border," as told by Western family members. East German pupils, on the other hand, rather blend personal "reminiscences of original history" and local patriotism into the historical narrative, while they tend to trivialize the context of the dictatorship.[43] Such memory disparities point towards a still ongoing process of German re-unification and identity building, in which memory making does play a prominent part. Accordingly, the memory discourse on the socialist past of Eastern Germany continues to be a worthwhile research agenda in unified Germany.[44]

---

40 Sabrow, "Zeitgeschichte als Aufarbeitung," 28–29.
41 For further information see https://www.bundesstiftung-aufarbeitung.de/.
42 The corresponding study was based on more than 200 interviews with school pupils from Lower Saxony, as well as Western and Eastern Berlin; see Sabine Moller, "Diktatur im Familiengedächtnis: Anmerkungen zu Widersprüchen im Geschichtsbewusstsein von Schülern," in *Aufarbeitung der Aufarbeitung: Die DDR im geschichtskulturellen Diskurs*, ed. Saskia Handro (Schwalbach: Wochenschau-Verlag, 2011), 140–141.
43 Moller, "Diktatur," 149.
44 This agenda may be exemplified by studies on the emergence and maintaining of East German identities even after 1990 and its representation in memory literature; for instance see Bernd Blaschke, "Erzählte Gefühle und Emotionen des Erinnerns: Ostdeutsche Identitätsliteratur der in den 1960er und 1970er Jahren Geborenen," in *Ostdeutsche Erinnerungsdiskurse nach 1989: Narrative kultureller Identität*, ed. Elisa Goudin-Steinmann and Carola Hähnel-Mesnard (Berlin: Frank & Timme, 2013). See also Regine Criser, "Zwischen Anpassung und Instrumentalisierung: Hybride Lebensnarrative in der Literatur nach 1989," in ibid. For an overview of GDR-related research, see Ulrich Mählert, *Die DDR als Chance: Neue Perspektive auf ein altes Thema* (Berlin: Metropol, 2016).

In the case of Mozambique, colonialism and the post-independence transition to state socialism have an outstanding relevance for the country's history and, accordingly, also its educational development. Still it seems that state socialism as a postcolonial development phase (around 1975–1990) tends to be overlooked in current memorial debates and in research on Mozambican history of education.[45] Instead, remembering the struggle for independence and an education system in the FRELIMO-run "liberated zones" during the 1960s are points of interest in the country's current politics of remembrance.[46] Thus, expectations on how to deal with the socialist past are quite different in post-socialist Mozambique and Germany.

The prerogative of interpreting the Mozambican past until today remained with FRELIMO. Since independence, FRELIMO continues to exercise control over the "mechanisms of engaging with the past and writing the national narrative of the war" as ruling party.[47] This would also include muzzling unwanted memories. However, sporadic explosions of remembrance in public debates accompany FRELIMO's channeled politics of forgetting. For example, the former warring factions FRELIMO and RENAMO would maintain general silence on the civil war on most occasions, and thereby follow the "the imperative for attaining peace and political stability."[48] Still, both parties occasionally use public memory debates to reinvigorate old rivalries with their former war opponents. Election campaigns are used to accuse the other side of respective war crimes, and regular "interruptions of silence" in the Mozambican parliament occur during these periods.[49] But outside of the public space, an unspoken silence agree-

---

45 Many Mozambican and international publications on the socialist period came out during exactly that time and were marked by "sentiments of solidarity and sympathy;" see Michael Cross, *An Unfulfilled Promise: Transforming Schools in Mozambique* (Addis Ababa: OSSREA 2011), 12. More recent publications discuss education during state socialism on few pages only, e.g. Mouzinho Mário et al., Higher Eduaction in Mozambique: A Case Study (Oxford: James Currey, Maputo: Imprensa & Livraria Universitária UEM, 2003), 7–10. Also Patricio Vitorino Langa, *Higher Education in Portuguese Speaking African Countries: A Five Country Baseline Study* (Cape Town: African Minds 2013), 63, accessed January 5, 2020, www.africanminds.co.za/wp-content/uploads/2014/02/AM-HE-in-Lusophone-Africa-Text-and-Cover-web.pdf.
46 See for instance Salvador André Zawangoni, *A FRELIMO e a Formação do Homem Novo (1964–1974 e 1975–1982)* (Maputo: CIEDIMA, 2007); Joel das Neves Tembe, História da Luta de Libertação Nacional (Maputo: Ministério dos Combatentes, Direcção Nacional de História, 2014). The corresponding "liberation script" in public memory debates was analyzed in Coelho, "Politics," 21.
47 Victor Igreja, "Memories as Weapons: The Politics of Peace and Silence in Post-Civil War Mozambique," *Journal of Southern African Studies* 34 (2008): 544.
48 Igreja, "Memories as Weapons," 540.
49 Ibid, 545–550.

ment seems to prevail, as explained by a parliamentary deputy of RENAMO: "the people that insult one another in the parliament, when they meet in a *barraca* [a hut where alcohol is sold] they don't talk about the bad things of the past."[50]

Did the educational history marked by socialism in Mozambique fall into oblivion, because the same time period was overshadowed by civil war, or was it simply no longer important? It seems that FRELIMO nowadays has little interest to dwell on memories of the socialist past.[51] Although street names such as Karl Marx Avenue or Mao Tse Tung Avenue shape Maputo's urban landscape and are clear reminders of the socialist past, this same past seems to have no positive or negative place in official memory.[52] Pitcher considers in this regard that "[w]ith the implementation of structural adjustment in 1987 and major constitutional changes since 1990, the government has dropped most reference to socialism."[53] At the same time, the scientific interpretation of Mozambique's socialist phase seems to move within "narratives of triumph and failure"[54]: while post-independence literature tended to glorify the socialist development, the same phase was generally declared as failure in writings after the system change. Contrary to both extremes, Pitcher demands that "scholars need to come to terms with the socialist period in Mozambique"[55] and eventually move away from both antithetical interpretations.

---

50 Ibid, 551. Such attempts to break the collective amnesia have been the subject of academic debates in Mozambique, for instance, in the "Philosophical Ateliers" organized by the prominent Mozambican philosopher Severino Ngoenha. These ateliers take place in the "Garden of the Madgermanes" (a term referring to the former Mozambican workers returned from the GDR in Maputo; see Machava, this volume). In this context, discussions have often been associated with the theme of revisiting the past to construct national reconciliation and to activate citizenship. Meetings are announced via social media channels like Facebook in a group named "Atelier Filosófico"; see group content on Facebook Inc., accessed July 26, 2020, https://www.facebook.com/Atelier-Filos%C3%B3fico-2217100891889370/.
51 Igreja, "Memories as Weapons," 554; Anne M. Pitcher, "Forgetting from Above and Memory from Below: Strategies of Legitimation and Struggle in Postsocialist Mozambique," *Journal of the International African Institute* 76 (2006).
52 Igreja, "Memories as Weapons," 545.
53 Pitcher, "Forgetting from Above," 95.
54 Pitcher, "Forgetting from Above," 106.
55 Pitcher, "Forgetting from Above," 106.

Remembering Each Other: Mozambican Memory and "Remembering Mozambique" in (East) German Memory Literature

After briefly recapitalizing the collective memory making on the socialist era in both countries, we would like to focus on the personal memories of Mozambicans and East Germans about each other. From the preceding section we conclude that neither Mozambique plays a central role in German historiography, nor does East Germany appear to be central to Mozambican memory debates. Nevertheless, we found pieces of common memories of socialist times in German as well as Mozambican memory literature. Such memories were recollected by East Germans and published with a focus on "remembering Mozambique" and the authors' mission in Africa, as well as by Mozambicans who published personal testimonies about their lives in the GDR.[56]

Although the chosen memory sources are written from the perspective of temporary migrants and therefore "outsiders" to the given society, they may be of complementary relevance for each other, for at least two reasons. First, we would maintain that memory literature published by Mozambicans contributes to include non-German perspectives into memory spaces connected to the GDR.[57] Remarkably enough, non-German remembering of the GDR occasionally results to be rather benevolent when compared to the inner-German debates.[58] From time to time even a breeze of nostalgia seems to fly through Mozambican memories of the GDR.[59] The bitter sweetness of remembering an adolescence as worker trainees in East Germany can be traced by the rousing stories of Mozambican returnees popularly known as "Madjermanes."[60] Second, we hold that selected East German memory books preserved a wide range of memories of the People's Republic of Mozambique. Associated memories of socialist Mozambi-

---

56 All consulted memory sources are listed in the bibliography section.
57 For further reading on non-German perspectives consult Kunze and Vogel, *Ostalgie international*.
58 West-German novelists, for instance, tend to present a "negative portrayal of the GDR." Stuart Parkes, "Literary Portrayals of the GDR by Non-GDR citizens," in *The GDR Remembered: Representations of the East German State Since 1989*, ed. Nick Hodgin and Caroline Pearce (Camden House: Boydell & Brewer, 2011), 66.
59 Tanja Müller, *Legacies of Socialist Solidarity: East-Germany in Mozambique* (London: Lexington, 2014); Marcia C. Schenck, "Ostalgie in Mosambik: Erinnerungen ehemaliger mosambikanischer Vertragsarbeiter in der DDR," *Südlink* 172 (2015).
60 See contributions of Machava, and Alberto and Schenck, this volume.

que mostly emerged in the context of East German working visits. Such visits were rather rare and only designated GDR citizens were allowed to travel to foreign countries in the 1970s and 1980s.[61] The same is true for most Mozambican citizens at that time. It seems though that especially that exceptionality of Afro-European contacts between nominally socialist partners contributed to the intensity of emotional memories on such encounters.[62] In this regard, we found the cooperation in education between the GDR and PRM to be a productive ground for recollecting common as well as unique memories of such encounters. What we found were memories of former colleagues, teachers or students, memories of educational institutions, memories of pedagogic settings, and, most remarkably, of the everyday life in a socialist world – a world that for both Mozambican and East German memory bearers disappeared in the early 1990s.

Interpretation of Memory Literature and Memories of Cooperation in Education

While reviewing the available memory literature by Mozambicans on socialist Germany and by East Germans on socialist Mozambique, it became apparent that publications connected to educational cooperation are few in number, but still rich in content.[63] The following section is devoted to the multifold memories of everyday life in both countries as represented in published memoires of former expatriates or students in their respective professional and private settings.[64]

---

61 Jens Niederhut, *Die Reisekader: Auswahl und Disziplinierung einer privilegierten Minderheit in der DDR* (Leipzig: Evangelische Verlagsanstalt, 2005).
62 Gertrud Lehnert, "Raum und Gefühl," in *Raum und Gefühl: Der Spatial Turn und die neue Emotionsforschung*, ed. Gertrud Lehnert (Bielefeld: Transcript, 2011).
63 Further memory literature by international educators who have worked in Mozambique during the 1970s and 1980s is available in English: Chris Searle, *We're Building the New School: Diary of a Teacher in Mozambique* (London: Zed Press, 1981); John S. Saul, *Revolutionary Traveller: Freeze-Frames from a Life* (Winnipeg: Arbeiter Ring Publishing, 2009).
64 Following our research interest, we identified 16 publications referring to contexts of educational exchange between the GDR and Mozambique. From that data corpus, we chose five memory books and five articles from edited volumes for in-depth analysis and used them as textual framework for carving out traces of common memory on both countries. Although almost all texts were published in German, four narrators are of Mozambican origin. To counterbalance this perspectival distortion in favor of written testimonies in the German language, we would like to recommend the relevant chapters in this volume that primarily rely on oral history sources from former Mozambican worker trainees and were actually conducted in Portuguese (see Machava; Alberto and Schenck, this volume).

Packing Bags and Imagining "the Other"

To begin with, it is worth mentioning that both Mozambican and East German memory texts extensively comment on the other society from the perspective of a guest or migrant. The first impressions upon arrival were relatively dominant for the perception of the other country. But the phase before arrival is also often described, because authors started to imagine the country of destination in their home country already. Especially in the arrival context, authors realized that they had eventually deemed themselves somewhat closer to paradise then reality in the host country would allow. Although the term paradise seems a bit exaggerated, we read that for both Mozambicans and East Germans the respective other country offered a notion of paradise—or at least of adventure and escape—in the phase before their arrival. Nevertheless, there was a slightly different emphasis on what paradise might mean for East Germans compared to Mozambicans. We will elaborate on these nuances of paradise—or Promised Land—while following the memories of Frank and Ibraimo. The GDR citizen Frank is the protagonist of a German memory fiction book.[65] Mozambican-born Ibraimo is the author of his own autobiography.[66] While Frank travelled southwards to work as educational advisor for the Mozambican government and being a professionally experienced adult,[67] the young man Ibraimo traveled northwards to pursue further education, but found himself as a contract worker in the GDR.

---

65 The novel's author himself has worked in Mozambique in the education sector; Helmut Dora, *Kokos und bitterer Tee: Tage und Nächte in Mosambik* (Rostock: BS-Verlag, 2009). We categorized this novel as a memory fiction book, because it combines elements of Mr. Dora's autobiographical experience of working in Mozambique with fictional elements, like the use of alter egos for the characters in the book. The use of alter egos certainly was meant to protect his former colleagues' identities and their private life, but also gave the author more freedom for interpreting his own past – with all its delicate details, like a love affair or other drama. The novel's protagonist, for instance, was renamed to "Frank", but the main storyline of the books is actually built around Mr. Dora's own experience in Mozambique. We were able to reconstruct this insight, because Mr. Dora was willing to recall parts of his life story to one of the authors during an interview in 2014.
66 Ibraimo Alberto, *Ich wollte leben wie die Götter: Was in Deutschland aus meinen afrikanischen Träumen wurde* (Köln: Kiepenheuer & Witsch, 2014).
67 We were shocked to discover that Dora uses the n-word in his book. It seems that the author uses the racist terminology more often when it comes to the description of people from rural Mozambique. This selectivity is worth noticing, because then the racialized imagery not only encompasses a black and white dualism, but also employs categories like rural and urban, educated and uneducated, or colleague and stranger, when it comes to racist terminology. Nevertheless, in at least one story he refers to a colleague and friend of his as "the strong n****." Dora, *Kokos*, 69. Having this in mind, one could argue that title and subtitle also refer to

For Frank, like for most East Germans at that time, working in Mozambique offered the opportunity to work and travel abroad, which was a great privilege at a time when cross-border movement was strongly regulated or even impossible for most GRD citizens. The East German imaginary world of faraway lands can be exemplified by the daydreaming of Frank. Although Frank was not sure where to locate Mozambique on a globe, his thoughts started traveling there as soon as the employment offer was announced to him by a GDR ministry.[68] His daydreaming was harshly criticized by his wife Rita:

> Well. So, you have already accepted the job? [...] Without even knowing anything about this country, your thoughts are already there. We have our kids here. What should we do with them? [...] Maybe there is racism, or maybe people are shooting there. Probably it's also very hot. We know nothing – and then, such adventures![69]

Yet, despite her concerns about their children, her discomfort to leave her "interesting job," and the worries concerning the overall situation in Mozambique, she decides to join Frank on his mission, as she did years before when both migrated to Cuba.[70] Both protagonists mention their sense of solidarity as an important motive to participate in Mozambique's post-socialist reconstruction, meaning the idea of building a socialist utopia abroad may also have played a part in their vision of faraway Mozambique.

A similar adventure spirit may be observed in the storyline of young Mozambicans, who preponderantly were not able to travel to Europe due to economic stratification in the post-independence period. Therefore, educational and vocational programs abroad were embraced as an opportunity to travel. The notion of the GDR as the Promised Land for foreign students is vividly described by the former Mozambican contract worker Ibraimo, who in his autobiographical record

---

these dichotomies. However, a literal interpretation is possible as well. "Coconut and Bitter Tea" might then refer to Dora's work with university students on coconut and tea plantations, which is described at length. Besides, we interpret that the main story behind the "bitter tea" was that usually staff and students got black tea with sugar for breakfast in the canteen, but in times when the civil war was getting worse there was a lack of sugar, even in Maputo. Thus, the coconut could stand for the exotic part of his teaching experience and the "notion of paradise" that many Easterners associated with the deployment in the Global South, while the bitter tea could represent the hardship of the situation. The subtitle "Days and Nights in Mozambique" seems to point towards the intensity of the experience.
68 Dora, *Kokos*, 12
69 Dora, *Kokos*, 14. All quotations from memory sources were translated by Piepiorka and Buanaissa.
70 Dora, *Kokos*, 15.

remembers that one day he and his fellow students found a scholarship announcement at school. The youngsters quickly decide to take their chance to go abroad and register on the application list:

> We conferred with each other for a few minutes, but the dice have been cast. [...] I couldn't imagine becoming a teacher [in Mozambique]. We wanted to get out, get away from the civil war. And then there was one more thing: In the GDR white people were living. The Gods. I took a pencil out of my pocket. [...] We were ready to travel to the land of Gods.[71]

Interestingly enough the initially positive notions on "the other" were based upon very little actual knowledge. In some narratives the main characters initially even had difficulties to locate the respectively other country on a map.[72] Preparations to fill in such knowledge gaps were organized by official authorities before embarkment, but a comparative glance suggests that training contents varied immensely in East Germany and Mozambique. Furthermore, students, teachers, blue-collar, and white-collar professionals from both countries reported that the content of their training courses did not necessarily meet the learners' needs. This can be illustrated in the recollections of Rita and Frank, who during preparatory training in the GDR were astonished that most of their Portuguese language teachers had never visited Mozambique themselves. Only one of them—upon request from the East German participants—shared some knowledge about colonial Mozambique. But his knowledge was limited to topics like architecture or general orientation in the capital city and did not cover cultural insights, which was registered by the participants with slight disappointment.[73]

Likewise, the Mozambican Ibraimo remembers that the training he and his fellows received did not really prepare them for what awaited them in the GDR, because it rather appeared to be a military camp than a preparations course for future workers and students. Instead of learning German vocabulary or intercultural habits, for instance, the prospective workers had to march about 40 kilometers per day. Ibraimo found this confusing, but accepted the military drill as he was convinced that it was for the sake of his future education.[74] An

---

[71] Alberto, *Ich wollte leben*, 77. Ibraimo's image of white people was strongly related to Portuguese colonialism. In his memory, white Portuguese acted like "Gods" who commanded over live and death in colonial Mozambique.
[72] This was also the case for Frank and Ibraimo: Dora, *Kokos*, 13–14; Alberto, *Ich wollte leben*, 77.
[73] Dora, *Kokos*, 17.
[74] Alberto, *Ich wollte leben*, 80–81.

East German physician confirmed to him during the application procedure that they were to study and even get interpreters until they learned German, so Ibraimo had no reason to wonder about the lack of language classes.[75] Furthermore, the Mozambican instructor in the military-like camp explained that the adolescents must exercise well in order to keep up with the GDR citizens, who in his account were working from dawn to night. According to Ibraimo, "the man was serious about that, and we believed him. The foreign GDR expanded into a myth. The people living there drudged from morning to night and put themselves in the service of communism."[76]

Apart from this, many participants in preparatory camps did not learn anything about cultural standards. They did not read books about the GDR, and received little further orientation concerning the GDR.[77] The adolescents and young adults thus discussed unverified stories "about a phenomenon called snow."[78] Nevertheless, the impending departure to unknown lands filled them with great expectations and excitement. It is striking that both Mozambican and East German narrators extensively describe their travel adventures, which were accompanied by stopovers in non-socialist countries,[79] or first-time flight experiences, as in the case of Ibraimo.[80]

Unpacking Reality and Meeting "the Other"

Another noteworthy aspect in Mozambican and East German memory texts is the way in which authors deal with realities shortly after arrival. In sections devoted to arrival, narrators deliberately integrate positive, ambivalent, and negative experiences made upon arrival into their overall storytelling. Mozambican narrators, for instance, reflected on the imbalances between their prior imaginaries and the irritating East German realities found upon arrival. East German narrators, on the other hand, rather focused on the exotic nature of the land and the

---

75 Alberto, *Ich wollte leben*, 86.
76 Alberto, *Ich wollte leben*, 80–81.
77 In biographical interviews, many Mozambican worker trainees stated that information on the GDR was "gathered through hearsay and rumors." Furthermore, prospective migrants rather relied on the "experiences of friends and family members" than on official written sources while planning their stay in the GDR; see Marcia C. Schenck, "From Luanda and Maputo to Berlin," 209.
78 Ibid.
79 Dora, *Kokos*, 19–21.
80 Alberto, *Ich wollte leben*, 100.

overall "newness" of the arrival situation, while postponing critical thoughts to later sections of their narrative.

To illustrate some critical moments of arrival in the GDR, we borrow memories from António, a Mozambican student of economy in der GDR. António remembers the adjustment to the new climate and food customs but considers such adjustments as minor problem. What really discomforted him though was the lack of contact to German locals. As he has previously got to know GDR citizens in Mozambique, he hoped to find "the same sort of people" in the GDR itself. But to his disappointment the East German residents were not as "open and sociable" as their compatriots working in Mozambique. António describes a "certain distance" that GDR citizens displayed in social interactions, which deeply puzzled him.[81] Gabriel, a Mozambican teacher at the School of Friendship in Staßfurt, even remembers false allegations against Mozambicans and shares a memory that reveals racist prejudice and a notion of envy for material goods on part of East German locals: "In a youth fashion store there were merely 100 pairs of jeans on offer. Five Mozambican pupils were also queueing there, and maybe two of them bought jeans. But as we were black, we attracted attention, so in the end people would say 'The blacks again bought out everything'. And this again led to tensions."[82] In search for explanation, Gabriel concludes that probably the local people were overwhelmed with receiving 900 foreigners at once in a small place like Staßfurt.[83]

On the other hand, many books contain positive memories of first encounters with GDR citizens. The Mozambican adolescent Eusébio, for instance, was delegated to the GDR in the 1980s to work as a translator in East German engine plants, where Mozambican citizens received vocational training or were employed as contract workers.[84] Eusébio recalls some "sympathetic Germans" willing to take care of newly arrived Mozambicans. In his view, "some of them hung out with us out of curiosity to meet a black person for the first time; others wished to find out more about our culture."[85] Eusébio arrived in the GDR in Decem-

---

[81] Renate Gudat and Abdul Ilal, "Erfahrungen von mosambikanischen Studenten in der DDR: Interviews," in *Engagiert für Afrika: Die DDR und Afrika II*, ed. Ulrich van der Heyden, Ilona Schleicher, and Hans-Georg Schleicher (Münster: Lit, 1994), 222, 224.
[82] Gudat and Ilal, "Erfahrungen," 217.
[83] For discussion of racism against non-white East German citizens, see Anna Ransiek, "Anders-Sein in der DDR – Narrative Bezüge nach der Transformation," in *Ostdeutsche Erinnerungsdiskurse nach 1989: Narrative kultureller Identität*, ed. Elisa Goudin-Steinmann and Carola Hähnel-Mesnard (Berlin: Frank & Timme Verlag, 2013).
[84] Eusébio João Dembe, "Os privilegiados da década 80," in *Moçambique-Alemanha, Ida e volta / Mosambik-Deutschland, Hin und zurück*, ed. ICMA (Maputo: ICMA, 2005).
[85] Dembe, "Os privilegiados," 65.

ber, and while playing in the snow, he made his first contacts with fellow East German teenagers, who taught him how to ride a sledge. In return he taught a German friend to dance "a dance from Africa."[86]

A generally positive memory landscape was outlined by Dieter, an East German exchange student at Eduardo Mondlane University in Maputo. Dieter's narrative stresses a high spirit of camaraderie on the part of his Mozambican fellow students, who helped him to integrate in the academic life after arrival. Dieter recalls that together they organized excursions to nearby beaches and various parties. In Dieter's memory, everyone enjoyed the pleasures of the weekend and only occasional quarrels disturbed the overall friendly atmosphere in the Mozambican student dorm. However, not all GDR citizens in Mozambique had this kind of contact with locals, and Dieter even remembers notions of envy from fellow GDR citizens in this regard.[87]

The arrival situation was rather different for East German cooperators who traveled to Mozambique as contracted personnel. On arrival at Eduardo Mondlane University, Frank and Rita were welcomed to the university's guesthouse, where they spend three months, before receiving an apartment for the rest of their stay in Mozambique. In their remembrance, the basic conditions such as water, light, and necessary utensils for everyday life were minimally provided.[88] But what seemed more exciting for them was meeting their neighbors from the Netherlands, France, Russia, or Portugal, who also worked as international cooperators at the university and shared the guesthouse with them.[89] Therefore, the first sensation of meeting "the other" in the case of Frank was rather related to observing other international cooperators than to meeting his Mozambican colleagues.[90] It is interesting, for instance, that Frank's description tends to exoticize his French neighbors in terms of sensuality.[91] Beyond the university's guesthouse, the environment of Maputo is described at length as being beautiful and exotic. First contacts with the local population occurred during a long walk

---

86 Dembe, "Os privilegiados," 65.
87 Dieter Hebestreit, "Als DDR-*Student* in *Mosambik*," in *Engagiert für Afrika: Die DDR und Afrika II*, ed. Ulrich von der Heyden, Ilona Schleicher, and Hans-Georg Schleicher (Münster: Lit, 1994), 227–228.
88 Dora, *Kokos*, 23.
89 International cooperators from various countries were contracted in the Mozambican education sector in the 1970s and 1980s. FRELIMO's international recruitment strategy, in the first place, served to substitute the Portuguese professionals who left Mozambique shortly after independence, but also aimed at a quick qualification of national cadres by these international cooperators.
90 Dora, *Kokos*, 29, 34–35.
91 Dora, *Kokos*, 35.

through the city, while Frank and his wife explored the streets of Maputo and constantly got lost. Since after independence most street names had been changed, they needed to ask locals for directions, because their city map proved to be outdated. Indeed, Maputo's streets were renamed after prominent figures of socialism such as Karl Marx, Vladimir Lenin, or Mao Tse Tung. Such personalities should have sounded familiar to Frank and Rita. In practice, however, they needed a while to get used to the Mozambican pronunciation of Friedrich Engels as "Federico Enschles," until they understood which path to follow.[92]

Overall it seems that former GDR cooperators' expectations were exceeded during their first weeks in Mozambique, because all East German narrators describe the beauty of nature and friendliness of people at length. An impressive example is delivered by Hans, a GDR advisor who worked at the teacher training institute in Maputo during the 1980s. Hans devotes a generous amount of text to his non-work activities in Mozambique and personal highlights like seeing a turtle, a dolphin, or a shark for the first time in his life (interestingly enough, Hans was responsible for the training of Mozambican biology teachers, amongst other duties).[93] His first encounter with the Indian Ocean in particular "seemed like paradise" to him and his wife.[94]

Solidarity as Motive in International Cooperation in Education

Solidarity was the official motive for cooperation in education between the GDR and the PRM in the 1970s and 1980s.[95] But how did this somewhat overused term manifest in the practice of everyday cooperation? In the memory books we found a rather high spirit of solidarity in travelers from both sides. But it seems that East Germans interpreted their stay in Mozambique in connection to tasks like an "internationalist duty"[96] or spreading Marxist ideals, while Mozambicans re-

---

92 Dora, *Kokos*, 26–27.
93 Hans Bruchsteiner, "Vom Lernen und Lehren – als Berater in der mosambikanischen Volksbildung," in *Wir haben Spuren hinterlassen! Die DDR in Mosambik: Erlebnisse, Erfahrungen und Erkenntnisse aus drei Jahrzehnten*, ed. Matthias Voß (Münster: Lit, 2005), 444–448.
94 Bruchsteiner, "Vom Lernen," 445.
95 Alexandra Piepiorka, "Exploring 'Socialist Solidarity' in Higher Education: East German Advisors in Post-Independence Mozambique (1975–1992)," in *Education and Development in Colonial and Postcolonial Africa: Policies, Paradigms, and Entanglements, 1980s–1980s*, ed. Damiano Matasci et al. (Cham: Palgrave Macmillan, 2020), doi:10.1007/978-3-030-27801-4_11.
96 Rainer Grajek, *Berichte aus dem Morgengrauen: Als Entwicklungshelfer der DDR in Mosambik* (Grimma: Ute Vallentin, 2005), 51. For further information on Grajek's deployment in Mozambique see also Katrin Bahr in this volume.

ferred to goals like building the nation state when explicating their educational missions in the GDR. Besides the slight difference in the long-term goal formulation, it seems that solidarity in practical terms was understood as loyalty and friendship. This may be exemplified by the narrative of East German journalist Peter Spaček,[97] who accompanied a FRELIMO commander on a rally to a village in Central Mozambique shortly after independence. Although the villagers never experienced contact to FRELIMO members before, Peter recalls that thousands had gathered to hear the announcements. The journalist intended to observe the meeting from the background, but the FRELIMO commander asked him to come on stage and included the foreigner into his speech:

> 'This comrade fought for us,' he said. Some of the listeners laughed. A white person? The audience busted out laughing as he grabbed and raised my pen. 'And this is his weapon.' But then he raised a Kalashnikov and pointed towards a nearby tree. 'With this weapon I can shoot as far as there. But with this one,' now again pointing at the pen, 'this comrade can reach out to the world.'[98]

In his further speech, the FRELIMO commander established a connection between the author's pen and the solidarity services of socialist countries to Mozambique, stressing the education of Mozambicans in the GDR, amongst others.

Over time, this heroic notion of solidarity, which was connected with the liberation struggle and also with the general reputation of the GDR, diminished in Mozambique. This, in part, happened due to rather bureaucratic shortcomings during the actual post-independence collaboration between the two countries. This may be demonstrated using the example of the East German cooperator Udo, who was delegated to the statistical office of Mozambique in 1979, where he helped organizing countrywide censuses and supported his counterparts and trainees in statistical planning and evaluation. His supervisor did express his satisfaction with Udo's work on several occasions and wished to prolong the cooperator's contract. Nevertheless, it seems that GDR authorities were not

---

[97] Peter Spaček was the first East German press correspondent, who visited the FRELIMO during the struggle for Mozambican independence. Already in 1970 he accompanied FRELIMO-troops into "the bush" and interviewed Samora Machel as well as other high-ranking FRELIMO-members. He published a positive report on his voyage to the FRELIMO-run "liberated areas" of Northern Mozambique in the international press and made FRELIMO's struggle known to a wider public; Peter Spaček, *War ich wirklich in Moçambique? Als DDR-Korrespondent auf vier Kontinenten* (Berlin: Edition Weisse Seiten, 2005), 100–103. For medial representation of Mozambique and FRELIMO in the GDR see also Bodie in this volume.
[98] Spaček, *War ich wirklich*, 123–124.

willing to let Udo go for any longer than a few months.[99] Due to his only short-term contracts, Udo used to travel back and forth between the GDR and Mozambique for five years, very much to the dismay of his Mozambican supervisor Rodrigues. After writing several requests for prolonging Udo's contract, Rodrigues eventually received a negative or only partly approving response from GDR authorities. Instead of Udo another East German cooperator was chosen to take over the job – a person who, in Rodrigues' view, did not possess the necessary skills to support the bureau's work during the next census. Resignedly, he turned to Udo: "Alas! No one makes life as hard for us as the countries we are friends with!"[100] And further he complained: "From other countries [...] people come voluntarily, with goodwill and ready to help us. With you we do have a friendship agreement, but every time there is a huge struggle to receive the requested support."[101] Such dialogues between the protagonist Udo and his Mozambican counterparts point towards a trust-based communication style between the colleagues. At the same time, the practical limits of state-organized socialist solidarity are addressed quite frankly here.

Learning to Understand Each Other

Intercultural or local learning can be traced back by small episodes told in the memory books of East German *cooperantes* (cooperators) in Mozambique. One such episode is recalled by Rainer, a history and arts teacher who worked as advisor in the department for teacher training for the Mozambican Ministry of Education between 1981 and 1986. On one occasion, Rainer is invited by a Mozambican colleague to meet some local artists and to visit the *Núcleo de Arte*, Mozambique's first art association. Among other works they discuss a painting showing a *curandeira* (healer), a traditional medicine woman performing a healing ritual. While examining the painting, Rainer wonders why the persons lying at the feet of the *curandeira* opened their mouths. The artist Mankeu explains that "their illness had made them sad. Sadness seals the mouth. The open mouth therefore symbolizes that sadness has escaped."[102] Deeply impressed by the African artwork, Rainer concludes in his book that this artist was like an embodiment of the Mozambican people.

---

[99] Udo Heiland, *Unter Moçambicanern: Arbeit – Leben – Abenteuer 1979 bis 1985* (Leipzig: Engelsdorfer Verlag, 2011), 320.
[100] Heiland, *Unter Moçambicanern*, 309.
[101] Heiland, *Unter Moçambicanern*, 349.
[102] Grajek, *Berichte*, 257.

But intercultural learning also occurred in the context of work – sometimes even in a classroom setting. During a practical lesson, one of Rainer's pupils, a future instructor of Marxism-Leninism named Senhor V., covered the October Revolution in Russia. Apparently, the term Bolsheviks was not familiar to all of his audience, so upon request Senhor V. explained: "You know, here in the South [of Mozambique] we have the Ronga tribe. Many Ronga are workers, peasants, or soldiers. Likewise, back then in Russia there was a tribe called Bolsheviks; many of them were also workers, peasants, soldiers."[103] We strongly assume that the East German instructors of Marxism-Leninism must have disagreed with this interpretation. Despite the misinterpretation of the historical role of the Bolsheviks in Russia, the topic was not discussed further in Rainer's recollection. Nevertheless, it seems surprising that Senhor V. relied on the tribe as a figurative example to illustrate the role of the Bolsheviks in Russia, because the example contradicted FRELIMO's discourse against tribalism in Mozambican society to a large extent. Apparently, while FRELIMO's politics aimed at overcoming tribal bonds on the national level, in a small teacher training institute in Nampula the tribe served as useful reference to interpret the role of Marxist-Leninist parties in revolutionary processes, by simply picturing them as leading tribes with many workers, peasants, and soldiers. This rather creative interpretation of "a tribe called Bolsheviks" by a future Mozambican instructor of Marxism-Leninism may serve as a good example of the ideological entanglements between Africa and the East, as it shows how local actors reclaimed the historiography of socialism by adapting it to local meanings.

Learning to Deal with Contradictions and Disappointments in State Socialism

Mozambicans who lived in the GDR often express mixed feelings when they reflect on East German state socialism in their narratives. Apparently, the self-representation of the country did not resonate with everyday life as experienced by foreigners. All Mozambican narrators did experience xenophobia or racism at some point, although the GDR government claimed that the East German society was guided by anti-racist ideals. Thus, racism rarely occurred in the workplace of the Mozambican migrants, but racist assaults often occurred in spheres where state control tended to be absent, namely in bars or discotheques.[104] In order

---

103 Grajek, *Berichte*, 80.
104 See Machava, this volume.

not to hurt the comfort of the GDR population and its leadership, the Mozambican teacher Gabriel learned to control what should and should not be said. In other words, he learned to control and manage his silence. He further mentioned that in the beginning his motivation for maintaining silence was not to hurt his East German hosts. But with time he learned that "the things that were not being said, turned out to be the most important ones, in a way."[105] Regarding the issue of freedom of expression in East German state socialism, Gabriel recollects that after a while he understood the informal rules of political communication: "There were things that you would say in a private setting. There you could express your opinion, discuss with people and express criticism. And then, there were official settings, where you would say the things which were expected to be said."[106] In this example, Mozambican narrators clearly work out the contradiction between the democratic self-representation of the GDR and the rather undemocratic practice of silencing political debates among citizens – or in this case foreigners. At the same time, Gabriel's memory demonstrates how foreigners adopted certain cultural practices that were common among GDR citizens.

East German observers also take up the topic of contradictions with state socialism when narrating about their experience in Mozambique. On the one hand, they recall situations in which they disagreed with the behavior of fellow GDR cooperators in Mozambique, and on the other hand, they observe contradictions in Mozambican state socialism as another noteworthy phenomenon. This may be illustrated by the autobiography of Udo, who was contracted by the Mozambican government to work on the population census and to qualify Mozambican statisticians. He and his intern from Eduardo Mondlane University were analyzing statistical data on Mozambique's industry sector from the years 1979 and 1980. A German cooperator called Micha shared the office with them, but did not show very much passion for this work. In Udo's recollections Micha affirmed that his contract was only valid for two years and that he would not stay in Mozambique for a single day longer, a stance that differed greatly from the official motive of internationalist solidarity as propagated in the GDR. Apart from that, this colleague used to speak German with Udo on all occasions, although it was obvious that none of their Mozambican colleagues would understand any German. As Udo recalled, this behavior was at least impolite if not highly offensive to their Mozambican colleagues, and Micha's attitude embarrassed him. Udo re-

---

105 Gudat and Ilal, "Erfahrungen," 218.
106 Gudat and Ilal, "Erfahrungen," 219.

counts that many other cooperators from the GDR behaved likewise and that the Mozambican partners repeatedly complained about such behavior.[107]

On the other hand, GDR citizens were sometimes overwhelmed by the challenges that awaited them at their workplace. The East German educational advisor Rainer, for instance, was delegated to contribute to the history curriculum for the teacher training institutes in the country. The "expert group" in charge of curriculum planning consisted of international educators, amongst others from Brazil and Portugal,[108] which led Rainer to speculate about their unwillingness to collaborate with him. Although "good sounding terms like 'socialist Mozambique', 'scientificity', and 'historical materialism'" were dropped by his international colleagues during team meetings, Rainer's version of socialist awareness was rather ignored in the curriculum planning process itself[109]: "You know, Mr. Grajek, we are all from different countries – we all have very different perceptions of the term awareness."[110] Facing such statements Rainer had to leave the final decision to their Mozambican supervisor, who—in this case—chose to opt in favor of Rainer's concept of "socialist awareness."[111]

What astonished East German authors was the contrast between the official appraisal of the Soviet Union as the mother state of socialism, and a seemingly minor popularity of Soviet cooperators among the Mozambican population. The East German statistician Udo remembers that during a visit to a fishermen's village at the Niassa Lake local women were uncertain if he would like to join them for lunch. Puzzled about their uncertainty, Udo asks for the reason of the women's concern and gets an upfront answer: a few weeks before his visit some "*soviéticos*" (Soviets) passed by the place to evaluate if a village cooperative could be founded there. The Soviet visitors chose to bring cans of tinned food instead of enjoying local food and did not cook together with the villagers. The latter concluded from this behavior that the *soviéticos* might have feared for their health, because they even brought water with them. Udo retrospectively regards such behavior as highly counterproductive to socialist goals like solidarity and friendship: "You cannot convince people with propaganda and beautiful

---

107 Heiland, *Unter Moçambicanern*, 74.
108 It was not unusual that international cooperators from Western countries and the Eastern bloc had to work together within the Mozambican education system. As a common language facilitated communication with Portuguese and Brazilian citizens, the Mozambican government frequently employed educational experts from both countries. See Piepiorka, "Exploring Socialist Solidarity," 290, 297.
109 Grajek, *Berichte*, 70.
110 Ibid.
111 Grajek, *Berichte*, 71.

speeches alone. How do they want to agitate for friendship, when they isolate themselves like that? It's a mystery to me."[112]

In addition to critically observing the behavior of Soviet cooperators, Mozambicans frequently mentioned national problems when talking to their East German colleagues and friends. Independence has raised great hopes among the Mozambican population and socialism was officially praised as the sure road to national development. But with the growing economic crisis and an ongoing civil war during the 1980s a severe lack of goods and services became manifest. In spite of this dramatic setting, East German cooperators occasionally observed a rather elitist or even selfish behavior on part of some FRELIMO party cadres, which did not correspond to the official agenda of socialism for the ordinary people. One of such unpleasant memories is mentioned by young journalist Peter Spaček, who recounts a meeting with an old FRELIMO friend "from the bush" (meaning the armed struggle).[113] Meanwhile his friend turned governor in the province capital of Tete invited Spaček for an opulent dinner. To Spaček's astonishment the new governor had taken over the former Portuguese governor's estate, including the butler. But what really caught the journalist's attention were the delicious prawns on his old friend's dining table. Such fancy foods were almost unavailable on the coast itself, but the dinner took place 400 kilometers inland and the governor apparently did not mind flying them in. He even boasted of the "solidarity" between governors that allowed him to organize such extravagances.[114] Downhearted Spaček came to the conclusion that it was not worth appealing to his old friend's socialist ideals from the guerila times: "As the idea failed in our own homes in Europe, why should it work exactly here, in faraway Africa?"[115]

When it came to consumer goods, some East German cooperators also observed a comparable decline in socialist ideals in the ranks of their own higher-ranking SED cadres. For instance, the biochemistry lecturer Holger, who worked at Eduardo Mondlane University, recalls an opulent reception in Maputo organized for a high-ranking SED delegation during their visit to the fifth FRELIMO Congress in 1989. What caught his attention at this reception were the boring speeches as well as the Western drinks, namely bottles of Evian water and the

---

112 Heiland, *Unter Moçambicanern*, 277.
113 Spaček has visited FRELIMO-controlled areas during the independence struggle and got to know many FRELIMO-leaders, who at that time were guerila fighters and lived in rather spartan conditions. Thus, the post-independence luxurious lifestyle of former comrades "from the bush" may have strongly contrasted with his earlier experience with FRELIMO-officials.
114 Spaček, *War ich wirklich*, 153.
115 Ibid.

soft drink Fanta on the tables. Later he learned from a colleague that these and many other Western products had been flown in especially for this government delegation and that the official airline of the GDR, *Interflug*, was responsible for the transport.[116] Although such memory details may seem insignificant, they show very well the awareness of privilege in both socialist societies, because the privileged access to scarce or exceptional goods was often tied to higher ranks in the state apparatus. Thus, while Mozambican governors and East German government representatives may have enjoyed fancy drinks and prawns every now and then, the ordinary people (including the authors of the memory sources) were rather used to queuing for basic goods like meat or even water[117] in times of shortage.

Such contradictions within state-socialist societies may be summed up in a political joke told by Mozambicans to their East German colleague during an annual works outing. The joke reads as follows: two Mozambicans want to eat fish. In the whole city they cannot get any, so they decide to go fishing at the river. After a while they catch a fair-sized fish and get out a pan to fry it. "I don't have oil," says one of them. "Well, me neither," comments the other, "so, let's fry it without oil! But I don't have any matches." The first is disappointed: "I also don't have any. Man, let's just throw the fish back into the water." In this moment the fish turn up his head and shouts: "Viva a FRELIMO!" – Long live FRELIMO.[118] In the 1980s, disillusionment about the ongoing economic crisis and the connected lack of consumer goods became widespread even among party cadres, who indeed found themselves in a relatively privileged situation within the distribution system of the FRELIMO-led state. Among the less privileged parts of the Mozambican population the "popular jokes in Maputo became increasingly bitter about the deteriorating situation."[119]

Although the joke blatantly made fun of the government's failure to provide the Mozambican population with basic supplies, all those present join in a hearty laugh.[120] The fact that this political joke was told in front of the East German colleague points to a relationship of trust, because the state censorship did

---

116 Holger Hegewald, "Berlin, Maputo, und zurück – Dozent an der Eduardo-Mondlane-Universität 1989–1990," in *Engagiert für Afrika: Die DDR und Afrika II*, ed. Ulrich van der Heyden, Illona Schleicher, and Hans-Georg Schleicher (Münster: Lit, 1994), 472–473.
117 Dora, *Kokos*, 34, 54–55, also 158–159. In Dora's novel Frank's wife Rita used to queue for meat and other groceries in line with other inhabitants of Maputo city.
118 Heiland, *Unter Moçambicanern*, 305.
119 Jason Sumich, *The Middle Class in Mozambique: The State and the Politics of Transformation in Southern Africa* (Cambridge: Cambridge University Press, 2018), 86.
120 Heiland, *Unter Moçambicanern*, 305.

not joke with unpleasant anecdotists – neither in the GDR nor in Mozambique.[121] At the same time, it is remarkable that all the protagonists on site immediately understood the joke and the underlying humor, which points to a common understanding of the poor condition in party-led economies. Jokes with a similar undertone were also popular in the GDR and other Eastern bloc countries.[122] Such anecdotes served as an outlet for annoyed or disappointed citizens in socialist societies around the globe who were promised prosperous socialist development but who at the same time regularly experienced a shortage of basic consumer goods. The circumstance that ordinary people—living in nominally people-led economies—suffered from the lack of basic supplies like matches or oil found expression in a particular genre of humor, the "communist joke".[123] These jokes illustrate a common horizon of dealing with scarcity in socialist societies and the experience of addressing it ironically or subversively.

Concluding Remarks

After recapitulating selected aspects of East German and Mozambican memory literature, we wonder whether it is reasonable to speak about a transnational memory space between these two formerly socialist populations. Although memories on overall socialist realities seem to coincide in Mozambican and East German narrations about "the other", the personal realities of the narrators and their memories vary considerably. Generally speaking, East German realities seem somewhat privileged as compared to the Mozambican storytelling. This may result from the positions narrators occupied in the overall system of educational exchange between the GDR and the PRM. Most East German narrators came to Mozambique as educators or advisors. Only one East German narrator

---

121 For the surveillance of political jokes within the GDR see Bodo Müller, *Lachen gegen die Ohnmacht: DDR-Witze im Visier der Stasi* (Berlin: Ch. Links, 2016). For the context of Mozambique see Richard D. Lewis, *Humor Across Frontiers, Or, Round the World in 80 Jokes* (Warnford: Transcreen Publishing, 2005), 100.
122 For instance, in the GDR, the lack of certain goods manifested itself in the form of long queues that formed in front of shops that were said to have the desired goods. Nevertheless, the supply of goods often did not meet the needs of East German consumers or ran out before everyone in the queue was served. A joke dealing with the routine of rumors about queuing for consumer goods reads as follows: One housewife says to another: "I hear there'll be snow tomorrow!", to which the other one replies: "Well, I'm not queuing for that"; see Ben Lewis, *Hammer And Tickle: A History of Communism Told Through Communist Jokes* (London: Phoenix, 2009), 132.
123 See Lewis, *Hammer And Tickle*, 11–21.

came to Maputo for study purposes, namely to learn the Portuguese language. On the other hand, most Mozambican narrators came to the GDR as prospective students or trainees. This implies that the divergent positions of the East Germans and Mozambicans in their destination countries may have resulted in very different memories, and a rather divided memory space.

At the same time, it seems that regardless of their position within the system, all narrators picture themselves as learners in a very broad sense. Both Mozambican and East German authors tell stories about encounters with new habits, new rules, new socialist realities abroad. And many passages are devoted to the intercultural understanding of one another, resulting in new socialist entanglements. Furthermore, socialist ideals seem to be valued in both Mozambican and East German memory texts. A common tone is also palpable in passages that criticize the negative aspects of state socialism in the respectively other country. In sum, a nostalgic but ambivalent consensus on the socialist project in both countries seems to manifest in the written testimonies of its former protagonists. In that sense, we found a notion of "sharedness" in post-socialist memories that originated in very different geographical and temporal spaces, expressed through temporary moorings. As a result, we see a delightful mosaic of Euro-African storytelling on educational exchange under socialist conditions, assembled by "Mozambican-*Ossis*"[124] (Mozambican "Easterners") and *muzungu*-Mozambicans (foreign Mozambicans). This post-socialist memory mosaic naturally remains open to further interpretation.[125]

Bibliography

Memory Sources

Alberto, Ibraimo. *Ich wollte leben wie die Götter: Was in Deutschland aus meinen afrikanischen Träumen wurde*. Köln: Kiepenheuer & Witsch, 2014.

Bruchsteiner, Hans. "Vom Lernen und Lehren – als Berater in der mosambikanischen Volksbildung." In *Wir haben Spuren hinterlassen! Die DDR in Mosambik: Erlebnisse, Erfahrungen und Erkenntnisse aus drei Jahrzehnten*, edited by Matthias Voß, 434–462. Münster: Lit, 2005.

---

[124] Grajek, *Berichte*, 268. Depending on the context, "Ossi" may be a colloquial or pejorative term for a person originating from Eastern Germany (or the former GDR).
[125] We want to send a cordial *obrigado* and *Danke* to Anne Dietrich and Marcia C. Schenck, who accompanied us in our journey through post-socialist memory landscapes with incredible patience and invaluable advice in the process of writing.

Dembe, Eusébio João. "Os privilegiados da década 80." In *Moçambique-Alemanha, ida e volta: vivências dos Moçambicanos antes, durante e depois da estadia na Alemanha / Mosambik-Deutschland, hin und zurück: Erlebnisse von Mosambikanern vor, während und nach dem Aufenthalt in Deutschland*, edited by ICMA, 63–70. Maputo: ICMA, 2005.

Dora, Helmut. *Kokos und bitterer Tee: Tage und Nächte in Mosambik*. Rostock: BS-Verlag, 2009.

Grajek, Rainer. *Berichte aus dem Morgengrauen: Als Entwicklungshelfer der DDR in Mosambik*. Grimma: Ute Vallentin, 2005.

Gudat, Renate, and Abdul Ilal. "Erfahrungen von mosambikanischen Studenten in der DDR: Interviews." In *Engagiert für Afrika. Die DDR und Afrika II*, edited by Ulrich van der Heyden, Illona Schleicher, and Hans-Georg Schleicher, 215–225. Münster: Lit, 1994.

Hebestreit, Dieter. "Als DDR-*Student* in Mosambik." In *Engagiert für Afrika: Die DDR und Afrika II*, edited by Ulrich van der Heyden, Illona Schleicher, and Hans-Georg Schleicher, 226–229. Münster: Lit, 1994.

Hegewald, Holger. "Berlin, Maputo, und zurück – Dozent an der Eduardo-Mondlane-Universität 1989–1990." In *Engagiert für Afrika: Die DDR und Afrika II*, edited by Ulrich van der Heyden, Illona Schleicher, and Hans-Georg Schleicher, 463–480. Münster: Lit, 1994.

Heiland, Udo. *Unter Moçambicanern: Arbeit – Leben – Abenteuer 1979 bis 1985*. Leipzig: Engelsdorfer Verlag, 2011.

Spaček, Peter. *War ich wirklich in Moçambique? Als DDR-Korrespondent auf vier Kontinenten*. Berlin: Edition Weisse Seiten, 2005.

Secondary Literature

Achille, Etienne, Charles Forsdick, and Lydie Moudileno, eds. *Postcolonial Realms of Memory: Sites and Symbols in Modern France*. Liverpool: Liverpool University Press, 2020.

Assmann, Aleida. *Erinnerungsräume: Formen und Wandlungen des kulturellen Gedächtnisses*. Munich: C.H. Beck, 1999.

Aleida Assmann. "Memory, Individual and Collective." In *The Oxford Handbook of Contextual Political Analysis*, edited by Robert E. Goodin and Charles Tilly, 210–224. Oxford: Oxford University Press, 2006.

Assmann, Aleida. "Wem gehört Geschichte? Fakten und Fiktion in der neueren deutschen Erinnerungsliteratur." *Internationales Archiv für Sozialgeschichte der deutschen Literatur* 36 (2011): 213–225.

Blaschke, Bernd. "Erzählte Gefühle und Emotionen des Erinnerns: Ostdeutsche Identitätsliteratur der in den 1960er und 1970er Jahren Geborenen." In *Ostdeutsche Erinnerungsdiskurse nach 1989: Narrative kultureller Identität*, edited by Elisa Goudin-Steinmann and Carola Hähnel-Mesnard, 245–263. Berlin: Frank & Timme, 2013.

Cesari, Chiara de, and Ann Rigney, eds. *Transnational Memory: Circulation, Articulation, Scales*. Berlin: De Gruyter, 2014.

Coelho, João Paulo Borges. "Politics and Contemporary History in Mozambique: A Set of Epistemological Notes." *Kronos* 39 (2013): 20–31.

Creet, Julia. "Introduction: The Migration of Memory and Memories of Migration." In *Memory and Migration: Multidisciplinary Approaches to Memory Studies*, edited by Julia Creet and Andreas Kitzmann, 3–26. Toronto: University of Toronto Press, 2011.

Creet, Julia, and Andreas Kitzmann, eds. *Memory and Migration: Multidisciplinary Approaches to Memory Studies*. Toronto: University of Toronto Press, 2011.

Criser, Regine. "Zwischen Anpassung und Instrumentalisierung: Hybride Lebensnarrative in der Literatur nach 1989." In *Ostdeutsche Erinnerungsdiskurse nach 1989: Narrative kultureller Identität*, edited by Elisa Goudin-Steinmann and Carola Hähnel-Mesnard, 199–212. Berlin: Frank & Timme, 2013.

Cross, Michael. *An Unfulfilled Promise: Transforming Schools in Mozambique*. Addis Ababa: OSSREA, 2011.

den Boer, Pim, ed. *Europäische Erinnerungsorte: Europa und die Welt*. 3 vols. 3. Munich: Oldenbourg, 2012.

Eigler, Friederike. *Gedächtnis und Geschichte in Generationenromanen seit der Wende*. Berlin: Erich Schmidt, 2005.

Erll, Astrid. "Travelling Memory." *Parallax* 17 (2011): 4–18. Accessed January 31, 2020. doi:10.1080/13534645.2011.605570.

Erll, Astrid. *Kollektives Gedächtnis und Erinnerungskulturen: Eine Einführung*. 3rd ed. Stuttgart: J.B. Metzler, 2017.

Fonseca, Ana Margarida. "(Re)Configurations of Identity: Memory and Creation in the Narrative of Mia Couto." In *Mozambique on the Move: Challenges and Reflections*, edited by Sheila P. Khan, Maria P. Meneses, and Bjørn E. Bertelsen, 135–152. Leiden, Boston: Brill, 2018.

François, Etienne, and Hagen Schulze, eds. *Deutsche Erinnerungsorte – Eine Auswahl*. Munich: C. H. Beck, 2005.

Geissler, Gert, and Ulrich Wiegmann. *Schule und Erziehung in der DDR: Studien und Dokumente*. Neuwied: Hermann Luchterhand, 1995.

Göschl, Regina. *DDR-Alltag im Museum: Geschichtskulturelle Diskurse, Funktionen und Fallbeispiele im Vereinten Deutschland*. Münster: Lit, 2019.

Graf, Herbert. "Vor der Unabhängigkeitserklärung Mosambiks – Erinnerungen und Reflexionen." In *Wir haben Spuren hinterlassen! Die DDR in Mosambik: Erlebnisse, Erfahrungen und Erkenntnisse aus drei Jahrzehnten*, edited by Matthias Voß, 61–129. Münster: Lit, 2005.

Grammes, Tilman, Henning Schluß, and Hans-Joachim Vogler. *Staatsbürgerkunde in der DDR: Ein Dokumentenband*. Wiesbaden: VS, 2006.

Gratzemann, Andreas. *Die Erziehung zum "neuen" Menschen im Jugendwerkhof Torgau: Ein Beitrag zum kulturellen Gedächtnis*. Münster: Lit, 2008.

Gronenthal, Mariell C. *Nostalgie und Sozialismus: Emotionale Erinnerung in der deutschen und polnischen Gegenwartsliteratur*. Bielefeld: Transcript, 2018.

Hahn, Hans Henning, Robert Traba, and Peter Oliver Lowe, eds. *Deutsch-Polnische Erinnerungsorte*. 5 vols. Paderborn: Schöningh, 2012–2015.

Halbwachs, Maurice. *Das kollektive Gedächtnis*. Stuttgart: Enke, 1967.

Handro, Saskia, ed. *Aufarbeitung der Aufarbeitung: Die DDR im geschichtskulturellen Diskurs*. Schwalbach: Wochenschau-Verlag, 2011.

Harisch, Immanuel Rafael. "Bartering Coffee, Cocoa and W50 Trucks: The Trade Relations of the GDR, Angola and São Tomé in a Comparative Perspective." *Global Histories* 3 (2017): 43–60. Accessed October 31, 2019. doi:10.17169/GHSJ.2017.135.

Hodgin, Nick, and Caroline Pearce, eds. *The GDR Remembered: Representations of the East German State Since 1989*. Camden House: Boydell & Brewer, 2011.

Honecker, Erich. *Aus Meinem Leben*. Berlin: Dietz, 1981.

Igreja, Victor. "Memories as Weapons: The Politics of Peace and Silence in Post-Civil War Mozambique." *Journal of Southern African Studies* 34 (2008): 539–556.

Klinge, Sebastian. *1989 und wir: Geschichtspolitik und Erinnerungskultur nach dem Mauerfall*. Bielefeld: Transcript, 2015.

Kunze, Thomas, and Thomas Vogel, eds. *Ostalgie international: Erinnerungen an die DDR von Nicaragua bis Vietnam*. Berlin: Ch. Links, 2010.

Langa, Patricio Vitorino. *Higher Education in Portuguese Speaking African Countries: A Five Country Baseline Study*. Cape Town: African Minds, 2013. Accessed October 15, 2019. www.africanminds.co.za/wp-content/uploads/2014/02/AM-HE-in-Lusophone-Africa-Text-and-Cover-web.pdf.

Lehnert, Gertrud. "Raum und Gefühl." In *Raum und Gefühl: Der Spatial Turn und die neue Emotionsforschung*, edited by Gertrud Lehnert, 9–25. Bielefeld: Transcript, 2011.

Lewis, Richard D. *Humor Across Frontiers, Or, Round the World in 80 Jokes*. Warnford: Transcreen Publishing, 2005,

Lewis, Ben. *Hammer and Tickle: A History of Communism Told Through Communist Jokes*. London: Phoenix, 2009.

Lüdeker, Gerhard Jens. *Kollektive Erinnerung und nationale Identität: Nationalsozialismus, DDR und Wiedervereinigung im deutschen Spielfilm nach 1989*. Munich: Ed. Text + Kritik, 2012.

Mählert, Ulrich, ed. *Die DDR als Chance: Neue Perspektive auf ein altes Thema*. Berlin: Metropol, 2016.

Matasci, Damiano, Miguel Bandeira Jerónimo, and Hugo Dores, eds. *Education and Development in Colonial and Postcolonial Africa: Policies, Paradigms, and Entanglements, 1980s-1980s*. Cham: Palgrave Macmillan, 2020.

Millei, Zsuzsa, Iveta Silova, and Susanne Gannon. "Thinking Through Memories of Childhood in (Post)Socialist Spaces: Ordinary Lives in Extraordinary Times." *Children's Geographies* (2019), 1–14. Accessed January 24, 2020. doi:10.1080/14733285.2019.1648759.

Moller, Sabine. "Diktatur und Familiengedächtnis: Anmerkungen zu Widersprüchen im Geschichtsbewusstsein von Schülern." In *Aufarbeitung der Aufarbeitung: Die DDR im Geschichtskulturellen Diskurs*, edited by Saskia Handro, 140–151. Schwalbach: Wochenschau-Verlag, 2011.

Mouzinho Mário, Peter Fry, Lisbeth A. Levey, and Arlindo Chilundo. *Higher Education in Mozambique: A Case Study*. Oxford, Maputo: James Currey; Imprensa & Livraria Universitária UEM, 2003.

Müller, Tanja. *Legacies of Socialist Solidarity: East-Germany in Mozambique*. London: Lexington, 2014.

Müller, Bodo. *Lachen gegen die Ohnmacht: DDR-Witze im Visier der Stasi*. Berlin: Ch. Links, 2016.

Niederhut, Jens. *Die Reisekader: Auswahl und Disziplinierung einer privilegierten Minderheit in der DDR*. Leipzig: Evangelische Verlagsanstalt, 2005.

Nora, Pierre, and Lawrence D. Kritzmann, eds. *Realms of Memory: Rethinking the French Past.* 1–3. New York: Columbia University Press, 1996–1998.
Parkes, Stuart. "Literary Portrayals of the GDR by Non-GDR Citizens." In *The GDR Remembered: Representations of the East German State Since 1989*, edited by Nick Hodgin and Caroline Pearce, 54–68. Camden House: Boydell & Brewer, 2011.
Piepiorka, Alexandra. "Exploring 'Socialist Solidarity' in Higher Education: East German Advisors in Post-Independence Mozambique (1975–1992)." In *Education and Development in Colonial and Postcolonial Africa: Policies, Paradigms, and Entanglements, 1980s-1980s*, edited by Damiano Matasci, Miguel B. Jerónimo and Hugo Dores, 289–318. Cham: Palgrave Macmillan, 2020.
Pitcher, Anne M. "Forgetting from Above and Memory from Below: Strategies of Legitimation and Struggle in Postsocialist Mozambique." *Journal of the International African Institute* 76 (2006): 88–112.
Ransiek, Anna. "Anders-Sein in der DDR – Narrative Bezüge nach der Transformation." In *Ostdeutsche Erinnerungsdiskurse nach 1989: Narrative kultureller Identität*, edited by Elisa Goudin-Steinmann and Carola Hähnel-Mesnard, 79–95. Berlin: Frank & Timme, 2013.
Reuter, Lutz R., and Annette Scheunpflug. *Die Schule der Freundschaft: Eine Fallstudie zur Bildungszusammenarbeit zwischen der DDR und Mosambik.* Münster: Waxmann, 2006.
Ritschel, Susanne. *Kubanische Studierende in der DDR: Ambivalentes Erinnern zwischen Zeitzeuge und Archiv.* Hildesheim: Georg Olms, 2015.
Roos, Hans-Jochen. "Unterricht unter Palmen: Als Biologielehrer an der FRELIMO-Schule in Bagamoyo." In *Wir haben Spuren hinterlassen! Die DDR in Mosambik: Erlebnisse, Erfahrungen und Erkenntnisse aus drei Jahrzehnten*, edited by Matthias Voß, 407–425. Münster: Lit, 2005.
Rudnick, Carola S. *Die andere Hälfte der Erinnerung: Die DDR in der Deutschen Geschichtspolitik nach 1989.* Bielefeld: Transcript, 2011.
Rupprecht, Tobias. *Soviet Internationalism after Stalin: Interaction and Exchange between the USSR and Latin America during the Cold War.* Cambridge: Cambridge University Press, 2015.
Sabrow, Martin, ed. *Erinnerungsorte der DDR.* Munich: C. H. Beck, 2009.
Sabrow, Martin. "Zeitgeschichte als Aufarbeitung: Der Fall DDR." In *Aufarbeitung der Aufarbeitung: Die DDR im geschichtskulturellen Diskurs*, edited by Saskia Handro, 21–36. Schwalbach: Wochenschau-Verlag, 2011.
Saul, John S. *Revolutionary Traveller: Freeze-Frames from a Life.* Winnipeg: Arbeiter Ring Publishing, 2009.
Schenck, Marcia C. "Ostalgie in Mosambik: Erinnerungen ehemaliger mosambikanischer Vertragsarbeiter in der DDR." *Südlink* 172 (2015): 21–23.
Schenck, Marcia C. "From Luanda and Maputo to Berlin: Uncovering Angolan and Mozambican Migrants' Motives to Move to the German Democratic Republic (1979–1990)." *African Economic History* 44 (2016): 202–234. Accessed February 12, 2020. doi:10.1353/aeh.2016.0008.
Schenck, Marcia C. "A Chronology of Nostalgia: Memories of Former Angolan and Mozambican Worker Trainees to East Germany." *Labor History* 59 (2018): 352–74. Accessed October 30, 2019. doi:10.1080/0023656X.2018.1429187.

Schleicher, Ilona. "Berufsbildung und Wirtschaftsbeziehungen DDR – Mosambik." In *Engagiert für Afrika: Die DDR und Afrika II*, edited by Ulrich van der Heyden, 179–195. Münster: Lit, 1994.

Schmieder, Ulrike. "Orte des Erinnerns und Vergessens: Denkmäler, Museen und historische Schauplätze von Sklaverei und Sklavenhandel." *Comparativ* 22 (2012): 60–94.

Searle, Chris. *We're Building the New School: Diary of a Teacher in Mozambique*. London: Zed Press, 1981.

Sengupta, Indra. "Introduction. Locating Lieux De Mémoire: A (Post)Colonial Perspective." In *Memory, History, and Colonialism: Engaging with Pierre Nora in Colonial and Postcolonial Contexts*, edited by Indra Sengupta, 1–8. London: German Historical Institute, 2009.

Sengupta, Indra, ed. *Memory, History, and Colonialism: Engaging with Pierre Nora in Colonial and Postcolonial Contexts*. London: German Historical Institute, 2009.

Siewert, Stephanie. "Die Topographie der Melancholie in transnationaler Perspektive." In *Raum und Gefühl: Der Spatial Turn und die neue Emotionsforschung*, edited by Gertrud Lehnert, 216–228. Bielefeld: Transcript, 2011.

Silova, Iveta, ed. *Post-Socialism Is Not Dead: (Re)Reading the Global in Comparative Education*. Bingley: Emerald Group Publishing, 2010.

Silova, Iveta, Nelli Piattoeva, and Zsuzsa Millei, eds. *Childhood and Schooling in (Post) Socialist Societies: Memories of Everyday Life*. Cham: Springer International Publishing, 2018.

Silova, Iveta, Noah W. Sobe, Alla Korzh, and Serhiy Kovalchuk, eds. *Reimagining Utopias: Theory and Method for Educational Research in Post-Socialist Contexts*. Rotterdam: Sense Publishers, 2017.

Sumich, Jason. *The Middle Class in Mozambique: The State and the Politics of Transformation in Southern Africa*. Cambridge: Cambridge University Press, 2018.

Tedesco, Maria do Carmo Ferraz. "Reconfiguração da Moçambicanidade nos romances de Mia Couto e Paulina Chiziane." *Revista Mosaico* 3 (2010): 81–91.

Tembe, Joel das Neves, ed. *História da Luta de Libertação Nacional*. Maputo: Ministério dos Combatentes, Direcção Nacional de História, 2014.

Tippner, Anja, and Anna Artwińska, eds. *Narrative of Annihilation, Confinement, and Survival: Camp Literature in a Transnational Perspective*. Berlin, Boston: De Gruyter, 2019.

Todorova, Maria, and Zsuzsa Gille, eds. *Post-Communist Nostalgia*. Oxford: Berghahn, 2010.

Traverso, Enzo. *Left-Wing Melancholia: Marxism, History, and Memory*. New York: Columbia University Press, 2016.

Tullner, Mathias. "Die Zusammenarbeit der DDR und Mosambiks auf dem Gebiet der Bildung und die Tätigkeit der Bildungsexperten der DDR in Mosambik." In *Wir haben Spuren hinterlassen! Die DDR in Mosambik: Erlebnisse, Erfahrungen und Erkenntnisse aus drei Jahrzehnten*, edited by Matthias Voß, 388–406. Münster: Lit, 2005.

van der Heyden, Ulrich, Wolfgang Semmler, and Ralf Straßburg. *Mosambikanische Vertragsarbeiter in der DDR-Wirtschaft: Hintergrund – Verlauf – Folgen*. Münster: Lit, 2014.

Vogel, Wolf-Dieter, and Verona Wunderlich, eds. *Abenteuer DDR: Kubanerinnen und Kubaner im deutschen Sozialismus*. Berlin: Karl Dietz, 2011.

Wandel, Malte. *Einheit, Arbeit, Wachsamkeit: Die DDR in Mosambik*. Heidelberg: Kehrer Verlag: 2012.

Welzer, Harald. *Das kommunikative Gedächtnis: Eine Theorie der Erinnerung*. Munich: C. H. Beck, 2002.
Zawangoni, Salvador André. *A FRELIMO e a formação do Homem Novo (1964–1974 e 1975–1982)*. Maputo: CIEDIMA, 2007.

List of Contributors

Ibraimo Alberto
Ibraimo Alberto is a former Mozambican contract worker who currently resides in Berlin. He co-authored his biography together with Daniel Bachmann, *Ich wollte leben wie die Götter* (KiWi 2014). Moreover, Alberto works as a social education worker in the fields of anti-racism and intercultural communication. Contact: ibraimo.alberto@yahoo.de

Christian Alvarado
Christian Alvarado is a Ph.D. Candidate in the History of Consciousness Department at the University of California, Santa Cruz. His current research examines the history and historiography of Kenya's Mau Mau within a transnational intellectual framework. His work aims to show how different interpretations of Mau Mau interfaced with contemporary historiographical, political, and cultural contexts by drawing on the semiotic and material landscapes upon which these understandings were articulated. More generally, Mr. Alvarado studies how shifting historical and popular narratives of anti-colonial struggles in Africa have over time been re-worked within diverse sets of discourses embedded in broader power structures. He is also interested in the role of translation and interaction between traditionally-siloed imperial networks, and conducts research across Anglophone, Francophone, and Lusophone boundaries. Contact: chdalvar@ucsc.edu

Eric Angermann
Eric Angermann is writing his doctoral thesis at the Georg-August-University of Göttingen on neo-Nazi groups in both the Federal Republic of Germany and the German Democratic Republic and their practices and modes of organization from 1983 to 1991. He is a fellow of the Hans-Böckler-Stiftung and undertakes historical-political educational work. Contact: e_angerman@gmx.net

Katrin Bahr
Katrin Bahr is a Visiting Assistant Professor of German Studies at Centre College, Kentucky. She received her Ph.D. at the University of Massachusetts in September 2020 with her dissertation examining the everyday life of East Germans in Mozambique during the 1980s. She is the co-founder of the Third Generation Ost network in the United States and has published articles on the East German third generation, East German memory and the cultural relationships between East Germany and Mozambique. She also curated the exhibition East Germany in Mozambique: Private Photographs of a Forgotten Time, which was shown in the United States, Germany, and Mozambique. Contact: katrin.bahr@centre.edu

George Bodie
George Bodie is currently a visiting lecturer in World History at the École Supérieure de Commerce de Paris. He received his Ph.D. from University College London in 2020. His thesis was entitled "Global GDR? Sovereignty, Legitimacy and Decolonization in the German Democratic Republic, 1960–1989." Contact: g.bodie.12@ucl.ac.uk

Eduardo Felisberto Buanaissa

Eduardo Felisberto Buanaissa is Mozambican and a university researcher and lecturer. As a research associate, he is currently doing his Ph.D. in Policy and Philosophy of Education at the University of Gießen, under the supervision of Prof. Dr. Ingrid Miethe. He has experiences in research and teaching in different departments at the Pedagogical University of Maputo-Mozambique, and is guest lecturer at the University of Magdeburg, in the Department of International and Intercultural Educational Research. Since 2017 he is also a member of the research group "Contemporary Africa: from nation building to Political Identity", based at the Pontifical Catholic University of Rio Grande do Sul in Porto Alegre, Brazil. Contact: ja.edu@hotmail.com

Thomas G. Burgess

Thomas G. Burgess' Ph.D. dissertation (Indiana University, 2001) and many of his subsequent publications have centered on various aspects of the Zanzibari Revolution. While initially his interest was primarily on the politics of youth and generation, he later sought to situate Zanzibar within a global history of socialism, and all of its attendant exchanges of knowledge, mobilities, and diasporas. After serving as Assistant Professor for five years at Hampton University, Burgess is currently an Associate Professor in the Department of History at the US Naval Academy, in Annapolis, Maryland. Contact: gburgess@usna.edu

Eric Burton

Eric Burton is Assistant Professor of Global History at the University of Innsbruck. He has published journal articles on the entangled histories of socialism, development, and decolonization in the *Journal of Global History*, *Cold War History* and *Journal für Historische Kommunismusforschung*, among others. The Ph.D. dissertation on which his forthcoming monograph (*In Diensten des Afrikanischen Sozialismus. Die globale Entwicklungsarbeit der beiden deutschen Staaten in Tansania, 1961–1990*) is based has been awarded the Walter Markov Prize 2019–20 by the European Network in Universal and Global History (ENIUGH). Special issues edited by him include *Socialisms in Development* (JEP/Austrian Journal of Development Studies, 2017) and *Journeys of Education and Struggle. African Mobility in Times of Decolonization and the Cold War* (Stichproben. Vienna Journal of African Studies, 2018). Contact: eric.burton@uibk.ac.at

Jörg Depta

Jörg Depta studied German as a Foreign Language (DaF) and Eastern European Studies at Leipzig University. He is currently finishing his Ph.D. thesis "Das Herder-Institut und die DDR-Sprachenpolitik im Ost-West-Konflikt 1951 bis 1972" at Leipzig University and working as a researcher and consultant at demos – Brandenburgisches Institut für Gemeinwesenberatung in Frankfurt (Oder) and the districts of Eastern Brandenburg. Contact: joerg-depta@posteo.de

Anne Dietrich

Anne Dietrich is currently finishing her Ph.D. thesis "Tropische Genüsse in der DDR" at Leipzig University and works as a project coordinator, lecturer, and museum educator. Her research focuses on the provision and consumption of coffee, sugar, and tropical fruits in the German Democratic Republic (GDR), focusing on supply shortfalls and trade relations with socialist-leaning countries in the Global South. She is the author of several book chapters on Eastern European and East German consumer culture and the GDR's foreign trade relations with countries of the Global South. Peer-reviewed articles have appeared in *Comparativ* and the *Austrian Journal of Development Studies*. She curated a permanent exhibition in Leipzig's Arabian Coffee Tree Museum and led the historical researches for the immersion show *Boomtown* at the Kunstkraftwerk Leipzig, which shows the development of industrial culture in the west of Leipzig in the nineteenth and twentieth centuries. As a museum educator, she regularly guides visitors through the Zeitgeschichtliches Forum Leipzig and is currently preparing the educational program for the Kunstkraftwerk Leipzig. Her research interests include the global history of the Cold War, the history of global commodities, Ethiopian and Cuban history, and the industrial history of Leipzig. Contact: anne.dietrich@uni-leipzig.de

Immanuel R. Harisch
Immanuel R. Harisch is a Doctoral Candidate in History at the research platform "Mobile Cultures and Societies" at the University Vienna, Austria, working on the topic of African trade unions and labor education in the East, West and South during the Cold War. He holds Master degrees in both African Studies and Development Studies with a term abroad at the University of Dar es Salaam. He has published journal articles on East-South encounters in the fields of trade and education, African socialisms, as well as on Walter Rodney and knowledge production at the University of Dar es Salaam. Since 2019 he is an co-managing editor of the open access journal *Stichproben – Vienna Journal of African Studies*. Contact: immanuel.harisch@univie.ac.at

Anne-Kristin Hartmetz
Having studied African studies and history with a focus on East European and global history, Anne Hartmetz is currently finishing her Ph.D. project on relations between Ghana and the Soviet Union during the Cold War. Her research interests include South-East relations during the Cold War, transnational history, global aspects of socialism, and economic aspects of Cold War history. She is a member of the Collaborative Research Center (SFB) 1199 "Processes of Globalisation under the Global Condition" at Leipzig University. Contact: anne-kristin.hartmetz@uni-leipzig.de

Francisca Raposo
Francisca Raposo lives in Chimoio, Mozambique. She studied in Staßfurt in Saxony-Anhalt at the School of Friendship (Schule der Freundschaft) between 1982 and 1989, where she became trained as a salesperson for clothes (Bekleidungsfacharbeiterin). In 2014 she finished her studies at the Universidade Pedagocica in Chimoio in environmental studies and community development (Licenciatura). Currently, she is writing a book about her memories preliminarily titled "To Germany and Back" ("Nach Deutschland und zurück"). Mrs. Raposo works as director of a student dormitory in Chimoio and is actively involved in projects about gender parity, access to education, and school food programs. Contact: francisca_raposo@yahoo.com

Fernando Agostinho Machava
Fernando Agostinho Machava has founded a consultancy in Maputo, Mozambique, assisting researchers with archival work and interviews. Previously, he worked as a historian in collaboration with the Presidency of the Republic Museum in Maputo where he was responsible for the elaboration of the historical content for an exhibition called *The Lives and Work of the Presidents of the Republic*. Originally from Maputo, Machava studied history at the Faculty of

Arts and Social Sciences, Eduardo Mondlane University. During his studies, he was partially supported by a Ministry of Education scholarship and came second in the SADC National School Composition Contest in 2012. He also worked as a research assistant for national and international researchers for two Ph.D.s and one M.A. thesis on different aspects of Mozambican history, ranging from the social history of post-independence Mozambique and the impact of the Civil War and military aid from Mozambique to neighboring countries to the former Mozambican migrants in the German Democratic Republic. He has meanwhile explored this area in his own work, resulting in a "Licenciatura" thesis titled "The Madjermanes and their Impact on the City of Maputo 1990 – 1997." He is interested in Mozambican history, the history of migration with a focus on reintegration of returnees from the GDR. Contact: fmachava00@gmail.com

Alexandra Piepiorka
Alexandra Piepiorka is a lecturer and researcher at the Institute for Educational Science, University of Giessen, Germany. Her ongoing Ph.D. project focusses on socialist cooperation in higher education between the former GDR and post-independent Mozambique. Contact: alexandra.piepiorka@erziehung.uni-giessen.de

Franziska Rantzsch
Franziska Rantzsch studied history and philosophy at the University of Erfurt. Since October 2018 she is a research associate at Erfurt University, at the history department. Since April 2017 she is a Ph.D. student at the Chair of Global History of the 19th Century, University of Erfurt. Her Ph.D. project has the working title "Die Vertragsarbeiterpolitik der DDR: Interessen – Konzeptionen – Entwicklung". Contact: franziska.rantzsch@uni-erfurt.de

Marcia C. Schenck
Marcia C. Schenck is the Professor of Global History at the University of Potsdam. Her most recent book project combines the history of development with the history of humanitarianism in a study about refugee management in Africa in the second half of the twentieth century. Previously, she was a visiting research scholar at Princeton University (2019), a lecturer at the Friedrich-Meinecke-Institut at Freie Universität Berlin (2018 – 19), and a Guest of the Director at the re:work Institute at the Humboldt Universität zu Berlin (2017 – 18). She received her Ph.D. in history from Princeton University in September 2017 and holds a M.Sc. in African Studies from the University of Oxford. Her dissertation *Socialist Solidarities and their Aftermath: Histories and Memories of Angolan and Mozambican migrants to the German Democratic Republic, 1975 – 2015* traces the migration experience and migrant memories of Angolan and Mozambican migrants to East Germany. Peer-reviewed articles have appeared in *Africa*, *African Economic History* and *Labor History*, among others. Her research interests include the history of refuge seeking, migration history, labor history, African history, global history, and oral history. Contact: marcia.schenck@uni-potsdam.de

Paul Sprute
Paul Sprute is a research associate and Ph.D. candidate at the Leibniz-Institut für Raumbezogene Sozialforschung Erkner in the research project "Conquering (with) Concrete: German Construction Companies as Global Players in Local Contexts" within the Freigeist program of the Volkswagenstiftung. He holds a B.A. in Political Science and History of the Universität Bremen and an M.A. in Global History of the Freie Universität and Humboldt-Universität in

Berlin. During his M.A. studies, he worked as a student assistant and was responsible for Global Histories: A Student Journal at Freie Universität. Paul Sprute's research focus was on the GDR's international solidarity and he wrote his Master's thesis on "The Afterlives of Solidarity: The *Solidaritätsdienst International* and its Re-Interpretation of the GDR's Programs of Global Development in Re-Unified Germany." Contact: paul.sprute@leibniz-irs.de

Index

Abdulrazak, Gurnah   30, 171, 181, 185, 189
Accra   5, 22, 65, 194, 196, 272
African Labor College, Kampala   198
African National Congress   30 f.
– see also ANC   30, 32, 42, 272, 123
Afro-Asian Committee   25, 123, 126, 128 f., 133
Afro-Shirazi Party   173
– see also ASP   173–175, 177, 188
Agbetrobu, Benoît   124
Agreement on Economic and Scientific-Technical Cooperation   147, 150, 153
Agriculture   28, 35, 188, 294, 300, 331
– Agricultural Machinery   33, 149, 302
Alberto, Ibraimo   44, 209, 229, 247–249, 252, 255 f., 345, 364
Alexandria   62, 74, 76, 79
Algeria   23, 28, 39, 143, 266
Alvarado, Christian   8, 13, 18 f., 28, 236
Alves, Nito   307
Amateur   252 f., 255, 258, 323–325, 330, 352
America   6, 10 f., 28, 30, 32 f., 142 f., 150, 180 f., 282, 295, 326, 344, 356, 122
Angermann, Eric   8, 13, 18 f., 25 f., 195 f., 198, 236, 115, 117, 120
Angola   7, 13, 15, 19 f., 28, 30 f., 33–35, 37, 39–42, 140, 147, 149, 152, 223, 272, 293–297, 299–312, 314 f., 319, 325, 336, 351
Anti-imperialism   4, 24, 65, 74, 76, 83, 297, 307, 315
Apartheid   30, 41 f., 266
Armed Forces (Angola)   302
Armed Forces (Mozambique)   161, 208, 212
Autobiography   175, 247 f., 364, 374
Axen, Hermann   32, 147, 267, 277

Babu, Abdulrahman Mohamed   43, 169, 173, 175 f.
Bahr, Katrin   7, 13, 19 f., 40, 161, 251, 280, 303, 319, 370
Bassa, Cahora   274

Beira   149, 243, 332, 335 f., 342, 344
Berlin TLC (Sports Club)   255
Berlin Wall   202, 209, 217, 265, 358
Bernau   1, 23, 25 f., 193, 195, 197 f., 115–119, 121, 126, 128–130, 132 f., 135 f.
Bernau College   25, 195, 236, 115, 132
Birmingham, David   301
Bissay, Luc   129, 133
Bolshevik   373
Boxing   44, 251–258, 260
Brandenburg   200, 257, 271, 130
Brandt, Willy   274
Brazil   375
Brigade Diaries   13, 295 f, 303, 308,
Buanaissa, Eduardo F.   7, 45, 149, 187, 213, 248, 295, 322 f., 332, 351, 365
Budapest   6, 256, 265
Burgess, Thomas G.   6 f., 13, 19, 29 f., 169, 172–180, 189
Burton, Eric   1–3, 22 f., 27 f., 65, 140, 169, 177 f., 187–189, 193, 247, 272, 282, 293 f., 296, 300, 303, 329

Cabo Delgado   243
Cairo   22, 27, 40, 61–73, 75, 79, 82, 161, 172, 272
Camara, Daouda   123 f., 127 f.
Cameroon   124, 129, 133
Capitalism   3 f., 16, 24, 147, 196, 298, 312, 319, 121
Carnation Revolution   34, 276, 319
Cassimo, Alberto   154–156, 163
Childhood   37, 207, 240, 258, 353, 357
China   4, 13, 21, 29, 39, 42, 170, 172, 176–178, 189
Chongo, Amandio   154
Civil War   34, 146, 149, 157, 208, 210, 212, 218 f., 222, 227, 243, 289, 301, 303, 315, 331, 360 f., 365 f., 376
Coffee   6, 28, 33–35, 185, 301 f., 310
Cold War   1–6, 9–13, 15–17, 21–23, 25–28, 34, 36, 39, 42, 44, 62–67, 74, 79, 82 f., 140, 142, 146, 163, 169–171,

174 f., 177, 180, 184, 187–189, 196, 198, 211, 215, 266, 270, 272, 274, 276, 282, 293–295, 297–301, 307, 315 f., 322, 327 f., 339, 356, 116, 122, 125, 128
Colonialism 5, 11, 17 f., 22 f., 40, 44, 145 f., 170 f., 174, 178, 185 f., 212, 237 f., 240, 267, 274, 282, 297, 312, 315 f., 319 f., 323, 326 f., 329, 342, 355, 360, 366
Commercial Coordination Division 148, 160 f.
– see also Bereich Kommerzielle Koordinierung 33, 148
– see also KoKo 33 f., 148
Communication 171, 181, 185, 296, 341, 372, 374 f.
Congo, Democratic Republic of 130
Congo, People's Republic 34, 267
– see also Congo-Brazzaville 7
Consumer Goods 250 f., 376–378
Contract Labor Accord 141 f., 148, 150 f., 153, 157–159, 320
Contract Worker 8, 19, 36, 41, 45 f., 140 f., 143, 151 f., 155, 158–162, 211, 248, 320, 345, 368
Convention People's Party 194
– see also CPP 194, 196, 199–201
Cooper, Frederick 10, 14, 17 f., 22, 195, 297
Copenhagen 256
Council for Mutual Economic Assistance 33
– see also CMEA 21, 34
– see also Comecon 32 f., 39, 43, 257
Council of Heads of Delegation 119, 125 f., 128, 131
– see also Rat der Delegationsleiter 198, 119, 135
Cuba 15, 24, 29, 31, 34, 36 f., 39, 42 f., 141, 143, 170, 175, 235, 243, 260, 280, 301 f., 365
Culture 4, 8, 20, 27, 31, 68, 171, 173, 179, 185, 189, 196, 209, 221, 223, 227, 239, 243, 266 f., 270, 280, 289, 323, 352, 355, 368, 134

Dangereux, Daniel 303, 307
Dar es Salaam 1, 22, 31, 65, 169, 176, 180, 235, 272 f., 300, 320

Decolonization 10, 15–18, 21–26, 30, 34, 43, 65, 142, 171, 187, 195, 272, 327, 116
Depta, Jörg 13, 18 f., 21, 27, 40, 61, 236, 116
Deubner, Rolf 132–134
Deutschland, Heinz 193 f., 196, 119 f., 124 f., 128 f., 131, 133, 136
Development 2, 10, 17, 24, 27, 31, 38–41, 64 f., 73, 80–83, 139, 141 f., 145, 148–150, 152 f., 159, 162, 170, 177, 179, 187, 189, 195, 201, 214, 236, 248, 250, 260, 269, 278 f., 283, 306, 319, 321 f., 326, 328 f., 332, 360 f., 376, 378, 123
Diallo, Hamidou 128 f.
Dietrich, Anne 1, 32–35, 43, 149, 379
Diplomacy, cultural 62 f., 68–70, 79 f.
Disappointment 29, 230, 251, 255, 366, 368
do Nascimento, Lopo 35
Dresden 32, 184 f., 199, 215, 255, 304
Dynamo Berlin (Sports Club) 255

East German Foreign Office 69
– see also MfAA 69, 71, 77, 141, 147, 150 f., 156, 159, 301, 335
East German Society 18, 254, 344, 373
East-West 35, 83, 162, 248
Eastalgia 46, 356, 358
Economy 1 f., 5, 8, 10, 32–35, 42 f., 140, 144–146, 148, 150–152, 155, 160, 162, 169, 195, 210, 212, 222, 226, 228, 265, 301, 305, 307, 310, 314, 320, 326, 368
Eduardo Mondlane University 45, 369, 374, 376
Egypt 13, 23, 27, 61–69, 71 f., 74–77, 79–83, 172, 277
Eisenhüttenstadt 200
El-Borolos, Abdul Wahab 77
El-Hefny, Mahmoud 69
Employment 140, 143, 145, 147, 150–160, 162, 212, 214, 219, 226, 228 f., 257, 300, 334, 365
Encounters 5, 7 f., 10 f., 13, 15 f., 18, 20, 27, 36, 44–47, 62, 139, 169–171, 184, 187, 209, 235, 238, 275, 294, 296 f., 302, 304–306, 308 f., 314, 320, 322, 327, 339, 342, 344, 352, 363, 368, 379, 116

Engineer 21, 35, 69, 199, 212, 321
Entangled Labor History 142
Entanglements 1, 4 f., 20, 27, 282, 322, 370
Ethiopia 3, 6, 16, 20, 31, 34 f., 41, 147, 265, 267, 299
Everyday Life 266 f., 319, 321 f., 324, 326, 330–332, 341, 344, 357–359, 363, 369, 373, 118, 133
Exploitation 1, 18, 30, 32, 148, 170, 203, 239 f., 281, 319 f.

Fanon, Frantz 330, 342
Federal Foreign Office (FRG) 70, 72 f., 80, 140
Federal Republic of Germany 70, 213, 259, 345
– see also FRG 70, 78, 80, 269, 271, 274, 284
– see also West Germany 21, 27, 39, 62–64, 66 f., 69–77, 79–83, 146, 175, 189, 202, 217, 259, 269, 273 f., 122, 136
Film 6, 28, 73, 268–270, 273, 275, 285–287, 331, 340
First World 203
Fischer, Oskar 147, 160
Forças Armadas Populares de Libertação de Angola 302
– see also FAPLA 302, 305, 307
– see also Armed Forces (Angola)
Foreman, George 255
Forquilha, Abílio 213 f.
Free German Youth 27, 72, 139, 149, 294, 304, 321, 327
– see also FDJ 27 f., 35, 72, 139, 149, 294 f., 299 f., 302, 304–308, 311, 313, 321, 325, 327, 329, 336, 116
– see also Freie Deutsche Jugend 72, 139, 177, 294, 327
Freedom 15–17, 22, 31 f., 34, 170, 199, 202, 220, 237, 261, 278, 301, 307, 364, 374
Frente de Libertação de Moçambique 19, 30, 144, 319, 351
– see also FRELIMO 15, 19, 30–32, 37, 40, 144–146, 152–156, 162 f., 208, 219, 235, 237 f., 268 f., 272–283, 286 f., 289, 319 f., 338, 351, 360 f., 369, 371, 373, 376 f.
Friendship 13, 19 f., 27 f., 32, 34–37, 40, 45, 62, 79, 139, 147, 162, 170, 177, 212, 235, 237, 240, 244, 271, 293 f., 297–300, 302, 304 f., 307–309, 320, 325, 327, 329, 332, 336, 351, 368, 371 f., 375 f., 129
Friendship Brigades 19 f., 27 f., 35 f., 40, 297, 325, 327, 329, 336

Gabela 302 f., 305, 311, 313
Gaza 144, 243
Gentsch, Martin 178
German as a Foreign Language 18, 27, 63 f., 77, 79, 81–83
– see also DaF 61, 63 f., 77–79, 81
German Reunification 44, 203, 257
Ghana 3, 15, 20, 23, 26, 28 f., 193–196, 199–201, 203, 116, 131
Ghana Trades Union Congress 195
– see also TUC 193–196, 199, 201
Gleijeses, Piero 34, 42, 175, 301, 307
Global History 4–6, 9–11, 13 f., 18, 22, 26, 247
Goethe Institute 27, 61 f., 69–72, 74–76, 79, 81 f.
Grajek, Reiner 332–334, 370, 372 f., 375, 379
Guinea 3, 13, 23, 28, 30, 81, 182, 272, 277, 319, 325, 123 f.
Guinea Bissau 30, 272, 277, 319

Hallstein Doctrine 21, 23, 62 f., 65–67, 72, 146, 175 f., 320, 116
Hard currency 33
Harisch, Immanuel R. 1, 7, 25 f., 28, 33–35, 149, 187, 193 f., 196, 207, 240, 247, 293 f., 296, 300–303, 308, 329, 351, 115, 117, 120 f., 128, 131
Hartmetz, Anne-Kristin 13, 18 f., 21, 27, 40, 61, 236, 116
Hassan, Mustafa 71
Helbig, Gerhard 68 f., 73, 81 f.
Herder Institute 25, 27, 61, 69, 73, 80–82, 236
Historiography 4, 16, 283, 358, 362, 373

Hlabukana, Gilbert   123, 125
Hoepner, Lutz   154
Hollender, Julian   147, 154
Honecker, Erich   31f., 147, 153, 211, 265, 267, 271, 276, 284, 287, 302, 351
Housewife   337, 378
Huhn, Reinhold   202f.
Hungary   141, 143, 171, 185

Ideology   2f., 44, 63, 189, 199, 201, 269, 297, 315, 323, 339, 116, 130
Independence   7, 19, 24, 30–32, 42, 144–146, 148, 152, 162, 172–174, 212f., 235, 243, 266, 275, 278, 286, 301, 319f., 327, 351, 360f., 365, 369–371, 376, 121
Industrial Relations Act   194
– see also IRA   194
Industrial Revolution   236
Industrialization   145, 250, 297
Inhambane   243
Integration   14, 38, 45f., 152, 161, 194, 216, 229, 253, 258, 302, 304, 321, 134, 136
Intercultural Exchange   45, 254
Intercultural Understanding   248, 258, 379
International Monetary Fund   42
– see also IMF   16, 42
International Solidarity   142, 147f., 150, 153, 161f., 237, 265, 271, 274, 293–296, 298f., 311, 315, 320–323, 329, 116, 118, 125
Internationalism   3, 6, 11, 18, 20f., 24, 39, 170f., 187, 201, 269, 282f., 285, 297, 316, 339, 356, 132
Isolation   23, 46, 169, 188f., 209, 271, 131
Israel   66, 70, 72, 74f., 82

Jacobs, Ernst-Otto   154
Juventude do Movimento Popular de Libertação de Angola   302
– see also JMPLA   296, 302, 304–309

Kaindoah, Salvatory   1–3
Kampfert, Karl   1, 193, 125, 132f.
Karl Marx   25, 61, 68, 271, 361, 370
Karume, Abeid   29, 175–180, 188f.

Kenya   4, 28, 173, 177, 185
Kenya Students Union   28

Labor Advisor   199
Labor Movement   148
Lake Müritz   202
Lake Plauen   202
Lamberz, Werner   146, 268
Liberation Struggle   17, 22, 31, 35, 280, 300, 320, 117
Libya   31, 146f.
Lichinga   331
Lieux de Mémoire   354
Living Condition   46, 219f., 223f., 321, 339, 117f.
Lobito   303, 306, 308
Luabo   241
Luanda   34, 160, 208, 302f., 309, 312, 352, 367

Macajo, Fernando António   249
Machava, Fernando Agostinho   7f., 19, 38, 45, 141, 207, 215–227, 257, 345, 356, 361–363, 373
Machel, Graça   238, 280
Machel, Samora   37, 139, 146, 229, 235, 276, 282, 286f., 329, 371
Madjerman   38, 46, 207–211, 219–221, 223–231, 362
Maé, Alto   208
Magdeburg   36, 236, 240, 248, 255
Maher, Antoum Chalaby   71, 76
Makonde   238, 280
Makosch, Ulrich   18, 31, 40, 265, 268, 270, 274–276, 285, 287f.
Makua   238
Malanje   303
Mali   25, 28f., 325, 116, 128
Maluana   214
Manhiça   214
Manica   243, 253, 279
Mao   172, 174, 177, 361, 370
Maputo   8, 38, 45, 140, 147, 152, 154–158, 160f., 163, 207–209, 211f., 214f., 217–222, 224–226, 230, 237f., 243f., 276, 287, 321, 330, 332f., 335, 338f., 343f.,

351f., 355, 360f., 365, 367–370, 376f., 379
Marxism-Leninism 3f., 34, 332, 373, 115f., 128, 136
Mbaitjongue, Osée 124
Memory Fiction 364
Memory Literature 45f., 352–354, 356, 359, 362f., 378
Memory Space 45, 352–356, 358, 362, 378f.
Middle East 30, 63, 66, 189, 283
Migrant 39, 44, 144f., 173, 207–213, 215–217, 219–224, 229, 237, 240, 250, 258, 260, 352, 354f., 362, 367, 373
Migration, Labor 9, 38, 140, 142–145, 148f., 158, 163, 208, 211, 240, 260
Military 16, 22f., 31, 34, 40f., 154, 175f., 210, 213, 235, 260, 266, 273, 277, 280, 305, 366f., 121
Ministry of Foreign Affairs (GDR) 140, 147, 150f., 301
Ministry of Foreign Trade (GDR) 147, 150, 160
Ministry of Labor 142, 154f., 158, 163
Ministry of State Security (GDR) 143
– see also MfS 143, 150–160, 358, 127
– see also Stasi 19, 143, 180, 287, 358, 378
Mittag, Günter 33, 147, 212, 295, 301–303
Mittag-Kommission 33
Moatize 139f., 149, 158, 302, 335f., 341, 344
Mobility 6, 23, 43, 172, 187, 249, 255, 117
Modernity 4, 18f., 21, 26, 200, 328
Modernization 16, 29, 35, 82, 142, 196, 297, 309, 314–316
Moorings 6–8, 22, 47, 142, 170, 238, 303, 343, 379
Mopeia 241
Movimento Popular de Libertação de Angola 30, 296, 302
– see also MPLA 15, 30, 32, 34f., 272, 296, 300–302, 305f., 309, 312, 314
Müller, Rudolf 202f.
Mutual Benefit 12, 148, 163

Nampula 243, 373

Nasser, Gamal Abdel 27, 62–67, 70, 79, 82f., 172f., 277
N'Dalatando 302, 312
Negotiation 10, 139, 141f., 151, 153–157, 176, 249, 294, 320
Neto, Agostinho 35, 272, 302, 307
New Man 208, 220, 235, 237, 328
Niassa 40, 243, 375
Nigeria 21, 27, 120, 130f.
Nkrumah, Kwame 17–19, 29, 194, 196, 199f.
Noack, Ingolf 154
Non-aligned 34, 66, 83
Non-Aligned Movement 65
– see also Bandung Conference (1955) 22, 172
– see also NAM 65
Nostalgia 46, 186, 211, 215, 222, 314, 356, 362
Nyerere, Julius 3f., 173, 176, 272

October Revolution 373, 135
Osei, J. A. 26, 193f., 203, 121f.
Osei-Opare, Nana 15f., 193, 196, 201

Pan-Africanism 5, 17f., 22, 65, 176, 178, 200, 121
Pan-Arabism 65, 70
Paternalism 183, 127, 135
Photograph 20, 40, 188, 247, 251, 273, 303, 321–345
Photographer 40, 273, 324–326, 330, 336
Photography 273, 324–327, 340, 344
Piepiorka, Alexandra 7, 15, 19, 27, 45, 149, 187, 213, 248, 295, 321–323, 332, 351, 365, 370, 375
Poland 38, 141, 143, 257, 357
Political Joke 377f.
Politics of Forgetting 360
Population 30, 38, 74, 144, 169, 174, 178, 180, 202, 226, 229, 239, 242, 257, 266, 268, 283, 286, 289, 305, 326f., 329, 331, 341, 369, 374–377, 118, 132, 134
Portugal 30, 146, 226, 273f., 277, 301, 319, 351, 369, 375
Potsdam 203, 216, 258

Poverty 46, 181, 210, 230, 238, 269, 312 f., 326
Privilege 3, 15, 43, 188, 210, 212 f., 221 f., 227, 255, 306, 311, 336, 339, 341, 344, 365, 377 f.
Pugach, Sara 21, 28, 44, 196, 198, 125

Quelimane 238, 240, 242 f.

Raase, Werner 115 f., 119
Racism 13, 18, 44 f., 170, 215 f., 229, 237, 240, 253, 255, 258–261, 267, 294, 320, 323, 342, 365, 368, 373, 123, 129 f., 132 f.
Rantzsch, Franziska 8, 19, 38, 139, 208, 211, 213, 249, 320
Raposo, Francisca 37, 210, 235 f., 238–240, 249
Resistência Nacional Moçambicana 39, 146, 303, 336
– see also RENAMO 39, 146, 149, 303, 336, 360 f.
Returnee 38, 45 f., 161, 207, 210 f., 215, 218–230, 355, 362
Rhodesia 30, 36, 121
Russia 11, 44, 46, 177, 257, 369, 373

Santos, Marcelino dos 147, 212, 274
São Tomé and Príncipe 30, 32 f., 294
Schenck, Marcia C. 1, 8, 12, 20, 35–37, 44, 46, 140 f., 160, 187, 193, 207–217, 221 f., 228 f., 235, 237, 240, 247, 249, 278, 307, 314, 345, 352, 356, 362 f., 367, 379
Schlack-Golodkowski, Alexander 33, 148, 160 f.
Schleicher, Hans-Georg 12, 22–24, 31, 35, 146, 198, 276, 300, 320 f., 336, 368 f., 377
Schleicher, Ilona 12, 22 f., 28, 35, 198, 276, 300, 320 f., 336, 352, 368 f., 116, 124
Schule der Freundschaft 36 f., 235–238, 351
– see also SdF 36 f., 235–240
Second World 5, 11, 18, 41, 64, 180, 200, 319, 327

Second World War 5, 18, 41, 64, 180, 200, 319, 327
Secretariat for Labor and Wages 142, 150 f., 154–159
Shangaan 238
Shona 238
Shubin, Vladimir 34, 294, 301
Six-Day War 27, 64, 74–77
Slavery 43, 238, 319
Slobodian, Quinn 12, 28, 44, 198, 215, 266, 299, 322, 327, 339, 116, 125
Snapshot 321, 323, 325, 341
Socialism 1–5, 9 f., 14, 18, 24, 26, 29, 31 f., 35 f., 41, 44, 46 f., 65, 146 f., 170 f., 174, 185, 187–189, 200, 203, 220, 229, 235, 239, 250, 270, 282–284, 289, 297, 310, 312, 319 f., 324, 328 f., 339, 353, 356–358, 360 f., 370, 373–376, 379, 116, 120, 122, 135 f.
Socialism, scientific 3, 188, 237, 361, 375
Socialist Economic Aid 148
Socialist Education System 351 f., 357
Socialist Unity Party of Germany 211, 267, 326
– see also SED 2, 8, 18, 23, 27, 31–33, 35, 44, 68, 72, 143, 146 f., 150, 153–155, 162, 219, 236, 267–269, 271, 276, 282, 285, 287, 299, 309, 320, 324, 326, 359, 376, 118 f., 127, 130, 132, 135
– see also Sozialistische Einheitspartei Deutschlands 2, 143, 118
Sofala 40, 218, 243
Solidarity Committee (GDR) 30, 149 f., 320, 326, 329
– see also Afro-Asian Solidarity Committee 25, 273
Sölle, Horst 147
Sontag, Susan 324, 326, 340
South Africa 6, 23, 36, 39, 42, 142, 144–146, 162, 209, 213, 218, 223, 229, 301, 121
South African Mining Industry 208 f.
South West Africa People's Organisation 30
– see also SWAPO 12, 30, 32, 187, 271 f., 299, 321, 122
Soviet Cooperator 375 f.

Soviet Union   2, 7, 11, 15, 17f., 21, 27, 29, 31, 41f., 64, 72, 77, 79, 154, 172, 175, 177, 182, 194, 260, 267, 270, 277, 301f., 327, 339, 345, 356, 375, 130
Specialist   69, 180, 303, 320–323, 327–332, 334–337, 339–341, 344, 125
Sprute, Paul   7, 13, 19f., 35, 293, 325
Stoph, Willi   147
Student Exchange   236
students, African   8, 25, 28, 36, 44, 187, 195, 198, 115f., 119, 121f., 126, 130
students, East German   45, 124
System competition   76, 81, 83

Tanganyika   1f., 26, 169, 173, 176, 122
Tanzania   1–3, 16, 20, 22f., 28, 42f., 154, 169, 173, 176, 180, 189, 266, 272, 277, 320
Tarraf, Nureddin   61, 69
Teacher   3, 30, 71, 73f., 78, 83, 171, 177, 183, 189, 239, 244, 321, 332, 336f., 351, 363, 366, 370, 115, 117, 122, 131
Television   19, 31, 73f., 207, 216, 221, 224–226, 228, 230, 268–271, 282–285, 288, 327
Tete   139, 243, 268, 275, 376
Tettegah, John K.   199
Third World   4, 11f., 18, 22f., 34, 39, 41, 43, 62, 65f., 79, 83, 142, 146, 169f., 172, 175, 180, 198, 266f., 295
Timm, Klaus   68
Trade Union   6, 22–25, 29, 193, 195, 198, 201f., 302, 115–120, 122f., 128–130, 132, 134–136
Trade Union College Fritz Heckert   1, 22, 25, 193, 195, 197f., 115f.
Travel   7, 19f., 26, 81, 155, 157, 174, 186, 213, 218, 237, 239f., 243, 248, 251, 256, 265, 271, 311, 323, 332, 334f., 339–341, 345, 357, 363, 365–367, 370, 372, 115
Treaty of Friendship and Cooperation   147, 162

Tribalism   237, 320, 373
Twala, Abdul Aziz   178

Uíge   302, 311f.
Ulbricht, Walter   61f., 64, 67–69
Umma Party   173

Vanguard   29, 46, 171, 174, 229, 236, 239, 115, 117, 119–121, 134f.
Vietnam   9, 15, 29f., 34, 38f., 46, 141, 278, 302, 356
Violence   39, 45, 170, 173f., 182, 184, 209, 215, 230f., 239, 254, 261, 282, 121, 135
Vocational Training   23, 28, 37, 150, 152, 157, 160, 162f., 235, 300, 310, 351, 368

W50 Truck   33, 149, 300f., 351
Weis, Toni   12, 35, 187, 271, 299, 315, 321, 122
Westad, Odd Arne   11, 34, 39, 64, 74, 79, 146, 294f., 297, 315
Wiriyamu Massacre   275
Witkowski, Gregory   266, 272, 276, 298f., 322, 327, 116
Wolf, Markus   175f., 179
Working Class   23, 25, 37, 229, 235, 117, 119f., 129, 134
Working Condition   215, 230, 240

Yugoslavia   13, 28, 186, 258, 269

Zambézia   242f.
Zambia   3f., 7, 31, 147, 274
Zanzibar   2, 6, 13, 28f., 169–181, 187–189, 325
Zanzibar Nationalist Party   172
– see also ZNP   172–175
Zeleza, Paul Tiyambe   16, 195
Zimbabwe   30, 32, 42
Zimbabwe African People's Union
– see also ZAPU   16
Zimbabwe African People's Union   30
– see also ZAPU   30, 42, 272

www.ingramcontent.com/pod-product-compliance
Lightning Source LLC
Chambersburg PA
CBHW071809230426
43670CB00013B/2409